W9-BNY-102

The Literature of Destruction

The Literature of Destruction

Jewish Responses to Catastrophe

EDITED BY **DAVID G. ROSKIES**

 THE JEWISH PUBLICATION SOCIETY

PHILADELPHIA · NEW YORK · JERUSALEM 5748 / 1988

Wingate College Library

*The publication of this book was made possible
by a generous grant from the Wolfman Fund.*

Copyright © 1989 by The Jewish Publication Society
First edition   All rights reserved
Manufactured in the United States of America
Library of Congress Cataloging in Publication Data
The literature of destruction: Jewish responses to catastrophe/
  edited by David G. Roskies.—1st Edition
    p.   cm.
  Bibliography: p.
  Includes index.
  ISBN 0-8276-0314-2
    1. Jews—Persecutions—History—Sources.   2. Jewish literature.
3. Holocaust, Jewish (1939–1945)—Literary collections.
I. Roskies, David G., 1948–   .
DS102.L54 1988
909'.04924—dc19   *88-2774*
                                                          CIP

Designed by Adrianne Onderdonk Dudden

לזכרון
דעם לערער בחסד עליון
שמשון דונסקי

Contents

The Literature of Destruction

Introduction

We are still captive to the myth that ours is an age of unprecedented violence, that "we are on a more brutal standard now," in the words of Moses Herzog, "a new terminal standard, indifferent to persons." Herzog also rails against the "wasteland mentality" that is everywhere reinforced: in the media; in popular music; in the cinema; in philosophy, poetry and fiction. Appearing against this backdrop, a new anthology titled *The Literature of Destruction* would seem to highlight the temper of our times.

The subtitle, however, tells a different story. For this anthology follows the *Jewish* response to recurrent historical catastrophes and reveals the extent to which Jewish collective memory has remained a vital resource, even in the modern era. Through their literature of destruction, Jews perceive the cyclical nature of violence and find some measure of comfort in the repeatability of the unprecedented.

Yiddish poet Moyshe-Leyb Halpern ended his apocalyptic vision of World War I with the words "No one's seen me here, ever. / I've not been here, never" (**55**).° Some twenty-five years later, Yankev Glatshteyn echoed this sentiment with the identical words: "Here I Have Never Been." When had the individual felt more overwhelmed by the disappearance of conscience than in 1919? When had a Jewish survivor ever surveyed so empty a world as in the wake of the Holocaust? Even the apocalypse, then, took its place on the continuum of Jewish experience.

Boldface numerals in the text refer to the numbered selections throughout the book.

Through the centuries and across numerous dispersions, the Jewish response has been governed by the same four components: a founding document, the Hebrew Bible, in which the covenantal scheme was laid out for all times to come; a set of historical archetypes, some biblical, some postbiblical, that could be reapplied to all future events; sanctioned vehicles for expressing one's rage both against God and against the gentiles; and an evolving set of rituals designed to rehearse all catastrophes and persecutions.

The Jewish literature of destruction was part of a three-way dialogue that engaged the writer, the people and the God of Israel. The basis for that dialogue was the covenantal ideal of sin-retribution-and-restoration. This covenantal ideal was laid out explicitly in the biblical exhortations of Moses and the Prophets to the Israelites. If the Israelites observed the commandments, the Land would yield its fruit; if they sinned, the Land would spew them forth. But exile did not mean abandonment, for if Israel returned to the ways of God, He would return them to their Land. Although nowhere in the Five Books of Moses were the threats actually carried out and although the Prophets added further conditions, warnings and consolations after the fact, the saga of the Judges and Kings showed the curses come true. Now it was the recurrent plot of a backsliding judge-king-prophet-nation returning to the ways of the Lord and restored to former glory that bore out the covenantal ideal. Because the terms of the contract were laid out in no uncertain terms, both sides were equally accountable: God, too, could be "reminded" of His promises.

Through the use of archetypes destruction could be made to fit into the covenantal scheme. When chroniclers and poets expressed their anguish or their rage, they used the archetypes of exile, destruction, martyrdom and redemption that were fixed in the ancient, immutable texts. These archetypes were events or images, rooted in sacred history, that established the precedent for all times to come. Though punctual and never superseded, the archetypes were understood transtemporally; that is to say, they could be reenacted throughout time and place. "Ask and see," wrote the Crusade chronicler Solomon bar Simson (**23**), "were there ever so many sacrifices like these from the days of Adam? Were there ever a thousand one hundred sacrifices in one day, all of them like the sacrifice of Isaac the son of Abraham?" When faced with the unprecedented spectacle of Jews killing themselves en masse rather than convert to Christianity, the survivor might have exclaimed: "This is the end! This event admits of no analogies. Here I have never been!" Instead, the Jewish response was to proclaim: "This event is so terrible, nothing like it has ever happened since." Through that linkage, however tenuous and inadequate, the particular archetype of destruction—in this case, the sacrifice of Isaac on Mount Moriah—was reinterpreted and reinforced.

Archetypes were the very basis of Jewish collective memory. No matter how long the list of martyrs grew to be, and no matter how many disasters crowded the memorial calendar, they ultimately confirmed the covenantal relationship between the Jews and the God of history.

So long as the dialogue remained an internal, Jewish matter and God was the sole addressee of the survivor's complaint, facts and figures were never important, save to embellish an account with formulaic numbers ("a thousand one hundred sacrifices") or to provide the other survivors with an occasional date to aid in their memorial rites. But when, in the modern era, the victims sought recompense from the world at large, they had to resort to quantifiable data. True to the mandate of scientific socialism, the Jewish Labor Bund corrected the casualty figures for the Kishinev pogrom in its proclamation of 1903 (**44**). Besides, there were now competing covenants under whose terms the Jews could hope for an end to the terrors of history: Jewish socialists placed their hope in global workers' solidarity, Jewish nationalists fought for political sovereignty and the rest looked for civil equality within democratic states.

In these modern times, the use of archetypes persisted despite the absence of faith in the old covenantal scheme of sin-retribution-and-restoration. History itself became a moral reference point for secular Jews who no longer attended synagogue or accepted the claims of Jewish sacred chronology. Those chiefly responsible for keeping group memory alive were secular intellectuals writing primarily in Hebrew and Yiddish. They made their presence felt at just the moment when both the scope and nature of anti-Jewish rhetoric and violence were drastically changing. New literary forms were needed to keep pace with the ever-growing cycles of violence—psychological short stories, realistic novels and historical dramas, heroic ballads and hymns, personal memoirs and calls to arms. Through these literary forms, new to Jewish literature, the concrete particulars of history were once again reshaped into larger patterns of meaning, whether by disassembling the recent events into their recognizable parts (a neoclassical approach) or by enlarging them against an apocalyptic landscape. So vast had this new Literature of Destruction become that it could no longer be contained within a single volume or be recited at a single ritual.

In traditional Jewish society, one rehearsed the catastrophes of old at set times in the liturgical calendar, according to fixed rites of mourning and penitence. If there ever existed a formal anthology of Jewish responses to catastrophe, it was the collection of *kinot* (dirges) for the Ninth of Av, the official date when the First and Second Temples were destroyed. In addition to the full text of Lamentations, these *kinot* included supplementary poems that reflected on later disasters in Jewish history (**27**). They ended with a cycle of poems on the Land of Israel, thus looking ahead to the abrogation of history with the coming of the Messiah. This juxtaposition of mourning and celebration, of fasting and feasting, was the operative principle of Jewish collective memory.

The present anthology chronicles some remarkable continuities in the Jewish response to destruction, as rabbis and writers, religious and secular intellectuals have bridged the historical abyss across some 2,500 years.

Although no individual text or genre is necessarily unique to the Jews, among no other people can one find these cumulative, unbroken and internally consistent memorial traditions. The memorial imperative was further strengthened in the modern era, from the 1880s onward, when secular texts became a kind of guiding scripture. The self-defense movement that arose among politically active Jews in eastern Europe owed as much to Bialik's "Poems of Rage" (**46–47**) as to the proclamations of the Jewish political parties. In Nazi-occupied Warsaw in 1940, the Zionist youth movement Dror issued a mimeographed anthology called *Suffering and Heroism in the Jewish Past in the Light of the Present.* Included in its 101 pages were excerpts from the Crusade chronicles (**23**), Nathan Nata Hanover's *The Abyss of Despair* (**35–36**) as well as the recent work of Bialik and Lamdan (**65**). In 1943, three years after its publication, this record of martyrdom became the blueprint for revolt.

Historians, too, played a vital role in shaping Jewish collective memory. While Yosef Yerushalmi concludes his provocative study *Zakhor* by lamenting the split between modern Jewish historiography and Jewish memory, Jewish historians in eastern Europe saw themselves as the vanguard of a new secular culture. S. Ansky was both a signatory to a call for historical chronicling during World War I (**52**) and the author of the most important Jewish chronicle to issue from that war (**53**). His *Khurbm Galitsye (The Destruction of Galicia)*, in turn, inspired the young engagé historian Emanuel Ringelblum to organize a team of archivists who collected, evaluated and preserved the record of perfidy and martyrdom in the very midst of total destruction (**71**).

It is the business of anthologies to create a "tradition" even where none may have existed before. Assembling a normative anthology has turned out to be much more difficult than I anticipated because it has meant following two contradictory mandates: one literary, the other historical. As a student of literature born and raised in North America after World War II, I naturally sought the most well-wrought, expressive and unique specimens. Especially where violence was concerned, the modern critics to whom I was indebted stressed the principle of commensurability: the greater the violence, the more it should have called forth a verbally brutal, syntactically disjointed and apocalyptic response. T. S. Eliot's *The Wasteland* was the prooftext most often cited. Throughout my career I have served that school of thought by presenting the ideologically radical side of Jewish culture, by favoring the more sophisticated and inaccessible writers over the popular, "sentimental" ones. I meant to dispel my students' naïve notions about Yiddish as a culture of the shtetl and to show them instead how "modern" or rebellious Jewish writers could be. But the historian's mandate required that I choose either those texts that had been most widely read and recited or those that represented the prevailing *Zeitgeist*. A work that was sui generis had no place here. Thus, some of my very favorite texts simply had to go: Israel Rabon's picaresque but virtually unknown novel *The Street*, Abraham Sutzkever's elegant but obscure sequence of prose poems called *Green Aquarium*. Conversely, some literarily unimpressive texts had to be included because of their enormous influence on the people themselves.

The Anglo-Saxon modernist bias is also unkind to expressions of "sentimentality." Ironic understatement is considered the better part of valor, and high rhetoric is tolerated only in politicians and evangelists. But norms of sentimentality differ from one culture to another. To English ears, Shayevitsh's *Lekh-lekho* (**91**) may very well sound self-pitying, and even a classic of Hebrew modernism such as Alterman's *Joy of the Poor* (**70**) seems less than suitably stoic. To Yiddish-Hebrew ears, however, both poets are models of epic control, indeed, of defiance. I can scarcely convey the impact of hearing *Lekh-lekho* declaimed at a memorial gathering organized by the Jewish Labor Bund in Montreal many years ago. It seemed to me then (as it still seems to me now) a work of heroic proportions. As for Alterman's classic, its power to forge a sense of collective destiny among secular Israelis has hardly diminished over the years.

To gauge the popularity of a given work, I was guided by whether and how often it was translated from one Jewish language to another. Thus, Solomon Ibn Verga's *Shevet Yehudah* (*The Scepter of Judah*, **30–33**), which describes the plight of Iberian Jewry, later became a Yiddish folkbook and probably enjoyed even greater currency in Yiddish than in Hebrew. On the other hand, early apocalyptic texts such as the Book of Enoch had been preserved only in *non Jewish* languages, so that as much as they represented an important moment in Jewish history, they were all but totally suppressed by the rabbinic leadership and could not influence subsequent generations until they were retranslated into Hebrew or otherwise made accessible to modern, secular Jews.

Until World War I, Hebrew and Yiddish coexisted in a kind of symbiotic relationship. After the war, Hebrew became the language of the Zionist revolution and of the new Jewish settlement in Palestine, and Yiddish was left to stake its claim in the European Diaspora. Two normative traditions thus arose that were esssentially the same; but because one Jewish center was secured and the other was destroyed, the underlying unities could be retrieved only through an act of editorial will.

It should be obvious that Jewish writers who were born into the same culture, received the same traditional education and faced the same set of historical upheavals would not produce a radically different response just because they adopted a different Jewish language. Yet Jewish culture has become so fragmented after the Holocaust that the obvious must not only be stated but also vigorously defended. As surprising as it may seem, Glatshteyn and Alterman have never before rubbed shoulders in any anthology, though their evolution as "national poets" is so remarkably similar, just as I. B. Singer and S. Y. Agnon, whose responses to the Holocaust complement one another, have never been brought together. By the same token, Jewish folklore and highbrow literary culture coexisted and interpenetrated even in such large urban centers as Kiev, Warsaw, Lodz and New York to an extent hardly imaginable today. Mordecai Gebirtig's stirring prewar hymn (**67**), which was sung throughout Nazi-occupied Europe, owed as much to Bialik as it did to the street ballads of an earlier era (cf. **42**).

In compiling this anthology, I could not be guided by what was already available in English translation because Jewish languages and English do not share much common ground. What gets translated and published in English seems to be governed by the pressures of academic publishing and by the mutable logic of the marketplace. Why, for instance, has Joseph Hakohen's dry-as-dust chronicle of Jewish suffering, *Be'emek habakha* (*The Vale of Tears*), been rendered into English, whereas translators have ignored Ibn Verga's eminently readable and enormously influential *Shevet Yehudah*? Conversely, the Holocaust as described in western European languages is deemed more accessible to the English reader than the Holocaust as described in Yiddish, Hebrew and Polish. (How vastly different are the views expressed in these languages will be evident from chapters XV to XIX.) This "tyranny of translation" was something I tried to avoid when making my own choices. One happy result of my decision was that some two thirds of the selections included here have never appeared in English before or have been retranslated for this volume.

When it came to achieving accuracy in translation, I again found myself caught at cross-purposes—on the one hand, wanting to present the most fluent and readable translations; on the other hand, wanting to emphasize the frequently allusive, coded quality of this literature. It was principally through the use and abuse of Scripture, liturgy and rabbinic texts that Jewish writers were able to highlight the spiritual meaning of destruction. Sometimes I emended an existing translation to bring out these allusive or parodic layers; most often, I relied on marginal comments.

As it turned out, therefore, by creating a normative anthology of aboveground traditions of Jewish response to catastrophe, I had achieved a radical thrust of my own. The very idea of treating mass death and modern violence as part of a religious tradition goes against the apocalyptic temper of our times. Language, we are constantly being told, is inadequate to describe the horrors of Nazism. We are warned that the dead are unredeemable and that the search for analogies to Auschwitz is itself obscene (see, most recently, Irving Howe, "Writing and the Holocaust," *The New Republic*, October 27, 1986). Those who insist on lifting the Holocaust out of history and human culture will not take kindly to the notion of a highly conservative literature bridging the historical abyss. Those who deny that the dead have died by conjuring them up as scholars, mystics and saints will be equally revulsed by the internal rage and recrimination that come through in so many of the contemporary records. Even the notion of a *normative* Jewish response has, since Gershom Scholem's pioneering work on Jewish mysticism and radical messianism, come under increasing attack. With the focus of modern Jewish historians still fixed on the behavior of individuals in post-Enlightenment Germany, France and England, the whole area of Jewish *collective* behavior must seem a dangerous anachronism.

Therefore, let apocalyptists and sentimentalists beware: I intend this anthology to revive the dialogue between history and literature and to present the Holocaust within the ongoing saga of a living people.

Chapters XIII and XV, the two longest in this anthology, are thematically linked to the collective aspect of this saga. Together they unlock a central chapter in Jewish cultural history: the use of the shtetl (the Jewish market town in eastern Europe), and later of the Nazi ghetto, to describe Jewish collective behavior in extremis. The literary image of the shtetl, a product of the nineteenth and twentieth centuries, incorporates (and parodies) the concept of *Kehillah Kedoshah*, a "holy community" united under God, with its medieval legacy of Jewish self-government. At the beginning of the twentieth century, when this hallowed concept had been rendered obsolete by the political fragmentation of the Jewish community and by the flood of migration to the West, the literary image of the timeless shtetl arose as a surrogate for the ancient covenantal bond. It was through the shtetl myth that modern writers could reflect most profoundly on what, if anything, would remain of that solidarity following the onslaughts of war and revolution. The shtetl as collective hero (or heroine) is one of the lasting achievements of modern Jewish fiction and six of its major exponents are amply represented here: Abramovitsh, Sholem Aleichem, Weissenberg, Warshawski, Hazaz, and Kipnis.

Then, in one of those bizarre instances of life imitating art, the Nazis turned back the clock of history and reinstituted the medieval ghettos, complete with "self-governing" Jewish councils and, for the first time, Jewish police. As a result, the ghetto residents experienced a profound sense of déjà vu, although every Jew must have known that this was not the kind of autonomy the Jews had ever hoped for. The ghetto became at once a surrogate shtetl and a demonic City of God, the last ingathering of European Jewry before their final destruction. The literary creativity produced under these conditions of terror and enforced autonomy staggers the mind. Logically, the starving, terrorized populace should have been reduced to anarchy, anomie and despair. Instead, the chronicling of destruction—in sermon and song, in story and diary—became for many a means of combating despair. For me, the retrieval of this literature is a sacred task.

Sacred, because the destruction of European Jewry was so total. Sacred, because the literature of the Holocaust will soon be our only link to that terrible ending. Sacred, because that literature, as opposed to the writing *on* the Holocaust that will go on being written for generations to come, is finite. Sacred, because of its insistence on the knowability of the destruction. Sacred, because in the reading of it, one discovers the ultimate value of life.

Yet even that does not mark the end. Indeed, the most controversial aspect of this anthology may be its two endings: chapter XIX illustrates the viability of earlier traditions in responding to the Holocaust, and the final chapter (XX) explores some hidden continuities of response in the nascent State of Israel. I admit that an equally strong case could be made for the breakdown of the popular tradition. Many, indeed, are the signs of dissolution: (1) the all but total loss of Yiddish and of internal Jewish bilingualism (the use of *two* Jewish languages for full self-expression); (2) the attempt to start the clock of Jewish history all over again, beginning in 1948, with the establishment of the State of Israel; (3) the centrality of the works of Elie Wiesel, who stands for the incommunicability of the Holocaust, for the imposition of silence, and for the privileged position of an apostle of the destruction.

Because for many readers of this anthology, Jews and non-Jews alike, Wiesel would seem to embody the very essence of the traditional Jewish response to catastrophe, it may be instructive to dwell a moment on his literary career and compare it with that of a contemporary. Wiesel's *Night* first appeared in Yiddish in 1956 as part of an impressive series of books dedicated to the Holocaust and to the memory of prewar Polish Jewry. The readers of this series, published in Argentina, were already familiar with the landscape of the death camps thanks to another writer, named Mordecai Shtrigler, whose harrowing account of his own experiences had appeared earlier: *Maidanek* (1947) and *In the Death Factories* (1948). Shtrigler was seven years older than Wiesel; otherwise, their lives were almost identical. Both had been talmudic prodigies, products of ultra-orthodox homes. Both ended up in Paris after the war and took up Yiddish and Hebrew journalism. But once Shtrigler had said what he had to say about the Holocaust, he went on to other topics, notably Zionism. Shtrigler never made the Holocaust the touchstone of his writing; he did not even draw on his experiences to invest his other causes with moral authority. There was much for a Jewish intellectual to do after the war, in a period of national rebuilding. Shtrigler's was the normative Jewish response to catastrophe, one that was viable so long as one worked for the benefit of the old constituency. Wiesel, in contrast, became different things for different people: the survivor as Christ figure for those, like François Mauriac, whose own Christian faith was faltering; a priest and prophet for those who would not put their trust in secular officialdom; a traditional storyteller for those who had no other link to the past. For all that, however, Wiesel carried the normative Jewish response to catastrophe one crucial step further: He turned the internal dialogue outward, now demanding a world reckoning for the Jewish blood so many nations had spilled and covered over.

Indeed, what is most novel in the world we now inhabit is that the record of Jewish pain and persecution has gone public—Anatoly-Natan Shcharansky defying his Soviet prosecutors from the dock in Moscow; Arab terrorists gunning down their civilian victims in Istanbul, Paris or Ma'alot; Wiesel and the American Jewish community castagating the President of the United States for the politic decision to honor the German war dead. Increasingly, it is the world media, rather than Jewish-language writers, that shape Jewish self-perception.

Given the amount of attention lavished by the media on the State of Israel, one would have thought that nothing about the Israeli experience had escaped the western eye. Yet even the most perceptive and even-handed reporter fails to see the workings of collective memory beneath the public image of bravado and belligerence. Since 1912, a memorial literature has come into being to commemorate the young men and women who fell in defense of the country. By now, these diaries, memoirs, albums and anthologies number thousands of volumes, most of them housed in a special library in the industrial quarter of Tel Aviv. Israeli high schools have memorial shelves set aside for their own alumni; many adult Israelis keep a few such volumes in their private libraries. They are accorded the same respect as are *sforim*, sacred tomes. These volumes are rarely offered for sale; they are almost never translated. They are eloquent testimony that the War of Independence was only the end of the beginning. Twenty years later, when the generation of 1948 sent its own children into war, it rediscovered the *'Akedah* motif all over again.

Perhaps this anthology will mark the closing of the European canon. Perhaps it will be seen as a last-ditch effort to inspire a cohesiveness that can never be (and probably never was) achieved, now that most Jews no longer speak their own languages, are no longer organized into organic communities and no longer share the same collective myths. Perhaps the whole subject of Jewish catastrophe will someday be rendered arcane, in which case this book may serve as a reminder of how Jews once used the word of God, in infinite permutations, to wrest meaning from a violent world.

As I have already presented my views in *Against the Apocalypse: Responses to Catastrophe in Modern Jewish Culture* (Cambridge, MA: Harvard University Press, 1984), I have limited my chapter introductions to commenting on the relevant texts. Still, one omission needs to be explained. Jewish women play a marginal role in this anthology because, until the modern period, they had little opportunity to contribute to the Literature of Destruction. Appropriate texts from books designed *for* women, such as the prayers for women known as *tkhines*, are derivative of the better-known texts. The Literature of Destruction is a male creation. Female figures inside that creation usually play a symbolic role, like the figure of Rachel weeping for her children or of Zion as a woman in mourning. Even in the modern period, when women took an increasingly active role in Jewish political life, they tended as writers to stay away from this traditionally male domain. (The earliest exception I know of is Rokhl Feigenberg, who wrote several documentary novels and plays about the Ukrainian massacres of 1918 to 1919.) Thus, the emergence, so late in the story, of a distinct woman's voice, such as Rachel Auerbach's (**78**), may suggest how much was lost to this literature because of the unbroken sexual barrier.

This is not to say that women are not featured prominently *within* the literature. They are certainly exploited as victims, as early as in the Mosaic Curses (**1**) and are frequently looked to as martyrological figures, most notably in the Book of Maccabees (**10–11**). In the Midrash on Lamentations (**16**), the fact that Mother Rachel's intercession finally wins the day, after all the Great Men of the Bible failed, is evidence not only that the rabbis were playing to the women in the congregation but also that the plight of women carried special weight in the covenantal scheme of things.

Finally, it is my pleasure to thank all those men and women who made this anthology possible: my host of excellent translators; Dvora Shurman, who edited parts of the manuscript while transcribing it onto diskettes; my colleagues Edward Greenstein, Avraham Holtz, Ivan Marcus and Burt Visotzky, who helped me with difficult references; my students Zvia Ginor, Joram Navon and Robert Wolf; Michael Fishbane, who reviewed the biblical material; Mordkhe Schaechter, who knew the words that no one else knew; Lucjan Dobroszycki, who explained many details about the Warsaw Ghetto; Dina Abramowicz, who helped with the *Oyneg Shabbes* materials; Zippora Weiss, who identified some of the names in Gradowski's chronicle; C. K. Williams, for his extraordinary labor of love; my gracious editor, Sheila F. Segal at The Jewish Publication Society; and, as always, and I hope for years to come, my friend Hillel Schwartz, who collaborated on most of the translations of Yiddish poetry and songs and reviewed every jot and tittle of the manuscript, measuring it against his exacting standard. Robert Wolf prepared the biographies through a research assistantship funded by the Jewish Theological Seminary.

Work on the manuscript was begun during the year I was a Guggenheim Fellow. I also received a generous grant from the Abbell Research Fund of the Jewish Theological Seminary of America. None of the writers included in this anthology was ever so fortunate.

New York City
October 2, 1987
Erev Yom Kippur 5748

I

Gahut/Exile

In the Book of Deuteronomy, the theological nerve center of the Bible, there is a long list of Curses known in Hebrew as the *Tokheḥa*, or Rebuke. It follows and partially echoes a shorter and less detailed list of blessings. (Another version appears in Lev. 26.) So terrible are these Curses, so vengeful is their image of God, that they are chanted quickly and quietly when it comes time to read them. Though the Curses form part of a larger covenantal scheme, every congregant from ancient times to the present is made to feel the elemental force of God's wrath.

The power of these Curses is partially derived from their source: They are kin to the "vassal treaties" used by conquerors in the Ancient Near East to instill fear and loyalty in the tribes and peoples they had subjugated. Both the specific imagery and the seemingly random order of the Curses have their direct parallel in contemporary ancient documents, such as the vassal treaty of Esarhaddon (VTE) from 672 B.C.E. (from Moshe Weinfeld, *Deuteronomy and the Deuteronomic School* [Oxford: Clarendon Press, 1972], pp. 117–18):

Deut. 28:23: The skies above your head shall be copper and the earth under you iron.

VTE 528–31: May they [the gods] make your ground like iron so that no one can plough it. Just as rain does not fall from a brazen heaven, so may rain and dew not come upon your fields and pastures.

Deut. 28:26–35
V. 27: The Lord will strike you with the Egyptian inflammation, with . . . boil-scars, and itch, from which you shall never recover.

VTE 419–20: May Sin [name of a god] . . . the light of heaven and earth clothe you with leprosy;

Vv. 28–9: The Lord will strike you with madness, blindness, and dismay. You shall grope at noon as a blind man gropes in the dark; you shall not prosper in your ventures, but shall be constantly abused and robbed, with none to give help.

VTE 422–4: May Shamash . . . not render you a just judgment; may he deprive you of the sight of your eyes (so that) they will wander about in darkness.

V. 26: Your carcasses shall become food for all the birds of the sky and all the beasts of the earth. . . .

VTE 425–7: May Nintura . . . fell you with his swift arrow; may he fill the steppe with your corpses; may he feed your flesh to the vulture (and) the jackal.

V. 30a: If you pay the bride-price for a wife, another man shall enjoy her.

VTE 428–9: May Venus, the brightest of stars, make your wives lie in your enemy's lap while your eyes look (at them).

V 30b: If you build a house, you shall not live in it. . . . V. 32: Your sons and daughters shall be delivered to another people. . . .

VTE 429–30a: May your sons not be masters in your house.

V. 33: A people you do not know shall eat up the produce of your soil and all your gains. . . .

VTE 430b: May a foreign enemy divide all your goods.

No less striking, however, are the differences between these texts: Whereas the Assyrian treaty formulations emanate from a pantheon of deities, the Mosaic Curses are the work of the Lord; and whereas the former are timeless, the latter contain specific references to earlier, biblical history (vv. 27, 59–60, 68).

Thus, in the earliest texts of the Literature of Destruction, the terror of history is both mitigated and intensified by the revolutionary concept that the Lord is the God of history. For however angry God may be, He never withdraws from the covenant. Destruction and exile spell not abandonment by God but punishment, and if the people return to the ways of the Lord, He will return them not to Egypt but to the Promised Land:

When all these things befall you—the blessing and the curse that I have set before you—and you take them to heart amidst the various nations to which the Lord your God has banished you, and you return to the Lord your God, and you and your children heed His command with all your heart and soul, just as I enjoin upon you this day, then the Lord your God will restore your fortunes and take you back in love. He will bring you together again from all the peoples where the Lord your God has scattered you. (Deut. 30:1–3)

On the other hand, because all national and natural calamities are the work of God's all-powerful will, there is no escape. One's claim to the land, as to life itself, is contingent upon the performance of His commandments.

This, then, is the relentless sequence of punishment that follows immediately upon the sin and the stern lesson of redemption that comes only upon true repentance. Both were driven home to the People of Israel even before they began their perilous journey through history.

1 The Mosaic Curses

(Deut. 28:15–69)

Reversal of Deut. 28:3–8, 10–13.

The sixth plague of Egypt; see Exod. 9:9–10.

Reversal of Deut. 20:5–7; cf. also Isa. 65:21–23 where the same images are invoked as a source of consolation.

¹⁵But if you do not obey the Lord your God to observe faithfully all His commandments and laws which I enjoin upon you this day, all these curses shall come upon you and take effect:

¹⁶Cursed shall you be in the city and cursed shall you be in the country.°

¹⁷Cursed shall be your basket and your kneading bowl.

¹⁸Cursed shall be the issue of your womb and the produce of your soil, the calving of your herd and the lambing of your flock.

¹⁹Cursed shall you be in your comings and cursed shall you be in your goings.

²⁰The Lord will let loose against you calamity, panic, and frustration in all the enterprises you undertake, so that you shall soon be utterly wiped out because of your evildoing in forsaking Me. ²¹The Lord will make pestilence cling to you, until He has put an end to you in the land which you are invading to occupy. ²²The Lord will strike you with consumption, fever, and inflammation, with scorching heat and drought, with blight and mildew; they shall hound you until you perish. ²³The skies above your head shall be copper and the earth under you iron. ²⁴The Lord will make the rain of your land dust, and sand shall drop on you from the sky, until you are wiped out.

²⁵The Lord will put you to rout before your enemies; you shall march out against them by a single road, but flee from them by many roads; and you shall become a horror to all the kingdoms of the earth. ²⁶Your carcasses shall become food for all the birds of the sky and all the beasts of the earth, with none to frighten them off.

²⁷The Lord will strike you with the Egyptian inflammation,° with hemorrhoids, boil-scars, and itch, from which you shall never recover.

²⁸The Lord will strike you with madness, blindness, and dismay. ²⁹You shall grope at noon as a blind man gropes in the dark; you shall not prosper in your ventures, but shall be constantly abused and robbed, with none to give help.

³⁰If you pay the bride-price for a wife, another man shall enjoy her. If you build a house, you shall not live in it. If you plant a vineyard, you shall not harvest it.° ³¹Your ox shall be slaughtered before your eyes, but you shall not eat of it; your ass shall be seized in front of you, and it shall not be returned to you; your flock shall be delivered to your enemies, with none to help you. ³²Your sons and daughters shall be delivered to another people, while you look on; and your eyes shall strain for them constantly, but you shall be helpless. ³³A people you do not know shall eat up the produce of your soil and all your gains; you shall be abused and downtrodden continually, ³⁴until you are driven mad by what your eyes behold. ³⁵The Lord will afflict you at the knees and thighs with a severe inflammation, from which you shall never recover—from the sole of your foot to the crown of your head.

³⁶The Lord will drive you, and the king you have set over you, to a nation unknown to you or your fathers, where you shall serve other gods, of wood and

stone. ³⁷You shall be a consternation, a proverb, and a byword among all the peoples to which the Lord will drive you.

Vv. 38–42: agricultural blights more local in character. Cf. Joel 1:2–8, 17–20 and Amos 4:6–11, where these images are invoked as a source of consolation.

³⁸Though you take much seed out to the field, you shall gather in little, for the locust shall consume it. ³⁹Though you plant vineyards and till them, you shall have no wine to drink or store, for the worm shall devour them. ⁴⁰Though you have olive trees throughout your territory, you shall have no oil for anointment, for your olives shall drop off. ⁴¹Though you beget sons and daughters, they shall not remain with you, for they shall go into captivity. ⁴²The cricket shall take over all the trees and produce of your land.

⁴³The stranger in your midst shall rise above you higher and higher, while you sink lower and lower: ⁴⁴he shall be your creditor, but you shall not be his; he shall be the head and you the tail.

⁴⁵All these curses shall befall you; they shall pursue you and overtake you, until you are wiped out, because you did not heed the Lord your God and keep the commandments and laws that He enjoined upon you. ⁴⁶They shall serve as signs and proofs against you and your offspring for all time. ⁴⁷Because you would not serve the Lord your God in joy and gladness over the abundance of everything, ⁴⁸you shall have to serve—in hunger and thirst, naked and lacking everything—the enemies whom the Lord will let loose against you. He will put an iron yoke upon your neck until He has wiped you out.

Vv. 47–57: curses relating to the enemy's invasion and onslaught.

⁴⁹The Lord will bring a nation against you from afar, from the end of the earth, which will swoop down like the eagle—a nation whose language you do not understand, ⁵⁰a ruthless nation, that will show the old no regard and the young no mercy. ⁵¹It shall devour the offspring of your cattle and the produce of your soil, until you have been wiped out, leaving you nothing of new grain, wine, or oil, of the calving of your herds and the lambing of your flocks, until it has brought you to ruin. ⁵²It shall shut you up in all your towns throughout your land until every mighty, towering wall in which you trust has come down. And when you are shut up in all your towns throughout your land that the Lord your God has given you, ⁵³you shall eat your own issue, the flesh of your sons and daughters that the Lord your God has given you, because of the desperate straits to which your enemy shall reduce you. ⁵⁴He who is most tender and fastidious among you shall be too mean to his brother and the wife of his bosom and the children he has spared ⁵⁵to share with any of them the flesh of the children that he eats, because he has nothing else left as a result of the desperate straits to which your enemy shall reduce you in all your towns. ⁵⁶And she who is most tender and dainty among you, so tender and dainty that she would never venture to set a foot on the ground, shall begrudge the husband of her bosom, and her son and her daughter, ⁵⁷the afterbirth that issues from between her legs and the babies she bears; she shall eat them secretly, because of utter want, in the desperate straits to which your enemy shall reduce you in your towns.

⁵⁸If you fail to observe faithfully all the terms of this Teaching that are written in this book, to reverence this honored and awesome Name, the Lord your God, ⁵⁹the Lord will inflict extraordinary plagues upon you and your offspring, strange and lasting plagues, malignant and chronic diseases. ⁶⁰He will bring back upon you all the sickness of Egypt which you dreaded so, and they shall cling to you. ⁶¹Moreover, the Lord will bring upon you all the other diseases and plagues that

This verse will be invoked throughout The Literature of Destruction to convey a sense of unprecedented calamity.

are not mentioned in this book of Teaching, until you are wiped out.° ⁶²You shall be left a scant few, after having been as numerous as the stars in the skies, because you did not heed the command of the Lord your God. ⁶³And as the Lord once delighted in making you prosperous and many, so will the Lord now delight in causing you to perish and in wiping you out; you shall be torn from the land which you are about to invade and occupy.

⁶⁴The Lord will scatter you among all the peoples from one end of the earth to the other, and there you shall serve other gods, wood and stone, whom neither you nor your ancestors have experienced. ⁶⁵Yet even among those nations you shall find no peace, nor shall your foot find a place to rest. The Lord will give you there an anguished heart and eyes that pine and a despondent spirit. ⁶⁶The life you face shall be precarious; you shall be in terror, night and day, with no assurance of survival. ⁶⁷In the morning you shall say, "If only it were evening!" and in the evening you shall say, "If only it were morning!"—because of what your heart shall dread and your eyes shall see. ⁶⁸The Lord will send you back to Egypt in galleys, by a route which I told you you should not see again.° There you shall offer yourselves for sale to your enemies as male and female slaves, but none will buy.

⁶⁹These are the terms of the covenant which the Lord commanded Moses to conclude with the Israelites in the land of Moab, in addition to the covenant which He had made with them at Horeb.

Deut. 17:16; cf. also Exod. 14:13.

II

Ḥurban/The First Destruction

For Jews, the *Ḥurban,* or Destruction, of Solomon's Temple in 587 B.C.E., has been the primal event of national catastrophe. The categorical response to this calamity evolved over time. As retold many centuries later, the story is rather cut and dried: The Temple was destroyed and the notables of Judah were exiled because King Zedekiah rebelled against the king of Babylon (**2**). In the early aftermath, however, when the shock of the Destruction was still too strong, at a time when neither the official cult nor most of the prophets had made provisions for such disaster, there was great need to mourn but few sources of consolation. Such contemporaneous texts as Psalm 137 (**3**) and the Book of Lamentations (**4**) were almost devoid of hope. Their main goal was to give voice to the enormity of the loss that had just occurred. Through the personification of Jerusalem as a woman in mourning, through the orchestration of individual and collective, male and female, voices and through such mnemonic devices as the alphabetical acrostic, the survivors were able to standardize the sins and the punishments so that both became archetypal in the popular mind.

In blaming the catastrophe on the false prophets who, among their other sins, whitewashed the prevalent injustice (Lam. 2:14), the author(s) of Lamentations sought to vindicate the true prophets of Israel. Indeed, with the collapse of the Temple cult and the abrogation of the monarchy, it was the prophets alone—by virtue of their rhetorical as much as their oracular powers—who could rouse the people from despair.

Given the bleak reality of exile, the prophets had to work overtime to shape a vision of personal, not to speak of communal, restoration. None succeeded more brilliantly than Ezekiel, a prophet and a priest, who arrived in Babylon as a refugee from Jerusalem. With great pathos and extraordinary skill, Ezekiel shaped his prophetic message into images that would remain forever fixed in the Jewish imagination.

With the image of God replacing the heart of stone in each Jew with a heart of flesh (Ezek. 36:26), Ezekiel expressed at least two radical notions at once: first, that nothing less than a creative intervention on the part of God was needed to make possible any fresh hearing or acceptance of His prophecy; second, that a new covenant was about to be forged between God and *every single member* of His people (**5**). Then Ezekiel envisaged a valley of dry bones to proclaim a national liberation from the desolation of exile (**6**).

Most inventive and astonishing was Ezekiel's scenario of a cataclysmic war (**7**). First, he conjured up an image of the Israelites living peaceably, prospering in the mountains of Israel after having rebuilt the dwelling places destroyed in earlier days (Ezek. 38:11–12). Thanks to the prophecies of Jeremiah, however, the people had been forewarned that an enemy would come to destroy them from the north (Ezek. 38:15). Ezekiel now identified that enemy as Gog from the land of Magog, which had not been mentioned since Gen. 10:2. More incredible still, this king named Gog would have to be dragged, kicking and screaming, to do battle with the peaceable Israelites. Once aroused, however, he would quickly turn hungry for blood and plunder. Israel, meanwhile, would be totally defenseless, though elsewhere Ezekiel had described the walled cities of Israel restored. God therefore would have to defeat the enemy single-handedly. So carried away was Ezekiel by this scenario of God vindicating His honor through a spectacular victory that he overlooked an obvious problem: Israel, too, would be destroyed in the ensuing cataclysm! The apocalyptic vision had a logic all its own in which the simultaneous piling up of images of destruction was far more important than maintaining a sequential order.

Some fifty years into the exile (550–539 B.C.E.), another prophet, whom we now call Second Isaiah, arose in Babylon (**8**). (The first had lived two hundred years earlier.) He presented a more lyrical vision of restoration, one in which the gentile nations would acknowledge God's greatness without bloody acts of divine retribution. Rather than generate new myths, Second Isaiah revived the Exodus as the paradigm of renewal, as the historical axis of God's might. In a reordering of biblical history, Second Isaiah dramatized the everlasting power of the Exodus. His "typological" method was stunning in its simplicity: God's former deeds and prophecies—both the great redemptive acts and the prophecies of doom—were proof that He would now restore His people. Whereas once, at the Exodus, God split the mighty waters, now, at the Return, He would irrigate the desert. This time God would act unilaterally, "for His own sake alone," without requiring a prior act of penance on the part of Israel. Furthermore, He would wipe the slate clean, going all the way back to Creation, to Adam's primordial sin in Eden.

Both Ezekiel and Second Isaiah went beyond the Sinaitic formula of sin-retribution-restoration by picturing a universal sovereign who would finally be forced to vindicate His own honor before the nations of the world; a God who now entered into a personal covenant with each member of His people; a deity who was so impatient with Israel's unbroken record of sins that He would start the tally all over again in a magnanimous and utterly miraculous act of national restoration. Without the fervent words of mourning and the brilliant words of consolation, it is doubtful whether any of the Babylonian exiles would ever have returned to begin the arduous task of rebuilding the ruins.

2 The Fall of Jerusalem

(2 Kings 25:1–21) [For alternate accounts, see 2 Chron. 36:11–21 and Jer. 52.]

I.e., Zedekiah's.

Zedekiah rebelled against the king of Babylon. ¹And in the ninth year of his° reign, on the tenth day of the tenth month, Nebuchadnezzar moved against Jerusalem with his whole army. He besieged it; and they built towers against it all around. ²The city continued in a state of siege until the eleventh year of King Zedekiah. ³By the ninth day [of the fourth month] the famine had become acute in the city; there was no food left for the common people.

⁴Then [the wall of] the city was breached. All the soldiers [left the city] by night through the gate between the double walls, which is near the king's garden—

Hoping to escape across the Jordan.

the Chaldeans were all around the city; and [the king] set out for the Arabah.° ⁵But the Chaldean troops pursued the king, and they overtook him in the steppes of Jericho as his entire force left him and scattered. ⁶They captured the king and brought him before the king of Babylon at Riblah; and they put him on trial. ⁷They slaughtered Zedekiah's sons before his eyes; then Zedekiah's eyes were put out. He was chained in bronze fetters and he was brought to Babylon.

⁸On the seventh day of the fifth month—that was the nineteenth year of King Nebuchadnezzar of Babylon—Nebuzaradan, the chief of the guards, an officer of the king of Babylon, came to Jerusalem. ⁹He burned the House of the Lord, the king's palace, and all the houses of Jerusalem; he burned down the house of every notable person. ¹⁰The entire Chaldean force that was with the chief of the guard tore down the walls of Jerusalem on every side. ¹¹The remnant of the people that was left in the city, the defectors who had gone over to the king of Babylon—and the remnant of the population—were taken into exile by Nebuzaradan, the chief of the guards. ¹²But some of the poorest in the land were left by the chief of the guards, to be vinedressers and field hands.

¹³The Chaldeans broke up the bronze columns of the House of the Lord, the stands, and the bronze tank that was in the House of the Lord; and they carried the bronze away to Babylon. ¹⁴They also took all the pails, scrapers, snuffers, ladles, and all the other bronze vessels used in the service. ¹⁵The chief of the guards took whatever was of gold and whatever was of silver: fire pans and sprinkling bowls. ¹⁶The two columns, the one tank, and the stands which Solomon provided for the House of the Lord—all these objects contained bronze beyond weighing. ¹⁷The one column was eighteen cubits high. It had a bronze capital above it; the height of the capital was three cubits, and there was a meshwork [decorated] with pomegranates about the capital, all made of bronze. And the like was true of the other column with its meshwork.

¹⁸The chief of the guards also took Seraiah, the chief priest, Zephaniah, the deputy priest, and the three guardians of the threshold. ¹⁹And from the city he took a eunuch who was in command of the soldiers; five royal privy councillors who were present in the city; the scribe of the army commander, who was in charge of mustering the people of the land; and sixty of the common people who were inside the city. ²⁰Nebuzaradan, the chief of the guards, took them and brought

them to the king of Babylon at Riblah. [21]The king of Babylon had them struck down and put to death at Riblah, in the region of Hamath.

Thus Judah was exiled from its land.

3 By the Rivers of Babylon

(Ps. 137)

By the rivers of Babylon,
    there we sat,
    sat and wept,

I.e., Jerusalem.   as we thought of Zion.°

[2] There on the poplars
    we hung up our lyres,
    [3]   for our captors asked us there for songs,
    our tormentors, for amusement,

Pss. 46, 48, 133.   "Sing us one of the songs of Zion."°

[4] How can we sing a song of the Lord
    on alien soil?

[5] If I forget you, O Jerusalem,
    let my right hand wither;
    [6]   let my tongue stick to my palate
    if I cease to think of you,
    if I do not keep Jerusalem in memory
    even at my happiest hour.

[7] Remember, O Lord, against the Edomites
    the day of Jerusalem's fall;
    how they cried, "Strip her, strip her

Cf. Lam.   to her very foundations!"°
4:21 22. [8] Fair Babylon, you predator,
    a blessing on him who repays you in kind
    what you have inflicted on us;
    [9]   a blessing on him who seizes your babies
    and dashes them against the rocks!

4 Lamentations

1 א Alas!
Lonely sits the city
Once great with people!

She that was great among nations
Is become like a widow;
The princess among states

Introduces the
personification of
Is become a thrall.°

ב ² Bitterly she weeps in the night,

Zion as a woman
Her cheek wet with tears.

in mourning; cf.
There is none to comfort her

vv. 15–17.
Of all her friends.
All her allies have betrayed her;
They have become her foes.

ג ³ Judah has gone into exile
Because of misery and harsh oppression;
When she settled among the nations,
She found no rest;
All her pursuers overtook her
In the narrow places.

ד ⁴ Zion's roads are in mourning,
Empty of festival pilgrims;
All her gates are deserted.
Her priests sigh,
Her maidens are unhappy—
She is utterly disconsolate!

Fulfillment of
ה ⁵ Her enemies are now the masters,°

Deut. 28:44
Her foes are at ease,

(1).
Because the Lord has afflicted her
For her many transgressions;
Her infants have gone into captivity
Before the enemy.

ו ⁶ Gone from Fair Zion are all
That were her glory;
Her leaders were like stags
That found no pasture;
They could only walk feebly
Before the pursuer.

ז ⁷ All the precious things she had
In the days of old
Jerusalem recalled
In her days of woe and sorrow,
When her people fell by enemy hands
With none to help her;
When enemies looked on and gloated
Over her downfall.

ח ⁸ Jerusalem has greatly sinned,
Therefore she is become a mockery.
All who admired her despise her,
For they have seen her disgraced;
And she can only sigh

And shrink back.

ט ⁹ Her uncleanness clings to her skirts.
She gave no thought to her future;
She has sunk appallingly,
With none to comfort her.—

י See, O Lord, my misery;
How the enemy jeers!
¹⁰ The foe has laid hands
On everything dear to her.
She has seen her Sanctuary
Invaded by nations
Which You have denied admission
Into Your community.°

Reversal of Deut. 23:4: "No Ammonite or Moabite shall be admitted into the congregation of the Lord; none of their descendants, even in the tenth generation, shall ever be admitted into the congregation of the Lord."

כ ¹¹ All her inhabitants sigh
As they search for bread;
They have bartered their treasures for food,
To keep themselves alive.—
See, O Lord, and behold,
How abject I have become!

ל ¹² May it never befall you,
All who pass along the road!
Look about and see:
Is there any agony like mine,
Which was dealt out to me
When the Lord afflicted me
On His day of wrath?

First mention of God as a gladiator.

מ ¹³ From above He sent a fire
Down into my bones.
He spread a net for my feet;°
He hurled me backward;
He has left me forlorn,
In constant misery.

נ ¹⁴ The yoke of my offenses is bound fast,
Lashed tight by His hand;
Imposed upon my neck,
It saps my strength;
The Lord has delivered me into the hands
Of those I cannot withstand.

ס ¹⁵ The Lord in my midst has rejected
All my heroes;
He has proclaimed a set time against me
To crush my young men.
As in a press the Lord has trodden
Fair Maiden Judah.

ע ¹⁶ For these things do I weep,
My eyes flow with tears:
Far from me is any comforter

Who might revive my spirit;
My children are forlorn,
For the foe has prevailed.
פ ¹⁷ Zion spreads out her hands,
She has no one to comfort her;
The Lord has summoned against Jacob
His enemies all about him;
Jerusalem has become among them
A thing unclean.

צ ¹⁸ The Lord is in the right,
For I have disobeyed Him.
Hear, all you peoples,
And behold my agony:
My maidens and my youths
Have gone into captivity!
ק ¹⁹I cried out to my friends,
But they played me false.
My priests and my elders
Have perished in the city
As they searched for food
To keep themselves alive.
ר ²⁰ See, O Lord, the distress I am in!
My heart is in anguish,
I know how wrong I was
To disobey.
Outside the sword deals death;
Indoors, the plague.
ש ²¹ When they heard how I was sighing,
There was none to comfort me;
All my foes heard of my plight and exulted.
For it is Your doing:
Oh, bring on them what befell me,
And let them become like me!
ת ²² Let all their wrongdoing come before You,
And deal with them
As You have dealt with me
For all my transgressions.
For my sighs are many,
And my heart is sick.

2   כ ¹¹ My eyes are spent with tears,
My heart is in tumult,
My being melts away
Over the ruin of my poor people,
As babes and sucklings languish
In the squares of the city.
ל ¹² They keep asking their mothers,

"Where is bread and wine?"
As they languish like battle-wounded
In the squares of the town,
As their life runs out
In their mothers' bosoms.

מ ¹³ What can I compare or liken
To you, O Fair Jerusalem?
What can I match with you to console you,
O Fair Maiden Zion?
For your ruin is vast as the sea:
Who can heal you?

נ ¹⁴ Your seers prophesied to you
Delusion and folly.
They did not expose your iniquity
So as to restore your fortunes,
But prophesied to you oracles
Of delusion and deception.°

Therefore, the Destruction vindicates the true prophets.

3 א I am the man whom the Lord has shepherded with
The rod of His wrath;
² Me He drove on and on

Parody of Ps. 23.

In unrelieved darkness;°
³ On none but me He brings down His hand
Again and again, without cease.

ב ⁴ He has worn away my flesh and skin;
He has shattered my bones.
⁵ All around me He has built
Misery and hardship;
⁶ He has made me dwell in darkness,
Like those long dead.

ג ⁷ He has walled me in and I cannot break out;
He has weighed me down with chains.
⁸ And when I cry and plead,
He shuts out my prayer;
⁹ He has walled in my ways with hewn blocks,
He has made my paths a maze.

ד ¹⁰ He is a lurking bear to me,
A lion in hiding;
¹¹ He has forced me off my way and mangled me,
He has left me numb.
¹² He has bent His bow and made me
The target of His arrows:

ה ¹³ He has shot into my vitals
The shafts of His quiver.
¹⁴ I have become a laughingstock to all people,
The butt of their gibes all day long.
¹⁵ He has filled me with bitterness,

Sated me with wormwood.

ו ¹⁶ He has broken my teeth on gravel,
Has ground me into the dust.
¹⁷ My life was bereft of peace,
I forgot what happiness was.
¹⁸ I thought my strength and hope
Had perished before the Lord.

ז ¹⁹ To recall my distress and my misery
Was wormwood and poison;
²⁰ Whenever I thought of them,
I was bowed low.

²¹ But this do I call to mind,
Therefore I have hope:

ח ²² The kindness of the Lord has not ended,
His mercies are not spent.
²³ They are renewed every morning—
Ample is Your grace!
²⁴ "The Lord is my portion," I say with full heart;
Therefore will I hope in Him.

ט ²⁵ The Lord is good to those who trust in Him,
To the one who seeks Him;
²⁶ It is good to wait patiently
Till rescue comes from the Lord.
²⁷ It is good for a man, when young,
To bear a yoke;

י ²⁸ Let him sit alone and be patient,
When He has laid it upon him.
²⁹ Let him put his mouth to the dust—
There may yet be hope.
³⁰ Let him offer his cheek to the smiter;
Let him be surfeited with mockery.

כ ³¹ For the Lord does not
Reject forever,
³² But first afflicts, then pardons
In His abundant kindness.°
³³ For He does not willfully bring grief
Or affliction to man,

ל ³⁴ Crushing under His feet
All the prisoners of the earth.
³⁵ To deny a man his rights
In the presence of the Most High,
³⁶ To wrong a man in his cause—
This the Lord does not choose.

מ ³⁷ Whose decree was ever fulfilled,
Unless the Lord willed it?
³⁸ Is it not at the word of the Most High,
That weal and woe befall?

Verses 31–39 articulate the covenantal theology.

³⁹ Of what shall a living man complain?
Each one of his own sins!

ג ⁴⁰ Let us search and examine our ways,
And turn back to the Lord;
⁴¹ Let us lift up our hearts rather than our hands
To God in heaven:
⁴² We have transgressed and rebelled,
And You have not forgiven.
ס ⁴³ You have clothed Yourself in anger and pursued us,
You have slain without pity.
⁴⁴ You have screened Yourself off with a cloud,
That no prayer may pass through.
⁴⁵ You have made us filth and refuse
In the midst of the peoples.
ע ⁴⁶ All our enemies loudly
Rail against us.
⁴⁷ Panic and pitfall are our lot,
Death and destruction.
⁴⁸ My eyes shed streams of water
Over the ruin of my poor people.

פ ⁴⁹ My eyes shall flow without cease,
Without respite,
⁵⁰ Until the Lord looks down
And beholds from heaven.
⁵¹ My eyes have brought me grief
Over all the maidens of my city.
צ ⁵² My foes have snared me like a bird,
Without any cause.
⁵³ They have ended my life in a pit
And cast stones at me.
⁵⁴ Waters flowed over my head;
I said: I am lost!

ק ⁵⁵ I have called on Your name, O Lord,
From the depths of the Pit.
⁵⁶ Hear my plea;
Do not shut Your ear
To my groan, to my cry!
⁵⁷ You have ever drawn nigh when I called You;
You have said, "Do not fear!"
ר ⁵⁸ You championed my cause, O Lord,
You have redeemed my life.
⁵⁹ You have seen, O Lord, the wrong done me;
Oh, vindicate my right!
⁶⁰ You have seen all their malice,
All their designs against me;
ש ⁶¹ You have heard, O Lord, their taunts,

All their designs against me,
⁶² The mouthings and pratings of my adversaries
Against me all day long.
⁶³ See how, at their ease or at work,
I am the butt of their gibes.
ת ⁶⁴ Give them, O Lord, their deserts
According to their deeds.
⁶⁵ Give them anguish of heart;
Your curse be upon them!
⁶⁶ Oh, pursue them in wrath and destroy them
From under the heavens of the Lord!

5 God Will Vindicate His Honor

(Ezek. 36:16—38)

Literally, Son of man.

¹⁶ The word of the Lord came to me: ¹⁷ O Mortal,° when the House of Israel dwelt on their own soil, they defiled it with their ways and their deeds; their ways were in My sight like the uncleanness of a menstruous woman. ¹⁸ So I poured out My wrath on them for the blood which they shed upon their land, and for the fetishes with which they defiled it. ¹⁹ I scattered them among the nations, and they were dispersed through the countries: I punished them in accordance with their ways and their deeds.

²⁰ But when they came to those nations, they caused My holy name to be profaned, in that it was said of them, ''These are the people of the Lord, yet they had to leave His land.'' ²¹ Therefore I am concerned for My holy name, which the House of Israel have caused to be profaned among the nations to which they have come.

²² Say to the House of Israel: Thus said the Lord God: Not for your sake will I act, O House of Israel, but for My holy name, which you have caused to be profaned among the nations to which you have come. ²³ I will sanctify My great name which has been profaned among the nations—among whom you have caused it to be profaned. And the nations shall know that I am the Lord—declares the Lord God—when I manifest My holiness before their eyes through you. ²⁴ I will take you from among the nations and gather you from all the countries, and I will bring you back to your own land. ²⁵ I will sprinkle clean water upon you, and you shall be clean: I will cleanse you from all your uncleanness and from all your fetishes. ²⁶ And I will give you a new heart and put a new spirit into you: I will remove the heart of stone from your body and give you a heart of flesh; ²⁷ and I will put My spirit into you. Thus I will cause you to follow My laws and faithfully to observe My rules. ²⁸ Then you shall dwell in the land which I gave to your fathers, and you shall be My people and I will be your God.

²⁹ And when I have delivered you from all your uncleanness, I will summon the grain and make it abundant, and I will not bring famine upon you. ³⁰ I will make the fruit of your trees and the crops of your fields abundant, so that you shall never again be humiliated before the nations because of famine. ³¹ Then you shall recall your evil ways and your base conduct, and you shall loathe yourselves for your iniquities and your abhorrent practices. ³² Not for your sake will I act— declares the Lord God—take good note! Be ashamed and humiliated because of your ways, O House of Israel!

³³ Thus said the Lord God: When I have cleansed you of all your iniquities, I will people your settlements, and the ruined places shall be rebuilt; ³⁴ and the desolate land, after lying waste in the sight of every passerby, shall again be tilled. ³⁵ And men shall say, "That land, once desolate, has become like the garden of Eden; and the cities, once ruined, desolate, and ravaged, are now populated and fortified." ³⁶ And the nations that are left around you shall know that I the Lord have rebuilt the ravaged places and replanted the desolate land. I the Lord have spoken and will act.

³⁷ Thus said the Lord God: Moreover, in this I will respond to the House of Israel and act for their sake: I will multiply their people like sheep. ³⁸ As Jerusalem is filled with sacrificial sheep during her festivals, so shall the ruined cities be filled with flocks of people. And they shall know that I am the Lord.

6 The Valley of the Dry Bones

(Ezek. 37)

Vv. 1–10: the vision.

The hand of the Lord came upon me. He took me out by the spirit of the Lord and set me down in the valley. It was full of bones. ² He led me all around them; there were very many of them spread over the valley, and they were very dry. ³ He said to me, "O mortal, can these bones live again?" I replied, "O Lord God, only You know." ⁴ And He said to me, "Prophesy over these bones and say to them: O dry bones, hear the word of the Lord! ⁵ Thus said the Lord God to these bones: I will cause breath to enter you and you shall live again. ⁶ I will lay sinews upon you, and cover you with flesh, and form skin over you. And I will put breath into you, and you shall live again. And you shall know that I am the Lord!"

⁷ I prophesied as I had been commanded. And while I was prophesying, suddenly there was a sound of rattling, and the bones came together, bone to matching bone. ⁸ I looked, and there were sinews on them, and flesh had grown, and skin had formed over them; but there was no breath in them. ⁹ Then He said to me, "Prophesy to the breath, prophesy, O mortal! Say to the breath: Thus said the Lord God: Come, O breath, from the four winds, and breathe into these slain, that they may live again." ¹⁰ I prophesied as He commanded me. The breath entered them, and they came to life and stood up on their feet, a vast multitude.

Vv. 11–14: the
interpretation.

¹¹ And He said to me: O mortal, these bones are the whole House of Israel. They say, "Our bones are dried up, our hope is gone; we are doomed." ¹² Prophesy, therefore, and say to them: Thus said the Lord God: I am going to open your graves and lift you out of the graves, O My people, and bring you to the land of Israel. ¹³ You shall know, O My people, that I am the Lord when I have opened your graves and lifted you out of your graves. ¹⁴ I will put My breath into you and you shall live again, and I will set you upon your own soil. Then you shall know that I the Lord have spoken and have acted—declares the Lord.

Vv. 15–28: the
reunification of
Israel and Judah.
Vv. 16–18: the
symbolic act.

¹⁵ The word of the Lord came to me: ¹⁶ And you, O mortal, take a stick and write on it, "Of Judah and the Israelites associated with him"; and take another stick and write on it, "Of Joseph—the stick of Ephraim—and all the House of Israel associated with him." ¹⁷ Bring them close to each other, so that they become one stick, joined together in your hand. ¹⁸ And when any of your people ask you, "Won't you tell us what these actions of yours mean?" ¹⁹ answer them, "Thus said the Lord God: I am going to take the stick of Joseph—which is in the hand of Ephraim—and of the tribes of Israel associated with him, and I will place the stick of Judah upon it and make them into one stick; they shall be joined in My hand." ²⁰ You shall hold up before their eyes the sticks which you have inscribed, ²¹ and you shall declare to them: Thus said the Lord God: I am going to take the Israelite people from among the nations they have gone to, and gather them from every quarter, and bring them to their own land. ²² I will make them a single nation in the land, on the hills of Israel, and one king shall be king of them all. Never again shall they be two nations, and never again shall they be divided into two kingdoms. ²³ Nor shall they ever again defile themselves by their fetishes and their abhorrent things, and by their other transgressions. I will save them in all their settlements where they sinned, and I will cleanse them. Then they shall be My people, and I will be their God.

Vv. 19–22: the
interpretation.

²⁴ My servant David shall be king over them; there shall be one shepherd for all of them. They shall follow My rules and faithfully obey My laws. ²⁵ Thus they shall remain in the land which I gave to My servant Jacob and in which your fathers dwelt; they and their children and their children's children shall dwell there forever, with My servant David as their prince for all time. ²⁶ I will make a covenant of friendship with them—it shall be an everlasting covenant with them— I will establish them and multiply them, and I will place My sanctuary among them forever. ²⁷ My Presence shall rest over them; I will be their God and they shall be My people.° ²⁸ And when My sanctuary abides among them forever, the nations shall know that I the Lord do sanctify Israel.

Vv. 24–28: The
repetition of forever
and for all time
stresses the
irreversibility of
the new
dispensation.

Echoes Lev.
26:11–12.

7 The Battle of Gog

(Ezek. 38)

Vv. 1–9: first
announcement of
the summoning of
Gog.

The word of the Lord came to me: ² O mortal, turn your face toward Gog of the land of Magog, the chief prince of Meshech and Tubal. Prophesy against him ³ and say: Thus said the Lord God: Lo, I am coming to deal with you, O Gog, chief

I.e., Gog has to be dragged by violence like some wild beast toward the goal willed by the Lord.

prince of Meshech and Tubal! [4] I will turn you around and put hooks in your jaws,° and lead you out with all your army, horses, and horsemen, all of them clothed in splendor, a vast assembly, all of them with bucklers and shields, wielding swords. [5] Among them shall be Persia, Cush, and Put, everyone with shield and helmet; [6] Gomer and all its cohorts, Beth-togarmah [in] the remotest parts of the north and all its cohorts—the many peoples with you. [7] Be ready, prepare yourselves, you and all the battalions mustered about you, and hold yourself in reserve for Me. [8] After a long time you shall be summoned; in the distant future you shall march against the land [of a people] restored from the sword, gathered from the midst of many peoples—against the mountains of Israel, which have long lain desolate—[a people] liberated from the nations, and now all dwelling secure. [9] You shall advance, coming like a storm; you shall be like a cloud covering the earth, you and all your cohorts, and the many peoples with you.

Vv. 10–13: Gog's own plans.

[10] Thus said the Lord God: On that day, a thought will occur to you, and you will conceive a wicked design. [11] You will say, "I will invade a land of open towns, I will fall upon a tranquil people living secure, all of them living in unwalled towns and lacking bars and gates, [12] in order to take spoil and seize plunder"—to turn your hand against repopulated wastes, and against a people gathered from among nations, acquiring livestock and possessions, living at the center of the earth.° [13] Sheba and Dedan, and the merchants and all the magnates of Tarshish will say to you, "Have you come to take spoil? Is it to seize plunder that you assembled your hordes—to carry off silver and gold, to make off with livestock and goods, to gather an immense booty?"

I.e., the People of Israel have a unique importance for the nations of the world.

[14] Therefore prophesy, O mortal, and say to Gog: Thus said the Lord God: Surely, on that day, when My people Israel are living secure, you will rouse yourself [15] and you will come from your home in the farthest north,° you and many peoples with you—all of them mounted on horses, a vast horde, a mighty army—[16] and you will advance upon My people Israel, like a cloud covering the earth. This shall happen on that distant day: I will bring you to My land, that the nations may know Me when, before their eyes, I manifest My holiness through you, O Gog!

Vv. 14–16: additional proclamation of God's purpose. Cf. Jer. 1:13–14. What was just seen as a future event is now brought to fruition by the word of the prophet.
Vv. 17–23: The destruction of Gog. Refers to Jeremiah's early prophecies.

[17] Thus said the Lord God: Why, you are the one I spoke of in ancient days through My servants, the prophets of Israel, who prophesied for years in those days that I would bring you against them!°

[18] On that day, when Gog sets forth on the soil of Israel—declares the Lord God—My raging anger shall flare up. [19] For I have decreed in my indignation and in My blazing wrath: On that day, a terrible earthquake shall befall the land of Israel. [20] The fish of the sea, the birds of the sky, the beasts of the field, all creeping things that move on the ground, and every human being on earth shall quake before Me. Mountains shall be overthrown, cliffs shall topple, and every wall shall crumble to the ground. [21] I will then summon the sword against him throughout My mountains—declares the Lord God—and every man's sword shall be turned against his brother. [22] I will punish him with pestilence and with bloodshed; and I will pour torrential rain, hailstones, and sulfurous fire upon him and his hordes and the many peoples with him. [23] Thus will I manifest My greatness and My holiness, and make Myself known in the sight of many nations. And they shall know that I am the Lord.

8 God's Former and Future Deeds

(Isa. 43)

But now thus said the Lord
Who created you, O Jacob,
Who formed you, O Israel:
Fear not, for I will redeem you;
I have singled you out by name,
You are Mine.
² When you pass through water,
I will be with you;
Through streams,
They shall not overwhelm you.
When you walk through fire,
You shall not be scorched;
Through flame,
It shall not burn you.
³ For I the Lord am your God,
The Holy One of Israel, your Savior.
I give Egypt as a ransom for you,

Whatever price is necessary to redeem Israel, God is prepared to pay.

Ethiopia and Saba in exchange for you.°
⁴ Because you are precious to Me,
And honored, and I love you,
I give men in exchange for you
And peoples in your stead.

Future deeds.

⁵ Fear not, for I am with you:
I will bring your folk from the East,
Will gather you out of the West;
⁶ I will say to the North, "Give back!"
And to the South, "Do not withhold!
Bring My sons from afar,
And My daughters from the end of the earth—
⁷ All who are linked to My name,
Whom I have created,
Formed, and made for My glory—
⁸ Setting free that people,
Blind though it has eyes
And deaf though it has ears."

⁹ All the nations assemble as one,
The peoples gather.
Who among them declared this,
Foretold to us the things that have happened?
Let them produce their witnesses and be vindicated,

Emet, here used as a technical term to denote that these prophecies can be relied upon. I.e., your life experience is the proof.

Veta'aminu li echoes the emet of v. 9.

That men, hearing them, may say, "It is true!"°
¹⁰ My witnesses are *you*°
—declares the Lord—
My servant, whom I have chosen.
To the end that they may take thought,
And believe in Me,°
And understand that I am He:
Before Me no god was formed,
And after Me none shall exist—
¹¹ None but Me, the Lord.
Beside Me, none can grant triumph.
¹² I alone foretold the deliverance
And I brought it to pass;
I announced it,
And no strange god was among you.
So you are My witnesses
—declares the Lord—
And I am God.
¹³ Ever since day was, I am He;
None can deliver from My hand.
When I act, who can reverse it?

Vv. 14–21:Poems of promise.

Of her prison.

¹⁴ Thus said the Lord,
Your Redeemer, the Holy One of Israel:
For your sake I send to Babylon;
I will bring down all [her] bars,°
And the Chaldeans shall raise their voice in lamentations.
¹⁵ I am your Holy One, the Lord,
Your King, the Creator of Israel.

Former deeds: the Exodus.

Mayim 'azim echoes the Song of the Sea, Exod. 15:10.

Because the new wonder will supersede the old.

Future deeds:

¹⁶ Thus said the Lord,
Who made a road through the sea
And a path through mighty waters,°
¹⁷ Who destroyed chariots and horses,
And all the mighty host—
They lay down to rise no more,
They were extinguished, quenched like a wick:
¹⁸ Do not recall what happened of old,
Or ponder what happened of yore!°
¹⁹ I am about to do something new;
Even now it shall come to pass,
Suddenly you shall perceive it:
I will make a road through the wilderness
And paths in the desert.
²⁰ The wild beasts shall honor Me,
Jackals and ostriches,
For I provide water in the wilderness,
Rivers in the desert,

Cf. Exod. 17:1–7.

To give drink to My chosen people,°

Allusion to Song of the Sea, Exod. 15:13, 16.

²¹ The people I formed for Myself°
That they might declare my praise.

²² But you have not worshipped Me, O Jacob,
That you should be weary of Me, O Israel.°

You never tested or called upon Me in the past, so why do you weary Me now? Cf. Jer. 2:4–8.

²³ You have not brought Me your sheep for burnt offerings,
Nor honored Me with your sacrifices.
I have not burdened you with meal offerings,
Nor wearied you about frankincense.
²⁴ You have not bought Me fragrant reed with money,
Nor sated me with the fat of your sacrifices.
Instead, you have burdened Me with your sins,
You have wearied Me with your iniquities.

Unilaterally, without requiring Israel to repent.

²⁵ It is I, I who—for My own sake°—
Wipe your transgressions away
And remember your sins no more.

In a technical sense: Help me remember if you have anything to justify yourself. Adam in the Garden of Eden. Ambiguous. A reference to Israel. Herem, used in a cultic sense.

²⁶ Help me remember!°
Let us join in argument,
Tell your version,
That you may be vindicated.
²⁷ Your earliest ancestor sinned,°
And your spokesmen° transgressed against Me.
²⁸ So I profaned the holy princes;°
I abandoned Jacob to proscription°
And Israel to mockery.

III

Kiddush Hashem/ Martyrdom

Few concepts in Judaism have undergone so profound a shift in meaning as *Kiddush Hashem.* When Ezekiel addressed his fellow exiles in Babylon (**5**), he prophesied that the Lord would sanctify His own Name because of the repeated *Hillul,* or Desecration, of His Name on the part of Israel. During the next five centuries, however, the whole equation was reversed: The agent of desecration became the gentile rulers, and the ones to enforce God's sanctity became the Jews. The revolutionary impact of Hellenism probably had as much to do with this turnabout as the effects of prolonged subjugation under the (Greek-speaking) Seleucids. For while the earliest tales of monotheists suffering martyrdom were told about exemplary Jews who defied the evil decrees of Antiochus IV, the record of their martyrdom was kept in Greek by a hellenized Jew named Jason of Cyrene (**9–10**). Moreover, the heroes and heroine of his story all behaved and spoke in a manner strikingly similar to that in Plato's account of the trial and death of Socrates (see Jonathan Goldstein's translation of 2 Maccabees in the Anchor Bible series [Garden City, NY: Doubleday & Company, 1983], pp. 282, 304.)

The term *Kiddush Hashem* appears nowhere in Jason's chronicle. The first martyr, Eleazar the priest (**9**), is described as a pietist who will not violate the Torah, but neither will he rebel against the king. The implication of his parting speech is that God knows his innocence and will punish his tormentors—a thoroughly traditional stance. The death of the next martyrs, the nameless mother and her seven sons (**10**), is given a somewhat broader religious significance. In their opening and closing speeches, they invoke Moses' great hymn (Deut. 32) as a prophetic text, explicitly, in the opening exhortation from Deuteronomy 32:36, and implicitly, in the youngest son's prayer for the fulfillment of the Deuteronomic promise of revenge and resurrection. Indeed, the belief in resurrection is the focal point of all their speeches and rests upon another passage imbedded in the same hymn: ". . . I [God] deal death and give life; I wounded and I will heal . . ." (Deut. 32:39). This explains the mother's philosphical excursus in the very midst of her sons' torture: She must prove that resurrection is *more conceivable* than the Creation and than human reproduction. When all is said and done, however, this First Family of martyrs hallows God's Name for rather personal reasons. Though their deaths may ultimately purchase mercy for all of Israel and will presumably pave the way for the military victories yet to come, their immediate goal is to gain forgiveness for their *own* sins so that they will merit a new life after death. As for Antiochus, he is nothing but a tool of God, the rod of His wrath, as were the kings of Babylon and Assyria before him.

A more coded way of developing the same analogy (and a method favored by apocalyptists) was to cast Antiochus in the role of Nebuchadnezzar and to place the hopes for deliverance in the mouth of a hero who lived generations before. Thus, the Book of Daniel came into being, and it alone, among all the works of Jewish apocalyptic literature, was preserved in the biblical canon. The part of this difficult book that enjoyed the greatest popularity was the story of three young men who were forced to hallow the wrong king by bowing down to his idol (**11**). Though their confidence in God was less than total, they did not succumb. When the young men emerged intact from the fiery furnace, the real point of the story became clear: God had sanctified His own Name by performing a miracle. The human drama was but part of God's self-dramatization—exactly as in earlier biblical prophecy.

The importance of these stories can hardly be overstated. These stories, rather than any legal tradition, set up the martyrological response to catastrophe. And Jews were by no means their only audience. The story of the mother and her sons became the cornerstone of Christian martyrology, and their purported grave—in Antioch—became a pilgrimage site for Christians. Meanwhile, though the rabbis relegated both the First and Second Books of the Maccabees to apocryphal status, the nameless Hellenistic widow turned up in rabbinic sources as the well-known martyr named Miriam (B. Gittin 57b; Midrash on Lamentations), and the Greek setting was updated to reflect the more recent Roman subjugation.

Now that the desecrators became the Greek or Roman rulers and the sanctifiers became the Jews, a second major shift occurred: the assumption of innocence on the part of the martyrs. Hananiah, Mishael and Azariah were rescued by God precisely because they were blameless; otherwise God would never have staged a miracle through them to proclaim His greatness to the world (*Kiddush Hashem*). Men like Pappus and Julianus, on the other hand (**12**, par. 15), who saw themselves as marked to die by the heavens, would never presume to be rescued by God. The only thing they could show for their deaths was that they, like the heroes of 2 Maccabees, knew how to challenge their executioners. Now the "real" Pappus and Julianus had indeed been sinners, at least in rabbinic eyes, for they had tried to lead a rebellion against Rome. But how could one explain the execution and death of the major rabbis of their generation under the draconian rule of Hadrian (135–138 c.e.)?

In the martyrological stories collected in Tractate "Mourning" (usually given the euphemistic title "Celebrations"), the confusion between arrogance and innocence is quite apparent. When Rabban Simeon and Rabbi Ishmael are about to be executed, one finds fault with the other. Perhaps, argues the first, his friend had been derelict in his rabbinic duties (**12**, par. 8). Is it not arrogant to think that one is blameless in the eyes of God? The eulogy delivered by their colleagues, however, makes a very different point: that Rabban Simeon and Rabbi Ishmael died because they were innocent, the death of the righteous being the first sign of impending evil. In the next story this point is made explicit. "Rabbi Akiba has been executed *only* as a sign," proclaim his surviving colleagues. He himself was completely clear of all wrongdoing.

Presumably, then, Akiba's blameless death would establish the new principle: that God had a special relationship with spiritual men such that their innocence need not be seen as arrogance. But in the very next story Rabbi Hanina is seized for "heresy" and is sentenced to the stake. What this heresy might have been is explained elsewhere in the Talmud (B. 'Avodah Zarah 18a): He publicly taught how to pronounce the ineffable Name of God. And so even he is being punished by God through the agency of the Romans.

The third stage in the evolution of the idea of martyrdom comes to be associated with the name of Rabbi Akiba. In the brilliantly told legend of Rabbi Akiba's martyrdom (**13**), Akiba is credited with accepting suffering with love as the highest expression of piety. The angels then push for an additional lesson: that dying directly through the hand of God is the reward for unconditional self-sacrifice. The ultimate reward, as announced directly from heaven, is that Akiba has merited eternal life in the world to come.

With all these components in place—a legacy of historical precedents, a firm theological rationale and a body of exquisite stories—one would expect a full-blown martyrological tradition to have taken hold in Judaism. Yet this was not the case, both because Christianity usurped and greatly expanded the Jewish martyrological sources and because rabbinic Judaism was much more concerned with regulating the internal life of the Jews than dictating their political behavior (and martyrdom was the supreme act of public piety). If the rabbis collected and preserved these stories at all, it was not to promote martyrdom but simply to show how the pious should face death and how eulogies should be delivered. Similarly, the Akiba legend was imbedded within a larger talmudic discussion of the requirement to bless God for the evil in the same way as for the good.

Just how reluctant the rabbis were to promote the martyrological tradition can be seen from the legal discussion recorded in the Babylonian Talmud (Sanhedrin 74a–b). Here the rabbis strictly limited the applicability of *Kiddush Hashem* to a "time of [religious] persecution"; otherwise, Jews were required to sacrifice their lives only if forced to commit idolatry, adultery or murder. Even idolatry, it was argued, could be practiced under duress, so long as it was not performed in public (defined as the presence of ten other Jews). Try as they might, however, the rabbis could not shake themselves free of the martyrological tradition, perhaps because it was so dear to the hearts of the Jewish laity, who loved nothing better than a good story.

9 Eleazar the Priest

(2 Maccabees 6)

In 167 B.C.E.
An Athenian
expert on the
Jews.

The Samaritan
temple.

Either practice or
petition, in
reference to the
Samaritans.

Either admitting
to practicing
Judaism or reciting
the Shema^c.

6 ¹ Not long thereafter,° the king sent Geron the Athenian°° to compel the Jews to depart from their ancestral laws and to cease living by the laws of God. ² He was also to defile both the temple in Jerusalem and the temple on Mount Gerizim° and to proclaim the former to be the temple of Zeus Olympios and the latter (in accordance with the . . .° of the inhabitants of the place) to be the temple of Zeus Xenios. ³ The execution of the wicked project brought suffering and indignation to all. ⁴ The gentiles filled the temple with debauchery and revelry, as they lolled with prostitutes and had intercourse with women in the sacred courts and also brought forbidden things inside. ⁵ The altar was filled with prohibited offerings excluded by the laws. ⁶ No one was allowed to observe the Sabbath or to keep the traditional festivals or even to confess he was a Jew.° On the monthly birthday of the king Jews were cruelly compelled to partake of the meat of pagan sacrifices. When a festival of Dionysus was celebrated, they were forced to put on wreaths of ivy and march in the procession in honor of the god. ⁸ A decree was published in the neighboring Greek cities, on the proposal of the citizens of Ptolemais, that they proceed against the Jews in the same manner and compel them to partake of the meat of pagan sacrifices ⁹ and that they butcher those Jews who refused to go over to the Greek way of life.

It was clear that a time of trouble had come. ¹⁰ Two women were brought to trial for having circumcised their children. Their babies were hanged from their breasts, and the women were paraded publicly through the city and hurled down from the walls.° ¹¹ Other Jews hastily assembled nearby in the caves to observe the Sabbath in secret. On being denounced to Philip they were all burned to death because they refrained from defending themselves, out of respect for the holiest of days.

Vv. 10–31:
Martyrs are
classified according
to the principles
for which they
gave up their lives.
In Jerusalem,
hurling from a
height may have
been a preferred
method for
executing women.

¹² I beg the readers of my book not to be disheartened by the calamities but to bear in mind that chastisements come not in order to destroy our race but in order to teach it. ¹³ If the ungodly among us are not left long to themselves but speedily incur punishment, it is a sign of God's great goodness to us. ¹⁴ With the other nations the Lord waits patiently, staying their punishment until they reach the full measure of their sins. Quite otherwise is His decree for us, ¹⁵ in order that He should not have to punish us after we have come to the complete measure of our sins. ¹⁶ Consequently, God never lets His mercy depart from us. Rather, though He teaches us by calamity, He never deserts His people. ¹⁷ Let this be enough as a reminder to my readers. Now we must quickly return to our story.

¹⁸ One of the leading sages was Eleazar, a very handsome man, now of advanced age. Repeatedly they tried to force him to open his mouth and eat pork. ¹⁹⁻²⁰ He, however, preferred death with glory to life with defilement. He spat, as one should when standing fast to resist the temptation to let love of life bring him to taste what religion forbids, and of his own free will he began to march to the whipping drum. ²¹ The meat was part of a sacrifice, and to eat it was a

violation of the Torah. The men appointed to compel him to do so had known Eleazar for many years. They took him aside and in secret urged him to fetch meat which he was permitted to eat, prepared by himself, and pretend that he was eating the meat from the sacrifice as ordered by the king, [22] for in so doing he would escape death and would receive from them the kindness due an old friend. [23] Eleazar came to a lofty resolution, one worthy of his years, worthy of the authority of old age, worthy of his conspicuous well-earned white hair, and of his way of life, which had been exemplary from childhood. More important, it was worthy of the sacred legislation established by God. Eleazar showed himself consistent: he told them to send him off to the netherworld without delay. [24–25] "Such pretense is unworthy of my advanced age. My pretense for the sake of a brief transitory span of life would cause many of the younger generation to think that Eleazar at the age of ninety had gone over to the gentile way of life, and so they, too, would go astray because of me, and I would earn the defilement and besmirching of my old age. [26] Indeed, even if I should be released for the present from punishment at the hands of men, alive or dead I would not escape the hands of the Almighty. [27] Therefore, if I now bravely give up my life, I shall show myself worthy of my old age, [28] as I leave to the young a noble example of how to go eagerly and nobly to die a beautiful death in the defense of our revered and sacred laws." Having spoken those words, he went straight to the torture instrument.

[29] What he had just said turned the men who shortly before had shown him friendship into enemies, because they viewed it as perversity. [30] As he was about to expire under the lashing, he groaned forth, "The Lord, Who possesses sacred knowledge, perceives that, though able to escape death, in my body I submit to cruel torment under the lash, and that yet in my soul I am glad to suffer it, out of reverence for Him." [31] So he died, leaving his death as an example of nobility and as a precedent of valor to be remembered not only by the young but by the multitudes of his nation.

10 The Mother and Her Seven Sons

(2 Maccabees 7)

7   [1] At that time seven brothers, too, with their mother were arrested, and the king tortured them with whips and thongs in an effort to force them to partake of pork contrary to the prohibitions of the Torah. [2] One of them as spokesman for all said, "What do you expect to learn from questioning us? We are ready to die rather than violate the laws of our forefathers." [3] The king, enraged, ordered griddles and cauldrons to be heated red-hot. [4] As soon as they were red-hot, the king gave the order to cut out the tongue of the one who had acted as spokesman and scalp him and cut off his hands and feet while his brothers and his mother look on. [5] The body was now completely helpless, but the king ordered that he be

brought, still breathing, to the fire and fried. As the odor of frying began to spread widely, the brothers and their mother exhorted one another to die nobly, saying, [6] "The Lord God looks on and truly is relenting concerning us, as Moses declared in the Song Which Confronts as a Witness:° 'And He will relent concerning His servants.' "°

[7] When the first of the brothers had passed away in this manner, they brought the second to be wantonly tortured, and after ripping off his scalp by the hair, they asked him, "Will you eat before your body is torn limb from limb?" [8] He answered in the language of his forefathers, "No!" And so, he, too, in turn was tortured. [9] With his last breath he said, "You, you fiend, are making us depart from our present life, but the King of the universe will resurrect us, who die for the sake of His laws, to a new eternal life."

[10] After him, the third was subjected to wanton torture. On demand, he promptly put forth his tongue and cheerfully held out his hands. [11] His words were noble: "I received these from Heaven, and for the sake of His laws I hold them cheap. From Him I hope to receive them back." [12] The king himself and his men were astonished at the spirit of the young man who set torments at naught.

[13] When he, too, had passed away, they tormented the fourth with similar tortures. [14] At the point of death, he said, "Better it is to pass away from among men while looking forward in hope to the fulfillment of God's promises that we will be resurrected by Him, for you shall have no resurrection unto life."°

[15] Forthwith they brought the fifth and began to torture him. [16] Gazing at the king, he said, "You wield power among men and work your will, but you are mortal. Think not that God has abandoned our people. [17] You wait and see His great might when He puts you and your seed to the torture!"°

[18] Thereafter they brought the sixth, and as he was about to die, he said, "Do not indulge in vain delusions! Through our own fault we are subjected to these sufferings, because we have sinned against our God. They pass belief! [19] You, however, think not to escape unpunished after having dared to contend with God!"

[20] Most remarkable was the mother. She deserves to be held in glorious memory, for she looked on as her seven sons perished in the course of a single day and bore it bravely because of her hopes in the Lord. [21] Each one of them in turn she exhorted in the language of their forefathers. Filled with noble resolution, she took her womanly thoughts and fired them with a manly spirit, as she told them, [22] "I do not know how you came to be in my womb. It was not I who gave you spirit and life, nor did I determine the order of the composition of the elements of each of you.° [23] Surely, then, the Creator of the universe, Who shaped man's coming into being and fathomed the fashioning of everything,° with mercy will restore spirit and life to you, inasmuch as you now hold your very selves cheap for the sake of His laws."

[24] Antiochus sensed he was being treated with contempt. The reproachful voice roused his hostility. Nevertheless, there was still the youngest, and Antiochus not only addressed appeals to him again and again, he even made repeated promises on oath to make him rich and prosperous and admit him to the Order of the King's Friends and entrust important functions to him, provided he would depart from the ways of his forefathers.

[25] When the youth paid him no heed, the king called upon the mother and urged

Title of the song derived from Deut. 31:21.
Quoted verse from Deut. 32:36, which ends ". . . when He sees that their might is gone."

Based on Dan. 12:2.
Vv. 16–19 allude to Dan. 8:24–25.

Antiochus IV suffered a wasting illness and had a miserable death. His son was executed.

Paraphrase of Eccles. 11:5.
Eccles. 8:17.

her to give the lad the advice that would save his life. ²⁶ In response to his insistent urgings, she consented to convince her son. ²⁷ She bent over him, and with scorn for the cruel tyrant, she said in the language of her forefathers, "My son, have pity on me who carried you in my womb for nine months and nursed you for three years and reared you and brought you to your present age. ²⁸ I ask you, my child, to look upon the heaven and the earth and to contemplate all therein. I ask you to understand that it was not after they existed that God fashioned them, and in the same manner the human race comes to be.° ²⁹ Do not fear this executioner, but be worthy of your brothers and accept death, so that in His mercy I may recover you along with your brothers."

The mother's argument for creation ex nihilo justifies the belief in resurrection.

³⁰ She was still speaking the last of these words when the youth said, "What are you waiting for? I refuse to obey the king's command; I heed the command of the Torah given through Moses to our forefathers. ³¹ You, who have devised all evil against the Hebrews, shall surely not escape the hands of God. ³² As for us, we are suffering for our own sins. ³³ If our living Lord has for a short time become angry with us in order to chastise and teach us, He will again become reconciled with His servants. ³⁴ You, however, you impious wretch, most bloodstained of all men, do not soar with vain delusions as false hopes° give you the insolence to lift your hand against the children of Heaven. ³⁵ You have not yet escaped the judgment of Almighty God, Who watches over us. ³⁶ My brothers, having borne pain for a short while, now have inherited eternal life under the terms of God's covenant,° whereas you shall suffer through the judgment of God the just punishment for your arrogance. ³⁷ I, following my brothers' example, give up my body and soul for the sake of the laws of our forefathers, praying to God that he speedily have mercy upon our nation. May you through being afflicted and scourged come to acknowledge that He alone is God. ³⁸ With me and my brothers may the Almighty put an end to the rightful anger inflicted upon our entire people." ³⁹ Enraged, the king, in his resentment over being mocked, treated him still worse than the others. ⁴⁰ So he perished undefiled, having put his trust entirely in the Lord. ⁴¹ And last, after her sons, died the mother. ⁴² Let us end here the stories of compulsion by extreme torture to partake of the meat of pagan sacrifices.

Allusion to Isa. 14:12–14: Antiochus is the latter-day king of Babylon and Assyria. Probably a reference to Isa. 55:2–3: ". . . Hearken, and you shall be revived. And I will make with you an everlasting covenant. . . ."

11 Hananiah, Mishael and Azariah

(Dan. 1:1–7; 3:13–33)

1   In the third year of the reign of King Jehoiakim of Judah, King Nebuchadnezzar of Babylon came to Jerusalem and laid siege to it. ² The Lord delivered King Jehoiakim of Judah into his power, together with some of the vessels of the House of God, and he brought them to the land of Shinar to the house of his god; he deposited the vessels in the treasury of his god. ³ Then the king ordered Ashpenaz, his chief officer, to bring some Israelites of royal descent and of the nobility—

[4] youths without blemish, handsome, proficient in all wisdom, knowledgeable and intelligent, and capable of serving in the royal palace—and teach them the writings and the language of the Chaldeans. [5] The king allotted daily rations to them from the king's food and from the wine he drank. They were to be educated for three years, at the end of which they were to enter the king's service.

[6] Among them were the Judahites Daniel, Hananiah, Mishael, and Azariah. [7] The chief officer gave them new names; he named Daniel Belteshazzar, Hananiah Shadrach, Mishael Meshach, and Azariah Abed-nego. . . .

3   [13] Then Nebuchadnezzar, in raging fury, ordered Shadrach, Meshach, and Abed-nego to be brought; so those men were brought before the king. [14] Nebuchadnezzar spoke to them and said, "Is it true, Shadrach, Meshach, and Abed-nego, that you do not serve my god or worship the statue of gold that I have set up? [15] Now if you are ready to fall down and worship the statue that I have made when you hear the sound of the horn, pipe, zither, lyre, psaltery, and bagpipe, and all other types of instruments, [well and good]; but if you will not worship, you shall at once be thrown into a burning fiery furnace, and what god is there that can save you from my power?" [16] Shadrach, Meshach, and Abed-nego said in reply to the king, "O Nebuchadnezzar, we have no need to answer you in this matter, [17] for if so it must be, our God whom we serve is able to save us from the burning fiery furnace, and He will save us from your power, O king. [18] But even if He does not, be it known to you, O king, that we will not serve your god or worship the statue of gold that you have set up."

[19] Nebuchadnezzar was so filled with rage at Shadrach, Meshach, and Abed-nego that his visage was distorted, and he gave an order to heat up the furnace to seven times its usual heat. [20] He commanded some of the strongest men of his army to bind Shadrach, Meshach, and Abed-nego, and to throw them into the burning fiery furnace. [21] So these men, in their shirts, trousers, hats, and other garments, were bound and thrown into the burning fiery furnace. [22] Because the king's order was urgent, and the furnace was heated to excess, a tongue of flame killed the men who carried up Shadrach, Meshach, and Abed-nego. [23] But those three men, Shadrach, Meshach, and Abed-nego, dropped, bound, into the burning fiery furnace.

[24] Then King Nebuchadnezzar was astonished and, rising in haste, addressed his companions, saying, "Did we not throw three men, bound, into the fire?" They spoke in reply, "Surely, O king." [25] He answered, "But I see four men walking about unbound and unharmed in the fire and the fourth looks like a divine being." [26] Nebuchadnezzar then approached the hatch of the burning fiery furnace and called, "Shadrach, Meshach, Abed-nego, servants of the Most High God, come out!" So Shadrach, Meshach, and Abed-nego came out of the fire. [27] The satraps, the prefects, the governors, and the royal companions gathered around to look at those men, on whose bodies the fire had had no effect, the hair of whose heads had not been singed, whose shirts looked no different, to whom not even the odor of fire clung. [28] Nebuchadnezzar spoke up and said, "Blessed be the God of Shadrach, Meshach, and Abed-nego, who sent His angel to save His servants who, trusting in Him, flouted the king's decree at the risk of their lives rather than serve or worship any god but their own God. [29] I hereby give an order that [anyone of] any people or nation of whatever language who blasphemes the God of Shadrach,

Meshach, and Abed-nego shall be torn limb from limb, and his house confiscated, for there is no other God who is able to save in this way."

³⁰ Thereupon the king promoted Shadrach, Meshach, and Abed-nego in the province of Babylon.

³¹ "King Nebuchadnezzar to all people and nations of every language that inhabit the whole earth: May your well-being abound! ³² The signs and wonders that the Most High God has worked for me I am pleased to relate. ³³ How great are His signs; how mighty His wonders! His kingdom is an everlasting kingdom, and His dominion endures throughout the generations."

12 Rabbinic Martyrs

(from Tractate "Mourning," chap. 8)

8   When Rabban Simeon and Rabbi Ishmael were seized and sentenced to be executed, Rabbi Ishmael wept.

"Son of the noble," said Rabban Simeon to him, "you are but two steps away from the bosom of the righteous,° and you weep?"

"Is it because we are about to be killed that I weep?" he replied. "I weep because we are being executed like murderers and like Sabbath breakers."°

Rabban Simeon then said to him: "Perhaps while you were dining or while you were sleeping, a woman came to ask for a ruling about her menses, her defilement, or her cleanness, and the servant told her, 'He is sleeping.' Whereas the Torah states: *If thou afflict them in any wise. . .* (Exod. 22:22). And what is written after this? *My wrath shall wax hot, and I will kill you with the sword. . .* (ibid. 22:23)."°

Some say: "It was Rabban Simeon who wept, and it was Rabbi Ishmael who spoke to him in this way."

When the news reached Rabbi Akiba and Rabbi Judah ben Baba that Rabban Simeon and Rabbi Ishmael had been killed, they rose, girded their loins with sackcloth, rent their clothes, and said: "O Israel, our brethren, hear us! If good has been destined to come to the world, the first to receive it would have been Rabban Simeon and Rabbi Ishmael. But now that it has been revealed to Him° who spoke and the world came into being, that dire punishments are ultimately destined for the world, they, therefore, have been taken from the world."°

The righteous perisheth, and no man layeth it to heart, and godly men are taken away, none considering that the righteous is taken away from the evil to come (Isa. 57:1).

And it also says: *He entereth into peace, they rest in their beds, each one that walketh in his uprightness* (ibid. 57:2).

9   When the news that Rabbi Akiba had been executed in Caesarea reached Rabbi Judah ben Betera° and Rabbi Hanina ben Tardion, they rose, girded their loins with sackcloth, rent their clothes, and said: "O Israel, our brethren, hear us! Rabbi

Martyrological term.

Mishnah Sanhedrin, 7:4, 9:1.

Rabban Simeon suggests that Rabbi Ishmael was perhaps inadvertently derelict in his rabbinic duties.

I.e., God foresaw the consequences.

They were punished not for their sins but as a warning to the world.

Variants read Judah ben Baba.

Akiba has been executed not because he was suspected of robbery or because he did not put all his strength into the study of Torah. Rabbi Akiba has been executed only as a sign. For it is written: *Thus shall Ezekiel be unto you a sign, according to all that he hath done shall ye do; when this cometh, then shall ye know that I am the Lord God* (Ezek. 24:24)."

"In a short time from now no place in the Land of Israel will be found where bodies of the slain have not been cast. For it is written: *Speak: Thus sayeth the Lord—And the carcasses of men fall as dung upon the open field* (Jer. 9:21)."

Not long thereafter, it is said, Roman armies attacked and put the entire world into chaos. Within twelve months the councils of Judah came to an end. For it is written: *Tremble, ye women that are at ease. Be troubled, ye confident ones* (Isa. 32:11). *Ye women that are at ease* refers to the councils. *Ye confident ones* refers to the circuses.

It is said that twelve months had not gone by before everything that had been foretold happened to them.

12 When Rabbi Hanina ben Tardion was seized for heresy, they sentenced him to the stake; his wife, to the sword; and his daughter, to life in a pavilion of harlots.

"To what did they condemn the poor woman?" said he to them.

"To the sword," they replied. At this point he cited these verses for her: *The Lord is righteous in all His ways, and gracious in all His works* (Ps. 145:17). *The Rock, His work is perfect, for all His ways are justice* (Deut. 32:4).

"To what did they condemn the master?" said she to them.

"To the stake," they replied. At this point she cited this verse for him: *Great in council, and mighty in work, whose eyes are upon all the ways of sons of men, to give every one according to his way, and according to the fruit of his doing* (Jer. 32:19)

At the time of his execution, they wrapped him in a Torah Scroll and set fire to him and to the Torah Scroll, while his daughter, throwing herself at his feet, screamed: "Is this the Torah, and this its reward?"

A fire not fanned by man is the fire of Gehenna.

I.e., the scroll is mere flesh, but its spirit is indestructible. See 11.

"My daughter," he said to her, "if it is for me that you are weeping and for me that you throw yourself to the ground, it is better that a fire made by man should consume me, rather than a fire not made by man.° For it is written: *A fire not blown by man shall consume him* (Job 20:26). But if it is for the Torah Scroll that you are weeping, lo, the Torah is fire, and fire cannot consume fire. Behold, the letters are flying into the air, and only the parchment itself is burning."°

"His" eyes presumably refers to Trajan, whose head, according to another variant, was thereupon bashed in by deputies who arrived from Rome.

15 Now when Trajan executed Pappus and Julianus, his brother, in Laodicea, he said to them: "If you are from the nation of Hananiah, Mishael, and Azariah,° let your God come and rescue you the way He rescued them."

They said to him: "Hananiah, Mishael, and Azariah were perfectly righteous men, and Nebuchadnezzar was a proper king. Because of him it was fitting that a miracle should be performed. But you are a wicked king, and for you it is not fitting that a miracle should be performed. As for us, we have incurred the death penalty before the Lord. If you do not kill us, the Lord has many executioners, the Lord has many destroyers: many bears, many tigers, many lions, that can fall upon us and kill us. The Holy One, blessed be He, delivered us into your hands, however, only because He intends to exact payment for our blood at your hands."

Nevertheless Trajan ordered them killed. It is said that they hardly stirred from there before they saw his eyes being gouged out.°

13 Rabbi Akiba

(B. Berakhot)

I.e., Rome.

Our Rabbis taught: Once the wicked Government° issued a decree forbidding the Jews to study and practice the Torah. Pappus ben Judah came and found Rabbi Akiba publicly bringing gatherings together and occupying himself with the Torah. He said to him: "Akiba, are you not afraid of the the Government?" He replied: "I will explain to you with a parable. A fox was once walking alongside of a river, and he saw fishes going in swarms from one place to another. He said to them: From what are you fleeing? They replied: From the nets cast for us by men. He said to them: Would you like to come up on to the dry land so that you and I can live together in the way that my ancestors lived with your ancestors? They replied: Art thou the one that they call the cleverest of animals? Thou art not clever but foolish. If we are afraid in the element in which we live, how much more in the element in which we would die! So it is with us. If such is our condition when we sit and study the Torah, of which it is written, *For that is thy life and the length*

Deut. 30:20.

of thy days,° if we go and neglect it how much worse off we shall be!"

It is related that soon afterwards Rabbi Akiba was arrested and thrown into prison, and Pappus ben Judah was also arrested and imprisoned next to him. He said to him: "Pappus, who brought you here?" He replied: "Happy are you, Rabbi Akiba, that you have been seized for busying yourself with the Torah! Alas for Pappus who has been seized for busying himself with idle things!"

It is related that when Rabbi Akiba was taken out for execution, it was the hour for the recital of the *Shema'*, and while they combed his flesh with iron combs, he directed his mind to accepting upon himself the kingship of heaven

I.e., reciting the Shema' (Deut. 6:4–9).
Deut. 6:5.
"One" in Hear, O Israel. . . .

with love.° His disciples said to him: "Our teacher, even to this point?" He said to them: "All my days I have been troubled by this verse, '*And thou shalt love the Lord thy God with all thy soul*,'° [which I interpret,] 'even if He takes thy soul.' Now that I have the opportunity shall I not fulfill it?" He prolonged the word *ehad*° until he expired while saying it.

The ministering angels said before the Holy One, blessed be He: "Such Torah, and such a reward? [He should have been] *from them that die by Thy hand, O*

Ps. 17:14.
Ibid.
Oracular voice.

Lord."° He replied to them: "*Their portion is in life*."°

A *bat kol*° went forth and proclaimed, "Happy art thou, Rabbi Akiba, that thou art destined for the life of the world to come."

IV

Rabbinic Theodicy in Midrash

After the destruction of Herod's Temple in 70 c.e., the touchstone of reality became, once and for all, God's word as recorded in Scripture and as interpreted by the rabbis. Whereas the practical application of the Torah to everyday life was debated among the scholars in the houses of study, its moral application was the subject of rabbinic sermons delivered in the new synagogues. Because sermons and Torah readings were linked to the cycle of Sabbaths and Festivals, it should come as no surprise that the Midrash on Lamentations should contain some of the most vivid and theologically radical rabbinic responses to the trauma of history, since it was a fifth- to seventh-century distillation of hundreds of sermons given during the summer months, when the destruction of the Temple is commemorated. In this Midrash the rabbis spoke openly of the pathos of God. They imagined Him weeping and finding no solace, calling on all the patriarchs to help Him mourn and they, in turn, taking up the defense of Israel (**14**). Soon the entire heavenly host, a gallery of patriarchs, matriarchs and prophets, and even the letters of the alphabet were drawn into the act (**15–16**). History was personalized. Abstract concepts of guilt-retribution-restoration were translated into dramatic vignettes. And the time-bound chronicle of Lamentations was systematically reread as a time-less document of Jewish suffering.

The simplest way of personalizing history was to fill in some of the missing characters: the Roman villains Vespasian, Hadrian and Trajan (**17–18**) and the victims, usually drawn from the Jewish aristocracy (**19**). One biblical prooftext, " . . . For these things do I weep . . . " (Lam. 1:16), could cover these and many other tales of gratuitous cruelty and exemplary heroism.

One of the central functions of Midrash was, in fact, to fill in the gaps in the biblical account, and especially in Lamentations proper, where nothing was so glaring as the almost total absence of God. The rabbis' favorite way of implicating God without touching the text was through royal parables in which the king (patterned, ironically enough, on the Roman emperor) was an obvious stand-in for the divine ruler. Through a subtle parable of a king and his *ketubbah* (**20**), the rabbis sought to prove that the Torah bound God to Israel even when He absented Himself without cause. And the words of that *ketubbah*, if properly interpreted, were still the ultimate and only proof of God's mercy—even in defiance of the physical ruins (**21**). (For more on this Midrash, see Alan Mintz, *Hurban: Responses to Catastrophe in Hebrew Literature* [New York: Columbia University Press 1984], chap. 2.)

The rabbis cut history down to manageable size by disassembling the Great Destruction into archetypes and moral lessons and by coding the memory of catastrophe into the liturgical calendar. Once ritual practice and the conceptual guidelines were in place, they left ample room for further elaboration. The *payyetanim*, or liturgical poets, adapted the themes and methods of the Midrash for synagogue use and their *kinot* for Tish'a b'Av became a veritable anthology of Jewish liturgical responses to catastrophe (**27**). Meanwhile, at the end of the Byzantine period in Palestine, a group of mystics drew together all the disparate sources on martyrdom to create a coherent Midrash of their own (**22**). In this radical retelling, rabbis, scribes and high priests who had lived at different times were imagined as dying together at the hands of an archetypal tyrant. The real drama, moreover, was shifted from this world to the next as the story's hero, Rabbi Ishmael the High Priest, ascended to heaven to argue his case before God. There, in heaven, he was shown an altar where the souls of the righteous were sacrificed daily. He learned that the Ten Martyrs, including himself, were to die for the purification of Israel as a vicarious atonement. This doctrine, so strikingly close to that in Christianity, could have been conveyed only through mystical fancy and elaborate storytelling. A motley of rabbinic heroes was recast into a mythical group of intercessors whose memory was invoked at the most solemn moment in the calendar—on Yom Kippur morning, in the *Seder Ha'avodah* section of the liturgy.

14 Jeremiah and the Patriarchs

(Midrash on Lamentations)

Isa. 22:12.

The messianic era.

Isa. 2:3.

Hos. 5:15.

Archangel who
defends the
interests of Israel.

Jer. 13:17.

See Gen. 17:14.

Another interpretation of *And in that day did the Lord, the God of hosts, call to weeping and to lamentation*:° at the time when the Holy One, blessed be He, sought to destroy the Temple, He said, "So long as I am in its midst, the nations of the world will not touch it; but I will close My eyes so as not to see it, and swear that I will not attach Myself to it until the time of the end° arrives." Then came the enemy and destroyed it. Forthwith the Holy One, blessed be He, swore by His right hand and placed it behind Him. So it is written, *He hath drawn back His right hand from before the enemy.*° At that time the enemy entered the Temple and burnt it. When it was burnt, the Holy One, blessed be He, said, "I no longer have a dwelling-place in this land; I will withdraw My *Shekhinah* from it and ascend to My former habitation; so it is written, *I will go and return to My place, till they acknowledge their guilt, and seek My face.*"°

At that time the Holy One, blessed be He, wept and said, "Woe is Me! What have I done? I caused My *Shekhinah* to dwell below on earth for the sake of Israel; but now that they have sinned, I have returned to My former habitation. Heaven forfend that I become a laughter to the nations and a byword to human beings!" At that time Metatron° came, fell upon his face, and spake before the Holy One, blessed be He: "Sovereign of the Universe, let me weep, but do Thou not weep." He replied to him, "If thou lettest Me not weep now, I will repair to a place which thou hast not permission to enter, and will weep there," as it is said, *But if ye will not hear it, My soul shall weep in secret for pride.*°

The Holy One, blessed be He, said to the Ministering Angels, "Come, let us go together and see what the enemy has done in My house." Forthwith the Holy One, blessed be He, and the Ministering Angels went, Jeremiah leading the way. When the Holy One, blessed be He, saw the Temple, He said, "Certainly this is My house and this is My resting-place into which enemies have come, and they have done with it whatever they wished." At that time the Holy One, blessed be He, wept and said, "Woe is Me for My house! My children, where are you? My priests, where are you? My lovers, where are you? What shall I do with you, seeing that I warned you but you did not repent?" The Holy One, blessed be He, said to Jeremiah, "I am now like a man who had an only son, for whom he prepared a marriage-canopy, but he died under it. Feelest thou no anguish for Me and My children? Go, summon Abraham, Isaac and Jacob, and Moses from their sepulchres, for they know how to weep." He spake before Him: "Sovereign of the Universe, I know not where Moses is buried." The Holy One, blessed be He, replied to him: "Go, stand by the bank of the Jordan, and raise thy voice and call out, 'Son of Amram, son of Amram, arise and behold thy flock which enemies have devoured.'"

There and then Jeremiah went to the cave of Machpelah and said to the patriarchs of the world:° "Arise, for the time has come when your presence is required before the Holy One, blessed be He." They said to him, "For what purpose?" He

began to speak before the Holy One, blessed be He, saying, "Sovereign of the Universe, when I was a hundred years old Thou gavest me a son, and when he reached years of discretion and was a young man of thirty-seven, Thou didst order me, "Offer him as a sacrifice before Me." I steeled my heart against him and I had no compassion on him; but I myself bound him. Wilt Thou not remember this on my behalf and have mercy on My children?" Isaac began, saying, "Sovereign of the Universe, when my father said to me, *'God will provide Himself the lamb for a burnt-offering, my son,'*° I raised no objection to the carrying out of Thy words, and I willingly let myself be bound on the top of the altar and stretched out my neck beneath the knife. Wilt Thou not remember this on my behalf and have mercy on my children?" Jacob began, saying, "Sovereign of the Universe, did I not stay twenty years in Laban's house? And when I left his house, the wicked Esau met me and sought to kill my children, and I risked my life on their behalf.° Now they are delivered into the hands of their enemies like sheep to the slaughter, after I reared them like chickens and endured for their sakes the pain of child-rearing. For throughout most of my days I experienced great trouble on their account. Now, wilt Thou not remember this on my behalf to have mercy on my children?" Moses began, saying, "Sovereign of the Universe, was I not a faithful shepherd to Israel for forty years, running before them like a horse in the desert? When the time arrived for them to enter the promised land, Thou didst decree against me that my bones should fall in the wilderness. Now that they are exiled, Thou hast sent for me to lament and weep over them. This bears out the popular proverb, 'I derive no benefit from my master's good fortune, but suffer from his bad fortune.' "

Gen. 22:8. According to Gen. Rabba 56:4, Isaac knew that he was to be sacrificed.

Based on Gen. 33:2.

16 Moses and Rachel

(Midrash on Lamentations)

Thereupon Moses said to Jeremiah, "Walk before me, so that I may go and bring them in and see who dares to touch them." Jeremiah replied, "It is impossible for me to walk along the road because of the slain."° He said to him, "Nevertheless let us go." Forthwith Moses went, Jeremiah leading the way, until they arrived at the rivers of Babylon. When the exiles beheld Moses, they said one to another, "The son of Amram has come from his grave to redeem us from the hand of our adversaries." A *Bat Kol* issued forth and announced, "This is a decree from Me."° Moses at once said to them, "My children, it is not possible to take you back [now] since it is so decreed, but the All-present will soon cause you to return"; and then he left them. Thereupon they lifted their voices in loud weeping, until the sound of it ascended above. So it is written, *By the rivers of Babylon, there we sat down, yea, we wept.*°

When Moses came to the patriarchs of the world, they asked him, "What did the enemy do to our children?" He replied, "Some of them they killed; the hands

As a priest he could not have physical contact with the dead.

That they remain in captivity.

Ps. 137 (3).

of others they bound behind their backs; others were fettered with iron chains; others were stripped naked; others died by the way and their carcasses were food for the birds of the heaven and the beasts of earth; and others were exposed to the sun, hungry and thirsty." Forthwith they all began to weep and utter lamentations: "Woe for what has befallen our children! How have you become like orphans without a father! How you had to sleep at noon during summer without clothing and covering! How you walked over rocks and pebbles stripped of shoes and without sandals! How were you laden with heavy bundles of sand! How were your hands bound behind your backs! How were you unable to swallow the spittle in your mouths!"

Moses lifted up his voice, saying, "Cursed be thou sun! Why didst thou not become dark when the enemy entered the Temple!" The sun replied, "By thy life, O Moses, faithful shepherd, how could I become dark when they did not permit me and did not leave me alone? But they beat me with sixty whips of fire and said to me, 'Go, pour forth thy light.' " Moses again lifted up his voice, saying, "Woe to thy brilliance, O Temple, how has it become obscured! Woe that its time has come to be destroyed, for the edifice to be reduced to ruins, for school children to be massacred, and their parents to go into exile and captivity and perish by the sword!" Moses again lifted up his voice, saying, "O captors, I charge you, if you kill, do not kill with a cruel death; do not make a complete extermination; do not slay a son in the presence of his father nor a daughter in the presence of her mother; because a time will come when the Lord of heaven will exact a reckoning of you." But the wicked Chaldeans refused to comply with his request, and they brought a son into the presence of his mother, and said to his father, "Arise, slay him!" His mother wept, and her tears fell upon him, and his father hung his head.

He further spake before Him: "Sovereign of the Universe, Thou hast written in Thy Torah, *Whether it be a cow or ewe, ye shall not kill it and its young both in one day;*° but have they not killed many, many mothers and sons, and Thou art silent!" At that moment, the matriarch Rachel broke forth into speech before the Holy One, blessed be He, and said, "Sovereign of the Universe, it is revealed before Thee that Thy servant Jacob loved me exceedingly and toiled for my father on my behalf seven years. When those seven years were completed and the time arrived for my marriage with my husband, my father planned to substitute another for me to wed my husband for the sake of my sister. It was very hard for me, because the plot was known to me and I disclosed it to my husband; and I gave him a sign whereby he could distinguish between me and my sister, so that my father should not be able to make the substitution. After that I relented, suppressed my desire, and had pity upon my sister that she should not be exposed to shame. In the evening they substituted my sister for me with my husband, and I delivered over to my sister all the signs which I had arranged with my husband so that he should think that she was Rachel. More than that, I went beneath the bed upon which he lay with my sister; and when he spoke to her she remained silent and I made all the replies in order that he should not recognize my sister's voice. I did her a kindness, was not jealous of her, and did not expose her to shame. And if I, a creature of flesh and blood, formed of dust and ashes, was not envious of my rival and did not expose her to shame and contempt, why shouldest Thou, a King Who liveth eternally and art merciful, be jealous of idolatry in which there is no reality, and

Lev. 22:28.

exile my children and let them be slain by the sword, and their enemies have done with them as they wished!"

Forthwith the mercy of the Holy One, blessed be He, was stirred, and He said, "For thy sake, Rachel, I will restore Israel to their place." And so it is written, *Thus saith the Lord: A voice is heard in Ramah, lamentation and bitter weeping, Rachel weeping for her children; she refuseth to be comforted for her children, because they are* Jer. 31:15.   *not.*°

This is followed by, *Thus saith the Lord: Refrain thy voice from weeping, and thine eyes from tears; for thy work shall be rewarded . . . and there is hope for thy future,* Jer. 31:16-17.   *saith the Lord; and thy children shall return to their own border.*°

17 The Fate of the Survivors

(Midrash on Lamentations)

Lam. 1:16.
9–79 C.E.; *Roman emperor* 70–79.

For these things do I weep.° Vespasian°° filled three ships with eminent men of Jerusalem to place them in Roman brothels. They stood up and said, "Is it not enough that we have provoked Him to anger in His Sanctuary, that we shall do so also outside the Holy Land [by consenting to immoral practices]!" They said to the women [of Jerusalem who were in the ships], "Do you desire such a fate?" They replied, "We do not." They then said, "If women who are formed by nature for coition refuse, how much more must we [refuse to be used for an unnatural purpose]! Think you, if we throw ourselves into the sea, will we enter into the life of the world to come?" Immediately the Holy One, blessed be He, enlightened their eyes with this verse, *The Lord said: "I will bring them back from Bashan, I will* Ps. 68:23   *bring them back from the depths of the sea."*° "I will bring them back from Bashan," i.e., I will bring them back from between the teeth of (*bein shinnei*) lions; "*I will*

I will bring them back to life at the resurrection. Ps. 44:21.

Ps. 44:23.

Ps. 44:22.

bring them back from the depths of the sea" is to be understood literally.°

The first company [in the first ship] stood up and said, "*Surely we had not forgotten the name of our God, or spread forth our hands to a strange god,*"° and they threw themselves into the sea. The second company stood up and said, "*Nay, but for Thy sake are we killed all the day,*"° and they threw themselves into the sea. The third company stood up and said, "*Would not God search this out? For He knoweth the secrets of the heart,*"° and they threw themselves into the sea. Then the Holy Spirit cried out, "For these things do I weep."

Hadrian the accursed set up three garrisons, one in Emmaus, a second in Kefar
Strategic points in preventing Jews from escaping the country. Lekatia, and the third in Bethel of Judea.° He said, "Whoever attempts to escape from one of them will be captured in another and vice versa." He also sent out heralds to announce, "Wherever there is a Jew, let him come forth, because the king wishes to give him an assurance [of safety]." The heralds proclaimed this to them and so captured the Jews. That is what is written. *And Ephraim is become like*
Hos. 7:11.   *a silly dove, without understanding.*° [The heralds taunted the captured Jews with

these words,] "Instead of trying to restore the dead to life, pray that those still living shall not be seized." Those who understood [the ruse] did not come out [from their hiding places], but those who did not understand it all gathered in the valley of Beth Rimmon.° [Hadrian] said to the captain of his army, "By the time I eat this slice of cake and the leg of this fowl, I must be able to look for a single person of all these [alive] without finding him." He immediately surrounded them with his legions and slaughtered them, so that their blood streamed [to the coast and stained the sea] as far as Cyprus. Then the Holy Spirit cried out, "For these things do I weep."

Cf. 2 Kings 5:18.

Those Jews who were hidden [in the caves] devoured the flesh of their slain brethren. Every day one of them ventured forth and brought the corpses to them which they ate. One day they said, "Let one of us go, and if he finds anything let him bring it and we shall have to eat." On going out he found the slain body of his father which he took and buried and marked the spot. He returned and reported that he had found nothing. They said, "Let somebody else go, and if he find anything let him bring it and we shall have to eat." When he went out he followed the scent; and on making a search, he discovered the body [of the man who had been buried]. He brought it to them and they ate it. After they had eaten it, they asked him, "From where did you bring this corpse?" He replied, "From a certain corner." They then asked, "What distinguishing mark was over it?" He told them what it was, and the son exclaimed, "Woe to me! I have eaten the flesh of my father!" This is to fulfill what was said, *Therefore the fathers shall eat the sons in the midst of thee, and the sons shall eat their fathers.*°

Ezek. 5:10.

18 The Irrational Hatred of the Goyim

(Midrash on Lamentations)

Ca. 53–117 C.E.; Roman emperor 98–117.

The wife of Trajan° the accursed gave birth to a child on the night of the Ninth of Av while all the Israelites were mourning [the destruction of the Temple]. The child died on Hanukkah. The Israelites said, "Shall we kindle the lights or not?" They decided to light them and risk the consequences. They lit the candles, and persons slandered them to Trajan's wife, saying, "When your child was born the Jews mourned, and when it died they kindled lights!" She sent a letter to her husband, "Instead of subduing the barbarians, come and subdue the Jews who have revolted against you." He boarded a ship and planned to do the voyage in ten days, but the winds brought him in five. On his arrival he found the Jews occupied with this verse, *The Lord will bring a nation against thee from far, from the end of the earth, as the vulture swoopeth down.*°

Deut. 28:49 (1).

He said to them, "I am the vulture who planned to come in ten days, but the wind brought me in five." He surrounded them with his legions and slaughtered them. He said to the women, "Yield yourselves to my troops, or I will do to you what I did to the men." They replied to him, "Do to the inferiors what you did to the superiors." He forthwith surrounded them with his legions and slaughtered them, so that their blood mingled with that of the men, and streamed [to the coast and stained the sea] as far as Cyprus. Then the Holy Spirit cried out, "For these things do I weep."

19 The Children of the High Priest

(Midrash on Lamentations)

Zadok, whose life straddled the end of the first century B.C.E. and the beginning of the next, is reputed to have fasted for forty days to prevent the Destruction that he foresaw; known to have officiated at the Temple. Joel 4:3.

It is related that the two children of Zadok° the High Priest, one a boy and the other a girl, were taken captive, each falling to the lot of a different officer. One officer resorted to a harlot and gave her the boy [as a slave]. The other went to a store-keeper and gave him the girl for wine; to fulfill the text which is written, *And they have given a boy for a harlot, and sold a girl for wine.*°

After a while the harlot brought the boy to the shopkeeper and said to him, "Since I have a boy who is suitable for that girl, will you agree that they should marry and the issue will be divided by us?" He accepted the offer. They immediately took the two of them and placed them in a room. The girl began to weep, and the boy asked her why she was crying. She answered, "Should I not weep when the daughter of a High Priest is given in marriage to a slave?" He inquired of her whose daughter she was and she replied, "I am the daughter of Zadok the [High] Priest." He then asked her where she used to live and she answered, "In the upper market-place." He next inquired what was the sign above the house and she told him. He said, "Have you a brother or sister?" She answered, "I had a brother and there was a mole upon his shoulder; and whenever he came home from school I used to uncover and kiss it." He asked, "If you were to see it, would you know it?" She answered that she would. He bared his shoulder and they recognized one another. They embraced and kissed until they expired. Then the Holy Spirit cried out. "For these things do I weep."

20 The Parable of the Ketubbah

(Midrash on Lamentations)

Lam. 3:21.

This I recall to mind, therefore I have hope.° Rabbi Abba ben Kahana said: This may be likened to a king who married a lady and made a large settlement upon her (lit., wrote her a large marriage contract [*ketubbah*]), "So many state-apartments

I am preparing for you, so many jewels I am preparing for you, and so much silver and gold I give you." The king left her and went to a distant land for many years. Her neighbors used to vex her saying, "Your husband has deserted you. Come and be married to another man." She wept and sighed, but whenever she went into her room and read her *ketubbah* she would be consoled. After many years the king returned and said to her, "I am astonished that you waited for me all these years!" She replied, "My lord king, if it had not been for the generous *ketubbah* you wrote me then surely my neighbors would have won me over."

So the nations of the world taunt Israel and say to them, "Your God has no need of you; he has deserted you and removed his Shekhinah from you. Come to us and we shall appoint commanders and leaders of every sort for you." The Children of Israel enter their synagogues and houses of study and read in the Torah, *"I will look with favor upon you, and make you fertile and multiply you. . . . I* Lev. 26:9–11.   *will establish My abode in your midst, and I will not spurn you,'*° and they are consoled. In the future when the redemption comes the Holy One Blessed Be He will say to Israel, "I am astonished that you waited for me all these years." And they will reply before the Master of All Worlds, "If it had not been for the Torah which you gave us . . . the nations of the world would have led us astray." That is what is written, *"If the Torah had not been my delight, I should have perished in my afflic-* Ps. 119:92.   *tion.'*° Therefore it is stated, "This do I recall to mind and therefore I have hope."°
Lam. 3:21.

21 Akiba's Laughter

(Midrash on Lamentations)

Lam. 5:18.   *For the mountain of Zion which is desolate.*°

Once Rabban Gamliel, Rabbi Joshua, Rabbi Elazar, Rabbi Azariah, and Rabbi Akiba came up to Jerusalem. When they reached Mount Scopus, they tore their clothes. When they reached the Temple Mount, they spied a jackal coming out of the Holy of Holies. They began to weep, yet Rabbi Akiba laughed. Rabban Gamliel said to him, "Akiba, you always astonish us. Here we weep and you laugh!" He replied, "Why do you weep?" Rabban Gamliel said to the others, "Look what Akiba asks us! A jackal emerges from the place about which it is written *Any* Num. 1:51.   *common man who encroaches upon it shall be put to death,*° and we should not weep? It is precisely through our situation that the verse is fulfilled: *Because of this our hearts are sick, / . . . Because of Mount Zion, which lies desolate, / Jackals prowl over* Lam. 5:17–18.   *it.'*° Replied Akiba, "For the same reason I rejoice. It is written, *I shall call reliable* Isa. 8:2.   *witnesses, Uriah and Zechariah son of Jeberechiah.*° Now what connection has Uriah with Zechariah? [Uriah lived in the time of the First Temple, while Zechariah lived in the time of the Second! But note well] what Uriah said and what Zechariah said. Uriah prophesied:

Zion shall be plowed as a field,
Jerusalem shall become heaps of ruins,
Jer. 26:18.   And the Temple Mount a shrine in the woods.°
Zechariah prophesied:
Thus said the Lord of Hosts: There shall yet be old men and women in the squares
of Jerusalem, each with staff in hand because of their great age. And the squares of
Zech. 8:4–5.   the city shall be crowded with boys and girls playing in the squares.°

The Holy One Blessed Be He said, 'Behold, I have two witnesses; if the words of
Uriah are fulfilled then so will be the words of Zechariah. If the words of Uriah
prove vain then so will be the words of Zechariah.' I have rejoiced because since
the words of Uriah have come true then the words of Zechariah will also come
true in the Future Time." [The rabbis] replied to him in these words: "Akiba, you
have consoled us. May you be consoled by the heralds of the redemption!"

22 The Ten *Harugei Malkhut*

(Midrash *Eileh Ezkerah*)

When the Holy One, blessed be He, created the trees, they grew haughty because
they were so tall, and they raised themselves ever higher and higher. But once the
Holy One, blessed be He, created iron, the trees humbled themselves, saying, "Alas!
The Holy One, blessed be He, has created the instrument that will fell us."

Likewise, after the destruction of the Temple, the arrogant members of that
generation boasted, "So what if the Temple has been destroyed! There are still
sages among us, and they can instruct the world in the study of the law and the
observance of the commandments."

Thereupon, the Holy One, blessed be He, set it in the mind of the Roman
emperor to study the Torah of Moses directly from the sages and the elders. The
emperor began with the Book of Genesis, and he studied until he reached the
Exod. 21:1.   chapter in Exodus that begins, "*And these are the rules,*"° When he came to the
verse, "*He who kidnaps a man—whether he has sold him or is still holding him—shall
Exod. 21:16.   be put to death,*"° he immediately ordered his palace to be filled with shoes,° and
Cf. Amos 2:6.   summoned the ten foremost sages of Israel. They came before him, and he seated
them upon thrones of gold, and said, "There is a grave matter of law about which
I must question you. Tell me the law, only the law, and the truth."

"Speak," the sages said.

"If a man has kidnapped one of his brothers from the children of Israel, and
treated him cruelly and sold him," the emperor asked, "what is the law concerning
that man?"

"According to the Torah," the sages answered, "that man must surely die."

"If so," the emperor said, "you are guilty of death."

"Tell us why," they asked.

"Because of Joseph," the emperor answered, "whom his brothers kidnapped and sold. If his brothers were still alive, I would judge them. Since they are not, you will bear the sin of your forefathers."

The sages beseeched the emperor, "Grant us three days' reprieve. If we can find a merit by which to acquit ourselves, then good. And if we can't, do as you wish."

They agreed upon this. The sages departed, and persuaded Rabbi Ishmael, the High Priest, to pronounce the Ineffable Name and thereby to ascend to heaven in order to learn whether the decree against them had been issued by the Holy One.°

Rabbi Ishmael purified himself through ritual immersion. He wrapped himself in his prayer-shawl and in his phylacteries, and distinctly pronounced the Ineffable Name of the Lord. Immediately, a wind bore him to the sixth heaven. There he met the angel Gabriel who said to him, "Are you Ishmael in whom your God prides Himself every day? Because He has a servant on earth who so resembles His own brilliant countenance!"

Ishmael replied, "I am that man."

Gabriel questioned him, "Why have you ascended here?"

He answered, "Because the wicked kingdom has decreed that ten sages of Israel must die. I have therefore ascended to learn whether that decree has gone forth from the Holy One, blessed be He."

Gabriel asked, "If the decree has not been signed, can you nullify it?"

"Yes," Ishmael answered.

"How?" Gabriel asked.

"[By pronouncing] the Ineffable Name."

"Blessed art thou, children of Abraham, Isaac, and Jacob!" Gabriel immediately exclaimed. "For to you the Holy One, blessed be He, has revealed matters He has not disclosed even to the angelic host."

It was said about Rabbi Ishmael, the High Priest, that he was one of the seven most handsome men in the world, and that his face resembled an angel's. When Rabbi Yosi, Rabbi Ishmael's father, reached the last days of his life, his wife said to him, "My dear husband and master, why do I see that many people manage to have children, while we have not? For we have no heir, neither a son nor a daughter."

Rabbi Yosi replied, "The reason is this: When other men's wives leave the ritual bathhouse, they watch themselves very closely. If anything unseemly happens to them, they return to the bathhouse and immerse a second time, and so they succeed in having children."

His wife said, "If this is what has prevented me, then I promise to be very scrupulous in these matters."

The next time she went to immerse herself, after she left the ritual bathhouse, a certain dog crossed her path. So she returned to the bathhouse, and reimmersed herself. [But when she left] the dog crossed her path again: she returned once more and reimmersed herself. Eight times this happened, until the Holy One, blessed be He, said to Gabriel, "How much trouble this righteous woman takes upon herself! Go and appear to her in the form of her husband."

Gabriel immediately went and sat at the door of the ritual bathhouse, where he appeared to the woman in the form of her husband, Rabbi Yosi. He took her

Rabbi Ishmael ben Elisha, along with Rabbi Akiba, founded the two most important exegetical schools in the first half of the second century C.E. Here he is conflated with an earlier figure by that name whom the Talmud (B. Berakhot 7a) identifies as a High Priest.

[by the hand] and led her home. That same night she conceived Rabbi Ishmael, and he was as handsome as Gabriel himself.

For this reason, Gabriel encountered Rabbi Ishmael when he ascended to heaven. The angel said to him, "Ishmael, my son, I swear to you that I overheard from behind the heavenly partition: ten sages are to be handed over to the wicked kingdom to be executed."

"For what cause?" Ishmael asked.

Justice, literally the principle of justice (midat hadin), is an attribute of God in rabbinic literature alongside His parallel attribute of mercy (midat haraḥamim).

"[As atonement] for the transgression Joseph's brothers committed when they sold him. Every day Justice° argues in accusation before the Throne of Glory, saying, 'Hast Thou written in Thy Torah a single superfluous letter? And yet, the fathers of the tribes sold Joseph, and Thou still hast not punished them or their descendants!' It has therefore been decreed that ten sages must be handed over to the wicked kingdom to be executed."

"And till now," Rabbi Ishmael asked, "The Holy One, blessed be He, could find no way to exact punishment except through our lives?"

Gabriel answered, "I swear to you by your own life, Ishmael my son! From the day his brothers sold Joseph [until now] the Holy One, blessed be He, has not found ten men in a single generation so righteous and pious as the fathers of the ten tribes. Because of this, the Holy One, blessed be He, will exact payment through your lives. But the truth is with you."

Samael-Satan; Guardian angel of Rome.

Guardian angel of Israel.

When Samael,° the wicked angel, realized that the Holy One, blessed be He, was about to seal His signature upon the decree to hand over the ten sages to the wicked kingdom, he rejoiced and boasted, "I have triumphed over the archangel, Michael."°

The Holy One, blessed be He, thereupon burned with anger against Samael, and said, "Samael! If you wish, you may release the ten sages from death, or you must agree to suffer leprosy for all time to come. But one of these [decrees] you must accept."

Samael the wicked replied, "I refuse to release those ten sages from death. Let me accept the other decree just as you have spoken."

Metatron-Enoch; records deeds of mankind.

Esau-Edom-Rome.

The Holy One, blessed be He, immediately raged in fury, and even before Samael had finished speaking, He summoned Metatron,° the master scribe and archangel, and commanded him, "Write this and seal it: for six whole months, plague and leprosy, tumors, sores, burning inflammations, jaundice, every sort of evil boil, shall afflict Edom° the wicked. Brimstone and fire shall fall upon man and beast alike, on their gold, their silver, and all they own, until a man shall say to his neighbor, 'I will give you Rome and everything in it for free!' and the other will answer him, 'What do I need these things for? There is no profit in them for me.'"

When Rabbi Ishmael heard this decree, his mind was finally set at rest. He began to stroll to and fro in heaven when he saw an altar next to the Throne of Glory. "What is this?" he asked Gabriel.

"An altar for sacrifice," the angel told him.

"What sort of sacrifice do you offer upon it each day?" Ishmael asked. "Are there bullocks and sacrificial animals here?"

"Every day we sacrifice the souls of the righteous on this altar," Gabriel answered.

"Who offers the sacrifices?" Ishmael asked.

"The archangel Michael," Gabriel responded.

Rabbi Ishmael thereupon descended to earth, and told his fellow sages that the decree against them had already been issued, written down, and sealed. On the one hand, his colleagues felt that they had been wronged to have such a grievous decree issued against their lives. On the other hand, they rejoiced that the Holy One, blessed be He, had judged them to be equal to the fathers of the tribes in righteousness and piety.

This was the order in which the sages sat in pairs: RABBI ISHMAEL and RABBI SHIMEON BEN GAMLIEL; RABBI AKIBA and RABBI HANINA BEN TERADION;° RABBI ELIEZER BEN SHAMUA' and RABBI YESHIVAV THE SCRIBE; RABBI HANINA BEN HAKHINAI and RABBI YUDA BEN BABA; RABBI HUTZAPIT THE TRANSLATOR and RABBI YUDA BEN DAMA.

The Roman emperor now entered, with all the noblemen of Rome following him. He addressed the sages, "Who shall be executed first?"

Rabbi Shimeon ben Gamliel spoke, "I am patriarch, son of a patriarch, descendant of David, the king of Israel, may he rest in peace. I shall be executed first."°

Rabbi Ishmael the High Priest spoke, "I am High Priest, son of a High Priest, descendant of Aaron the Priest. I shall be executed first—and not see my colleague die."

Said the emperor, "This one has said, I shall be executed first, and this one has said, I shall be executed first. If so, cast lots between them."

The lot fell upon Rabbi Shimeon ben Gamliel. The emperor ordered his head cut off, and his servants decapitated Rabbi Shimeon ben Gamliel. Then, Rabbi Ishmael the High Priest took the head and, placing it between his thighs, he lamented with a bitter heart, "Where is Torah? Where is its reward? Here lies the tongue that once explained the Torah in seventy languages! And now it licks the dust!"

So Rabbi Ishmael mourned and wept over the body of Rabbi Shimeon ben Gamliel. The emperor said to him, "What is this? You, an old man, weeping over your fellow sage! You should be weeping over yourself!"

Rabbi Ishmael replied, "I *am* weeping over myself! For my fellow sage was greater than me in knowledge of Torah and wisdom. And now he has joined the heavenly academy before me. This is why I am weeping."

While Rabbi Ishmael was still giving voice to his grief, weeping as he lamented, the daughter of the emperor looked out her window and saw how handsome Rabbi Ishmael the High Priest was. Compassion for him seized her, and she sent to her father asking him to grant her one request. He sent back to her, "My daugher, whatever you ask I shall do—so long as it does not concern Rabbi Ishmael and his colleagues." She sent back, "I request you to allow him to live." The emperor replied, "I have already taken an oath." She responded, "Let me then request that you order to have the skin stripped off his face that I may have it to use instead of a mirror to look upon myself."

The emperor immediately ordered his servants to strip the skin off Rabbi Ishmael's face. When they reached the spot on his forehead where he used to place his phylacteries, Rabbi Ishmael groaned with such terrible bitterness that the heavens and the earth trembled. He groaned a second time, and the Throne of Glory trembled. The host of angels spoke before the Holy One, blessed be He, "A righteous man like this, to whom Thou hast revealed all the mysteries of the upper world and the secrets of the lower one—shall this man be murdered cruelly by so wicked a man? *This* is Torah? *This* is its reward?"

Also spelled Tardion. Head of the yeshiva at Sikhinin in the Galilee. Cf. 12.

Probably a conflation of Shimeon ben Gamliel I and II, both of whom occupied the office of patriarch, or Nasi. The first, according to the Tractate on "Mourning" (12), died a martyr; the second survived the Bar Kochba revolt.

The Holy One, blessed be He, answered, "Leave him to his fate. The merits of his deeds shall stand for the generations following him." Then He added, "What can I do to help my children? The decree has gone forth, and there is no one to annul it."

Bat kol.
An oracular voice° declared from heaven, "If I hear one more word in protest, I shall destroy the entire universe and return it to chaos and void!"

When Rabbi Ishmael heard this, he became silent. The emperor said to him, "Until now you never wept or cried out. Yet now you do!"

Rabbi Ishmael replied, "Not for my own soul am I crying out—but for [the privilege of observing] the precept of laying phylacteries [upon my forehead], which now is lost to me."

"Yet you still trust in your God!" said the emperor.

Job 13:15.
"Let Him kill me if He will," said Rabbi Ishmael. *"I shall still hope in Him."°* Thereupon, his soul departed from Rabbi Ishmael.

50–135 C.E.; cf.
12–13, 21.
Next they brought forth Rabbi Akiba, the son of Joseph.° Rabbi Akiba was able to offer interpretations for the crownlets upon the letters of the Torah, and he revealed meanings in the Torah just as they had been transmitted to Moses at Sinai. When they brought him forth to be executed, a letter to the emperor arrived informing him that the king of Arabia had invaded his territory. The emperor hastened to depart, and ordered that Rabbi Akiba be imprisoned until his return from war. After he returned, he ordered Rabbi Akiba to be brought forth, and they carded his flesh with steel combs. Each time the steel comb entered his flesh, Rabbi Akiba proclaimed, *"Righteous is the Lord. The Rock!—His deeds are perfect; yea, all*

Deut. 32:4.
His Ways are just; a faithful God, never false; true and upright is He."°

An oracular voice came forth and declared, "Blessed art thou, Rabbi Akiba. For you were righteous and just, and now your soul has departed you, righteous and just."

Akiba's student,
who attended his
teacher while he
was in prison and
was present when
Tinneius Rufus
condemned Akiba
to death. See B.
Eruvin 21b.
After he died, Elijah the prophet, of blessed memory, took Rabbi Akiba's corpse on his shoulders and carried him a distance of five parasangs. On the way, Elijah met Rabbi Joshua the Grits-Dealer.° He asked Elijah, "Are you not a priest?" Elijah answered, "The corpse of a righteous man does not impart impurity." Rabbi Joshua the Grits-Dealer accompanied Elijah until they came to a certain cave of extraordinary beauty. They entered the cave and found inside it a handsome bed and a burning candle. Elijah, of blessed memory, lifted Akiba by his head, and Rabbi Joshua the Grits-Dealer took him by his feet, and they laid the body upon the bed. For three days and for three nights the angelic host wept over Rabbi Akiba. Afterward, they buried him in that cave, and the following day Elijah, of blessed memory, took Rabbi Akiba and brought him to the heavenly academy where he interpreted the meaning of the crownlets upon the letters of the Torah. And all the righteous and pious souls gathered to hear Rabbi Akiba's interpretations.

After Rabbi Akiba, Rabbi Hanina ben Teradion was brought forth. It was said about Rabbi Hanina ben Teradion that his behavior was equally becoming to the Holy One, blessed be He, and to his fellow men. Never did a curse against his neighbor rise upon his lips. When the Roman emperor forbade the study of Torah, what did Rabbi Hanina ben Teradion do? He arose, convoked public assemblies, and sat in the marketplace of Rome where he taught and occupied himself with interpreting Torah. The emperor commanded that Rabbi Hanina be wrapped in the scroll of the Torah and burned. The executioner seized Rabbi Hanina. He wrapped him in the Torah scroll, kindled the fire, and took tufts of sheep's wool which he soaked in water and placed upon Rabbi Hanina's heart so that he would not die too quickly. Rabbi Hanina's daughter was standing nearby, and cried to her father, "Oh, oh, father! Must I watch you [die] this way?"

He answered her, "It pleases me, my daughter, to have you see me now."

His students stood next to him, and asked, "Our teacher, what do you see?"

He replied, "I see scrolls of parchment aflame and letters flying up [through the air]." Then he began to weep, and his students asked him, "Why are you weeping?"

He answered, "If I alone were being burned, it would not grieve me. But the scroll of the Torah is now being burned with me."

The executioner addressed Rabbi Hanina. "Rabbi! If I were to remove the tufts of wool from above your heart and let you die quickly, would you promise to bring me to eternal life in the world-to-come?"

Rabbi Hanina answered, "Yes."

The executioner said, "Swear to me." Rabbi Hanina took an oath, and as soon as he had, the executioner fanned the flames, removed the tufts of wool, and Rabbi Hanina's soul departed him. Likewise, the executioner threw himself upon the flames and was consumed by the fire.

An oracular voice thereupon declared, "Rabbi Hanina and his executioner have both gained entrance to eternal life in the world-to-come."

About this incident, Rabbi Judah lamented,° "Some men gain eternal life for themselves in a single moment, like that executioner, while others work all their lives to win this reward and then lose it in a single moment, like Yohanan the High Priest who served in the High Priesthood for eighty years and became a Sadducee at the very end of his life."°

Next they brought forth Rabbi Yuda ben Baba.° From the time he was eighteen years old until he was eighty, Rabbi Yuda never tasted the pleasure of sleep for longer than a nap. The day he was brought forth for execution was a Friday, late in the afternoon, and Rabbi Yuda beseeched his captors, "Wait for me just a little until I fulfill one precept the Holy One, blessed be He, has commanded me."

They said to him, "You still trust in your God!"

He answered, "Yes."

"Does this God in whom you trust," they asked Rabbi Yuda, "still have any strength left him?"

"Great indeed is the Lord," he replied, *"and very exalted, and to His greatness there is no end of searching."*°

"If your God still has strength," they asked, "then why has He not saved you and your colleagues from this kingdom?"

Rabbi Yuda answered, "A great and awesome king requires our deaths. He has merely handed us over to your ruler so as later to requite our blood from his hands."

Those men went and told the emperor what Rabbi Yuda had said. The emperor summoned him and asked, "Is it true or not what my men have told me you said?"

Rabbi Yuda replied, "It is true."

Judah the Prince, redactor of the Mishnah.

Hasmonean King John Hyrcanus. A second-century sage, known for his piety.

Ps. 145:3.

The emperor said, "How insolent you people are! You stand upon the threshold of death, and you still keep up your insolence!"

Rabbi Yuda responded, "O Caesar! Wicked man! Son of a wicked man! Did the Lord not see His temple destroyed, His righteous and pious servants murdered? And yet He did not make haste to avenge them at once."

Rabbi Yuda's students said, "Our teacher, you should have flattered the emperor with words of cajolery."

He answered, "Have you not learned that any one who flatters a wicked man is destined to fall into his hands." Then he said to the emperor, "By your life, Caesar, permit me to fulfill one commandment. Its name is the Sabbath, and it is [like] the world-to-come."

The emperor replied, "Was it to fulfill *this* request I agreed to listen to you!"

Rabbi Yuda at once began to sanctify the Sabbath with the verses, *"The heaven and the earth were completed,"* and so forth.° He uttered them in a pleasing and loud voice, and all who stood around him were amazed. But when he reached the end of the last verse, "Which in creating God had done," they did not let him complete it. The emperor ordered that Rabbi Yuda be executed, and his servants executed him. Rabbi Yuda's soul departed him just as the sage pronounced "God."

An oracular voice came forth and declared, "Blessed art thou, Rabbi Yuda! You resembled an angel, and your soul departed you with the name of God."

The emperor gave his servants commands. They cut Rabbi Yuda's limbs apart and threw them to the dogs, and Rabbi Yuda was never brought to funeral or given burial.

After him, Rabbi Yuda ben Dema was brought forth.° That day was the eve before the holiday of Shavuot,° and Rabbi Yuda said to the emperor, "Upon your life! Grant me a short reprieve until I can fulfill the commandments of Shavuot. Allow me to sanctify the day in order to praise the Holy One, blessed be He, who gave us the Torah."

The emperor said to him, "Do you still hold trust in the Torah and in the God who gave it?"

"Yes," Rabbi Yuda replied.

"What reward will you receive for this Torah of yours?" the emperor asked.

"It is what David, may he rest in peace, said," the sage answered. *"How great is Your goodness, reserved for those who fear You."*°

The emperor exclaimed, "No fools in this world are like you people—if you believe in a world-to-come!"

"And no fools in the world are there like *you*," Rabbi Yuda responded, "who deny the Eternal Lord. Oh, oh! The shame, the disgrace *you* will feel when you see us united with the Holy Name in light eternal, while you reside in the lowest, deepest depths of hell!"

The emperor burned with anger against Rabbi Yuda, and ordered that he be tied by the hair upon his head to the tail of a horse and dragged through Rome in all its expanse. After this was done, he gave orders for the sage to be cut up limb by limb.

Elijah, of blessed memory, then came, gathered Rabbi Yuda's limbs, and buried him in a certain cave near the river that descends to Rome. For thirty days, the Romans all heard the sound of lament and weeping from inside that cave, and they went and informed the emperor.

Gen 2:1.

Lived in mid–second century. Celebrates the giving of the Torah at Sinai.

Ps. 31:20.

He said to them, "Even if the entire universe were to be turned back to chaos and void I will not rest, not until I have satisfied myself with those ten sages just as I have sworn to do."

One of the wise men of Rome happened to be present, and he said to the emperor, "My lord, O Caesar! Recognize the folly of your acts, how completely you have erred in sin by sending forth your hand against the people of God without compassion. Know that a bitter end awaits you, for it is written in the Jewish Scriptures, *God is compassionate and gracious, slow to anger;* yet it is also written there, *But He instantly requites with destruction those who reject him.'*°

Exod. 34:6; Deut. 7:10.

When the emperor heard this, his anger burned against that elder and he ordered him to be strangled to death. When the elder heard this, he immediately rushed to circumcise himself, and once he had been strangled, his corpse vanished and could not be discovered anywhere.

Cf. Isa. 5:25, 9:11 and elsewhere. Lived at beginning of second century. Called "the translator" because as the official spokesman of Rabban Gamliel of Yavneh, he transmitted the sage's opinions to the public.

The emperor was seized with violent trembling. Nonetheless, he did not relent in his anger, and his hand was still stretched forth.°

Rabbi Hutzapit the translator was brought out next.° About Rabbi Hutzapit, it was said that he was a hundred and thirty years old the day he was brought to be executed, yet he was so handsome in appearance he resembled an angel of the Lord of Hosts. [The emperor's] men went and told him about Rabbi Hutzapit's beauty and old age, and said, "We beseech you, our lord, pity this old man."

The emperor asked Rabbi Hutzapit, "How old are you?"

The sage answered, "Tomorrow I will be a hundred and thirty years old. Allow me, I beseech you, to complete my days."

The emperor asked, "What difference does it make if you die today or tomorrow?"

Rabbi Hutzapit responded, "The chance to observe two more precepts."

"And which commandment do you wish to observe now?" the emperor asked.

"The recitation of the *Shema'* in the evening and in the morning," Rabbi Hutzapit replied, "whereby I will crown as king over me the name of the great, awesome, and sole Lord."

The emperor exclaimed, "Shameless and greedy people! How long will you trust in your God? He has no power to rescue you from my hands. My ancestors destroyed His temple. They strewed the corpses of His servants around Jerusalem. No one was there to bury them. And now your God Himself is old, He has no more strength to save you. For if He had any strength, would He not already be avenging Himself, His people, His temple, as He once did to Pharaoh, Siserah, and all the kings of Canaan?"

When Rabbi Hutzapit heard this, he let out a terrible cry of lament, seized his clothes, and rent them in mourning over the blaspheming of the blessed name and its shame. "Woe unto you, Caesar," he said. "What will you do on the final day when the Blessed One judges Rome and your gods?"

The emperor said, "Am I to haggle with this man forever?" He commanded that Rabbi Hutzapit be executed, and his servants stoned him to death and hung him. Later, the emperor's officers and counselors came and beseeched him to permit Rabbi Hutzapit to be buried because they had taken pity upon the sage's elderly age. The emperor allowed the sage to be buried, and Rabbi Hutzapit's students came and buried him, making a great and solemn lament over their teacher.

A student of
Akiba's who lived
in the late second
century.

Next they brought forth Rabbi Hanina ben Hakhinai.° That day was Friday, the Sabbath eve, on which Rabbi Hanina used to sit in fasting from the time he was twelve until now when he was ninety-five. His students asked him, "Our teacher, do you wish to taste something before your execution?"

He said, "All my life until now I have fasted [on this day], never eating or drinking. And now that I do not know where I am going, you tell me to eat and drink!" He began to recite the blessing that sanctifies the Sabbath day, *"The heaven and the earth were completed,"*° until he reached *"and He made it holy,"* but even before the sage was able to complete that verse, he was executed.

Gen. 2:13.

An oracular voice came forth and proclaimed, "Blessed art thou, Rabbi Hanina ben Hakhinai! For you were holy, and now your soul has departed you in holiness just as you pronounced the word 'And He made it holy.' "

A colleague of
Akiba's who lived
in the latter half
of the second
century.

After Rabbi Hanina, they brought out Rabbi Yeshivav the Scribe.° It was said that Rabbi Yeshivav was ninety years old on the day he was brought forth to be executed. His students came and asked him, "Our teacher, what will be the fate of the Torah?"

Rabbi Yeshivav replied, "It is destined that the Torah will be forgotten from Israel because this wicked nation has shamelessly plotted to destroy our most precious jewels [the sages] among us. If my death could only serve as atonement for our generation! Yet I behold [this vision]: No street in Rome will be without a corpse slain by the sword. For this wicked nation is fated to shed the innocent blood of Israel."

His students asked, "And what will be our fate, our teacher?"

He answered, "Hold fast to each other. Love peace and justice, perhaps there will be hope."

The emperor asked Rabbi Yeshivav, "Old man, what is your age?"

Rabbi Yeshivav replied, "This day I am ninety years old, and even before I came forth from my mother's womb, it was decreed by the Holy One, blessed be He, that my colleagues and I would be handed over into your hands so as to avenge our blood from them."

"And does there exist another world [when this act of vengeance against me will take place]?" the emperor asked.

"Yes," the sage answered. "And woe to you! Woe to your shame when He will requite the blood of His righteous creatures from your hands."

The emperor commanded, "Quickly kill this one, too. And let me behold the power and strength of this God. Let me see what He will do to me in another world." So he commanded, and they burned Rabbi Yeshivav to death.

One of Akiba's
last pupils. He
was ordained by
Judah ben Baba
and lived in the
middle of the
second century. It
is doubtful
whether he was
actually martyred.

Rabbi Eleazar ben Shamu'a was brought forth next.° On that day, it was said, Rabbi Eleazar was a hundred and five years old, and from his infancy until the end of his life no one had ever heard him utter a frivolous word, nor had he once quarreled with his neighbor, not in word or in deed. He was a humble and modest man, and he had fasted for eighty years of his life.

The day of Rabbi Eleazar's execution was Yom Kippur. His students came to him and asked, "Our teacher, what is it you behold?"

He answered, "I behold Rabbi Yuda ben Baba whose bier is raised aloft, and the bier of Rabbi Akiba ben Joseph is next to it. The two are disputing with each other over a point of law."

"And who is there to decide the law between them?" Rabbi Eleazar's students asked.

"Rabbi Ishmael the High Priest," he replied.

"And who wins the dispute?" they asked.

"Rabbi Akiba," the sage said. "Because he has toiled with all his strength over the Torah." Then he said to them, "My children, I also behold the soul of each and every righteous creature purifying itself in the water of Shiloah in order to enter the heavenly academy in purity this day and to hear the sermons that Rabbi Akiba ben Joseph will preach on the matters of the day. Each and every angel will bring golden thrones upon which the righteous souls will all sit in purity."

The emperor ordered the sage to be executed. Then an oracular voice came forth and proclaimed, "Blessed art thou, Rabbi Eleazar ben Shamu'a! You were pure and your soul has departed you in purity."

V

History as Liturgy in Ashkenaz

If for a thousand years following the destruction of Herod's Temple, history was imploded, abstracted and incorporated into myth and liturgy, then the Crusades of the eleventh and twelfth centuries lent a new sense of concreteness to the subject of catastrophe. The unprecedented spectacle of Jewish mass martyrdom in response to the Crusaders' missionary zeal called for something new in the way of a literary response—a concern for names, dates and specific events. Indeed, the Hebrew Crusade chronicles were a novel form in the Literature of Destruction, though here, too, there were stronger links to the past than meet the eye. The chronicles, as Ivan G. Marcus has shown, present two competing scenarios, one political, the other martyrological (see "From Politics to Martyrdom: Shifting Paradigms in the Hebrew Narratives of the 1096 Crusade Riots," *Prooftexts* 2 [1982]: 40–52). In the first, men of political authority in the Jewish and Christian world use conventional strategies in a this-worldly power struggle. The model is the Purim story of Esther in King Ahasuerus's court. At a critical point in the narrative attributed to Solomon bar Simson (**23**), marked by a liturgical outburst, it becomes clear that the political option has failed, that there will be no Purim in Germany. Then the focus shifts to individual members of the Jewish community—men, women and children, scholars and laity—arming themselves for an other-worldly struggle. Their acts of cultic homicide draw not on political expediency but on every conceivable religious precedent: the sacrifice of Isaac (the *'Akedah*); the death by fire of Aaron's sons Nadav and Avihu; the suicide of Saul; the trial of Hananiah, Mishael and Azariah; the Temple sacrifice; Akiba's grand improvisation, dying with the *Shema'* on his lips. All this yielded a new model of collective action: *Kiddush Hashem* as mass martyrdom. No wonder the survivors compared Mainz to Jerusalem!

Yet for all their fierce piety and local patriotism, the Jews of Ashkenaz (the traditional name for Franco-German Jewry and their descendants) did not accept the chronicling of history in so bold a form. Though the chronicles captured both the political and spiritual dimensions of the catastrophe, the rabbinic strategy of highlighting the timeless, cyclical nature of the event ultimately triumphed. The chronicles were never made part of the liturgy or ever circulated other than in a few manuscript copies. Instead, the Crusades were linked up with the existing liturgical calendar. A new day was set aside for the commemoration of the martyrs—the Sabbath before Shavuot, the anniversary of the start of the First Crusade—and a new prayer was composed for the occasion (**26**). The names of the local martyrs were also read aloud in the synagogue. (For the fullest account of Jewish responses to the Crusades, see Robert Chazan, *European Jewry and the First Crusade* [Berkeley: University of California Press, 1987], esp. chaps. 4, 5.)

The new waves of catastrophe intensified the survivors' rage—mainly against the Christians (**24**), but also against God. "There is none like You among the dumb," wrote Isaac bar Shalom in bitter response to the Second Crusade of 1146, "keeping silence and keeping still in the face of those who aggrieve us" (**26**). The intensity of the complaint was new even if the form was not. Survivors of the First Destruction had expressed their anger at God through a parody of Psalms: "I am the man whom the Lord has shepherded/ with the rod of His wrath" (**4**). Thenceforward, a method of sacred parody had developed whereby the sacrilege that had been perpetrated against the Jews on the plane of history was mimicked by doing violence to the sacred texts.

Isaac bar Shalom's plaint was lifted from a talmudic response to the destruction of the Second Temple. After describing how Emperor Titus had defiled the Holy of Holies in 70 C.E. and then blasphemed against God, a second-century sage named Abba Hanan is reputed to have said, in open parody of Psalm 89:9: "Who is like You, mighty in self-restraint? You heard the blasphemy and the insults of that wicked man, but You kept silent!" (B. Gittin 56b). This acclamation of God's might from the Book of Psalms was itself a rephrasing of Exodus 15:11: "Who is like You among the gods?" Changing the word *elim* ("gods") to *illemim* ("mute"), someone from the School of Rabbi Ishmael took the parody one step further: "Who is like You, O Lord, among the dumb?" (B. Gittin 56b). Precisely how radical this response was intended to be is difficult to gauge, for the trick of adding a single Hebrew consonant was typical of rabbinic wordplay. In Isaac bar Shalom's mind, however, there could be no doubt that the rabbis had expressed their impatience with the silent God who seemed impervious to His people's fate. And so he added his own, almost blasphemous, voice to the choir: "Do not keep silence!" he repeated at the end of each stanza.

To ensure a place for his poem in the liturgy, Isaac bar Shalom wrote it as *zulat,* that is, a poem inserted in the benediction after the morning *Shema'* (Hear, O Israel, the Lord our God, the Lord is one) between the proclamation "There is no God beside You" and the affirmation "You have been the help of our fathers from old." Numerous threads within the poem itself tied history and the liturgy together: the reference to the martyrs who died with the *Shema'* on their lips (lines 31–32); acts of *Kiddush Hashem* described in terms of the sacrificial cult, climaxing in line 45, "All Israel weeps for the burning," which reinterpreted the death by fire of Nadav and Avihu as an act of voluntary martyrdom; and the final line of the poem that tied into the fixed liturgy, "arise for our *help*. . . ." Indeed, the poem occupied just this place in the morning service for the first Sabbath after Passover, the period of commemoration for the Jews of Ashkenaz.

Another space for accommodating liturgical poems on historical themes was in the *kinot* for the Ninth of Av. Here, too, there was room for subtle parody as an expression of anger. To complete the liturgical movement from past destruction to future redemption, the medieval editors of the *kinot* had added Judah Halevi's exquisite "Ode to Zion" at their conclusion, thus encouraging a host of imitators. Among them was Rabbi Meir of Rothenburg, who used Judah Halevi's famous opening line, "O Zion, will you not ask how your captives are . . . ," as a parodic point of departure for his own angry response to the public burning of the Talmud in Paris (**27**).

And so the Jews of Ashkenaz, through new rites of commemoration and new expressions of rage, strengthened but did not alter the structure of collective memory. What changed was the intensity or style of collective memory, not its basic mode. Even the gruesome hallmark of Ashkenaz— *Kiddush Hashem* as *mass* martyrdom—was standardized into the symbolic medium of prayer. At a time of relative tranquillity for European Jews, Rabbi Isaiah Horowitz (the Sheloh) composed a prayer that asked God for the ability to sustain one's faith during the pain of torture (**28**). Martyrdom had been incorporated as yet another *mitzvah,* a commandment, and as such, it required a blessing. *Kiddush Hashem* was well on its way to being viewed as the Jewish way of death.

23 The Crusade Chronicle of Solomon Bar Simson

Now I shall recount the development of the persecution in the rest of the [Jewish] communities that were killed for the sake of his unique Name and how they cleaved to the Lord God of their ancestors and declared his unity unto death itself.

The spring months of 1096.

It came to pass in the year 4856,° the year 1028 of our exile, in the eleventh year of the two hundred and fifty-sixth cycle, during which we had hoped for salvation and comfort according to the prophecy of the prophet Jeremiah: "Cry out in joy for Jacob, shout at the crossroads of the nations!"° Instead it was turned into "agony and sighing,"° weeping and crying. Many evils designated in all the [passages of] rebuke—written and unwritten°—passed over us. For then rose up initially the arrogant, "the barbaric,"° "a fierce and impetuous people,"°° "both French and German. They set their hearts to journey to the Holy City, which had been defiled by "a ruffian people,"° in order to seek there the sepulcher of the crucified bastard and to drive out the Muslims who dwell in the land and to conquer the land. "They put on their insignia"° and placed an idolatrous sign on their clothing—the cross—all the men and women whose hearts impelled them to undertake the pilgrimage to the sepulcher of their messiah, to the point where they exceeded the locusts on the land—men, women, and children. With regard to them it is said: "The locusts have no king."°

Jer. 31:6. The first word of the verse is Ranu, the numerical value of which is 256.
Isa. 35:10, 51:11.
See 1, esp. v. 61.
Ps. 114:1.
Hab. 1:6.
Ezek. 7:22.
Ps. 74:4.

Prov. 30:27.

It came to pass that, when they traversed towns where there were Jews, they said to one another: "Behold we journey a long way to seek the idolatrous shrine and to take vengeance upon the Muslims. But here are the Jews dwelling among us, whose ancestors killed him and crucified him groundlessly. Let us take vengeance first upon them. 'Let us wipe them out as a nation; Israel's name will be mentioned no more.'° Or else let them be like us and acknowledge the son born of menstruation."

Ps. 83:5.

Now when the [Jewish] communities heard their words, they reverted to the arts of our ancestors—repentance, prayer, and charity.° The hands of the holy people fell weak and their hearts melted and their strength flagged. They hid themselves in innermost chambers before "the ever turning sword."° They afflicted themselves with fasting. They fasted three consecutive days—both night and day,° in addition to daily fasts, until "their skin shriveled on their bones and became dry as wood."° They cried out and gave forth a loud and bitter shriek. But their Father did not answer them. "He shut out their prayer"° and "screened himself off with a cloud, that no prayer might pass through."° "The tent [of prayer] was rejected"° and he banished them from his presence."°° For a decree had been enacted before him from [the time when God had spoken] of a day of accounting,° and this generation had been chosen as his portion, for they had the strength and valor to stand in his sanctuary and to fulfill his command and to sanctify his great Name in his world. Concerning them David said: "Bless the Lord, O his messengers, mighty men who do his bidding, ever obedient to his bidding."°

This is the three-part formula that dominates the liturgy of Yom Kippur.
Gen. 3:24.
Esther 4:16.
Lam. 4:8.
Lam. 3:8.
Lam. 3:44.
Ps. 78:67.
2 Kings 17:18.
Exod. 32:34.
Ps. 103:20.
April 10, 1096.
April 25–26, 1096.
May 3, 1096.

That year Passover fell on Thursday° and the new moon of Iyyar on Friday.°° On the eighth of Iyyar,° on the Sabbath, the enemy arose against the [Jewish] community of Speyer and killed eleven saintly souls who sanctified their Creator on the holy Sabbath day and refused to be baptized. There was a notable and pious woman who slaughtered herself for the sanctification of the [Divine] Name. She was the first of those who slaughtered themselves in all the communities. The rest were saved by the bishop° without baptism, as has been written above.

Bishop John of Speyer (1090–1104). May 18, 1096. Jer. 5:6; Zeph. 3:3.

On the twenty-third of Iyyar,° they rose up against the [Jewish] community of Worms. The community divided into two groups. Some stayed in their homes and some fled to the bishop. Then "the wolves of the steppes"° rose up against those that were in their homes and pillaged them—men, women, and children; young and old. They tore down the stairways and destroyed the houses. They plundered and ravaged. They took the Torah and trampled it in the mud and tore it and burned it. "They devoured Israel with a greedy mouth."°

Isa. 9:11.

May 25, 1096.

Seven days later, on the new moon of Sivan,° the day of the arrival of Israel at Sinai in order to receive the Torah, those who still remained in the chambers of the bishop were subjected to terror. The enemy assaulted them, as they had done to the earlier group, and put them to the sword. They [the Jews] held firm to the example of their brethren and were killed and sanctified the [Divine] Name publicly. They stretched forth their necks, so that their heads might be cut off for the Name of their Creator. There were some of them that took their own lives. They fulfilled the verse: "Mothers and babes were dashed together."° Indeed fathers also fell with their children, for they were slaughtered together. They slaughtered brethren, relatives, wives, and children. Bridegrooms [slaughtered] their intended and merciful mothers their only children. All of them accepted the heavenly decree unreservedly. As they commended their souls to their Creator, they cried out: "Hear O Israel! The Lord is our God; the Lord is one."° The enemy stripped them and dragged them about. There remained only "a small number"° whom they converted forcibly and baptized against their will in their baptismal waters. Approximately eight hundred was the number killed, who were killed on these two days. All of them were buried naked. With regard to them Jeremiah laments: "Those who were reared in purple have embraced refuse heaps."° I have mentioned their names above. May God recall them beneficently.

Hos. 10:14.

Deut. 6:4.

Isa. 10:25, 16:14, 29:17.

Lam. 4:5.

When the saintly ones, the pious of the Almighty, the holy community in Mainz—"a shield and buckler"° for all the [Jewish] communities, whose reputation spread throughout all the provinces—heard that some of the community in Speyer had been killed and that the community in Worms [had been attacked] twice and that the sword had reached them, their hands fell weak and "their hearts melted and turned to water."° They cried out to the Lord with all their heart and said: "Lord God of Israel, are you wiping out the remnant of Israel?"° Where are all your awesome wonders about which our ancestors told us, saying, 'Truly the Lord brought you up from Egypt and from Babylonia?'° How many times have you saved us? How have you now abandoned and forsaken us, O Lord, leaving us in the hands of wicked Christendom that they might destroy us? Do not distance yourself from us, for tragedy is near and there is none to aid us."°

Pun on Ezek. 38:4, 39:9, with Magenza, the Hebrew name of Mainz. Josh. 7:5. Ezek. 11:13.

Judg. 6:13.

Ps. 22:12.

The notables of Israel gathered together to give them good counsel, so that they might be able to be saved. They said to one another: "Let us choose of our elders and let us decide what we shall do, for this great evil will swallow us up." They agreed on the counsel of redeeming their souls by spending their moneys and bribing the princes and officers and bishops and burghers. The leaders of the com-

Archbishop
Ruthard of Mainz
(1089–1109).

munity, notable in the eyes of the archbishop,° then rose and came to the archbishop and to his ministers and servants to speak with them. They said to them: "What shall we do about the report which we have heard concerning our brethren in Speyer and in Worms who have been killed?" They said to them: "Listen to our advice and bring all your moneys to our treasury. Then you, your wives your sons and daughters, and all that you have bring into the chamber of the archbishop until these bands pass by. Thus will you be able to be saved from the crusaders." They contrived and gave this counsel in order to gather us and to surrender us

Eccles. 9:12.
B. Bava Batra
138a.

into their hands and to seize us "like fish enmeshed in a fatal net"° and to take our moneys, as they ultimately did. The end result proves the original intention.° In addition, the archbishop gathered his ministers and servants—exalted ministers, nobles—in order to assist us. For at the outset it was his desire to save us with all his strength. Indeed we gave him great bribes to this end, along with his ministers and servants, since they intended to save us. Ultimately all the bribery and all the

Prov. 11:4.

diplomacy did not avail in protecting us "on the day of wrath"° from catastrophe.

Hos. 4:12.

At that time a duke arose, Godfrey by name—may his bones be ground up— harsh in spirit. "A fickle spirit moved him"° to go with those journeying to their idolatrous shrine. He swore wickedly that he would not depart on his journey without avenging the blood of the Crucified with the blood of Israel and that he

Josh. 8:22; Jer.
42:17.
Isa. 58:12.

would not leave "a remnant or residue"° among those bearing the name Jew. His anger waxed against us. To be sure, "a protector"° arose—the exemplar of the generation, the God-fearing, offered up on the innermost altar, R. Kalonymous

A designation for
the leader of the
community.
In point of fact,
Emperor Henry IV
was in northern
Italy from
1090–1097.
Esther 1:22.

the *parnas*° of the community of Mainz—who immediately sent an emissary to Emperor Henry in the kingdom of Apulia, where he had tarried for nine years.° He told him of all these events. Then the anger of the emperor was aroused, and he sent letters throughout all the provinces of his empire,° to the princes and bishops, to the nobles and to Duke Godfrey—messages of peace and [orders] with regard to the Jews that they protect them so that no one harm them physically and that they provide aid and refuge to them. The wicked duke swore that it had never occurred to him to do them any harm. Nonetheless we bribed him in Cologne with five hundred silver *zekukim*. They likewise bribed him in Mainz. He swore on his staff to behave peacefully toward them. But [God] "who truly makes

Isa. 45:7.

peace"° turned away from them and hid his eyes from his people and consigned them to the sword. No prophet or seer nor any man of wisdom or understanding

Num. 23:10.

can fathom the essential issue—how could the sin of "the innumerable people"° be so heavy and how could the souls of these saintly communities be so destructive,

Jer. 11:20.

as though shedding blood. Except that surely [God] is "a just judge"° and we bear the shortcomings.

Ps. 124:5 referring
to baptism.
2 Kings 17:9.
Cf. Acts of the
Apostles 5:30.
Cf. Matthew
27:25.

Then "the seething waters"° gathered. "They heaped up unfounded charges"° against the people of God. They said: "You are the descendants of those who killed our deity and crucified him.° Indeed he said: 'A day will surely arrive when my children will come and avenge my blood.'° We are his children and it is our responsibility to avenge him upon you, for you are the ones who rebelled and transgressed against him. Indeed your God was never pleased with you. While he sought to do well by you, you did evil before him. Therefore he has forgotten you

Exod. 32:9, 33:3
and elsewhere.
Job 37:1.

and no longer desires you, for you have been 'stiffnecked'° with him. He has separated himself from you and has shown favor to us and has taken us as his portion." When we heard this, "our hearts quaked and were distressed."° "We

Ps. 39:3.
Ps. 143:4; Lam. 3:6.
Lam. 3:50.
Job 2:1.
Pope Urban II at Clermont on November 27, 1095.
I.e., Christians.
Isa. 57:14.
Words missing in the manuscript.
Gen. 22:17; 1 Kings 5:9.
Isa. 29:6.

Gen. 45:26.
Josh. 2:11.
Isa. 19:1.
Jer. 40:3.
Ps. 78:60.
Ezek. 11:16.
I.e., the synagogue.
Lev. 26:33.
Isa. 30:17.
Ps. 78:61.
Lam. 2:20.
Isa. 42:22.
Lam. 1:21.
2 Kings 21:12.
Jer. 48:17.
Lam. 4:2.

Albert of Aix, in his closing pejorative note on the popular crusading bands, cites the veneration of a goose that was seen as inspired by the Holy Spirit.

Exod. 16:3, there uttered by the rebellious Israelites seeking to return to Egypt.

were struck silent."° We sat in darkness "like those long dead,"°° until "the Lord might look down and see from heaven."°

"Then Satan also came"°—the pope of wicked Rome—and circulated a pronouncement° among all the gentiles who believe in the offshoot of adultery, the children of Seir,° that they congregate together and ascend to Jerusalem and conquer the city "on a way built up"° for pilgrims and that they go to the sepulcher . . .° whom they accepted as a deity over them. Satan came and mingled among the nations. They all gathered as one man to fulfill the commandment. They came "as the sand on the seashore,"° with a noise like the rumbling of "a storm or a tempest."° It came to pass that, when the embittered and poor had gathered, they took evil counsel against the people of God. They said: "Why are they occupied with doing battle against the Muslims in the vicinity of Jerusalem? Indeed among them is a people which does not acknowledge their deity. What is more, their ancestors crucified their god. Why should we let them live? Why should they dwell among us? Let our swords begin with their heads. After that we shall go on the way of our pilgrimage." "The hearts of the people of God went numb"° and "their spirits departed."°°

They came and pressed their entreaty before the Lord. They fasted and diminished their blood and flesh. "The hearts of Israel melted inside them."° Indeed "God did as he had said, for we sinned before him."° He forsook "the tabernacle of Shiloh,"° "the diminished sanctuary,"°° which he had placed among his people in the midst of the nations. His anger waxed against them and "he unsheathed the sword against them,"° until "what was left of them was like a mast on a hilltop, like a pole upon a mountain."° "He let his might go into captivity"°° and trampled it underfoot. "Look O Lord, and behold, to whom have you done thus?"° Is not Israel, "a people plundered and despoiled,"° your special portion? Why have you lifted the shield before his enemies? Why have they become mighty? "They hear how I sigh."° All those who hear about me . . . "both their ears will tingle."° "Alas the strong rod is broken, the lordly staff,"°° the saintly congregation "valued as gold,"° the community of Mainz. For there was a divine edict in order to test those who fear him, that they suffer the yoke of his pure awe.

It came to pass on a certain day that a gentile woman came and brought with her a goose that she had raised since it was a gosling. This goose went everywhere that the gentile woman went. She said to all passersby: "Behold this goose understands that I intend to go on the crusade and wishes to go with me."° Then the crusaders and burghers and common folk gathered against us, saying to us: "Where is your source of trust? How will you be saved? Behold the signs that the Crucified does for them publicly in order to take vengeance on their enemies." Then all of them came with swords to destroy us. Some of the high-ranking burghers came and stood opposite and would not allow them to harm us. At that moment the crusaders stood united against the burghers and one side smote the other until they killed one of the crusaders. Then they said: "All these things the Jews have caused." Then they almost gathered against us. They spoke harshly, [threatening] to assault and attack us. When the saintly ones saw all these things, their hearts melted. When they heard their words, they said, both great and small: " 'If only we might die by the hand of the Lord,'° rather than die by the hands of the enemies of the Lord. For he is a merciful God, unique in his universe."

They left their houses empty and came to the synagogue only on the Sabbath

May 24, 1096.
Deut. 26:5, 28:62
(**1**).

before the new moon of Sivan,° the last Sabbath prior to our destruction, when "a few"° entered to pray. Rabbi Judah ben Rabbi Isaac entered there to pray as part of that quorum. They wept copiously, to the point of exhaustion, for they saw that this was the decree of the King of all kings and that no one might annul it. There was there a venerable scholar, Rabbi Baruch ben Rabbi Isaac, and he said to us: "Know truly and surely that a decree has been enacted against us from heaven and we will not be able to be saved. For tonight we—I and my son-in-law Judah—heard the souls which were praying at night in the synagogue loudly, like a cry. When we heard the sound, we thought that perhaps some of the community came from the courtyard of the archbishop to pray in the synagogue at midnight, in anguish and bitterness. We ran to the door of the synagogue to see who was praying. The door was closed. We heard the sound and the loud wail, but we could comprehend nothing of what they were saying. We returned home shaken, for our house was close to the synagogue." When we heard these words, we fell on our faces and said: "You, O Lord God—are you wiping out the remnant of Israel?"° They went and recounted these events to their brethren in the court-yard of the burgrave and in the chambers of the archbishop. They too knew that a decree had been issued by the Lord and they wept copiously and accepted divine judgment and said: "You are righteous, O Lord, and your rulings are just."°

Ezek. 11:13.

Ps. 119:137.
May 25, 1096.
Count of
Leiningen.

It came to pass on the new moon of Sivan° that Count Emicho,°° the persecutor of all the Jews—may his bones be ground up between iron millstones—came with a large army outside the city, with crusaders and common folk in tents. The gates of the city were locked beore him. He also had said: "It is my desire to go on the crusade." He became head of the bands and concocted the story that an emissary of the Crucified had come to him and had given him a sign in his flesh indicating that, when he would reach Byzantium, then he [Jesus] would come to him [Emi-cho] himself and crown him with royal diadem and that he would overcome his enemies. He was our chief persecutor. He had no mercy on the elderly or on young women; he had no pity on the infant and the suckling and the sickly. He made the people of the Lord "like dust to be trampled."° "Their young men he put to the sword and their pregnant women he ripped open."° They camped outside the city for two days.

2 Kings 13:7.
2 Kings 8:12.

At the time when the wicked one came to Mainz on his way to Jerusalem, the elders of the people came to their archbishop, Ruthard, and bribed him with two hundred silver *zekukim*. It had been his intention to go to the villages which belonged to the archbishops. But the [Jewish] community came, when they bribed him, and begged him, so that he stayed with them in Mainz. He brought all the community into his inner chambers and said: "I have agreed to aid you. Likewise the burgrave has said that he wishes to remain here for your sakes, to assist you. You must therefore supply all our needs until the crusaders pass through." The [Jewish] community agreed to do so. The two—the archbishop and the burgrave—agreed and said: "We shall either die with you or live with you." Then the community said: "Since those who are our neighbors and acquaintances have agreed to save us, let us also send to the wicked Emicho our moneys and our letters, so that the [Jewish] communities along the way will honor him. Perhaps the Lord will behave in accord with his great loving-kindness and will relent against us. For this purpose we have disbursed our moneys, giving the archbishop and his ministers and his servants and the burghers approximately four hundred silver *zekukim.''* We gave the wicked Emicho seven gold pounds so that he might assist us. It was of no avail, and to this point no balm has been given for our affliction. For we were unlike Sodom and Gomorrah. For them ten [righteous] were sought in order to save them.° For us neither twenty nor ten were sought.

It came to pass on the third day of Sivan,° which had been a day of sanctity and setting apart for Israel at the time of the giving of the Torah—on that day when Moses our teacher, may his memory be blessed, said: "Be ready for the third day"°—on that day the [Jewish] community of Mainz, the pious of the Almighty, were set apart in holiness and purity and were sanctified to ascend to God all together. "Cherished in life, in death they were not parted."° For all of them were in the courtyard of the archbishop. The wrath of the Lord was kindled against his people and he fulfilled the counsel of the crusaders and they were successful. All wealth was unavailing, along with fasting, self-affliction, wailing, and charity. There was no one "to stand in the breach"°—neither a teacher nor a prince. Even the holy Torah did not protect those who study it. "Gone from Zion are all that were her glory,"° namely Mainz. The sound of "the lords of the flock"°° ceased, along with the sound of "the valorous who repel attacks,"° "who lead the many to righteousness."° "The glorious city, the citadel of joy,"°° which had distributed untold sums to the poor. One could not write with "an iron stylus"° on a whole book the multitude of good deeds that were done in it of yore. In one place [were found] Torah and power and wealth and honor and wisdom and humility and good deeds, taking innumerable precautions against transgression. But now their wisdom had been swallowed up and turned into destruction, like the children of Jerusalem in their destruction.

It came to pass at midday that the wicked Emicho, persecutor of the Jews, came—he and all his army—to the gate. The burghers opened the gate to him. Then the enemies of the Lord said to one another: "Behold the gate has been opened before us. Now let us avenge the blood of the Crucified." When the children of the holy covenant—the saintly ones, the God-fearing who were there saw the huge multitude, the army as large "as the sand on the seashore," they cleaved to their Creator. They donned armor and strapped on weapons—great and small—with Rabbi Kalonymous ben Rabbi Meshullam the *parnas* at their head. But from their great anguish and from the many fasts undertaken, they did not have sufficient strength to stand up before the enemy. They then came in battalions and companies, sweeping down like a river, until Mainz was filled completely. The enemy Emicho made an announcement to the citizenry that they surrender and remove the enemy [the Jews] from the city. "A great panic from the Lord fell upon them."° The men of Israel strapped on their weapons in the innermost courtyard of the archbishop and all of them approached the gate [of the courtyard] to do battle with the crusaders and the burghers. They did battle against one another at the gate. Our sins brought it about that the enemy overcame them and captured the gate. "The hand of the Lord lay heavy"° upon his people. Then all the gentiles gathered against the Jews in the courtyard, in order to destroy them totally. The hands of our people wavered, when they saw that the hand of wicked Edom had overcome them. Indeed the men of the archbishop, who had promised to help them, fled immediately, in order to turn them over to their enemies, for they were "splintered reeds."° Even the archbishop himself fled from his church, for they intended to kill him as well, since he has spoken up on behalf of Israel.

Gen. 18:23–32.
May 27, 1096.

Exod. 19:15.

2 Sam. 1:23—
David's dirge for
Saul and
Jonathan.

Ps. 106:23.

Lam. 1:6 (4).
Jer. 25:34.
Isa. 28:6.
Dan. 12:3.
Jer. 49:25.
Jer. 17:1; Job
19:24.

Zech. 14:13.

1 Sam. 5:6.

2 Kings 18:21;
Isa. 36:6.

May 27, 1096.
Zeph. 1:15.
Job 3:5.
Job 3:4.
Gen. 22:17.

The enemy entered the courtyard on the third of Sivan, on the third day of the week,° "a day of darkness and gloom, a day of densest clouds."°° "May darkness and day gloom reclaim it";° "may God above have no concern for it; may light never shine upon it."° Woe for the day when we saw the anguish of our souls. Stars, why did you not cover your light—was not Israel compared to the stars?° The twelve constellations, like the number of the tribes of Jacob, why did you not extinguish your light from shining on the enemy that intended to blot out the name of Israel?

When the children of the sacred covenant saw that the decree had been enacted and that the enemy had overcome them, they entered the courtyard and all cried out together—elders, young men and young women, children, menservants and maidservants—to their Father in heaven. They wept for themselves and their lives. They accepted upon themselves the judgment of heaven. They said to one another:

The four modes of capital punishment in Jewish law are by stoning, burning, strangulation and sword.

"Let us be strong and suffer the yoke of the sacred awe. For the moment the enemy will kill us, but the easiest of the four deaths is by sword.° We shall, however, remain alive; our souls [shall be] in paradise, in the radiance of the great light forever." They said unreservedly and willingly: "Ultimately one must not question the ways of the Holy One, blessed be he and blessed be his Name, who gave us his Torah and the commandment to put to death and to kill ourselves for the unity of his holy Name. Blessed are we if we do his will. Blessed are all those who are killed and slaughtered and die for the unity of his name. They are destined for the world to come and shall sit in the circle of the righteous, Rabbi Akiba and

See 23.

his associates, 'the pillars of the universe,' who were killed for his Name.° What is more, a world of darkness will be exchanged for a world of light, a world of pain for a world of happiness, a transitory world for a world that is eternal and everlasting." Then they all cried out loudly, saying in unison: "Now let us tarry no longer, for the enemy has already come upon us. Let us go quickly and sacrifice ourselves before the Lord. Anyone who has a knife should inspect it, that it not be defective. Then he should come and slaughter us for the sanctification of the unique [God] who lives forever. Subsequently he should slaughter himself by his throat or should thrust the knife into his belly."

The enemy, immediately upon entering the courtyard, found there some of the perfectly pious with Rabbi Isaac ben Rabbi Moses the dialectician. He stretched out his neck and they cut off his head immediately. They had clothed themselves in their fringed garments and had seated themselves in the midst of the courtyard in order to do speedily the will of their Creator. They did not wish to flee to the chambers in order to go on living briefly. Rather, with love they accepted upon themselves the judgment of heaven. The enemy rained stones and arrows upon them, but they did not deign to flee. They struck down all those whom they found

Esther 9:5.

there, with "blows of sword, death, and destruction."°

Those in the chambers, when they saw this behavior on the part of those saintly ones and that the enemy had come upon them, all cried out: "There is nothing better than to offer ourselves as a sacrifice." There women girded themselves with strength and slaughtered their sons and daughters, along with themselves. Many men likewise gathered strength and slaughtered their wives and their children and

Deut. 28:56 (1).
Jer. 31:20.

their little ones. "The tenderest and daintiest"° slaughtered "their beloved children."° They all stood—men and women—and slaughtered one another. The young women and the brides and the bridegrooms gazed through the windows and cried out loudly: "Behold and see, our God, what we do for the sanctification of your holy Name, rather than deny you for a crucified one, a trampled and wretched and abominable offshoot, a bastard and a child of menstruation and lust."° "The precious children of Zion,"°° the children of Mainz, were tested ten times, like our ancestor Abraham and like Hananiah, Mishael, and Azariah.° They offered up their children as did Abraham with his son Isaac.° They accepted upon themselves the yoke of the fear of heaven, of the King of kings, the Holy One, blessed be he, willingly. They did not wish to deny the awe of our King or to exchange it for [that of] "a loathsome offshoot,"° a bastard born of menstruation and lust. They stretched forth their necks for the slaughter and commended their pure souls to their Father in heaven. The saintly and pious women stretched forth their necks one to another, to be sacrificed for the unity of the [Divine] Name. Likewise men to their children and brothers, brothers to sisters, women to their sons and daughters, and neighbor to neighbor and friend, bridegroom to bride, and betrothed to his betrothed. They sacrificed each other until the blood flowed together. The blood of husbands mingled with that of their wives, the blood of parents with that of their children, the blood of brothers with that of their sisters, the blood of teachers with that of their students, the blood of bridegrooms with that of their brides, the blood of cantors with that of their scribes, the blood of infants and sucklings with that of their mothers. They were killed and slaughtered for the unity of the revered and awesome Name. At such reports "the ears of those who hear must surely tingle." "For who has heard the like? Who has ever witnessed such events?"° "Ask and see."°° Were there ever so many sacrifices like these from the days of Adam? Were there ever a thousand one hundred sacrifices on one day, all of them like the sacrifice of Isaac the son of Abraham? For one the world shook, when he was offered up on Mount Moriah, as is said: "Hark! The angels cried aloud!"° The heavens darkened. What has been done [this time]? "Why did the heavens not darken? Why did the stars not withdraw their brightness?"° . . . and light—"why did they not darken in their cloud cover,"° when one thousand one hundred holy souls were killed and slaughtered on one day, on the third day of Sivan, a Tuesday—infants and sucklings who never transgressed and never sinned and poor and innocent souls? "At such things will you restrain yourself, O Lord?"° "For your sake they were killed"°—innumerable souls. "Avenge the blood of your servants that has been spilled"° in our days and before our eyes speedily. Amen.

That day the crown of Israel fell. Then the students of Torah fell and the scholars disappeared. The honor of the Torah fell, as is written: "He threw down from heaven to earth the glory of Israel."° Those who fear sin ceased. Men of good deeds disappeared, along with the splendor of wisdom and purity and abstinence and the splendor of the priesthood and men of trust and "those who repair the breach"° and those who turn back evil decrees and the anger of their Creator. Those who give charity in secret diminished. "Truth was absent"° and preachers ceased, along with the revered and the luster of old age. [Woe for] the day upon which many troubles befell us.° "There was nowhere to turn, either right or left,"°° "because of the rage of the oppressor."° For from the day that the Second Temple was destroyed there were none like them in Israel and after them there will be no more. For they sanctified and declared the unity of the [Divine] Name with all their heart and with all their soul and with all their might. Blessed are they and

Lam. 4:2.
Mishnah Avot
5:3.
9.
Gen. 22:1–19.

Isa. 14:19; i.e.,
Christ.

Isa. 66:8.
Jer. 30:6.

Isa. 33:7.

Joel 2:10.
Isa. 5:30.

Isa. 64:11.
Ps. 44:23.
Ps. 79:10.

Lam. 2:1 (4).

Isa. 58:12.
Isa. 59:15.

Allusion to Deut.
31:17.
Num. 22:26.
Isa. 51:13.

blessed is their portion, for all of them are destined for the life of the world to come. May my portion be with them.

24 Pour Out Thy Wrath

Passover Haggadah

Over the third cup of wine:
Blessed art thou, Lord our God, King of the universe,
who createst the fruit of the vine.
The door is opened:
(According to the Italian rite)

Ps. 79:6.

Pour our Your fury on the nations that do not know You,
upon the kingdoms that do not invoke Your name.

(According to the Sephardic and Yeminite Rites)

Ps. 79:6–7.

Pour out Your fury on the nations that do not know You,
upon the kingdoms that do not invoke Your name,
for they have devoured Jacob
and desolated his home.

(According to the Ashkenazic rite)

Pour out Thy wrath on the nations that do not know Thee,
upon the kingdoms that do not invoke Thy name,
for they have devoured Jacob
and desolated his home.

Ps. 69:25.

Pour out Your wrath on them;
may Your blazing anger overtake them.

Lam. 3:66.

Oh, pursue them in wrath and destroy them
From under the heaven of the Lord!

25 Commemoration of Martyrs

(Sabbath Prayer Book, Ashkenazic Rite)

May the Merciful Father, who dwells in heaven, in his abundant mercies remember compassionately the pious and righteous and pure, the sacred communities, who sacrificed themselves for the sanctification of the Divine Name. "Beloved and cher-

2 Sam. 1:23.
*David's dirge for
Saul and
Jonathan. King
Saul's heroic
suicide thus
becomes a
martyrological
paradigm.*
Deut. 32:43.
Joel 4:21;
*translation
modified to fit
the usage.*
Ps. 79:10.
Ps. 9:13.

Ps. 110:6–7.

ished in life, they were not parted in death."° They were swifter than eagles and stronger than lions in doing the will of their Creator and the desire of their Protector. May God remember them beneficently along with the other righteous of history. May he avenge the blood of his servants which has been spilled, as is written in the Torah of Moses, the man of God: "O nations, acclaim his people! For he will avenge the blood of his servants, wreak vengeance on his foes, and cleanse the land of his people."° By your servants the prophets it has been written: "When I establish innocence, I shall not excuse the shedding of their blood, and the Lord shall dwell in Zion."° In the Writings it is said: "Why should the nations say: 'Where is their God?' Before our eyes let it be known among the nations that you avenge the spilled blood of your servants."° It is likewise said: "For he does not ignore the cry of the afflicted; he who requites bloodshed is mindful of them."° It is likewise said: "He works judgment upon the nations, heaping up bodies, crushing heads far and wide. He drinks from the stream on his way; therefore he holds his head high."°

26 There Is None Like You Among the Dumb

ISAAC BAR SHALOM

B. Gittin 56b *on
Ps.* 86:8, *reading*
illemim *for the
text's* elim (gods).

Ps. 83:2.

Job 30:5.

There is none like You among the dumb,°
Keeping silence and being still in the face of those who aggrieve us.
Our foes are many; they rise up against us,
As they take counsel together to revile us.
"Where is your King?," they taunt us.   5
But we have not forgotten You nor deceived You.
    Do not keep silence!°

Those driven from the midst of men° became proud.
They crushed Your people with rigor.
Your enemies lifted up their head,   10
Those seekers of ghosts and of idols.
Our foes would judge us, and are saying:
"How now, you hapless Jews!"
    Do not keep silence!

"Be receptive to advice,   15
Lest you turn into disgrace.
Yea, to quarrel and to strife,
But, if you will be like us,
Turning to us, coming close,
One people we shall be."   20
    Do not keep silence!

In answer cried the smitten ones:

"From our God we turn not, nor shall we worship yours!

Deut. 7:26 in reference to the Canaanite cult.
'You shall utterly detest, and utterly abhor it.'°

Alive and enduring is our Redeemer,　　　　　　　　　　25

Him we shall serve, and Him we praise.

In time of trouble, He is our salvation."

　　Do not keep silence!

They made ready to slay their children,

Intending the blessing of sacrifice.　　　　　　　　　　30

"Hear O Israel, the Lord is our God,

Opening words of the Shemaʿ Deut. 6:4.
The Lord is One."° Let us proclaim His Unity!

For His Name's holiness are we slain,

Our wives and children are falling by the sword.

　　Do not keep silence!　　　　　　　　　　　　　　35

Terminology of animal sacrifice in Leviticus.
As priests for the slaughter of their holocaust,°

They bound the children and their mothers;

And, in the fire, they burned their skins,

Sprinkling the blood of sisters and brothers,

Offering as sweet savored sacrificial portions　　　　　40

The head and severed parts of flesh.

　　Do not keep silence!

A charred and overflowing pile,

Terminology of Sabbath laws. Lev. 10:6. Nadav and Avihu.
Like an oven both uncovered and unswept;°

All Israel weeps for the burning.°　　　　　　　　　　45

But those falling in God's fire

Are destined for His initiates' abode,

Like Hananiah, Mishael and Azariah.

　　Do not keep silence!

As refuse they treated Moses' Law,　　　　　　　　　50

According to tradition, the final redactors of the Talmud. 12, par. 12. Exod. 32:16.
The Talmud of Rabhina and Rabh Ashi.°

Can You, at this, restrain Yourself and keep Your peace?

Pages and parchments destroyed by flailing sword,

Yet holy letters flying up on high—°

God's writing on the tablets is engraved.°　　　　　　55

　　Do not keep silence!

The foe was strutting with his sword,

Destroyed my precious ones, made them to nought.

According to the Mekhilta Beshallah 5, Nahshon ben Amminadav jumped into the Sea of Reeds even before it parted. Israel, after Deut. 32:10. Nisan.
And he slew all who did my eye delight.

The year: four thousand nine hundred and seven,　　　60

When trouble closely followed trouble,

And, for my feet, they set a snare.

　　Do not keep silence!

The day when Nahshon hallowed God,°

The foe struck at the apple of His eye;°　　　　　　　65

On the twentieth day of the first month,°

They were dashed to pieces, the expounders of weighty
And light matters of the Law, and of analogous reasoning,
Of statutes, ordinance and teachings.
    Do not keep silence! 70

Almighty God, be zealous for Your Law.
Put on Your vengeance and Your zeal.

Ps. 80:3. Arouse Your mighty power—°

Reference to
Amalek-Rome. As You once rebuked the swinish beast°
With destruction and havoc and breaking. 75
Him and his people You smote with the plague.
    Do not keep silence!

Egypt. Your right hand once smote the monster of the Nile.°
Crush now with a hammer the skull of her

Isa. 47:8. That sits securely to her pleasures given.° 80

Conflation of Song
of Songs 5:10 and Bright and ruddy as You came from Seir,°
Isa. 63:1–3. Seir- Scatter with destructive storm the one who now does rule.
Edom. Like a tested warrior, do arouse Your zeal!
    Do not keep silence!

Make our remnants Your own once again. 85
Among crowds show us Your wonders.
Establish peace upon us!
Pity, O our Holy One, those whom You have dispersed;

Ps. 51:14. Let a willing spirit uphold us.°

Ps. 44:27. Arise for our help, and redeem us!° 90
    Do not keep silence!

ca. 1147

27 O Law, Consumed by Fire

MEIR OF ROTHENBURG

O [Law], consumed by fire, seek the welfare of those who mourn for you,

In the Land of   of those who yearn to dwell in the court of your habitation.°
Israel. Of those who yearn for the dust of the earth, who grieve
    and are horrified over the conflagration of your parchments.

Isa. 50:10. They grope in the dark, bereft of light,° 5
    indeed, they long for the daylight to shine upon them and upon you.
[Seek too] after the welfare of one who sighs and weeps with a broken heart;
    who always bewails the pangs of your agony—

And who howls like jackals and ostriches,
    and cries out bitter lamentation for your sake.   10

How was it that [the Torah] given [by God], the Consuming Fire, should be
    consumed by fire of mortals, and that the heathens were not singed through
    your burning coals?
How long will you lie [resting] in profound tranquillity, O, Edom,
    while the faces of my young ones° are covered with nettles?   15
You sit in arrant haughtiness to judge the sons of God in every cause,
    and to bring [us] before your tribunal.°

Moreover, you [O Law,] even decreed the burning of the edicts and the statutes
    [which were given] with fire,°
    therefore, blessed be he, who shall requite you.°   20
O [my Holy Law,] was it for this that my creator delivered you with lightning
    and fire,
    that at the end fire should blaze upon your skirt?
O Sinai, is it for this that God, rejecting the loftier [peaks], has chosen you,
    and [his glory] has shone in your confines?°   25
[Was that] to be an omen, that the Law would [one day] be humiliated
    and descend from its glory?° Behold, I will tell you a parable.
The parable is of a king who wept at his son's wedding feast,
    [for] he foresaw that he would die;° such was your fate, foretold in your own
    words.°   30

O Sinai, instead of putting on a [noble] mantle, cover yourself with sackcloth,
    change your garments [and] put on widow's clothes!
I will shed tears until they swell as a stream,
    and reach the graves of your two noble chiefs.
And I will enquire of Moses and Aaron, [who were] on Mount Hor: 35
    "Is there then a new Law, is that why they burnt your scrolls?"
In the third month [Israel was exalted] and the fourth turned conspirator
    to destroy your objects of delight,° and all the perfection of your beauty.
[Moses] mutilated the Tablets of stone and even repeated his folly
    by burning the Law in fire.° Is this [the fulfillment of] the double reward?°°40

My soul is amazed—How can ever again food be sweet to my palate
    after beholding what your plunderers have gathered?
Men whom you have rejected from entering the assembly, burnt the Law
    of the Most High in the midst of the market-square, like [the spoils of] a
    condemned [city].°   45
I can no more find any paved way,
    for the straight course of your highway is obscured.
For tears that shall be mingled with my drink shall be sweeter than honey,
    indeed would that your shackels be tied on to my own feet.
    It would be pleasant for my eyes to draw the waters of my tears, for all   50
    who clung fast to the hem of your skirt.
But they would dry up [as soon] as they run down my cheeks,
    for my heart burns over the absence of your Divine Master.

My priests.

I.e., God caused
us to be judged by
the enemy.
Exod. 17:18.
Ps. 137:8.

Midrash on Ps.
68:17.

When the Temple
was destroyed.

On the same day.
When the
Israelites
proclaimed: "We
will faithfully do
and obey!" (Exod.
24:7).

Moses smashed
the tablets of the
Law on the
seventeenth of
Tammuz.
Isa. 61:7.

Deut. 13:17.

The righteous whose good deeds protect the rest of Israel.

He took his treasure with him,°
    [and when] he went far away did not your [protecting] shade vanish?   55
And as for me, alone without your great one, I remain bereaved and forlorn,
    like a sole beacon on top of the mountain.
No more do I hear the voice of singing men and singing women,
    for the strings of your [wind] instruments are snapped.
I will clothe and cover myself with sackcloth, for your slain ones,   60

Jer. 15:8.

    whose lives were so very dear to me, have multiplied more [numerous] than the sand.°
I am indeed astonished that the day's luminary shines [bright]
    to everyone, but to me and you it grows darkness.
O cry to the Rock with a bitter voice, for your catastrophe   65
    and your anguish; O that he would remember the love of your betrothal-day!
Gird on garments of sackcloth for that devouring [fire]
    that burst forth to divide you [into many portions], and has utterly swept away your heights.
May the Creator comfort you according to the days of your affliction, and   70
    may he restore
    the captivity of the tribes of Yeshurun, and raise your meek ones [from their lowliness].
You will again adorn yourself with ornaments of scarlet;
    you will take up timbrel and lead the circling dance, and rejoice in your   75
    revels.
Then shall my heart be uplifted at that time when your Creator will afford you light,
    will brighten your darkness and illuminate your [sorrowing] gloom.

ca. 1242

28 The Martyr's Prayer

ISAIAH HALEVI HOROWITZ

The Martyr's Prayer

You are holy and your name is holy and the holy martyrs of Israel have sanctified and will again sanctify your name. They will suffer all manner of death and torture for the sanctification of your name and for the deliverance of the nation of Israel.

God, O Holy One, if it is your will to bring this test upon me, sanctify me and purify me; make my thoughts and my mouth proclaim the holiness of your name in public, as did the Ten Martyrs and the thousands and myriads of martyrs of Israel. . . .

Be near me so that the pain not confuse me and my thoughts continue to cleave to you, joyful in the hour of suffering.

Strengthen my power of speech that I may proclaim your holiness clearly and consciously and manifest to all.

Purify me of my sins, iniquities, and transgressions and let my portion be with the martyrs who cleave to your holiness.

VI

The Spanish Exile

Once the Jews of Ashkenaz definitively established *Kiddush Hashem* as an either-or proposition, as a matter of life or death, they set about celebrating and commemorating this apotheosis of self-sacrifice in poems, prayers and memorial rites. Such a model response to religious persecution left little room for instances of apostasy, though there was ample evidence of such at least since the eleventh century. Across the European continent, however, on the Iberian peninsula, the problem of forced conversion loomed very large, and the response that evolved over time became a unique feature of Sephardic Jewry: the tract of consolation addressed to those who were then living or had previously lived as Marranos, secret Jews.

Maimonides, the most celebrated of all Sephardic Jews, lived at a time of religious persecution in Muslim Spain. The country had recently been overrun by a fundamentalist Muslim sect called the Almohads, who adopted a policy of forced conversion to Islam. Many Jews were coerced into making a public affirmation that Muhammad was the prophet of God; others refused and suffered martyrdom. To avoid such a fate, Maimonides and his family fled to Fez, Morocco, and later to Egypt. While still in Fez, Maimonides learned of a *halakhic* ruling made by a rabbi to a forced convert. The latter had inquired whether he would gain merit by secretly observing as many commandments as he could. Outraged by the rabbi's negative reply, Maimonides wrote his own exposition on the meaning of martyrdom **(29)**.

Maimonides defended a nonheroic model of response. He did this by distinguishing between speech and action (what the Moroccan Jews professed in public and what they performed in private) and by defining

Kiddush Hashem as a convenantal framework for the relationship between God and Israel, which was always open to the possibility of *teshuvah*, repentance. As David Hartman recently explained it, Maimonides tried to strengthen the faith of the Moroccan Jewish community even as he tried to allay its guilt (*Crisis and Leadership: Epistles of Maimonides* [Philadelphia: The Jewish Publication Society, 1985], pp. 46–90). In the end, he counseled whoever could to settle elsewhere. Heeding his own advice, Maimonides then left for the Land of Israel and then settled in Egypt.

Three hundred years later, the entire Iberian-Jewish community suffered its ultimate catastrophe, this time at the hands of Christian rulers: the expulsion from Spain in 1492 and the forced conversion of Portuguese Jews, many of whom were Spanish refugees, in 1497. Those who remained on the Iberian peninsula either lived as New Christians or were ultimately flushed out by the Inquisition as Marranos. By 1507, when King Manuel of Portugal allowed the so-called New Christians to emigrate, the Iberian Peninsula was officially free of Jews.

The scattered remnant sought the key to its calamity in history itself. Two groups of Iberian-Jewish exiles were particularly concerned with the chronology and cause of recent events: those who saw the Exile as the culmination of past persecutions and those who looked to the coming of the Messiah to put an end to history.

Solomon Ibn Verga belonged to the first group. The extraordinary success of his *Shevet Yehudah (The Sceptre of Judah),* published posthumously by his son in 1553, showed that the chronicling of historical suffering could console future generations no less than the hope of imminent redemption.

Shevet Yehudah, as Yosef Yerushalmi has pointed out (*Zakhor: Jewish History and Jewish Memory* [Seattle, London, and Philadelphia: The University of Washington Press and The Jewish Publication Society 1982], p. 65), contained not a trace of messianism. Indeed, Ibn Verga saw the world as an unstable place where only a king could be trusted to protect the Jews, who were largely to blame for the violence and hatred unleashed upon them by the rabble. When Ibn Verga enumerated the seven causes for the persecution **(33)**, only the first presented the traditional attitude that Jews were being punished for the sins of old. Otherwise, the gentiles were guilty on one count—religious intolerance— while the Jews were guilty on five: for killing Jesus, for conspicuous wealth, for running after gentile women, for swearing falsely and for excessive pride. The historian of the Lisbon Massacre **(31)** made a similar point by holding up the rapacious tax collector named Mascarenhas for special blame.

What, then, was so consoling? It was the cumulative saga of so much suffering that had already been withstood, and the privileged place that the Spanish exiles occupied in the larger scheme of things. It was also Ibn Verga's ability to tell the story exceptionally well. Take, for instance, the fifty-second chapter, with which our selection begins **(30)**. Embedded within is the exquisite prayer of a bereaved father whose climactic cry— "A Jew I am and a Jew I shall remain"—surely bespoke the terrible dilemma of the Marranos, one of whom was the author himself. Although some of these stories of exiles and castaways were reminiscent of the Midrash on Lamentations **(17, 19)**, those that described the Inquisition were strikingly new. Through such juxtapositions, both the recapitulated and the unprecedented sorrows became part of an unbroken chain of Israel's history in exile.

The advent of printing helped the Iberian exiles, dispersed throughout Europe and North Africa, to forge an internally coherent response. As early as 1519, the Sephardic community of Venice incorporated in its liturgy a historical dirge by Judah ben David **(34)**, who took the measure of the disaster through standard poetic devices: an epic list of names (Seville, Aragon, Catalonia, Castile, Leon) and a repeated refrain to cover the incremental losses in incremental order (family, community, scholarship, chastity, faith, salvation, covenant, national glory, the divine presence, prayer, prophecy, Torah, the Sabbath and Festivals). What this dirge shared with Ibn Verga was a this-worldly focus that all but eliminated the hope of messianic intervention (see lines 39–40). More startling still, for a liturgical poem, was Ben David's openness about Jewish apostasy, bribery, betrayal and despair. These most controversial stanzas never appeared in the printed sources.

Messianic speculation was the other route taken by the Iberian-Jewish exiles. The most idiosyncratic exponent of this approach (who, for that reason, was excluded from the anthology) was scholar and statesman Don Isaac Abravanel (1437–1508). Exiled from the land where he had enjoyed so much power and privilege, Abravanel turned against the political life and the kings of flesh and blood to uphold instead the true Sovereign of History. In his biblical and aggadic commentaries, Abravanel laid out a three-act messianic drama, beginning with God's vengeance upon the Christians and Muslims, followed by the return of the Ten Lost Tribes, and culminating in the resurrection of the dead. The drama was supposed to begin in 1503 (or, alternatively, 1531). (See Benzion Netanyahu, *Don Isaac Abravanel: Statesman and Scholar*, 3rd ed. [Philadelphia: The Jewish Publication Society, 1972].)

As Abravanel had seen his own political life end so abruptly, he imagined that God would bring history itself to an absolute, cataclysmic end. About a century later, a new mystical teaching began to emerge from Safed that incorporated the endings of history—expulsion, mass conversion and foreign invasion—into a single, all-encompassing myth. This Lurianic myth declared that evil had its roots in a primal tragic flaw that occurred at the very creation of the cosmos itself (see Gershom Scholem, *Major Trends in Jewish Mysticism* [New York: Schocken, 1954], chap. 7). The task of the mystic was to redeem the sparks of holiness from the "shells" into which they had been thrust and to unify the sparks through acts of *tikkun*, or cosmic restoration. Isaac Luria of Safed (1534–1574), who formulated this teaching, was said to have held the key to the structure of the cosmos and to have effected such acts of *tikkun*.

Thus, two strategies were added to the arsenal of Jewish responses to catastrophe: the embrace of historical chronicles as a source of consolation and a new messianic scheme in which the mystic became the hero of history. Both were to have a profound impact on the new center of world Jewry—eastern Europe.

29 The Epistle on Martyrdom

MOSES MAIMONIDES

Maimonides is here exploiting his medical know-how in a metaphoric vein.

B. Sanhedrin 74a–b.

In the Talmud, Esther is cleared of her guilt for marrying a gentile king since she submitted to him passively.

During the Sassanian rule in Persia (226–651 C.E.), the Jews were required to heat the Persian places of worship; the authorities did this strictly for their own benefit. If the oppressor is not intent on conversion, the individual should yield under all circumstances and

Realizing this amazing matter that hurts the eyes, I undertook to gather pharmaceutics and roots from the books of the ancients, of which I intend to prepare medicine and salve helpful for this sickness, and heal it with the help of God.°

I think it right to divide what I have to say on this subject into five themes: 1. the class of the laws related to the time of forced conversion; 2. definitions of the desecration of God's name and the punishment; 3. the ranks of those who die a martyr's death, and those who are forcibly converted in a persecution; 4. how this persecution differs from others, and what is to be done in relation to it; and 5. a discussion of how advisable it is for one to be careful in this persecution, may God soon put an end to it. Amen.

Theme one, the distribution of the precepts during a time of duress, is divided into three classes: A. One class of precepts, those concerning idolatry, incest, and bloodshed, requires that whenever a person is forced to violate any of them, he is at all times, everywhere, and under all circumstances obliged to die rather than transgress. *At all times* means in a time of persecution or otherwise; *everywhere* means privately or publicly; *under all circumstances* means whether the tyrant intends to have him act against his faith or not; in these situations he is obliged to die rather than transgress. B. All the other commandments, any of which an oppressor may compel him to transgress, he is to judge. If the tyrant does it for his personal satisfaction, be it a time of persecution or not, privately or publicly, he may violate the Torah and escape death. Support of this procedure is found in the chapter on the wayward son:° "But the case of Esther was public! Yes, but she was always passive."° Rava maintained: "If it is for his personal satisfaction it makes a difference; otherwise how do we allow ourselves to give them the censers and the coal-containers?"° Clearly, it is because it makes a difference when it is for their personal satisfaction. In the case of Esther the similar difference exists: It is for their personal satisfaction. Rava is following his own reasoning, for he rules that if a non-Jew orders a Jew to cut the alfalfa on a Sabbath day and throw it before his beasts or he will kill him, he is to cut it and not have himself killed. But if he orders him to cast it into the river, he is to prefer death to obeying him, since he wants him to commit a sin. It is our principle to follow Rava's decision. It is clear that as long as the oppressor is doing it for his personal satisfaction he is to transgress and to shun death, even if it is in public and in the course of a persecution.° C. If it is the aim of the oppressor to have him transgress, it is for him to deliberate. If it is a time of persecution he is to surrender his life and not transgress, whether in private or in public, but if it is not, he should choose to transgress and not die if it is in private, and to die if it is in public.° This is how the sages formulate it: When Rabbi Dimi arrived he ruled in the name of Rabbi Johanan that even if it is not a time of persecution, he may transgress rather than die only in private; in public he may not violate even a minor rabbinic precept, *thus save his life. Since he is not serving as an example to others, he may yield to the oppressor.*

11.
22.
10.

Deut. 15:22–23.

1 Kings 12:20-33. *He is notorious as the man "who sinned and he led many to sin." Julianus and Pappus;* **12:15.**

Death by the sword, stoning, strangulation, burning, premature death, divinely caused death and lashes.

B. Pesaḥim 25b.

Maimonides is discriminating between a forced convert who is still guilty of profaning God's name and a deliberate sinner. On Lev. 10, in the section dealing with the people who dedicate their offspring to Molech.

even changing the manner of tying the shoes. *In public* is defined as a body of ten, all Israelites. . . .

Theme three is about the gradation of those who are martyrs for God's name and those whom persecution forces to convert. You have to realize that wherever the sages rule that one is to surrender his life and not transgress, one who was executed has sanctified God's name. If ten Israelites witnessed his death he has sanctified His name publicly. It includes Hananiah, Mishael, Azariah,° Daniel, the ten martyrs by government order,° the seven children of Hannah,°° and all the other victims of Israel, may God avenge their blood in the near future. It is to them that the verse refers: *Bring in My devotees, who made a covenant with Me over sacrifice* [Ps. 50:5]. To the rabbis this verse seemed appropriate: *I adjure you O maidens of Jerusalem, by gazelles or by hinds of the field* [Song of Songs 2:7], which means—*I adjure you, O maidens of Jerusalem,* the persecuted generations; *by gazelles,* those who did for Me what I desired, so I did what they desired; *by hinds of the field,* those who shed their blood for Me like the blood of the gazelles and the hinds.° To them this verse also refers: *It is for Your sake that we are slain all day long* [Ps. 44:23].

A person to whom God grants the privilege of ascending to this high rank, in other words, to suffer a martyr's death, even if he is as sinful as Jeroboam ben Nebat and his associates,° is surely one of the members of the world-to-come, although he may not be learned. The rabbis infer this from the tradition that no creature is qualified to attain the status of the martyrs by government order: "Is it Rabbi Akiba and his colleagues? But of course not! They are beneficiaries of learning and good deeds. No, it is the martyrs of Lydda."°

Now, if he did not surrender himself to death but transgressed under duress and did not die, he did not act properly, and under compulsion he profaned God's name. However, he is not to be punished by any of the seven means of retribution.° Not a single instance is found in the Torah in which a forced individual is sentenced to any of the punishments, whether the transgression was light or grave. Only he who acts voluntarily is subject, as Scripture directs: *But the person . . . who acts defiantly . . . that soul shall be cut off* [Num. 15:30], but not of one who was forced. The Talmud often says: The Torah rules that the forced individual is not culpable, *for this case is like that of a man attacking another and murdering him* [Deut. 22:26], and frequently the ruling is repeated; a forced individual is excused by the Torah.° He is not dubbed a transgressor, nor a wicked man, nor is he disqualified from giving testimony, unless he committed a sin that disqualifies him from serving as a witness. He simply did not fulfill the commandment of sanctifying God's name, but he can under no circumstance be named a deliberate profaner of God's name.

Therefore, anyone who claims or thinks that a person who transgressed is to be condemned to death, because the sages established the principle that one must surrender himself to death and not transgress, is absolutely wrong. It simply is not so, as I shall explain. True, it is upon him to surrender to death, but if he does not he is not guilty.° Even if he worships idols under duress his soul will not be cut off, and he is certainly not executed by court order. This principle is clearly stated in the Sifra:° The divine Torah rules regarding one who gives of his seed to Molech: *I Myself will set My face against that man* [Lev. 20:5], not if he was forced, nor if it was unwittingly, nor if he was taught wrong. Plainly then, if he was forced or was taught wrong his soul will not be cut off, although it will be if he does it presumptuously and voluntarily. It is even plainer that if he was forced to commit sins that, if presumptuously and voluntarily committed, are punished by forty lashes, he is not at all subject to this punishment. The law against profanation is stated prohibitively in the declaration of God, blessed be He: *You shall not profane My holy name* [Lev. 22:32].

Now it is known that a false oath is profanation, as we read in the Torah: *You shall not swear falsely by My name, profaning the name of your God: I am the Lord* [Lev. 19:12].° Yet the text of the Mishnah reads: "Men may vow to murderers, robbers, and tax-gatherers that what they have is heave-offering. . . ." The school of Shammai qualifies that they may confirm this with a vow; the school of Hillel broadens it to include even an oath. This is explicitly written. These matters are clear and in no need of supportive argument of any kind, for how can anyone suggest that the law with respect to a person who acted under duress and one who acted voluntarily is the same? And our sages ruled: "Let him transgress and surrender his life." So you see, this man° is of higher status than the sages, and more punctilious about the Law. By word of mouth and the use of his tongue, he surrenders himself to death and claims to have sanctified God's name. But by his actions he is a sinner and rebellious, and he makes himself guilty against his life, because God, exalted be He, established *by the pursuit of which man shall live* [Lev. 18:5], and not die.

Theme four deals with the difference between this persecution and others, and what a person should do. Remember that in all the difficulties that occurred in the time of the sages, they were compelled to violate commandments and to perform sinful acts. The Talmud lists the prohibitions, that they may not study Torah, that they may not circumcise their sons, and that they have intercourse with their wives when they are ritually unclean. But in this persecution they are not required to do anything but say something, so that if a man wishes to fulfill the 613 commandments secretly° he can do so. He incurs no blame for it, unless he set himself without compulsion to desecrate the Sabbath, although no one forced him. This compulsion imposes no action, only speech. They° know very well that we do not mean what we say, and that what we say is only to escape the ruler's punishment and to satisfy him with this simple confession. Anyone who suffered martyrdom in order not to acknowledge the apostleship of "that man,"° the only thing that can be said of him is that he has done what is good and proper, and that God holds great reward in store for him. His position is very high, for he has given his life for the sanctity of God, be He exalted and blessed. But if anyone comes to ask me whether to surrender his life or acknowledge, I tell him to confess and not choose death. However, he should not continue to live in the domain of that ruler.° He should stay home and not go out, and if he is dependent on his work let him be the Jew in private. There has never yet been a persecution as remarkable as this one, where the only coercion is to say something. When our rabbis ruled that a person is to surrender himself to death and not transgress, it does not seem likely that they had in mind speech that did not involve action. He is to suffer martyrdom only when it is demanded of him to perform a deed, or something that he is forbidden to do.

A victim of this persecution should follow this counsel: Let him set it as his objective to observe as much of the Law as he can. If it happens that he has sinned

---

The second half of the verse is the result of the first.

The rabbi who wrote the response to the convert.

Despite his insistence that these converts can continue to live as Jews, Maimonides is cautious enough to advise secrecy, lest the authorities not tolerate their public behavior as Jews.
The Moslems and their rulers.

Muhammad.

Maimonides' own departure from Spain, and later from Fez, may have resulted from his fear that he was in danger of being recognized as a Jew.

There are detailed rabbinic prohibitions against moving things back and forth from a home to a public area on the Sabbath.

When a person is guilty of a grievous sin or crime and incurs severe punishment, he must not be chastised for a minor offense.

1 Kings 12:28–33.

much, or that he has desecrated the Sabbath, he should still not carry what it is not allowed to carry.° He must not think that what he has already violated is far more grievous than what he observes;° let him be as careful about observance as possible. Remember, a person must learn this fundamental principle. Jeroboam ben Nebat° is chastised for making the calves, and for disregarding the regulations regarding the Sabbath that comes immediately after a holiday, or the like. None can claim that he was guilty of a more serious sin. This principle is applicable only in man-made laws in this world. God inflicts punishment for grievous sins and for minor ones, and He rewards people for everything they do. Hence it is important to bear in mind that one is punished for every sin committed and is rewarded for every precept fulfilled. Any other view of this is wrong.

What I counsel myself, and what I should like to suggest to all my friends and everyone that consults me, is to leave these places and go to where he can practice religion and fulfill the Law without compulsion or fear. Let him leave his family and his home and all he has, because the divine Law that He bequeathed to us is more valuable than the ephemeral, worthless incidentals that the intellectuals scorn; they are transient, whereas the fear of God is eternal. Moreover, when two Jewish cities are at one's elbow, one superior to the other in its actions and behavior, more observant and more concerned with the precepts, the God-fearing individual is obliged to depart from the town where the actions are not at their best, and move to the better township. We are guided by the admonition of the rabbis not to dwell in a city in which there are fewer than ten righteous residents.°

Cf. Pirkei de-Rabbi Eliezer, chap. 26.

They derive this from a dialogue between God and Abraham, which concludes the account of Sodom. *What if ten righteous people should be found there? And He answered: "I will not destroy, for the sake of the ten"* [Gen. 18:32]. This is the proper thing to do when both cities are Jewish. But if the place is gentile, the Jew who resides there must by all means leave it and go to a more suitable location. He must make every effort to do so although he may expose himself to danger, so that he can get away from this bad spot where he cannot practice his religion properly, and strive to reach a comfortable place. Indeed, the prophets have spelled out that a person who resides among nonbelievers is one of them,° and so King

Based on B. Ketubbot 110b.

David complained: *For they have driven me out today, so that I cannot have a share in the Lord's possession, but am told, "Go and worship other gods"* [1 Sam. 26:19]; he equated his dwelling among the gentiles with the worship of other gods. The pious and the God-fearing are required to despise evil and its doers, for so David declared: *O Lord, You know I hate those who hate You, and loathe Your adversaries* [Ps. 139:21]. He also announced: *I am a companion to all who fear You, to those who keep Your precepts* [Ps. 119:63]. Likewise, our father Abraham, we find, despised his family and his home and ran for his life to escape from the doctrines of the heretics.

This is the effort he must make to separate himself from the heretics when they do not coerce him to do as they do; he should leave them. But if he is compelled to violate even one precept it is forbidden to stay there. He must leave everything he has, travel day and night until he finds a spot where he can practice his religion. The world is sufficiently large and extensive. The appeal of the person who pleads his duties to his family and his household is really no excuse. *A brother cannot redeem a man, or pay his ransom to God* [Ps. 49:8]. I do not think it is right to make this plea in order to avoid the obligation and not flee to a reasonable place. He must under no circumstance continue to reside in the land of persecution. If he does, he is a transgressor, profanes God's name, and is almost a presumptuous sinner.

Those who delude themselves to think that they will remain where they are until the king Messiah appears in the Maghreb, and they will then leave for Jerusalem—I simply do not know how they will rid themselves of the present difficulties. They are transgressors, and they lead others to sin. The prophet Jeremiah's criticism: *They offer healing offhand for the wounds of My people, saying, "all is well, all is well," when nothing is well* [Jer. 6:14 and 8:11], fits them and others like them very well. There is no set time for the arrival of the Messiah that they can count on and decide that it is close or distant. The incumbency of the commandments does not depend on the appearance of the Messiah. We are required to apply ourselves to study and to the fulfillment of the precepts, and we must strive for perfection in both. If we do what we have to, we or our children or grandchildren may be privileged by God to witness the coming of the Messiah, and life will be more pleasant. If he does not come we have not lost anything; on the contrary we have gained by doing what we had to do. But it is wicked and hopeless and a renunciation of the faith for anyone to stay on in these places and see the study of Torah cease, the Jewish population perishing after some time, he himself unable to live as a Jew, but continue to say: "I will stay here until the Messiah appears and then I shall be relieved of the situation I am in."

Theme five is concerned with how a person should regard himself in this persecution. Anyone who cannot leave because of his attachments, or because of the dangers of a sea voyage, and stays where he is, must look upon himself as one who profanes God's name, not exactly willingly, but almost so. At the same time he must bear in mind that if he fulfills a precept, God will reward him doubly, because he acted so for God only, and not to show off or be accepted as an observant individual. The reward is much greater for a person who fulfills the Law and knows that if he is caught, he and all he has will perish. It is he who is meant in God's qualification: *If only you seek Him with all your heart and soul* [Deut. 4:29]. Nevertheless, no one should stop to plan to leave the provinces that God is wroth with, and to exert every effort to achieve it.°

It is not right to alienate, scorn, and hate people who desecrate the Sabbath. It is our duty to befriend them, and encourage them to fulfill the commandments. The rabbis regulate explicitly that when an evildoer who sinned by choice comes to the synagogue, he is to be welcomed and not insulted. In this ruling they relied on Solomon's counsel: *A thief should not be despised for stealing to appease his hunger* [Prov. 6:30]. It means do not despise the evildoer in Israel when he comes secretly to "steal" some observance.

Ever since we were exiled from our land persecution is our unending lot, because *from our youth it has grown with us like a father and from our mother's womb it has directed us* [Job 31:18].° But we frequently find in the Talmud, "a persecution is likely to pass."° May God put an end to this one, and may the prediction be realized. *In those days and at that time—declares the Lord—the iniquity of Israel shall be sought, and there shall be none; the sins of Judah, and none shall be found; for I will pardon those I allow to survive* [Jer. 50:20]. May it be His will. Amen.

Maimonides does not concede the right to transgress and make peace with the idea of continuing to live on enemy turf.

Maimonides applies Job's personal confession to the fate of the entire Jewish people.
B. Ketubbot 36.

30 The Fate of the Exiles

SOLOMON IBN VERGA

The Fifty-Second

I heard tell from aged exiles of Spain that a certain ship was struck with plague and that the ship's owner cast the passengers off onto uninhabited terrain. Most died there of hunger; only a few found the strength to proceed on foot in search of civilization.

Now among these was a certain Jew who struggled on with his wife and two sons. The wife, whose feet were untried, fainted and perished, leaving her husband, who was carrying the boys. He and his sons also fainted from hunger; when he awoke he found the two dead. In agony, he rose to his feet and cried, "Master of the Universe! You go to great lengths to force me to desert my faith. Know for a certainty that in the face of the dwellers of heaven, a Jew I am and a Jew I shall remain; all that You have brought upon me or will bring upon me shall be of no avail!" Then he gathered dirt and grasses, covered the boys, and went off in search of a settlement.

The group of Jews did not stand about waiting to die; but each one was so enmeshed in his own soul's sorrow that he gave no heed to his fellow.

The Fifty-Third

Those who went to Fez suffered His judgments, be He blessed, particularly keen hunger. Denied entry to the cities by their inhabitants, who feared that food prices would soar, they pitched their tents in the fields and there sought out wild plants, praying that they might find some—for drought had destroyed all the vegetation, leaving only roots. Many died in the field with none to bury them, so weakened were the survivors by hunger. On the Sabbath day they would forage only with their mouths, taking comfort in the fact that they plucked nothing with their hands.

Something unheard-of took place there: an Arab came along, saw a beautiful Jewish girl, possessed her in the sight of her mother and father and went his way. Some half an hour later he returned, spear in hand, and ran her through the belly. "Monster!" they called out. "Why have you done this?" He answered that he feared lest the girl might have become impregnated and that the child would have been raised in the Jewish faith. Oh, hear and see: has ever the like been seen or heard of in the whole world!?

There, too, a poor woman saw her son faint away. Having no means of subsistence and seeing that his death was certain, she lifted a stone and hurled it upon his head, and the boy died. Then she struck herself until she, too, expired.

The Fifty-Fourth

When the Jews were in the field near Fez, so intense was the famine in the land that a Jew would go to the city and sell his child into slavery for a loaf of bread. The king of Fez, however, was a just and kind king: at the famine's end he proclaimed that anyone who had bought a Jewish youth for bread had to release him to his father and mother.

The Fifty-Fifth

At another location near Fez there was a large vessel owned by the heathen, and the youths, Jewish youths, would approach that spot, called Saleh, to scavenge sustenance from the sea. Now the owner of the vessel met them on the seashore and gave each one of them a piece of bread. Seeing bread, the youths were overjoyed and brought the news to their fellows. On the day following this report, about one hundred and fifty youths arrived at the seashore. The shipowner told them to come on board and eat bread to their fill; but when they boarded he lifted anchor and sailed off with them all. Now when news of this reached the Hebrew camp, and particularly when the women heard it, they rushed to the shore and screamed, but there was none to save them. And there the mothers of those youths raised a din of shouting and weeping such as had never been heard before. And that cruel man set aside the brightest and handsomest of those youths and made a present of them to the country's rulers; the rest he sold in a foreign land.

The Fifty-Sixth

Exiled from Spain, some boats reached Italian territory, where the famine was also great. The plague was widespread on board ship and the poor people did not know what to do; finally they disembarked. The townspeople, however, barred their entry, so they journeyed on to the district of Genoa where they were allowed to enter the city even though the famine was strong there as well. The young men, however, unable to endure further privation, would go to the house of idolatrous worship to change their faith in order to receive a bit of bread. Many of the uncircumcised circulated in the marketplace, crucifixes in one hand and a morsel of bread in the other, saying to the young men of Israel, "Only bow to this—and have bread!" In this way many converted and were swallowed up amongst the nations.

The Fifty-Seventh

Some of the Jews who had come to Genoa, seeing that the famine was intense there, left on foot for Rome. The Jews of Rome, however, gathered to confer as to what action to take to prevent the entry of strangers into their midst who would damage their livelihoods. At once they collected a thousand florins to give the Pope as a gift that he might not welcome them into his domain. Now when this was all related to the Pope, he said, "Here is something new to me! I have heard tell that Jews normally pity one another; and look—these people act cruelly! Therefore I decree that they, too, shall be banished: no longer shall they dwell in my domain." The Jews of Rome had to collect two thousand additional gold florins as a gift to the Pope to let them be—and to let the foreigners enter the city. Then the poor exiles ate of the good of the land.

The Fifty-Eighth

The owner of one vessel bearing refugees from the Spanish expulsion intended to kill his passengers in order to rob them of their possessions. Now a just and kind merchant was on board, who said, "It would be a grave sin to shed the blood of innocents." That cursed man answered, "I come but to take vengeance for the blood of Jesus that they spilled!" The merchant replied, "He forgave the shedding of His blood in order to save mankind; shall you not offer forgiveness? My advice is to cast them off onto one of the islands: if they die, they die; but let not your hand be upon them." So that cruel man arose, stripped them naked and cast them off near a desolate promontory visited by no man.

Now all the poor, wretched castaways did not stir for very shame, for they were naked; only at night did they walk about in the dark. They drew water from the rocky crevices by the shore—sweet water—and drank it; and so three days passed. At the close of the third day they said to one another. "Let us climb this promontory for a view: perhaps we shall see a city or village and live!" With great difficulty they clambered to the top of that huge rock to seek rescue, but found a pride of lions, who leapt upon them. One man was torn apart; others cast themselves off the rock and were crushed. The poor Jews, hoping for rescue, plunged into the sea to escape the lions; and after the beasts returned to their lairs, swam back to shore and so survived for five days.

On the sixth day they sighted an approaching ship. The people on board, seeing human beings in the distance, were amazed, for they knew that the site was uninhabited and unsuitable for taking rest. The shipowner sent a man ashore to learn what had happened and the Jews told him the evil that had been done them. Moved, the captain had them brought aboard. Then he seized an old sail and ripped it into pieces, giving everyone a portion to cover his private parts; but to the women he gave whole garments in view of the requirements of modesty. Next he gave food and drink to all. Now when he came to a place inhabited by Jews he disembarked his poor passengers, who quickly sent a messenger to their fellow Jews, thinking that the man wanted to sell them. Soon the heads of the Jewish community boarded the vessel, only to be told, "I did not take these paupers captive by the sword in order to have them ransomed. Pay me what I have spent; that will be more than enough." That they did and made him a gift as well. Then the Jews stepped free, and they gave them clothing and drink, as befits the children of Israel.

So long as these poor people lived they prayed to God to lengthen the days of that shipowner and give him his due reward.

31 The Lisbon Massacre of 1506

SOLOMON IBN VERGA

The Fifty-Ninth

In 1493 Joao II deported Portuguese Jewish children to the island of Saint Thomas.

What can we say, what utter, to portray the savage decrees of Lisbon, the worst of which was the banishment of the youths to uninhabited, lost sea isles they called *Islas Perdidas*.° How the women wept and wailed when they were taken off by royal decree and put on board the boats: he who saw it never had witnessed moaning, grief and evil in his life! Pitier or comforter was there none, nor any advocate.

Now one woman had six children taken from her. When she heard that the king was going out to his house of prayer she went out to meet him and fell at his horse's feet, pleading that she be allowed to keep her littlest boy—but he would not hear, commanding his servants, "Get her away from me!" She, however, stubbornly persisted and the servants chastised her. Then the king said, "Let her be: she's like a bitch robbed of her pups!"

May God see and judge the oppression of the children of Israel!

A few hold that this is the reason for that decree: the expelled Jews of Spain promised the king a certain sum for permission to enter his kingdom; in the end, many did not make good, and this was the evil and bitter result.

Now some of those youths died on the boats from change of climate and diet; others, upon landing on the islands, were devoured by reptiles in the lakes and on the seashore. In the course of time it happened that a young man married his sister: some were aware of this and others not. One of their number returned home and wed his mother.

The Sixtieth

An apparent allusion to the massacre both within Lisbon and in the surrounding countryside.

Hebrew: Anusim.

In addition to the Black Death.

I.e., the Dominicans.

The Dominican convent in Lisbon.

The edict of slaughter in Lisbon: I was outside the city. When I returned, days later, I was told, "Not all mirrors are alike:° but truly what all suffered equally is this—the bitterest and most evil of fates. And now I shall set down what that old man told me.

On the first night of Passover Christians found Marranos° seated with matzoth and bitter herbs before them, according to the law of the Passover. They were brought before the king, who commanded that they be incarcerated until they should be tried. Now at that time there was a drought and famine in the land.° The Christians gathered and said, "Why has God treated us and our lands so—surely because of the guilt of these Jews!" Now when the preaching order of the *Predicadores*° heard this claim, they contrived to seek a ruse to help the Christians. One of their number rose in the church° and preached a stinging sermon against the seed of Israel. And devise a ruse they did: they fashioned a hollow icon, its case made of glass with an opening in the rear: inserting a lit candle, they said that fire sprang forth from the icon—whereat the people fell on their faces, crying, "See this great miracle! This teaches us that God had condemned all the seed of the Jews to fire!" Now one Marrano happened there; not having heard these remarks, he naively observed, "A pity the miracle is not of water, rather than fire, for it's water we need with this drought!" The Christians, hot for evil, rose and declared, "Look! He mocks us!" Immediately they took him out and killed him. His brother, hearing of this, came to the spot and cried, "Alas, my brother—who killed you?" At that a swordsman arose, cut off his head and flung it onto his brother's corpse. Following this all the priests arose, took wooden crosses of Jesus the Nazarene, proceeded to the city square and announced, "Anyone who kills a Jew shall receive one hundred days of atonement in the world to come!" At that a mob formed, armed with swords, and in three days killed three thousand souls,° dragging them and pushing them into the street and burning them. A few fetuses

The death toll was probably in excess of 1,000.

were tossed from windows to waiting spears below where the fetuses would jump a number of yards. And there were other barbarities and atrocities that it is not seemly to report.

A few opined that all the hatred of the Christians stemmed from their hatred of one Jew named Mascarenhas, an arrogant tax collector who lorded it over them and promulgated many regulations to their hurt. This theory is strengthened by the fact that as soon as Mascarenhas was found, the killing came to an end.° No blame can be laid to the judges of Lisbon for this affair, nor to its leaders and rulers, for this action was taken in the face of their opposition: they came out to save the Jews, but could not do so in the face of the mob, who moved to lay hands on them as well. Indeed, they had to flee to save their lives.

Now the king of Portugal,° a just and kind°° king, was not in the city at this time. When he heard what had happened he wept and shouted, and returned to the city at once.° Uncovering through investigation the priests' plot, he would have torn down the church whence the evil issued, but his ministers would not allow it. Then he meant to execute all the murderers, but the advisers showed him his crown law, whereby any offense committed by more than fifty people cannot be punished by death: only the instigators could be held accountable. Thereat the king commanded that the priests be arrested and ordered that they be burnt. Now, of old, Lisbon had been known as "the faithful city,"° but the king commanded that for three years it be called "the rebellious city."°

The New Christian Joao Rodrigues, who collected taxes and customs duties for the king. His death did not signal the end of the massacre.

Dom Manuel. Hebrew: Hasid.

Actually, he did not return at all.

Isa. 1:26.

Ezra 4:12, 16; Both names refer to Jerusalem.

32 The Inquisition

SOLOMON IBN VERGA

The Sixty-First

I have heard tell that a few persons in Spain fabricated a tale—that they had found a murdered boy in the home of a Jew, gashed over the heart; they claimed that his heart had been removed for ritual purpose. Don Solomon ha-Levi, a sage and a kabbalist, came and placed a (Divine) name under the boy's tongue. The lad awoke and told who it was who had killed him and had taken out his heart in order to calumniate the poor Jews.

I have not seen this story in writing: I only heard it.

The Sixty-Second

This quasi-magical ritual probably occurred around 1481.

In the great city of Seville lived Rabbi Judah Ibn Verga of blessed memory.° When the Inquisition arrived there the local residents declared that whoever wished to know which Marranos secretly practiced Judaism should arrest Rabbi Judah Ibn Verga, for he determined all matter of Jewish practice. Before he appeared before the Inquisition the rabbi, of blessed memory, knew precisely what he had to do. He set three pairs of doves in the window: the first were plucked and slaughtered, and he wrote on their necks, "These shall be the Marranos who shall leave last"; the second were plucked but not slaughtered, and he said, "These shall be the middle group"; the rest he left alive with their feathers upon them and wrote, "These will be first (to leave)." They, however, did not pay him any mind and suffered what they suffered. And many of the Marranos he passed through fire, so that the heavenly decree would be effectuated thereby. He then fled to Lisbon, where he was tortured mercilessly to disclose who practiced Judaism in secret. He, of blessed memory, withstood the trial and died of his tortures in prison. May the merit of all the martyrs ever stand with us!

33 The Causes of Persecution

SOLOMON IBN VERGA

Sixty-Third

Solomon declared, One is stunned, pondering these awesome tribulations, and asks, "Why is this great wrath? He has not done the like to any nation"—be they ever so more sin-laden than the Jews! All these and like questions are answered by a single verse from Scripture: "You alone have I known (from all the nations), oh children of Israel; therefore I visit all your sins upon you."° In addition there are seven things that brought about what we have endured. The first is the sins of our fathers, as our sages of blessed memory have revealed, saying, "But when I make an accounting, I will bring them to account for their sins."° "Now there is no accounting,"° etc. And the author of Lamentations declared, "Our fathers sinned and are not and we bear their iniquities."° The second reason is that when (our) merit is not great, the Exile continues of its own momentum, due to hatred of our religion as well as the ruler's urge to force them that enter the world to accept his faith and religion. As our sages of blessed memory have said, "Why was that mountain called Sinai? Because thence hatred (sin'ah) descended upon the world!"° And how much more so is this the case when our faith prohibits eating and drinking with them, which draws hearts together, as our sages of blessed memory have said, "Great is imbibement, which brings together them distant from one another."° And they have commented on "for you have done it."°° The third reason is the killing of Jesus the Nazarene. Not for naught did Moses say, "Lo, if we sacrifice the abomination of the Egyptians before their eyes shall they not stone us?"° The fourth: there are three great objects of envy and passion—religion, women and wealth; and in the case of Israel and the nations, all three obtain. In Spain they (the Jews) began to cast eyes on the women of the land, so accustomed were they to do so. Some of them even gave themselves dispensation, asserting

Amos 3:2.

Exod. 32:34.
B. Sanhedrin 102a: "No retribution whatsoever comes upon the world which does not contain a slight fraction of the golden calf."
Lam. 5:7.
B. Shabbat 89a.
B. Sanhedrin 103b.
Lam. 1:21 and Lam. Rabbah 1:56.
Exod. 8:22.

Thirty-nine lashes administered for transgressing a negative commandment. See B. Sanhedrin 81a.

A tosafist (talmudic commentator) and author of Sefer Mitzvot Hagadol. Zeph. 3:13.

Johannes Versoris, rector of the Sorbonne in 1458.

that this called only for the punishment of strokes.° They did not realize, however, that fanatics would attack them° on those grounds and that, for this behavior, tradition held them cut off from their people; and over and above all these sins— that if the woman were impregnated she would bear a devotee of idol worship. Envy of wealth: the Jews arrived with their trades and goods; and whenever one would be found stealing or thieving guilt would—typically—devolve upon them all, resulting in the desecration of God's name: for they maintain that we have no religion. As Rabbi Moses of Coucy wrote,° had our people been guilty only of this, it would have sufficed to prolong our exile; and we read in the prophets, "The remnant of Israel shall not commit iniquity nor speak falsely."° The fifth: the people's habit of swearing falsely. Ibn Ezra wrote that this alone would have sufficed to prolong our exile. The sixth: the excessive pride of some few of our people who would have ruled over the resident heathens of the land like lords. And as regards pride, it happened that in the year of the expulsion, on the eve of the Day of Atonement, an argument erupted in the synagogue, with everyone seizing one of the brands that stood before the synagogue to strike his fellow. And many such (offenses) are ours. The Lord is just!

Now inasmuch as these accounts break the heart, I have seen fit to adduce here a heartening matter, namely, the glory of the Temple in its restoration, as I have found written by the great Versoris,° who was turned to by the just and kind King Alfonso; I have translated it from Latin into our holy tongue.

ca. 1507

34 Know Judah and Israel

JUDAH BEN DAVID

Know, Judah and Israel, I am exceeding bitter;
Therefore I tremble for all my sins.

My heart revives within me when I hear weeping;
On seeing laughter I recoil, yes recoil.

Son, brother, sister, mother, all kin—   5
Weep you your families, gash you your flesh.

Good uncle, all men, all women, weep;
I, weeping, will make all men tremble, tremble.

Gone my song, gone my joy when I bring to my mind
Seville: it is lost, it is utterly lost.   10

Gone God's congregation and students of the Law.

Rise then, oh Judah; Israel—mourn.

My soul shrinks away, is lost for the loss
Of all my congregations—destroyed, destroyed.

My knowledge is gone through that which Time brought;   15
I despise song's notes and the whir of the dance.

Gone salvation's counsel from scholars' mouths:
The foe butchered their finest like sheep and wild asses.

Gone is God's pity, His mercies forgot;
Cruel now he seems; like my enemy.   20

Gone the patriarchs' merit, no more to defend
Their descendants: their stock expires, cut off.

The chasteness of all Jewish women is gone:
They are fallen to foes' hands and defiled, defiled.

Gone faith in my God when my people succumbed   25
To the ravager shouting, "Worship as I!"°

I.e., they converted to Christianity.
I.e., the New Testament has supplanted the Old.
Lines 27–48 missing from all printed versions.

Gone Sinai's faith when the foe declares,
"It is perished, supplanted."° Ah, how they revel!

Gone the crown of all Aragon Jewries; as well,
Catalonia's, subdued by the plundering foe.   30

Gone the bright crown of Castile and Leon;
My tears could fill vessels, weeping their woe.

Gone the hope in the coming of God's Messiah,
Yinon son of David, the fair, the fair.

Salvation is gone from the Hebrew folk;   35
Griefs spring up fresh as a blazing fire.

Gone the home of the Mishnah and Talmud, reviled
In foes' eyes: traitors betray it, betray!°

A veiled reference to the convert and Jew-baiter Geronimo. According to popular legend, the Messiah's arrival was stopped at the last moment.

Converted Jews are cut off from one another and from other Jews.

Mourning for those who have been killed.

We will not hear the call of Elijah, God's prophet:
Restrained in Heaven, he is told, "Stand fast!"°   40

Gone the covenant given to Israel as witness
All the length of our exile. Rebel you no more!

Gone the glory of each soul born to the Jews
As companionship cedes to the wind and the road.°

Gone fathers' joys seeing sons steeped in honor.   45
Fallen they see them—and weary of mourning.°

Gone comfort from Judah; now, in his heart,
Despair deeply roots, yes, roots and blooms.

Gone is God's rule over Jewry's killers;

His people are plundered, and drained through forced   50
    bribes.

Gone the truth of the Torah and God's command:
Through heathen rapine it is learned no more.

Sweetness has gone from the midst of his folk,
But bitterness lacks not—it visits with zeal.   55

Gone sweetness, gone goodness; the words of the wise
Have all taken leave, have rusted away.

My people call out; God gives no reply:
answer, pity, redress are there none.

The Presence is no longer found upon earth,   60
Not in Temple or folk: our Glory departs.

Gone the saying of *Kaddish* and "Bless ye the Lord!"
Gone are the synagogues, razed to the ground.

Gone the sound of God's names, *Tsur*/the Rock, *Adonai,*
Yah, Ehyeh/I shall Be, *Elohim, El Shaddai.*   65

Prophecy departs me, all visions are sealed;
No *Urim,*° no constructions of God's Holy Name.

Worn in the
breastplate of the
high priest and   Gone precentors and helpers, their sweet sounds are still;
used for   Rare poems and the reading of Prophets are gone.
divination; Exod.
28:30.   Gone the study of Torah from little ones' mouths.   70
You who live yet—take sackcloth and wrap your-
    selves round.

Sabbath and Holiday glory are gone:
Then take darkness, pitch darkness, for couch—and recline.

Gone Judah's bright rule until David's son reigns: 75
Oh may he revive, in all splendor, our folk!

VII

The Golden Age of Polish Jewry

In the Jewish scheme of things, great catastrophes worked to intensify existing modes of remembrance rather than supplant them with something more radical. This is perhaps the most difficult aspect of the subject for modern readers to grasp, trained as we are on the notion of commensurability. For us, especially looking back after the destruction of European Jewry in our century, the greater the catastrophe, the more it should challenge the basic theology of sin-retribution-restoration; the more it should undermine the standard rituals and liturgical formula. In fact, the opposite tendency can be seen throughout this anthology: the greater the catastrophe, the more it recalled the ancient archetypes; the more it brought to mind the calamity that had most recently been withstood. Later on, in the twentieth century, this would develop into a self-consciously *neoclassical* mode of response as distinct from the apocalyptic, radical school.

The Jews of eastern Europe could lay claim to all the traditions that had come before because they were becoming the main consumers and producers of Jewish learning. The mid-sixteenth to mid-seventeenth centuries could rightfully be called the Golden Age of Polish Jewry, a time of unprecedented corporate autonomy, economic privilege and religious creativity. All that came to a sudden end with the Cossack revolt under Bogdan Chmielnicki (pronounced *Khmel-nítski*) from 1648 to 1649, which ultimately left the Polish Empire in a permanent state of ruin. Yet even this great catastrophe did not generate anything new. It simply added new impetus to the earlier response: to the writing of historical chronicles and dirges and to the further standardization of *Kiddush Hashem* as the Jewish way of death. If Sabbatianism (the belief that Sabbetai Zvi was the Jewish Messiah) coincidentally arose soon thereafter, this radical movement found few adherents in Poland (see Bernard D. Weinryb, *The Jews of Poland: A Social and Economic History of the Jewish Community in Poland from 1100–1800* [Philadelphia: The Jewish Publication Society, 1972], chap. 10).

Just how conventional the Jewish response to the Chmielnicki uprising was can be seen from the most popular of the contemporary chronicles, Nathan Nata Hanover's *Yeven metsulah* (*The Deep Mire* or *The Abyss of Despair*). Despite his rational attempt to trace the causes of the revolt back to the end of the previous century, he began his chronicle by "proving" that the destruction had been preordained (**35**), thereby implying that the victims did not die for their sins. Politically, he stood exactly where Ibn Verga had stood before him, his faith in the king and the nobles unshaken (**36**). Like the rabbis of the Midrash, Hanover personalized the events of history to tell a dramatic and didactic story of good guys (the heads of the *Yeshiva* and the brave Polish nobility), bad guys (the treacherous Cossacks, the Tatars and the Ukrainian rabble) and martyrs (all the Jews who were killed, whether or not they tried to flee). Written for Jews inside and outside of Poland (the first edition was published in Venice), the chronicle also served a practical purpose: The author supplied the dates of the various massacres so that the survivors would know when to observe the *yortsayt* (anniversary of death) for their lost kin. Finally, the chronicle ended with an eloquent tribute to the Polish-Jewish community modeled on the six attributes of greatness enumerated in the Mishnah. No wonder, then, that in some communities Hanover's account was adopted as recommended reading prior to the fast of Tish'a b'Av.

Just as the Sephardic school of history writing was adapted for broad liturgical use, the esoteric teachings of Lurianic Kabbalah were popularized by Hasidism, the great religious revival movement in eastern Europe that traced its beginnings to Israel Ba'al Shem Tov (ca. 1700–1760). In the apocryphal legends that circulated about him, he was endowed with Isaac Luria's marvelous knowledge and powers.

In both the Lurianic and Hasidic versions, divine *tikkun*, or acts of cosmic restoration, could not be measured in terms of visible reality. Neither the trial nor the torture of the martyrs of Pavlysh (**37**) carried the weight of the story; the significant drama occurred in the midnight struggle of the *tsaddik*, or righteous person. And even the tsaddik's failure to gain divine intercession was testimony to his cosmic powers, for his actions were linked to those of Rabbi Ishmael in the legend of the Ten *Harugei Malkhut* (**22**). And so, on the very threshold of modernity—the tales of the Ba'al Shem Tov were first published in 1815—the Jews of eastern Europe had once again found archetypes and legends to mediate the manifestations of predictable evil.

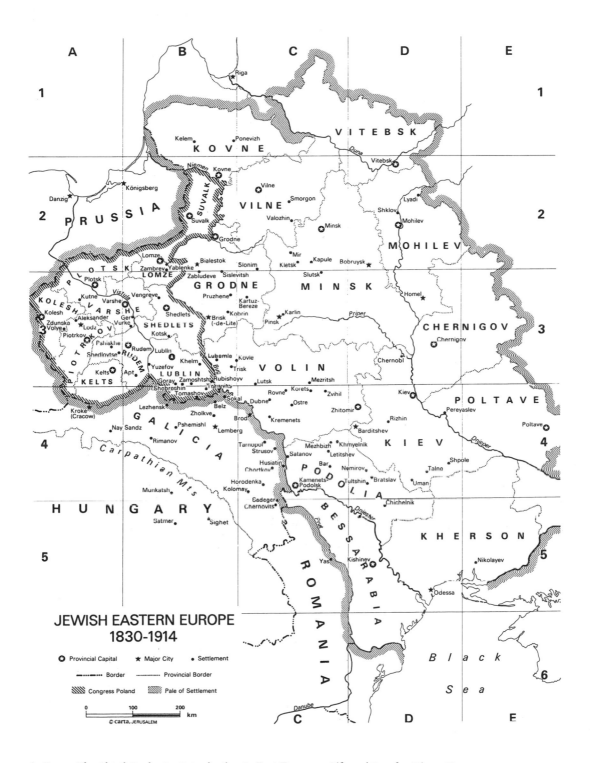

JEWISH EASTERN EUROPE
1830-1914

⊕ Provincial Capital   ★ Major City   • Settlement

–·–·–·– Border   ·········· Provincial Border

▨ Congress Poland   ▨ Pale of Settlement

0   100   200
km

© carta, JERUSALEM

1. From *The Shtetl Book: An Introduction to East European Life and Lore* by Diane K. Roskies and David G. Roskies (Ktav Publishing House, Inc., 2nd revised edition, 1979)

35 The Abyss of Despair

NATHAN NATA HANOVER

Author's Introduction

Lam 3:1 (4).

"I am the man that hath seen the affliction by the rod of His wrath,"° when God smote His people Israel, His first-born. From heaven unto earth He cast down the beautiful and glorious land of Poland, "oh fair in situation, the joy of the whole earth."° "The Lord hath swallowed up unsparingly the habitations of Jacob,"°° the lot of His inheritance,° and hath not remembered His footstool in the day of His anger.°

Ps. 48:3.
Lam. 2:2.
Deut. 32:9.
Lam. 2:1.

All this was foreseen by King David (peace be unto him), when he prophesied the joining of the Tartars and the Greeks° to destroy His chosen Israel, in the year zot° of the era of creation. The "Greeks," in their typical manner, offered the following ultimatum to the Jews: He that wishes to remain alive must change his faith and publicly renounce Israel and his God. The Jews, however, heeded not their words, but stretched out their necks to be slaughtered for the sanctification of His Holy Name. Among them were the land's leading scholars as well as the men, women and children; the whole community. May the God of vengeance avenge them and return us to His land.

Greek Orthodox.
ZOT = 408 = 1648 (each letter of the Hebrew alphabet has a numerical value).

This tragedy was forewarned by King David (peace be unto him), in Psalm 32, where it is said: "For this (*al "zot"*) let everyone that is godly pray unto Thee in a time when Thou mayest be found." (*l'et m'tso*) etc.,° so that no evil may come to pass. The letters of the words *l'et m'tso* (in a time when Thou mayest be found), have the same numerical value as those of *yavan v'kedar yahdav hubaru* ("Greek" and Tartar joined together). The dog and the cat made an alliance to uproot the people of Israel, which is likened to a straying lamb. This occurred in the year (408) of the era of creation (*zot*) omitting the first numeral. Psalm 69 also speaks of this tragic event.

Ps. 32:6.

There it is said: "Save me O God, for the waters are come in even unto the soul, *I am sunk in deep mire where there is no standing.* I am come into deep waters and the flood overwhelmed me . . . etc."° *Tav'ati b'yeven m'tsulah* (I am sunk in the deep mire), is of the same numerical value as *hmiel v'kedar b'yavan yahdav hubaru* (hmiel° and the Tartars joined together with the "Greeks"), the combined virus of a scorpion and a wasp. "*Shibbolet*" (the flood) is numerically equal to *Chmielecki, hayavan v'kedar* (Chmielecki,° the "Greeks" and the Tartars). *Shetafatni shetef* (anger and wrath overwhelmed me), for in the Polish language the name Chmielecki is associated with nobility,° while the Russians referred to him as Chmiel.

Ps. 69:3.

I.e., Chmielnicki.

Should be Chmielnicki.

He was made a member of the Polish nobility.

Rabbi Jechiel Michael, chief of the Jewish community, and head of the academy of the holy congregation of Nemirow, whose soul departed in purity, for the glorification of His Name, referred to the name Chmiel, as representing the first letters of the phrase *Hevle Mashiah yavi l'olam* (he will usher in the pangs of the Messiah).° And after him will come the feet of the messenger.

The trials and tribulations that portend the Messiah's coming.

I named my book *Yeven m'tsulah* (The Deep Mire), because the words of the

Psalmist allude to these terrible events, and speak of the oppressors, the Tartars and the Ukrainians as well as of the arch-enemy, Chmiel, may his name be blotted out, may God send a curse upon him. This book may thus be a chronicle to serve future generations.

I dwelt at length on the causes which led to this great catastrophe, when the Ukrainians and the Tartars united to revolt against Poland, although the two had always been enemies. I recorded all the major and minor encounters, as well as the evil decrees and persecutions; also the days on which those cruelties occurred, so that everyone might be able to calculate the day on which his kin died, and observe the memorial properly. In addition, I have also described the customs and practices of Polish Jewry which followed the path of goodness and righteousness. All this I did with a deep reverence for God. I based these upon the six pillars which support the world.° I have written it in a lucid and intelligible style, and printed it on smooth and clear paper.

According to Avot 1:2, 18: Torah, prayer, lovingkindness, judgment, truth and peace.

Therefore, buy ye this book at once. Do not spare your money, so that I may be enabled to publish the book *'Neta Sha'ashuim'* (Plant of Delights), containing homilies on the Pentateuch which I have authored. For this benevolence the Almighty God will keep you from all evil and distress, and will hasten the coming of the Messiah. Amen, so may it be the will of Him Who dwelleth in splendor.

These are the words of the author Nathan Nata the son of the martyred Rabbi Moses Hanover Ashkenazi (may the memory of the righteous be a blessing, may God avenge his blood) who dwelled in the holy community of Zaslaw, near the holy community of Ostrog in the province of Volhynia, in the land of Russia.

36 The Massacres of the Holy Community of Nemirow

NATHAN NATA HANOVER

The Oppressor Chmiel, may his name be blotted out, heard that many Jews had gathered in the holy community of Nemirow, and that they had a great deal of silver and gold with them. He knew that the holy community of Nemirow was distinguished for its great riches. It had been a great and important community replete with scholars and scribes, a city full of justice, the abode of righteousness, (but now they have been murdered).

June 10, 1648; the twentieth of Sivan was also the anniversary of the massacre at Blois in 1171; later adopted by Polish Jews to commemorate the Cossack uprising.

Accordingly, Chmiel sent a leader, an enemy of the Jews, and about six hundred swordsmen with him, to attack this noble community. In addition, he wrote to the city heads to help the band. The city leaders readily responded to aid them with all their might and main. This they did, not so much because of their love of the Cossacks but because of their hatred of the Jews.

And it came to pass on a Wednesday, the 20th of Sivan,° that Cossacks approached the city of Nemirow. When the Jews saw the troops from afar, their hearts trembled from fright, though they were not certain, as yet, whether they were Polish or Cossack. Nevertheless all the Jews went with their wives, and infants, with their silver and gold, into the fortress, and locked and barred the doors, prepared to fight them. What did those evil-doers, the Cossacks do? They devised flags like those of the Poles, for there is no other way to distinguish between the Polish and the Cossack forces except through their banners. The people of the city were fully aware of this trickery, and nevertheless called to the Jews in the fortress: "Open the gate. This is a Polish army which has come to save you from the hands of your enemies, should they come." The Jews who were standing guard on the wall, seeing that the flags were like those of Poland, believed that the people of the city spoke the truth. Immediately they opened the gate. No sooner had the gate been opened than the Cossacks entered with drawn swords, and the townspeople too, armed with swords, spears and scythes, and some only with clubs, and they killed the Jews in large numbers. Women and young girls were ravished,° but some of the women and maidens jumped into the moat surrounding the fortress in order that the uncircumcised should not defile them. They drowned in the waters. Many of them who were able to swim, jumped into water, believing they would escape the slaughter, but the Ukrainians swam after them with their swords and their scythes, and killed them in the water. Some of the enemy shot with their guns into the water, and killed them till the water became red with the blood of the slain.

Lam. 5:11.

The head of the rabbinical academy of Nemirow was also there. His name was, his excellency, our master and teacher, the rabbi; Rabbi Jechiel Michael, son of his excellency, our teacher, Rabbi Eliezer, of blessed memory. He knew the whole of Rabbinic writings by heart and was proficient in all the worldly sciences. On the Sabbath before the catastrophe he preached and admonished the people that if the enemy should come (God forbid) they should not change their faith, but rather be martyred for the sanctification of His Name. This the holy people did. He also jumped into the water believing that he would save himself by swimming when a Ukrainian seized him and wanted to slay him, but the scholar implored him not to kill him, for which he would compensate him with a great deal of gold and silver. The Ukrainian consented and he led him to the house, where his silver and gold were hidden, and the Cossack released him. The Rabbi then left that place with his mother, and the two hid in a certain house all that night till the morning dawn.

On the morrow, the 22nd of Sivan, the Ukrainians searched the houses, suspecting that Jews might be hidden there. The Rabbi and his mother then fled to the cemetery. Thus, should they be killed they would receive burial. But it so happened that when they came near the cemetery, a Ukrainian shoemaker, one of the townspeople, pursued the Rabbi with club in hand and inflicted on him wounds. The Rabbi's mother pleaded with the Ukrainian to kill her instead of the son but the latter paid no attention and proceeded to kill first the Rabbi and then the mother, may God avenge their blood. Three days after the massacre the Rabbi's wife buried him, for in the town where the slaughter took place the majority of the women were spared, except for the old and feeble who were killed.

It happened there that a beautiful maiden, of a renowned and wealthy family, had been captured by a certain Cossack who forced her to be his wife. But, before they lived together she told him with cunning that she possessed a certain magic and that no weapon could harm her. She said to him: "If you do not believe me, just test me. Shoot at me with a gun, and you will see that I will not be harmed." The Cossack, her husband, in his simplicity, thought she was telling the truth. He shot at her with his gun and she fell and died for the sanctification of the Name, to avoid being defiled by him, may God avenge her blood.

Another event occurred when a beautiful girl, about to be married to a Cossack, insisted that their marriage take place in a church which stood across the bridge. He granted her request, and with timbrels and flutes, attired in festive garb, led her to the marriage. As soon as they came to the bridge she jumped into the water and was drowned for the sanctificaton of the Name. May God avenge her blood.° These, and many similar events took place, far too numerous to be recorded. The number of the slain and drowned in the holy community of Nemirow was about six thousand. They perished by all sorts of terrible deaths, as has already been described. May God avenge their blood. Those of the holy community of Nemirow who escaped the sword fled to the holy community of Tulczyn, for there, outside the city, was a very strong fortress.

For similar motifs, see 17.

1653

37 The Martyrs of Pavlysh

(Shivḥei haBesht, tale 137)

In 1753 twenty-four Jews were charged with the murder of a four-year-old Christian boy. Twelve of the Jews were tortured and executed; the rest saved their lives by converting to Christianity.

Besht is the acronym for the Ba'al Shem Tov.

There was a blood libel in the holy community of Pavlysh.° The rabbi of the holy community of Korostyshev, whose name was Rabbi David, escaped. He wanted to flee as far as the provinces of Walachia. All the important people in the area around Pavlysh were afraid that a libel would be made against them as well. When Rabbi David arrived at the holy community of Medzhibozh, the Besht° stopped him and told him several times that the people would be saved. But they were killed, and afterwards a letter reached Rabbi David telling him about the horrible and painful tortures that each of them had suffered. He brought this letter to the Besht who became grief-stricken. That day was Sabbath Eve, and the Besht went to the mikveh and cried bitterly. He prayed Minḥah with great bitterness until his followers could not lift up their heads.

They said: "Perhaps when he will begin welcoming the Sabbath, he will do it joyfully."

But the Besht also prayed the Reception of the Sabbath prayer and the Maariv with a bitter heart. He sanctified the wine as he wept. He washed his hands, sat at the table, and then went to sleep. In his room he stretched himself out on the floor and lay there for a long time. The members of his household and the guests waited until the candles began to die out.

His wife went to him and said: "The candles will soon die out and the guests are waiting."

He said to her: "Let them eat, recite the blessing over the food, and go."

His wife also went to the room where the Besht was and lay down on her bed. The Besht was still lying down on the floor with his arms and legs outstretched.

Rabbi David stood at the door to watch what would happen, but he became weary of standing, and he took a bench and sat at the door. At about midnight he heard the Besht say to his wife: "Cover your face."

At that very moment the room became brightly lit, and the light shone through the cracks. The Besht said: "Welcome Rabbi Akiba." And he also welcomed the martyrs whose names no one knows. Rabbi David recognized Rabbi Akiba by his voice.°

It is unclear whose voice is meant.

The Besht said to the martyrs: "I decree that you go and take revenge on the enemy, the persecutor." The martyrs answered: "Do not let these words pass from your lips again, and let what you have said be nullified. You, sir, are not aware of your power. When you, sir, upset the Sabbath, there was a great tumult in paradise and we fled from the palaces as though we were running before the sword. Even when we reached an upper palace we found that all had to flee from there as well, though they knew not why. Finally, we came to an upper palace where they understood the cause, and they shouted at us: 'Hurry and go to quiet the Besht's tears.' Let us tell you, sir, that all the suffering man has to endure in life is like the skin of a garlic clove° in comparison to the suffering we endured as martyrs for His blessed and lofty name. Nevertheless, the *yetser hara'*° played its role and confused our thoughts just a hair. In spite of the fact that we completely spurned the *yetser hara'* we had to suffer a half an hour in Gehenna. After we entered paradise we began to argue that we wanted to take revenge upon our enemies. They answered us: 'Since he is still living if you want to take revenge, you will have to become reincarnated.' We said, 'Thank God that we sanctified ourselves and became martyrs for His name and had to suffer the pain of Gehenna, and that half an hour in Gehenna makes all other suffering seem like the skin of a garlic clove in comparison. What would become of us if we were to be reborn again in this world? We might commit sins, God forbid, from which we would not have any redemption. It is better for us not to take revenge and not to be reincarnated.' Therefore, it is our request that you, sir, cancel what you have said."

Idiomatic expression for something insubstantial. Evil inclination.

The Besht asked them: "Why did those in heaven mislead me and not reveal to me that you were destined to be martyrs?"

They answered him: "If you had known of it you would have prayed a great deal and canceled the decree, and it could have caused great trouble, God forbid. Therefore, they did not inform you, sir."

I heard from the rabbi of our community that the Besht said that in heaven they had promised him to cancel the decree, but a [Jewish] preacher gave a sermon in the holy community of Brody exploiting the plight of the prisoners and in so doing caused strife which resulted in the death of the prisoners because of our many sins.

1815

VIII

Protest and Parody in Tsarist Russia

The partitions of Poland at the close of the eighteenth century did not bode well for the Jews of eastern Europe. Austria took Galicia in the south and offered its Jews a degree of civil liberties that their brethren to the north and east would not enjoy for another 150 years. Galicia, however, was the heartland of Hasidism, and the Hasidim did all they could to resist the carrot of emancipation. Meanwhile, the tsarist empire, which took the lion's share of Poland, administered the stick: It banished Jews from within a fifty-mile radius of its western borders (ostensibly to curtail smuggling); it expelled Jews from the villages (ostensibly to curtail the sale of vodka); and it began drafting them into the army (ostensibly to equalize their standing with other groups). This last was the severest blow of all—first, because the Jewish quota was proportionately higher than for any other group (the comparable Polish quota was a short-lived punitive measure); second, because the twenty-five-year stint (yes!) was preceded by special training in so-called Cantonist battalions for minors; third, because it was the responsibility of the *kahal,* the local Jewish community council, to find the young men to fill the quota. The *kahal* often hired *khapers* (snatchers) to kidnap Jewish children for the Cantonist brigades. At least half of the child conscripts, if they lived long enough, were forcibly converted to Christianity.

Although Jews were by no means the only group in the tsarist empire to protest the draft, Yiddish folk songs (**38–39**) reveal the nature of their peculiar plight: the machinations of the *kahal* to fill the quota from among the poor and dispossessed; the flagrant violation of the recruits' religious freedom; the attempt on the parents' part to intensify the religious education of their sons as a buffer to conversion, or in the hope that the *kahal* might spare the better students. As late as 1901, when many of these songs were first published, whole stanzas of anti-Christian sentiment were expunged by the tsarist censor. Most of the anger, nonetheless, was directed inward at those who collaborated with the enemy, and most of the appeals were (still) directed to the One who used the Tsar as the rod of His wrath.

The political fragmentation of eastern Europe into Austrian, Prussian, Russian and Polish spheres (*Congress Poland* was the name given to the area not swallowed up by everyone else) was mirrored by the fragmentation inside the Jewish community. While the *kahal* was never to regain its legitimacy after the Cantonist period, which ended in 1856, even rabbinic leadership was now up for grabs. This, at least, is what the tsarist regime intended when it created government-supported rabbis for each municipality within the Pale of Settlement (that area of the Russian empire to which Jews were confined). These men, graduates of the two newly established rabbinical seminaries, were barely tolerated by the very communities they were supposed to serve. From their ranks, however, soon emerged a significant cadre of *maskilim*, western-oriented intellectuals. Their main arena of influence was not the synagogue, the Hasidic *shtibl* or the *kahal* chamber, but the Jewish periodical press publishing in Russian, Polish, Hebrew and Yiddish. Here secular literature finally came into its own in the form of serialized novels, topical poems, essays and, most favorite, satiric feuilletons. The towering figure of this literary renaissance was Sholem Yankev Abramovitsh (1836–1917).

Abramovitsh came of age as a *maskil* during the reign of Tsar Alexander II, a time of high hopes for liberals of every stripe. But when Alexander II was assassinated in 1881, heralding the first wide-scale pogroms in Russian history, the advocates of reform suffered a crisis of faith. Unlike the majority of disillusioned *maskilim*, Abramovitsh did not seize upon one or another of the radical solutions to "The Jewish Problem"—socialist revolution, mass immigration to America or a return to Zion—because he had come to see the fate of the Jews as bound up with social, economic and political factors both within Russia and without. For him, the forces of fragmentation were inherent in society at large. Only a comprehensive effort at self-improvement and self-help would rebuild that which was about to be destroyed.

Had Abramovitsh presented this message in his own analytic voice, it would not have been heard above that of other intellectuals who were scrambling to make sense of the expulsions, pogroms and mass migration in the midst of the collapse of the Russian feudal economy. Instead, Abramovitsh resurrected Mendele the Bookpeddler, his old standby, who now addressed his audiences in Hebrew as well as in Yiddish. Through the dual nature of his character—at once blasphemer and consoler—Mendele embodied the contradictions of the Jewish predicament. In a new, synthetic

Hebrew that echoed the glorious national past even as it depicted the debased anarchic present, Mendele emerged as a Jewish Grand Inquisitor.

"Shem and Japheth on the Train" (**40**) can be read as a sermon because of the way Abramovitsh used biblical archetypes to cut the monsters of modernity—trains, secular ideologies and the nation-state—down to manageable size. Abramovitsh took his cue from the midrash on Noah's two sons, Shem and Japheth, who represented the future division of the world into Jews and gentiles. The rabbis envisioned the two sitting together under the same tent, studying Torah. Abramovitsh showed how Jewish-gentile relations had been severed almost beyond repair by the modern division of the world into S[h]emites and anti-S[h]emites. Despite the odds, he offered in conclusion an ironic Torah of Survival to all victims of Europe's rising xenophobia.

What made the story so unique for its time was that it could also be read as a vicious, no-holds-barred parody of all of Jewish sancta. Much of the parodic venom, however, operated on an allusive level, which is well-nigh impossible to translate. Easiest to appreciate are the prooftexts—scriptural passages, in the main—that characters cited to bolster their positions: Reb Moshe's (i.e., Moses') speech was studded with common biblical references and talmudic constructions as befit a man of simple faith; Japheth had recourse to the standard texts of his traditions, the Suffering Servant passages from Second Isaiah and the Gospel According to Luke.

Altogether different (and exceedingly difficult to render) is Mendele's sacrilegious wordplay. The story begins with a celebrated line that links the hectic scene at the Ksalon train station to the Israelites' frenzied dancing in front of the Golden Calf. Hallowed Exodus-related phrases (God took us out of Egypt *with a mighty and outstretched arm;* and the Israelites went into the sea on dry ground, the waters forming a wall for them *on their right and on their left*) are then used to describe the mad dash for a seat in the third-class train compartment. There follows an outrageously funny analysis of the two kinds of sweat that plays off a particularly juicy passage in the Talmud. Through such display of almost demonic erudition, the sancta of Judaism are viciously undercut.

Abramovitsh's pervasive form of parody went far beyond those earlier stylized inversions that had been meant to open up but never to supplant the traditional meanings of the sacred text. Through Mendele, Abramovitsh was calling for a new norm of collective behavior, one that would repudiate any passive acceptance of the Jewish fate or facile recourse to redemptive analogies.

Abramovitsh made the facile recourse to archetypes the subject of an entire story (**41**). The people of Beggarsburgh, Mendele's native town, represent the parasitic legacy of the past, which Mendele challenges as being irrational, self-serving and counterproductive. In a delicious parody of what Salo Baron would later term "lachrymose historiography," Mendele shows us a society so fixated on disaster that it cannot tell the good news from the bad. It *relies* upon catastrophes to structure its conception of time and place. Thus, the Great Fire in Beggarsburgh (itself a parody of the *Ḥurban*) triggers an automatic recourse to biblical citations designed to prove, as always, that the catastrophe was preordained in heaven. This sends Mendele into one of his famous tirades; he appeals for constructive, human intervention on behalf of the fire victims and prophesies incalculable losses if they fail to mobilize.

Until the revolt of the *maskilim,* suffering had always been linked to sin, and every calamity might become a source of collective comfort by invoking the right set of archetypes. Now, for the first time, writers who shared the burden of suffering refused to buy into the system. Instead, they issued a call for Jewish self-determination. To drive the message home, they began to use the archetypes of destruction as a warning and a threat.

38 Songs of the Cantonist Era (1827–1856)

The Streets Flow with Our Tears

The streets flow with our tears
You can bathe in the blood of children dear.

O what a terrible calamity!
Will there ever be a remedy?

Little children are torn from their lessons
And pressed into coats with soldiers' buttons.

Our rabbis, our bigshots are in cahoots
Teaching our children to be recruits.

Zushe Rakover has seven healthy sons
Not one will be forced to carry a gun.

But widow Leah's only kid will be
A scapegoat for the *kahal*'s treachery.

It's a *mitsvah* to round up the simple folk:
Who cares if they're swaddled in army cloaks.

But lousy little Lord Fauntleroys
Are never taken as one of the boys!

For Twenty Miles I Ran and Ran

For twenty miles I ran and ran
until a house I came upon.

"Sir! Give me a piece of bread.
Look at me: I'm pale as death."

"Quick, before eating, get washed and proper;
They're checking for passes at every door."

On bread, on bread I make a blessing—
later I'll figure out the mess I'm in.

After the bread you must say Grace.
But snatchers are prowling around the place.

I'd already washed and the blessing been said
when in walked a snatcher after my head.

Says he: "Where are you going?"
Say I: "To buy seeds for sowing."

"No, that's not why you're on the run.
It's your fate you're escaping from."

To the draft board he drags me, his claim;
Everyone lowers his head in shame.

They put me through the physical test—
then announce: "A soldier, one of the best!"

Andante

Tsvan - tsik   mayl   bin   ikh   ge - lo - fn—

Hob— ikh   a   shti - bl   on - ge - tro - fn.

Tra - la - la - la - la,   Tra - la - la - la - la - la,   Tra -

la - la - la - la - la,   Tra - la - la - la - la.

O, Merciful Father

O, merciful Father who dwells in heaven,
You're the protector of all the orphans!

Better to study Bible and Rashi
than to eat the soldiers' mush.

Better to lie on a Study House bench
than to make a friend in a trench.

Better to wear a *tallis* and *kitl*
than to sport a sword around your middle.

Better to eat hard doughy *kneydlakh*
than to be beaten in a barracks.

Better to study Gemora for years
than to shed so many tears.

Better to sweat over talmudic codes
than to stand guard for hours in the cold.

[Last stanza censored.]

39 Song of the Balta Pogrom (1882)

Misfortune, terror and fury
We've never been without—
Now as in each century—
And whither they come we know not.
Shout Jews, shout loud as you can,
So loud your shout reaches on high
And wakes up the Old Man.
His sleep is just a lie.
What's He trying to put over?
What are we, flies in the wind?
Is there nothing in our favor?
Enough! It's got to end.

All of us beaten hair and hide,
Our belongings tossed hither and thither,
Grooms taken from their brides,
Children from their mothers.
Shout, children, shout loud as you can,
So loud your shout reaches on high
And wakes up the Old Man.
His sleep is just a lie.
Listen, and You'll hear the babies
In their cradles cry again.
They plead with You that You might say:
Enough! It's got to end.

Everything in blithers and smithers,
Brides, canopies and clothes.
Not a single feather
Left in the bedding or pillows.
Fly you feathers, fly as you can,
'Til you reach the One on High.
Wake up the Old Man.
His sleep is just a lie.
All we own is smashed to bits,
The last cup crushed and bent.
It's time You Yourself took pity.
Enough! It's got to end.

Um-glik shrek un moy-res mir vey-sn nit fun__ va-nen Oykh
haynt vi in a-le doy-res Zay-nen mir oys-ge-
shta-nen. Shrayt yi-dn shrayt a-royf! Shrayt he-kher__ a-hin__
dort. Vekt ir dem al-tn oyf. Vos shloft__ er__ kloy-mersht__
dort? Ve-men vil er gor ge-vi-nen?
Vos zay-nen__ mir a flig?_____ Loz er undz a
skhus ge-fi-nen. Oy, es zol__ shoyn__ zayn__ ge-nug!

Record it for all time to come,
The murder and the dread.
Torah scrolls were cut open,
Sacred parchments torn to shreds.
Fly you parchments, fly aloft,
'Til you reach the One on High.
You can wake old Moses up.
His sleep is just a lie.

<table>
<tr><td>I.e., the Torah scrolls.</td><td>We were unable to protect them,°
Who could have known what would descend?
Let Moses plead our case before Him.
Enough! It's got to end.</td></tr>
</table>

40 Shem and Japheth on the Train

SHOLEM YANKEV ABRAMOVITSH

I

Exod. 32:18: the Golden calf.

Jer. 31:15: Ruchel weeping for her children.

Ezek. 34:21.

Deut. 4:34.

It is not the voice of them that flee from a fire, neither is it the voice of them that run from armed bandits—it is the noise of Jews° who congregate upon the train station of Ksalon [Foolstown] that is heard on high.° There, in haste and confusion, our brethren press on, with bundles of every size and shape in their hands and on their shoulders; women, too, encumbered with pillows and bolsters and wailing infants; all jostling one another with side and with shoulder° as they perilously hoist themselves up the ladder to the third-class compartments, where a fresh battle will be fought with a mighty and outstretched arm° for places in the congested train. And I, Mendele the Bookseller, burdened with my goods and chattels, join manfully in the fray: I climb, stoop, and jostle my way through as one of the crowd. Yet, while we Jews hustle and work ourselves into a state of frenzied irritability, lest, Heaven forbid, someone should get ahead of us in the crush, and while we gaze beseechingly upon the railway employees, as if the fact that we are traveling at all indicates an unrequited act of grace on their part—all this while, the gentile passengers are strolling up and down the hallway in front of the station with their luggage and waiting until the bell rings for a second or even a third time, when they will mount the train at leisure, and each proceed to his appointed place.

After the hubbub outside, there is a renewed scramble for seats. Some lucky ones find places straightaway; others trail up and down in a fruitless quest. A stout, loquacious female is thrust forward, pushing baskets and bags ahead of her. She trips over them and falls headlong. Lying there, she looks for all the world like a goose bought in the market before Passover, after it has been taken home and the strap untied from its legs. It collapses on the floor with its tail and wings outspread, gazing up in terror, and gasping for air. Now, another woman appears in the doorway, clutching her bedding and bits of old clothes, shrilly urging her children to bustle along behind. This is the woman it has pleased the Lord to

Gen. 24:43.

Exod. 14:22.

designate° as my traveling companion, together with her husband and her numerous offspring: it is in their compartment that I shall sit, wedged in with the maximum of discomfort between bundles of household goods and bedding that mount up on my right and on my left.°

All this business of a railway journey is new to me. Never in my life have I experienced it, and I am surprised at everything I see. My place is so cramped that I am unable to stir, but can only sit cooped up and perspiring. Formerly, when I used to travel by coach through all the lands of Jewry, I did not mind being hemmed in by bundles of my own books and—needless to say—it was a special joy to perspire. (Everyone knows this who has chanced to be on the road in the month of Tammuz, when the blessed Lord puts forth such insufferable heat at noon that no bird flies, no ox lows to his fellow in the stall,° the forest does not stir, the very leaves on the trees cease their whispering: then, when the world is hushed and mute, one slumps back in the carriage seat and enjoys, as I have done, the most timely sweating of all.) But now it is quite otherwise: perspiration brings no solace, and the constriction only saps my strength. I begin to think that for my sins my innate Jewish character has somehow been transformed, so that I am no longer able to appreciate these same two privileges of the Seed of Abraham.

Based on a midrashic description of the giving of the Torah at Sinai.

But the treatment the railway officials accord to the passengers, and the passengers to one another, together with the experiences I have just undergone, combine to persuade me that the change is not in my own disposition, but in this strange mode of travel. For a coach journey in former times was quite unlike today's journeys by train. Then a man was his own master and free to choose for himself. Even if the travelers were crowded in, two facing two with one extra for makeweight, so that their legs were jammed together like herrings in a barrel— well, they could always get out and take a walk, there was nothing to stop them, and they had the world at their feet. Indeed, this very fact that they had a free choice would mitigate their discomfort, so that their afflictions became, as it were, the trials of love. But in the train there is no feeling of independence. One is like a prisoner, without a moment's respite from durance vile. And that, of course, is why this perspiring is so unpleasant: for an imposed sweat is altogether unlike the majestic sweating of a free man.° Consider, moreover, that the passengers in a coach are set apart from the common populace; they make up a little colony, a corporate entity of their own. Time flows on for them, evening and morning, one day° . . . a second day . . . a third. . . . There is world enough and time to meditate on all things, to satisfy every desire in the course of their travels. The sky is a tent over their heads, the earth spreads its bounty before them, they watch the glorious pageant of God's creation, they rejoice in its variety—yes, and if sometimes the coach is upset, this is not so bad either: for the earth like a kindly mother merely receives her children back into her lap. But in contrast the railway train is like a whole city in motion, with its multitude and its uproar, its population split into classes and sects, who carry with them their hatred and envy, their bickerings and rivalries and petty deals. Such passengers may traverse the whole world without regard to the grandeur of nature, the beauty of mountains and plains, and all the handiwork of God. . . .

Cf. Ketubbot 39b: One who is forced to have intercourse cannot be compared to one who acts willingly.

Gen. 1:5.

The guard blew his whistle and the train started. Our people were now able to relax. They began to take notice of one another, and to make their inquiries as to each man's trade, and his occupation, and whence he came, and whither he was heading; as is right and natural for our people. Strangers fraternized and addressed one another by their first names, as if they had been friends since childhood. And so Chaim opened the goodly treasures° of his knapsack and produced a bottle of wine, drank from it and passed it on to Shmuel while Shmuel broke off a piece

Deut. 28:12: there attributed to God.

of his loaf for Chaim, offering it with some cucumber and onion from his bag, and so they feasted together. In the same spirit Shmerl slipped a sum of money to Anshel with the request that he be so good as to pass it on to an in-law whose business was in the town where Anshel would be staying; and Reuven gave documents and bills to Shimon for Levi the produce-dealer; and the whole compartment became a hucksters' mart. We of Israel are preoccupied with the problems of making a living; no wonder that the winds of petty commerce raged mightily.° My own business instincts awoke too, and I bethought me of trying to sell some books. But I was obliged to abandon this project. My belongings were submerged in a great wave of other people's possessions, and it would have been impossible to salvage them save by very strenuous effort; in fact, cooped up as I was, this was altogether beyond my power. So I continued to sit in idleness perched on the edge of the seat, contemplating without relish the passengers who shared my compartment.

Ps. 50:3.

An unattractive-looking woman with a bleak nose faced me, propped up on a large pillow, from which feathers were constantly escaping and floating out into the world. Her eyes were timid, her lips dry and compressed, and her whole countenance shriveled like a baked apple. Since her arrival she had not had a moment's rest from her children, who pestered her continually with their questions and bickerings. The three smaller ones kept exchanging places and disturbing her as they bobbed up and down. In her lap a baby was drowsing now, after having wailed for some time; it snored in its sleep; a tear still stood on its cheek, which seemed utterly bloodless. And beside me sat her husband: a tall, spare man, his back somewhat bowed, with a lean neck, a long nose, and a stunted beard. Sorrow lurked in his eyes, and his lips carried the suggestion of a bitter smile. To the right of him his grown-up daughter sat in a kind of sad trance, with two small girls leaning against her.

Literally, "I must make mention today of my offenses (Gen. 41:9).

Literally, that they had "known affliction under the rod of His wrath" (Lam. 3:1).

I sinned in my heart, I must confess,° for I resented these companions from the start of the journey. Their presence irked me, and I silently cursed my ill luck that had placed me in the same compartment with such odd and vexatious folk. But as I considered them more carefully I began to view them in a new light. Their dress, their appearance, their wan expression, testified to extreme poverty° and roused my pity. The mother's intermittent sighs moved me; and even more, the excessively humble attempts of the father and children to avoid getting in my way. But what touched me most deeply was the sight of the infant, who had fallen asleep out of sheer weakness, after pouring out his woes on his mother's lap. All this led me to paint in my fancy a grim enough picture of the life of that poor family. My imagination drew me into further speculations as to the many families among our people in a similar plight, who bear in silence their poverty and distress. I was sunk in these reflections when one of the children began to plead with his mother for something to eat. To soothe him she answered:

"See, Yankele, it's still daylight: now isn't the time for food; you must wait a bit longer!"

"Hush, Yankele," added his father, crooking his lips into a smile, "Bismarck made rules against eating."°

Here and elsewhere the father undercuts Bismarck's cruel edicts with pseudolegal

"Is your child ill, then?" I asked the father in a gentle, sympathetic tone for I felt a strong urge now to enter into speech with him.

language. Mendele takes the ironic gesture literally.

"Ill? God forbid! He's perfectly sound in mind and limb. I wish I had the weight in gold of the food he can put down at any time of the day!"

"Then who is this Bismarck of yours, who makes rules to keep a healthy boy from eating?" I was all ready for a heated polemic against this man.

"Don't you know who Bismarck is? I'm astonished!"

"And what if I don't? He's some doctor, to be sure; and in Ksalon, my hometown, let me tell you, there are hundreds of smart doctors and bloodletters of his type. We have a common saying, that no man, if he followed the doctor's orders, would live out his year."

I laughed across at this man and his daughters, and they smiled back tolerantly. Taking this as a mark of their approval, and an encouragement to further eloquence, I laughed again in my complacency, and was about to reveal further depths of wisdom and discernment in a series of anecdotes about the physicians of my town, when the ticket inspector, accompanied by other railway employees, entered our compartment, and the conversation came to a halt.

After these had departed without incident, and such folk as had made themselves scarce during the visit had popped up again (in the usual way) from under the benches, the pillows and other paraphernalia were heaped up once more. Suddenly a strange individual appeared from beneath the seat opposite me.° He was bareheaded and dressed in outlandish gentile fashion, with ragged trousers and a Polish cape that fastened with brass hooks across the chest and fell short to the knees. His face was chalk-white, his cheeks sunken, and his moustache formed thin fringes whose ends dropped like lizards' tails from the sides of his mouth. As he stood up on his feet he belched, yawned and stretched himself, like a man who has just come out of his sleep. All my companions, old and young, greeted him in the most friendly fashion, and he in turn gazed smilingly upon them. For my part I was quite amazed, and could not explain to myself the connection between this Pole and the poor family with whom I was traveling, so Jewish in every detail. Many conjectures came into my head, of which the most probable seemed to be that the stranger was that Bismarck of whom my neighbors had already spoken. But at once I found that I was mistaken, for the woman now addressed him by name, in a mixture of Polish and Yiddish:

Here "Japheth" is introduced who, in serving "Shem," also bears out the biblical role of Canaan; see Gen. 9:26–27.

"Why are you standing, Panie Przecsczwinczicki?° Sit down here in our Itsik's place, and Itsikl will go over and sit in with his father."

His long last name is mildly satirical.

"Please don't put yourselves out for me, Chaya dear," answered the man with the seventeen-lettered name. "I can take Itsik on my knee. Reb Moshe, I see, has already too many children squeezed in with him on one seat." He spoke the same queer mixture of Polish and Yiddish.

Prov. 4:2.

"Did you sleep sweetly under the bench, Panie Japheth?" asked Reb Moshe with a smile of affection. "You see now, that I gave you good advice,° and you followed my instructions perfectly! Lucky fellow! As for me, after the next stop it will be *my* turn to lie under the luggage."

"Take me on your knee too, Reb Japheth!" begged Yankele; and he went over and seated himself together with Itsikl, while the stranger affectionately clasped them both.

I gaped at Reb Moshe, quite unable to grasp the situation, but he seemed to read my thoughts, and turning to me said:

"This man you see before you is of pure Polish stock, and his birthplace is a little town in Poland."

"Why do you call him Japheth, then?"

"Because his real name, Przecsczwinczicki, is such a jawbreaker. And besides, the name Japheth fits him perfectly, and nowadays he well deserves it."

"Your explanation, I'm afraid, only confuses me the more. You are like those exegetes who twist their texts to make them the more cryptic to the ordinary man. Tell me your story, please; but let it be a connected account, and not cut up in bits and snippets."

"Not cut up! I am a tailor by trade, and the tailor's way is to stitch the pieces of his cloth together with a needle. But when he has to deal with words, he cuts up the seams of the narrative, patches on digressions, and tears his story into remnants. All the same, I shall try, so far as I am able, to do as you ask. . . . But I have forgotten my manners. Let me say first, in common politeness, *Sholom Aleichem*, my dear sir, and may I have the pleasure of knowing your name?"

Reb Moshe greeted me, after the fashion of our people, by rising a little from his seat, and I returned his greeting (doing my best to budge myself likewise) and informed him of my name and occupation.

II

Moshe the Tailor was by nature one of those "happy paupers" of whom we have many in our midst. Poverty, it seems is unable to break their spirit; and its train of afflictions does not lead them to rail, like melancholiacs, at the ways of the world. The notion is fixed in their minds that they have received their deserts, and that it is their inexorable lot to pass their years in squalor and privation: therefore it is not for them to desire, or even to depict in their fancy, those pleasures of life which were created for their more fortunate superiors. They bow their heads submissively before storms, and when they recount their troubles, they spice the story with a touch of humor, and seem to deride even themselves.

"I take it," Reb Moshe began, "that you are not contemplating any marriage negotiations so there is no need for me to trace my pedigree back to Father Abraham, or to relate the entire history of my life since the day I was born. It is enough to say that my story is a familiar one, and repeats the experience of our race. So I shall pass over many things which may be taken for granted and avoid all needless ornamentation.

"I was born in Lithuania. As a young man I migrated to Prussia, where for many years I supported myself and my wife, who is also a Lithuanian, together with our children, by the work of my trade. All this time I and my family were Jews. I plied my needle and we ate our bread without fear. True it is that the title 'Jew' brought me no great honors, and did not raise me to the rank of princes and peers. Yet it was not exactly held to be a crime, and did not prevent me from earning a living of sorts. . . ."

"What is all this?" I cried in dismay. "Do you mean that now you are *not* a Jew?"

"I am a Jew no longer, for there are no Jews left anymore," answered the tailor with a smile. "It seems you do not know what age we are living in."

"How can I fail to know? Look, here is my calendar, which I have had printed at my own initiative and cost. Today is Wednesday, this week's portion of the Law

*Num.
16:1–18:32,
relevant, perhaps,
in that Korah
rebelled against
Moses and was
punished.*

is about Korah,° it is the year five thousand six hundred and forty—by the full reckoning." I recounted the number of years and days back to the creation of the world in a high voice and all in one breath. And taking out one of the little calendars I carry in my breast pocket. I flourished it in front of Reb Moshe, implying by this that I could sell him a copy.

"But the Germans think otherwise," said Reb Moshe quietly. "The Germans, who perform miracles of science, have turned the clock back a thousand generations, so that all of us at this day are living in the time of the Flood. Nowadays they call the Jew 'Shem,' and the gentile 'Japheth.' With the return of Shem and Japheth the customs of that far-off age have returned too, and the earth is filled with violence. The non-Semites are hostile toward the Semites; they discover imaginary wrongs, and in particular—do you know what?—in the matter of eating and drinking! For in this the Semites behave like other human beings, and such conduct is regarded as tantamount to treason and theft. Others find fault with the sons of Shem because they reproduce their kind—if you will pardon the phrase—like other men. At first these reactionaries were derided by their neighbors, and held to be madmen, but the madder they became, the more followers they found, until this lunacy struck root in the minds of people and rulers alike, and seemed to be a right and proper attitude. As the animosity spread, many hardships befell us daily, until their great Count Bismarck arose and decreed the expulsion of all the sons of Shem who were not of German nationality.° And so thousands of unfortunate people were deprived of their living and turned into a helpless rabble. As for my dear Yankele," he ended with a bitter smile, "this stubborn child refuses to obey the decrees of his rulers. He is hungry, so he will cry for bread. He has a stomach and wants to fill it—the wicked rebel!"°

*There were a
series of expulsions
of Polish nationals
from Prussia in
the years
1884–87. While
these orders
applied to Jew and
non-Jew alike,
they contained an
anti-Semitic
element.
1 Sam. 20:30.*

"So now you have come from Prussia?" I asked.

"It is nine months since we left Prussia, just as it is nine months since this child of our old age was born," he replied, pointing to the baby asleep in his mother's lap. "When the police came to expel us, my wife Chaya was brought to bed of our Leyzerke here. They informed me that I was required to leave the state at once. I told them that my wife was in childbirth, and I begged them to grant us three months' stay until she had recovered and the summer season had come round. But the police gave me visible proofs—using the strong arm of the law, not to mention its fists—that the exigency of driving Jews across the frontier is so great that it takes precedence over care for human life, and that even to be naked and barefoot in the rain, to be dangerously ill or on the point of death, does not exempt one from this decree.° When I saw that my plea was rejected and they had the law on their side, I took my staff in my hand, slung my knapsack over my shoulder, and we all went forth, on a cold day of falling snow. Thus we left the town I had lived in from the time of my youth until now when I am in the years of decline. The police escorted us with a guard of honor for we Israelites are, after all, the sons of kings!

*Talmudic
terminology.*

"And so," he went on, "Reb Moshe the Tailor and his family went on their travels, from town to town, through all the lands of the Exile. Our clothes wore out, we were left without money or possessions, there was not a coin in our pockets save what came to us in the way of charity from our own people. But unfortunately our Jewish poor, who wander in search of bread, are all too numerous. They come from all points of the compass, from Prussia and Yemen, from Persia and Morocco,

B. Bava Metsia
71a.

and throng the gates of the charitable, so that there are not enough alms to go round, and the local poor must have priority over strangers.° Thus we wandered long, I and my dependents, exhausting ourselves in the search for a resting place but finding none. And at this time I have come from Galicia.''

Literally,
Leyzerke's voice
was heard from on
high (Jer. 31:15).

Profoundly affected by this story, I sat staring at the floor and could think of no word to reply. But as I sighed to myself at the fate of our homeless people, the infant Leyzerke awoke from sleep, and raised his voice in loud lament.° For me, his weeping made up a dirge on the misfortunes he had brought forth with him from the womb, on the poverty that preceded his birth, and on the world from which he had been exiled even before his eyes had beheld it. His wails mounted into a crescendo of accusation, directed against this world that had embittered his life from the hour when he first saw daylight, and had deprived him even of the allotted period of rest in his mother's body that is the natural right of all creatures.°

Here the
Enlightenment
seeps into
Mendele's
language.

His mother rocked and caressed him, beguiling him with false promises of sweets and all manner of good things in time to come, but he complained the more loudly, as if to prevail over her blandishments, crying, so it seemed to me: *Woe is my lot that you have borne me, O my mother, to see toil and sorrow, and to waste away my*

Jer. 15:10.

days in the vain hope of promises and pledges!° His father, too, in his ironic way, sought to console the child. ''Put your finger in your mouth and suck it,'' he said. ''It is not for Jews to complain, my dear Leyzerke, nor to make their voices heard, even if their bellies are empty and their flesh grieves them. If they do, a great bear will come and gather them into his sack.'' But the little Jew, Leyzerke, only grew more indignant; he kicked out angrily, waved his fists and glared wrathfully at his father, as if to reply: *Wretched beggar and sycophant that you are, father of mine! Why did you beget a luckless soul like me, with as many sorrows as the hours of my life—with as many doors for you and me to knock on in our exile as there are hairs to my head!* Thus Reb Moshe and the infant Leyzerke answered one another, while the mother sighed, the daughters grieved, and I pondered bitterly until the Pole stood up and took the child in his arms. He caressed him, dandled him, and Leyzerke at last grew quiet.

With mounting curiosity, I turned to Reb Moshe:

''Tell me please, who is this Pole, and what have you to do with one another?''

''He is an old disciple of mine—not in the tailor's art, for he is a cobbler by trade—but in the art of being a Jew. Have a little patience,'' he added, noting my surprise, ''for I will explain everything.

''This Polish cobbler and I lived for many years in the same town in Prussia. Each of us practiced his trade, and we were at peace with one another. On holidays we used to drink together in the tavern, and ask each other's advice about our problems and those of our fellow workers. In times of need we would help each other, in a brotherly way. True, we used to have our disagreements now and then, as people do, and especially would we dispute about matters of religion. He would take sides for his own faith, I for mine, and each of us would quote chapter and verse for his opinions. He would never allow me to say a word against pigs— naturally, I find them abominable—but he would act as devil's advocate, praising these animals and telling me how good they were to eat. I, for my part, would spit in disgust and retort that they were such ugly, nauseating brutes, that nothing could make them any better, not even the butcher's knife. That is how we used to carry on with each other, but always the argument would end with a 'Well, let's leave it at that,' and we would part as friends.

"He told me once that he thought the Jewish way of cooking fish and making puddings was better than theirs. He also thought that our Jewish girls were prettier and more attractive than those of his own people. And he said quite emphatically, that as far as he was concerned, he saw nothing wrong with the Jews being given a small share of the next world for themselves to which I answered, just as generously, that I would not put any obstacle in the way of gentiles eating pork, if they wanted to, and was ready on my side to rail off a corner of the lower paradise reserved for good *goyim*.° In fact, since we were both in a mood for concessions, I went so far as to say that I would let them have all *this* world as well—on condition only that they set apart a small share of it for us. So we stayed on good terms, and drank a toast to our friendship, he filling his glass and crossing himself over his heart, and I filling mine and saying the blessing for ale—while we both put the drink down in one draught.

The two levels of Paradise are a popular concept in rabbinic lore and Jewish mysticism.

"So it was in those days. But when they brought back the times of the Flood, and chaos returned to the world, human nature changed also. Friends became estranged, and my old comrade's bearing toward me was not as it had been. If he chanced to see me in the marketplace, he would behave like a stranger, neither greeting me nor returning my greeting to him. He no longer drank with me in the tavern, but each of us would choose his own corner. The time came when I saw him there with a set of men who were abusing the Jews in loud voices with the object of baiting me. I let them rage on as if I had heard nothing and when they realized that I was ignoring them and treating them like the stupid cattle that they were, their anger blazed up. They began aiming personal remarks in my direction, they insulted me in their drinking songs, at last they laid hands on me and shouted at me to clear out. At this point the innkeeper came up and with cunning excuses to save his face, expelled me without too much loss of dignity. So I went out, sick at heart.

"This experience was mental torture for days after, and in my bitterness I would dispute with God. 'God of heaven,' I would say, 'Thou who hast chosen us from all peoples, and cherished us, why have I and Thy people Israel come to this degradation and shame?° If such is the portion of those whom Thou lovest, would then that Thou hadst *not* loved us, and hadst *not* desired us above all other nations. It is said, indeed, that the Creator, blessed be He, will reward all mankind according to their deserts. But I find no comfort in this. For what profit is it to me, Moshe the Tailor—the son of Thy people—whose days are brief and full of sorrow—whose soul is trodden down like dust under the feet of the impious—if, at some date in the far-off future, Thou wilt keep faith with my sons' sons and work their salvation? And what if, at the end of days, the descendants of the impious receive the punishment that their forefathers deserved? Then neither the oppressors nor the oppressed will have received their due. The former will not have been punished, nor the latter rewarded, and what purpose is served by settling accounts, when neither debtor nor creditor remain alive?' Yes, indeed I sinned greatly in these thoughts, and even at the time I feared them, for they were nothing but the prompting of evil, and blasphemy and defiance against the heavens. But all my efforts to suppress them were useless, for they rose up of their own accord, against my conscious will.

Reb Moshe's point of departure is the fourth of the Eighteen Benedictions in the Festival 'Amidah.

"Once I was walking in one of the streets of our town, very low in spirits, for hardships were accumulating, and for lack of customers my livelihood was dwindling away—when suddenly I saw my old companion coming toward me. His head was in the air, his moustache was waxed proudly, and there was a look of scorn on his face. By some impulse, as if the devil had prompted me, I stood in his way, and humbly greeted him, as if nothing had happened.

" 'Nowadays there is no getting away from these nuisances!' he replied provocatively, meaning to insult both me and my people at the same time.

" 'Panie Przecsczwinczicki!' I said imploringly. 'What harm do you find in me, that you have become a stranger?'

" 'What creature is this?' he cried angrily, and averted his glance. I realized from this curt reply what hatred he nursed in his heart, to the point where he could turn his eyes away from his fellow-man and refuse to acknowledge a friend. Nevertheless I made yet another attempt.

" 'Don't you recognize me, your true old friend and comrade? Again I ask you, what harm have I done? How have I sinned?'

" 'You are tainted with the sin of your nation° for they are always robbing and plundering people!'

Isa. 53:8: the *Suffering Servant.*

" 'Whom have I robbed? And whom have I oppressed? Don't you know full well that I have no property, and no money, and if you were to search my house from floor to ceiling, what would you find, but a few threadbare bits of bedding, a table, and two or three rickety chairs that still, by some miracle, stand on their legs? You should know better than anyone how poorly I live; how the potatoes cooked by my wife Chaya, God bless her, are the only dish to be seen on my table, and that is as much as I have got from all my labor. Do I have to tell you that I am a workingman, and toil away at my trade by day and night?'

" 'I know that well enough!' he answered scornfully. 'That's exactly the point— that you toil at your trade by day and night! It's your work that takes work away from us. So all your labor is to cause other people loss.'

" 'My trade and yours are completely different,' I said in self-justification. 'I work with a needle and you with an awl, and nobody else has lost anything on my account, either, for I am, thank God, a first-class tailor—you yourself have paid me all sorts of compliments about the trousers I made you. The chief thing is that I don't put up my charges like others in the trade. Now look here,' I said with a friendly smile, 'stop being foolish. Come to my place and we'll have potatoes and fried onions again, as my wife Chaya knows how to cook them. . . . I see that your trousers are torn. They've done you good service for something like three years. . . . And the shoes I'm wearing are down at heel and fairly ask to be mended. Can't you see that we need one another? But if we helped each other, then I would patch your trousers, and you would repair my shoes, so each would be the gainer.'

"Like a man whose objections have all been met, my companion stood silent and bewildered. I could see from his face that he was inwardly considering what to do next, and judging that this was the right moment to win him over, I went on:

" 'Yes indeed, Panie . . . you are not as simple as you look, and in your heart, I'm sure, you think other than what you say aloud. You have been playing the fool too long, brother. Now tomorrow happens to be Friday, so what about your coming over for the Sabbath evening, and enjoying some good fish with us?'

" 'You wouldn't touch my pork, would you? So you can keep your rotten fish!' he retorted, flushing in anger.

" 'So it's the pork you want to pick a quarrel about!' I cried, perceiving what was at the root of his fanatical hatred. 'Just because I won't defile myself with what is forbidden me by my faith, you are ready to persecute me and destroy me! Well, well, I shall only say that I can't understand you, for you are acting like a lunatic. Tell me the truth, Panie: Are you quite sound in body and mind?'

"My companion's only response to this question was to thrust out his hard fist—and in a flash he had slipped away out of sight.

"From that time on I did not see him again. But from what I heard, he was one of the rioters in the city of Stettin, when they burned the synagogue there, and he took part in that exploit."

III

While Reb Moshe was telling his story, his grown-up daughter would sigh from time to time and tremble convulsively. Suddenly her face turned white. She got up from her seat and went to the door of the compartment for air. Her mother followed her, with tears in her eyes, while the father's face clouded over and he became silent. Sensing after a while that some explanation was called for, he leaned forward and whispered to me. It appeared that his eldest daughter, named Brayndl, was betrothed to an admirable young man who was a carpenter's apprentice in the Prussian town where they used to live. This young man loved her dearly, and she returned his love with all her heart. Accordingly Reb Moshe in his capacity as father had promised a dowry of two hundred silver marks, to be paid in cash before the nuptials to his future son-in-law, Zelig. The young man would thus have the means to fit up a workshop with the tools of his trade. The date of the wedding was provisionally fixed for such time as his apprenticeship would come to an end and he would qualify for a diploma from his master. Anxiously these lovers waited for the arrival of their wedding day, and only three months lay between them and their happiness, when the decree of banishment was promulgated. According to its provisions, Reb Moshe and the members of his household went into exile, and the lovers were parted.

"This is the worst burden I have to bear," the father concluded sadly. "My feelings for my daughter are such that I would give my life for her happiness. What a calamity it is, Reb Mendele, that I must watch her grieving day and night for her lover! The whole world has grown dark for her."

So now I understood why this girl had sighed and trembled while Reb Moshe was recounting their experiences; and I could have wept, myself, in sheer compassion.

The train stopped at a small station on the way. The Pole took up the jugs that were under the seat, and raced off to draw water from the pump. He quickly returned, and passed the jug round, first to Brayndl, then to Leyzerke, and then to the rest of the children, so that they all were able to refresh themselves. I felt a strong impulse to thank him for this, and was all the more desirous of an explanation to the whole enigma. How came this man to attach himself to Reb Moshe and his family, after all that had passed between them?

Almost as soon as the train began to move again, the tailor made a gesture dismissing, as it were, the sorrows of his mind, and went on again with his story, telling it in his usual ironic fashion.

"It was once upon a time, in Galacia. I was wandering by night in the street of a small town there when I came upon a tavern, a dim tumble-down place whose lamp did not serve to light up the ends of the room. As I entered I glimpsed the shapes of men scuffling in a dark corner, and heard the voices of a man and a woman yelling curses and abuse. The person they were insulting lay on the floor, begging for mercy and crying: 'Have pity on me! You are human beings too! Hunger and thrist drove me to it, and that's why I ate your bread and drank your wine, though I haven't a penny in my pocket.' But his enemies kept up their abuse, and threatened to tear the clothes from his back and the cap off his head by way of compensation. I perceived that this cruel pair were the innkeeper and his wife, and that all their rage was because a man had not the money to pay for his meal. Familiar, as a Jew, with every aspect of poverty and hunger, I sympathized with this poor wretch and came forward to rescue him. I entreated the keepers of the tavern to show mercy, speaking fair words and quoting the Bible, which declares that he who commits a crime for the sake of bread° has acted under duress and should be dealt with leniently. When this produced no result, I paid them the price of the meal out of my own pocket. They were then silent and slunk away.

Prov. 28:21.

"The poor man I had saved was just beginning to thank me feverently, when, coming from the dark corner into the full light of the lamp, we caught sight of one another's face, and each of us started back in dismay. I recognized this humble wretch as—who do you think—Przecsczwinczicki!

"As tailors do, I looked first at his clothes, and found them torn and ragged.° His shoes were worn through; the cap on his head was creased like a rag, and scarcely improved his appearance. As for his body, it was shrunken to mere skin and bones, while his face had the livid, unnaturally bloated look of starvation. For some moments we stood speechless. At last, moved by pity for my old companion in his misery, I found words.

Note that Shem and Japheth clothed the naked Noah (Gen. 9:23).

" 'What has become of you, Panie Przecsczwinczicki?' I asked. 'How do you come to be in such a state?'

"He hung his head, and slowly the answer came, in a still, small voice:

" 'They've issued the same decrees for us Poles as they did for you Jews. So now I have to wander about like you, and beg for my bread.'

" 'I really am sorry for you,' I said, shaking my head at his plight.

" 'How can you possibly be sorry for me?' he answered bitterly. 'Why don't you show how much you hate me? You, especially, after I've treated you like dirt, and plagued you all for nothing!'

Prov. 28:13.

" 'He who confesses and gives up his faults will find mercy,' I quoted.° God will not remember our past iniquities.'

" 'But I cannot forget my own for it's my fate to stand now in your shoes, I have learned what lies the well-fed tell about the hungry, and the citizens of a country about aliens, and the strong about the weak. . . . It has been a lesson to me, what happened here in this tavern. Oh, if only those pampered fools could have the same experience, they might learn some sense, and then there'd be less trouble in the world. Well, you may forgive me if you wish, but I only feel the more ashamed of myself.'

" 'Be that as it may, you *are forgiven,*' I said to him. 'Say no more about it, for you are not the only one to have done wrong, brother. Many have sinned like you—in every generation. And now, let us sit down together and drink to our old friendship.'

"We made a good evening of it there, and talked our hearts out. It was like the old times we used to have together back in Prussia. We called to mind those days, when we lived in peace and followed our own trades, and then we told one another of all the hardships we had been through since we were driven out of that land. I let him know the troubles that were on my mind, and he told me of his. He had been wandering about for a long time and could not make a living among strangers. There was no work, and no one to give him a helping hand. Calamity, panic, and frustration lay on all that he undertook°—for such was the competition in every trade nowadays that each man had only time to think of himself. And so this ex-cobbler had spent all his small savings on the road, and sold his few belongings to buy food, and now had nothing left but the clothes he sat in. It was three days since he had spent the last coin he had, and his position was desperate.

Deut. 28:20 (1).

"I cheered him up with glass after glass for it is written, 'the laborer is worthy of his hire,'° or, as I read the text, 'a man in trouble deserves a drink.' And the drink lit him up so that he flung his arm around me lovingly, and we forgot all about the old quarrel and were very happy together, till in the end the innkeeper came round to tell us that it was long past bedtime.

Prov. 31:6.

"It was a fine, clear night, and the full moon shone in all its beauty. The marketplace was deserted, the whole town slept, and we walked on in silence, each man thinking his own thoughts. Not a sound could be heard except the tramp of our own footsteps and the occasional barking of dogs in the distance. When we reached the crossroads, and it was time to part from my friend, I took his hand—to find it was trembling and cold as ice.

" 'My lodgings are up this lane,' I said to him. 'Which way do you go?'

" 'Wherever my feet take me,' he answered with a sigh.

" 'But have you no place to stay the night?'

It appeared not. "Birds, it is written, have their nest, and foxes their holes—but I, the Son of Man, have nowhere to lay my head."°

Luke 9:58 incorporating Ps. 84:4.

" 'Are there no wealthy folk among you?' I asked him. 'Does nobody help the poor?'

" 'Our idea of charity is different, and our wealthy folk are different too. A man may be poor and a stranger, but if he is able-bodied, then no one is sorry for him. The houses of the rich are not open to all comers, and there are porters to keep the poor away from the courtyards.'

" 'Listen,' I said to my friend. 'Life in exile—this precious gift from God's store—belongs only to the Jews, His chosen people. It is ours alone, for no other nation or race in the world has the strength to take it and to bear its weight. And since you, my friend, seem to have won a share in this gift, there is no remedy for you but Judaism.'

" 'What!' he cried in terror. 'Are you telling me that I must become a Jew?'

" 'No, you fool! The God of the Hebrews is in no hurry to acquire more souls: He is content with the Jews he already has. In fact, he is sufficiently burdened with His own Jewish paupers, whom He has to care for and sustain by miracles each day and hour. No, I am not trying to convert you. Stay a Christian as you have always been, and keep your religion in your own way, but there is one thing you must do. You must come to master the Jewish art of living, and cleave to that, if you are to preserve yourself and carry the yoke of exile. At first this will be hard for you, but in the course of time you will learn through suffering—for pain begets endurance. Do you believe that the Jews from the beginning of their history were such as I am today? You are wrong, friend! For long ages they went through every kind of affliction and retribution. They tried out many ways of life until they became as they are now. It is exile that has given them special characteristics that mark them off from all other peoples, has taught them special contrivances to gain a living, and has set a special stamp upon their charity, too, from the point of view

2 Sam. 7:23.

of both giver and receiver. *Who is like Thy people Israel, a unique nation in the world!°* which is skilled in ways of procuring its needs; which must, by the very nature of its being, maintain itself in the teeth of all oppressive laws and decrees that seek to prevent this. What nation in the world has such strange customs as we? Our paupers constantly return to the same doors; they *demand* alms, as if they are collecting a debt that is due to them. And our wealthy benefactors do not scrutinize

After B. Bava
Batra 9a.

each case.° They give, again and again, freely to all comers, even if these are healthy and able-bodied. Not only this, but of their own accord they invite these paupers as guests to their table, on weekdays, not to mention Sabbaths and festivals, so that the poor are as members of the household. Such is the law of the Exile, with all its six hundred and thirteen prohibitions and exactions. Yes, we know how to keep this law; and we have the strength of rocks to bear the burden of it, and to endure it, and to live by it.' "

"You have spoken the truth Reb Moshe," I said in reply. "How many qualities of body and soul are peculiar to us Jews, solely as the result of our dispersion among the nations and our precarious position in the world! Indeed, these very qualities have given us the strength to bear up, to satisfy our needs, and to survive in the Exile. The story goes back to ancient times. The chronicle of our people's livelihood is one long record of miracles—from the harsh fate of our forty years' wandering in the wilderness to the bread of affliction in our present exile—wherefore every son of Israel reads in his morning prayers the portion of the law relating to the manna, which is appropriate to all occasions and has its permanent spiritual significance. But let us come back to your own story. Proceed, Reb Moshe, for I am eager to hear more."

"There is very little left to tell. After I had spoken, my friend, the Pole, stared hard at me, and said:

" 'See now, you say to me: learn to master the Jewish way of living. But you have not told me what I must do. You have talked such a lot, Panie Moshe, but I can't understand a single word of it all.'

" 'Don't let that trouble you. I shall teach you the rules—the things a man must do if he is to live in the Exile, and which if he neglects, he will certainly perish. From now on you are adopted into my family, and will come with us along the way until we find some resting place. Be brave, my son, to take upon you the

Avot 4:2: in
reference to the
Torah.

afflictions of the Jews, and be faithful to my teaching!'°

Avot 4:2.

"From the hour my friend joined us and came under my wing, I have educated him in the ways of poverty, and given him good counsel° to ward off evil and to share our kind of life. I have taught him to be content with but little food and drink, to withstand the clamor of the belly, and to punish it at times by fasting. I have revealed to him the mysteries of the art of begging, and have taught him how to bow his head before calamities, as well as how to prevail over obstacles and hindrance in obtaining, by all manner of devices, his essential needs. All these things I have taught him, and, I thank God for it, my labor has not been in vain. At the beginning it was hard for this disciple of mine to face up to such trials, and it seemed preferable to die a speedy death than to draw out his life amid the sufferings and misfortunes of our strange people. But little by little he grew accustomed to them, and made great strides in his studies, until he attained the proficiency standard in penury and endurance, in humility and submission, in mortification of the body and the soul. He became like a real Jew, and is now fully adapted to exile, and trained to welcome its strokes and afflictions.

"Happy man!" concluded Reb Moshe with a contented smile. "And happy too am I, his teacher, that I am privileged to see this!"

I looked across at the Pole, and observed him playing cheerfully with the infant Leyzerke. He was entertaining him with a series of imitations of animal and bird calls: now he crowed like a cock, now mooed like a cow, neighed like a horse, croaked like a frog, or growled like a bear—and all this as quietly and unobtrusively as possible, lest he disturb the other passengers. The children romped round him merrily, Yankele on one side, Itsikl on the other. Even the unfortunate maiden Brayndl forgot her beloved Zelig sufficiently to smile, and her mother, perceiving it, for the moment seemed transformed into a happy matron.° As for Moshe, he delighted in the whole spectacle, and beaming with pleasure, cried:

"Rejoice, children of mine, for I have lived to see Japheth in the tents of Shem! May you prosper, Panie Japheth, and acquit yourself well in your studies, for your own good as well as for the good of your master, who has taught you to be of such service. So may you flourish and go from strength to strength!"°

I had many more questions to put to Reb Moshe, but there was no time left to ask them for now the train had stopped at a main junction, where I had to take leave of him and cross to another line.

As I left the compartment carrying my luggage, I saw the Pole standing outside and whispering to one of the train employees in a most humble and ingratiating manner, while he pressed a coin into his hand. I understood at once what this mystery signified, and what the disciple of Reb Moshe was requesting. . . . And raising my eyes aloft, with a sigh that came from the depths of my heart, I said:

"Lord of the universe! Grant us but a few more such disciples—and Shem and Japheth will be brothers—and peace will come to Israel!"

1890

41 Burned Out

SHOLEM YANKEV ABRAMOVITSH

The story I am about to tell you, gentlemen, took place in the first year after the Great Fire of the Holy Community of Beggarsburgh.°

That conflagration is inscribed in the chronicles of the community, and the

Side notes:

Ps. 113:9.

Hebrew ḥazak ḥazak venithazeik, the formula recited when one completes the reading (or writing) of a sacred text.

Kabzeel in Hebrew, from Josh. 15:21.

Beggarsburghers date every event in their lives from it. They say, for example: "So and so was born, or such a one was married and buried in this or that year of the Great Fire; the yarmulka decree, the decree on ordination and elementary education, the death of children because of the sins of the city, the stinking mildew, the scraping of the ritual bath and of the polluted river—all took place in this or that year of the Great Fire." There are still old men and women in these precincts from the time of the Great Fire, and sometimes, when they sit by the stove in the House of Study at twilight, the young people thirstily drink in their words, and their eyes are flooded with tears.

Gen 12:9: and Abraham journeyed.

I myself was not in town during the Great Fire. I was far afield, wending my way from place to place° in my wagon laden with books. In those days there were no newspapers among the Jews as there are today, no writers, no glib stylists, no composers of articles, and the like. They didn't publicize the plight of abandoned wives, they didn't eulogize the dead, and they didn't write up fires in high tones. Husbands deserted their wives, the dead died and were buried in secrecy, and homes and bathhouses burned to the ground with no one to proclaim it to the world. Therefore Beggarsburgh burned down, and I knew nothing of it.°

Gen. 28:16: Jacob's dream.

One day it chanced I was slowly proceeding alongside my horse, who was taking small steps at the side of the road, tearing off clumps of grass and munching complacently. It was Lag b'Omer, the one summer day when a Jew mustn't mourn, and all of lovely creation, in its splendor, crowned with great glory, is permitted for his enjoyment. Behold, I was raising my feet, walking, and regarding the gracious trees and plowed fields,° meadows, vegetables gardens, and grain. The mandrakes gave forth their fragrance,° and winged creatures sang sweetly to me in exultation. I listened and imagined violins and timbrels, flutes and trumpets, the shepherd's pipe and the cymbal—musical instruments giving voice for grooms and brides today in all our settlements, wherever Jews live. There I was, sharing their joy and sending them greetings and blessings from afar, wishing that their matches be good ones, that they flourish and multiply, just like the grass of the field. While I was contemplating the Lord's bounty in the world of the living and enjoying it within my heart, bands of people appeared before me, walking along the road, staffs in their hands, bundles on their shoulders,° having the appearance of absolute beggars. True, it is common enough to encounter beggars on the road, and it is a law for Israel° for all eternity that beggars must constantly wander through the towns within their confines, but such a huge abundance of beggars, in such long processions—that was a great astonishment, even greater when I got a close look and saw they were Beggarsburghers, my fellow townsmen!

Avot 3:7: rabbinic injunction not to interrupt one's study to contemplate nature.

Song of Songs 7:14.

Exod. 12:11: the Exodus from Egypt.

Ps. 31:5: in reference to blowing the shofar on the New Moon.

Joel 2:16: the Day of the Lord.

"Alas! Beggarsburgh is on the march!" I called out, frightened and confused at what I saw, that great horde of men and women, children and suckling babes,° all of them with their clothes torn, barefoot, hungry and thirsty, their faces as sooty as the bottom of a pot. "What is this, my brothers, and what is the cause of it?"

"Alas, our city has been destroyed," they all answered at once. "We are Beggarsburghers, but Beggarsburgh is no more!"

Isa. 13:6.

"Devastation hath come from the Lord,° a decree of heaven!" The sound of weeping came from among the women.

Zech. 1:2.

"The Lord hath waxed sorely wrathful° against Beggarsburgh!" the people lamented.

"In the multitude of our sins," the city notables began recounting, "For our sins the soot in a chimney caught on fire. . . ."

"In Naftali the Redhead's chimney," others interrupted them, "it wasn't swept, and it wasn't trimmed, and the fire was borne on the wings of the wind,° it spread to the thatched roofs and piles of straw, and to the low walls of the wooden houses, jammed close together, and they all burned at once. A great outcry rose in the city,° turmoil and great confusion°°—and no one extinguished the blaze. Alas, what has happened to us'° The Lord hath not had mercy on the dwellings°° of Beggarsburgh, from on high He sent fire and burned our city!"

"Brothers," I waxed furious and began arguing vehemently against them, "you began by talking about a fire in Naftali the Redhead's chimney and ended with fire from on high! What do flames from heaven have to do with it?"

"Fire from heaven descended upon us by means of the Redhead's chimney," my brethren replied ingenuously. "They are one and the same. Here's proof: how many years has his chimney stood unswept and untrimmed? Nevertheless, by the Grace of the blessed Lord, nothing ever happened. . . . Certain simpletons explain the fire, saying it came because of the sin of building houses close together, cheek by jowl till there was no room left, and for the sin of thatched roofs and faulty stoves, and for the sin of the firemen, of whom there is neither hide nor hair in our township, but those fools have neither understood nor set it in the tablets of their hearts that Beggarsburgh passed many years as it was, and from the time it was first built it knew no evil. . . . The truth is, as it is written, 'If the Lord preserveth not a city, in vain shall the guardian labor,'° 'If the Lord sendeth fire from on high,° even many waters shall not extinguish it.' ''°°

No wisdom, no understanding, and no argument can stand before the written Word,° hence I bent my head and kept my peace.

The Beggarsburghers were tired and weary, trudging and stumbling as they went, and my knees too failed me with the travails of the road, so we stopped to rest a bit by a grove of trees near a small pond. The Beggarsburghers hung their bundles and rags from the willows by the water,° and they prostrated themselves upon the earth.° The men moaned and groaned,°° provoking one another, and arguing about the situation. The women lamented, cursing their day° and making their voices ring. Suckling babes groped for their mothers' breasts, seeking milk to restore their souls, and there was none°—the breasts were withered. Young children asked for bread and wept. There was Leyzril, the perennial village idiot of Beggarsburgh, for he too was among the exiles° of his congregation. His clothes were tattered and his hair unkempt,° his hat was all awry, slipping down over his neck. He wandered about, going up to one person after another like a cow seeking her calf, with his mouth wide open, staring, occasionally making strange noises through his nostrils, not saying a word. I sat silently among the downtrodden Beggarsburghers, distraught and mournful about their great disaster, and the lovely world of the Holy One, blessed be He, was darkened for me. Alas, what good does that creation do for me now, with all its beauty? It gives its glory to the others, not to us Jews. The sun's warmth no longer restores my soul, for it is a blazing fire. The fresh air has become a pestilence for me, and the fragrant incense of the harvest and the mountain plants is acrid smoke in my nose. Flames blaze in my

Ps. 104:3.

Exod. 12:30: death of the Egyptian firstborn.

Isa. 22:5.

Kinot for Ninth of Av.

Lam. 2:2.

Ps. 127:1.

Lam. 1:13.

Song of Songs 5:7.

Prov. 21:30.

Ps. 137:2 (3).

Num. 11:32: quails in the wilderness.

Ezek. 9:4.

Job 3:1.

Based on Isa. 41:17.

Based on Ezek. 1:1.

Lev. 13:35: the leper.

Ps. 39:4.

Job 30:31.

thoughts.° I see a vision of fire, wind, and pillars of smoke. The birds' song becomes mourning, and their melody the sound of weeping!°

"Where will you go, my brothers?"I opened my mouth after a long silence and spoke with great pity.

"Where can burned out Jews go?" replied the members of the band with a nod of their head and a sigh. "Where all our paupers go, to the settlements of our merciful Jewish brethren. We have certificates signed by the Chief Rabbi of our holy congregation, granting us the right and privilege of begging for alms from door to door. The community leaders worked diligently in behalf of the burned out people and divided the cities of Israel among them by lot.° Many groups wandered off in the other direction, and we've taken this one. Now we must make a further division among ourselves, as to who will go where, but there is dissension in our ranks. Some of us wish to go one place, but all the rest do too. So we're clinging to each other in one big bunch, arguing, irritated, and angry on our way.° Everyone vexes his companion and annoys him. Perhaps, Reb Mendele, you might act as judge and decide for us!"

Num. 26:55: division of the Land among the twelve tribes.

Gen. 45:24: Joseph to his brothers.

"Scatter, beggars!" I told the Beggarsburghers gently. "Split up for your own benefit and pleasure. Why are you bunched together, crowded up, fighting, squabbling, and annoying each other? You're only harming yourselves. Everyone is interfering with everybody else, and too many poor souls are picking at the same crust of bread. You'll manage yet to stir up an outcry. People will complain that you're descending like locusts,° and you'll be a burden on the community. Spare yourselves and split up, Jews!"

When I saw my words were going unheeded, I ceased addressing them. I shook my head and said to myself: "Not even fire will separate you, Jews!"

Nahum 3:16.

I.e., Idletown, as poverty stricken as they, will be slim pickings.

Deut. 12:12.

Chesalon in Hebrew, from Josh. 15:10.

"They're fobbing off the Idletown District on us,° and they're skimming off the cream, Foolsville and its surroundings. We too have a share and a holding° in Foolsville!"° they cried out.

"We won't forfeit our right. We too have Jewish souls, and our lineage is as good as yours!" the others shouted.

"Drop dead!"

"A curse on your ancestors!"

Based on 1 Sam. 10:11–12: Is Saul also among the prophets?

"Sweet Jews," I said to the Beggarsburghers who were shouting loudest, "Are you too among the burned out?° You were never householders."

"What difference does it make whether we were householders or tenants? Now we're all destitute," they responded sensibly. "We owned no homes, but we had dwellings. We used to live in Yankev-Shimshon's basement, a man and his children in his own corner, and when his house burned down, we were deprived of our dwelling. Now where shall we go?"°

Gen. 37:30: Reuben to his brothers.

"I used to live in the House of Study," shouted Azriel the idler, "and since it was burned down, I have nowhere to sleep, and I am like everyone who was burned out."

If fleas could talk, they would lodge the same complaint, I thought to myself, for they too live in people's houses and beds.

"The fire murdered me and throttled me at the same time," complained Dovid-Yehuda the storekeeper. "In normal times, when the Beggarsburghers lived in their houses, I would rent a store, and customers would come my way.

Ps. 109:66.

With the destruction of Beggarsburgh, my luck turned bad, and my livelihood was lost."

"I'm a miserable, poor man, as you can plainly see," explained Nochum the teacher, speaking tastefully and intelligently.° "When there were householders, I used to teach their sons in my schoolroom, and I barely scraped by. Now that there are no householders, where will pupils come from? Without pupils, there can be no schoolroom, without a school and Torah, there's no flour."

Rolled parchment with texts from Deuteronomy on one side and the name of God on the other that is affixed to the doorpost of Jewish homes.

Pious male Jews hired to recite psalms in times of illness or mourning.

Num. 27:17.

Based on Isa. 3:6.

Lam. 5:1.

2 Sam. 13:20: the rape of Tamar.

"Just what I say: if there are no houses, there are no mezuzas."° Yoysef-Shimshon the scribe spoke downheartedly. "When Beggarsburgh stood, I used to write parchment scrolls for mezuzas, and now, since there are no houses, who needs scrolls?"

"And we," put in several Beggarsburghers, known among us as clerics: beadles and cantors, public functionaries, their helpers, and their relatives and the relatives of their relatives, various sorts of office-holders, marriage brokers, grave-diggers, students of Mishnah and professional reciters of psalms° in honor of the dead, orators and the like from the burial society. "Now we are like shepherds with no flock,° like moss with no wall, like fish with no fry. Woe is us, and alas for our children and babes, there is neither food nor clothing, no householders and no governors.° We are for the Lord, and now our eyes are turned to our relatives and redeemers, our acquaintances and generous donors. Let them take care of our children, let them support us until the Almighty takes pity on Beggarsburgh and rebuilds our city so we can return to our livelihood."

"There is no sorrow like ours," lamented Shloyme the windbag, pouring his heart out to me. "My sorrow is that of a daughter! Look ye and see my shame,° my devastated daughter Hinda-Rochel over there.° She was engaged to a man, and the wedding was set, according to the prenuptial agreement, for this Lag b'Omer. Everything was in order between the parents-in-law. What did the Holy One blessed be He do? The Holy One blessed be He made a great fire in the city, and quite a few people suffered damage, including me. One mustn't question the Holy One blessed be He and ask why He did that, and He certainly knows what He's doing. Since I suffered damage, it goes without saying that I became a pauper, and I couldn't carry out my part of the agreement. Not that I didn't wish to do my part, perish the thought, but simply because my hands are absolutely empty. And what did the groom say, that splendid lad? The groom said, 'I want out. If the *main thing* is lacking, what do I want your daughter for?' He stood there and ripped up the prenuptial agreement. As a result my daughter wasn't married, and she's gone back to being a maiden as before. There she is, sitting in shame and disgrace, shedding tears and weeping, and my wife, may she live long, is shedding tears too, wailing and reproaching me, 'Thief, why did you let the groom go! Thief, why don't you take pity on your daughter? All her friends are married already and giving suck to children, and she, you thief, is still a maid! Whither shall I take

2 Sam. 13:13.

my disgrace?'° Today is Lag b'Omer, the wedding day according to the agreement, and her weeping is loudest of all, as on Tish'a b'Av. The one cries, the other cries,

Lam. 1:22.

they both cry, and as for me, my heart is perishing.° Alas, if only a dog licked my heart and I went mad on the spot! What shall I do? What can I do? I'm prepared to go this far: let my wife and children go on their own to ask for help with all the others who were burned out, and I'll set forth by myself to beg for dowry money in Jewish towns. What do you think, Reb Mendele?"

"What can I tell you?" said I to Shloyme the windbag. "Dowries are certainly good merchandise, a fine business, of even higher importance to the Jews than burned-out people."

While the men of Beggarsburgh were talking to me, the womenfolk added their own spice, seasoning their husbands' talk with lamentations and groans, with oaths and curses, as is their way. Even the frogs raised their voices and croaked in the pond, and the cicadas and crickets chirped from among the stalks of grain. There was great noise and shouting, hubbub and wailing in the camp.

Isa. 14:29.

Nothing softens my heart and arouses a multitude of elevated sentiments, feelings of love and pity, yearnings, and many more which cannot be defined or named, than the face of an innocent child asleep, especially when he drowses in weakness or scourged by the rod that smiteth him.° One wretched child, a weak, frail boy, came up to me while I was engaged in conversation, lay his head upon my knees, and dozed off—and I did not know. After I stopped talking, I noticed him, and my mercy was aroused,° and a powerful flood of emotions stirred within me. I looked at his sweet, thin face, which was without a drop of blood, and his parched lips, which were slightly open, and his thin, weak arms. One arm lay on his chest, which was swelling and rising, and the other hung loosely. His features were all imbued with a spirit of grace and pleading, and a note of sadness could be heard in them: lamentations and woe for suffering and pain, forgiveness, pardon, and pleas for mercy, relief, and rescue.° I looked, and my soul flowed out of me.° I was filled with mercy and exalted feelings of sanctity. I wished to weep, to embrace that poor waif, all my suffering townsmen, and all my oppressed brethren, my fellow Jews, and to kiss them all with my lips.° I looked from that innocent child to the Beggarsburghers, bitter in soul and full of anger, oppressed, downtrodden, and crushed, and I was crazed by what my eyes saw.°

Gen. 43:30: Joseph takes pity on Benjamin.

Esther 4:14.
Job 30:16.

Song of Songs 1:2.
Deut. 28:34 (1).

"Oh you heavens," my heart cried out to the Lord, "how afflicted are the Jews and how different the way they live, their food, and the satisfaction of their needs, from all the other nations of the earth! Who is like thee, O Israel, one nation in the world?° Its people are like the limbs of a body, attached and dependent upon each other, influencing each other, supporting each other, maintaining each other, perishing and lost with one another. Misfortune comes to some of them, and many are in distress. Flames attack Beggarsburgh, houses are burned down, and all the children of Israel weep for the fire!° All the people of Beggarsburgh cry out, even those who never had houses in their lives. The town's idlers and teachers, judges and clerics, cantors and slaughterers, marriage brokers, grooms, and brides, storekeepers and hucksters, traders, and all its many beggars.

2 Sam. 7:23.

Lev. 10:6: death by fire of Nadav and Avihu.

"My heart, my heart goes out to you, poor child!"

"Hannah, Hannah!" I heard the sleeping boy's father call to his wife, "Go and pick up Chaim-Yankele. He's sleeping on Reb Mendele's knees, and he will be a burden to him."°

Job 7:20.

"Alas for the mother, and alas for her soul!" cried out Hannah, full of love and great pity, as she stretched out her arms to take her son. "See how he's lying there, my precious one, the delight of my eyes. He is wrapped in the weariness of his soul,° his left hand beneath his head,°° sleeping like a bird. He's hardly tasted life, yet how many troubles has he seen in this world!"

Based on Jonah 2:8.

Song of Songs 2:6.

"Let him sleep! No matter, no matter, let him lie down and rest a little," I told his parents, engaging the boy's father in conversation. He was a good, honest man, and learned in Torah. "Tell me please, Reb Yehiel-Mordecai, how you found nourishment and sustenance in the bad times that rose up and beset you?"

"Blessed be our God, who has done miracles for us and sustained us, for in His goodness do we live," answered Reb Yehiel-Mordecai, raising his eyes to the heavens in praise and thanksgiving. "What does a Jew need for nourishment and to keep his soul alive? A bushel of potatoes from one sabbath eve to the next. We made do with little and trusted in His great name, may He be praised, and in the mercy of our Jewish brethren."

"And did our Jewish brethren come to your assistance from their homes and dwellings?"

"From one city and from the nearby villages they sent a few wagons full of bread right after the fire, and from the rest of the cities came nothing except some personal contributions, and they were few."

"Why were you not diligent in informing them of your troubles in writing, telling them you were in great distress?"

"We wrote, Reb Mendele, we wrote. We also sent special delegations to Jews all over, to gather contributions for us, and neither voice nor answer has come from them all!° When we saw that no help came from our brethren, and we could no longer sustain ourselves, we followed the maxim of our Rabbis, 'Judge not thy friend till thou art in his place,'° and now we are walking to our friends' place, with our children and our old people,° our sons and our daughters, and perhaps they will take pity on us. Perhaps they will have mercy. And what is your opinion, Reb Mendele? Will our journey succeed?"°

"Did you ever have a pain, Reb Yehiel-Mordecai, somewhere in your body at any time?"

"What kind of question is that, Reb Mendele? I have pains. My hips ache. May you be spared. Can't you see by looking at my face and body that I am a man in pain, oppressed by agonies?"

"And how did you cure it, Reb Yehiel-Mordecai?"

"When my hips first began hurting me, when I could still do something for my own relief, I made an effort to distract myself from them. I did nothing else, hoping silently that God would deliver me.° Now that the pains are very severe, I have nothing, even if I wished, and I am even doubtful whether remedies would be effective. For now I have pains not only in my hips but in every one of the 248 members of my body. I am like a broken vessel, may such a thing never happen to you. But Reb Mendele, what does that have to do with what we were talking about?"

"What does it have to do with it?" I asked bitterly. "It's just like the burned-out Beggarsburghers and all sorts of other wretched and destitute folk. They are all mortally ill, infected members of the body of the Jews! If only our fellow Jews were wise and intelligent,° they would make every effort to find a remedy and cure their weakened limbs, to strengthen and restore them in counsels and knowledge, to keep the illness from becoming worse, so that the pain shall not be eternal and the blow not mortal, refusing to be cured,° spreading and harming the entire body. If only our brethren took part in the troubles of the Beggarsburghers, in their time of woe,° and the men of their city each gave a penny to help, the pennies would add up to a great sum, so that in a short time they could rebuild their ruins

1 Kings 18:26: idols of Baal.

Avot 2:4.

Exod. 10:9.

Gen. 24:42, 56: Eliezer upon meeting Rebecca.

Based on Lam. 3:15.

Deut. 32:29.

Jer. 15:18.

Job 21:17.

and return to their work as before. Then they would not be driven from their homes into exile, wandering and lost in the world.

"Now listen, Reb Yehiel-Mordecai, and I shall tell you what will befall you and those like you, the lost and rejected, and our brethren from here too in the end of days.° The Beggarsburghers, abandoned and neglected,°° will be like other unfortunate and poverty-stricken folk, shoved out of their homes. Once they have started to fall, they will fall lower and lower,° never to rise up and return to their former state. Along the way they'll eat whatever comes to hand, and in the end they'll be wandering beggars, penniless and a sore affliction on the house of Israel. That ulcer will spread through the whole body of our people, bringing rot to its bones° and causing pains and grave suffering. Since our brethren did not support all those among them who fell, willingly and voluntarily giving a little right away when their feet stumbled,° in the end they shall be forced to give a great deal more, but to no avail. The poor and destitute will beg forever from door to door, collecting from them no matter what. They will give and give again as to a bag with holes in it,° whatever they can afford and more than they can afford. Against their will they will establish alms-houses for poor and wayfaring guests; they will be obliged to scatter their money to miserable idlers, to the weak and downtrodden, both to the lazy and to the disabled. Against their will they will support widows and feed orphans; against their will, poor kinsmen and kinswomen will live with them, and they shall not turn away from their own flesh.° Against their will they shall give charity and much else, without limit, until they can do no more. Then they'll consume less and spend less, they'll do less business, and their livelihood will suffer greatly. They too will become poor, and new indigents will be added to the first. The poor of that place will then go elsewhere and do what was done to them, and so the scab shall spread through Israel,° and poverty, penury, and destitution will increase.

"Do you see, Reb Yehiel-Mordecai, what that frog does by hopping into the pond? When he leaped he made a circle of waves in the water, and those waves made more waves around them, and they produce more and more waves, spreading everywhere without cease. That tiny little cause had many effects, going on and on. A fire broke out in Beggarsburgh, bringing many evil consequences. In the end of days *all of the House of Israel will weep for the fire!*"

"Our Sages have said that before you," said Reb Yehiel-Mordecai, shrugging his shoulder and waving his arm. His lip had that twist typical of those who frequent the House of Study when they disparage what someone else says. "Since we find them in our rabbis, what's your new point? In the Midrash to the Song of Songs° our Sages said: 'Consider the walnut. If you take one away from the rest, they all fall down and roll away one after the other. So it is with the Jews. If you take one of them, they all feel it.' "

"So what's to be done, Reb Yehiel-Mordecai?" I asked bitterly. "In heaven's name, will the Jews always be behindhand in self-improvement and slow to better their lot, so that they won't fall down and roll away one after the other like so many walnuts?!"

Reb Yehiel-Mordecai put his hands on his face, sighed and moaned, and made no answer. We sat wordless, keeping silence, each sunk in his own thoughts.

Presently the Beggarsburghers moved on in noise and confusion, setting forth on their way with their women and children, and Leyzril the madman trailed

Gen. 49:1: Jacob to his sons.

Job 4:20.

Esther 6:13.

Hab. 3:16.

Deut. 32:35.

Hag. 1:6.

Isa. 58:7.

Lev. 13:8.

Song of Songs Rabba 6:11.

along behind them. I went with them on my horse and wagon to see them off. When we reached the crossroads I parted company with them tearfully and went my own way.

I never saw those miserable Beggarsburghers again in my life, and I don't know what happened to them in the end. Doubtless they rolled about like walnuts with the rest of the destitute Jews until they vanished from the face of the earth. I did run into Leyzril one day in Foolsville. He was walking through the street like the village idiot, and little boys ran after him, mocking him: "Up the madman! Up the madman!"

1897

IX

Oracles of Kishinev, 1903

With fatal predictability, the next cycle of violence erupted during Passover, the time for blood libels in Christian Europe. The place was Kishinev—provincial capital of Bessarabia (in the southwestern part of the Russian empire) and a center of anti-Semitic agitation. What earned the Kishinev pogrom so prominent a place in Jewish collective memory, however, was its timing on the secular calendar, the fact that it happened at the very beginning of "that century in which humanity boasts of its civilization, its progress, its education and culture," in the words of the Bundist proclamation (**44**). What's more, even the Jews of Russia, who were schooled in violence, were not prepared for outright murder. Not merely feathers and plundered property were strewn about the streets. Forty-nine Jews were murdered in Kishinev in 1903—more than in all the pogroms of 1881 to 1882 combined.

One response was totally precedented. Simon Frug, who had come of age as a poet during the previous wave of pogroms, spoke for the majority of Jews when he described Kishinev as one episode in a timeless tale of misfortune and called for a massive relief effort on behalf of the victims (**43**). This sentimental poem became so popular among the masses that it was set to music by an American-Jewish composer, Henry Russotto, during World War I and was cited as late as March 1942 in a private appeal for aid written in the Lublin ghetto.

To a new generation of Jews raised on Marxist ideology, on the other hand, the root of all evil was capitalism, which fostered class conflict and ethnic animosities to further its own designs. To the Jewish Labor Bund of Russia and Poland, the solution was nothing short of socialist revolution. Until that day, working-class Jews should look to "international proletarian solidarity" for support (**44**).

Finally, the ad hoc Union of Hebrew Writers occupied a middle ground between the panhistorical and radical-activist positions (**45**). Though it began its proclamation by invoking the memory of Chmielnicki and Gonta, it went on to argue that hatred of the Jews was endemic to the system of tsarist repression, not native to the gentile population of eastern Europe. In this dog-eat-dog environment, only Jewish solidarity across ideological and class lines would make a difference.

Because the competing ideologies had to go public in their search for a solution to The Jewish Problem, each party was vitally concerned with marshaling the correct facts and figures. Furthermore, if the government, as everyone believed, had colluded with the rioters, then the victims would have to gather their own data that would stand up as evidence in Russian courts, or before the Court of History. And so it was that the Union of Hebrew Writers sent thirty-year-old poet Hayyim Nahman Bialik to Kishinev to collect photographs and eyewitness accounts. Yet for all this new concern with documentation, it was Bialik's poetic record of the pogrom—which deliberately falsified the data he himself had collected—that transformed Kishinev into a crucible of heaven and earth.

Bialik's "Upon the Slaughter" (**46**), written on the eve of his trip to Kishinev, brought the Poem of Wrath into the Literature of Destruction. However angrily a medieval poet complained about the silence of God (**26**), no synagogue poet had ever arrogated to himself the voice of the prophet. Bialik used the prophetic voice to rage against the Lord and His Chosen People. Instead of ending with a plea for divine intercession, Bialik concluded his Poems of Wrath by uttering a curse. The force of Bialik's subversion was already evident in the poem's title, a play on the blessing pronounced by the ritual slaughterer before he slit the animal's throat. Here, by implication, it was the powerless human victim who pronounced the blessing upon himself! As for God's justice, it was too little, too late.

"In the City of Slaughter" (**47**), Bialik's most sustained Poem of Wrath, redefined the pogrom poem for all time to come. Bialik's prophet-speaker launched a two-pronged attack: against the Jews, who had acted like cowards and *shnorrers* in the face of the enemy's onslaught, and against God, who had abdicated His throne. To intensify his anger at Jewish passivity and powerlessness, Bialik ignored the cases of sporadic resistance to the rioters. Beginning with the voice of a reporter, the poet surveyed the physical and psychic ruins in graphic detail—an account more carefully designed to shock Jewish sensibilities than anything heard before—and this pseudoreportage reached its climax with the description of the cowardly husbands running off to the rabbi to ask whether they could sleep with their ravaged wives (lines 108–111). But it suddenly became clear that the speaker of the poem was none other than God Himself, who all along had been sharing His anger with the prophet (lines 127ff). Ultimately, God was to call on the prophet to "demand the retribution for the shamed / of all the centuries and every age! / Let fists be flung like stone / against the heavens and the heavenly Throne!" (247–250). Failing that, there was nothing left for the prophet to do than to stifle his rage and to flee unavenged into the wilderness.

Thus, even in an age of newspapers and photojournalism, of mass rallies and political action, the most allusive and "coded" response reverberated loudest and longest. The enemy was all but relegated to oblivion so as to fix attention on the Jewish archetypal responses: on martyrdom, resurrection, divine retribution, confession and mourning. The facts of the pogrom, including the sporadic self-defense, were suppressed to highlight the crisis of Jewish powerlessness in the face of recurrent violence. And when the censor changed the title to "The Oracle at Nemirow" before he would allow its publication, that, too, created a powerful resonance, forever linking the first major pogrom of the twentieth century with the massacres 250 years earlier—in particular, with the perfidy of the gentile rulers who, then as now, conspired with the murderers against the Jews (cf. **36**).

42 Pogrom Songs

The Kishinev Pogrom

On the first day of Pesaḥ
Jews revelled and were joyous.
On the last day of Easter
Kishinev was in chaos.

Kishinev encircled like a barrel
girded by an iron hoop.
Fathers, mothers, and children
fell in a single group.

Oh, You God in heaven—
won't You look this way?
Listen to our shouting,
for the goys have had their holiday.

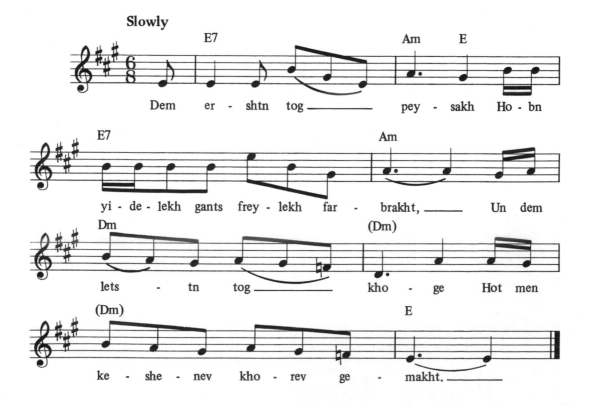

Slowly

Dem er - shtn tog ____ pey - sakh Ho - bn
yi - de - lekh gants frey - lekh far - brakht, ____ Un dem
lets - tn tog ____ kho - ge Hot men
ke - she - nev kho - rev ge - makht. ____

Oh, Have You Read in the Papers

Oh, have you read in the papers
about the famous city of Odessa?
What a calamity befell it
in the course of two or three days.

Suddenly someone cried:
Hey, beat the Jews with all your might!
Through the windows bullets began to fly.
In a moment the pogrom was at its height.

Murderers flew through the streets
with axes and knives sharp and hot,
and whenever they found a Jew
they killed him on the spot.

There in her wedding gown
lies a beautiful bride.
Oh, near her stands a murderer,
his dagger poised to strike.

There lies a handsome woman,
she lies crumpled in the dust.
Near her lies a little babe
sucking her cold, dead breast.

43 Have Pity!

SIMON FRUG

1

Streams of blood and rivers of tears
Deep and wide they flow and roar. . . .
Our misfortune, great and timeless
Has laid its hand on us once more.

Do you hear the mothers moan
And their little children cry?
In the streets the dead are lying;
The sick are fallen down nearby.

Brothers, sisters, please have mercy!
Great and awful is the need.
Bread is needed for the living,
Shrouds are needed for the dead.

2

From afar it's hard to feel it:
Distant tears—a stranger's moan,
The tragedy is someone else's,
The blood of strangers—oh, brothers, no!

A thousand hearts—a single sorrow,
A thousand streets—a single house;
We are all a single victim,
Orphaned is each one of us.

Brothers, sisters. . . .

3

Streams of blood and rivers of tears
Deep and wide they flow and roar. . . .
Deathly fear stares through the window
And hunger drum-beats at the door.

How weak our hand is to do battle,
How great and heavy is our woe—
Come and bring us love and comfort
Jewish hearts, we need you so!

Brothers, sisters. . . .

[First published on the front page of the St. Petersburg *Fraynd*, no. 82, April 1903]

Andante

Shtro-men blut un tay - khn

tre - rn zi - dn fli sn tif _ un breyt, un - dzer

al - ter groy-ser um-glik hot _ zayn hant ___ oyf undz far -

shpreyt;   Hert_ir dort   vi mu - ters klo-gn   un _ fun

kin - der   dos_ ge - shrey   toy - te li - gn   oyf_ di

ga - sn   kran - ke fa - ln   ne - bn_ zey.

Git de— toy - te oyf takh-ri - khim   Git di le-be-di-ke broyt.

D.C. 3 times

rit.

44 Proclamation of the Jewish Labor Bund

The Russian Social Democratic Workers' Party
The General Jewish Workers' Bund in Lithuania, Poland and Russia

To All Jewish Workers Male and Female!

°*The casualty figure, as is well known, was higher. The proclamation was written when the full extent of the pogrom was not yet known. [Editorial note in the original.]*

On the sixth and seventh of April a pogrom took place in Kishinev! A band of Christians attacked the Jewish townspeople and with the greatest cruelty they destroyed Jewish homes, stores, study houses and brought to ruin a large number of Jewish families. Up to forty-one people° were felled at the hands of this wild force!

The Kishinev pogrom is a terrible and tragic fact in the twentieth century, that century in which humanity boasts of its civilization, its progress, its education and culture. But however deeply this fact may touch our human feelings, the spilled blood and the whole tragic picture of the pogrom must not be allowed to dim our vision, or blur our understanding, or obstruct the essential and profound factors that brought this fact about, and that bring about thousands of other such tragic facts.

Anti-Semitism, the hatred of Jews that finds occasional expression in pogroms, is only one kind or species of the hatred that generally exists between different nations. This hatred, however, does not lie in the nature of people; as surely as it blossoms only under specific social conditions, so will other conditions destroy it. In the struggle for existence, it often happens that different groups are thrust into competition with one another, and this is what gives rise to the hatred between them. And when these competing parties also belong to different nationalities, then the hatred becomes a racial and national struggle.

Capitalism increases the competition both among individual capitalists and among the bourgeois classes of different nations who strive to displace one another from this or that market. The hatred between different classes can exist among the nationalities that inhabit a single land as well as those that inhabit different countries.

The entire capitalist world that trembles before the international force of the united proletariat tries through all possible means to undermine this unity and solidarity: by arousing national animosities among the workers; by inciting the basest instincts of a people against a foreign people and thereby diverting its attention from its real concerns, from the revolutionary socialist struggle. And in those countries where the people is especially ignorant and enslaved, all these efforts meet with great success.

Anti-Semitism, as we said before, is but one form of national hatred; it finds most of its following among the petty bourgeois strata of society. The evolutionary course of capitalism is such that small capital is increasingly swallowed up by large capital, and as it loses its footing, it seeks to save itself by destroying its Jewish competition. Agitation begins against the Jewish competition, against Jewry in general, and this agitation, falling as it does on the fertile ground of ignorance and superstition, has a particularly great effect.

Here in Russia, the tsarist regime plays the lead role in national agitation and persecution. The powerful labor movement, the peasant unrest, the student unrest, and the whole revolutionary current sweeping over all of Russia make the autocracy unsure of its existence so that it will use all means at its disposal—hanging, flogging, exile to Siberia; exploiting every possible occurrence to turn the Russians against the Poles and both against the Jews—in order to weaken the revolutionary spirit among the people, to confound its political understanding. The tsar's lackeys keep the people in ignorance, propagate the wildest superstitions in its midst; the anti-Semitic papers, supported by the government, spread the old wives' tales about blood libels and try to convince the people that the Jews are the sole cause for its terrible, forlorn state. And the ignorant, debased masses, who already carry hatred and protest in their hearts, who do not understand the true causes of their plight, spill all their rage upon the innocent Jews.

What do we see in the Kishinev pogrom?

A month earlier a Christian boy was killed in Dubosar, not far from Kishinev. The murderers were not found and the anti-Semitic paper *Bessarabets* disseminated the rumor that Jews had murdered the boy to use his blood for religious purposes. The anti-Semitic press did not cease from inciting Christians against the Jews, to awaken all those base feelings and instincts among the folk, and the utterly debased mob began to attack Jews with a frenzy. The huge mass of police and Cossacks who descend like locusts on workers at every demonstration, at every battle with the capitalists and the government, who rout the demonstrators in an instant, couldn't restrain a few hundred angry rioters (there are more than three hundred policemen, three army regiments, three brigades and a battalion of reserves stationed in Kishinev). The government did not step in because it didn't want to, because it has a vested interest in such things as pogroms.

How can we overcome the causes that bring about national hatred, anti-Semitism and pogroms, and what can we do when pogroms break out?

The so-called "Friends of the Jewish People" spill rivers of tears over the new Jewish calamity: the [St. Petersburg daily] *Fraynd* [Friend] wrings its hands in despair; the [Warsaw weekly] *Yidishe Folkstsaytung* [Jewish People's Paper] instructs us to be as still as the waters, as low as the grass, while the Zionist poet [S. Frug] laments, "How weak is our hand to do battle, how great and heavy is our woe."°

(43)

Only slaves can talk this way, people who are accustomed to enduring all acts of violence submissively, who don't believe in their own powers and who always await salvation from other quarters—from God, from friends, from the government.

This is not the way we, Jewish workers, think. The struggle that we've been waging for so many years has convinced us that help lies in us alone. Our unity has increased our power; our solidarity and readiness to protect our interests at all times have instilled fear in our enemies.

Ignorant, debased and enraged masses took part in the Kishinev pogrom. The intelligent, class-conscious Christian worker is our comrade; he fights together with us under a single flag, under the flag of international socialism. Spreading class consciousness, aiding the growth of the socialist movement that will destroy the whole capitalist order—this is the best and only way to bring an end to anti-Semitism and the pogroms.

What, then, should we do during the pogroms themselves?

We must answer violence with violence, no matter where it comes from. Not with sweet words but with arms in our hands can we prevail upon the frenzied pogromists. We mustn't hide in attics but must go out face to face, "with a mighty arm,"° to fight these beasts.

Deut. 4:34.

Let not the Kishinev pogrom weaken our faith in our sacred ideal. With hatred and with a threefold curse on our lips let us sew the shrouds for the Russian autocratic regime, for the anti-Semitic band of swindlers, for the whole capitalist system. May the number of conscious and active fighters for socialism keep growing; may the solidarity with our fellow workers of other nations keep on growing!

Down with anti-Semitism!

Down with Tsardom!

Long live international proletarian solidarity!

Long live socialism!

Central Committee of the Bund
April 1903

45 Proclamation of the Hebrew Writers' Union

Brothers!

The slaughter and plunder in Kishinev, the likes of which have not descended upon us since the days of Chmielnicki and Gonta°—command us to open our eyes

Cossack commander responsible for the massacre of

thousands of Jews
and Poles in the
city of Uman in
June 1768 at the
hands of the
Ukrainian
Haidamacks.

and see our status in this country as it is, so that we can choose our path and cease to delude our souls in vain consolations and useless hopes. And, as *Jewish writers,* who hold the state of their people so dear to heart, we ask your permission to present you with our views on this matter.

The Kishinev event is not an isolated episode, and we cannot attribute all blame to the wickedness of some individuals. Indeed, a few wicked individuals who incite the masses against us and take the lead, are always the *immediate* cause in such cases, but not in them will we find the source of evil; rather in our situation *in general.* Had we not been deprived of fundamental human rights, had the masses not seen, day in and day out, our humiliation in this country, the hatred and contempt that are poured down upon us *from on high*—the power of a few agitators would not have been so great as to lead the masses to robbery and murder in broad daylight. But as we are degraded and oppressed endlessly by the very laws of the land; as we are always being trampled on by anyone who has feet, and our enemies continuously molest us and all that we hold sacred without anyone's protest; as we are in such a lowly state and the boorish masses see our degradation and hear our shame day in and day out—it is only natural that this constant education implants a strong belief in the hearts of the rabble that a Jew is not human, and there is no obligation to treat him justly, like other human beings; that not only his property and his honor, but his life, too, is disowned, and his blood is unaccounted for.

Even if we assume that the government does not wish for slaughter and plunder and desires to protect us from these actions, which disturb the peace in the land, in general, it too has no power to undo the *results,* so long as the *conditions* hold firm. It is impossible to break the barrel yet keep its wine. The effect that continuous daily acts have is much greater than that of a single command sent from above, even in the most pressing manner, if trouble is nigh or has come already.

The local clerks in the town, who have long been accustomed to receive orders and warnings against the Jews, and to execute those orders without pity or mercy, will be unable to turn from foe to friend for one hour, upon a sudden decree, and to feel, in times of danger, any obligation to side with the Jews against their own brothers and countrymen. And when they perform their duty against their own wishes, it should come as no surprise that it will be performed halfheartedly, falsely, or even—as we have witnessed in Kishinev—by losing control themselves and by joining hands with the perpetrators.

And the investigation and inquiry, the sentence and the punishment that follow later on—can we trust that they will thwart the masses from daring to attack us once again? We shall not discuss herewith the common, known phenomenon that even the severest of punishments is not potent enough to wipe out the sinners from the face of the earth where there are internal causes that lead to the birth of such sinners. We have no need for this general rule, seeing as we already know, from our twenty years of experience, the results of all these investigations and sentences on the issue of riots against Jews; how many are punished and what their punishments are. This, too, is no cause for wonder. After all—the investigators of justice and the judges themselves are only human and have difficulty controlling their own feelings. To the hatred and contempt that they feel toward Jews at any time a suppressed anger is now added, for being forced to testify against their own people and to punish brothers for harming Jews. All of this motivates them to incline instinctively toward mercy as they treat the guilty and to diminish the image of truth at the time of investigation and the image of justice at the time of sentencing.

What, then, can we depend on, brothers, so that the tragedy does not spread again throughout the land, as it did twenty years ago, and even more violently now, judging from the beginnings in Kishinev? And why should we expend energy and degrade our pride by asking for help and rescue from the *outside,* so long as our condition in the land remains as it is—and indeed will so remain for the foreseeable future? Tears and pleadings—these were the only means we used since the pogroms began and until now. They did not avail us nor rescue us from the present tragedy, the slaughter in Kishinev, which is the answer to our tears and pleadings.

Do we still intend to be contented with tears and supplications in the future?

It is a disgrace for five million human souls to unload themselves on others, to stretch their necks to slaughter and cry for help, without as much as attempting to defend their own property, honor and lives. And who knows whether it is not this very disgrace that is the principal reason for our contemptible state in the eyes of the rabble, for whom we are like dust? Among the many and different peoples residing in this land, there are none but us who lend their bodies to their assailants and their honor to shame and do not resist with their last remaining might. Only the one who can defend his honor is honored by others. If the citizens of this land saw that there is a limit even to our suffering, that we, too, though we cannot and do not wish to match their plunder, violence and cruelty, are ready and able, when necessary, to defend that which we hold dear and sacred to our last drop of blood— had they witnessed this in action, then they would not assault us so readily; then a few hundred drunkards would not venture to close in on a large Jewish community of forty thousand, sticks and axes in hand, ready to kill and plunder to their hearts' desire.

Brothers! The blood of our brethren in Kishinev cries out to us! Shake off the dust and become men! Stop weeping and pleading, stop lifting your hands for salvation to those who hate and exclude you! Look to your own hands for rescue!

A *permanent organization* is needed in all our communities, which would be standing guard and always prepared to face the enemy at the outset, to quickly gather to the place of riots any men who have the strength to face danger. We also believe that the government should recognize our just cause in asking for one thing alone: that they let us defend ourselves with our own hand. If the lack of human rights has led us to these straits, where even our blood is unprotected in the eyes of the people of this land—would they also wish to deprive us of the natural right of every living creature to defend itself inasmuch as it is able?

Obviously, this matter requires further consideration on how it can be carried out, and it was not our intention to go into detail. Our purpose was only to awaken your heart to the general principle upon which we must establish our future actions, so that our lives will not forever be endangered. But in order to organize the matter in all its detail, we believe that a general assembly must be called by representatives of the main communities in our land. Such an assembly is urgently needed and should not be delayed. Because in addition to the fundamental issue to which we have already alluded, other weighty issues arise in light of the change that occurred in our condition. Thus, for example, the question of emigration, which to date suffered from a lack of order, would most certainly soon become even more complicated, since fear is great in the Pale of Settlement and particularly in the southern towns, and one can foresee that emigration will increase more than ever.

Various issues in our life demand resolution now, and the assembly will have to attend to them and seek solutions in wisdom and intelligence.

Ps. 102:14. Awake, brothers, since the time has come!° The time has come! And with our strong hope that among the leaders of the community and others who deal in public affairs there will be found people who understand the value of this hour in our lives, and devote their energy to implement our proposal, we sign,

With brotherly greeting,

The Union of Hebrew Writers

[Ahad Ha'am, Simon Dubnow,
Ben-Ami, Y. Ch. Ravnitsky,
Hayyim Nahman Bialik]

P.S. We hereby ask that the content of this letter be made known to enlightened people and men of action everywhere (and those of them who will kindly write to us at this address of their opinions on the matter will do us a service).

April 20, 1903

46 Upon the Slaughter

HAYYIM NAHMAN BIALIK

*Title: from
the blessing
pronounced by the
ritual slaughterer.
Avodah Zarah
17a: the words of
Eleazar ben
Dordia, the
fornicator.*

Pss. 13:12, 94:3.

*Parody of Ps.
89:14 ("Yours is
an arm endowed
with might.") and
Eleazar ben
Kallir's yotser for
Rosh Hashanah
Melekh azur
gevurah, which*

Heavenly spheres, beg mercy for me!°
If truly God dwells in your orbit and round,
And in your space is His pathway that I have not found—
Then you pray for me!
For my own heart is dead; no prayer on my tongue;   5
And strength has failed, and hope has passed:
O until when? For how much more? How long?°

Ho, headsman, bared the neck—come, cleave it through!
Nape me this cur's nape! Yours is the axe unbaffled!°
The whole wide world—my scaffold!   10
And rest you easy: we are weak and few.
My blood is outlaw. Strike, then; the skull dissever!
Let blood of babe and graybeard stain your garb—
Stain to endure forever!°

*begins by
describing the ten
garments of God.*

*Lanetsaḥ (forever)
also echoes
Kallir's poem; here
rhymed with
retsaḥ (slaughter),
line 12.*

*Repudiation of
Ps. 89.*

*Judg. 6:14: God's
statement to
Gideon.*

Ezek. 16:6.

*Echoes Yevamot
92a: Let the law
pierce the
mountain.*

If Right there be,—why, let it shine forth now!   15
For if when I have perished from the earth
The Right shine forth,
Then let its Throne be shattered, and laid low!°
Then let the heavens, wrong-racked, be no more!
—While you, O murderers, on your murder thrive,°   20
Live on your blood,° regurgitate this gore!

Who cries *Revenge! Revenge!*—accursed be he!
Fit vengeance for the spilt blood of a child
The devil has not yet compiled . . .
No, let that blood pierce world's profundity,   25
Through the great deep pursue its mordications,°
There eat its way in darkness, there undo,
Undo the rotted earth's foundations!

May 1903

47 In the City of Slaughter

HAYYIM NAHMAN BIALIK

*Gen. 12:1: kum
lekh-lekha, God's
command to
Abraham.*

Deut. 3:27.

Arise and go now° to the city of slaughter;
Into its courtyard wind thy way;
There with thine own hand touch, and with the eyes of thine head,°
Behold on tree, on stone, on fence, on mural clay,
The spattered blood and dried brains of the dead.   5
Proceed thence to the ruins, the split walls reach,
Where wider grows the hollow, and greater grows the breach;
Pass over the shattered hearth, attain the broken wall
Whose burnt and barren brick, whose charred stones reveal
The open mouths of such wounds, that no mending   10
Shall ever mend, nor healing ever heal.
There will thy feet in feathers sink, and stumble

Jer. 13:16.

On wreckage doubly wrecked,° scroll heaped on manuscript,
Fragments again fragmented—

Lev. 19:16.

Pause not upon this havoc,° go thy way.   15
The perfumes will be wafted from the acacia bud
And half its blossoms will be feathers,
Whose smell is the smell of blood!
And, spiting thee, strange incense they will bring—

Num. 11:20.

Banish thy loathing°—all the beauty of the spring,   20

The thousand golden arrows of the sun

I.e., the rays of Will flash upon thy malison;°
the spring sun will The sevenfold rays of broken glass
pierce your body Over thy sorrow joyously will pass,
like darts; cf. For God called up the slaughter and the spring together,°—   25
Prov. 7:23. The slayer slew, the blossom burst, and it was sunny weather!

The pogrom began Then wilt thou flee to a yard, observe its mound.
on April 19, Upon the mound lie two, and both are headless—
1903. A Jew and his hound.

The self-same axe struck both, and both were flung   30
Unto the self-same heap where swine seek dung;
Tomorrow the rain will wash their mingled blood
Into the runnels, and it will be lost
In rubbish heap, in stagnant pool, in mud.

Gen. 4:10. Its cry will not be heard.°   35
It will descend into the deep, or water the cockle-burr.
And all things will be as they ever were.
Unto the attic mount, upon thy feet and hands;
Behold the shadow of death among the shadows stands.
There in the dismal corner, there in the shadowy nook,   40
Multitudinous eyes will look
Upon thee from the sombre silence—
The spirits of the martyrs are these souls,
Gathered together, at long last,
Beneath these rafters and in these ignoble holes.   45
The hatchet found them here, and hither do they come
To seal with a last look, as with their final breath,
The agony of their lives, the terror of their death.
Tumbling and stumbling wraiths, they come, and cower there
Their silence whimpers, and it is their eyes which cry   50
Wherefore, O Lord, and why?
It is a silence only God can bear.
Lift then thine eyes to the roof; there's nothing there,
Save silences that hang from rafters
And brood upon the air: 55
Question the spider in his lair!
His eyes beheld these things; and with his web he can
A tale unfold horrific to the ear of man:

Lines 59–65 in A tale of cloven belly, feather-filled;°
the Hebrew Of nostrils nailed, of skull-bones bashed and spilled;   60
original all begin Of murdered men who from the beams were hung,
with ma'aseh And of a babe beside its mother flung,
be- . . . (a tale Its mother speared, the poor chick finding rest
of . . .). Upon its mother's cold and milkless breast;
Of how a dagger halved an infant's word,   65

Literally, its soul Its *ma* was heard, its *mama* never heard.°
expired with O, even now its eyes from me demand accounting,
'Mama' instead of
with the Shema';

a play on Akiba's
martyrdom (13).

For these the tales the spider is recounting,
Tales that do puncture the brain, such tales that sever
Thy body, spirit, soul, from life, forever!   70
Then wilt thou bid thy spirit—*Hold, enough!*
Stifle the wrath that mounts within thy throat,
Bury these things accursed,
Within the depth of thy heart, before thy heart will burst!
Then wilt thou leave that place, and go thy way—   75
And lo—

Literally, spills its
rays on the
ground, echoing
Onan's spilling his
seed; Gen. 28:9.

The earth is as it was, the sun still shines.°
It is a day like any other day.
Descend then, to the cellars of the town,
There where the virginal daughters of thy folk were fouled,   80
Where seven heathen flung a woman down,
The daughter in the presence of her mother,

Based on midrash
on Hos. 10:14:
"When mothers
and babes were
dashed to death
together."

The mother in the presence of her daughter,°
Before slaughter, during slaughter, and after slaughter!
Touch with thy hand the cushion stained;   85
Touch the pillow incarnadined:
This is the place the wild ones of the wood, the beasts of the field
With bloody axes in their paws compelled thy daughters yield:
Beasted and swined!

1 Sam. 24:11.

Note also do not fail to note,°   90
In that dark corner, and behind that cask
Crouched husbands, bridegrooms, brothers, peering from the cracks,
Watching the sacred bodies struggling underneath
The bestial breath,
Stifled in filth, and swallowing their blood!   95
Watching from the darkness and its mesh
The lecherous rabble portioning for booty
Their kindred and their flesh!

Jer. 3:25.
Esther 5:9.
Judg. 16:21,
Samson's story.

Crushed in their shame,° they saw it all;
They did not stir nor move;°   100
They did not pluck their eyes out;° they
Beat not their brains against the wall!
Perhaps, perhaps, each watcher had it in his heart to pray:

Jer. 5:12.

A miracle, O Lord,—and spare my skin this day!°
Those who survived this foulness, who from their blood awoke,   105
Beheld their life polluted, the light of their world gone out—
How did their menfolk bear it, how did they bear this yoke?
They crawled forth from their holes, they fled to the house of the Lord,
They offered thanks to Him, the sweet benedictory word.
The *Kohanim* sallied forth, to the Rabbi's house they flitted: 110

According to
rabbinic law, the
wife of a Kohen
(descendant of the
priesthood) must
abrogate relations
with her husband

Tell me, O Rabbi, tell, is my own wife permitted?°
The matter ends; and nothing more.
And all is as it was before.

Come, now, and I will bring thee to their lairs

The privies, jakes and pigpens where the heirs   115
Of Hasmoneans lay, with trembling knees,
Concealed and cowering,—the sons of the Maccabees!
The seed of saints, the scions of the lions!°
Who, crammed by scores in all the sanctuaries of their shame,
So sanctified My name!   120
It was the flight of mice° they fled,
The scurrying of roaches was their flight;
They died like dogs, and they were dead!
And on the next morn, after the terrible night
The son who was not murdered found   125
The spurned cadaver of his father on the ground.
Now wherefore dost thou weep, O son of man?°

Descend into the valley; verdant, there
A garden flourishes, and in the garden
A barn, a shed,—it was their abbatoir;   130
There, like a host of vampires, puffed and bloated,
Besotted with blood, swilled from the scattered dead,
The tumbril wheels lie spread—
Their open spokes, like fingers stretched for murder,
Like vampire-mouths their hubs still clotted red.   135
Enter not now, but when the sun descends
Wrapt in bleeding clouds and girt with flame,
Then open the gate and stealthily do set
Thy foot within the ambient of horror:
Terror floating near the rafters, terror   140
Against the walls in darkness hiding,
Terror through the silence sliding.
Didst thou not hear beneath the heap of wheels
A stirring of crushed limbs? Broken and racked
Their bodies move a hub, a spoke   145
Of the circular yoke;
In death-throes they contort;
In blood disport;
And their last groaning, inarticulate
Rises above thy head,   150
And it would seem some speechless sorrow,
Sorrow infinite,
Is prisoned in this shed.
It is, it is the Spirit of Anguish!°
Much-suffering and tribulation-tried   155
Which in this house of bondage binds itself.
It will not ever from its pain be pried.
Brief-weary and forespent, a dark Shekhinah°
Runs to each nook and cannot find its rest;
Wishes to weep, but weeping does not come;   160
Would roar; is dumb.

Marginal notes:

if she has been raped.

Literally, grandchildren of the lions in Av harahamim (25) and the seed of the martyrs: references to 1096 and 1648.

Play on "Fleeing as though from the sword" (Lev. 26:36). Used throughout Ezekiel.

Ruah dakka.

Internal allusion to earlier poems of Bialik such as Levadi.

Its head beneath its wing, its wing outspread
Over the shadows of the martyr'd dead,
Its tears in dimness and in silence shed.
And thou, too, son of man, close now the gate behind thee;   165
Be closed in darkness now, now thine that charnel space,
So tarrying there thou wilt be one with pain and anguish
And wilt fill up with sorrow thine heart for all its days.
Then on the day of thine own desolation
A refuge will it seem,—   170
Lying in thee like a curse, a demon's ambush,
The haunting of an evil dream,
O, carrying it in thy heart, across the world's expanse
Thou wouldst proclaim it, speak it out,—
But thy lips shall not find its utterance.   175
Beyond the suburbs go, and reach the burial ground.
Let no man see thy going; attain that place alone,
A place of sainted graves and martyr-stone.
Stand on the fresh-turned soil.
Such silence will take hold of thee, thy heart will fail   180
With pain and shame, yet I
Will let no tear fall from thine eye.
Though thou wilt long to bellow like the driven ox
That bellows, and before the altar balks,
I will make hard thy heart, yea, I   185
Will not permit a sigh.
See, see, the slaughtered calves, so smitten and so laid;
Is there a price for their death? How shall that price be paid?
Forgive, ye shamed of the earth, yours is a pauper-Lord!
Poor was He during your life, and poorer still of late.   190
When to my door you come to ask for your reward,
I'll open wide: See, I am fallen from My high estate.
I grieve for you, my children. My heart is sad for you.
Your dead were vainly dead; and neither I nor you
Know why you died or wherefore, for whom, nor by what laws;   195
Your deaths are without reason; your lives are without cause.
What says the Shekhinah? In the clouds it hides
In shame, in agony alone abides;
I, too, at night, will venture on the tombs,
Regard the dread and weigh their secret shame,   200
But never shed a tear, I swear it in My name.
For great is the anguish, great the shame on the brow;
But which of these is greater, son of man, say thou—
Or liefer keep thy silence, bear witness in My name
To the hour of My sorrow, the moment of My shame.   205
And when thou dost return
Bring thou the blot of My disgrace upon thy people's head,
And from My suffering do not part,
But set it like a stone within their heart!

Turn, then, to leave the cemetery ground, 210
And for a moment thy swift eye will pass
Upon the verdant carpet of the grass—
A lovely thing! Fragrant and moist, as it is always at the
coming of the Spring!
The stubble of death, the growth of tombstones!
Take thou a fistful, fling it on the plain 215
Saying,

Conflation of Isa. 40:7 and Job 14:7; also refers to Jewish burial practice of plucking grass and throwing it back as a symbol of rebirth; this practice, in turn, is based on Ps. 72:16.

"The people is plucked grass; can plucked grass grow again?"°
Turn, then, thy gaze from the dead, and I will lead
Thee from the graveyard to thy living brothers,
And thou wilt come, with those of thine own breed, 220
Into the synagogue, and on a day of fasting,
To hear the cry of their agony,
Their weeping everlasting.
Thy skin will grow cold, the hair on thy skin stand up,
And thou wilt be by fear and trembling tossed; 225
Thus groans a people which is lost.
Look in their hearts—behold a dreary waste,
Where even vengeance can revive no growth,
And yet upon their lips no mighty malediction
Rises, no blasphemous oath. 230
Are they not real, their bruises?
Why is their prayer false?
Why, in the day of their trials
Approach me with pious ruses,
Afflict me with denials? 235
Regard them now, in these their woes:
Ululating, lachrymose,

Ezek. 27:32.
Crying from their throes,°

Ritual confessions of Yom Kippur.
We have sinned! and *Sinned have we!*—°
Self-flagellative with confession's whips. 240
Their hearts, however, do not believe their lips.
Is it, then, possible for shattered limbs to sin?
Wherefore their cries imploring, their supplicating din?
Speak to them, bid them rage!
Let them against me raise the outraged hand;— 245
Let them demand!
Demand the retribution for the shamed
Of all the centuries and every age!
Let fists be flung like stone

Based on Isa. 66:1.
Against the heavens and the heavenly Throne!° 250

And thou, too, son of man, be part of these:
Believe the pangs of their heart, believe not their litanies:
And when the cantor lifts his voice to cry:
Remember the martyrs, Lord,
Remember the cloven infants, Lord, 255

Based on the
Avinu malkeinu
prayer recited on
fast days.

Consider the sucklings, Lord,°
And when the pillars of the synagogue shall crack
At this his piteous word
And terror shall take thee, fling thee in its deep,
Then I will harden My heart; I will not let thee weep!   260
Should then a cry escape from thee,
I'll stifle it within thy throat.

Literally,
desecrate.

Let them assoil° their tragedy,—
Not thou—let it remain unmourned
For distant ages, times remote,   265
But thy tear, son of man, remain unshed!
Build thou about it, with thy deadly hate
Thy fury and thy rage, unuttered,

Jer. 1:18.

A wall of copper,° the bronze triple plate!
So in thy heart it shall remain confined   270

Isa. 11:8.

A serpent in its nest°—O terrible tear!—
Until by thirst and hunger it shall find

Ezek. 26:12.

A breaking of its bond.° Then shall it rear

Deut. 32:33.

Its venomous head, its poisoned fangs,° and wait

Based on Isa.
10:6.

To strike the people of thy love and hate!°   275

Leave now this place at twilight to return
And to behold these creatures who arose
In terror at dawn, at dusk now, drowsing, worn
With weeping, broken in spirit, in darkness shut.
Their lips still move with words unspoken.   280
Their hearts are broken.
No lustre in the eye, no hoping in the mind,
They grope to seek support they shall not find:
Thus when the oil is gone,
The wick still sends its smoke;   285
Thus does the beast of burden,
Broken and old, still bear his yoke.
Would that misfortune had left them some small solace

Ruth 4:15.

Sustaining the soul, consoling their gray hairs!°
Behold the fast is ended; the final prayers are said.   290
But why do they tarry now, these mournful congregations?
Shall it be also read,
The Book of Lamentations?
It is a preacher mounts the pulpit now.
He opens his mouth, he stutters, stammers. Hark   295

Sanhedrin,
beginning of chap.
11, in a discussion
of those who have
no portion in the
world-to-come.

The empty verses from his speaking flow.°
And not a single mighty word is heard
To kindle in the hearts a single spark.
The old attend his doctrine, and they nod.
The young ones hearken to his speech; they yawn.   300

Ezek. 9:1.

The mark of death is on their brows;° their God
Has utterly forsaken every one.

And thou, too, pity them not, nor touch their wound;
Within their cup no further measure pour.
Wherever thou wilt touch, a bruise is found.   305

Job 14:22.
Their flesh is wholly sore.°
For since they have met pain with resignation
And have made peace with shame,
What shall avail thy consolation?
They are too wretched to evoke thy scorn.   310
They are too lost thy pity to evoke,
So let them go, then, men to sorrow born,
Mournful and slinking, crushed beneath their yoke.
Go to their homes, and to their hearth depart—
Rot in the bones, corruption in the heart.   315
And when thou shalt arise upon the morrow
And go upon the highway,
Thou shalt then meet these men destroyed by sorrow,
Sighing and groaning, at the doors of the wealthy
Proclaiming their sores, like so much peddler's wares,   320
The one his battered head, t'other limbs unhealthy,
One shows a wounded arm, and one a fracture bares.
And all have eyes that are the eyes of slaves,

Ps. 123:2.
Slaves flogged before their masters;°
And each one begs, and each one craves: 325
Reward me, Master, for that my skull is broken
Reward me for my father who was martyred!
The rich ones, all compassion, for the pleas so bartered

Barukh
shepetarani,
father's blessing
over his son upon
his bar mitzvah.
Lines 333–49
written ca. 1906.
Extend them staff and bandage, say *good riddance,*° and
The tale is told: 330
The paupers are consoled.
Avaunt ye, beggars, to the charnel-house!
The bones of your fathers disinter!
Cram them within your knapsacks, bear
Them on your shoulders, and go forth   335
To do your business with these precious wares
At all the country fairs!
Stop on the highway, near some populous city,
And spread on your filthy rags
Those martyred bones that issue from your bags,   340
And sing, with raucous voice, your pauper's ditty!
So will you conjure up the pity of the nations,
And so *their* sympathy implore.
For you are now as you have been of yore
And as you stretched your hand   345
So will you stretch it,
And as you have been wretched

Vekha'asher
shnorartem
tishnoreru, a
Hebrew doubling
So are you wretched!°

What is thy business here, O Son of man?

of the Yiddish
shnorn, to beg.

Rise, to the desert flee!   350
The cup of affliction thither bear with thee!
Take thou thy soul, rend it in many a shred!
With impotent rage, thy heart deform!
Thy tear upon the barren boulders shed!
And send thy bitter cry into the storm!   355

(First published in *Hazman* [The Times], St. Petersburg, July–September 1904)

X

Anatomies of Revolutionary Violence

Something was happening to the insular mode of Jewish response to catastrophe. Ever since Reb Moshe enlightened Mendele about the edicts of Bismarck and the nature of anti-Semitism (**40**), there was a shift to a more outer-directed, politically motivated form of group behavior. By the time of the Kishinev pogrom thirteen years later, the Jewish socialists and Zionists were already squaring off over the proper response to tsarist repression. Both sides called for self-defense, but the Bund threw in its lot with the "workers of the world," whereas the Union of Hebrew Writers saw national self-determination as the only way to secure Jewish life. In the literature, however, these radical solutions were still transposed into an internal debate between the prophet and his people, the prophet and his God.

Not so in the wake of the Revolution of 1905, which began and ended with a bloodbath. For only one day of that fateful year, October 17, was there rejoicing in the streets. On that day the tsar granted Russia its first constitution promising a degree of civil liberty. It was followed, on October 18, by a wave of counterrevolutionary pogroms.

Jewish life in Russia exploded, first with the hope of salvation, then with the terror of mob violence. How this centrifugal force was played out in the collective and individual Jewish psyche is graphically illustrated in the three prose works that follow. Weissenberg's Yiddish novella (**48**) appeared within a year of the events described, yet the work actually telescoped a decade of radicalization in the shtetl, or Jewish market town, of eastern Europe. Weissenberg's nameless shtetl, modeled on his native Zelechow, was especially prone to outside influence for two reasons: first, it specialized in the production of ready-made boots in factories whose primitive working conditions had not changed for centuries; second, these boots were produced for export to the nearby city of Warsaw, the political nerve center of Poland. Sholem Aleichem's Heysen (**49**), in contrast, was vulnerable by virtue of its being linked by rail to other towns in the Ukraine, and the counterrevolution appealed most readily to the landless peasants who worked the railroad. Shapiro's setting (**50**), finally, was the most modern. In his "big city in southern Russia" (Yekaterinoslav, perhaps), a Jew had become so estranged from his family and community that he joined a Russian revolutionary cell and fell in love with its non-Jewish leader. Brutally reminded of his Jewishness by the pogrom, the hero—in the most shocking way—turned his anger on himself.

Because these stories were written at a time of great uncertainty in Russia, each writer was particularly hard-pressed to know how the story should end: Would the present period of political reaction give way to new reforms, or was this the beginning of the end?

Weissenberg viewed the shtetl as a microcosm of the community at large, corrupt and class-ridden. He was interested in exploring how violence begat more violence until both the shtetl oligarchy and the young workers were sucked into the maelstrom. Ultimately, their failure was eclipsed by the failure of the shtetl as a whole. So small and isolated a place could never be master of its own fate. Enemy forces were always waiting on the sidelines to quash any signs of autonomy. This is why Itchele's point of view in the story deserves special attention, as he alone foresees the outcome.

For Sholem Aleichem, the trains and telegrams merely masked the age-old plot of a last-minute "miracle" that thwarted the evil designs of local patriots and their debased lackeys. The real hero of the story was the narrator, the lively down-to-earth merchant from Heysen, whose upbeat manner of narration already bode well for the outcome. Meanwhile, that marvelous train, the Slowpoke Express, behaved as unpredictably as history itself. That a "miracle" could still be wrested out of secular violence was final proof of the story's desire for affirmation.

What is most startling about Sharpiro's story, and what most troubled readers when it was first published in Yiddish in New York City, is that it, too, ends on a positive note that is meant to be taken seriously. It proclaims the birth of a Nietzschean man who has freed himself of all inhibitions and all the victimizations of his past, who has escaped from politics and civilization to return to something elemental and basic. His story, told through two narrators in a totally detached manner, is the story of a purgation. And it is the cross—the symbol that Jews have learned to fear the most—that marks his salvation: The cross is the *shel rosh*, the frontlet on his forehead, commanding him to remember; the cross is the symbol of the suffering Christ, and thus of his victimization; and the cross is the sign of Cain, the mark of a murderer. In psychological and graphic detail unprecedented in Jewish fiction, Shapiro has drawn a man who has freed himself through violent action, who has successfully conquered that which was weak in him. Through the pogrom, an alienated intellectual has become a man of iron.

The symbol of the cross is only the most obvious subversion of religious imagery that occurs in these stories. Weissenberg sets the opening of his novella (not included here) during the twilight hour in the House of Study. Traditionally, this is the mellowest time of the day, when Jewish men gather round to tell stories and swap the latest news. Instead, it marks the first confrontation between the shtetl establishment and the young workers. And the fight breaks out about Passover, no less, the upcoming spring festival, which this year will usher in revolution instead of joy. Indeed, from this point onward, the ritual calendar, with its comforting flow of sacred time, will counteract the unpredictable violence of historical time. Everything comes together on the eve of Yom Kippur, in a brilliant description of ritual violence—the slaughtering of the atonement roosters—that harkens back to what has just happened in the shtetl proper and foreshadows the pogroms still to come from the world outside. Finally, Yekl returns to the scene of his initial defeat, this time to oust the rabbi with the shout: "No psalms! . . . Only arms, real arms!" The inner sanctum, where the recitation of Psalms is a sign of simple piety, has been violated by the enemy within. Then comes the enemy from without to put an end to the whole charade.

Sholem Aleichem's subversion is typically more subtle and playful than that. It operates solely on the level of language. When the Cossacks arrive in the eleventh hour, they do so, according to the witty narrator, *"uksomim beyodom,* with whips in their hands." But the Hebrew phrase actually means "with divination in their power (hand)" (Num. 22:7), which harks back to another ambiguous threat to the safety of the Jewish people, that which Balak tried to deliver through the mouth of Balaam. What a perfect analogy to the sight of Cossacks arriving in town not to wreak havoc themselves, but as instruments of the law!

48 A Shtetl

I. M. WEISSENBERG

Meanwhile the news coming from Warsaw and the other big cities was not good—Baku was in flames, Tatars were slaughtering people in the streets, and even in the immediate area there was talk of something in the wind . . . something planned for "this Sunday."

Sunday came. Red-faced peasants in coarse woolen coats, dark caps with shiny peaks, and high-heeled boots, poured in from all the surrounding villages. Priests from neighboring parishes came with their flocks. Heavy chanting and deep organ tones issued forth from the high arcades of the church and spilled over the silent shtetl rooftops, filling the air with a fearsome sound.

At noon, the churchgoers emptied into the enclosed yard. First came a holy icon topped by a golden orb that flashed in the sunlight, dazzling the eye with millions of tiny golden darts. It was followed by a banner depicting a white-headed eagle that older folks remembered having last seen some thirty years before.° Then a red and white striped flag, and further back another banner showing a crèche. The banners could be seen fluttering above the wall as the procession moved around the churchyard, like Jews circling the synagogue on Simḥat Torah with the scrolls of the Law. A soft, muted chanting was heard. Gradually the banners neared the open gates and a moving mass of faces appeared, row upon row of people walking shoulder to shoulder, the men bareheaded, the women with red and white kerchiefs tied under their chins. They swarmed through the narrow gates and onto the wide gravel road that led through the verdant fields.

Row upon row of shoulders and heads moved into the distance, while more and more kept emerging from the open gates in a seemingly endless flow. A light dust rose from beneath the thousands of shuffling feet as the sea of rustling gray coats flowed steadily onward. The rows of heads rose and fell like waves along the strand. Banners waved. Ahead walked the priests in their white breastplates and square black velvet miters. Behind them came the folk, a submissive multitude of thousands, moving with bowed heads to the strains of a deep and steady chant. The long procession drew farther and farther away toward the spot on the horizon where the banners waved and beckoned across the field.

Then Jewish women and girls began to appear on the hilltop outside the shtetl where they used to gather yellow sand to sprinkle on the floors for the Sabbath. Shtetl workers in their shirtsleeves came too, to observe the goings-on: at least they, thank God, were not the target! The women praised God for His great bounty, of which they were undeserving, and cheerfully watched the receding procession: let there be banners, idols, stones, bones . . . as long as Jewish children were left in peace. Blue skies sprawled overhead; nature itself seemed to have declared a holiday, opening every door and gateway to summon the world out into the fields.

Itchele, Yekl,° and the PPS°° man were out on the hill with the others watching the distant happenings. They saw only a sea of men's bare heads and red and white kerchiefs scattered like flowers among the flowing multitude. The banners

A symbol of Poland's independence; the Poles staged an abortive uprising against the Tsar in 1863.

Yekl is the leader of the shtetl Bundists.

The Polish Socialist Party, which combined socialism with an appeal to Polish national aspirations.

fluttered and unfurled and finally came to rest before a tree where the entire peasant mass stopped. There, where the roads parted, a cross stood under the tree, deep in the shadow of its branches. The chanting grew deeper and the people grew still. And then they kneeled. The entire multitude, from one end to the other, sank to its knees like grain in a great field when the wind bends it groundward. In one sweeping motion all their backs bent over, and their faces bowed to the ground. The chanting seemed to soften, to grow more hushed as though soon all the motionless heads would be lulled to sleep. A sweet rapture embraced the countryside. The fields were bathed in a sea of light, and the golden sun shone steadily on the silent congregation below. A soft breeze caressed the blond hair of the silent bowed heads. Banners waved, the golden orb glittered, piercing the sunlight with its thousands of fiery darts, but the sun sat unperturbed, staring thoughtfully into space.

Abruptly the chanting ceased. At the far end, people were beginning to stand up. Then the chanting was resumed as the congregation surged forward along the road into the green field. And all the while the housewives and girls and some of the young men of the shtetl stood watching from the yellow sandy hill. The procession receded farther into the distance, where the broad gravel road was no more than a narrow path slithering and snaking uphill and down among the green fields. Soon it was almost out of sight, a thin black stripe across a green landscape.

The spectators started back to town, but Itchele stayed, gazing thoughtfully into the distance.

"Let's go back," suggested the PPS man.

"Tell me," Itchele asked, snapping out of his reverie, "what sort of a march was this?"

"A procession," replied the PPS man.

"A religious procession," added Yekl for clarification.

"Didn't you tell us that a Christian was coming down from Warsaw to make a speech, and that we would all march together?"

"Shoulder to shoulder," added Yekl.

"Oh yeah," shrugged the PPS man, "But this was something different. These are the 'Narodovtsi.' . . ."°

The explanation was irksome. It seemed to Itchele that the PPS man had deliberately used a fancy term like "Narodovtsi" to avoid answering the question.

From narod, the people; a right-wing Polish populist movement, at times aggressively anti-Semitic.

"Liar!" he cried, "You know very well you're lying!"

The PPS man laughed aloud. This only angered Itchele the more, but he decided that it hardly made any difference. Since the death of Lazar the shopkeeper, he had lost all interest in this business.

He started back to town, heavyhearted, but once back in the shtetl he felt even worse. Looking around the marketplace at the peaceful little houses with their windows half open, he sensed something he had never sensed before: there, beyond the shtetl, lay such a vast multitude, and here everything was so small, so puny, held together by just a dab of spit. . . . It occurred to him that if the thousands out there suddenly decided to have a bit of fun—just a simple bit of peasant fun— if each of them took from the houses of the Jews no more than a couple of rotting floor boards apiece and carried them off under his arm, nothing would remain of the shtetl but an empty plot of land.

After that Sunday, the young men wanted a banner of their own. The PPS man, when he became aware of it, was afraid that Yekl might take the initiative, just as Yekl was afraid that the PPS man might do the same. Overnight in the teashop two flags were readied, and by morning a crowd had gathered in front of the glass door—handsome scrubbed youths with freshly brushed caps and a festive sparkle in their eyes. The crowd grew until the street was black with people. Where was the PPS man, they wanted to know. All at once he arrived, carrying a flag with Polish letters embroidered in silver. His face was drawn and his eyes were blood-shot from lack of sleep, but the flag fluttered and waved overhead to the great joy of the crowd. He was greeted excitedly and surrounded by a circle of upturned, eager faces.

Soon after, Yekl appeared waving a second flag just as lovely and every bit as bright as the other. He walked steadily, looking straight into the crowd with a serene and devout expression, but Itchele, who waltzed alongside him, grinned broadly at everyone. They stopped in front of the crowd and Yekl nodded:

"Good morning, friends."

Then he stood quietly, his flag facing the PPS man's. This was not at all as he had foreseen. He had intended to lead his followers separately behind their own banner. But now that everyone was standing together it was too late. The PPS man hadn't anticipated this either. So the two men stood glumly face to face, raising their heads occasionally only to drop them again.

The youths craned their necks to get a look at the flags, Yekl's too, with its simple, homey Yiddish words in the familiar alphabet: what a thrill it was to see both flags waving together!

"Well, why are we standing here?" Yekl asked after a long silence.

"Go ahead, what do you want of me?" countered the PPS man, shrugging off the question. Though Yekl made no reply, Itchele was not to be cowed:

"Listen, you blockhead! Don't take us for a bunch of suckers."

"Who said anything like that?" the PPS man protested. "The only reason I'm standing here is because I sent some men out to cut the telegraph wires and I have to wait for them to come back."

"That's different," conceded Itchele. But the explanation made Yekl even glum-mer: the PPS man always seemed to be taking the initiative. Yekl had the feeling that he too had meant to do something of the kind, but it had slipped his mind.

A couple of youngsters came running up, breathless with excitement, their caps askew. They pushed their way into the circle and whispered into the PPS man's ear.

"So where are they?" he asked.

"They're on their way. They'll soon be here. They really cut it right through. The wire made a terrible sound. B-r-r-r!"°

And soon the youths themselves appeared with smiles of triumph. Their leader wore a jacket and boots and a red kerchief around his neck and carried a white stick. As he came toward them, he signalled by raising the stick in the air with the curved end upward, then leaped up as though grabbing hold of something. Finally he sliced the air with the edge of his hand and nodded decisively: it was done!

Among the crowd an uneasy murmuring began and faces grew troubled. The soldiers would soon be on their way. The provincial officer would hear of it. But the PPS man was delighted with his deed. Now the work was complete! He smiled

The telegraph wires were cut to disrupt communication.

to himself and he and Yekl moved forward with the flags, side by side, followed by the rest of the crowd.

The street emptied as though in their honor; all the stores closed down. The crowd marched behind the flags, faces aglow with collective joy. A song started up, growing louder and bolder till it flooded the entire street.

The ranks of the marchers kept swelling as new recruits joined in. Slogans and counter-slogans broke through the singing. Finally, they reached the mayor's garden and the town hall. The crowd came to a stop and the leaders shouted out their demands, which were caught up and repeated by the vast sea of voices. After that, they all moved back into the street. Unnoticed by anyone, the mayor, half hidden by the shrubs, conferred with the excise officer, the Police Chief, and a couple of gray-coated woodcutters with axes in their hands who kept an eye on the demonstrators from afar. The PPS man marched jubilantly out in front but Yekl, right beside him, considered *himself* the leader. The further they marched, the noisier the cheers became, until the street seemed ready to explode. On and on they marched, until they reached their destination—the marketplace!

But the square was empty when they got there. The stands of baked goods were bare. A pale, frightened face peeked out from a crack in a doorway, threw one confused look at the flags and the dense crowd, and shut the door tightly.

In a flash the PPS man was atop one of the stands, waving his flag, and Yekl the carpenter with his flag was on another. The crowd settled quietly around the two stands and looked up expectantly at its leaders. Since Yekl appeared to have nothing to say, the PPS man launched into an oration and spoke with such energy that his hat almost fell off. He spoke at length, tossing his head and flexing his arms and legs like a horse. The crowd, dazzled by this hailstorm of words, stared directly upward at the face trembling with emotion and the eyes burning like torches. Housewives ran out, their sleeves rolled up above their elbows and their hands sticky with dough. Girls with tangled hair carrying babies in their arms, and young children with bagels in their hands, joined the outer circle of the crowd. As soon as the PPS man noticed these new additions to his audience, he shifted his tone, like a comedian, and began to call to his comrades in a higher, sharper voice:

"*Bratshe, tovarishtshe!*"° he exclaimed, his mouth chopping the words like lettuce for a salad.

Far back in the crowd some of the Gentiles exchanged twisted smiles under their blond moustaches. One of them pushed in behind the girls and women at the back, poked his head in toward the center, feigned an expression of dumb innocence and stammered fearfully: "The soldiers are coming! The soldiers!"

The women nearest him panicked. There was a hushed moment of suspense; then like an electric charge the message shot through the crowd and with an abrupt jolt the whole mass suddenly erupted.

"Stay where you are!" Yekl screamed with all his might. Itchele jumped up beside him and yelled even louder, waving his arms, but the pandemonium only spread. The men at the center stood fast, but at the edges, everyone was already on the run. It was impossible to restrain the women and the girls; they bolted, tripping and stepping over bodies that lay in their way. The hard knot of men at the center kept shouting: "Stay where you are! Stay where you are!" but to no avail. The turmoil only increased. Hands and feet and disheveled heads tumbled in a mass on the ground. Each tried to extricate himself by clutching at someone

Russian for
"brothers,
comrades."

else: grasping fists and fingers refused to relax their grip and the crowd melted into a tangle of protruding arms and legs. At last a path was cleared, and within minutes the women and girls and many of the youths had fled. Only the staunchest of the men remained, the elite. The PPS man turned to them once more and waited for them to settle down.

By this time the woodcutters had nothing more to do. So they turned into the market lane and walked idly back to the town hall.

By evening the shtetl knew that the telegraph wires had been cut. By morning there were soldiers in town. They arrested Yekl the carpenter and took him off to the provincial jail. His neighbors turned their heads as he was led from his house under guard. Only the tobacconist watched the proceedings with a frown: Yekl still owed him two rubles for cigarettes. . . .

The PPS man, according to one of the local coachmen, had made off by train in the middle of the night.

The sun went on shining anyway. Everything was bathed in light. The upper-story windows of the shops peered out into the marketplace. Householders began to gather: Isaac Feyge-Libes with his son-in-law Hershele; Dovidl Rosenzweig with his cap pulled over his forehead, hands behind his back, and paunch protruding slightly; then little clusters of prominent Jews with beards. The largest group gathered at the water pump where Dovidl was holding forth, gesticulating wildly and talking very heatedly, probably about the union men who were nowhere to be seen. Presumably they were all lying low.

But suddenly Itchele the bootmaker appeared across the marketplace, eyes downcast as though he were fed up with the world and preferred to look at the tips of his patent leather shoes. His hands were folded behind him, making his broad shoulders and back appear somewhat sunken, and his eyes were visibly moist. As he took a quick look at the clusters of householders, his cheekbones trembled; but he kept coming closer. Among one of the groups he recognized Chaim Yosele, a journeyman shoemaker who was now evidently a convert to respectability. Itchele walked by, feigning disinterest, but aware of the eyes watching him. Voices overtook him:

"There's no Tsar, they claim, there's no God either!"

"There are only fighters!" he heard Chaim Yosele titter.

Itchele turned sharply and glowered at Chaim Yosele who only two days before had been one of those "fighters" himself! The blood rushed to his cheeks and his eyes blazed with anger. The onlookers froze. Dovidl hurried toward Itchele with outstretched arms:

"Just look at you now! Look how angry you are! You get angry without even waiting for an explanation. He was talking about the PPS man. . . . You can see his point, after all, you're a clever fellow yourself. If you have to do something like that, at least cover your tracks. You don't have to leave a calling card! If you don't tweak the Tsar's nose, you won't have to go into hiding. The whole thing is so ugly. You know what people are saying now? That he's flown the coop. He just took off and left you holding the bag. He's probably the one who put you up to it, isn't he?"

The shaft hit home. Itchele bit his lips and hung his head. Without saying a word, he shrugged his shoulders and walked away—the plague take them all, and the PPS man too! He clenched his fists but then remembered something he had decided a while ago: what difference did it make? Since the death of Lazar the shopkeeper he was through with the movement anyway.

Meanwhile Dovidl returned to his circle of listeners and began haranguing in earnest:

"I really let him have it! I showed him how stupid their ideas were. Their whole movement's as good as buried!"

"And I was afraid he was going to come over and sock me!" Chaim Yosele giggled.

"Why should he make a fool of himself? He knows we would have made mincemeat out of him. Besides, with a hefty father-in-law like yours, and your father-in-law's two brothers, why should you be worried about Itchele? It's not like before. There are no more Jewish cossacks!"

"Come on. Let's go somewhere we can talk," said Isaac Feyge-Libes the shoe manufacturer, and he moved away, his son-in-law at his heels.

Dovidl agreed, pulling Chaim Yosele along behind him.

At a slow, leisurely pace they strolled along the street single file, their hands clasped behind their backs. Chaim Yosele tried to imitate their gait. One blond sidecurl stuck out foolishly from behind his ear, his cap had slipped dangerously to one side, but he strutted along, jacket unbuttoned, like a real somebody, as if to say: make way for me. All the time he kept glancing around to see whether anyone saw him—there he was, with Isaac Feyge-Libes, the biggest shoe-man in town; with his son-in-law Hershele, a genius who at thirteen had conducted services in the tailor's congregation—the women would peek through the cracks to get a look at him. There he was in their company, on his way to Dovidl Rosenzweig's house. . . .

The four of them sat down around the table in Dovidl's office. Isaac Feyge-Libes took a ruble from his wallet and tossed it on the table with a request for shnapps. Chaim Yosele was about to pick up the coin and fetch the refreshments himself when Dovidl grabbed him by the elbow and held him back. He rang his little bell and immediately the door swung open and Dovidl's son rushed in:

"What is it, father?"

"Bring us some shnapps and a couple of beers," he ordered, handing him the coin.

Some minutes later, when the bottles and glasses were already on the table, Dovidl got up to lower the window blinds.

"We'll show them, those ignoramuses!" he remarked, with a meaningful look at the manufacturer.

"We'll serve them up for stew!" Isaac Feyge-Libes chipped in, tugging at the twin tips of his beard.

"We'll form an association to oppose theirs!" Hershele proposed.

"We can draw up a list and get all the householders to sign," Dovidl added, showing off his talent for organization.

"As for you, my fine young man," Isaac turned to Chaim Yosele, who was still finding it hard to believe in whose company he sat, "how is it that you never come to see me, as though I weren't in the business at all? Some people have all the luck. But when I need a worker, a craftsman, I have to go begging for one. . . ."

"To tell the truth, Reb Isaac," Yosele puckered his fat lips as though cooling a steaming plate of kasha, "I've been thinking that I'd like to go to work for you."

"Naturally! You're like one of us, after all," Dovidl chimed in with an expressive twinkle for Isaac's benefit, "and your father-in-law is certainly one of us!"

And so the matter was settled. Chaim Yosele went to work for Reb Isaac. In the factory, Reb Isaac would slap him warmly on the back. "You go right on out and strike with the others, Chaim Yosele," he would say, pointing to the workers with a sinister little smile, "you be a fighter like the rest of them, do you hear?"

"Chaim Yosele," the clever son-in-law would call out mockingly, in the presence of the other workers, "our district officer is such a fool. What sort of match are his soldiers for these brave warriors of ours?"

"The 'fighters' are going to get it, all right!" Chaim Yosele declared self-importantly.

Some of the workers lowered their eyes. Others smiled sheepishly at their three "judges." They were well aware that the slightest whisper in the provincial officer's ear nowadays would be enough. . . .

Chaim Yosele spent more and more of his time conferring with Hershele. One evening Hershele suggested to him, "See if you can take care of that tall beanpole with the red bandana around his neck."

So Chaim Yosele hung around the synagogue courtyard between *minḥa* and *ma'ariv*, and when he saw the gangling youth, he ripped the red bandana from his neck and provoked a fight.

His father-in-law reproached Chaim Yosele for getting into so many bloody rows. But Chaim Yosele puffed out his cheeks and exclaimed:

"They don't let you earn a living—these strikers!"

Since the captain of the gendarmes had now begun to frequent the shtetl, Dovidl and his son were always to be seen rushing down the street in their Sabbath caftans to pay a call. When someone asked the son why, he was told bluntly:

"Whom else would the captain send for? It's a town of animals, after all. Did the captain have anyone else to talk to when he came?"

The workers now sat at their benches as meekly as lambs. The more resigned they became, the greater Chaim Yosele's daring. Every evening he would beat up the gangling youth, and every morning he was greeted by Dovidl with a big hello.

Early one morning when the ground was still wet with dew, and the scattered sawdust and straw of the marketplace lay bleached in the sun's early glare, Chaim Yosele's father-in-law stood haggling with a peasant and two other prospective Jewish buyers over a wagonload of fruit. Suddenly a woman came running up to him with several others close behind, screaming:

"Help! Come quickly! They're beating up your son-in-law!"

"Woe is me!" the poor man cried in confusion, "so early in the morning?" He set out at a run, still in his apron, and headed straight for the "beanpole's" house. A group of people stood there looking up at the second-story windows; Dovidl too was watching from his own doorstep across the street. In the middle of the crowd stood Chaim Yosele, his face and head smeared with blood. As soon as Dovidl saw the father-in-law rushing up the street, he smiled to himself and turned back into the house.

At the sight of his father-in-law, Chaim Yosele lunged toward the front door. But the father-in-law, who was even more distraught than he, shoved the boy behind him, broke through the door, and started up the stairs. A hail of wooden boards came crashing down the stairs to block his way. The gangling youth stood with his mother behind a pile of wood, frantically hurling down one board after another. Through the open door came the shrieks of small children and the screams of the father who kept running over to the window in a frenzy and then back to the aid of his wife and son. The boards flew in mad confusion down the stairs, but Chaim Yosele's father-in-law continued climbing, shielding his head with his hands. In a flash the gangling youth ran inside, grabbed something from over the chimney, and oblivious to what he held in his hands, rushed out again to attack.

Chaim Yosele's father-in-law felt a single blow under his heart. For a moment he remained motionless, with a dazed glassy-eyed look, staring at his antagonist in a trance. Then he began to stagger, and making a grab for the railing, stumbled weakly down the stairs. At the bottom he shot an uncomprehending look up at the sky, and then opened his mouth wide, in a great gasp for air. Desperately he looked around him, his eyes flickering with doubt. Some hidden force drove him back toward the door. He pushed against it with both hands, and trembling violently, was able to force it open. As he lifted his foot to step over the boards a stream of blood gushed from his boot. . . .

The crowd looked on, dumb with shock. Someone let out a woeful cry and stepped forward with fists raised and teeth clenched as though restraining some fierce emotion.

"Help! Help!" people shouted from all sides. But the man was already spinning blindly in a circle, leaning more and more to one side until he thudded to the ground.

"He's dead!" went up the cry.

"Take off his boot!" someone yelled, and there was a sudden rush for his foot. The boot came off with a jerk; a pool of black blood poured out as though from a butcher's pail.

The dead man's glazed eyes stared upward one final time and the brows trembled slightly. Right in the center of the heart there was a hole the size of an egg. Warm blood still oozed from the wound, soaking the man's body and all his clothing.

The body was lifted and carried off. Someone supported the head, which bobbed behind like the head of a slaughtered goose. The face was waxen, the mouth somewhat twisted and clenched from pain, and the eyes half-open, bulging. The bearers walked unsteadily, a little wedge of men with a body in their arms, and Chaim Yosele ran behind, beating himself on the head and bellowing: "My father-in-law!" But the rest of the crowd remained on the scene, yelling up at the windows: "Down! Down! Bring them down!"

Ladders were set up against the wall.

All at once Ephraim, one of the men who helped carry off the body, came running back in a sweat:

"What is there left to live for? The organization has killed!" he screamed dramatically, then offered himself by the throat, "Go ahead, go ahead and kill me, too!"

"The organization . . . the organization, . . ." sobbed the women, choking on their tears, "a father of eight little children."

Without warning, the Police Chief suddenly appeared. His blond moustache quivered, and his eyes flew over the heads of the crowd to the windows above.

The cap with its badge sat firmly on his head, and he kept a tight grip on the sword in his belt as though he were about to draw.

The crowd grew more agitated. Angrily, they glared up at the windows. Ephraim, followed by several of the others, stormed the ladders, screaming upward with blood-red faces.

Shrieks from inside the house pierced the heavens. But several hands were already reaching out to smash the windows. The shattering of the panes was drowned in a roar of voices, as splinters of glass rained down over the sea of blazing faces below. Only black silhouettes were visible in the windows. Some of the men climbed inside; others stood on the ladders trying to get in, while the bottom rungs were being contested by ever greater numbers of volunteers. At the same time a mob broke through the outer door and rushed the stairs.

"Bring them down! Down!" the cries sounded across the yard. The crashing of boards merged with frenzied human screams and filled the air with madness and chaos. In the narrow doorway the crowd pushing inward was halted by those starting back down. The boy's father, pale and stunned, was shoved through the door by fifty hands. Then the son, his face quite unrecognizable, blood streaming over his hair and face. He was pushed against a wall with his head slumped forward. Boards began to rise and fall over his head, and the mob, like a compressed mass with a thousand flailing limbs, raged and beat him savagely until the boy sank under the blows. He was no longer visible, but a few kicks were added for good measure. The Police Chief tried to force his way through, the veins bulging in his neck, and his eyes fierce with determination as he tried to push people back with his arms. But the mob was a solid mass, united in a single raging passion that burned in every face. A naked sword flashed suddenly in the policeman's hand, held straight up over their heads. The mob fell back as if hit by a splash of cold water. Terrified, they watched with bated breath. . . .

"Move back!" shouted the Police Chief. He lifted the youth who lay on the ground gasping, and shielded his bloody head with both his hands. Supporting the boy under the arm, the officer told those around him to see to the father, who was also stretched out on the ground, tearing at his hair with mournful cries. Some of the men dragged the father along as the crowd set out after the Police Chief and the boy, who huddled against him and tried to bury his head under the officer's arm. But the mob ran loose like a wild herd, brandishing wooden slats and trying to hit the boy anywhere they could. Ephraim threatened the youth with a club, which he held upraised over his head, but each time the weapon began to fall the father would leap forward and pull it away. Ephraim dodged and looked for another opening; when he saw his chance, he took aim at an eye and swung with all his might. The boy pitched forward with a terrible cry. In that same moment the father threw himself over the boy, covering him with both hands and pressing his whole shuddering body over him like a shield. The crowd felt it had had enough. The officer drew his sword again and the boy lurched to his feet, stumbled and staggered onward. His eye fell out of his face, large as a potato, coated in black. Pieces of hair and flesh had been ripped from his scalp, and blood ran down over his neck and shoulders. They barely made it to the town hall.

Now the mob prowled the streets looking for "strikers." Men with blackened faces and matted beards ran headlong down the street brandishing their wooden boot-supports as clubs. They found a boy hiding under the bridge. By the time they were through with him he lay bruised and battered on the soft earth, his face so badly swollen that the eyes could not be seen.

Suddenly word spread that the brothers of the murdered man were on their way! . . . They had been traveling with their partners to Warsaw, but were intercepted at a stop along the way by a telegram from the shtetl. The mob awaited them impatiently: now the action would really begin! At noon a couple of horses came clattering down the street into the center of town, pulling a wagonload of men. The passengers jumped down; among them were older men in fedoras, and youths in shiny peaked caps and leather jackets, the brothers of the dead man, his partners, and a few who had come along for the ride. Knives and revolvers glinted sharply in their hands as they ran into the marketplace shouting: "Our brother! Our brother!"

Their first stop was the dead man's house. A white sheet covered the corpse, which lay on the floor with candles burning at its head. The widow and a floorful of children lay prostrate around the dead man, burying their heads against his body. The brothers took one look at the scene, a quick look at their brother's face under the sheet, and hurled themselves to the floor. They beat their foreheads, crying: "Our brother! Our brother!" The house resounded with weeping and heartrending cries. Slowly, with knives bared, the partners began edging toward the door, but the widow ran to block their way:

"Even if you slaughter the whole town," she sobbed, "you still won't bring my husband back to life!"

Out of pity for her, they turned away and stuck their weapons in their pockets. But once back out in the courtyard, they picked up boards and clubs and rushed into the street.

Then blows echoed through the streets for fair, as workers were pulled from their benches and dragged from their lofts. Inflamed and bloodthirsty, the men chased down their victims, and soon blood began to spurt afresh from heads already steeped in gore. The cobblestones were bathed in blood. The sky shuddered. The sun burned red, the air was thick and red. Like a great slaughterhouse, the marketplace lay smashed and bloodied.

It was then that Itchele appeared in the square with an iron bar that he had pried loose from one of the storefronts. He marched across the square with iron-firm steps. Quickly he slid into the lane and turned into a side street where he stopped before the open window of Isaac Feyge-Libes's workshop.

"Where are the boys?" he asked Hershele when he saw the empty workbenches.

"What boys?" the other replied, turning pale as a sheet.

"Have they run away?"

"Run away? . . . yes . . . with their paring knives. . . ." Hershele slowly regained his composure and threw out his arms as though a tragedy had befallen him.

With a grimace of disgust, Itchele threw the iron bar to the ground and took to his heels. But all at once he stopped, turned back, retrieved the weapon, and fled a second time as if someone were tearing him by the hair. . . .

He paused at another window farther along the street, but found no one there either. By now he was a little calmer. Slowly, he strode away, hanging his head, with both hands clutching the iron bar behind his feet. As he passed a house on the next street he heard a scream and a terrible racket coming from behind the front door. He ran over to the entrance and stood transfixed: the whole gang from Warsaw was in the yard with their clubs and revolvers, menacing someone at an upper window. A moment later he saw Tevel, a boy of about eighteen, being dragged from his workbench, his sleeves still black from the dye. The boy shot one desperate glance toward the door to the yard before blows began raining down on him. With a sharp sigh, as if someone had knocked him off balance, Itchele grabbed hold of the doorpost for support. His face contorted with pain as he watched the butchery. Then he staggered into the street, a beaten man, poisoned to the very last drop of his blood.

He went home and threw himself down on the bed, tossing and groaning. His mother and younger brothers and sisters watched from across the room, holding their breath. For a full day and a night he lay in the same spot. The following day his first words as he finally rose from the bed were to ask his mother about Tevel. She told him it wasn't known for certain whether the boy would live. The expression in Tevel's eyes as he looked toward the door haunted Itchele still. Could a living person look like that? As he recalled the scene, Itchele's eyes grew damp with moisture. . . .

But when he stepped outside, Itchele learned from the barber-surgeon that Tevel was actually on the mend. The sun greeted him full in the face. A splendid brightness flooded the marketplace, and Itchele was forced to squint, unable to keep his eyes open. Everything was very still, much too still it seemed to him. The shops were open, and the storekeepers stood in their usual spot in the doorways. But their bearing was stiff, unnatural. The sky too was motionless, perfectly blue and clear. The sun shimmered and glared off the whitewashed walls of the shops. The stillness was ominous, like after a funeral. Suddenly Itchele saw a few tailors scurrying by with their sewing machines on their backs, their heads pressed so low by the heavy load that the tips of their beards stuck straight out from their chests, and the ends of their long coats swept the ground behind them. Itchele turned away from the sight; he was reminded of Menashe the ironmonger's death . . . even before he was buried his daughters were stealing the good china from the attic, behind each other's back. But now, Itchele thought, he would settle for anything—as long as Tevel was all right. . . .

That evening when Itchele sat down for a bite and a glass of tea—after his long fast, his mother insisted on the glass of tea—a boy burst into the house:

"Itchele," he whispered breathlessly, "some fellows are down from Warsaw . . . workers . . . with guns . . . they're waiting just outside the shtetl. . . ."

He slammed the glass down on the table and followed the boy outside.

Before long a bunch of young men had gathered in the marketpace—Itchele and about eighteen others. The atmosphere was charged. Storekeepers stood in the entrances of their shops, watchful and waiting, with one foot ready to slam the door.

As it happened, there was no trouble that night. The funeral had been held the evening before, and right afterward the men responsible for the beatings had all left town. Only the brothers themselves remained, and as Itchele put it, "They are his brothers, after all. . . ." By the next day not a trace of the Warsaw visitors remained. They were said to have fired some shots into the air before driving off in their wagon.

Things returned to normal, and everyone knew that Itchele was now in charge of the organization. Once again Dovidl Rosenzweig slunk around like an orphan. Sometimes, out of sheer loneliness, he would sidle up to one of the union-men and mention an item he had read in the papers—about the strikers in Bialystok or the revolutionaries who had set the fires in Baku—and praise them to the skies.

The summer dragged on. As the days shortened, people began to buckle down: the year promised to be a prosperous one, somewhat hectic perhaps, but with jobs for everyone. As for military consignments—there was work enough to drown in! Almost unnoticed, the days passed, the sun moved further aslant, and the wind shifted, bringing a fresh new tang to the air and a whisper of strange new secrets. . . . The sun's rays shed a redder, cooler light over the earth with intimations of something cold and unfamiliar. Each day, the sun grew more thoughtful and silent, as though regretting something lost. It took the birds till noon to begin testing their wings and pecking at their underfeathers. Then, stretching their wings, they hopped tentatively over the synagogue roof, no more than a shingle at a time, twittering piteously; there was much longing in that sound.

And the evenings were different too. Night fell ever more abruptly, and before you knew it the sun was setting in a corner of the horizon behind some red clouds that were trying to find a night's lodging in back of the woods. A red glow spread over the synagogue roof with its tiny attic window staring raptly into the distance. Far away, in silent yearning, the sun went down. Shadows stretched noiselessly across the street. The shops looked like dark bakers' ovens. Market-women with their baskets and stools under their arms shuffled homeward, chilled to the bone, their faces pinched and wrinkled, and their lips blue.

The nights kept getting colder.

Lights shone gently from all the houses and stores. The shopkeeper's white face in the doorway stood out sharply against the dark night, and his yawn rolled into the empty marketplace like a hollow echo. Overhead, the sky was a crystal plate decorated with sharp-edged, glittering stars that seemed to be burrowing deeper and deeper into the recesses of the night. One by one, the lights in the windows went out. Heavy footsteps resounded through the square as the watchman made the rounds of the shuttered stores, making known his desire for a new fur coat in a series of strange sounds and endless mutterings. . . .

At dawn thick white dew shrouded the marketplace from rooftop to ground. The cold red sunrise ushered in a ruddy, cold day. The High Holy Days were approaching. Boys and study-house benchwarmers played hide-and-seek with the shofar, and every morning after the first prayers the sexton had to conduct an angry inquiry into its whereabouts. Every morning the well-heated ritual bath hissed with steam. In the early dawn, shutters rang as the sexton rushed from house to house, waking the men for the penitential prayers. Like a demon he flew through the streets and alleys, rapping loudly at each house, then rushing on to the next.

The older Jews became more serious and subdued; the youths, paler and more gaunt. The synagogue courtyard was quiet during the day, the house of study dozed, and its moldy green windows gave off a restful bluish glow in the sunlight. But at night they were ablaze with red. Inside, the congregation prayed fervently; the groans and sighs blended with the heartrending chant of the petitioners, and then flowed into the muffled darkness outside. At daybreak, when skies began to clear, the lights in the synagogue were extinguished and sallow faces appeared in the windows to look out at the sober new morning. Across the square the treetops of the barrel-maker's garden rustled and nodded, as if they had been privy to a secret that night. The sky paled in the east and a bright stripe of clouds stretched across the horizon, but the rest of the sky remained ashen, and in the cool morning air one could almost hear a sigh: "Remember the Covenant." The people recited and remembered, aware that the night of nights would soon be upon them. . . .

And it came—the eve of Yom Kippur.

Roosters used for the atonement ceremony of kapparot are then slaughtered on the eve of Yom Kippur.

That morning the roosters wakened not to crow but to lament, with bitter, mournful cries.° "There is no judge and no judgment," their voices called as they were dragged from their roosts, roused from the sweetest of dreams, for the slaughterer in his broad-sleeved smock with the slaughter-knife in his teeth was passing from house to house. There was a flurry of feathers and a flapping of wings against the ground. Stifled cries were silenced, and a final gasp or flickering glance was crushed beneath an indifferent boot.

A red morning trembled in the east. Fearsome and blood-stained, it heralded an afternoon more awe-inspiring still. Shops were bolted; the wax memorial candles shining through the windows were enough to fill one with dread. Choked cries emanated from the houses, punctuated by the groans and sobs of men and women. Soon the shutters were closed and the Jews of the shtetl, dressed all in white, their eyes red with weeping, walked down the street in the direction of the synagogue.

After Yom Kippur the sky grew changeable. Winds began to whistle and clouds like runny gray mold chased across the sky, rotting the heavens. The birds awoke in a fright, and quickly banding together flew forth in V formation, like two ribbons stretching back from a single head, until they disappeared among the distant clouds.

The trees took fright and yellowed. A rustling was heard through the woods, and leaves began falling to the ground, blanketing the earth like a yellow shroud. As the wind howled through the trees the branches, now naked, began to beat themselves and groan, deafening the heavens with the sounds of their mourning.

It was almost Sukkot, and everyone was busy banging together his booth, hammering boards into the wooden posts under his windowsill. Once again the wagon came clattering over the bridge, carrying visitors from Warsaw who jumped down as it came to a stop, grabbed their parcels, and ran homeward, keeping their heads tucked into their collars against the damp chill wind.

Throughout the entire holiday week the sky remained overcast and it rained steadily. But for Simḥat Torah, the holiday of the Rejoicing of the Law, the weather improved. Youths moved into the streets and staged a stormy demonstration during the procession of the scrolls in the synagogue. It was a demonstration that did them proud; as Itchele said, a real "smash!"

Called in October 1905.

And that was the way things went for the rest of the winter. Since there was a general strike on,° no one left the shtetl. The citified sons stayed home, and the town declared a Sabbath of its own: a local strike was called on a local scale. Only later was it discovered from the underground newspapers and proclamations that this was part of the general strike which workers everywhere were waging.

Gangs of young men roamed the streets daily like packs of hungry wolves. The door of the teashop swung open and shut as youths inside and out tried to put the bite on someone—maybe a "brother" would stand them to a meal or lend them a little money to tide them over—anything to still their hunger. Later on, when they were back at work, they would have no use for such behavior, but in the meantime it was either beg or starve. . . . It was in this spirit that some thirty youths set out for Aaron the butcher's.

When he saw the calamity bearing down on him, the butcher edged back into a corner and blinked out in terror. His wife, a rather chubby woman, got the hiccups and made abrupt crowing noises to the delight of the gang, which imitated her every sound like a cantor's choir. They raised such a row that people came running in off the street and peered through the windows. Meanwhile one of the boys found a very large loaf of black bread in one of the cupboards, and within minutes it was plucked apart like a rooster. At least they keep their hats on while eating, the butcher thought to himself, beginning to breathe a little easier:

"What is it you want, my young friends?" he asked finally.

"What we want," several voices cried in unison, "we'll tell you what we want. You can keep your gizzards and giblets and drumsticks. . . . All we want is bread!"

"If it's only bread you want, that shouldn't be too difficult," said the butcher, coming a little closer. "Tell me, about how much do you want me to give you for bread?"

"Ten rubles," someone blurted out.

"Ten! Ten!" chimed in the chorus.

"It's impossible," the butcher protested, "you want to ruin me?"

"Who wants to ruin you? All we want is enough for a bit of bread and herring for each of us!"

His wife had been standing in the chimney corner, her mouth twisted into an unpleasant grimace, and her lips visibly trembling.

"Yocheved," the butcher summoned her, "these Jews want bread, and we'll just have to get them some. . . . Go borrow ten rubles from the neighbor."

She moved toward the door, but turned before leaving to throw a lingering glance in the direction of her poor husband: to what fate was she abandoning him? In fact her husband was quite capable of rustling up the ten rubles himself, but he didn't want to give the gang any wrong ideas.

The youths received their money in cash and tore into the street, cheering lustily. Afterward the teashop was very lively. Youths jumped over the benches and tables, and Itchele cheered them on:

"Good for you, boys! If you know how to take care of yourselves, that's half the battle!"

From the newspapers and from rumors the shtetl learned more and more about the strikers in the cities. No one cared a damn any more for Victoria's° constitutional reforms—why, here, even the railroads were on strike!

And then suddenly there was news of pogroms . . . long lists of towns and cities . . . horrible accounts of the Black Hundreds° cutting open human bellies . . . crushing the heads of suckling babes. The news struck terror into the heart of young and old alike. There were rumors that thugs were on their way, that they were already in Warsaw. Four thousand men were said to have come by the Terespol train. Reb Avrom Feinberg lost no time having his door nailed up with thick iron bars. His neighbors, scarcely one of whom had a door of his own, just a wife and

I.e., Queen Victoria, England.

Popular name for the hundred-man paramilitary units of the League of the Russian People, supported by Tsar Nicholas II to "preserve public order." The

Black Hundreds initiated many brutal pogroms against the Jews.

children and a rickety table, wanted to declare a day of fasting. Faces turned black as the earth. Even Itchele was dejected.

Evenings, clouds bobbed in the leaden skies like gray clay pots in dirty water. Windows looked somberly out at the street. Care-worn Jews, their heads bowed to the ground, crept toward the synagogue for *minḥa* and *ma'ariv*.

In the study-house one evening, the congregation discussed the latest events. Cigarette smoke rose to the ceiling, and the candle lights flickered as if in a fog. The reader, pausing between prayers, stood facing the congregants with his back to the lectern. At that moment the Gentile bath attendant appeared in the doorway, a fur cap on his head and the corner of his dirty undershift showing under his heavy cotton vest. His eyes glittered like a tomcat's, and his lips, which usually were turned up in a foolish smile, now seemed to be sucking at something. Stach, the bath attendant, had news to report: thugs were on their way. They had been seen on the Warsaw road. The men's jaws trembled.

Later that same evening, Chanele, the women's bath attendant, returned to town from a village near the station where she had accompanied one of the women back home from the ritual bath. She told her neighbors what the women had seen: Russians in red shirts and long peasant blouses were hanging around the station that morning . . . the thugs everyone was talking about! By now maybe there were as many as a hundred of them. . . .

Her neighbors listened, groaning "Merciful God," and wringing their hands. When they slipped out of the bath-house, one by one, instead of going straight home they dropped in on other neighbors who passed the word along until it reached even the study-house of the Blendiver Hasidim. By then it was a grizzly tale: a hundred villainous hoodlums with swords and knives were massed at the station, waiting to attack.

People began closing their shutters. The street remained dark and deserted. Occasionally, someone would run nervously by, stopping at every corner for a frightened look and then fly on with coattails flapping in the wind. Where would such a Jew be running to, unless to the bath-house, to hide in the loft, under the birchbrooms?

The teashop was still filled with young people, but a mood of silent dejection hung over the room. All at once Itchele burst in like a thunderbolt:

"Why are you sitting around?" he cried. "Don't you know what's happening?"

He was greeted by stares.

"So what are we supposed to do?"

"Who'll come with me to the ironmonger's for scythes?"

They were ready, to a man, to follow Itchele wherever he might lead. He selected a handful and in a little while they were back carrying scythes tied in bundles. Everyone grabbed a weapon. Their faces brightened with excitement as the curved blades of the scythes sparkled in their hands.

But a look around the room suggested there were still too few of them and they sent for the tanners to join them. A moment later the messengers were back with a little girl who seemed to be bursting with joyfulness. It was Yekl's sister, bringing news of her brother's return.°

A political amnesty was declared as part of the new constitution.

"Yekl is back!" There was a flurry of excitement.

Scythes in hand, the crowd surged into the street and made straight for Yekl's house, where they swarmed around him like bees. Overwhelmed, Yekl raised his hands for silence. Noticing the scythes, he asked what was going on. It took a moment before the men remembered their mission and explained about the thugs.

"Phooey!" Yekl spat, "It's a lie! It's a provocation! I've just come from the station, haven't I?"

The scythes were put away. With a rousing song, Yekl was escorted into the marketplace while some boys ran off to the Charity for Poor Brides to fetch huge red lanterns which they lit and mounted on tall poles to brighten the whole market square. Singing lustily, the young crowd accompanied Yekl from store to store. The lanterns' reddish light flooded the walls, and their reflection blazed in the upstairs windows like fires in the night. The confused sounds of shouting and singing echoed through the shtetl.

From the two householders who came over to extend Yekl a welcome, the town learned, to its relief, that the rumors of hoodlums were utterly false. Grateful to God for His mercy, everyone went off to bed.

By early morning, Yekl was already out in the square near the public wall; the Chief Police Officer was with him, and they were playing a little game: Yekl pasted up copies of a proclamation and the officer tore them down. A lick of the tongue, a proclamation mounted, and then torn down. Another proclamation pasted up, another torn down. They stood side by side, looking one another right in the eye, as if the whole thing had been prearranged, until the pile of proclamations had passed from Yekl to the officer. At that point they looked one another in the eye again, as if to say: Well, how about that? . . .

Men and women stood by and smiled at Yekl's audacity: the Tsar's new Constitution must really be in effect after all!°

The Imperial Manifesto of October 17, 1905, granting civil liberties.

Meanwhile the rabbi in his nightcap, with his long earlocks and padded satin coat, was on his way to the study-house with a group of followers to recite the psalms. When Yekl saw them, he quickly rounded up some of his gang and marched in behind.

Up front the recitation had already begun. The reader was standing at the lectern, chanting, "A psalm of David . . ." and the congregation was swaying and singing along. The rabbi's cap swayed back and forth against the wall; the other worshippers sat around the tables over their open psalters, wrapped in prayer-shawls, chanting mournfully, hardly in the usual hasidic manner at all. Yekl and his gang mounted the platform. Startled, the rabbi and congregation raised their heads.

"What good are the psalms?" Yekl shouted with a bang on the table. "This is no time for psalms!"

The congregation was dumbfounded.

"This is the time, not for psalms, but for arms! For fighting with weapons!"

"Help! Arms!" screamed the rabbi, tearing himself by the hair. "Help! Arms! There are no arms . . . only psalms! Psalms!"

"No psalms!" Yekl outshouted him, "only arms, real arms! Pistols! Revolvers!"

"Help! Revolvers!" screamed someone in the congregation, an impassioned Jew with eyes radiating heavenly devotion. He jumped up on the rabbi's table and faced Yekl, his long beard atremble with the emotion of his effort.

"You're just a thief!" Yekl hollered him down, waving a finger in front of his face. "Your scale is false. You put your foot on it whenever you're weighing anything. You short-change the farmers!"

"Jews, kill me . . . I'm ready to die for the sanctification of the Name!" the Jew shrieked in a high quavering voice. He tore open his clothes at the breast and fixed the congregation with a fiery stare.

"Get down! Get down!" went up the cry around the podium. Faces burned in anger and fists rose in the air.

"Psalms! Psalms!" cried the congregation from all sides, and the devout Jew with the long beard suddenly burst out with a cry: "A psalm of David. . . ."

"Quiet!" Yekl's gang pounded on the podium, and then one of them pulled a gun.

"Help!" screamed the crowd. Hands stretched upward to grab the Jew down from the table. The men's faces were contorted with fear as they looked up at the platform.

The gang on the podium made a move for the stairs, and in a flash the congregation threw open the windows and began to leap out. Within a minute the study-house was empty. There remained only the rabbi, who sat in his corner with his face to the wall, crying like a small child, and some elderly Jews in prayer-shawls, sitting at the back tables as if petrified, looking fearfully at their rabbi. . . .

A breeze blew in through the open windows, and sent the curtain of the Ark billowing outward, as if it too were trying to tear loose through the window. Outside there were wild shouts of triumph. Like a stampeding herd, the youths began running through the street. Even Itchele could not hold them back, though he spread his arms and he and Yekl tried to stop them, yelling "Enough! Enough!" But by now the boys were in a fever of excitement. One after another the shops were locked up, but the youths ran headlong, screaming at the top of their lungs.

All at once some boys dashed up breathlessly:

"Listen . . . hurry . . . get down to the courthouse. They're trying to oust the judge . . . there are *goyim* there too, and others. . . . Hurry! Hurry!"

"Come on now, let's put an end to it!" Yekl cried with the rest.

"An end to it! An end to it!"

"Long live the revolu. . . ."

"Hurrah! Hur-r-a-a-a-h!"

And they surged forward.

Like a thick black cloud they descended on the courthouse, where a group of Gentiles awaited them. The two groups merged and stood together looking up at the courthouse windows, until some of the men moved forward to enter the building, and the crowd swept in after. In a short while the judge rushed out, looking quite distraught and glancing back nervously over his shoulder. Uncertain where his safety might lie, he hurried down the street as if driven by a storm, bareheaded, the tails of his coat flying out behind him.

The crowd raised a triumphant cheer and watched him scurry out of sight down the end of the street, where the bailiff lived.

That same night the youths were dragged from their beds; by morning the rooftops were shrouded in fog, and it was quiet, except for the occasional echo of an iron rod against a wall. Householders came out to exchange news about the events of the night. Pale mothers with tear-stained eyes appeared in the street; their sons stood at the town hall, bound in chains, surrounded by soldiers: soldiers in greatcoats with rifles over their shoulders. Itchele and Yekl were there, with almost all their friends. There were only two who didn't belong: a Jew of about forty with a black beard and an intense expression on his face who had been arrested because he didn't let a soldier inspect the cupboard where his wife's jewelry was kept; and a peasant in a gray coat, with a very ordinary face and big innocent eyes, who had lingered in the tavern till rather late the previous night, and on his way home had indulged in some caroling. . . .

"Pavel," asked one of the locals when the guards had moved slightly apart, "How did you get into this?"

"My dear friend," said the peasant, helplessly, a sour look on his face, "I was enjoying a drink, at my very own expense too . . . and now even that's not allowed!"

Several dozen reinforcements came galloping up. Wagons, driven by peasant-coachmen, drew up behind them and the officer motioned for the youths to climb aboard. They crowded into the wagons. The horses, growing impatient, tossed their heads and pawed the ground until the wagons finally began to move, surrounded by a circle of soldiers on horseback.

As he rode into the main street, the officer in charge signalled to his men. Smartly, they slapped their hands against their scabbards and drew; the glare from their naked swords flashed like a bolt of lightning. The procession ambled through town, the shame-faced prisoners in the wagons and the horsemen swaying gently in the saddle. Everything was hammered shut. But for the thud of horses' hooves and the jangle of spurs the street seemed uncommonly still, silent as a tomb. A dreadful fear gripped the heart; what if the street should die, just so, behind its locked shutters, as they were passing through?

Not until they had crossed the bridge did the soldiers urge their steeds to a trot. Gray morning mist enveloped them as they receded into the countryside. From a distance it looked as though a wandering black smudge had set out to roam the wide gray world.

1906

49 The Wedding That Came Without Its Band

SHOLEM ALEICHEM

"I do believe I promised to tell you about another of our Slowpoke's miracles, thanks to which, don't you know, we were saved from a horrible fate. If you'd like to hear about it, why don't you stretch out on this seat and I'll lie down on that one. That way we'll both be more comfortable."

So said my friend, the merchant from Heysen, as we were traveling one day on the narrow-gauge train called the Slowpoke Express. And since this time too we were all by ourselves in the car, which was rather hot, we took off our jackets, unbuttoned our vests, and made ourselves right at home. I let him tell his story in his jovial, unhurried manner, making a few mental notes as he did so that I could write it down later in his own words.

"Once upon a time . . . it happened a while ago, back in the days of the Constitution,° when we Jews were getting the glad hand. Actually, though, we in Heysen were never afraid of a pogrom. Shall I tell you why not? For the simple reason that there was no one to do the job. Of course, I don't mean to suggest that if you looked hard enough, you couldn't have found a few public-spirited citizens who would have welcomed the chance to dust off a Jew or two, that is, to break all our bones—the proof of it being, don't you know, that when the glad tidings began to arrive from other places, some of our local patriots° dashed off a secret message to whoever they thought it might concern: seeing as how, they wrote, it was time to stand up and be counted in Heysen too, where there was a dearth of volunteers, could they please be sent reinforcements in a hurry. . . . And don't you know that twenty-four hours hadn't gone by when word reached us Jews, and again in strictest secrecy, that the reinforcements were already on their way. Where were they coming from? From Zhmerinka, and from Kazatin, and from Razdyelne, and from Popelne, and from a few other places that were equally famous for their roughnecks. How, you ask, did we get wind of such a top secret? The answer, don't you know, is that we had a hidden agent, a fellow called Noyach Tonkonog. Who was this Tonkonog? I'll try to describe him for you, because being a traveler in these parts, you may run into him some day.

"Noyach Tonkonog is a Jew who grew more up than out. And since God gave him a pair of long legs, he learned to put them to good use. He's always on the run and hardly ever at home. He's got a thousand irons in the fire, most of them not his own. His own business, that is, is a printshop. And because it's the only one in Heysen, he rubs elbows with government officials, and with our local gentry, and with all kinds of people in high places.

"It was Noyach who broke the good news to us. That is, he personally spread it around town by whispering in everyone's ear, 'This is strictly for your private consumption, because I'd never tell anyone else. . . .' Before long the word had traveled like wildfire that hooligans were being brought in to attack the Jews. We even knew the exact hour of the attack and the direction it would come from—it was all planned like a military operation. Well, there was great gloom in Heysen, don't you know! And it was the poor who panicked the most. That's not what you'd normally expect, is it? After all, it makes more sense for a rich Jew to be scared to death of such a thing, because he's liable to be cleaned out of house and home. If you own nothing to begin with, on the other hand, why worry? What's there to lose? Still, you should have seen them drop everything, grab their children, and run pell-mell for cover. . . . Just where, you ask, does a Jew hide in Heysen? Either in the cellar of a friendly Russian, or in the attic of the town notary, or wherever the owner puts you in his factory. And in fact, everyone managed to find a place. There was only one Jew who didn't bother, and you're looking at him right now. I'm not trying to boast, mind you, but you'll see if you think about it that I had logic on my side. In the first place, what good does it do to be afraid of a pogrom? You either live through it or you don't. . . . And secondly, even assuming that I'm no braver than the next man, and that, when push comes to shove, I'd like to be someplace safe myself, where, I ask you, is safe? Whose word do I have that, in all the excitement, the same friendly Russian, or town notary,

*Euphemistic
reference to the
pogroms of 1905.*

*Literally, the few
[Polish] squires.*

or factory owner isn't going to . . . do you follow me? And besides, how can you just go and abandon a whole town? It's no trick to skedaddle—the whole point is to stay and do something! . . . Of course, you may object, that's easy to say, but what exactly can a Jew do? Well, I'll tell you what: a Jew can find a string to pull. I suppose there's someone with the right sort of influence where you come from, too. In Heysen he's called Nachman Kassoy, a contractor with a round beard, a silk vest, and a big house all his own. And because he builds roads, he was on good terms with the prefect of the district, who even used to have him over for tea. This prefect, don't you know, was quite a decent goy. In fact, he was a prince of a goy! Why do I say that? Because he had his price, if you paid it through Nachman Kassoy. That is, he was perfectly willing to accept gifts from anyone (why be rude, after all?), but he liked getting them from Nachman best of all. There's something about a contractor, don't you know. . . .

"In short, I fixed things via Nachman, drew up a list of donors, and managed to raise the funds—and a tidy little sum it was too, don't you know, because you couldn't cross a prefect's palm in such a matter without giving it some good scratch . . . in return for which, he did his best to reassure us that we could sleep calmly that night because nothing would happen to us at all. Fair enough, no? The only trouble was that we still had our secret agent, whose reports went from bad to worse; the latest of them, which he of course passed on in such strict confidence that it was all over town in no time flat, was that he, Noyach Tonkonog, had personally seen a telegram that he very much wished he hadn't. What was in it? Just one word, but a most unpleasant one: *yedyem,* it said—here we come! Back to our prefect we ran. 'Your Excellency, it looks bad!' 'How come?' 'There's a telegram.' 'From whom?' 'The same people.' 'What's in it?' *'Yedyem!'* You should have heard him laugh. 'You're bigger fools than I thought,' he said. 'Why, just yesterday I ordered a company of Cossacks from Tulczyn for your protection. . . .' Well, that put some spunk in us, don't you know: a Jew only needs to see a Cossack to feel so courageous that he's ready to take on the whole world! It was nothing to sneeze at, a bodyguard like that. . . .

"In short, there was just one question: who would arrive first, the Cossacks from Tulczyn or the roughnecks from Zhmerinka? It stood to reason that the roughnecks would, since they were traveling by train while the Cossacks were on horseback. But we had our hopes pinned on our Slowpoke: God was great, and the only miracle we asked of Him was to make the train a few hours late, which it usually was anyway, in fact, nearly every day. . . . Yet for once, don't you know, as though out of spite, the Slowpoke was right on time: it pulled in and out of each station like clockwork. You can imagine how it made our blood run cold to hear from our secret agent that another *yedyem*egram had arrived from Krishtopovka, the last station before Heysen—and this time, for good measure, the *yedyem* had a *yahoo* after it. . . . Naturally, we went right to the prefect with the news, threw ourselves at his feet, and begged him not to count on the Cossacks from Tulczyn and, if only for appearances' sake, to send a detachment of police to the station so that the hooligans shouldn't think the only law was that of the jungle. His Excellency didn't let us down. In fact, he quite rose to the occasion. What do I mean by that? I mean, he put on his full dress uniform with all its medals and went off to the station with the entire police force to meet the train.

"But our local patriots, don't you know, weren't caught napping either. They had also put on their best clothes and their medals, taken along a pair of priests for good luck, and gone off to meet the train at the station—where, in fact, they asked the prefect what he was doing there, which was the exact same question he asked them. A few words were exchanged, and the prefect made it clear that they were wasting their time. As long as he was in charge, he said, there would be no pogroms in Heysen. He read them the riot act, but they just grinned back at him and even had the cheek to answer, 'We'll soon see who's in charge around here. . . .' Just then a whistle was heard. It made our hearts skip a beat. We were all waiting for it to blow again, followed by a loud 'Yahoo!'—and what that 'Yahoo!' meant, don't you know, we already knew from other towns. . . . Would you like to hear the end of it, though? There was a second whistle, all right, but there never was any 'Yahoo.' Why not? It could only have happened on our Slowpoke. Listen to this.

"The driver pulled into Heysen station, climbed out of the engine full of prunes, and headed straight for the buffet as usual. 'Just a minute, old man,' he was asked. 'Where's the rest of the train?' 'What rest of the train?' he said. 'Do you mean to say you didn't notice,' he was asked, 'that your engine wasn't pulling any cars?' That driver, he just stared at them and said: 'What do I care about cars? That's the crew's job.' 'But where's the crew?' he was asked. 'How should I know?' he answered. 'The conductor whistles that he's ready, I whistle back that I am too, and off I go. I don't have eyes in the back of my head to see what's following behind me. . . .' So he said, the driver—there was nothing wrong with his logic. In a word, it was pointless to argue: the Slowpoke had arrived without its passengers like a wedding without its band. . . .

"As we found out later, that train was carrying a merry gang of young bucks, the pick of the crop, each man jack of them, and in full battle gear too, with clubs, and tar, and what-have-you. They were in a gay old mood, don't you know, and the vodka flowed like water, and when they reached their last station, that is to say, Krishtopovka, they had themselves such a blast that the whole train crew got drunk too, the conductor and the stoker and even the policeman—in consequence of which, one little detail was forgotten: to hitch up the locomotive again. And so, right on schedule, the driver took off in it for Heysen while the rest of the Slowpoke, don't you know, remained standing on the tracks in Krishtopovka! Better yet, nobody—neither the roughnecks, nor the other passengers, nor even the train crew—noticed what had happened. They were all so busy emptying glasses and killing bottles that the first they knew about it was when the station-master happened to look out the window and see the cars standing by themselves. Did he raise Cain! And when the rest of the station found out, all hell broke loose: the pogromchiks blamed the train crew, and the train crew blamed the pogrom-chiks, and they went at it hot and heavy until they realized that there was nothing to do but shoulder their legs and tote them all the way to Heysen. What other choice did they have? And that's exactly what they did: they rallied round the flag and hotfooted it to Heysen, where they arrived safe and sound, don't you know, singing and yahooing for God and country. Shall I tell you something, though? They got there a little too late. The streets were already patrolled by mounted Cossacks from Tulczyn, who clearly had the whip hand—and I do mean whips! It didn't take those hooligans half an hour to clear out of town down to the last man. They vanished, don't you know, like a pack of hungry mice, or like snow on a hot summer's day. . . .

"Well now, suppose you tell me: shouldn't our Slowpoke be plated with gold, or at least written up in the papers?"

1909

50 **The Cross**

LAMED SHAPIRO

1

How shall I describe him? A giant of a man, huge bulk, broad shoulders, but not stout. Indeed he was gaunt. His countenance dark, sunburned, with high cheekbones and black eyes. His hair was completely gray, yet made him seem youthful—thick, shaggy, slightly curly. A child's smile on his lips contrasted with an old man's tiny wrinkles around his eyes.

Then I saw his wide forehead. It was marked with a sharply cut brown cross, a shallow wound—two knife cuts, crossing each other.

We met on the roof of a railroad car racing along on the East Coast of the United States. Since the two of us were tramping across the country, we decided to team up until we got fed up with each other's company. I knew he was a Russian Jew, like myself; I asked no further questions. No passports are necessary for the kind of life we lead.

That summer we saw almost every state in the Union. During the day we usually walked, cutting across forests, bathing in rivers we found on the way. We got food from the farmers. Some we were given and some we stole—chickens, geese, ducks, which we roasted over a campfire in a forest or on the prairie. But some days we had no choice; we had to make do with gooseberries we picked in the woods.

We slept wherever we happened to be at nightfall—out in the open fields or under a tree in a grove. On dark nights we sometimes "hopped" a train, climbing on top of a railroad car to hitch a ride. As the train sped along, a stiff wind blasted into our faces, carrying smoke from the locomotive, fumes and puffs dappled with great sparks. The prairie glided and rambled around us, breathing deeply, speakingly softly and quickly, with sundry sounds in many tongues. Distant galaxies sparkled over our heads, and thoughts drifted across our minds—such strange thoughts, as wild and free as the voices of the prairie. They seemed disconnected, and yet they seemed intertwined, linked and chained together. In the cars beneath us people were sitting or lying, many people whose paths were marked out and whose thoughts were closed off. They knew where they were coming from and where they were going; they told these things to one another, yawned and went to bed, unaware that two untrammeled "birds" were perched above them, resting briefly from their travels. Travels from where to where? At dawn we jumped to the ground, stole a chicken or fished with makeshift poles.

One day in late August I was lying naked on the sandy bank of a deep, narrow river, drying myself in the sun. My friend was still in the water, as noisy as a gang of school boys. Then he climbed up the bank, fresh and glistening from head to foot; the brown cross on his forehead stood out sharply. For a while we lay wordlessly on the sand side by side. I wanted yet did not want to ask him about that mark on his forehead. Still I finally asked that question.

He lifted his head from the sand, eyed me curiously and a bit derisively.

"You won't be frightened. . . ? I've been an outsider for years now."

"Tell me," I said.

2

My father died when I was only a few months old. From the things I heard about him I gathered he was someone special, a man from a different world. I carry his image—a fantasy image—in my mind because, as I've said, he was *someone special.* But that's not what I want to talk about.

My mother was a tall, thin woman with broad shoulders, with a cold and gloomy nature. She ran a store. She fed me, paid my school fees and often beat me because I didn't turn out the way she wanted.

What did she want? I'm not quite sure. She probably wasn't quite sure either. She had fought with my father all the time. When he died she was only thirty-two, but she refused all marriage offers.

"No, after him there's no other. I don't need anyone—and how can I take a stepfather for my child?"

She never remarried. I had to be my father's replacement, but without his faults. He had been completely impractical; she said he was too hot-headed. In any case, she used to beat me relentlessly. Once when I was about twelve she hit me with the iron rod she used to bar her store shutter on the inside. I was so furious that I hit her back. She froze, her face blanched; she gaped at me. She never beat me again.

The atmosphere in our home became even colder and tenser than before. Six months later I went out into the world.

It would take me too long to tell you everything, and it wouldn't be all that interesting, so let me get to the main point. Fifteen years later I was living in a large city in southern Russia. I was a medical student and survived by giving private lessons. I had brought my mother there, but she was not dependent on me. She lived with me but supported herself by peddling old clothes in the marketplace. She wasn't ashamed of her work, but she was contemptuous of the other junk dealers: Who were they compared to her?

She was as cold to me as ever, at least outwardly, and I was just as cold to her. I think I even hated her a little. Beyond that she didn't concern me. I lived in an entirely separate world.

3

It was a trivial matter: we had to remake the world—first Russia, then the rest of the world. Meanwhile, we were still working on Russia.

All of Russia was feverish with agitation. Group after group, the masses were being sucked into the torrent; over their heads their individual heroic deeds would blaze with the burning red fire of rockets. One person after another, of high birth and low, fell in the struggle. The old order responded; it responded well—with such things as pogroms. The pogroms made no special impact on me. We had a term: *counterrevolution*; it explained everything very precisely. Of course, I had never experienced a pogrom, but our city would have its turn.

I was on the local committee of a political party, but that was too little for me. A thought as sharp as a knife was cutting deep into my brain, slowly but surely. What it was I didn't really know. I didn't want to know. But I felt as if my muscles were getting stiff, more cramped. Then one day—I didn't know why—my grip broke the arm of a chair in the home I was tutoring in. I froze, bewildered. Another time one of my pupils asked me in astonishment, "Who's Minna?" and I realized I had inadvertently said her name, *Minna*. I also realized that even though it was a random thought, Minna was a girl I knew, her image constantly in my thoughts. I would hear the sound of her name, *Minna*, feel that strange sense of significance that was always in the air when Minna was present.

There were four other men and one girl in our committee. I didn't remember the eyes of the men, but Minna's eyes were blue, light blue. Yet at certain moments they would darken, get darker, until they were black and deep as an abyss. Her hair was black, her figure average, lovely; and there was something slow and serious in her movements.

She seldom joined in the debates at our meetings. In two or three terse phrases she would make a suggestion or state an opinion. She would then remain silent and attentive, narrowing her myopic eyes. Very often, after heatedly debating an issue, cleansing it, ridding it of all misunderstandings, we were amazed to see that we had reached the same conclusion that Minna had already formulated in her two or three terse phrases.

All we knew about her was that she was the daughter of a Russian official of high position. Once we passed through the door of our underground cell each of us shed his personal life, like an overcoat in the vestibule.

4

Now the cloud of a pogrom was looming over our city. Strange sounds were audible, soft, sharp sounds, like the hissing of a snake. People went about with their ears atuned, with swift, sidelong glances. They twitched their noses as if sensing a suspicious smell, quietly, grimly.

One hot afternoon our committee had an emergency session in Minna's apartment, which was the meeting place of our underground cell. It wasn't a long meeting: just brief discussions, no debates, and a resolution. We were to organize some kind of self-defense as fast as possible. Several times during the meeting I caught Minna gazing at me and, when the other members began filing out one by one, she signaled to me to stay.

I stopped in my tracks, my hat on my head, my back and my hands leaning against a table. Minna, with her head lowered and her arms on her chest, was pacing up and down. We both remained silent. Then she raised her head, paused and looked right at me. She was pale, very pale, but her eyes were deep black, as only Minna's eyes could be.

I felt cold. All at once, as if illuminated by a strong, sudden burst of fire, I saw the light. I had to be one of the "rockets" that light up the path of the revolution—and pay the price.

Minna was the first to understand. She had seen it on my face even before it became clear to me. How had she known?

"Have you made your decision?" she asked after a while, her voice choked.

"Yes," I replied, calmly and firmly, feeling as if I had made my decision that very instant.

She gazed at me for a while, then began pacing up and down again. In a few minutes she was as calm and serious as ever.

"We're sure to meet again," she said, shaking my hand.

Walking back to my home, to my mother, I felt my whole body vibrating. I thought how strange a person's destiny was, his path in life probably very short, going from a woman he almost hated to a woman he was starting to love.

Before stepping inside my apartment, I glanced around at the city. The sun was setting, and a translucent golden veil of peace was draping its soft folds over the streets and houses. How lovely our city was.

5

We were too late. The pogrom erupted that very night, suddenly, like an exploding mine, and in my own neighborhood.

The first screams came to me confused, in a hazy dream. Then it dawned on me what was happening. I jumped out of bed, lit a lamp and threw on my clothes. At that moment my mother sat up in her bed, looking at me strangely. Her look gave me chills. It was cold and ironic, as if the pogrom were aimed at me and not her. I stood there for a moment, half dressed, eyeing her in bewilderment, and all those minutes the house was shaking, as if in the eye of a storm.

Then the windows shattered, one door burst open after another. Like a foaming wave, with disconnected shrieks and cries, a gang of pogromists crashed into the house.

I'm a strong man, but before that night, I had never had to fight seriously, angrily. I had never known real anger before that night, anger that intoxicates you like wine; real anger boiling up deep in your blood, seething through your body, crashing into your head, sweeping away all thoughts. And when the pogromists—every variety, young, old, with homemade weapons or none at all—when they jumped on me, I defended myself coldly. Yet I was dazed. I didn't seem to understand what they wanted from me. But suddenly something minor happened—I think someone smashed my writing implements on the floor. An intense heat burned through my body; my mind was whirling; my arm flew up, of its own accord. I confronted a short Christian of indeterminate age. His face was gaunt, bloodless, with a bristly red moustache and small, beady eyes full of icy brutality. I think I bashed my fist into that ugly face, and I couldn't help bellowing like a raging bull. Then everything was spinning, around me and inside me, whirling fast and hot, as I felt a bizarre pleasure.

I don't know how long it went on. My fury and my pleasure grew as my strength encountered resistance and overcame it. At the same time, something reached me from far away, an annoying, monotonous voice like the buzzing of a mosquito, and disjointed Russian words: "Don't . . . don't . . . tie . . . tie . . . tie. . . ." Their resistance to me grew swiftly, more swiftly than my strength, on all sides, over me, under me. Then it suddenly solidified around my body, like a stone membrane. My pleasure vanished. And fury, sheer infernal fury, burned my chest and dried my throat. Little by little my fury cooled, frozen, and remained on my heart like a sharp, heavy chunk of ice. I came to.

I was lying on the floor, tied up, almost wrapped, in rope, covered with wounds, bleeding. The short Christian was dancing around me, the one with the piercing eyes. But his face was horribly bloody and altered. And there was blood on the faces of the others crowding around me.

They picked me up from the floor like a sack and tied me to the foot of my mother's bed.

My mother! This was the first time I had remembered she was there. She had jumped off the bed, obviously to help me. Now they dragged her back to the bed I was tied to.

I almost didn't recognize her. She was wearing a nightshirt on her broad, gaunt frame. Her hair was wildly tousled, her eyes flashing, her teeth clenched, and she was mute. They hurled her into the bed opposite me.

6

Imagine a single gray hair torn from a head. It is nothing, absolutley nothing. Two hairs? A clump of hair, torn out at one time, many clumps of long, gray hair. Forget it—nothing, nothing at all.

When you break bones they crack. But when you break twigs, dry wood, goodness knows what else, it all cracks, a "natural phenomenon."

Imagine two old, shrunken breasts. Flesh, matter consisting of certain elements. Just ask a chemist. And if they're your mother's breasts, two chaste breasts that once nursed you, that you've never seen bared since childhood. And dirty fingers rip them to shreds before your eyes.

Tell me, please. What does nature, what does the universe know about filth and shame? There are no such things in the universe as filth and shame.

Oh, certainly. Never, not ever, has a human body, the fine body of a man or woman, been spit at like that and humiliated. But what should I care. After all you can be sure: there are no such things in nature as filth and shame.

A year passed, two, ten, one hundred and two hundred. How is it possible? How can it be that I could live that long? Can a human being really live that long?

Mother! Scream! Scream! Damn you, what do you think? That you're back in the days when you used to beat me so brutally, so silently! Just one scream! Just one scream! Oh, God!

Years upon years . . .

Can you see the bloody face, the first human face I saw when my life began? A severe, gloomy face, the first face I ever saw in my life. The woman with that face used to beat me, and I hated her. I still hate her even now, even more than before, and my hatred chokes me, strangles me. For why, if it wasn't out of hatred, did I gaze so eagerly as the face changed from minute to minute? Why didn't I shut my eyes? Why did they bulge so painfully, with such burning curiosity? Good, dear people, poke out my eyes! What do you care? One slash with a knife and they'll ooze out, bubbles of liquid, these two accursed globes of liquid that I should not have. Goddamnit! You're laughing! You're happy people, very happy, but poke them out, what do you care?

Years and years.

7

The short Christian said: "The old bitch still don't wanna scream. Let me at her!"

It took a while, but then I heard a sound. It was a groan, a sob, a shriek—everything at once, and words in the shriek. Although the voice was hoarse and totally changed, the words echoed in my ears, clear and sharp, like the slow, distinct peals of a bell: "Oh, my son!"

For the first time in her life.

The sweat rained from my forehead and filled my eyes. I wrenched my body with all my strength, and the rope cut deeper into my flesh. God took pity on me for a while: my head whirled and I blacked out. But I had time to hear laughter all around me.

I came to for a moment. Again the short Christian was speaking: "That's enough. Let her die slowly, right before his eyes. And I'll make the sign of the cross on him to save his kikey soul from hell."

I felt two deep cuts in my forehead, one crossing the other, and again I heard laughter. A warm, narrow trickle ran from my forehead, down my nose and into my mouth.

I blacked out again.

8

Total blackness. Total silence. Nothing coming from the outside, no fixed point on the inside. Only a disquiet, a deep disquiet and a tremendous effort to find some sort of fixed point.

A word came wandering into this world of chaos: "What?" Then three times: "What? What? What? . . . " Then twenty times: "What. . . . " The word grew, it spread out and multiplied. It became: "What is here? What is around? . . . What is myself, and what is outside myself?" Suddenly, a sharp brightness and intense pain in my head. Three words stuck in my brain like a long, thin needle reaching from one ear to the other: "Oh, my son!"

I recovered my wits.

It was night. The lamp had gone out, or else *they* had put it out before leaving. I was still tied to the bed. I felt a wound on my forehead, burning intensely, making me forget all the other wounds. All kinds of noise came from the city. The city was shrieking in the night, a dull shriek with sudden, sharper outbursts from time to time, like a distant blaze. Near me, on the bed, something was writhing in the darkness.

"Mother!"

Silence.

"Mother?"

No answer. My voice couldn't reach that far, reach that world of agony haunted by her strict, harsh ghost. "Oh, my son," she had called to me. Yes, her son. Every drop of blood she was losing flowed along invisible paths into my veins, igniting an infernal fire. "Oh, my son!" A heavy hammer went up and down, slow and incessant, falling on my head each time. Whole worlds collapsed in ruins.

9

"What's that on your forehead?"

"It's supposed to save my soul from the suffering of hell," I replied.

They shook their heads and began to disperse. I became nervous, "Wait," I said. "I'll explain it to you."

They shook their heads again and vanished.

"I am the Lord God who took you out of Egypt."

"Thou shalt have no other gods but me."

"I am a jealous and vengeful God, and I demand of you: 'Be something.'"

The gusts of the tempest stormed over the shaken masses. The bodies, enslaved, shook as if being whipped. But the dark, gaunt faces and the feverish black eyes ignited with the crimson fire that crowned the head of the mountain.

"Oh, my son!" she said. Those were her very words, "Oh, my son."

Daybreak. My head was swollen and empty, like a barrel. I should have fled. Yes, fled, but—aha—the ropes. You can find some device. There has to be some device, some . . . kind of . . . device. . . .

I strained to put my thoughts into some kind of order. An iron nail. In the footboard of the bed I was tied to was a twisted nail with a broad head. What was a nail doing there? It didn't matter. With the nail you can . . . what can you do with the nail?

I twisted and struggled until I managed to push one of the ropes onto the nail. Then I started rubbing the rope across the sharp iron head of nail.

Hours dragged by, and my head grew numb. I barely knew what I was doing. But I kept on working, as precise and obstinate as a machine. Eventually the ropes yielded slightly. A little more effort and, bit my bit, torn, frayed ropes were lying at my feet. Shattered fragments of gods were lying at my feet.

10

I leaned over the bed. There was definitely something there, feverish, bearing no resemblance to a human being. The moaning was already so faint that my ear could barely catch it. I softly murmured, "Mother. . . ." My breath reached the raw wound that had once been a face, and I repeated, "Mother."

A stirring ruffled over the wound, and something opened. I peered hard; it was an eye. One eye; the other had run out. The remaining eye was blood-soaked, but still glowing, like an ember.

Did it recognize me? I don't know, but I felt it did. I felt it was looking at me with a question and a severe demand. "Yes, yes, it will be all right," I said, loud and earnest, not really knowing what I was talking about.

Then I looked around the room. Among the pieces of shattered furniture I spotted a broken table leg, thick, cylindrical, well turned. It would be just right.

I picked it up. With all my strength I swung it down upon the glowing eye. The bloody something twitched a single time, then remained motionless as a stone. The glowing eye was gone.

I heard a short sob, followed by a strange bellow that was immediately stifled. It was something unwilled, I assure you. And the voice was so alien that I still am not certain it was mine.

When I went outside the sun was setting, the ancient sun, which had spun its golden orb over this place a thousand years ago. Who says a thousand years are more than twenty-four hours? I was a thousand years old.

11

Then came the darkest days of my life, as the city suffered through a state of fever. Fire, slaughter. Bloody fighting, shooting in the streets. The Jews had organized a self-defense under the very blaze of the pogrom.

What did I do? I don't know. I found myself now in the ranks of the defense organization, now in the mobs of pogromists. I felt like a leaf wafted by the storm. The cross burned on my forehead. The words "Oh, my son" echoed in my ears.

If I'm not mistaken, I once ran into *my* Christian, the one that belonged to me alone. I felt as if I could grab him and drop him into my pocket. He turned pale, unable to move, but I didn't grab him. He aroused nothing in me. I simply patted his back and winked at him cheerfully. I didn't notice whether it inspired more courage in him.

Another episode remains in my memory.

An old Jew was running down the street chased by a young Christian, about sixteen years old, with an ax in his hand. The boy caught up with the old man and, with one stroke, he split his skull. As the old man fell, the boy pushed the split head together with his boot.

Instantly, gun in hand, a young Jew darted up, a pale young man, with a gaunt face and glasses. They ran, and I ran after them. The young Jew shot, but missed. The Christian left the broad, open street and ran into a courtyard. My foot got caught in something, and I fell.

By the time I ran into the courtyard, the Christian was standing in a corner, his back to a fence. His childlike face was green, his gray eyes gaped and bulged, his teeth chattered in a rapid rhythm. The young Jew stood right in front of him, with the gun in his raised hand, but his face was even paler than before. He stared at the wild terror of young flesh and blood, stared for some time. Then he put the gun to his own head, and fired.

The last light of reason vanished from the Christian's eyes. He sat down beside the body twitching at his feet, rose. Then, with an insane shriek, he leaped over the corpse and ran out of the courtyard.

A wild laugh erupted from inside my throat. My foot rose, of its own accord, and kicked the bloody carcass, lying twisted on the ground like a trampled worm.

12

It went on for days and nights; I don't know how long.

One evening, I stood at a door, knocking in a special way, a sign indicating I was a friend. What kind of signal was it? What was its purpose; how did I know it? I didn't ask myself those questions, just as you don't ask such questions in a dream. The door opened, and I saw Minna.

Lightning flashed in my brain; for a moment I was terror-stricken. I realized now where I was and what I was going to do, and calmed down instantly.

She didn't recognize me right away. Then she shuddered, grabbed my hand and pulled me into the room. I let myself down into a chair. She looked at my head, at my forehead where the cross burned, and she said nothing. Then, in a hushed voice, she spoke:

"Tell me everything."

I told her. I told her willingly and calmly—everything. Told of my mother's agony, with shameful details. Her face turned from red to yellow. When I was through, I bowed to her with a pleasant smile. She barely noticed; she buried her face in her hands. When she looked up again it was covered with tears, real tears. I swear it: wet, soft, and—I'd bet anything—warm tears! She knelt before me and took my hand, as my smile broadened. This time she noticed, quickly stood up, and began pacing up and down the room, glancing at me nervously. I kept on sitting and smiling—very pleasantly, I thought.

Finally, she resorted to what she considered an extreme measure. She sat down on the chair across from me and asked softly: "What about your decision?"

My decision? What decision? . . . Wait a moment . . . Yes, years ago, many years ago, I made a decision, a very important one, but—about what? . . . And suddenly I remembered.

I burst out laughing. I laughed in her face. But soon I became serious again, and looked into her eyes. She had turned as white as linen, and she leaped up from the chair. I stood up slowly and calmly.

I raped her.

She struggled, as my mother had struggled. But what use was her strength against the man with the cross on his forehead? Her face alternately changed in fright from blazing redness to corpselike pallor. She didn't scream. She bit her lower lip, chewed it, swallowed the blood. And I did my work, with all the humiliating touches. It took a long time.

Then I strangled her, quickly and tempestuously. I dug my fingers, long, bony fingers, into her white throat. She turned red, blue, and then black. It was over.

I collapsed on a chair, falling asleep almost that very instant, as if sinking into deep water—no dreams.

13

When I awoke I noticed that the tallow candle on the table had not grown much shorter. I probably hadn't slept for more than fifteen minutes, but I was fresh, alert and calm.

That moan, "Oh, my son!" still haunts me today, but from that day on it became softer, more maternal. My mother's soul had found its rest.

Our secret meeting place was furnished comfortably, almost elegantly, to avert any suspicion. I went into the bathroom and washed my head and my hands. The mirror showed me that I was gray. And at last I saw the cross that I had felt all that time. The wound no longer hurt; it merely itched slightly.

At first I wanted to take a knife and cut a swath off my forehead, in order to erase the cross. Then I changed my mind. Let it stay: "A frontlet between thine eyes." Ha! Is this the kind of "frontlet" that our dear, old God meant?

14

I now owed nothing to anyone, nor did I want to pay anything. I left our city that same night. Two days later I crossed the German border and set sail for America.

The ocean embraced me with its endless vastness, with strong winds, with its sharp, salty breath. It talked to me about wonderful things. It spoke out loud, it spoke silently. I listened to it with joy and amazement, and I have no words to express what it told me.

Soon after I arrived in America I began to wander across the country, and the prairies began to translate into its language what the ocean had said to me. Oh, the nights and days on the prairie!

I've been wandering for three years. And I feel like a newborn child, feel that I'm strong enough now. Soon I'll return to civilization. And then . . .

I gave him a sidelong glance, but he had stopped speaking. He had clearly forgotten me.

And I, an outsider for years, mused: "A generation of iron men will come, and they will rebuild what we have allowed to be destroyed."

1909

XI

World War I

World War I, the Great War, brought to an abrupt end the old Europe of interlocking monarchies, open borders and grand tours. The impact of the war on Jewish life in eastern Europe was no less profound: For the first time, Jews in huge numbers were forced to take up arms against their fellow Jews. Cities, towns and villages on the eastern front were laid waste, and the traditional structures of the community were destroyed.

At first Jews themselves were unaware of their special plight. For Jewish soldiers, the world of trenches and gas warfare was no more horrifying than for their non-Jewish comrades-in-arms (**51**). On the home front, the sight of refugees, breadlines and forced labor battalions was equally shocking to all. But gradually a more focused picture came into view: of a Russian army that expelled 600,000 Jews along its *own* borders and carried out brutal pogroms each time it advanced or retreated over enemy terrain; of a Jewish civilian population that was caught between the hatred of local Poles or Ukrainians and the vengeance of the conqueror; of Jewish soldiers treated with suspicion and cruelty even in their own ranks.

How this tragedy became known is a story in and of itself. It was essentially through the work of a few intellectuals. When Peretz and his two close friends Yankev Dinezon and S. Ansky issued their appeal to collect materials about the Great War (**52**), they could not have guessed that within seven months no Hebrew or Yiddish printed matter would be allowed to pass through the Russian mails or that the Jewish press would be forced to close. Against this backdrop, S. Ansky's singular achievement looms even larger. He not only defied the news blackout by systematically collecting the pertinent data and documents, not only traveled through the war-torn areas, single-handedly organizing a relief effort on behalf of the civilian Jewish population, but also wrote a monumental diary-memoir in the process.

The Destruction of Galicia, subtitled *The Jewish Catastrophe in Poland, Galicia and Bukovina, from a Diary, 1914–1917,* occupies a unique place in the Literature of Destruction (**53**). For one thing, it is the work of an insider among Jews and Russians alike. From 1911 until the outbreak of the war, Ansky had led the first Jewish ethnographic expedition through the *shtet-lekh* of the Ukraine and Galicia, giving him primary access to Jewish folk art, legend, song and custom. The war brought him back to many of the same places. Second, Ansky was thoroughly at home in the world of Russian liberal and radical politics. From 1894 to 1905 he had lived and worked among Russian emigrés in Paris, and upon his return to Russia in 1905, he maintained a high political profile. It was thanks to these connections, his impeccable Russian and his aristocratic demeanor that he could penetrate the Russian military bureaucracy and travel unhindered throughout the war zone. Finally, Ansky was a seasoned writer—a poet, playwright, storyteller and scholar.

Combining these perspectives, Ansky provided a detailed eyewitness account of his mission and also consistently tried to draw the timeless significance out of the raw data of experience: He analyzed the symbolic meaning of the Shma' Yisrael legend; he ruminated on the implications of the Hasidic manuscript whose letters had all vanished from the parchment. Ansky was equally critical of Russian-Jewish doctors who betrayed their Jewishness as of Galician Jews who seemed to capitulate to defeat and degradation. Yet for all that, Ansky's memoir was remarkably self-effacing. He gave little indication of how important he himself had been in orchestrating the events described. This is what made *The Destruction of Galicia* so very traditional: It highlighted the collective saga and down-played the role of the individual.

Through the manipulation of language, Sholem Aleichem was able to create highly individuated voices that also bespoke the collective experience. He shaped the trials of a nation caught up in a world torn apart into quintessential folk monologues. As a long-time observer of Jewish life, all Sholem Aleichem needed was to meet one informant on board a ship of refugees bound for America, and one man's tale of horrors was turned into an encyclopedic compendium of "Tales of 1001 Nights" (**54**), which in Yiddish carries the additional meaning of "Tales of Woe." We have already seen Sholem Aleichem's talent for cutting the traumatic events of history down to manageable size. Now we come in on Yankel Yunever's monologue as the town of Krushnik is about to change hands for the second time and the brutal discipline of the Germans is about to be displaced by the anarchic terror of the Russians. Because Yankel has the knowledge of hindsight as he recounts how he lost two sons in the war and because he is a man steeped in traditional learning (a middle-class version of Tevye the Dairyman), he can pinpoint for us exactly how different this war is from any previous catastrophe: All the time-tested methods of intercession break down and the delegation to the German commandant is rendered speechless. This time the Cossacks arrive not to save the town but to slaughter its Jewish inhabitants. Prayer offers but momentary respite.

In the writings of Sholem Aleichem and Ansky we see a neoclassical response to catastrophe. Both writers begin with the assumption that the tablets have been broken, that traditional Jewish life has been irrevocably altered, that the Jewish people will never again be united behind a single vision of sin-retribution-redemption. The mandate of the writer, therefore, is to reimpose a sense of order on the shattered past, to explore and reexamine the full thrust of the classical traditions so as to arrive ultimately at a new restorative vision of faith and community. This accounts for the encyclopedic impulse in their writing on Jewish catastrophe, why every personal and collective memory is brought to bear on the war and its victims. The literary monument is designed to replace the physical and spiritual ruins and to become, in turn, a source of meaning.

Moyshe-Leyb Halpern's "A Night" (**55**) represents a countermovement in east European Jewish culture. In this bleak view, Jewish catastrophe is but a sign of the world apocalypse, the end of civilization per se. Specific national or redemptive claims are rendered meaningless by the universal scope and impersonal nature of the violence. And so the writer's task is to create a language and a logic commensurate with this new violence—the more bleak and blasphemous, the better.

Why this apocalyptic view should first have taken hold in America is not hard to surmise. Through the American-Yiddish press, the immigrant masses knew exactly when and how their native towns went up in flames. Suddenly they saw themselves less as immigrants to the New Land as exiles from the Old. Locally, meanwhile, the Jewish community was divided over which side to support: the Germans, who alone could bring down the hated Tsar, or their Russian compatriots, who were locked in battle with the "Huns." Halpern, an East Side Yiddish poet of extraordinary talent, sent a plague on both their houses.

"A Night" was Halpern's vision of three circles of hell: (1) the collapse of European civilization as refracted through (2) the pogroms in his native Galicia; and the pogroms as refracted through (3) the embattled consciousness of one of the survivors, the speaker of the poem. The rapid-fire movement of the poem is fueled by *mentshele*, the demonic "little man," the double, the comic impresario who parodies both the dreamer and his dream. Nothing is sacred in his cabaret routine: not the memory of childhood (since the "I" of the poem was a stranger in his own home); not the mutilated remains of his father; least of all, the grand messianic schemes in whose name nations have always slaughtered other nations.

All of history, in *mentshele*'s scheme, is conjured up as "a funeral cortege that stretches a thousand leagues." In this way Halpern reduces all of history to its darkest side and repudiates the very attempt to find meaning in history through national sagas and lamentations. "A Night" is Halpern's answer to Bialik, for Bialik's anger presupposed a nation accountable to God, whereas Halpern's nightmare eliminates all mention of God and denies all human attempts at transcendence. At the climax of Halpern's vision, all past victims of atrocity, themselves once swayed by messianic dreams, themselves so faithfully memorialized, call down an eternal curse on the speaker/poet. In the end, the individual's only hope is in death.

51 Song of the Mobilization

The first day of the mobilization
People began to wail and cry;
The second day of the mobilization
They closed down all the factories.

Oh God, you God in heaven,
Why this punishment upon your people?
You bring together the multitudes,
Then herd them off like so many sheep!

Woe to the father and woe to the mother
Who have a son in the reserves.
He's fitted out in soldiers' clothes
And shipped off to war. Heaven preserve us!

No sooner was I rushed to the station
Than I stood for hours awaiting the train.
Farewell, my dearest parents,
God knows if I'll ever come home again!

No sooner did us soldiers board the train
Than we embraced each other, desperate.
By the time we arrived at the front—
Three months in the same old shirt.

No sooner did we reach the front
Than we were stationed in a trench.
A piece of shrapnel flew right by
And I fell right down with a crunch.

There in the middle of the field,
Oh mother, I felt as bitter as death!
By the time the medic ran up to me,
I lay in my own bloodbath.

No sooner did the medic reach me
Than he gave me a transfusion.
Until they got me to the hospital,
Oh, I suffered terrible pain.

There I lay on my little cot:
Deaf, you understand.
And I could write to you, dear parents,
That they'd cut off one of my hands.

The right hand of mine I'd lost,
I'd never go to the front again;
And I could write to you, dear parents,
That I'd be back home in a snap, yes ma'am.

No sooner was I in the door
Than mother beat her fists against her head.
When she saw me with only one hand
How many tears she shed!

Without a right hand it's very bad,
I can't earn enough for a stump of bread.
Dear God, snatch me away from the land of the living
And send me death instead!

Dem er-shtn tog fun der mo-bli - za-tsye Iz ge-vo-rn a yo-mer a ge-veyn. Dem tsvey-tn tog fun der mo-bli - za-tsye Zay-nen a - le fa-bri-kn ge - bli - bn shteyn. Dem bli - bn shteyn.

52 Appeal to Collect Materials About the World War

We are living through an extraordinarily important historical moment without precedent in world history.

No matter how the war we are now living through may end, it will bring about an upheaval in the life of people and nations, both in the economic-political and spiritual sense. Boundaries of countries will be redrawn. Worldviews will be fundamentally altered, whether in terms of the interests or ideals of nations. Much will be destroyed and much rebuilt; much will be uprooted and much will take root. New life forms sprout from the very fields that are being so well irrigated with blood.

We are living through an extraordinarily painful global process in which the life of man, the life of hundreds of thousands is reduced to a speck of dust that falls onto one side of the gargantuan scale that weighs the histories of nations and races.

A large proportion of our people has just recently suffered through the war of the Balkan nations. Now a second, even larger proportion has been dragged into a world war.

Each drop of our shed blood, each tear, each act of suffering and sacrifice must be entered into our historical account. Whoever sows blood has the right to reap!

We must become the historians of our part in the process. We and you who are living through this now must put away for the near and distant future each sign that the historical process inscribes upon our people. Otherwise our account will be empty, and neither people nor history will owe us anything, and our name will be erased from the page on which the world records its terrible and painful process as entitlement for better times. . . .

And that is not all.

Worse still is that others—total strangers—will write for us and in our names! And among those strangers we have so few friends. And our enemies will stop at nothing: no means that won't justify the end of blackening the Jewish name. And not merely will our entitlement to rights and to righteousness be obliterated for a long, long time to come, but the factory of lies and fabrications and the wildest accusations will be working overtime. And our page in the account of this great process will be black. Not only will our spilled blood be of no use to us at all, and our tears flow in the darkness and run into oblivion, but they [our enemies] will draw up a new bill of indictment against us, and out of our pain, suffering and sacrifice a new yoke will be woven around our necks and new chains forged for our feet.

And when a friend appears who will want to defend us, who will want to reveal the truth, he will lack for material with which to flesh out the truth.

Woe to the people whose history is written by strange hands and whose own writers have nothing left but to compose songs of lament, prayers and dirges after the fact.

Therefore, we turn to our people that is now and evermore being dragged into the global maelstrom, to all members of our people, men and women, young and old, who live and suffer and see and hear, with the following appeal:

BECOME HISTORIANS YOURSELVES! DON'T DEPEND ON THE HANDS OF STRANGERS!

Record, take it down, and collect!

See to it that nothing is lost or forgotten of all that happens in our life during and because of the war: all the upheaval, the sacrifice, the suffering, the acts of valor, all the facts that illuminate the attitude of Jews to the war and of others toward us; all the losses and philanthropic efforts—in short, record everything, knowing thereby that you are collecting useful and necessary material for the reconstruction of Jewish history during this horribly important and vitally important moment. Whatever can be recorded should be recorded, and whatever can be photographed should be photographed. *Material evidence* should be collected, and all this should be sent (C.O.D., if necessary) to the Jewish Ethnographic Society in Petrograd [address supplied in Cyrillic letters], either directly, through a Jewish newspaper or through one of the undersigned.

We hope that our appeal will not be a call in the wilderness but will resound within every Jewish heart and that it will awaken the activity that can only be hoped for.

> I. L. Peretz
> (Warsaw, aleje Jerozolimskie 83)
> Yankev Dinezon
> (Warsaw, Mila 15)
> S. Ansky-Rapoport

[Published in the Warsaw Yiddish daily *Haynt*, January 1, 1915]

53 The Destruction of Galicia

S. ANSKY

1

At the very outbreak of the war, when the Russian army occupied Galicia—so swiftly that within two or three weeks it stretched from Prague in the West to Hungary in the South—news began to arrive, unclear, as if it had been stifled, about gruesome acts of violence that the Russian military, especially the Cossacks and Cherkassians, were perpetrating against the defenseless local Jewish population. In retaliation for a provacative gunshot, a large part of the city of Brody was burned down, the Jews were robbed, some killed. Austrian Husiatyn and Belz were razed to the ground, and there had been a bloody pogrom with many victims in Lemberg. Rumors spread about violence in many other cities and towns. It also appeared that the Jewish population within the conquered territory, devastated and cut off from both their own land and from Russia, were simply dying of starvation.

The most horrible thing about all the reports was that they arrived by chance, like obscure rumors, and had an alarmingly indefinite quality: a letter from the front that slipped accidentally past the censor, a tale of a wounded and emaciated Jewish soldier and the like. All other routes for news from over there had been closed. No private person could enter or leave Galicia. Even the random letters and stories represented a cry of despair rather than a systematic transmission of facts.

"My hands lose their strength and my eyes become red with tears of blood," writes a Jewish soldier, "when I remember the horrors it has been my lot to see in Galicia, when I remember the acts of savagery that the Cossacks have carried out against Jews. There is murder and robbery, women are raped in the streets, the breasts of old women are cut off and the wretched people are left to die. . . ."

A second soldier writes:

"We came to a small Jewish town in Galicia. The military discovered a wine cellar, broke it open and began getting drunk. I also drank and became drunk like the others. But when I left the cellar and saw what was happening in the town, what the soldiers were doing to Jews, I soon became sober."

And nothing more.

A third, a soldier who later lost his sanity as a result of what he had seen in Galicia, relates:

"Wherever the army passes through, the Christians place icons in their windows and on their doors. Where there are no icons, the house is Jewish and can be pillaged with impunity. When our company was going through some village, one of the soldiers spotted from a distance a house on a hill, and told the captain that he thought it was a Jewish house. The captain allowed him to go and look. He soon returned in high spirits with the news that Jews lived there. They opened the door and saw that there were as many as twenty Jews in the house, half-dead with fear. The Jews were led out of the house and the captain issued a command: '*Koli! Rubi!*' (Stab! Chop!). I didn't see what happened next. I started to run, until I fell in a faint."

These and dozens of other cries of despair gave the impression that in Galicia something was happening that went beyond the human imagination. A great Jewish territory with a population of a million Jews, who only yesterday had all human and civil rights, was surrounded by a fiery ring of blood and iron: cut off from the world and delivered to the full power of Cossacks and soldiers who were enraged like wild beasts. It seemed that a whole Jewish tribe was perishing!

Our first pressing need was to come into contact with the Jews of Galicia and above all bring them whatever material help we could. But this was not easy. During the first months of the war, our rich men weren't willing yet to consider organizing a broad campaign for the Jewish war victims. They wanted to make do with the large donations that they were giving for the general requirements of the war, and they maintained that the Jews "should not separate themselves" from everyone else—that this could appear "unpatriotic." With such an attitude toward the sufferings of the Jews, and with such "patriotic" fervor, they naturally did not want to hear about the Jews of Galicia. When an important Russian official, coming from Galicia, approached a Jewish millionaire of Kiev, well known for his civic work, with the question: "Why aren't you organizing any help in Galicia for your brothers who are dying of hunger?" the millionaire replied:

"Your Excellency! We look upon the Jews of Galicia not as brothers, but as enemies, against whom we are waging war!"

But I must add that within a short time there was a change in the attitude of even the patriotically minded rich Jews toward the Jewish war victims, even toward the Galician Jews.

When the news from Galicia showed clearly what kind of holocaust [*khurbm*] was taking place, I determined to make every effort to get there, somehow or other, to travel through the ruined towns, establish the extent of the catastrophe and the magnitude of the need and, returning with factual data, no longer to request but demand help for the Jews of Galicia.

It was not easy for me to carry out my plan. For three whole months I had to knock at different doors before I obtained legal permission to travel to Galicia.

At first I hoped to obtain a pass as a merchant, planning to journey with the wagons of flour that Brodsky° was sending to Galicia—and later, with a party carrying sugar. When this did not work out, I approached the then-mayor of St. Petersburg, Count Ivan Ivanovitsh Tolstoy, and asked to be taken along with whatever medical division was being sent from there to Galicia.

Lev Brodsky (1852–1923), Jewish industrialist and philanthropist.

Tolstoy, a true friend to the Jews, responded very warmly to my request. As there was at that time no detachment leaving St. Petersburg for Galicia, he gave me a letter to the mayor of Moscow, Tshelnokov, the head of the All-Russian Municipal Union. Tshelnokov sent me with a letter to the head of the Union of Provincial Councils [Zemsky Soyuz], Prince George Lvov, who was, for his part, also unable to be of assistance to me, and advised me to get a letter from Tolstoy to Gutshkov,° who was then in Warsaw and able to give me a special mission pass for Galicia. Upon returning to St. Petersburg, I received a telegram from Moscow, saying that Prince F. D. Dolgorukov was organizing a detachment to Galicia and agreed to take me along. I traveled once more to Moscow—but Dolgorukov's detachment had been given an order not to go to Galicia, but to Riga. Another detachment was formed by Konovalov, but for bureaucratic reasons Konovalov would not take me with him. In short, everyone professed warm sympathy with my task, expressed his readiness to help me—and sent me to someone else.

Russian minister of war.

Finally I decided to make my way to Galicia via Warsaw. With a letter from Count Tolstoy to Gutshkov and a recommendation from Prince Lvov to the Chief of the Warsaw Branch of the Provincial Union, V. V. Virubov, I traveled to Warsaw on the 21st of November.

2

The devastated Jewish population, which had no possibility of fighting either the cruel persecutions and murders or the most shameful libels, responded as it had in the past—by weaving from its own sighs and tears legends that afforded it strength and comfort. In one place it was whispered that "the Rebbe is writing a megillah about the war, which will surpass everything that has been written until now, and when he ends it, redemption will come for the Jews." In other places there was much talk about the *kets* [end of the Exile]. It was looked for in old sacred books, and it was calculated that these were, indeed, the days of the Messiah that were drawing nigh. Most of all, legends were created about the espionage libels. The people's imagination worked in the same way as in the case of blood libels. In each blood libel the people saw not a made-up story, but a crime committed by others in order to put the blame on the Jews. Of course, the legends were, like all folk legends, suffused with a deep optimism—that eventually the truth would be revealed.

The most widespread libel was about secret telephones, through which Jews were supposed to be passing all the information to the enemy. The people's creativity responded to this with a series of legends, which were partly associated with Zamosc. One legend told simply that as the result of a libel about a telephone, several Jews were hanged and several more were about to be hanged. But a priest with a cross came to the judge and swore that not the Jews but the Poles were guilty. And as soon as he had proved this, the Jews were set free and the Poles were hanged—sixteen in all.

The second legend was more poetic:

The Poles in Zamosc [falsely] informed against the Jews, saying that they were helping the enemy. Several Jews were arrested. When the magistrates sat down to try them and the Jews were on the point of being sentenced to death, a Russian woman teacher and a Russian civil judge came up, fell on their knees and begged that the sentence not be carried out until they had been heard. The magistrates consented. The judge and the teacher swore that the Jews were not guilty. "If you want to know who is really guilty," they said, "then come with us." So they went with them. They led the magistrates to the Count's manor house and led them down into a deep cellar. There they found the Countess Zamioska standing and talking on the telephone to the Austrians. She was hanged at once.

This legend I heard in Minsk. I heard another, similar one in Lublin, which concluded as follows: They went down to the Countess Zamioska in the cellar, and found there a whole group of Jews in long coats, in skullcaps, with long earlocks, standing and talking on the telephone to the Austrians. The magistrates were surprised. It certainly showed that the Jews were guilty! But the Russian judge cried out: "Take them in for questioning!" This was done, and it appeared that they were Poles who had put on the Jews' clothing so that, if they were caught, suspicions would fall on the Jews.

There were still other legends, about a commander (in another variant, a governor) who found out that a Polish soldier was urging other soldiers to make a pogrom against the Jews. He called the soldier to him, tore off his insignia and said: "I would shoot you, but I do not want to soil my hands with unclean blood."

Another told that a Polish officer drove all the Jewish soldiers out of the trenches into the field that was in the line of fire. One Jewish soldier grabbed the officer's sword and wounded him. When the commander found out about this, he ordered the Jewish soldier to be released and said he was right.

The legend most widespread about Jews in the present war concerned the meeting of two Jewish soldiers on the battlefield. One ran the other through with his bayonet and heard him cry out as he died, *"Shma Yisroel!"* [Hear, O Israel . . .].

While traveling before the war through Volhynia and Podolia to collect folklore, I encountered a very widespread legend about a betrothed pair whom Chmielnicki had murdered while they were being led to the wedding canopy. In fifteen or sixteen small towns I was shown a small grave near the synagogue, and everywhere I was told the same legend about the betrothed couple. This is almost the only legend from the time of Chmielnicki that is still so widespread. After the persecutions of 1648, the existence of the Jewish people was endangered, the whole Jewish people was on the point of being massacred and the people symbolized this in the legend of the betrothed pair who were murdered at the moment of their union, which was to have perpetuated their families and generation. A symbol, as it were, of a tree cut down in its moment of blossoming.

In the present war, the people is not threatened with disappearance; but it is one of the terrible tragedies that can occur in the history of a people, that brother should fight brother. And from the first moment, the people dwelt on the tragedy that was symbolized in the legend of the *"Shma Yisroel."*

I heard this legend in all kinds of variants: without exaggerating, in eight or ten localities, in St. Petersburg, Moscow, Minsk, Kiev, Warsaw; in short, everywhere I met Jewish soldiers or homeless people. It is typical that almost everywhere it was told not as a story but as a fact, which had happened to such and such a person.

3

In Moscow I visited a Jewish "lazarette" [military hospital], which, it seemed, was the only one in all of Russia. It was Jewish not only because it was run with Jewish money but principally because almost all the wounded soldiers who were looked after there (ninety to ninety-seven) were Jews, as were the doctors, nurses and orderlies.

The lazarette was founded by Shoshana Persitz. She instituted a kosher kitchen for the few Jewish soldiers who were there originally. As it became well known, the doctors and orderlies of other lazarettes began to send Jewish soldiers there who ate no *treif*. Thus a Jewish lazarette was gradually formed.

It was a big wooden house. Clean, well lit, large rooms with dozens of beds. A number of severely wounded soldiers are still in bed. The rest, in robes and shoes, walk about. Elderly Jews, bearded, with bent backs; young men, youths, with pale sickly faces, with bandaged heads, arms in slings, on crutches, look like old men. Only two or three are tall, sturdily built and fresh in appearance. Some walk deep in thought from room to room; others stand in knots chatting; still others sit by their little tables, writing letters or reading. A young man sits apart, immersed in a Gemara. The young man was a rabbi in a small town.

At first glance they are not recognizable as soldiers. Ordinary but sick Jews, in pain; shopkeepers, artisans, teachers, sons of good families. But as I looked, I noticed—or more correctly, felt—something new about them, something unusual in their movements, in the tone of their speech, in their glances. A stern hermetic look, as if they bore a heavy secret. It was as if all of them were swathed in a deep, silent grief.

And I remembered that all these ordinary Jews, the young rabbi, the storekeeper with the red beard, the carpenter, the Hebrew teacher, had all seen before them the Angel of Death, endured the storm of death, received in their bodies its poisonous bite, themselves sowed death around them, and took into their souls something of "the other side" that cannot be grasped by thought or expressed in words but that leaves an eternal mark on the soul.

They answer my questions willingly but quietly; reserved, serious, without superfluous words, without complaining at all about the inhuman sufferings that they have undergone.

I asked if they experienced fear during the battle.

The rabbi answered with a sad smile:

"We were frightened by the terror of war, but not by the war itself. As soon as the battle started, bullets flew and we ourselves had to shoot, run, pursue. Then the fear would vanish. In any case, terror cannot last for long, you get used to it. To such a degree that I slept soundly at the moment when the battle was raging. And when I awoke, two dead soldiers were lying near me.

"Once," he relates further, "when I was in a place in the trenches, about twenty Jewish soldiers gathered, deliberated among themselves, and under the enemy's very eye put on *tefillin* and stood up to pray with a *minyan*. The commander of the regiment approached, but when he found out that we were praying he exclaimed to the Russian soldiers: 'See how Jews pray under fire! God will surely listen to such a prayer!' "

Stories are told of bloody battles, fields littered with dead, rivers of blood, screams, sighs of people and groans from the earth. Stories of burned, destroyed, ruined villages, cities and small towns. About the Jewish population, which was writhing in mortal fever between two conflicting armies.

A soldier tells how his regiment was positioned for four days near his native townlet where his parents, brothers, sisters and relatives still lived. The Austrians occupied his town, and his regiment fired on them. They saw the town from a distance. They could see where the shrapnel fell. He knew every house in the town, who lived where, and he saw how one house after another, one street after another burned, was shattered. When the Austrians were chased out and the Russians entered the town, he found nothing but ruins. Of his father's house only the walls remained intact; he found no living being either in his house or in the entire town, and to this day he does not know whether they went to join the Austrians or whether they are wandering about, hungry and helpless.

Then stories are told about the war in Galicia. What terrible things have happened there, what terrible sights it has been their lot to see.

The soldiers begin to tell their tale and break off halfway, wave their hands in a gesture of resignation: it is difficult to conclude, difficult to convey the dreadful impressions.

4

In Lemberg Dr. Hoyzner told me about a gruesome incident: it is difficult to relate it, impossible to remain silent about it.

Once someone came to him from a Russian lazarette and summoned him to a fatally wounded Jewish soldier, who wanted to make a confession. He went to the lazarette and found the soldier already dying.

"Rabbi," said the soldier to him, "I cannot die. . . . I have a great sin on my conscience, and I beg you to grant me forgiveness for it."

"What does your sin consist of?" asked the rabbi.

"Our regiment occupied a small Jewish town," the dying man began to relate. "As usual, a pogrom started. The soldiers broke into a wine cellar and began drinking. I drank with them, got drunk and went through the town with them to rob Jews. I ran into a house and found there an old man with a *shtrayml°* and long sidelocks. As I later discovered, he was the rabbi. I grabbed him by the *grud* [chest] and yelled: *'Zhid, davay horoshi'* ['Kike, gimme money']. He replied that he had no money." The dying man fell silent.

"What happened next?" asked the rabbi.

The soldier was silent for a while and then said quietly:

"I stabbed him to death."

He began to sob and beg: "Rabbi, grant me forgiveness, so that I may die in peace."

Rabbi Hoyzner was so shocked that he did not know what to reply. He promised the dying man that he would think about it and give him an answer later. But in two hours he was told that the soldier was dead.

This dreadful deed that Rabbi Hoyzner told me about was of course out of the ordinary, but unfortunately not unique. In the terrible atmosphere of war-maddened instincts there could not but occur such nightmares, that the weaker and less ethically developed of the Jewish soldiers gave in to the general intoxication of savagery, and, along with their Russian comrades, perpetrated the most shameful deeds—even against Jews. I was told the following by Dr. Lander:

In a small town that their troops entered, a pogrom began. Lander went to the colonel and insisted he take measures to stop the pogrom. The colonel sent an officer and several soldiers to accompany Lander. They went to the town. Hearing voices from inside a house, they went in and encountered two soldiers who ran out of the house with plundered objects. The soldiers were at once arrested. To his great shock, Lander saw that both soldiers were Jews!

But however many such deeds occurred, they represent, of course, a rare exception. From everything I heard and saw during my travels through Galicia, I can state with perfect confidence that the attitude of the Jewish soldier to the Jewish population in Galicia was almost always brotherly, and often steeped in true self-sacrifice. The Jewish soldier was the only element that could defend the robbed and plundered Jews during the invasion of the Russian military. As devoid of rights as the Jewish soldiers were in the Russian army, they were often able to save a small town, or individuals, from pogroms and violence. Into an atmosphere of deepest despair, the Jewish soldier brought to the population a certain moral support, and often material support as well.

In spite of the stern prohibitions against meeting and having relations with the

Fur-rimmed hat worn by hasidic men.

local Jewish population, the Jewish soldiers, risking their lives, visited Jews on the sly, gave them advice on how to behave and helped them in every way they could. In many places Jewish soldiers became family friends in Jewish households. I know of cases in which Jewish soldiers sacrificed themselves for their Galician brothers. When the maddened Cossacks raped Jewish women in a small town, in the middle of the street, several dozen Jewish soldiers scattered behind the houses, shot at the Cossacks, laying many of them out on the ground.

Another incident: During the pogrom in Sokol, Jewish soldiers either took goods from the stores together with the Cossacks or asked the Cossacks for part of the plunder and quietly, via back streets, returned them to the robbed house-holders. In some places where the population was suffering severely from hunger, Jewish soldiers shared their last crusts of bread with the local Jews. In the small town of Lukhatov I was told a great deal about a Jewish soldier name Yisrolik Vaysbard, who supported almost the whole town for half a year, providing it with money and foodstuff. Entire legends about this soldier were created in the town. Some told that his father had come to him in a dream and commanded him to give all he had to support the town. Others simply expressed the opinion that this was the Prophet Elijah.

To my great regret, I cannot say the same about Jewish military doctors as about Jewish soldiers. In the Russian army there were several thousand Jewish doctors. Their position was incomparably more privileged than that of the Jewish soldier. Not a few Jewish doctors have the rank of colonels and regimental commanders. They were always in the company of officers and had access to the generals. The could, indeed, greatly help the persecuted and unprotected Jewish population. Unfortunately, however, as I became convinced, in many cases they displayed appalling indifference to their Galician brothers. I do not, of course, wish to accuse all Jewish doctors. It is sufficient to mention the name of Dr. Lander—who for an entire four years worked with the greatest self-sacrifice on behalf of the Galician Jewish population—in order to see that there were exceptions to this. Apart from Dr. Lander, I met only two or three doctors in Galicia (Dr. Helman, Dr. Szabad and a few others) who took some interest in the condition of the local Jews. All the other doctors whom I met during these few years in Galicia showed absolutely no interest in Jews. Some of the doctors simply made an effort to conceal their Jewishness and swallowed in silence all the insults and slanders that were rained upon Jews in their presence. I met a Jewish military doctor, Shabshayev from Orenburg. He related with great enthusiasm his deeds of military heroism. He had saved a whole division from captivity and performed other heroic deeds. The general liked him very much and had awarded him several medals. He had even been written up in the newspapers. When I asked him about the relationship of the military to Jews, he said that he knew of no terrible facts about this but added straight away:

"In any case, I wouldn't know much about it, because I avoided meeting local Jews in the occupied territory. I was even harsher to Jews than to Christians, so that I would not be suspected of sympathy with Jews."

He knew of no "terrible acts," and yet he himself related how they had removed all Jews from administrative offices, quarantine hospitals, military transports and other institutions and sent them to the trenches at the front. They had made a survey of Jewish soldiers, and there were, of course, few officers who dared to say a good word for the Jews. The following questions were in the survey: "Do Jewish soldiers have close relationships with the local Jews? How many of the dead, wounded and captured were Jews?" In Shabshayev's regiment there were 10 dead, 40 wounded and 190 captured Jews. The number of captured was proportionately not greater among the Jews than among the Russians. But no survey was made of the latter, and the number—190 Jews who surrendered—astonished everybody. The following incident occurred: ten soldiers were sent on a reconnaissance mission, and they were all captured. An ordinary matter. But among the ten soldiers was one Jew, so the whole blame was put on him, and the company commander is said to have been severely punished for sending a Jew on reconnaissance.

At the close of our conversation Dr. Shabshayev made this request: "Don't tell anyone what I have told you. Don't even say that you met me and, in particular, that we talked about Jews. That could do me harm."

Other doctors did not hide their Jewishness, but they had so little concern for the condition of the Jewish population that I could not get any information about it from them. Some doctors spent many months in Jewish *shtetlekh,* where their hospitals were stationed, and during this time they showed no interest in the condition of the local Jewish population. After great effort I was able to obtain from some Jewish doctors copies of official orders about edicts against the Jews. They knew how important it was to let the Jewish communal activists in St. Petersburg know about these orders but were afraid to let them get out in case, God forbid, it should become known who had informed about the document. More: upon meeting some doctors who were stationed with their hospitals in remote Jewish *shtetlekh,* where there was great hardship, and to which I could not travel, I asked them to accept several hundred rubles from me, take them to their shtetl and distribute them among the needy or give them to the local committee or the rabbi. Most of the doctors refused to do this. And those who agreed to take the few rubles did so unwillingly, as if they were thereby making a great sacrifice.

5

In Khoroskov I met two Jews, Rabbi Frenkel from Husiatyn and Reb Lipe Shvager. Both of them had had a great business in books, especially in old *sforim* [Jewish religious books], rare books and manuscripts. This was the greatest book trade in old *sforim* in Galicia. During the pogrom and the fire their whole book business was completely destroyed. They were able to save only a small quantity of manuscripts and old *sforim.* I took some of them with me and brought them to Petrograd, to be kept in the museum.

Reb Lipe Shvager, an intimate of the Rebbe of Kopyczynec, told me a wondrous story, which has the character of a mystic, symbolic legend. In fact, the legend has already taken shape and entered the cycle of Hasidic miracle tales.

When the war began, the Rebbe of Kopyczynec was in Hamburg, where he was taking a health cure. His whole family was there with him. Lipe Shvager was there too. When the Russians invaded Galicia, the Rebbe summoned Shvager and said to him:

"You should know that I have two letters handwritten by the holy Ba'al Shem himself. Now, in wartime, they could, God forbid, be destroyed. Go at once to Kopyczynec and save the letters. If you cannot return, hide them in a safe place. Know that many dangers lie in wait for you on the road. You could be killed by a bullet or executed on a libel charge, may Heaven preserve us, but the peril must not deter you from carrying out the sacred mission of saving the letters."

Shvager at once agreed to go, and asked the Rebbe:

"And what will happen to your property, Rebbe, the gold and silver and precious objects that you have in your court?"

It was said that there was property in the court in the value of several million crowns.

"All of it can go," replied the Rebbe calmly, "but the Ba'al Shem's letters must be rescued."

Shvager set off. He came to Kopyczynec several hours before the Russians entered the town. Obviously there could be no question of going back. But he had just enough time to save and conceal the letters. He put them in a box and buried them two meters deep in the wall of a cellar in the Rebbe's court. In the same cellar he buried some of the Rebbe's gold and silver. For three or four months after that he had no opportunity to go to the cellar. During this time he narrowly escaped death several times and was arrested on suspicion of spying. When he finally had a chance to get to the cellar, he found none of the precious objects that he buried there. Everything had been dug up and stolen. The wall in which the box with the letters was hidden had been demolished, and the box had disappeared.

The effect this had on Shvager can readily be imagined. He almost died of grief. But a few days later, when he again began to dig and search in the wall, he suddenly discovered the box intact. But when he opened it, he found to his great astonishment that all the characters had vanished from the letter, which was written entirely in the Ba'al Shem's hand (the second letter was only signed by him), and only a blank piece of paper remained.

To tell the truth, I didn't believe this story at all. I thought this was one of the common legends that were easily invented in time of war. So I asked Shvager to show me the letter. The letters were in Kopyczynec, hidden in an inner sanctum, and Shvager did not want to display them. But when I met him a few weeks later in Kopyczynec and was very insistent, he agreed, rather unwillingly. He brought the letters into the synagogue. They were wrapped in several papers. Shvager, with the greatest awe, not touching them with his hand, unwrapped them. I saw two very old sheets of paper laid together. One of them consisted of text written on both sides in a thin, close script—according to Shvager, in the handwriting of Reb Gershon Kitever° (the letter has already been published). On the second page, on the very edge, one could just detect the signature in sharp, long, thin characters: "Yisroel Ba'al-Shem." The second letter, which was half decayed (both were written in 1753), with soft spots from dampness or tears, was blank, without a trace of characters. Shvager gazed at the letter with a look of mystic contemplation and said quietly:

"They say the characters have disappeared because of dampness and can be restored by chemical means. But we Hasidim think differently, quite differently. . . ."

Looking at the letter of the "flown away" characters, I remembered the shard of the broken tablets [with the ten commandments] that I had found in the ruined and desecrated synagogue in Dembits. On it there remained only the words *TIRTSAḤ* . . . *TIN'AF* [thou shalt kill . . . thou shalt commit adultery]. Both sym-

° The Ba'al Shem Tov's father-in-law.

bolic occurrences came together for me in the rabbinic phrase: ''broken tablets and flying letters.''

The whole life of the Jewish population in Galicia appeared to me as a moral explanation of these two symbols.

On my first journey through Galicia in 1915, I followed closely in the path of the war, wandered among smoldering fires and saw fresh traces of the most horrible pogroms. The terror of death ruled in every corner. The mark of a drama lay on every town, every house, every object; and steeped in yet greater tragedy were the people who had recently lived through that deadly terror: they were shattered, almost mad with despair. At that time, the Jews [of Galicia] seemed to me like broken tablets, with blood flowing from every crack. Yet then the tragedy was still external, a consequence of the war. Hundreds and thousands of lives were cut off, fortunes ruined, great cultural treasures destroyed; but the storm had not yet touched the depths of the soul, not destroyed human dignity. When a former rich man or respected householder suddenly became impoverished and was dying of hunger, the thing that was as hard as death for him was to ask for alms, and many such people were indeed ready to go hungry rather than seek the help of strangers. The tragedy of the bleeding, ruined and degraded population was great, but in its greatness, in the sharpness of the pain, there was a harsh beauty, which elevated human suffering to the level of an epic folk tragedy.

Now, as I journeyed through towns big and small that were relatively intact, I no longer encountered this once lofty and beautiful drama. What had previously been a tragedy had now become an everyday phenomenon. The former heroes of folk tragedy had been transformed into professional beggars. People had forgotten the past, were afraid to look into the future and lived with the petty mendicant interests of today, worrying about a slice of bread, a handful of grits. People had become used to continual hunger, to the rags on their bodies, to standing for hours at the food stations. People wandered around, neglected, silent, sunken in despair, indifferent to their dreadful condition. The few intellectuals left had also become used to being isolated from culture, social life or intellectual fulfillment. And all these living corpses appeared to me no longer in the image of broken tablets, but as tablets whose letters had flown, tablets that had been stripped of the highest sanctity.

6

From Tlutsi I had to travel in Bukovina: to Zoloshtshik, Snyatin, Czernowitz. But Homelski, whom I met, suggested that I travel with him to Buczacz, where he had business to settle. I agreed.

The ranges of the Carpathians begin in this region: mountains and valleys. When we had traveled about halfway, we saw from far off, on a high mountain, a large, extremely massive and magnificent building. Drawing a little closer, we noticed that it was an old ruin, of which only the walls remained. As we later discovered, it was the ruin of a monastery.

I was arrested by this thought: why do ancient ruins, many hundreds of years old, possess such magnificence, such dramatic beauty, while new ruins look rejected with nothing dramatic about them? This is because around a new ruin there are random bits of half-burned, not quite ruined sections, which strike the eye, create a dissonance and blur the intrinsic drama. Old ruins that have survived hundreds of years preserve only those parts that are indestructible and that can stand up to time and all the elements of nature.

The same is true of human tragedy. At the moment when it occurs, there is much in it that is fortuitous, glaring, that drowns out and obscures its mysterious tragic core. Only when years have passed and all the trivialities and accidents, everything that is temporal and unimportant have been washed away by time, does the tragedy crystallize its true, splendid and tragic visage and become a theme for artists who create the great immortal tragedies of the world.

As we crossed the mountain, a frightful scene opened up before us. In the valley lay a dead town—a great town, with many streets and houses. But *all* the houses were burned down and smashed to pieces. They stood like battered, fossilized corpses. A kind of Pompeii stood before us. I had seen ruined towns before, but never had I seen the panorama of such a catastrophe.

We paused for a while. Neither I nor Homelski nor our waggoner knew of a big town on our route. Had we made an error in counting the kilometers? Was this already Buczacz, which was, indeed, a total ruin? Homelski, who had been to Buczacz before, looked and began to recognize it: yes, Buczacz.

We drove up to the town. Empty and dead. There was not a living creature to be seen anywhere. Then near the entrance we saw two soldiers coming out of a half-fallen little house that stood below the mountain, looking like a mountain cave. We stopped the soldiers and asked them the name of the town.

"Yazlovits," they replied.

And seeing us look at the ruins, they added:

"There were fierce battles here. In retreat our artillery pulverized the town."

"And what is that little house that you came out of?"

"A shop."

We entered the little house and there found a Jew and his household. The house was tiny, low, with an earthen floor. In one room was the household, five or six souls, and the second room was a kind of store. Soldiers bought cigarettes, rolls and notions.

We asked for something to eat. At first the storekeeper said he had nothing but rolls. But when he found out we were Jews he invited us into the other room. It was the Sabbath eve, and the mistress of the house was getting ready to bless the candles.

Sabbath stew.

"On the Sabbath we also have a little pot of *cholent*,"° she said. "We will give you half of it; you need to eat too."

We would have refused, but when we saw the "little pot," which was as huge as the head of Og, King of Bashan,° we stopped feeling embarrassed.

In Jewish folklore, a giant.

While we were eating the householder came in.

"Are there many Jews in this town?" I asked him.

"There is only one Jewish household—mine," he replied. "During the bombardment and the fires all the Jews ran away. Now they are not allowed back. I was favored, permitted to settle. This counts as outside the town. So we stay here, I buy and settle and earn my crust of bread."

"And the soldiers do not hurt you?"

"No. On the contrary. They are very glad to have a place where they can buy something in the town. Everything is dead, so to speak."

Part of the town could be seen through a small window in the house. Among the ruined and burnt houses I recognized a large, splendid stone synagogue, which was also ruined, roofless, with empty burnt-out windows.

"The synagogue burned too?" I automatically asked the householder.

"Yes. . . ." He sighed. "All the *sforim* were burnt." "What a synagogue that was," he resumed and paused. "Six hundred years old. They say it wasn't built; it was found already fully built under the earth."

I had already heard, in Volin and elsewhere, the legend about old synagogues, that they had been found fully built under the earth. But the householder added another feature to the legend.

"When they had unearthed the synagogue and gone inside, they found an old man there with a gray beard reaching to his belt, who was sitting and studying."

We came to Buczacz late at night. The appearance of the town was almost the same as in Yazlovits; dozens of large streets were thoroughly ruined and burnt. The few houses that remained intact were occupied by the military staff and hospital. The light of the big electric street lamps gave the dead town a yet more tragic look.

There were still Jewish families in the town, living in the cellars. I had no time to make inquiries; I had to start my return journey at dawn. But at night, on my way to the military hospital where I had lodging, I encountered an elderly Jew. I stopped him and began asking questions.

"What destruction [*khurbm*] there has been in your town!" I expressed my sympathy.

"Anything can be called 'destruction' [*khurbm*]," he answered with a sigh. "What you see is nothing, in comparison."

"With what?"

"With what! They destroyed the cemetery and scattered gravestones that were six hundred years old; they burned down the tombs of great scholars. In our town, you know, the Oreh Hayyim is buried."

I felt that for this Jew the destruction of the cemetery was a greater tragedy than the destruction of the town itself.

7

For many years Sadigure was the residence of a family of Hasidic rebbes who trace their descent to the Ba'al Shem's greatest pupil, Rabbi Ber of Mezritsh. The founder of the Sadigure dynasty, the grandson of Rabbi Ber, Rabbi Sholem Shakhne of Pogrebishtsh was a great kabbalist and a remarkable personality. He dressed in European style and led an expansive aristocratic life, in the style of the Polish magnates of the time. His son, the well-known Rabbi Yisroel of Ruzhin, who was the first of the dynasty to settle in Sadigure, excelled his father in both personal greatness and behavior. His court was like an emperor's; a band of twenty-four musicians played constantly near his table; he never went out to drive without six horses abreast. His son and grandson also adopted his way of life, and the court of Sadigure was renowned as the wealthiest and noblest of rebbes' courts.

The war, which laid waste so many Jewish treasures, also destroyed the court of Sadigure and its unique way of life, with its great antiquities that generations had collected—antiquities both material and spiritual.

Before the war, Sadigure had a population of about ten thousand souls, three quarters of them Jews. When the Russian army occupied Sadigure for the first time in September 1914, a terrible pogrom took place there. All the Jewish houses and stores were plundered and many Jews were wounded and murdered.

I traveled to Sadigure in a military vehicle, together with Dr. Ratni, a Jewish military doctor from a hospital in Czernowitz. I also took a Jew from Sadigure with me, a *melamed* [teacher] who had been in Czernowitz the whole time and never dared to enter Sadigure, since he was afraid of the soldiers and local gentiles. This Jew offered to sell me some old *sforim* that he had hidden in Sadigure. He knew that his little house at the end of the town had not been burnt, and he did not doubt that his books were still intact.

"I have hidden them in such a way that the Destroyer [Devil] himself would not find them," he boasted.

His little house was indeed undamaged but stood without doors and windows. Inside were straw and horse dung. The Jew looked in bewilderment at this house. He could hardly recognize it.

"Where are your books hidden?" I asked him.

"In the loft . . ." he answered in a subdued voice.

We got hold of a ladder and climbed up into the loft. Books? Even the chimney bricks had been taken.

The Jew stood in the loft, discouraged, depressed, and looked at a corner where he had hidden his books. He had covered them with bricks and not doubted that no one would find them there. He was badly shocked. His head bowed, he returned to Czernowitz on foot.

I went to the Rebbe's court, which is almost at the end of the town. Two castles in a medieval Moorish style, with round turrets at the sides, were ornamented artistically with ridged, pointed cornices. Their massive doors looked like gates. Both castles, one facing the other, were in exactly the same architectural style and of the same size and painted red. One was the Rebbe's dwelling, the other the synagogue.

Both buildings were still intact, but only the shells of the buildings. Inside, everything had been stolen, spoiled and horribly dirtied. A military hospital for typhus patients occupied both buildings.

A typical comic Russian incident happened to me there. As soon as Dr. Ratni and I drove up to the Rebbe's court in our military car and got out, both military doctors from the hospital rushed to meet us, together with several nurses and orderlies.

The doctors greeted us and showed great deference and willingness to be of help to us, especially to me. I couldn't understand why. But as we were driving away, Dr. Ratni burst into loud laughter and said: "What do you know! They took you for the new divisional general and were sure you had come to inspect the hospital. The senior doctor told me so before we left."

This was because my officer's epaulets resembled those of a general. Whatever the reason, the doctors took me everywhere, explained and showed everything to me.

We entered the building that had been the Rebbe's house. I shuddered at the destruction I saw there: empty, desolate rooms, hideously muddied, walls that had been spat upon and broken. In the biggest room there were benches near the walls. Here sick Rumanian soldiers who had just been brought in from their posts sat or reclined. Gaunt, dark, melancholy shadows of men, in torn, wet, muddy greatcoats, half barefoot, sitting hunched up, shivering with fever and groaning. In the next room the injured were having their wounds bandaged, and those who were sick with typhus were being completely shaved.

The third room was being used as a bathroom. A water heater had been installed, heated from below. In a dense steam and suffocating stench, dozens of naked, emaciated, sick soldiers wandered about.

As we stood in the first room, where the sick Rumanian soldiers had just been brought from the front, the senior doctor pointed at them and addressed me with an ingratiating smile:

"What do you say to these heroes, our brave allies? Ha, ha! No doubt they imagined that waging war is as simple as playing in a Rumanian band in an outdoor cafe."

And he added a little more quietly, as if telling me a secret: "Do you know what the Emperor said about Rumania? He said Rumania is not a nation but a profession. Ha, ha! A brilliant remark."

When we went outside the doctor stopped, pointed at the buildings and began to relate: "You see these palaces? Wonderful architecture, genuine castles! They belonged to a very great Jewish 'rabbin,' a kind of bishop whom the Jews worship. He was frightfully wealthy, owned hundred of millions, which he removed to Austria at a timely moment.

"This house" he indicated the Rebbe's dwelling, "is historic. Here a few years ago, the famous Beilis trial that shook the world was held."°

"What do you mean, Beilis's trial was held here?" I asked in surprise.

"Here, here!" he replied with a confident smile, like a person to whom a mystery is known. "I am quite sure of it."

"What are you talking about! The trial was held in Kiev."

"In Kiev," he gestured contemptuously. "That was just a performance. Puppets danced there, whose strings were pulled from here. The real trial was held here."

"How?" I began to listen with interest.

"The greatest Jewish 'rabbiners' and the richest bankers in the world met here, and under the chairmanship of the local bishop, the whole trial was carried out here, all the details were worked out, a large sum of money was agreed on for the necessary costs. Then all the directives and orders went from here to Kiev. And what had been decided on here took place there."

He said this with such certainty that I had no doubt that this old Russian intellectual, who even had a medical degree, seriously believed this fantastic legend.

"Here, in the other building,"—he pointed to the synagogue—"there was a Jewish temple. We have set up a hospital here, with all of eighty beds."

I entered the synagogue, which was large and very high. The first thing I noticed was the row of beds where, under military greatcoats, the sick and dying lay. The air was heavy, choking. Our entry attracted the gazes of the sick men—suffering, pitiful, imploring gazes that turned to us for help. From other beds we were met

A ritual murder trial against Mendl Beilis (1911–1913) that raised an international outcry against the tsarist regime.

by gazes that were heavy, earnest and cold, already hopeless, sunken into themselves. A whole gamut of gazes!

I looked around. Bare, cracked dirty walls, on which there no longer were any of the traditional pictures, lions or leopards or musical instruments. A costly but broken chandelier hung from the ceiling.

But then my glance fell on the eastern wall, and I trembled at what I saw. The rich decoration around the Holy Ark, with the tablets above, remained unharmed. But a large Eastern Orthodox icon had been placed inside the empty Ark.

Mishnah Taanit 4:6; cf. Against the Apocalypse, pp. 16–17.

Tselem beheikhal, "an idol in the sanctuary,"° flashed through my mind. And this startled me more than all the pogroms I had seen. An ancient feeling awoke in my heart, an echo of the destruction of the Temple. I stood and could not tear my eyes from the grotesque sight. I felt that a dreadful blasphemy had been perpetrated here, a desecration of both religions. The brutal hand of a crazed soldier had exacted the same reprisal from God as from man.

The doctor told me something, but I did not hear what he said.

When I returned to Czernowitz, I met a Jew from Sadigure, a Hasid. I told him what I had seen in the Rebbe's synagogue, but this did not surprise him. The same cold, stony expression remained on his embittered face.

"What is the synagogue, compared with what has been done to the Rebbe's grave!" he said with a sigh.

"What happened to the grave?"

"You don't know? They destroyed the whole cemetery. Dragged and broke the gravestones to bits. They tore down the tomb of Rabbi Yisroel of Ruzhin, dug up the grave and scattered the bones. They had been told that Jews bury money in graves, so they were looking for it. . . ."

Thinking about what I had seen and heard at the court at Sadigure, I remembered a legend I had heard about Rabbi Yisroel of Ruzhin. As is well known, the Ruzhiner was arrested on account of a libel (he was accused of ordering or permitting the murder of two Jewish informers), and even after he was set free he was still fiercely persecuted. When he escaped to Austria, the Russian government demanded that he be surrendered to them. With the help of Metternich and with great effort, he was able to persuade the Austrian government not to turn him over.

Against this background a legend grew about a gigantic battle between the Ruzhiner and Tsar Nicholas I. It tells that Nicholas was a bitter personal enemy of the Ruzhiner and persecuted him all his life. This greatly surprised the Russian ministers, and they once asked Nicholas:

"Why do you persecute the Ruzhiner? Is it worthy of a great monarch like yourself to spend his whole life chasing after a contemptible little Jew?"

Nicholas leapt up and shouted in rage: "What do you mean, contemptible little Jew? All my life I have been bending the world one way and he has been bending it the other. And I cannot get the better of him."

And Rabbi Yisroel of Ruzhin used to say: "I was born on the same day as he, but three hours later, and I cannot catch hold of him. If I had only been born a quarter of an hour earlier I would defeat him."

The Ruzhiner did not want to be revealed or to sit on the Rebbe's throne as long as Nicholas was Tsar. He made a condition: "Either I or he!"

There was an uproar in the heavens, and Nicholas was about to be cast down from his rule. But then Nicholas's angel intervened and began to protest:

"What is this—no law and no judge? If both of them were contending for the throne at the same time, there would be room to argue about who should cede to whom. But now, seeing that His Majesty Nicholas is already Tsar, how can he be deposed?"

So the heavenly court decided that Nicholas would remain king and that the Ruzhiner would yield and allow himself to be revealed. But in order to conciliate him, the Ruzhiner was allowed to go through all the heavens and take whatever he wanted. As he went through the Heaven of Song he took the most beautiful melody from it.

Nicholas has long been dead and forgotten, but the war between him and his opponent has not ceased. He has stretched his dead hand across three generations of Tsars. He has destroyed the Ruzhiner's court, desecrated his synagogue and cast up his bones from his grave. In their evil deeds "dead hands" are as terrible as living ones.

1914–1917

54 Tales of 1001 Nights

SHOLEM ALEICHEM

So we're at the point, aren't we, where my son Yekhiel was made mayor of Krushnik, and was running things, as they say, with an iron hand, and the Poles were scraping and digging, looking everywhere for lies to tell, spreading Haman's slanders against him and against all of us. Well, they kept at it, those Poles, may their names be blotted from memory, until finally the Germans began making "forays" into town. That is, they began searching and scavenging and shaking up people. And God helped them—they actually found something at Aba the *shohet*'s,° some hidden circumcision knives, along with a packet of circumcision powder, which looks a bit like gunpowder. And then the fun began—God Almighty!

Ritual slaughterer.

First off, they took the *schlimazel* (the *shohet*, I mean) and threw him into jail, solitary confinement, so that God forbid no evil should come near him, and no one disturb his rest. And the whole town became, what should I say, a very pit of desolation and bitter lament. And all at once they came running to me. "What's going on?" they said. "Yankel, why don't you speak up? Your son," they said, "is the mayor, isn't he? And you," they said, "you're such a big shot, if you said the word, that *schlimazel* (the *shohet*, that is) would be a free man."

Well, I tried to reason with them. "Get off my back," I said. "You're making a bad mistake, my dear friends. In the first place," I said, "I'm not the big shot you think me, and even if I am, let's say, that's no special advantage. On the contrary.

Just because," I said, "my Yekhiel is mayor, and because I'm pretty important around here—a big shot, as you say—just because of this," I said, "I'd do more harm than good. Because if you knew the Germans," I said, "like I know them, you wouldn't talk that way. I'll tell you exactly what a German is," I said. "A German hates flattery as much as a kosher Jew hates pork. A German won't stand for empty words, and as for bribery," I said, "forget it. A German's not a Russian who'll watch your hand to see if you've got a bribe there for him. A German," I said, "needs delicate handling, if you see what I mean."

You'd think that that would do it, right? But you're dealing with Jews. You say salt, they say pepper. So you say pepper, they say garlic. And all the while the *shohet's* wife and her children were standing off to one side, weeping and wailing, tearing their hair out. I don't know about you, Mr. Sholem Aleichem, but I have an odd habit—when I see tears, I'm struck dumb. I can't stand to see someone crying. I can't, that's all. I'm not bragging that I'm good-hearted; it's the power of tears, if you see what I mean. But in the long run all that made no difference anyway. As it turned out, I didn't have to be begged. The authorities ordered me

The rabbi appointed by the government.

to come. And not only me, but our rabbi too, and the *rabbiner,*° along with all the other first citizens of Krushnik. Our hearts sank, I can tell you, but we gathered up our courage and got ready to go. That is, we dressed in our Sabbath best, with top hats—very elegant, very fitting and proper. It was as if we weren't being sent for, but had decided on our own to go as a delegation.

Meanwhile, my wife saw me all decked out on a Wednesday afternoon. "Yankel," she said, "where are you off to?"

Naturally I didn't tell her they'd sent for us. Does a woman have to know everything? So I made up a story that we were going as a delegation to the Germans, to the commandant I mean, in order to save a poor Jew from the gallows.

Well, she wrung her hands and started wailing, "Yankel, you mustn't do it!" There was a terrible pain in her heart, she said. Lightning, she said, had struck her. Evil days were coming upon the children of Israel. . . .

As you'd expect, a wife. What does a woman know anyway? Though to tell the truth, my wife (may she rest in peace) was not as foolish as other women. In fact, she wasn't foolish at all. You might even say the opposite. She was clever, quite clever; and sometimes she could talk like a wise woman, a wonderfully wise woman! I don't say it because she was my wife or because she's now in heaven. After death, as they say, you become a saint on earth, but that's not why I praise her. I'm not like other men. Here's an example—if you'd go to Krushnik and ask around about Yankel Yunever's wife, Miriam Mirel, you'd hear only praise and praise and more praise! First, she was pious, and not just "respectable," God forbid, like other women who won't move an inch from the letter of the law. Besides that, she was religious, very religious! But who's discussing religion? We're talking about kindness, about the meaning of character. This was a woman! A vessel of

A good-natured person.

goodness! A person without a gall!° Well, maybe not *without* gall. Everyone has a gall, naturally, and if you step on it, it's got to burst, because a human being can't be more than a human being, if you see what I mean.

But I don't want to mix things up, and as you know I hate to brag. So I'll get right to the point. We are going, I and the rabbi and the *rabbiner,* and the other good men of Krushnik, to the head authority, the commandant, to hear him out. And we went confidently. After all, we made quite a show, as they say, with the father himself of Krushnik's mayor there—you can't just dismiss something like that with a wave of your hand! And on our way we discussed what we'd say to the commandant. We decided that I would begin and address him in the words Deut. 3:23–24. of Moses: "O Lord, you have begun to show your servants your greatness°—that is to say, you have been gracious toward us, Herr German, from the day you set foot upon our land." And more of that kind of high talk. Why should we wait until he'd start? It would be best to get in a few words first, and then by the way, if you see what I mean, we could throw in something about the *shohet*—explain who the *schlimazel* was, why he'd hidden the ritual knives, just what that packet of circumcision powder meant—a regular lecture.

But as they say, if it's fated to be a disaster, you lose your tongue. That's where my real story begins. When I think of it even now, it makes my hair stand on end. . . .

In short then, we arrived at the commandant's headquarters, and there we found the *schlimazel,* Aba the *shohet* himself, tied up in the courtyard, and two soldiers with loaded rifles, one at each side of him. The *shohet* was trembling like a leaf and muttering something, probably his last confession. We were going to cheer him with a word or two, something like "Aba, God is with you!" But the soldiers gave us a nudge with their rifles—meaning one word to him, the *shohet,* and we'd be shot dead. And if a German says he'll shoot, trust him, especially when the whole world has gone crazy. At the slightest whim they'd shoot. Do you see what I mean or not? For example, someone comes by and says, "Got some tobacco, pal? If you do, all right. If not, I'll shoot." He doesn't give you time to think it over, let alone to defend yourself, to explain that you never use tobacco. Your life wasn't safe, that's the kind of world it was—try and do something about it.

To make a long story short, I don't have to tell you how we Krushniker Jews felt when we saw the *shohet* tied up and making his last confession. You can imagine it for yourself. I could only think, great God Almighty, what's going to happen to this Jew? And what will happen to his wife, the poor widow, and to his children, the orphans, if God forbid we can't get them to listen?

As we were standing around like that, thinking, out came not the commandant, but some other devil—a redhead, fat, well-fed, a cigar in his teeth. He'd just had a good supper and apparently more than a few drinks to wash it down. Along with him came two other officers. They looked at us; we looked at them. We examined each other, that is, without words for a while. No one knew what would happen. Now if it had been the commandant himself, and if he'd received us like human beings in his house, not outside there in the courtyard, then it would have been a different matter altogether, and quite a different sort of conversation. But this way, nothing. We stood and were silent—I and the rabbi and the *rabbiner* standing right up front, in the firing line, if you see what I mean. The other Krushniker dignitaries were standing behind us and pushing us from behind to say something. But how can you say something if you can't talk? Besides I was waiting for the rabbi to start—he was older. And the rabbi was waiting for the *rabbiner*—he'd been appointed by the government.

When they saw what they had there—a speechless delegation, a feast without food—the fat one yelled out to us, "Who are you?" So I stepped forward, let happen what may, and introduced him to the old man. "This is our rabbi," I said. "And the younger one, he's the *rabbiner*, the rabbi appointed by the government, and as for me," I said, "I'm Yankel Yunever, the father," I said, "of the lord mayor of Krushnik."

You'd think, wouldn't you, that he'd be impressed? Not at all. He didn't move a muscle. So seeing that reputation didn't work, I began to plead, putting first things first, as they say. "We, the foremost citizens of Krushnik," I said, "come before you as a delegation," I said, "with a request, to beg mercy for this Jew"—and I pointed to the *schlimazel,* to Aba the *shohet,* that is.

The fat German heard me out, then motioned to the soldiers to take us away. So they took us, if you see what I mean, and put us into prison like real criminals, each in a separate cell. It all happened in a minute, much less time than it's taken me to tell you about it. Did they let us send word at least to our wives and children? No, they shoved us in, locked the doors, and that's that. Should we have asked them why? Useless! First, a German won't answer. That's one reason. Another is it could make things worse, God forbid. Wartime's a powderkeg. You have to watch what you say, if you see what I mean, because who knows which side will win and what the result will be? It could be that the top dogs will be turned out into the cold, and the winners wind up six feet below.

In short, we were in a tight spot. Although if you look at it another way, what could they have against us? After all, we were dealing with Germans, with gentlemen. But then again, this was a time when Germans weren't really German, or Frenchmen French, or Englishmen English. They were wolves, not men—human beings acting like animals, like wild beasts, a plague on them! It was worse now than at the time of the flood; it was the end of the world. You probably think they fined us or beat us with whips. Well, think again. But you'd never guess, not if you'd live nine lives, so don't trouble yourself. Give me a minute or two to catch my breath, and I'll tell you a pretty story. Then be so good as to tell *me* what it was—a joke? the real thing? or a dream? . . .

Let's call it a story about the new moon—I mean, a story about how we Krushniker Jews prayed to the new moon. You remember, don't you, where we left off? They had kindly seated us in prison, me and the rabbi and the *rabbiner* and the other good men of Krushnik, the town's pride and joy, because of the crime we'd committed—we'd taken the part of Aba the *shohet,* pleaded on his behalf, if you see what I mean, and tried to save a Jew from the gallows. So there we sat, each one of us in his own cell, not studying Torah and not sitting at work for ten rubles a week, but just sitting, like common thieves and drunkards, in prison. What could we do? We'd been seated, as they say, so we sat . . . sat one hour, sat two hours, sat three hours. . . . Soon it would be night—what were we sitting there for, I ask you? At home they didn't even know where we were, that's where it hurt! And besides, everything has to end sometime, as they say, so let it come, I thought, one way or another!

I tell you, my head was ready to burst. I kept thinking and thinking, and only of evil things, and of worse to come. I imagined, first, that they'd condemn us as criminals and sentence us according to the laws of war. Next they'd politely line us up—the finest Krushniker citizens, including the rabbi and the *rabbiner,* all in a row, and twelve soldiers would stand ready, rifles loaded, waiting for the good word. And then the commandant enters in person, so I imagine, and asks us to say our last prayers—he's a German, after all, a gentleman! At this I get a bit hot under the collar and I think, "Yankel, the end's approaching. It's only a minute to death anyway; why not ease your conscience, as they say, and give him a piece of your mind?" And I begin in the language of our fathers, speaking as Abraham spoke before the gates of Sodom: "My Lord, harken to me, and hear me out. Do not take offense, O German, but let your servant's words find favor in the ears of his lord and master"°—and so on, without putting the least emphasis on the fact that he's a German and a commandant and the conqueror of Krushnik.

Gen. 40:18.

And as I'm arguing with him (in my imagination, that is), the door opened and who do you think came in but a soldier with a loaded rifle. Once inside, he winked at me as if to say, "Be so kind as to follow me." Well, I could see there wasn't much choice, so I went. Outside it was pitch black. I looked around and saw the others were there, too—all of Krushnik's finest, the rabbi and the *rabbiner* included. Behind each of them stood a soldier, armed to the teeth.

Then the captain shouted "Forward!" and we went, the whole delegation, quietly, no words spoken, because talking wasn't allowed—strictly forbidden, as they say. Only sighs and groans that would break your heart, just like at Rosh Hashanah, during prayers before the *Shofar* is sounded.° Did you ever hear the groaning then? My heart ached, especially for our rabbi, an old man seventy years old. What am I saying, seventy? He must have been then, according to my calculations, at least seventy-five, and if you really want to know, maybe even eighty, because I can still remember him at my wedding in Yunev. I was married in Yunev, you know. They brought him down from Krushnik, and by that time he was already an old man. I mean, not an *old* man, but gray-haired. And since then it's been . . . let's see, to be exact . . . no doubt as much as—actually, I don't remember; and anyway, I don't want to get off the track. That weakens the point of the story, if you see what I mean. I might forget where I'm at. Though as for my memory— God keep it always as clear as it is now. And to prove it, I'll tell you where I left off.

The shofar is blown in three sequences during the musaf service, and forty blasts conclude the entire morning service.

I was telling you about the old man, our rabbi, how he was walking out in front, and we Krushniker dignitaries were walking behind him, sighing and moaning and not allowed to speak a word. If only our families knew where we were— if only we ourselves knew where they were taking us! But nothing doing; like sheep to the slaughter, as they say. No sign they might be taking us to something good, because if so why wouldn't the Germans tell us where we were going? And certainly no one was waiting there to heap honors upon us, because then they wouldn't be pushing and shoving us—"Forward, march! Forward, march!" Before we could look around we found ourselves on Death Street, which leads to the new cemetery. I say the new one because in Krushnik we had two cemeteries, thank God, an old one and a new one. Of course, the new one was already old enough, and well populated, one grave set snugly beside the other. Pretty soon we'd have to find space for a third cemetery, if only God would let us live, and put an end to the war, and let Krushnik remain Krushnik and Jews, Jews.

Well, I won't drag this out. As we were going along the moon came out, and we could see that we were at the cemetery. What was I to think? Had someone in town died, some important person, or were they bringing some dead person here from another town, to be buried in a Jewish grave? But then why should *we* be here, and why, for that matter, a funeral with soldiers? But then again what other reason could there be for marching us suddenly, in the middle of the night, to the burial grounds?

As we were thinking this over, we looked up and saw—there he was, too, the *schlimazel,* Aba the *shohet,* I mean. He, and two soldiers with him! What was *he* doing here? Nothing much—just standing there with a shovel in his hands, digging a grave, and weeping, tears streaming down his face. Well, we didn't like the looks of it. In the first place, who was he digging a grave for? Second, what sort of a gravedigger was Aba the *shohet?* And besides that, what was he weeping about? Any way you looked at it, it was a puzzle, if you see what I mean, a mystery of mysteries, incomprehensible.

But it didn't take long—maybe as long as it's taking to tell you this, maybe even less—and all questions were answered. The captain gave an order and there emerged from out of nowhere a group of soldiers carrying shovels, and they took us, if you see what I mean, and stood us several steps apart from each other. Then they handed each of us a shovel and asked us to be so good as to dig graves, every one on his own private plot, since in two hours at most, so they gave us to understand, we'd be shot.

You want to know how we felt when they told us the good news? I can't speak for the others; that's their business. But for myself I can say absolutely, and give you my oath, that I felt—nothing. Simply and truly nothing. What do I mean *nothing?* Take a healthy person, strong and able, with wife and children and suddenly put a shovel in his hand and order him to dig his own grave since he's about to be shot! I ask you, Mr. Sholem Aleichem, think it over carefully—do you have any idea of what that means? No, you have to go through it yourself. It's a waste of time to explain. Though actually it wasn't so complicated. If a person had brains and was level-headed and could think around and about, he could see it all plainly for himself and stop worrying himself so much. "After all," I said to myself, "what's so special here? It's the old story. As they say, if God wants you to die, don't be a smart aleck; you've got to die. You're not the only one. People are dying in the thousands, tens of thousands, falling like flies, like straws in the wind. So just imagine, Yankel Yunever, that you're a soldier and in the heat of battle. Fool! Who thinks of death in the heat of battle? Or rather who thinks of anything *but* death? Because if you get right down to it, what's war if not the angel of death? And what's the point of telling the angel of death, if you see what I mean, to fear death?" Think it over, Mr. Sholem Aleichem. You'll soon see how deep that is!

Still, what's the good of philosophy? You want to get to the point, right? Well, I can tell you this much—I know as much about what happened next as you do. Suddenly confusion broke out, a clamor from heaven, a drumming of drums, a chaos of soldiers running and horses galloping. Great God Almighty, I thought, what's going on? A revolution? The earth opening under Sodom and Gomorrah? The end of the world? In an instant the soldiers vanished, and we Krushniker Jews remained all alone on the new burial grounds, shovels in hand, and—silence.

It was then we understood—not that we *understood* anything (why should I lie to you?), but we felt with all our five senses, if you see what I mean, that something extraordinary had happened, a true and genuine miracle from heaven, and we'd been saved from disaster. But for all that, we just couldn't say a word to each other, not a word! We'd lost our tongues, and that was that. And like one man, as if we'd decided on it beforehand, we threw down the shovels, pulled ourselves together, and hit the road, as they say—slowly at first, then a little faster, and then we ran, but really *ran*, if you see what I mean, like you run from a blazing fire.

Where did we get the courage? And especially the old rabbi, where did he get the strength to run like that? But he didn't last long, poor thing, and when he couldn't go any further he stopped short, with his hand on his chest, barely breathing. So we stopped too—it's not decent to leave a rabbi by himself in the middle of nowhere. We still couldn't say a word, and we still didn't know what was happening. But we could hear the drumming and the galloping and the shooting. Something was going on, God only knows what, but as it's written, "God will provide, so keep quiet."° Quiet we were—we couldn't speak.

The first to say something was the old rabbi. "Children," he called to us, looking up toward the bright moon. "I can tell you that it's the Almighty," he said, "the Creator of heaven and earth who has done these things. God Himself," he said, "has taken pity on our wives and children and saved us from disaster. And so we owe it to God," he said, "to give thanks to His moon; it's the right time of the month." And without another word, he turned his face to the new moon—the rabbi, I mean—right there in the middle of town, and we stood around him. And the rabbi started chanting, "Hallelujah," cheerfully, and we all followed him, growing livelier as we went along, chanting, clapping, and leaping. By the time he got to "Let us dance in praise of His name," we were really dancing! Such a prayer to the new moon, believe me, Krushnik had never heard of since Krushnik was Krushnik. Never had and never will again. It was, as they say, a once-in-a-lifetime prayer to the new moon.

You can imagine we didn't know where we were, whether in this world or the next, when it came to the *"Sholem aleichem's."*° I heard someone blubbering, right into my ear, *"Sholem aleichem."* I answered, *"Aleichem sholem!"* and looked around. It was him, the *schlimazel*, Aba the *shoḥet*, I mean. How did *he* get here? Had he also been with us there at the burial grounds? A curse on it all! I'd completely forgotten—he'd been the first one! We must have been out of our minds, if you see what I mean. I only wanted to hug and kiss that *schlimazel*, and at the same time I wanted to hug the rabbi (may his memory stay with us always—he's now in another world, a better one). And the way he died! God Almighty! May it happen to all our enemies! You'll hear about it, don't worry; I won't leave out the details. That was a Jew! Where can you find Jews like him today?

But just think what a rabbi can do. Once we'd finished our prayer to the new moon, he wanted to say a few more words. He decided, if you see what I mean, to explain a passage from the Song of Songs. "The voice of my beloved," he began. . . . I hope he'll forgive me for saying this, but he had one fault, our rabbi: he loved to hold forth, to give lectures. So we took counsel and decided nothing doing. A prayer to the new moon was one thing, but a commentary on the Song of Songs, with interpretations and illustrations and exhortations, in the middle of town, late at night, after such horrors and such miracles and wonders—*that*, brother, we could leave for another occasion. So we tucked in our coattails, as they say, and ran for home, each one of us. And there we met with another happy scene, I mean a real celebration. By comparison, everything we'd been through was mere child's play. You'll say that yourself when you hear the story. . . .

You know, Mr. Sholem Aleichem, Jews brag about the town of Kishinev.

Literally, " 'The Lord will battle for you; you hold your peace!' " (Exod. 14:14).

Climax of the prayer for the New Moon; it also means "how do you do."

Kishinev, they say, was world-famous for its pogroms and its hooligans. Ha! I'd laugh at them if there were any Jews left there to laugh at. Kishinev! You call *that* a town? Kishinev was a dog compared to Krushnik. Do you hear me? Kishinev wasn't worthy of washing Krushnik's feet. Concerning the treatment of Jews, the Kishinever hooligans could have learned a lesson or two (if they don't mind me saying so) from our Russian Cossacks. To begin with, they didn't even have the right weapons. In Kishinev, if they felt like smashing a house, they'd have to gather up a hundred people, along with sticks and rocks and pebbles. But what good are such weapons?—if you can call them weapons. By the time you get something going, smash up a house or two, all the excitement's gone out of it and the party's over. Now in our town in Krushnik, there were dozens of good guns, or if you preferred there was a fine cannon. A few blasts of that cannon, and you've shot up the whole area, wiped out the marketplace with all its stores and stalls and the houses all around to boot. Do you see what I mean, or don't you? With one blow they wiped out all of Krushnik, didn't leave a shred behind, not a trace! They rooted us out from the bottom up, demolished everything Jewish, just as if it wasn't their own country they were in but the enemy's. As if Krushnik was some kind of fortress, another Paris, or a Warsaw! Though I must tell you that Krushnik was always, what should I say, a helter-skelter town, a town thrown open to the wind and the rain, without courtyards, without orchards, without gardens, without fences or walls—only houses and shacks, naked, bare Jewish homes; and these they smashed up, cut down, hacked apart, split in pieces, ground up, wiped out. Finished, no more Krushnik!

And was it only Krushnik, you think? The way it was with Krushnik, that's how it was with Rakhev, too, and with Mazel-Bozhetz, and with Bilgoray, and with every other Jewish town all around as far as Lublin. But not Lublin, of course—that was the provincial capital, and Poles lived there as well as Jews; and it was they, the Poles, who unleashed the furies. If not for them, if they hadn't poured oil on the fire with their lies, then maybe nothing would have happened.

The first to show up was the Honorable Mr. Pshepetsky, head of the administrative council. The morning after our prayer to the new moon, he ran to tell the Russian officials, personally, that we Krushniker Jews were hand in glove with the Germans. Proof was, he said, that no one wanted the job of mayor; only my Yekhiel, he said, would take it on.

Well, the Russians didn't have to hear more. They were furious, beside themselves with rage against all Jews, and especially against the mayor himself, against my Yekhiel. A summons was issued from headquarters that he should be taken— my Yekhiel, that is—dead or alive! And not only him. They were to take all of us, if you see what I mean, all the first citizens of Krushnik, along with the rabbi and the *rabbiner*, and bring us to Ivan, dead or alive—he desired to see us.

Don't you think I knew beforehand it would turn out that way? I knew! My word as a Jew I knew, and the proof is that I warned everyone. "Jews," I said, "as you love God, let's get out of here!" I told them in good time, too, that night, just as soon as we heard the Germans running and Ivan coming on with his Cossacks. Because I knew that where Ivan set foot no grass would grow. So I told them, "Let's get out of here, wherever our feet will carry us. Anywhere in the world," I said, "but not here."

Well, I almost convinced them—all but one. That was the old man, the rabbi.

He just dug in his heels and refused to budge. He didn't want, he said, to run for the sake of running. "If the God of Israel wants to preserve us," he said, "He'll preserve us, as He has up until now; and if not, God forbid, then it's a sure sign," he said, "that that's our fate. And if so," he said, "then let it at least be as it's written, 'I shall sleep with my ancestors,' "° In short, all he wanted was to be buried like a Jew and remain forever in his own Krushnik. The world's full of evil temptations. But he couldn't have even that satisfaction. Man thinks and God winks, as they say. He forgot to reckon, our rabbi, with those two-legged beasts.

Gen. 47:30.

If you remember, the whole business began during the night of the new moon. Ivan and his Cossacks set out to ransack our homes on the pretense of looking for runaway Germans, and in the course of things they did what they always do— what they did, for example, in Kishinev, in Bialystok, in Balta, in Kateri-Neshov, and in other Jewish towns. The only difference was that there they beat people and robbed them, while here they very methodically emptied our pockets, inquiring of each one of us, *"tshasiki? tshasiki?"* ("watches? any watches here?"), not meaning watches in particular: watchchains, rings, earrings, and money-purses would also do. Then when they'd taken it all, everything finished and done with— as the text has it, "emptied out Egypt,"° carried off all its treasures of wealth— then they proceeded to the people: bound them, beat them, stabbed them, shot them, and hanged them. Especially hanged them. They hanged so many of us there weren't any trees left for hangings. They had to place logs over the rooftops, and there on the logs they continued hanging the Jews of Krushnik, one by one.

Exod. 12:36.

Their first victim was our rabbi, the old man, blessed be his memory. The Cossacks broke into his house early, just at daybreak. He'd already put on his prayer shawl and phylacteries and was starting to pray, when they tore in like a flood. "Vodka!" they shouted—meaning they wanted whiskey. Why whiskey at daybreak? Simply out of hunger, if you see what I mean; they were faint and famished, poor men, and so they needed a drop of whiskey. But how would an old rabbi come by whiskey, especially at a time when it was, as they say, strictly forbidden? So he gestured with his hands (not wanting to interrupt his prayers) that he had no vodka to offer them. For that he received a healthy curse, along with a slap for good measure, so that his prayer book fell from his hands. When he bent to pick it up he received another blow to the head from behind. Then the Cossacks lifted him, unconscious, from the floor, wrapped him neatly in his prayer shawl and phylacteries, tied him to a horse (to the horse's tail, I mean), and dragged him through town into the marketplace. There they hanged him from a tree and set guard over him, with orders that he must hang like that for three days and three nights. No one should dare take him down.

So he hung there, the old rabbi, wrapped in his prayer shawl, beaten and bloodied, in the middle of the marketplace, swaying back and forth in the wind, as though standing in prayer. Whoever passed by stopped to look, then ran off shuddering to tell his neighbor, and the neighbor told *his* neighbor, and soon people all over town were whispering the news to each other, and then the crowd came running to see. Cows! Cattle! Why were they running? What was so special here? Hadn't they seen a hanged man before? And for that matter, what about me, old fool that I was—why did *I* run to see it? Don't ask how much health it cost me, how many sleepless nights. To this day I see him when I close my eyes— wrapped in his prayer shawl, his face petrified, blue and streaked with blood,

Hengt shimenesre; the moment of most intense devotion is the Eighteen

Benedictions, the so-called Standing Prayer.

swaying back and forth as he stood there saying his prayers. What am I saying? He wasn't standing, he was hanging, if you see what I mean, hanging in prayer!°

But let's not talk about it anymore. Silence is best, as they say. Let's talk of happier things. Wasn't there a pogrom in your town? Didn't they hang Jews there? And by the way, what country are *you* running from, Mr. Sholem Aleichem?

1915

55 A Night

MOYSHE-LEYB HALPERN

I

Ohay, oho—
Who calls this way? Who is the man who rode the slopes
At midnight down the mountain? At the wildest gallop
He came straight down the mountain, arms stretched long and wide,
As a host of horsemen hunted him down the cliffsides,   5
A nation of riders with whips held high in the air,
Flashing from clouds of smoke, sharp as lightning. Here, there,
Flames rose through the night like wild birds taking flight,
And echoing, echoing, the wild call crisscrossed the valley—
Ohay, oho, oho, ohay—   10

III

And bringing us all a world of rest and peace
Will come a king mounted on a snow-white steed.
Whether as a blessing, whether as a curse—
Thus it stands written in the sacred verse:
And it shall come to pass in the end of days.   5

While stars glowed and flowers into blossoms burst
And the bird lifted its song in the forest,
Life hung on, waiting an eternity
To make the king welcome when he rides by.
And it shall come to pass in the end of days.   10

This earth was brought to ashes through blood and fire.
And who among us has the sword ever spared?
On whom will his most holy radiance shine,
Pure and lucid as the sun, when he rides in?
And it shall come to pass in the end of days.   15

And you, my King, hallowed by generations,
For whom is your rest? For whom is your peace meant?
The blood spilled for you across these long centuries
Will come forward, demanding an answer for me.
And it shall come to pass in the end of days.   20

VIII

My eyes open wider. My head,
it becomes heavy as lead.
I don't know what I'm crying for.
The little man° comes once more,
And he's crying as I am.   5
He calls me over to him.
Who is to blame, my brother,
For your pain? he asks in whispers.
You yourself have been longing
To see how your father's hanging.   10
There he is before you, dangling
Soundless before your eyes, swinging.
You believe this is a dream?
Then put a finger on the tree
And touch your father's hands and feet.   15
You'll feel how cold he is. Feel.
See his eyes, how they bulge out,
And his tongue hanging out, bloated.
Pull the hair out of his beard,
He won't let out a word.   20
Take out your pocket knife, drive
The blade up through his belly.
Knock out the last of his teeth.
Set fire to his sunken cheeks.
Burn and broil him, pluck and pull.   25
No matter: he'll still dangle
On the rope, and at your pleasure
He'll swing one way or the other.
Why cry, brother? What do you gain?
Who is to blame for your pain?   30

X

When I yearn for my childhood,
Now some thirty years gone, out
Comes the little man, *mentshele*,
and he rises up on his heels.
My brother, he whispers to me,   5
Whatever you want shall be.
He spreads the neck of his sack
And pulls out an ancient cloak,
Long and wide, purple and red.

Mentshele, homunculus.

A couple of wings hang on it,   10
Dirty as old snow. *Mentshele*
crawls inside the cloak, wraps himself

A fur-trimmed hat
worn by Hasidic
Jews on the
Sabbath and
festivals.

Up, takes a shapeless *shtrayml*°
Trimmed with a wreath of green laurel
And puts it on, pulling it down   15
Over his ears. On the ground
Nearby he sets a red-stringed harp
Crusted with rust and dirt.
Tearful, gazing toward heaven,
His eyes pious and stricken,   20
He begins that old lullaby
Sung at my cradle long years gone by.

XI [The Lullabye]

If you pay your dues, brother,
You'll travel in fine phaetons,
Ay lyu-lyu, lyu-lyu.
If you don't pay up, brother,
You'll foot it on thorns and stones,   5
So make with the shut-eye, you.
Ay lyu-lyu, lyu-lyu.

You'll be driven from doorways
Like a dog, like a stray.
Ay lyu-lyu, lyu-lyu.   10
Wherever you pass your day,
In the night you won't stay.
So make with the shut-eye, you.
Ay lyu-lyu, lyu-lyu.

If you slouch down on some rock,   15
Blaming yourself, flailing away,
Ay lyu-lyu, lyu-lyu,

Cf. Jer. 31:15.   Mother Rachel will take stock°
And weep for your black fate.
So make with the shut-eye, you.   20
Ay lyu-lyu, lyu-lyu.

Her wailing will put an end
To the Messiah's patience.
Ay lyu-lyu, lyu-lyu.
He will shatter his chains,   25
Then hit his head on a stone.
So make with the shut-eye, you.
Ay lyu-lyu, lyu-lyu.

XII

Lyu, lyu, sings the little man,
And my eyes will not stay open.
I see myself a little kid

Inside my father's shoes and coat.
I don't want to go to heder;   5
I'm caterwauling on the floor.
Mama shoves me out of the house.
I stand by the wall. The wind blows
The cold snow all over me.
I feel the snow, how coldly   10
It melts, drips down along my face.
With my sleeve I wipe it away.

Probably the boy's From my hand falls the groshen.°
lunch money. In the snow by the wall I lie down,
so sorry that I can't be ill.   15

The porets, Polish The landowner° comes from the mill.
squire. His dog barks at me. I sneak back
Into the house and steal some bread
For the dog, who leaps, takes it in his teeth.
Then Mama comes out and screams—   20
Screams and curses me with death
For stealing the piece of bread
While my father goes off to work,
Slaves to the bone at the market,
Freezing in the ice and snow, poor fool,   25
Just so his son can go to school.

XIII

I hear how Mama swears at me,
How the dog barks as he leaps,
And the landowner laughs at the sight,
And it seems to me that it's night
And the landowner roars   5
Like an angry black bear
Spinning around and around
And dancing back and forth and
The landowner leaps and roars,
Dancing, singing with my mother.   10
Into their circle leaps the dog
And they dance leg to leg to leg.
A Jew comes running down the road,
Blood dripping from his head.
I see how he leaps with pain   15
As he weaves into their dancing.
Jews come one after the other
Bleeding with broken heads and arms.
Synagogue. Men come dancing from the *shul*°
Small synagogue And the *kloyz*,° and women too,   20
or study-house. Feathers flying from their bellies.
An old Jew on fire whirls before me,
a Torah cradled in his arms.

Into the round dance swirl the others
Not dead yet, not properly slaughtered.   25
In her arms a murdered child,
A raging woman comes flying,
Hair loose in the wind, eyes large and green.
The street dances with *kloyz* and house,
The river dances and overflows   30
Its banks with waves of blood and sludge.
The tree dances on the river's edge.

Red flags of the   My father dances on the rope.
socialist   In leap long-dead corpses
revolution.   Parading with their red flags,°   35

Blue and white   And mice with blue and white flags,°
flags of the   Hordes of mice, heaps of mice follow,
Zionist movement.   Leaping from the outhouse wall.
Whirling with their feet in blood,
Smoke and flame about their heads,   40
They surround me, all of them.
I want to scream, but I am dumb.
When I try to lift my hand,
I scratch a cold wall. Again,
I hear someone playing a harp,   45
Someone singing. My eyes open up.
By my bed stands *Mentshele*
In ancient cloak and *shtrayml*,
Rocking himself to rest, to
And fro, and singing lyu-lyu.   50

XVI

A travesty of   And spinning three times, the little man stands
"The Sermon on   Aloft on a table in preacher's threads.
the Mount."   And pointing at me he pours out his wrath:
An eye for an eye and a tooth for a tooth,
And when they have torched your roof and your bed,   5
Go wail by the porch like a dog on edge.
Worms devour the earth and birds devour the worms.
So, dog, go nab a bird in a snowstorm
Flapping frozen wings, hopping on frozen feet,
And split it with your brother, piece by piece.   10
And if he has no hands, as happens sometimes,
Chop an arm off your shoulder and give it to him.
And if your sister bears a bastard, shout
That the soldier's name was "Holy Ghost,"
And that the bastard is really a god-to-be   15
Who, like Jesus, brings us but love and mercy.
If they won't believe you, take the cross from your heart
And also the prayer shawl—half black and half white—
And set them together and spit on them both.

Then order all flags to be gathered on the spot   20
And braid them together like horsehair and hide
And hang yourself at your father's side
And swing in tandem back and forth, him and you,
Until the braided rope rots through,
Until a gentile buries your two corpses   25
In the ground with his dead horse.

XIX

An overview of   I'm at my wits' end,
Jewish history.   Don't know where I am.
                    The whole world—town and field—
                    Whirls in a fire-red wheel.
Sabbath stew.   Up springs a *cholent*° pot   5
                    And an ancient head crawls out,
                    Its beard, it seems, and its hair
                    Have seen a thousand years or more.

                    A mouse creeps from the floorplanks.
                    It grows as big as an elephant,   10
                    Nibbles the beard, gulps down the hair.
                    Someone gives me a flag to bear.
                    My father stares from the tree,
                    In his mouth the foam seethes,
                    And he beckons me with a wink.   15
Pushke, symbol of The holy almsbox° jingles,
the requirement to A funeral cortege
give charity.   Stretches a thousand leagues.
                    Alms clink, feet plod forward,
                    Tired as their thousand years.   20

                    It seems to me that someone sits
Prayer shawl.   In a blood-spattered *tallis*°
                    On a burial stretcher
                    And burns, a Torah in his arms.
                    As he rocks back and forth, afire,   25
                    I ask, "Who is this and why?"
                    It seems to me that it is I
                    Who rock on the stretcher and cry.
                    I wonder where I am and who
                    And where I'm from, where I'll go.   30
                    A chain stretches, glows
The golden chain   Like a snake wrought of gold.°
of Jewish   The chain spins, winding
tradition.   Round my arm seven times.°
Like the strap of I spring up by the Nile   35
the tefillin.   Where dwells the crocodile.°
Like Joseph in   There, I am undressed,°
Egypt.

Like Joseph, stripped twice: once by his brothers and once by Potiphar's wife.

Taken to the king's palace.
I hear the king yell—
Slaves and courtiers fall 40
On their faces before him.
He kicks them, beats them
With the flat of his sword.
A slave comes forward
With meat and wine on a tray. 45
He spits into the tray.
A naked woman is brought—
He whips her, cuts out her heart,
Sucks the blood from it. He sucks it dry
And still he is unsatisfied. 50
I am brought before him then

The enslavement of the Jews under Pharaoh.

As sorcerers spin around his throne.°

—King, if it's health you desire,
Have him beaten like a cur.

—King, if happiness you'd recall, 55

According to rabbinic legend, babies were used instead of bricks to make up the Egyptian quota.

Brick him into a wall.°

—King, for a joke and a smile,
Throw him into the Nile.

—King, a man of grace would
Draw a bath from his blood. 60
They brick me into the wall,
They throw me into the Nile,
They suck my heart dry.
What to do? I shout, I cry
And plead for death and leap 65
Into the sea to be free

Exod. 13:9–31: crossing of the Red Sea and the drowning of Pharaoh's army.

From these straits and this pain.°
I must be caught, the king ordains.
His men leap into the waters
With their swords and daggers, 70
Their horses and chariots of iron.

I watch them sink like one great stone.
This is awful punishment—
I await the same end.
A wave spirits me away 75
To a desolate place
Where there is no water
And the red earth is parched

Retelling of the forty years of wandering in the wilderness.

And yields no sustenance.°
My wandering drags on and on 80
For years across mountains
And steppes. I will turn to stone,

And I will never again
Reach a valley of men. . . .

XX

They come to a halt in a snowy field
And leave me by myself.
Here comes the little man again, on crutches,
Head bandaged, but it's still *mentshele*.

He kneels before me and calls me his king,   5
Asks me my wish and my desire.
I tell him, "Don't you see that I'm alone
And can't move a finger."

He gives a wink—presto, soldiers in hot pursuit
Corral a naked skeleton.   10
It raises its legs like a whore in a bar
At work in the middle of drunks.

It raises its legs and dances around me,
Dances and bellows and sings:
"So may death itself whirl around you,   15
Round and round in an endless ring."°

A host of women rises from the earth,
Laying a child on the fire like a log.
They divvy up its roasted hands and legs
And leave the head for the dogs.   20

Divvying done, they raise the bones
Aloft, then toss them to me:
"So may your flesh be eaten away
'Til all that's left is just as clean."

Trees huddle in on every side,   25
Corpses swinging high and low.
The wind throws itself against the branches,
Plasters the corpses with snow.

The corpses gather together in arcs
As if before a throne.   30
"May the same wickedness happen to you,
The same evil, as we have known.

"And may the earth go forever barren
Where you've been weaving your dream.
Each night, without a thread of explanation,   35
May a new corpse hang from your tree.

"And should you stretch your hand out longingly,
May the palsy strike your hand.
May you choke to death in the midst of the word

A grotesque version of the Mosaic Curses (1).

Ps. 137 (3): here
the homeland is
Galicia.

Should you invoke the homeland.°   40

"And may you stray and wander in your dying,
Your death always just around the bend,
For your daydream of a king drags us on
And on, from this land to that land."

When the corpses have done with their curses,   45
I curse myself up and down.
Their final AMEN tumbles over me
Like stone upon stone.

Comes a dray horse as white as the snow,
Pulling an empty wagon.   50
Icicles of blood hang from its muzzle,
Ice gleams from its mane.

I stretch out my hands toward the little man
Who gives me a look so cold. . . .
I see the wagon sinking in the snow,   55
And the horse as it drops and folds.

A voice drifts in through the wind, through the night,
Calling: Ohay! and Oho!
When I squint into the distance, the rustle,
I don't see a thing. Zero.   60

XXV

O hoist me high when I'm a corpse
And bind me tight upon a horse,
And let me ride the road alone
As dead as death, with no companion.
Then step by step I will decay,   5
Fall toward grass and stone and clay.
And you, who spent your life on me
So wastefully, so uselessly—
Up-end the last few signs around
Of one who can no longer be found.   10
Let's just say for the hell of it
A night-mare's come and gone. That's that.
No one's seen me here, ever.
I've not been here, never.

1916–1919

XII

The Self Under Siege

The violence of war, revolution and pogroms was intense and unforgiving. In the five-year period between 1914 and 1919, the Jews of Russia experienced all three in such rapid succession and over such a vast stretch of territory, that there seemed to be no escape. Palestine, too, was the scene of warfare between the Turks and the British. To the extent that Jews faced the knowable, organized violence within a communal setting, the communal structure itself could still absorb some of the blows. (This is the subject of the next chapter.) To the extent that Jews faced the ubiquitous, anarchic violence as *individuals*, whether as Red Army soldiers, Zionist pioneers or survivor-emigrés in some faraway European city, they had nothing but their own physical and psychic resources to fall back on. In the Literature of Destruction, a new genre was adopted, the psychological short story, to convey the impossibility of that contest.

For this genre to work, a new type of hero was needed as well. Certainly no stranger to German, French and Russian literature, this "dangling man," or *talush*, made his first appearance in the pages of Hebrew and Yiddish fiction in the last decade of the nineteenth century. His social-psychological profile—an alienated urban intellectual with nowhere to go, no one to love and too many competing ideologies to believe in—made him the perfect vehicle for conveying the embattled mind of the modern Jew. Even when directly involved in combat, these anti-heroes were acted upon but did not initiate any meaningful action. Even when identified with some ideology, their ultimate behavior belied the party line (recall the man with the cross on his forehead [**50**]).

In the modern Jewish scheme of things, who could be more heroic than a member of the Second Aliyah to Palestine? These were the architects of the Zionist infrastructure, the swamp drainers and road builders extolled in so much of the literature. Yet Brenner's portrait of a Zionist teacher in a pioneer settlement (**56**) was anything but rosy. While the war between the Turks and the British was drawing to a close, the teacher was engaged in his own struggle to reconcile the interests of the Jewish settlers with the needs of the Jewish refugees, the rules of hygiene with the dictates of conscience. In this ultimately futile arena of human endeavor, the best a person could do was bring an emaciated child to burial and face one's own senseless death with equanimity.

Meanwhile, back in Europe, another venue of heroic action was political assassination. Of all the unavenged crimes of that era, uppermost in Jewish minds was the wave of pogroms during the Civil War of 1918 to 1919 that had been carried out by the Ukrainian nationalists under the leadership of Simon Petlura. Would the nervous young man who appeared in the home of the celebrated author in Bergelson's story (**58**) be able to perform such an act? Judging from various signs, beginning with the young man's cheeks, he seemed incapable of overcoming even his own psychological fixations. Here, on closer inspection, was a man motivated solely by spite: "And for spite," he admitted to the writer, "you can do something ugly. For spite, you can do something lovely—it's all the same, as long as it's for spite." So much for the long-awaited act of national retribution.

How, indeed, could a normal, civilized human being become an agent of death? Nowhere in the Literature of Destruction was this question answered more brilliantly than in Lamed Shapiro's "White *Challah*" and in Isaac Babel's stories of the *Red Cavalry*.

For the first time in Jewish literature, Lamed Shapiro wrote a pogrom story from the vantage point of the non-Jew, a speechless and historyless peasant named Vasil (**57**). Note that Vasil was not born without feelings. As a child, when he saw the sharp edge of a bone pierce the skin of an injured dog, he cried. But soon thereafter his brutalization began—first at the hands of his family, then at the hands of his army officers, and finally in the throes of battle. Throughout his life, Vasil had one overriding passion: the Jews, "people who wore strange clothes, sat in stores, ate white *challah* and had sold Christ." When the war brought him face to face with the "real" enemy, he demanded his final due and closed both circles by turning cannibal. Had Shapiro merely wanted to present a case study in human pathology, the story would have ended here; instead he drew a universal landscape of desecration officiated over by the high priests of death who, in a horrible reversal of Christianity, now used the flesh of the Jew to substitute for the Host.

Unlike Vasil, the bespectacled narrator of Babel's stories came to the job endowed with analytic powers and fine ethical sensibilities. In the first story (**59**), later excised from *The Red Cavalry*, his allegiance was clearly on the side of the innocent victims, even if he depicted the Jewish P.O.W. in a grotesque light. In "The Rabbi's Son" (**60**), the new revolutionary ethos, which spared no one and nothing, was brilliantly conveyed by the grab bag of relics that Bratslavsky left behind, while the heightened, almost confessional tone of the narrator's voice bespoke his strong ties to traditional values. But there was one more story to go in the canonized version of *The Red Cavalry*. In that story, the Jewish intellectual narrator achieved his most fervent desire: to become a Cossack in every respect.

Through the prism of the mind, these writers dramatized the impossible contest between the individual will and the blind force of historical violence. Yet these stories were more than carefully crafted works of psychological fiction. Behind their descriptive approach there also lay a prescriptive program. By exposing the enormous psychic and cultural obstacles faced by the modern, politicized Jew, these anti-heroic stories could also inspire—or prefigure—real heroic action. Simon Petlura, the real-life counterpart to the man who lived behind door number five in Bergelson's story, was assassinated in Paris in May 1926, two years *after* the story was published. The assassin's name was Shalom Schwarzbard. At his trial, the atrocities were brought to light, and Schwarzbard was acquitted.

56 The Way Out

YOSEF HAYYIM BRENNER

I

Each morning, day in, day out, when the tiny train was due to arrive from Tulkarm to fetch wood to stoke the engine, the old pioneer teacher would go out onto the balcony of his attic room on the farm. Shading his eyes, he would peer into the distance to see whether they were coming.

They were sure to come. They could be expected any day now.

They would be on that little train that came to fetch the wood. They would be arriving from back there, from that nightmare-ridden waste, where the soil lay desolate, the trees hewn down and the dwellings in ruins; from that dead region where the handful of farmers who were left paid the soldiers billeted in their houses to chop the remaining almond trees into firewood; from the place where the only food was unground millet, to fill the belly and still the pangs of hunger; from the place where damp huts, infested with mice and vermin, soggy with filth and permeated with the accumulated stench of months, gave sorry shelter to women and children who were chilled to the marrow and contorted with disease; from the place where out of the surviving hundreds, half a dozen dead were carted away daily for burial; from the place where there was no longer any room to lay the scores of new victims that succumbed daily to the disease, nor a garment to cover them, nor even a sheet to spread under them; from the place whose denizens did nought to alleviate their plight—all they did was to listen to the guns firing, argue among themselves about military tactics, groan and grumble: "Oh, that Evacuation Committee has been our undoing! . . . it has been the end of us!"; from the place where those versed in the art of trickery and theft accumulated napoleons° and made a fortune, and the privileged few healthy young men who had come down from the north ate eggs and jam, played cards round the clock and merely waited for the "liberation" that was so late in coming.

"Did you hear that? They're shooting again!"

"It's our side° shooting. . . ."

"What are you talking about? Those aren't our guns. . . ."

"Then where do you think our side is stationed, and where is that shooting coming from. . . ?"

"And even if it is ours, it means that they° are advancing. . . ."

"The planes have been flying around here all day. . . ."

"This morning there was one flying around for almost two solid hours. . . ."

"And did you see the *golem*? . . . I saw it. . . ."

(The golem, or dummy, was what they called the military observation balloon.)

"It's the weather that's holding them back. . . ."

"No doubt about it. As soon as the rainy season's over, we'll be going back to Jaffa!"

But the rainy season went by, and Passover too, without unleavened or even leavened bread, and the wretched exiles, instead of returning to the south, to Jaffa,

The French gold twenty-franc piece was used as legal tender in Turkish Palestine.

I.e., the Turkish army.

I.e., the British forces under General Allenby. This was no indication of their sympathies, however, for they were eagerly awaiting the British victory that would deliver them from their desperate plight.

were again forced to pack their miserable rags and chattels and drag themselves wearily in the opposite direction, to the north.

What was going to happen to them? How would it all end? They were all broken in body and spirit, worn out, naked and starving, ravaged by contagious disease, and they would be coming here; they would be disgorged by the train to lie around out in the open, exposed to the scorching rays of the sun by day and to the chill and the dank dew by night, to be consumed by malaria, the dread swamp fever. Broken hollow shells of humans, hardly able to move, unable to do anything for themselves . . . who was going to feed them, give them drink, tend to them? What was going to happen to them?

II

As the days went by and they failed to arrive, the rumor went round that they had been sent straight to the Galilee and would not show up here. People began to breathe more freely and gradually went back to their everyday matters.

All of a sudden, one sweltering morning in June, the news struck like a thunderbolt:

"Forty-two of them!"

"Where?"

"Over there. Don't you see? In among the tree stumps, that's where they're lying around. . . ."

"In that case," it was the old pioneer teacher. "In that case," he stammered, confused, "surely we have to do something . . . water. . . ."

"They're filling a barrel with water already . . . take it out to them over there . . . they mustn't come here to drink our water . . . we've got our children to think of . . . the doctor from the colony said we mustn't have anything to do with them before everything's been disinfected first. It's only that the horses haven't come back yet . . . there's nothing to carry the water in. . . ."

But the old man in his excitement hardly heard what he was being told of this latest setback. "And what about bread?" he said. "We have to fetch them some bread, at least a few loaves for the meantime . . . something for breakfast. . . ."

The farm was small and had only one oven, and there was very little bread to go round. The teacher himself had two loaves. He put one loaf into a basket, broke a chunk off the other one and put it into the basket too, then went round to each of the houses on the farm—there were five in all—to "borrow" some loaves or even a few slices for the newly arrived refugees; there were forty-two of them after all. . . .

The housewives could not refuse, hard as it was to leave their families without any bread, for had not the exiles been breadless all through the long winter, and had just come in from their arduous trek, starving, thirsty and in a sorry state. The basket was soon filled with the loaves, half-loaves and crusts that the women scraped together, and the old man hurried to bring it to the newcomers. The drum of water had not yet been carted over; there were unaccountable delays.

III

Ghastly shadows. Old men and old women, sprawling inert near their meager bundles. Women in tattered blouses, their emaciated breasts exposed. Young girls, their shriveled faces long devoid of the bloom of youth. Seven or eight sickly orphans.

"Folks, don't snatch, don't crowd around him!" a short, yellow-bearded fellow rose to his feet and hurried over to the old man who had come up with his basket of bread. "It's got to be divided out properly, everyone gets an equal share, according to the list of names . . . sh . . . sh . . . here's the list . . . now let's share it out . . . not like that . . . you'll tear the old man to pieces. . . ."

"Why, there's bread!" An old woman refugee was jubilant. "This must be England, they're giving us bread."

"What about the wagons?" demanded a red-headed man, his hair providing the only spot of color among the exiles. He was standing next to a pile of five stout crates reinforced with steel hoops. "Is that all the committee sent us, the rogues? They're all rogues in that Evacuation Committee, everyone of them, damn them! In Kfar Sava they made us a lot of fine promises, and here they let us lie out in the open. Aren't they ever going to transfer us to the colony?"

The old pioneer teacher patiently explained that he was not from the Evacuation Committee of the neighboring colony, but had brought the bread on his own initiative from a nearby farm. He would be going into the colony very soon to notify the local evacuation committee of the new arrivals.

"And what can we get in the colony to go with the bread?" a young woman asked. "I myself divided out the bread in Kfar Sava . . . but they say there's honey here, plenty of honey . . . and butter . . . and how much would a pound of meat cost?"

"Suppose I wanted to settle in this colony?" asked the red-haired man's wife after receiving her ration of bread. She volunteered the information that she was the sister of the young woman who had doled out the bread in Kfar Sava. "Would I be able to find a place to live, nothing much, just a room with a ceiling over it? I don't want it for nothing, God forbid . . . I'm quite ready to pay whatever they might ask for it. I'm just sick of having no place to live. . . ."

"Oh, dear," complained the woman distributing the bread, "everybody knows I had such a fine flat in Kfar Sava."

Another woman fastened herself onto the old man. "A doctor," she said, "a doctor is what we need here. Please come and see for yourself . . . a baby's dying . . . can't eat any bread . . . two years old she is and looks like two months . . . her father stayed behind in Petah Tikva . . . hasn't even had a spoonful of water for two days . . . her mother hasn't eaten a thing, can't suckle the baby, has nothing to nurse her with." She begun tugging the old man. "Please come and see for yourself."

A young woman of about twenty sat alone among the trees apart from the others. She was barefoot and as thin as the dry twigs that lay around her. In her arms she rocked a naked child whose white body was covered with the bites of mosquitoes, lice, fleas, and other vermin and with festering sores. Inert and silent, the child stared out of wide-open glassy eyes.

"If only . . . a drop of milk . . ." the mother articulated the barely heard syllables.

"What we need here is a doctor, a doctor," insisted the woman who had called the old man over.

"D'you hear that!" A woman nearby flared up. "A doctor and milk they need, if you please, and my child hasn't even got any water. . . ."

"There's no milk to be had on the farm," the old teacher stammered in embarrassment. "But there's water there and they'll be bringing some very soon."

He turned to the harping woman, "Have you got a pot, or some other container? Come along with me and I'll let you have some water. It's only ten minutes' walk. . . ."

"There's water to be had much nearer," spoke up the officious little man with the list. "Over there near the bridge."

"Heaven forbid!" the old man exclaimed in alarm. "Don't you drink that water, it's swamp. On the farm we have good water . . . who's coming along with me to fetch some?"

Nobody offered to go with him. Who was going to walk all that distance? Furiously the young woman thrust a kettle into the hands of an orphan who had volunteered for the task and sent him over to the bridge to fetch some water for her baby. The water there was nearer.

IV

The office of the village council, which also dealt with refugee relief, was closed, but all around, throughout the colony, life went on as usual. Sitting on the veranda outside the office, the old pioneer teacher sensed, to his alarm, that the enthusiasm which had prompted him to run from the "station" near the farm into the colony was now beginning to wane, sobered by the closed door of the office. Not so long ago he had seen himself pounding the council table with his puny fist, shouting at them, even plunging his nails into the council chairman's beard, fulminating: "Murderers! Why don't you do something!" But now that he had been waiting outside the closed door for half an hour, he felt a kind of numbness creep over him. The janitor, who had passed by a little while ago, had told him that the head of the council was asleep but would be along shortly. But even when the head of the council came, what would he, the teacher, tell him, and what could the council actually do?

The head of the council arrived an hour later.

"I've come to tell you," the old man began in a low voice, "that some refugees, forty-two of them, have arrived. . . ."

"I know that," the head of the council replied curtly.

"Then what's going to happen?" the old teacher was embarrassed.

"Whatever's got to happen. I've given instructions that they aren't to be allowed into the colony before they've all undergone disinfection. Altogether, they'll be moving on from here . . . they've got nothing to do in the colony."

"Good, so they'll get the wagons today?" the teacher was pleased.

"I'm afraid it's a bad business about those wagons," said the deputy council head who had just come in. "It's the peak of the season right now, and who of the farmers will want to hire out his wagon? A wagon's worth its weight in gold at this time of the year."

"In any case, by tomorrow morning we'll have requisitioned two carts," said the head of the council importantly.

"Two carts for forty-two people?" protested the teacher.

"Well . . . to carry their belongings. The people will have to walk."

"But most of them are ill, diseased . . . there are children. . . ."

"We know all about that," the deputy broke in. "A wagon if we can get it, means a hundred and twenty gold francs."

The council head kept silent.

"And they'll spend tonight out in the open?"

The deputy did not reply. After a few minutes' silence he began telling the council head about his phone call to the central office of the Evacuation Committee. As there were Turkish Officers in the post office while he was making his call, he didn't want to say over the phone exactly how much money he wanted the committee to send to cover the cost of feeding the new arrivals, but he hinted at it by saying "twice as much as you sent the day before yesterday," which meant a hundred and fifty napoleons. The money had already arrived by special messenger.

"So we can buy the millet now?" asked the council head.

"They're asking thirty-nine medjidahs a bushel."

"Is that so?" exclaimed the head of the council. "Never mind, we've got to buy. We can't afford to be particular about the price right now."

"If I'm not mistaken," the deputy said to the council head, "you must also have a few bushels of millet for sale."

Very soon, the room was crowded with grain merchants and brokers. From time to time, the deputy would plunge his hands into his pockets and pour out streams of gold napoleons. One broker cracked a joke:

"Never mind. The refugees aren't pigs. They'll even eat this millet."

"But it's half sand!"

"*Malesh*, no matter!"

The old teacher tried to make himself heard above the din of the transactions. "So it's all decided then. They're to spend the night out in the open! And we'll be able to say" he quoted from the Bible, " 'Our hands have not shed this blood.' "°

Receiving no answer he flung another verse at them: " 'How have their hearts turned unto stone!' "°

"But they're used to it by now," one of the farmers who had been called in to see about hiring the carts tried to set his mind at rest. "They have spent the whole winter at Kfar Sava."

The head of the village council was apologetic. "As long as they haven't been disinfected, we mustn't have anything to do with them . . . doctor's orders. . . ."

"In that case you'd better be careful of me," shouted the old teacher. "I've been there, and I haven't been disinfected. I'm carrying all the germs!"

"That wasn't very clever of you," the deputy grew dead serious and stopped jingling the gold coins. "You shouldn't have come here, really."

"One doesn't play around with these things. . . ."

"You mustn't go against the rules of hygiene. . . ."

The negotiations were at an end.

Deut. 21:7: the ritual of the red heifer.

Not an actual verse.

V

The teacher stayed in the colony overnight, unwilling to go back to the farm. He was not at all sure that the carts would be sent in the morning, and if he was not there to push things, who else would?

At midnight the whole countryside was blanketed by a chill, dank mist. For a long time he stood outside watching the swirling vapors and shivering slightly, unable to go inside. No, he would stay out. All night long he roamed about the slumbering colony, and dawn found him standing outside the closed door of the village council office.

It was nine o'clock by the time the two carts set out for the timber-loading station. The mist had not yet lifted completely. Sitting on one of the lumbering carts, he reflected: if a new batch doesn't arrive today, those who came yesterday will manage somehow. The poorest ones will be packed off. Those who are better off—if they insist on staying and particularly if they indicate that they won't become a public burden—will probably be allowed to enter the colony after undergoing disinfection. But if a new batch should arrive today, what with the general mismanagement and indifference prevailing in the colony, all's lost!

As he drew near and peered through the mist at the shivering people, he saw to his relief that no new ones had arrived. His heart seemed to contract in a spasm and tears welled up in his eyes.

The red-haired man was ensconced in a makeshift hut he had thrown up with the help of two Yemenites; the hut was made of his crates, some canvas, and eucalyptus branches. All the others—men, women and children—lay huddled in the damp open field, panting with thirst and shivering.

"Sodom, that's what this colony is!" spat the little yellow-bearded fellow. He seemed to have shrunk even smaller during the night.

"And what are you going to feed us today?" the old teacher was accosted by the woman who had been so impressed by "England" the day before.

"They'll be bringing you some bread," the old man promised, feeling obliged to add "millet bread."

He looked about him for the sick child (he had brought her a can of milk, about half a pint, which he had finally managed to procure in the colony), but he did not see her anywhere. He was told her mother had taken her into the colony to the doctor, without being disinfected first, in defiance of the orders.

"What do you advise us to do?" the old man was bombarded with questions on all sides. "Should we stay here or go on?"

In the meantime, the red-haired man's crates had been loaded onto the carts with the help of the carters and the officious yellow-bearded little man. The crates, which contained bales of cloth, were extremely heavy and it was only by dint of a great deal of heaving and straining, grunting and puffing, that they were finally hoisted onto the carts. A new difficulty now arose. One of the carters, a Jew from the colony, stubbornly refused to accept any additional load, not even as much as a straw (there were only two crates on his cart). In the ensuing argument, the orphans were placed on the cart and removed a dozen times. The carter remained obdurate: he was not going to kill his pair of mules for the refugees, there were plenty of other carts in the colony, the Evacuation Committee could jolly well hire as many as were needed. The other carter, an Arab drayman, who did not understand all this talk about the all-powerful Evacuation Committee, was more amenable: he agreed to take, in addition to his three crates, a few bundles and an impatient old couple, who, in their eagerness to get away at all costs, boarded the cart like martyrs ascending the scaffold.

The carts lumbered off.

"Aren't they going to send us any more carts?" the refugees who had been left behind looked at one another in blank amazement.

"What about me and my children? Aren't we going to get a cart?" The woman who had demanded water the day before did not yet grasp what had happened.

Very soon there was a storm of protests, oaths, recriminations, and gnashing teeth, with violent plans of action followed by witty rejoinders, but all the refugees remained out in the field in the end.

A squabble broke out over possession of what was left of the red-haired man's hut. "I had it first!" "No, I did!" and as the argument raged hotly, the few poles and branches were pulled down and strewn about. The orphans sat playing with the branches and squirting water at one another—the good water that had at last been brought over from the farm.

The old teacher returned to the colony to report on the situation. Some of the younger men of the colony had not gone to work that day, having undertaken to see to the disinfection and to put up tents for the refugees in the colony, so that they should not have to spend another night out in the open. There was a serious hitch, however. The village council claimed that the authorities would not permit the refugees to be brought into the colony: this was an army depot—the deputy head of the council explained—and the authorities did not want the soldiers to catch the disease carried by the refugees. The tents were therefore left unpitched. The bathhouse-keeper firmly refused to allot his premises for the disinfection and another large boiler was not to be had at any price.

The refugees remained where they were and the old teacher stayed with them, tired and helpless. Exposed to the night's dew, he was seized by a violent fever. Next morning, the train from Tulkarm brought a new batch of 174 refugees. There was no way out.

VI

With the attack of fever still on him and overwhelmed by a sense of great loss, the old man rushed away from the refugee encampment in the direction of the colony. The way out lay across his path.

On the rise overlooking the colony, in among the trees, stood a knot of people—including some tattered, hungry scarecrows of Turkish soldiers—looking down at an emaciated woman who sat barefoot on the ground, with her dead child at her side.

The body of the child, stark naked the day before yesterday, was now dressed in a little frock.

"The doctor tried to pour a spoonful of milk into her mouth, but she couldn't swallow it. It was plain there was nothing to be done," said one of the bystanders.

The mother sat silent for some time. She looked just the same as she had looked two days ago. When she finally spoke, she said she wanted them to bury her dead baby, and that they should not forget to bring her the day's millet-bread ration. She was hungry, she said, and wanted to eat.

The child, too, apart from the frock it was wearing, looked the same as it had looked when alive: the mouth was closed, the eyes wide open, the cheeks just as hollow, and the sores still festering.

"Why don't they bury the child?" one of the bystanders protested.

"They've been over to the village council three times already," answered another. "There's nobody to talk to . . . nobody wants to call the burial society . . . they keep putting it off. . . ."

"I'll bury her," the old pioneer teacher announced. "Who can give me a hoe?"

They waited while some of the people went into the colony to fetch a hoe, asked for one at every house, and came back empty-handed.

A *small Turkish coin.*

Someone noticed that one of the soldiers carried a trench tool. Wordlessly, the old man took a bishlik° out of his pocket and held it out to the soldier, as if to say: "Will you come along with me?" The soldier nodded. The old man picked up the little corpse, and carrying it in front of him laid across his outstretched arms—the way a godfather holds a child at circumcision rites—he began walking in the direction of the cemetery.

For half an hour they trudged through the deep sand, the soldier with his tassel-less tarbush in front, the malaria-racked old man dragging after him, his strength flagging. No longer able to bear the child's body in front of him, he placed it under his arm, where the tiny corpse sagged and dangled limply.

The cemetery fence had been pulled up, and where the railings had been, the earth was now pockmarked with deep, narrow potholes.

The old corpsebearer was drenched with perspiration, as if he had taken a large dose of quinine to force the fever down. He could hardly carry his load any farther, though the tiny frail body weighed far less than the basket of bread he had brought to the refugees two days ago. He looked around him, eyes sightless with exhaustion. Hugging the little body, he murmured: "My little girl, my child. How beautiful you are. What a beautiful woman, a loving woman, you could have grown up to be. Who knows what happiness you are taking with you to the grave today? My little girl!"

His foot caught in one of the potholes. He extricated it without noticing that he had sprained the large toe of his left foot, and went on. Suddenly he stopped. "Here!" he said to the soldier.

The soldier unshouldered his trench tool and set to work simply, without asking any questions. He dug steadily for ten minutes, very much like an overgrown child playing in the sand, then raised his childlike eyes questioningly to his new commander, the old man who had given him the bishlik. The latter, who had meanwhile laid the body on the heap of sand, motioned him to dig deeper. "We can't have the dogs getting at the body," he thought.

The soldier obeyed, and when the grave was ready, he straightened his back and stood, waiting. The old man did what was necessary. Removing the child's frock, for some reason, he placed the poor little body, ravaged with starvation and mosquito bites, in the ground and began shoveling the damp earth over it with both hands. The soldier picked up the discarded frock and placed it under his tassel-less tarbush as an additional headgear, but immediately removed it from his head to tuck it into a gaping rent in his tunic where there had once been a pocket, and then helped the old man shovel the earth into the grave. With a strange devotion, he joined in the burial of this child of a faith alien to his.

They returned to the colony, now as comrades, united by the bond of their shared deed.

The old man was limping badly, the excruciating pain in his toe turning each hobbling step into torment. But he felt that his task was still unfinished, that he could not simply say good-bye to his dark-skinned friend, the Turkish soldier, without some further token of friendship. He wanted to offer him a glass of wine, drink with him, say to him: "Your health, fellow sufferer! Your good health, Anatolian peasant, who has known so much hardship!" But there was not a drop of wine to be had in the colony's only store: The Mukhtar° had taken it all for the Mudir° who was billeted in his house.

Village headman.

Turkish local military governor.

"That's all to the good!" thought the old man, remembering that Moslems are forbidden to take wine and that the soldier might have felt embarrassed if offered some. Instead, he bought him a packet of cigarettes and a chunk of hard cheese, pressed another bishlik on him, and warmly shook him by the hand. Full of gratitude and high spirits, the Turkish soldier went his way, the child's frock peeping out from the erstwhile pocket of his tattered tunic. The old man, however, was now unable to walk a single step. The jagged stump of the rail which had been torn out of the cemetery fence—for military purposes, no doubt—had made a deep, serious wound in his toe. Night had fallen by the time one of his laborer-students came to take him back to the farm on a donkey. At his request, the laborer-student brought a bowl of cold water to his room and then left.

He lay alone in the dark room. He had tried bathing his toe in the cold water, but the throbbing pain had become unbearable and he was no longer able to move, not even to ease himself. Yet he felt strangely relieved, completely absolved of all his obligations toward others. Relief had come.

He dimly made out the half loaf of bread lying on the table amid his books and soiled underwear, reminding him that he had not eaten a thing for three days— but the agonizing pain in his toe drove out all thought of eating. Obeying some obscure impulse, he stretched out his hand to finger the bread, saw that it had gone stale and hard, and was swept by remorse at not having taken the two whole loaves along with him. "What a great pity," he thought, "to let even a crust of bread go to waste right now. . . ." His sorrow quickly passed, however, to make way for the sense of relief that flooded him. Ten minutes' walk away, the ruthless night spread over the third batch of refugees. They had arrived unexpectedly that afternoon, his pupil told him on their way to the farm, sixty-nine of them. But they were no longer his concern, he would not go to them, he was unable to go. He felt relieved.

1919

57 White *Challah*

LAMED SHAPIRO

1

One day a neighbor broke the leg of a stray dog with a heavy stone, and when Vasil saw the sharp edge of the bone piercing the skin he cried. The tears streamed from his eyes, his mouth, and his nose; the towhead on his short neck shrank deeper between his shoulders; his entire face became distorted and shriveled, and he did not utter a sound. He was then about seven years old.

Soon he learned not to cry. His family drank, fought with neighbors, with one another, beat the women, the horse, the cow, and sometimes, in special rages, their own heads against the wall. They were a large family with a tiny piece of land, they toiled hard and clumsily, and all of them lived in one hut—men, women, and children slept pell-mell on the floor. The village was small and poor, at some distance from a town; and the town to which they occasionally went for the fair seemed big and rich to Vasil.

In the town there were Jews—people who wore strange clothes, sat in stores, ate white *challah*, and had sold Christ. The last point was not quite clear: who was Christ, why did the Jews sell him, who bought him, and for what purpose?— it was all as though in a fog. White *challah*, that was something else again: Vasil saw it a few times with his own eyes, and more than that—he once stole a piece and ate it, whereupon he stood for a time in a daze, an expression of wonder on his face. He did not understand it all, but respect for white *challah* stayed with him.

He was half an inch too short, but he was drafted, owing to his broad, slightly hunched shoulders and thick short neck. Here in the army beatings were again the order of the day: the corporal, the sergeant, and the officers beat the privates, and the privates beat one another, all of them. He could not learn the service regulations: he did not understand and did not think. Nor was he a good talker; when hard pressed he usually could not utter a sound, but his face grew tense, and his low forehead was covered with wrinkles. *Kasha* and borscht, however, were plentiful. There were a few Jews in his regiment—Jews who had sold Christ— but in their army uniforms and without white *challah* they looked almost like everybody else.

2

They traveled in trains, they marched, they rode again, and then again moved on foot; they camped in the open or were quartered in houses; and this went on so long that Vasil became completely confused. He no longer remembered when it had begun, where he had been before, or who he had been; it was as though all his life had been spent moving from town to town, with tens or hundreds of thousands of other soldiers, through foreign places inhabited by strange people who spoke an incomprehensible language and looked frightened or angry. Nothing particularly new had happened, but fighting had become the very essence of life; everyone was fighting now, and this time it was no longer just beating, but fighting in earnest: they fired at people, cut them to pieces, bayoneted them, and sometimes even bit them with their teeth. He too fought, more and more savagely, and with greater relish. Now food did not come regularly, they slept little, they marched and fought a great deal, and all this made him restless. He kept missing something, longing for something, and at moments of great strain he howled like a tormented dog because he could not say what he wanted.

They advanced over steadily higher ground; chains of giant mountains seamed the country in all directions, and winter ruled over them harshly and without respite. They inched their way through valleys, knee-deep in dry powdery snow, and icy winds raked their faces and hands like grating irons, but the officers were cheerful and kindlier than before, and spoke of victory; and food, though not always served on time, was plentiful. At night they were sometimes permitted to build fires on the snow; then monstrous shadows moved noiselessly between the mountains, and the soldiers sang. Vasil too tried to sing, but he could only howl.

They slept like the dead, without dreams or nightmares, and time and again during the day the mountains reverberated with the thunder of cannon, and men again climbed up and down the slopes.

3

A mounted messenger galloped madly through the camp; an advance cavalry unit returned suddenly and occupied positions on the flank; two batteries were moved from the left to the right. The surrounding mountains split open like freshly erupting volcanoes, and a deluge of fire, lead, and iron came down upon the world.

The barrage kept up for a long time. Piotr Kudlo was torn to pieces; the handsome Kruvenko, the best singer of the company, lay with his face in a puddle of blood; Lieutenant Somov, the one with girlish features, lost a leg, and the giant Neumann, the blond Estonian, had his whole face torn off. The pockmarked Gavrilov was dead; a single shell killed the two Bulgach brothers; killed, too, were Chaim Ostrovsky, Jan Zatyka, Staszek Pieprz, and the little Latvian whose name Vasil could not pronounce. Now whole ranks were mowed down, and it was impossible to hold on. Then Nahum Rachek, a tall slender young man who had always been silent, jumped up and without any order ran forward. This gave new spirit to the dazed men, who rushed the jagged hill to the left and practically with their bare hands conquered the batteries that led the enemy artillery, strangling the defenders like cats, down to the last man. Later it was found that of the entire company only Vasil and Nahum Rachek remained. After the battle Rachek lay on the ground vomiting green gall, and next to him lay his rifle with its butt smeared with blood and brains. He was not wounded, and when Vasil asked what was the matter he did not answer.

After sunset the conquered position was abandoned, and the army fell back. How and why this happened Vasil did not know; but from that moment the army began to roll down the mountains like an avalanche of stones. The farther they went, the hastier and less orderly was the retreat, and in the end they ran—ran without stopping, day and night. Vasil did not recognize the country, each place was new to him, and he knew only from hearsay that they were moving back. Mountains and winter had long been left behind; around them stretched a broad, endless plain; spring was in full bloom; but the army ran and ran. The officers became savage, they beat the soldiers without reason and without pity. A few times they stopped for a while; the cannon roared, a rain of fire whipped the earth, and men fell like flies—and then they ran again.

4

Someone said that all this was the fault of the Jews. Again the Jews! They sold Christ, they eat white *challah,* and on top of it all they are to blame for everything. What was "everything"? Vasil wrinkled his forehead and was angry at the Jews and at someone else. Leaflets appeared, printed leaflets that a man distributed among the troops, and in the camps groups gathered around those who could read. They stood listening in silence—they were silent in a strange way, unlike people who just do not talk. Someone handed a leaflet to Vasil too; he examined it, fingered it, put it in his pocket, and joined a group to hear what was being read. He did not understand a word, except that it was about Jews. So the Jews must know, he thought, and he turned to Nahum Rachek.

"Here, read it," he said.

Rachek cast a glance at the leaflet, then another curious glance at Vasil; but he said nothing and seemed about to throw the leaflet away.

"Don't! It's not yours!" Vasil said. He took back the leaflet, stuck it in his pocket, and paced back and forth in agitation. Then he turned to Rachek. "What does it say? It's about you, isn't it?"

At this point Nahum flared up. "Yes, about me. It says I'm a traitor, see? That I've betrayed us—that I'm a spy. Like that German who was caught and shot. See?"

Vasil was scared. His forehead began to sweat. He left Nahum, fingering his leaflet in bewilderment. This Nahum, he thought, must be a wicked man—so angry, and a spy besides, he said so himself, but something doesn't fit here, it's puzzling, it doesn't fit, my head is splitting.

After a long forced march they stopped somewhere. They had not seen the enemy for several days and had not heard any firing. They dug trenches and made ready. A week later it all began anew. It turned out that the enemy was somewhere nearby; he too was in trenches, and these trenches were moving closer and closer each day, and occasionally one could see a head showing above the parapet. They ate very little, they slept even less, they fired in the direction the bullets came from, bullets that kept hitting the earth wall, humming overhead, and occasionally boring into human bodies. Next to Vasil, at his left, always lay Nahum Rachek. He never spoke, only kept loading his rifle and firing, mechanically, unhurriedly. Vasil could not bear the sight of him and occasionally was seized with a desire to stab him with his bayonet.

One day, when the firing was particularly violent, Vasil suddenly felt strangely restless. He cast a glance sidewise at Rachek and saw him lying in the same posture as before, on his stomach, with his rifle in his hand; but there was a hole in his head. Something broke in Vasil; in blind anger he kicked the dead body, pushing it aside, and then began to fire wildly, exposing his head to the dense shower of lead that was pouring all around him.

That night he could not sleep for a long time; he tossed and turned, muttering curses. At one point he jumped up angrily and began to run straight ahead, but then he recalled that Rachek was dead and dejectedly returned to his pallet. The Jews . . . traitors . . . sold Christ . . . traded him away for a song!

He ground his teeth and clawed at himself in his sleep.

5

At daybreak Vasil suddenly sat up on his hard pallet. His body was covered with cold sweat, his teeth were chattering, and his eyes, round and wide open, tried greedily to pierce the darkness. Who has been here? Who has been here?

It was pitch-dark and fearfully quiet, but he still could hear the rustle of the giant wings and feel the cold hem of the black cloak that had grazed his face. Someone had passed over the camp like an icy wind, and the camp was silent and frozen—an open grave with thousands of bodies, struck while asleep, and pierced in the heart. Who has been here? Who has been here?

During the day Lieutenant Muratov of the fourth battalion of the Yeniesey regiment was found dead—Muratov, a violent, cruel man with a face the color of parchment. The bullet that pierced him between the eyes had been fired by someone from his own battalion. When the men were questioned no one betrayed the culprit. Threatened with punishment, they still refused to answer, and they remained silent when they were ordered to surrender their arms. The other regimental units were drawn up against the battalion, but when they were ordered to fire, all of them to a man lowered their rifles to the ground. Another regiment was summoned, and in ten minutes not a man of the mutinous battalion remained alive.

Next day two officers were hacked to pieces. Three days later, following a dispute between two cavalrymen, the entire regiment split into two camps. They fought each other until only a few were left unscathed.

Then men in mufti appeared and, encouraged by the officers, began to distribute leaflets among the troops. This time they did not make long speeches, but kept repeating one thing: the Jews have betrayed us, everything is their fault.

Once again someone handed a leaflet to Vasil, but he did not take it. He drew out of his pocket, with love and respect, as though it were a precious medallion, a crumpled piece of paper frayed at the edges and stained with blood, and showed it—he had it, and remembered it. The man with the leaflets, a slim little fellow with a sand-colored beard, half closed one of his little eyes and took stock of the squat broad-shouldered private with the short thick neck and bulging gray watery eyes. He gave Vasil a friendly pat on the back and left with a strange smile on his lips.

The Jewish privates had vanished: they had been quietly gathered together and sent away, no one knew where. Everyone felt freer and more comfortable, and although there were several nationalities represented among them, they were all of one mind about it; the alien was no longer in their midst.

And then someone launched a new slogan—"The Jewish government."

6

This was their last stand, and when they were again defeated they no longer stopped anywhere but ran like stampeding animals fleeing a steppe fire, in groups or individually, without commanders and without order, in deadly fear, rushing through every passage left open by the enemy. Not all of them had weapons, no one had his full outfit of clothing, and their shirts were like second skins on their unwashed bodies. The summer sun beat down on them mercilessly, and they ate only what they could forage. Now their native tongue was spoken in the towns, and their native fields lay around them, but the fields were unrecognizable, for last year's crops were rotting, trampled into the earth, and the land lay dry and gray and riddled, like the carcass of an ox disemboweled by wolves.

And while the armies crawled over the earth like swarms of gray worms, flocks of ravens soared overhead, calling with a dry rattling sound—the sound of tearing canvas—and swooped and slanted in intricate spirals, waiting for what would be theirs.

Between Kolov and Zhaditsa the starved and crazed legions caught up with large groups of Jews who had been ordered out of border towns, with their women, children, invalids, and bundles. A voice said, "Get them!" The words sounded like the distant boom of a gun. At first Vasil held back, but the loud screams of the women and children and the repulsive, terrified faces of the men with their long earlocks and caftans blowing in the wind drove him to a frenzy, and he cut into the Jews like a maddened bull. They were destroyed with merciful speed: the army trampled over them like a herd of galloping horses.

Then, once again, someone said in a shrill little voice, "The Jewish government!"

The words suddenly soared high and like a peal of thunder rolled over the wild legions, spreading to villages and cities and reaching the remotest corners of the land. The retreating troops struck out at the region with fire and sword. By night burning cities lighted their path, and by day the smoke obscured the sun and the sky and rolled in cottony masses over the earth,° and suffocated ravens occasionally fell to the ground. They burned the towns of Zykov, Potapno, Kholodno, Stary Yug, Sheliuba; Ostrogorie, Sava, Rika, Beloye Krilo, and Stupnik° were wiped from the face of the earth; the Jewish weaving town of Belopriazha went up in smoke, and the Vinokur Forest, where thirty thousand Jews had sought refuge, blazed like a bonfire, and for three days in succession agonized cries, like poisonous gases, rose from the woods and spread over the land. The swift, narrow Sinevodka River was entirely choked with human bodies a little below Lutsin and overflowed into the fields. On the ruins of Dobroslawa sat a madman, the sole survivor of the town, who howled like a dog.

The hosts grew larger. The peasant left his village and the city dweller his city; priests with icons and crosses in their hands led processions through villages, devoutly and enthusiastically blessing the people, and the slogan was, "The Jewish government." The Jews themselves realized that their last hour had struck—the very last; and those who remained alive set out to die among Jews in Maliassy, the oldest and largest Jewish center in the land, a seat of learning since the fourteenth century, a city of ancient synagogues and great yeshivas, with rabbis and modern scholars, with an aristocracy of learning and of trade. Here, in Maliassy, the Jews fasted and prayed, confessing their sins to God, begging forgiveness of friend and enemy. Aged men recited Psalms and Lamentations, younger men burned stocks of grain and clothing, demolished furniture, broke and destroyed everything that might be of use to the approaching army. And this army came, it came from all directions, and set fire to the city from all sides, and poured into the streets. Young men tried to resist and went out with revolvers in their hands. The revolvers sounded like pop guns. The soldiers answered with thundering laughter, and drew out the young men's veins one by one, and broke their bones into little pieces. Then they went from house to house, slaying the men wherever they were found and dragging the women to the marketplace.

7

One short blow with his fist smashed the lock, and the door opened.

For two days now Vasil had not eaten or slept. His skin smarted in the dry heat, his bones seemed disjointed, his eyes were bloodshot, and his face and neck were covered with blond stubble.

"Food!" he said hoarsely.

No one answered him. At the table stood a tall Jew in a black caftan, with a black beard and earlocks and gloomy eyes. He tightened his lips and remained stubbornly silent. Vasil stepped forward angrily and said again, "Food!"

But this time he spoke less harshly. Near the window he had caught sight of another figure—a young woman in white, with a head of black hair. Two large

Inversion of the Exodus from Egypt.

These are mostly fictional place names.

eyes—he has never before seen such large eyes—were looking at him and through him, and the look of these eyes was such that Vasil lifted his arm to cover his own eyes. His knees were trembling, he felt as if he were melting. What kind of woman is that? What kind of people? God! Why, why, did they have to sell Christ? And on top of it all, responsible for everything! Even Rachek admitted it. And they just kept quiet, looking through you. Goddamn it, what are they after? He took his head in his hands.

He felt something and looked about him. The Jew stood there, deathly pale, hatred in his eyes. For a moment Vasil stared dully. Suddenly he grabbed the black beard and pulled at it savagely.

A white figure stepped between them. Rage made Vasil dizzy and scalded his throat. He tugged at the white figure with one hand. A long strip tore from the dress and hung at the hem. His eyes were dazzled, almost blinded. Half a breast, a beautiful shoulder, a full, rounded hip—everything dazzling white and soft, like white *challah*. Damn it—these Jews are *made* of white *challah*! A searing flame leaped through his body, his arm flew up like a spring and shot into the gaping dress.

A hand gripped his neck. He turned his head slowly and looked at the Jew for a moment with narrowed eyes and bared teeth, without shaking free of the weak fingers that were clutching at his flesh. Then he raised his shoulders, bent forward, took the Jew by the ankles, lifted him in the air, and smashed him against the table. He flung him down like a broken stick.

The man groaned weakly; the woman screamed. But he was already on top of her. He pressed her to the floor and tore her dress together with her flesh. Now she was repulsive, her face blotchy, the tip of her nose red, her hair disheveled and falling over her eyes. "Witch," he said through his teeth. He twisted her nose like a screw. She uttered a shrill cry—short, mechanical, unnaturally high, like the whistle of an engine. The cry penetrating his brain maddened him completely. He seized her neck and strangled her.

A white shoulder was quivering before his eyes; a full, round drop of fresh blood lay glistening on it. His nostrils fluttered like wings. His teeth were grinding; suddenly they opened and bit into the white flesh.

White *challah* has the taste of a firm juicy orange. Warm and hot, and the more one sucks it the more burning the thirst. Sharp and thick, and strangely spiced.

Like rushing down a steep hill in a sled. Like drowning in sharp, burning spirits.

In a circle, in a circle, the juices of life went from body to body, from the first to the second, from the second to the first—in a circle.

Pillars of smoke and pillars of flame rose to the sky from the entire city. Beautiful was the fire on the great altar. The cries of the victims°—long-drawn-out, endless cries—were sweet in the ears of a god as eternal as the Eternal God. And the tender parts, the thighs and the breasts, were the portion of the priest.

Korbones—can also mean "ritual sacrifices."

1919

58 Among Refugees

DAVID BERGELSON

Returning home from the streets of Berlin one hot July day, I found my family tense and agitated. Their faces looked pale and very frightened.

They promptly informed me that a stranger had been waiting in my den for over three hours, a young man . . . a Jew.

"He's sort of. . ."

"Very impatient . . ."

They had informed the young man that I wouldn't be back before evening, but instead of replying, he had gone right into the den and sat himself down. They had made it clear to him: it would be better if he came back later on. At first he didn't take it in; then a bewildered look came over him. He had answered coldly:

"No, it's much better if they don't see me coming here and leaving too much. . . . You might have trouble with the police."

I went in to have a look at the young man. But he was a stranger to me too.

He seemed about twenty-six or -seven. He was sitting hunched over in a corner, in the farthest easy chair, as if drowsing.

His eyes were narrow, the shoulders hunched. His whole body reminded me of the gray dust on the far roads of small towns, and he seemed like someone who had breathlessly traveled a long distance.

I asked him whether he really wanted to see me. Not fully awaking, he answered as if in rebuke, "Of course, otherwise I wouldn't have come here. But please don't tell anyone. I have to do something here in Berlin. . . . I'm . . . Well, how shall I put it? . . . I'm a Jewish terrorist."

I didn't understand.

"Are you in a political party?" I asked.

"No," he made a face. "I hate political parties."

I clearly was dealing with someone who had come to me along confused and crooked roads. What could have brought him to me? I left him alone for a while. But, sitting at the table in the dining room, I couldn't put his face or his appearance out of my mind for even an instant. I couldn't help thinking what my family had said to me upon my return:

"He's sort of. . ."

"Impatient . . ."

There are people who look dusty even though you won't find a speck of dust on them—the young man was such a person: he had high cheekbones, which were uneven and made his cheeks look dissimilar. The right cheek was the same as on all faces—a cheek that wants to enjoy the world, that says, "I want to be with people."

And his left cheek was crooked; it looked as though it were his and yet. . . . It was like a cheek at war with the world—it had fallen out of favor with life, and therefore life had fallen out of favor with it. The left cheek made the young man look ugly, but apparently he had sided with it. He reminded me of a mother who has a beautiful child and a monster—for justice's sake he was on the side of the ugly left cheek and bore within himself its badness. Because of the ugly cheek he wore a mustache—he wanted it, no matter how slightly, to cover the crookedness. I saw the mustache instantly and thought, the right cheek isn't pleased with it because the mustache has an unusual color of dirty brass. It commands your attention and announces, "Don't bother me. I'm nasty. It would be better if you go your way, and I'll go mine."

All this was sharply pronounced on his face. Sitting in the other room, I was very ill at ease, I kept feeling his eyes on me through the thick wall.

When I went back, he was still sitting in the same place, indifferent. Two bright sparks were burning in his eyes—akin to the flames of memorial candles lit early in the evening, but they may have looked that way because of the sunset.

Outside, beyond the long curtains, I could feel the gigantic checkered streets beginning to come alive, to swarm, to give off the huge dry heat they had been breathing throughout the long day—a day like a year, a day like a long, long road. On a day like this, looking back, you think to yourself, you've walked a tremendously long distance. A day like this drives all the lonely eccentrics out into the streets, and they roam around, like mute, restless ghosts.

Once, on a day like this, in the park, a lonely person had sat down on my bench and started saying that you're never so lonely as when you're among people and that you're never so thoroughly "among people" as in a big city. I couldn't help remembering that incident as I gazed at my visitor. I asked him, "Are you a refugee?"

"A refugee."

"From where?"

He named a large city in the sandy parts of Volhynia. He glanced around to make sure the door behind us was tightly shut, and he showed me some documents to prove that he really came from that city and that he had been a pioneer in Palestine. Next, he mentioned the name of an infamous Ukrainian pogromist. He asked whether I had heard about the man's terrible butcheries. He glared hard at me with the blazing flames in his eyes, and I sensed that the difficult and terrible thing he had to tell me was beginning: so far, he had been polite—he had been speaking on behalf of his right cheek—now, he would be speaking on behalf of his left cheek, the crooked one. . . .

We sat facing one another in a remote corner of the room. He pronounced the name of the infamous pogromist and began with these words:

"Listen . . . he's here now . . . in Berlin."

He glared even harder at me and started telling me the whole story.

"Listen: For nearly three weeks, I've been living 'with him' here in this city in a cheap rooming house. I, in room number three. He, in room number five—our doors facing one another. I'm a stranger here. No one knows me. He doesn't know me either. But I know him very well.

"Sometimes:

"We meet in the hallway. At the entrance, there's a worn red doormat—both of us wipe the dust off our shoes. You understand—on the very same doormat. . . . And then: As he passes, he glances at me. I bolt into my room and I can still feel his gaze right here and here. . . . (The young man quickly slapped both his cheeks.) My eyes dart into the mirror. I wonder what he saw in me. A seedy young Jew. Sometimes I don't shave for days on end. I gaze with tired, bloodshot eyes. I'm often pallid like someone who's been fasting day after day. That's all, isn't it? What else can he possibly see in me?

"But I know *him* from back home. I've known him since my childhood; from every Jewish trouble, from a lot of different troubles. He aroused the populaces of four whole provinces; you think he's like Purishkevich,° like Krushevan?°° He's a lot worse. He led pogroms himself, the recent ones, the most terrible ones. He vanished each time and then resurfaced leading a new slaughter of Jews. He wore a beard, he spoke simply so the peasants would take him for one of their own and believe him. But here, abroad, he's shaved off his beard, and he dresses up. He's become an aristocrat again. He's strong, tall, his face is ruddy, full. His mustache is cheerfully twirled out. His eyes are nasty and they have a venomous twinkle. The venomous twinkle of his butcheries.

"Next to him, I'm pale and bent. Do you see? Not so much short as bent. Ever since childhood, my face has been squashed and crooked as though it had been run over. I wear a mustache, see. . . . I'm not attractive, especially in profile. . . . It runs in the family. . . . You think I don't realize? Of all the young men I know, I'm the ugliest. And I was the ugliest back home, in my town. That was why I lived apart from the other children, all alone, like an orphan. Picture me back then on summer evenings: a twelve-year-old schoolboy with brass buttons, a schoolboy running off to synagogue after his pious grandfather to say evening prayers, like a puppy finding refuge with him. And not because others are biting it, but because the other schoolboys never notice me. I can stand among them, and it's as if no one were standing among them. To go to synagogue, you have to walk along the Boulevard—that's the main street. On a summer evening, schoolboys, you know, like to get all dressed up and stroll about five or six abreast. The schoolboy running after his grandfather halts. He looks at the strollers, they don't notice him. The schoolboy takes fright and runs fast, fast, after his grandfather. . . . And I really was an orphan—from the age of eight. My grandfather's children died young. . . . He was small, gray, with a hairy face. Waxen features, with hair in his nose and his ears, with smacking lips and cold black little eyes, darting either way, like a monkey's eyes. But there was no hair growing from his eyes. When he spoke, very few people could understand what he said. They would seldom come to his home, but they did come to pay him money, interest. His house was big and deserted. . . . It stood on the Boulevard, at the very end. The only people living in it were Grandfather, myself and an elderly maid from way back. And Grandfather had an odd habit: every time a child of his died, he would buy a clock and set it up or hang it in one of the rooms. By the time I was fourteen or fifteen the clocks were everywhere; a clock in every room—all of Grandfather's children had died. At dawn, when Grandfather got up, he would first wind all the clocks, like a mother who starts by feeding all her children. He hums, he has no voice. When he sings, it's like a cat snorting under the table. Our whole family is like that. And so am I—I have no voice. Grandfather's hairy face is like a clock—the nose is the hand, the eyes are two numbers. The clocks strike, Grandfather hums.

"And right across the Boulevard, at the very end too, is where the Pinskys live. A large family, a merry one. Almost every week they enjoy some new success.

V.N. Purishkevich (1870–1920), leader of the anti-Semitic faction in the Russian parliament and founder of "the Black Hundreds."

P.A. Krushevan, editor of the anti-Semitic Bessarabets; chief instigator of the Kishinev pogrom.

They give banquets. And Pinksky's younger son Zorah lives right across from our windows, which are always shut. But the windows over there are always open, always merry; so are the balconies. Zorah has nothing but daughters, nothing but young girls, nothing but schoolgirls in dark-brown dresses with well-ironed white collars, nothing but lovely, charming, dark-haired girls. With the scent of Palmolive soap, especially the youngest, with a dimple below her two front teeth. You know? The way it happens sometimes. And right there, with that dimple below her two front teeth, it all begins, all the beauty in her face, her body, and her movements, when she rides her bicycle like all her sisters. They play piano over there. Even now, whenever I heard a piano being played somewhere, I remember: Ahhh! It's the Pinskys. They're having a birthday party, schoolboys arrive—we can see it on their balcony from Grandfather's window.

"In our house, the clocks are striking. Somewhere, in one of the rooms, Grandfather is humming over a holy book, snorting like an old cat. And I wander among the clocks. Every clock is a grave, a memorial candle. I am a schoolboy, I study hard, all day long, all summer long. And what do you think? What do I think about? I think about doing something for spite. . . . Do you understand? About doing something. A thing that no one across the way, over on the merry balcony, would do. And for spite, you can do something ugly. For spite, you can do something lovely—it's all the same, as long as it's for spite.

"Then the war caught up with me, but I didn't try to get out of it, like others, do you understand? . . . as though for spite. But right after the war ended, almost by itself, my feeling of spite also ended. I felt a sorrow at my loss:

"Where is my spite?

"That was why I was one of the first to leave my town after it was ravaged by a pogrom, and I became a common laborer in Palestine—as though for spite. But later on, when a lot of children from well-to-do families in my town started coming to Palestine, and some of the young Pinskys were among them, I left Palestine and came here, to this city. Here, at the very same time, I started to go hungry and to write. I thought to myself, 'People like me are the kind who want to blow up the world with dynamite. I won't let it happen. On the contrary: I'll break in on the other side.'

"I thought up a story, not about myself, but about someone else. The story begins by describing a certain Jewish pauper in our town. Every Thursday, the pauper goes begging among the rich Jews who live in the gentile neighborhood. The pauper is greatly despised by the Christian children there. They can't stand him. The moment they catch sight of him, they pelt him with stones and sic their dogs on him. Loud shouts arise all over the Christian neighborhood. The air is full of cries, a trampling of feet, a barking of dogs. The pauper is terribly afraid of dogs. His teeth chatter, yet he's glad, because the yelling and barking inform everyone that he's arrived in the Christian neighborhood. The alms are brought out to him from every Jewish home; he doesn't have to waste time knocking at every Jewish door individually. When the pauper arrives in the Christian neighborhood, he stops in the middle of the street and starts to cough so that the kids will see him and sic their dogs on him. . . .

"I wrote it all in one breath. Those were the first chapters and I instantly felt that the pauper was myself; do you understand? Again myself. . . . The Christian neighborhood—that was my town in disguise, my life, but no one is siccing dogs on me. They don't even bark at me, and yet I can feel them barking. My cough—that's my serving in the army, my going to war, my leaving for Palestine as a common laborer. . . . The act of spite that I've wanted to commit ever since my childhood—that's my way of begging for alms. . . . But since actually I want to give on my own . . . you understand? To be a rich man just once in my life, to cast out alms like this, with an open hand—just look. . . . And in those days, when I thought such things (I couldn't sleep night after night), I heard a slight noise early one morning in the corridor of my rooming house—the noise was mixed with the sharp sound of Ukrainian. I looked out into the corridor, and first I saw a chambermaid. She was carrying two heavy suitcases; and then I saw *him* in the flesh, with his cheerfully twirled mustaches. He was respectfully followed by some younger man.

" 'Oh yes?' he asked the younger man in Ukrainian, and sniffed the air with his nose, 'Aren't there any Jews here?'

"I was standing by my door. I watched the chambermaid take him right across from me, to room number five. I was stupefied. And suddenly a feeling of lightness came to me in my daze, as though I weren't alone anymore. Some portion of me had arrived. I felt so much lighter, although I still didn't know what this lightness was. It wasn't till later that I asked, 'Just why do I feel so joyous? Why?' "

There was a knock at the door of my den. They were calling me to the dining room. And then it began getting dark in my den as though evening were settling in. The young man asked for some water. He held the glass by its edge. His hand shivered slightly; he looked very pensively at his feet as though trying to see whether he had lost something down there, something of what he wanted to tell me. He said, "What was my purpose in telling you these things? I want you to understand who I am. . . . Now you'll believe me, because no one could make up such a story out of thin air. I don't think I've left anything out, have I? I've told you about Zorah Pinsky and about his daughter, haven't I? Yes, I have. That was everything, everything that happened to me back then, until I felt that I was going to kill *him*. You understand? Among so many Jews, I, of all people, I, to whom the whole story happened. Just think: Who else, if not I?"

In the darkness of the room I could see the two white spots in the corners of his mouth. White spots that come from much talking. He put down the glass.

We were sitting again face to face in the corner of the room. I asked him a question, and the two memorial candles in his eyes started going out and lighting up over and over again, like fires with which sailors signal at sea. He began talking again.

"Why do you ask, *When* did I decide to kill *him?* What difference does it make? And besides, does a man decide a thing like that? I remember the first thing I decided on was the place. . . . One day I left my room and went into the corridor, and I saw him: he was standing there, talking on the telephone. He was obviously hearing bad news. As he held the receiver to his ear, his eyes began to widen, the savage venom burned stronger in them. He asked, 'Whaaat?' And the 'what' was drawn out and terrified. I stool aside, and someone inside me thought: Right there by the telephone is the best place, right there, you could kill him with one shot. You understand? It wasn't I who thought so, but someone else.

"True, in one of the slaughters for which he alone was responsible, they killed my grandfather, the old man with the waxen face and the two cold eyes that dart right and left, like a monkey's eyes. But the pity I've always felt for my grandfather is not really mine either, it too belongs to someone else. . . . So then there:

"Right there by the telephone, I thought, there's no better place possible.

"And as I thought this, I felt myself filling up with joy. I suddenly wanted things to be joyful. I went to a restaurant and ate lunch, spending nearly all the money I possessed—a lunch with a glass of wine. I felt I was carrying around something in my heart that hadn't been in my heart earlier and that no one around me had. When I went outside, I saw, as though for the first time in my life, that it was a beautiful summer day. Lots of people were strolling about in the street, lovely people. . . . My feeling for them was like that of a man who has to go on a long journey and is having a difficult time taking leave of his family: he hasn't even managed to embrace them, as is proper, to hug them tight, as is proper, but he does have to leave. And that was how I felt about them all, all of them without exception—like shadows. I haven't really clasped them properly and I already have to leave them.

"I walked around a whole day with that feeling in my heart, and then, by the time I got home, it was already evening. Our two doors glared at one another severely. I tell you, the only doors that can glare at one another in that way are the doors in a rooming house where *that thing* has to happen. Door number three glared at door number five and seemed to be saying, 'My man, who lives behind me, is going to kill your man, who lives behind you.'

"Have you ever seen such doors? You sleep in your room all night long. You seem to be sleeping very soundly, but in your sleep you remember their numbers—number three glares at number five. . . .

"And then suddenly I woke very early, at sunrise. I peeped into the hallway and saw that our shoes had been put out to be shined: mine—at my door; and his—at his door. Mine—worn-out Jewish boots with sagging elastics (they've already been to Palestine)—and his—solid goyish boots with shafts that go up under the trousers.

"He's here, at home, I thought to myself.

"And I felt good at the thought, as though I weren't alone any more. I looked at the place by the telephone—the best place. . . .

"And again I wanted everything to be joyful around me. Back in my room I opened up the window facing the street.

"The sun was coming up.

"Empty streets.

"A few sleepy, freshly washed faces.

"Workers going to work, one by one.

" 'Tu-whit, tu-whit,' the whistling of a bird came into my room from a nearby tree, a whistle more reminiscent of life than any others; and at the sound of that 'tu-whit, tu-whit' I felt the same as I had felt the night before about people, as though I were about to go on a long journey, and we were having a difficult time taking leave of that 'tu-whit, tu-whit.'

"From then on, I began watching *him* in the rooming house.

"It was good to know that *he* was there in the room across from me, behind door number five, and I always felt desolate whenever *he* went off somewhere and his room remained empty. The hours would stretch out so, and the minutes too.

"I would wander around my room and through the corridor and I would feel: if he doesn't come, in the next minutes, my heart will explode. . . .

"I have to tell you:

"He signed his own name, personally, in the guest book of our rooming house. Under his name there's the flourish of a man who's satisfied with himself. He came from Copenhagen. A dead city. Copenhagen. Jews there are busy with their own bits of life. No one even hunted for *him*.

"I look at the flourish underneath his name, and I'm annoyed at his peace of mind. He would never dream of keeping up his guard. We're like bedbugs in his eyes—I, you, all the people he butchered.

"A lot of people visit him.

"The young Russian comes, the one who first brought *him* to the rooming house. Someone else comes, an older man, with a beard, and someone else, a young woman in black.

"And across the way you can hear him then:

"Snorting with a hard, cheerful laugh.

"And then, late at night, when I lie awake, I feel such a strong desire to go out into the corridor with a knife and do something. . . . Even if it's just cutting a hole in his boots there. Just like that. So that he'll know that someone's after him. It wouldn't disturb his peace of mind. . . .

"I don't do it—simply because that would ruin the whole thing, and because both of us are guarded by the *place* in the corridor at the telephone—the place now controls us both.

"He comes to the telephone several times a day, and I already know:

"The *thing* will take place by evening, at least no earlier than in the afternoon.

"Although I didn't think about it before. It came precisely, automatically, as though someone had given me an assignment and said, 'You have to do it by such and such a time, in such and such a place.'

"And that was why I didn't worry about anything, as though someone had prepared everything for me in advance. All I would have to do is accept and carry it out. And it was only then that I remembered, once, at night, 'I don't have anything to do it with.'

"You understand, don't you? A knife is no good. A knife often merely leaves a scratch. The surest thing is—a gun. I'm a veteran. I'm strong and I can shoot, but I'm a stranger in this city, this cauldron. There's no one I can get a gun from. And besides, I have very little money, just enough to live on for a few days. The money won't suffice, but even if I did have the money, where could I buy it? In a weapons store? That's no good. With someone of my appearance—just look at me—with someone like me, they would instantly realize that he's buying the gun with his last few pennies and that he wants to do something with it. Assuming you can buy firearms in stores, without a permit, I don't believe it, but in a city like this, a cauldron, the police certainly never stop looking for various 'elements' that are preparing to do something, and if they look for them anywhere, then what better place than a weapons store. Suppose they apprehend me there. They won't find anything on me, but there'll be a big commotion. As far as the police here are concerned, my papers aren't quite in order.

"They could come and inquire about me at the rooming house.

"*He* could find out and vanish.

"I could ruin the whole *thing*.

"I'm such a bungler!

"I have to find some sort of solution and do something, but it's already difficult for me to think. You understand? I thought quite a bit before I began preparing the *thing*. Now I'm like a drunk doing everything in his power so that no one will realize he's drunk. A man like that feels that with every move he makes, everyone around him will realize everything, everything. . . .

"What would you do in my place?

"Just imagine—you're sober. . . .

"You would certainly ask someone for help. But you have to realize: I have no family in the city—and no friends either.

"There are a few people here from my home town, but I never see them. I don't even know where they live.

"There's a fellow here from my town, Beryl Hum—that's what he was called back home, although his real name was Boris Blum. That's what he was called, because he was always buzzing around the Zionists and writing for their Russian newspapers. He's a capable man, he knows several languages, he always hits it off with perfect strangers, even Christians.

"He's already ingratiated himself with a few German newspapers, and now he's writing for them. He runs around with a briefcase under his arm.

"There's someone else here from my home town, Zorah Pinsky and his daughter. I've already told you about her. She was the most beautiful girl in town, and you can imagine what happened to her in the pogrom. . . . That's what people said, although no one ever heard it from the Pinskys.

"People said that among the Pinskys every swelling goes down; the Pinskys wipe their lips. I was told they came out unscathed. They've got their wits about them, even in times of pogroms. . . .

"The Pinskys are here now—I knew it even before I left Palestine. But I don't want to ask them for help. I don't even want them to know I'm here. Do you understand? It's more important to me than anything else. It's my secret.

"I go to the big park every day. I sit on a bench. I think about finding a solution. And when I sit there and think, I feel glad that the Pinskys don't know anything about it. They'll find out later as soon as I've done the thing. They'll find out about it at dusk, from the evening papers. It will be cloudy out. It will be raining. Or else the sky may be clear, the sun will be setting. No matter: every future moment of my life seems strange, every moment that will come later, after I do the *thing*. All people, whether strangers or from my native town, seem indifferently near and indifferently far. They're all mixed up in my mind with the vesper sounds of a faraway church, reaching me in the big park after I've sat on a bench all alone, through a long, long day, thinking that I'm going to do the *thing*.

"And, at such times, what do I care about this whole foreign cauldron of yours with its hubbub and with all the people running around in it and filling it up? What do I care about them, even if *she* is here—Pinsky's daughter—one of the people for whom I'm going to do the *thing*.

"All I care about is the days when I sit on and on in the city park.

"I can't tell you how long it went on. Perhaps, a whole week and more;

perhaps, just three or four days. I don't count the weeks anymore. Or the days. I've stopped. . . .

"But once, when I was sitting near a lively avenue in the park, who should pass by but Beryl Hum, or rather, Boris Blum, which is his real name. He walked by quickly with his briefcase under his arm, with the sweaty little forelock of a man who has to run all over the city cauldron thus every day. He turned to me with his darkly tanned face and with the white handkerchief in his lapel pocket, ready to wipe his wet forehead. He looked at me with those bewildered eyes, greeted me, and promptly sat down at my side and began asking, astonished:

" 'How long have you been in Berlin?'

" 'Not very long,' I said, 'not very long.'

" 'Why, I heard you were in Palestine.'

" 'I came here from Palestine.'

" 'You have a job here?'

" 'No,' I said, 'I don't have a job here.'

"I can't remember everything we talked about. I noticed him scrutinizing me in a bewildered way. He was staring at my clothes and the way I looked in general.

"I didn't like it. And that may have been the very reason why I started telling him everything I've told you up till now, but much more briefly. He remembered me very well from back home. He knew my grandfather, and he could believe every word I said.

"I told him that now the whole *thing* depends solely on him, and so our meeting should not remain a chance encounter, because the thing I'm going to do is not just *my* thing. Precisely because I have no one else to turn to, he himself will have to get everything for me, everything I need for the *thing*. And besides, he's always in Jewish groups here. He associates with them, and they associate with him. As a result, he has more responsibilities than a speculator, or a simple man in the street. Who should I turn to, if not him?

"I saw that even though he was very busy and very bewildered, he was nevertheless listening to everything I had to say, and not coldly either—there was sympathy in his large bewildered eyes.

" 'That's incredible!' he said. 'It's simply. . . . Why, in Palestine, if an Arab kills a Jew, then a few hours later you'll find a dead Arab, and here, among so many Jews, all these pogromists are running around scot-free, and there's not a single Jew around to get rid of even one of them. A strange people! What a strange people!'

"And he started looking at me again in bewilderment. He looked at my face, at my overall appearance, even at the shoes and hat I was wearing.

" 'It's simply incredible!' he said. 'Simply incredible! A knife certainly won't be of any use for a *thing* like that. A Jewish student once used a knife on a Jew-baiter, and all he did was scratch him. You really have to have a gun. Too bad . . . you were in the war . . . you know how to shoot . . . wait a moment . . . wait a moment. . . .'

"And he rested his chin on his hand and started thinking.

" 'Fine.' He suddenly got up from the bench and shook my hand. 'I'll take care of it. I'll get it for you. But wait a moment, when? Tomorrow. Give me your address. . . . Tomorrow morning you'll get a note from me. . . . OK? No, it would be better if we met somewhere. . . . Where? Right here in the park would be the best place, right here on this bench. Tomorrow afternoon, at the very same time, 3 P.M.'

"He hurried off with his briefcase under his arm. I saw him walk for a while and then look back at me. He walked again for a while, and then again he looked back at me. That's the way it was. . . .

"The next afternoon at the stroke of three, to the very minute, I was already sitting in the park on the very same bench. I waited for him for a very long time. I just sat there, waiting. I was sure he wouldn't come. But I still kept sitting there.

"Around five o'clock, he suddenly showed up on the promenade. He didn't come over to my bench.

" 'Come on,' he beckoned to me with his eyes, in passing. 'Follow me.'

"And we went off. Him first, and me a few yards behind him, as though we didn't know one another. He got into a streetcar, and so did I, still as though I didn't know him.

"He sat in one corner, and I in the other. We thus rode on, for a long, long time, and perhaps it only seemed long because I was so impatient.

"I thought to myself: Where is he taking me? We were already downtown, the streets were thronged.

"We kept going—the streets were still thronged.

"We got out, he first, I behind him. Again an unfamiliar street, a narrow one, and then another street. We stole into a courtyard, crept up a stairway. We entered through a door—a small, dark, dusty corridor.

"I instantly realized: it wasn't his home, it looked like some kind of commercial office where you don't work past 3 P.M., and then you lock up and leave it empty.

"In the second or third little room after the corridor, there were about five people sitting around a table, and by the way they were sitting there I could tell they had gathered especially because of the *thing* I was going to do. I understood that they were important men in the community, and that Beryl Hum had summoned them because he didn't want to take full responsibility by himself. They were no longer young. One of them had gray hair, a second one was tall and chubby, and he was completely bald, his sharp, bulging eyes stared severely, his chin jutted out, and he looked like a man who is always puffing his cheeks. Imagine: I was confused enough, but it suddenly struck me that he's always fighting with his wife—I mean the man with the bald head—I really don't know why, but it simply struck me that way, and he kept staring at me incessantly.

"And no one said anything to me. For a while, we sat around the table wordlessly. I waited. Any moment now, they would start talking to me.

"But instead of talking to me, they kept summoning one another into the next room to exchange secrets. From the very start, they kept whispering there in pairs, and then in groups of three and four, and all of them with Beryl Hum. They kept coming back and then summoning one another to talk in private. . . .

"I noticed: The group was slowly shrinking, they were leaving one by one.

"I heard: They were going into the corridor one by one and hurrying down the stairs.

"But why was Beryl Hum one of the first to vanish? I simply couldn't understand. . . .

"And when all of them were gone, the only one left with me in the room was the tall, chubby one with the bald head and the severe, bulging eyes.

"I noticed: He kept shifting closer and closer to me, his sharp eyes peered right into my face, and so severely that I could feel his bulging gaze in my eyes, in my heart; but he kept shifting closer and closer. And when his chest was already grazing mine, he suddenly said, 'Listen,' he said to me, 'I'm a doctor . . . a psychiatrist. . . .'

"He peered even more severely into my eyes and said more boldly, 'I'm a doctor . . . a psychiatrist. . . .'

"What could I answer him? I shifted away, and my heart began pounding, even though he was still talking to me.

"Then something pushed me toward him, and not so much me, as my hand . . . this very hand . . . do you see my hand? My arm is muscular . . . it was in the war . . . and it wasn't till later, when I was down in the street again, that I felt it hadn't helped me at all—I mean slapping his face so furiously. . . . Because if they think I'm out of my mind, then the fact that I slapped him will just convince them all the more . . . and besides . . . my sorrow won't be any the less for it.

"Beryl Hum really made a mess of things. A few big pot-bellied Jews got together—for what? For curiosity's sake? To have a look at me? One of them was Beryl Hum, who only yesterday had said, 'Incredible! It's really incredible! In Palestine, when an Arab kills a Jew, they promptly kill an Arab, even if he's a total stranger.'

"Why am I out of my mind if I want to kill a pogromist who is guilty of so much bloodshed?

"Walking all alone, I immediately began sorting out the words that the tall bald man had spoken when he had moved so close to me. He had said something about a sanitorium where I could 'rest' for a couple of weeks. . . . About well-to-do people from my town who were here now and had expressed their willingness to pay for my stay in the sanatorium. . . .

"But just who are these well-to-do people from my town if not Zorah Pinsky and his family? Does it mean that Beryl Hum had already discussed the thing with them too, that they too regard me as being that way? And suddenly I got so depressed, as never before in my life.

"I was pained by everything around me, everything my eyes saw along the way: the city, the street, the cars, the noise, and most of all, the hour pained me . . . the evening hour, 7 P.M. At this time of day, *he* stands there in the corridor, by the telephone, every day. . . . All last night I paced up and down my room. I was certain that today, finally, at this time, at the telephone, I would make an end of it. . . . What was there left to do?

"And I felt all the more strongly about doing the *thing*, so that people would read about it in the evening papers. Let them all read about it, all of them, the five important men, Beryl Hum, and the Pinskys—let her read about it. . . . She was one of the people for whom I was going to do the *thing*. . . .

"I began thinking: Isn't there a Jewish group around here somewhere, a group that would help me? I thought to myself, 'Is there anybody at all—possibly a writer? Writers, I thought, are the conscience of the nation. They are its nerves; they present their nation to the world. People read a writer's works because they want to find out how his nation lived in his time.

"And so I came to you. I've told you everything. You must know—tomorrow, or the day after, *he* may suddenly get up and vanish from the rooming house. And now that I've told you everything, you are as responsible as I am, and even more than I am, because you're a writer. . . . I've been sitting with you here, in this dark room, and for a long time now I've been wanting to ask you, Please turn on the light. I want to see your face. . . ."

Almost in a daze, I stood up to turn on the light. I did it as though the young man's last few words were no more than a joke, than the words of an eccentric with peculiar ideas. But I forgot these feelings the moment I turned on the light and saw the young man's face.

His crooked left cheek was burning as though with a dark steely fire. His right cheek was drowsy right up to the eye and was practically out of the running. It seemed lifeless; the burning left cheek was in control with its entire crookedness. And the young man himself was no longer speaking simply. It was as though he were quarreling with me, demanding his due from me. And the thing he was demanding was minor: a gun.

Staring at me with the fire that was in his drowsy left eye, he was arguing, fairly screaming. And I kept looking at the fires that were in his eyes.

The young man told me, "Listen, if you want to refuse, then don't refuse right away. Think it over first. I'll give you all night. If you decide to do as I ask, then send me the gun. I'll give you my address. I'll wait."

A few days later, I received a note from the young man with the crooked cheek:

"I've found a solution. Behind the mirror that hangs in my room, number three, in the rooming house, there is a hook. The rope on which the mirror hangs will be sufficient. . . . I understand the whole thing now: I am a refugee . . . among refugees. . . . I don't want to be one anymore. . . ."

1924

59 And Then There Were None

ISAAC BABEL

The prisoners are dead, all nine of them. I feel it in my bones.

Yesterday, when Corporal Golov, a worker from Sormovo, killed the lanky Pole, I said to our staff officer that the corporal was setting a bad example for the men and that we ought to make up a list of the prisoners and send them back for questioning. The staff officer agreed. I got a pencil and paper out of my knapsack and called Golov. He gave me a look of hatred and said, "You look at the world through those spectacles of yours."

"Yes, I do," I replied. "And what do you look at the world through, Golov?"

"I look at it through the dog's life of us workers," he said and, carrying in his hands a Polish uniform with dangling sleeves, he walked back toward one of the prisoners. He had tried it on, and it did not fit him—the sleeves scarcely reached down to his elbows.

Now Golov fingered the prisoner's smart-looking underpants. "You're an officer," Golov said, shielding his face from the sun with one hand.

"No," came the Pole's curt answer.

"The likes of us don't wear that sort of stuff," Golov muttered and fell silent. He said nothing, quivering as he looked at the prisoner, his eyes blank and wide.

"My mother knitted them," the prisoner said in a firm voice.

I turned around and looked at him. He was a slim-waisted youth with curly sideburns on his sallow cheeks. "My mother knitted them," he said again and looked down.

"She knits like a machine, that mother of yours," Andrushka Burak butted in. Burak is the pink-faced Cossack with silky hair who had pulled the trousers off the lanky Pole as he lay dying. These trousers were now thrown over his saddle. Laughing, Andrushka rode up to Golov, carefully took the uniform out of his hands, threw it over the saddle on top of the trousers, and, with a slight flick of his whip, rode away from us again. At this moment the sun poured out from behind the dark clouds. It cast a dazzling light on Andrushka's horse as it cantered off perkily with carefree movements of its docked tail. Golov looked after the departing Cossack with a bemused expression. He turned around and saw me writing out the list of prisoners. Then he saw the young Pole with his curly sideburns, who glanced at him with the calm disdain of youth and smiled at his confusion. Next, Golov cupped his hands to his mouth and shouted, "This is still a republic, Andrushka! You'll get your share later. Let's have that stuff back."

Andrushka turned a deaf ear. He rode on at a gallop, and his horse swung its tail friskily, just as though it was brushing us off.

"Traitor," Golov said, pronouncing the word very clearly. He looked sulky and his face went stiff. He knelt down on one knee, took aim with his rifle, and fired, but he missed.

Andrushka immediately turned his horse around and charged right up to the corporal. His fresh, pink-cheeked face was angry. "Listen, brother!" he shouted loud and clear and was suddenly pleased by the sound of his own strong voice. "Want to get hurt, you bastard? Why the fuss about finishing off ten Poles? We've killed them off by the hundreds before now without asking your help. Call yourself a worker? Make a job of it, then." And looking at us in triumph, Andrushka galloped off.

Golov did not look up at him. He put his hand to his forehead. Blood was pouring off it like rain off a hayrick. He lay down on his stomach, crawled over to a ditch, and for a long time held his battered, bleeding head in the shallow trickle of water.

The prisoners are dead. I feel it in my bones.

Sitting on my horse, I made a list of them in neat columns. In the first column I numbered them in order, in the second column I gave their names, and in the third the units to which they belonged. It worked out to nine altogether. The fourth was Adolf Shulmeister, a Jewish clerk from Lodz. He kept pressing up to my horse and stroked and caressed my boot with trembling fingers. His leg had been broken with a rifle butt. It left a thin trail of blood like that of a wounded dog, and sweat, glistening in the sun, bubbled on his cracked, yellowish bald pate.

"You are a *Jude*, sir!" he whispered, frantically fondling my stirrup. "You are—" he squealed, the spittle dribbling from his mouth, and his whole body convulsed with joy.

"Get back into line, Shulmeister!" I shouted at the Jew, and suddenly, overcome by a deathly feeling of faintness, I began to slip from the saddle and, choking, I said, "How did you know?"

"You have that nice Jewish look about you," he said in a shrill voice, hopping on one leg and leaving the thin dog's trail behind him. "That nice Jewish look, sir."

His fussing had a sense of death about it, and I had quite a job fending him off. It took me some time to come to, as though I had had a concussion. The staff officer ordered me to see to the machine guns and rode off. The machine guns were being dragged up a hill, like calves on halters. They moved side by side, like one herd, and clanked reassuringly. The sun played on their dusty barrels, and I saw a rainbow on the metal.

The young Pole with the curly sideburns looked at them with peasant curiosity. He leaned right forward, thus giving me a view of Golov as he crawled out of the ditch, weary and pale, with his battered head, and his rifle raised. I stretched out my hand toward him and shouted, but the sound stuck in my throat, to choke and swell there. Golov quickly shot the prisoner in the back of the head and jumped to his feet. The startled Pole swung around to him, turning on his heels as though obeying an order on parade. With the slow movement of a woman giving herself to a man, he raised both hands to the back of his neck, slumped to the ground, and died instantly.

A smile of relief and satisfaction now came over Golov's face. His cheeks quickly regained their color. "*Our* mothers don't knit pants like that for us," he said to me slyly. "Scratch one and give me that list for the other eight."

I gave him the list and said despairingly, "You'll answer for all this, Golov."

"I'll answer for it, all right!" he shouted with indescribable glee. "Not to you, spectacles, but to my own kind, to the people back in Sormovo! They know what's what."

The prisoners are dead. I feel it in my bones.

This morning I decided I must do something in memory of them. Nobody else but me would do this in the Red Cavalry. Our unit has camped in a devastated Polish country estate. I took my diary and went into the flower garden, which was untouched. Hyacinths and blue roses were growing there.

I began to make notes about the corporal and the nine dead men. But I was immediately interrupted by a noise—an all-too-familiar noise. Cherkashin, the staff toady, was plundering the beehives. Mitya, who had pink cheeks and came from Orel, was following him with a smoking torch in his hands. They had wrapped greatcoats around their heads. The slits of their eyes were ablaze. Myriads of bees were trying to fight off their conquerors and were dying by their hives. And I put aside my pen. I was horrified at the great number of memorials still to be written.

1923

60 The Rabbi's Son

ISAAC BABEL

Do you remember Zhitomir, Vasily? Do you remember the River Teterev, Vasily, and that night when the Sabbath, the young Sabbath crept along the sunset, crushing the stars beneath her little red heel?

The slender horn of the moon bathed its darts in the dark waters of the river. Queer old Gedali, the founder of the Fourth International, led us to Rabbi Motale Bratslavsky's for evening prayers.° Queer old Gedali shook the cock's feathers on his top hat in the ruddy haze of evening. The predatory eyes of lighted candles blinked in the Rabbi's room. Broad-shouldered Jews groaned dully, bent over prayerbooks, and the old buffoon of the Chernobyl *tsaddiks* jingled coppers in his frayed pocket.

The name is evocative of Nahman of Bratslav (1772–1810), the only tsaddik who left no heirs.

Do you remember that night, Vasily? Beyond the window, horses were neighing and Cossacks shouting. The wilderness of war yawned beyond the window, and Rabbi Motale Bratslavsky prayed by the eastern wall, digging his emaciated fingers into his talith. Then the curtain of the Ark was drawn aside, and we saw in the funereal candlelight the Torah rolls sheathed in covers of purple velvet and blue silk° and, bowed above the Torah, inanimate and resigned, the beautiful face of Elijah the Rabbi's son, last prince of the dynasty.

Either a memory lapse or poetic license: The Torah is not read at Friday night services.

Well, only the day before yesterday, Vasily, the regiments of the XII Army opened the front at Kovel. The conqueror's bombardment thundered disdainfully over the town. Our troops faltered, and mingled in confusion. The Political Section train started crawling over the dead backbone of the fields. And a monstrous and inconceivable Russia tramped in bast shoes on either side of the coaches, like a multitude of bugs swarming in clothes. The typhus-ridden peasantry rolled before them the customary humpback of a soldier's death. They jumped up on to the steps of our train and fell back, dislodged by the butt-ends of our rifles. They snorted and scrabbled and flowed on wordlessly. And at the twelfth verst, when I had no potatoes left, I flung a pile of Trotsky's leaflets at them. But only one man among them stretched a dead and filthy hand to catch a leaflet. And I recognized Elijah, son of the Rabbi of Zhitomir. I recognized him at once, Vasily. And it was so heartrending to see a prince who had lost his pants, doubled up beneath his soldier's pack, that we defied the regulations and pulled him up into our coach. His bare knees, inefficient as an old woman's, knocked against the rusty iron of the steps. Two full-bosomed typists in sailor blouses trailed the long, shamed body of the dying man along the floor. We laid him in a corner of the editorial office, on the floor, and Cossacks in loose red trousers set straight the clothes that were dropping off him. The girls planted their bandy legs—legs of unforward females— on the floor, and stared dully at his sexual organs, the stunted, curly-covered virility of a wasted Semite. And I, who had seen him on one of my nights of roaming, began to pack in a case the scattered belongings of the Red Army man Bratslavsky.

His things were strewn about pell-mell—mandates of the propagandist and notebooks of the Jewish poet, the portraits of Lenin and Maimonides lay side by side, the knotted iron of Lenin's skull beside the dull silk of the portraits of Maimonides. A lock of woman's hair lay in a book, the Resolutions of the Party's Sixth Congress, and the margins of Communist leaflets were crowded with crooked lines of ancient Hebrew verse. They fell upon me in a mean and depressing rain— pages of the Song of Songs and revolver cartridges. The dreary rain of sunset washed the dust in my hair, and I said to the boy who was dying on a wretched mattress in the corner:

"One Friday evening four months ago, Gedali the old-clothesman took me to see your father, Rabbi Motale. But you didn't belong to the Party at that time, Bratslavsky. . . ."

"I did," the boy answered, scratching at his chest and twisting in fever, "only I couldn't leave my mother."

"And now, Elijah?"

"When there's a revolution on, a mother's an episode," he whispered, less and less audibly. "My letter came, the letter B, and the Organization sent me to the front. . . ."

"And you got to Kovel, Elijah?"

"I got to Kovel!" he cried in despair. "The kulaks opened the front to the enemy. I took over the command of a scratch regiment, but too late. . . . I hadn't enough artillery. . . ."

He died before we reached Rowno. He—that last of the Princes—died among his poetry, phylacteries, and coarse foot-wrappings. We buried him at some forgotten station. And I, who can scarce contain the tempests of my imagination within this age-old body of mine, I was there beside my brother when he breathed his last.

1925

XIII

The Rape of
the Shtetl

The shtetl (the Yiddish word for small town) was presumably the last bastion of tradition in Jewish eastern Europe. There everything was still governed by Jewish law—time and place, home and market, not to speak of the myriad houses of prayer and learning. There the strict demarcation between the Sabbath and weekday, the sacred and profane, the Jews and the gentiles seemed utterly immutable. The less that was actually known about the shtetl—its demography, history, economy and collective mores—the more readily it functioned as a mythical place, as a *kehillah kedoshah* (holy congregation) bearing witness to God's presence in exile. The first to exploit this image of the shtetl were, as usual, the secular writers in Yiddish and Hebrew who, beginning in the 1860s, recognized the shtetl's potential as a fictional shorthand for the fate of the Jewish collective. Abramovitsh (**40–41**) laid the groundwork with Beggarsburgh, Foolsville and Idletown, parodically modeled on the sacred triad of Worms, Speyer and Mainz. Sholem Aleichem's Heysen (**49**) and Krushnik (**54**) were no more real for being locatable on the map. Their inhabitants still placed their faith in the power of language to rescue them from disaster. Weissenberg's nameless shtetl (**48**) exploded the myth of Jewish solidarity by exposing the violence and class conflict that lay just beneath the surface.

After World War I and the Bolshevik Revolution, when the physical collapse of the shtetl became visible for all to see, the writers seized anew on its symbolic landscape to convey their sense of utter desecration and upheaval. Oyzer Warshawski (**61**), a young protégé of Weissenberg's, reopened the assault on the myth of the shtetl with *Shmuglares* ("smugglers"

in Polish-Yiddish dialect). He chose a family of teamsters as his chief pro-
tagonists: Pantl, an inarticulate man of brute passions, and his two sons
Mendl and Urke. With an eye for the comic, Warshawski showed how
Pantl introduced a new economic order to the shtetl—this time without
the help of paid agitators from Warsaw. In fact, the shtetl in wartime was
in a favorable position vis-à-vis Warsaw, where there was no escaping the
German war economy. In the isolated shtetl, the profit motive still reigned
supreme. Respectable artisans and merchants joined forces with the low-
lives; Jewish men went into business with gentile women. And as for the
Germans—they were bought off with sexual favors.

Having totally disavowed the hallowed image of the shtetl, Warshawski
provided a countermyth instead, a self-contained culture of smugglers,
sentimental tales of the Good Ole Days and even a homegrown (Polish)
anthem. The two new settings of Jewish solidarity were Pantl's wagon en
route to Warsaw and the shtetl bedrooms where Jewish smugglers shacked
up with their gentile "partners."

Warshawski's method answered to the dictates of critical realism, with
its focus on the animal in man. He transcribed vulgar speech; he focused
on mass behavior instead of on a central hero; and he followed a naturalist
determinism that saw heredity and environment governing all of human
behavior. For the Jewish reader of the 1920s (and probably for present-
day readers as well), the most shocking scene comes in chapter 15 when
Raytshl is caught naked, wrapped in pieces of raw meat, a more lucrative
contraband than flour or salt. This is a pivotal scene because now it is one
human body being exploited for profit; soon outright forms of prostitution
are to be introduced into the shtetl. More profoundly, it is an image of
nakedness beyond the skin, an exposé of civilization itself.

In Warshawski's story, the shtetl survives, by hook or by crook. But in
the revolutionary upheaval that followed, east of the new Polish-Soviet
border, no amount of internal change could save the shtetl from extinction.
Despite the efforts of the younger generation of Jews to establish a brave
new shtetl world, complete with its own commune and militia, the en-
terprise was doomed from the start. This, at any rate, was the verdict of
twenty-six-year-old writer Hayyim Hazaz (**62**) who, like Warshawski,
launched his career by exploding the myth of the shtetl.

In one corner were the spokesmen of traditional society—passionate
old men who had only their wit and rabbinic writ to hold on to. Once the
chief providers of the shtetl economy, these petty merchants were now
deemed parasites by the new Soviet regime. In the other corner were their
sons and daughters, armed with guns and an unshakable rhetoric about
the dictatorship of the proletariat. Because the revolution had just begun
and Russia was still at war with Germany, there were competing revolutionary tactics to choose from. Polishuk stood for the iron will of bolshevism, and Soroka the anarchist (whose name means "magpie") went

around setting fire to the manor houses of the old aristocracy. Only the sworn counterrevolutionaries would not be countenanced, namely, the Bundists, the original standard-bearers of socialism among the Jewish masses of eastern Europe, because the Bund was aligned with the Social Democrats and fought for the "parochial" interests of the Jewish working class.

What makes *Revolutionary Chapters* so unusual as a work of shtetl fiction and as a chronicle of a particularly violent moment in Jewish history is Hazaz's way of breaking down the oppositions he has just drawn so forcefully. This happens on several levels at once. Read as a historical parable, the pivotal moment in the story comes in chapter 9 when Soroka's Jewish militia successfully thwarts a pogrom and immediately thereafter is forcibly demobilized by the army. Thus, Soroka's sudden return at the end of the story to announce the German approach is that much more ominous. The shtetl now stands defenseless before an enemy that does not differentiate between petty bourgeois Jews and revolutionary Jews.

One character in the story does try to bridge both worlds: Motl Privisker, the passionate Hasid who left his wife and children and begins to prophesy the End of Days. As the only character who reacts in a complicated way to the rapid course of events, Motl commands our attention, if not our sympathy. Just as there is no going back to a world of simple faith, so there is for Motl no real possibility of ever becoming a Bolshevik, much less of catching the eye of Reb Simcha's daughter, Henya, the romantic center of the story. Motl's despair and his flights of prophetic clairvoyance thus embody the madness of a revolution that would ultimately swallow up the world.

Despite the language of the story, an ornate and incongruous Hebrew, there is no single consciousness here to hold all the disparate parts of that language together. In a sense, the language epitomizes Motl's dilemma, for on the one hand, biblical and rabbinic locutions are used in bold juxtaposition with modern, colloquial expressions, and the sheer energy of the prose holds out some redemptive promise. On the other hand, this rapid linguistic montage throws even the most traditional-sounding phrase out of context, and the very foundations of Jewish culture seem to have been permanently uprooted.

The half-crazed characters in Hazaz's story inhabit a self-destructing world. Everything is in a state of turmoil, from the howling winds to the men in uniform. The judgment of history is still an open question. But with the knowledge of hindsight and from the perspective of his new home in Israel, Hazaz revised the story completely, once in 1956 and again in 1968. (For an English translation of this final version, see *Gates of Bronze* [Philadelphia: Jewish Publication Society, 1975].) It is precisely the finished quality of these later versions and the consistent narrative viewpoint that rob the work of its original vitality. In *Revolutionary Chapters,* style *is* content, and no style captures the apocalyptic frenzy of the Revolution as well as Hebrew Expressionism.

Itsik Kipnis's lyrical novella *Months and Days* (**63**) provides the very opposite viewpoint. On the surface, the work is a throwback to a prelapsarian image of the shtetl, to a place of social integration, eternal summer and abiding love. In opposition to the official Soviet line on the shtetl ("an ugly anachronism inimical to the interests of the working class"), Kipnis draws a vibrant, loving portrait of the shtetl that made this book a runaway bestseller among Soviet-Yiddish readers. The secret of Kipnis's success is the façade of naïveté he manages to maintain even while writing an extraordinarily detailed chronicle of terror.

To begin with, the twenty-two-year-old narrator named Ayzik resembles no one so much as Sholem Aleichem's child-hero Motl, the son of Peyse the Cantor. Unlike Motl, however, Ayzik is capable of growth, and as the terror mounts, we watch Ayzik literally and figuratively take over the reins in his desperate attempt to save the lives of his family.

The hero's struggle between innocence and awareness is brilliantly underscored by the dual nature of time. There is idyllic time, which is measured in months: the endless holiday of the newlywed couple, a time of fullness and joyous expectation. And there is tragic time, the time of encroaching terror, when every minute could be the last. The pogrom itself is referred to euphemistically as a "holiday," so that even the language maintains the façade of innocence. It is through the desecration of time—night and day are reversed, the pogrom reaches its peak on the Sabbath, and the hero finally loses track of time altogether—that the reader experiences the full impact of the violence.

Writing under Soviet rule, even Kipnis could not get away with rehabilitating the shtetl as a meeting ground between Jews and God. Without God, therefore, Kipnis had to look to human intervention to restore the moral order. And so he had the Red Army wreak vengeance upon the Ukrainian murderers, and he had Buzi give birth to a girl to compensate partially for the loss of so many lives. This last was the only fanciful touch to an otherwise faithful account: the "real" Buzi (Kipnis's young wife) died of typhus soon after the pogrom.

Today Kipnis's novella assumes the status of a classic in the Literature of Destruction for both literary and historical reasons. By drawing selectively on the Sholem Aleichem tradition that preceded him, Kipnis placed the Ukrainian pogroms within the recognized sequence of modern Jewish catastrophes. By approaching the horror through the innocent eyes of a man-child, Kipnis looked ahead to such works at Günter Grass's *The Tin Drum*, Uri Orlev's *Lead Soldiers* and, most recently, David Grossman's *See Under 'Love.'* Historically, the story he tells anticipates the fate of thousands, if not tens of thousands, of Jews who, under Nazi occupation, sought refuge among their erstwhile friends in the Polish and Lithuanian countryside. There are Holocaust memoirs, such as Leyb Rochman's *The Pit and the Trap,* that read like a replay of *Months and Days,* except that the scale and duration of the murder are so much more vast that almost no one comes out of the Holocaust alive. And because Soviet Jews were eventually silenced and because no one within their boundaries was allowed to mourn the Great Destruction, Kipnis's modest work must stand as the lone monument to the Jewish national catastrophe, made more terrible still by the singular barbarism of Soviet totalitarianism that robs a people even of its past.

Taken together, these three novellas show that the shtetl, portrayed realistically or idyllically, still held its own in the collective memory as the place where Jewishness was played out. In a sort of spiritual archeology, the shtetl became the last site (until the ghettos of World War II) where one could dig up the *kehillah kedoshah.* It was the site, also, at which the choice of covenants (old, new or none at all) was made with most pathos and in the increasing absence of God; wherefore the Chosen People came to mean not People Chosen by God as much as people victimized by the rest of the world.

61 Smugglers

OYZER WARSHAWSKI

7

Yitskhok-Yoyne was a patch tailor, but not like the others with their eager little laughs and their abusive melodies. He was a man with a fine gray beard and wore a cloth hat with a wide brim perched on his gray head. He always had a somewhat preoccupied smile on his bearded face and a packet of tobacco almost always in his hand as he recited a chapter from the Book of Psalms or hummed a prayer from the Days of Awe.

Yitskhok-Yoyne was also a prayer-leader in the town synagogue. When he came home from the synagogue, he washed his hands and wiped them slowly. And he took a full hour to eat. His two sons and a daughter, a young woman with red cheeks, worked in the front room.

The place fairly buzzed with work. The young people filled the house with their fine songs, and their voices mingled with the hoarse rattling of the machines that sounded like someone with seriously damaged lungs.

That, however, is how things used to be once. Once upon a time, during the good years when there was peace in the world and a pound of white bread cost five groschen. "Once upon a time there was a king." But, with the outbreak of war, that all disappeared, like magic; like a bad dream. "For our many sins," as Yitskhok-Yoyne, the patch tailor, put it. Today? Who has work to do today? Who earns anything? Dead—business of all sorts. Merchants sold their goods for practically nothing so that they might have the wherewithal to buy bread. As for working men—working men went about searching for peasant customers with lighted candles. Things were really as bad as they could be. One went about with nothing to do. The last ruble had been long since devoured. So, what was to be done? You considered one scheme, and then another, and the conclusion was that one had to make a still. This was all discussed in secret—all very hush hush. But no matter how softly it was whispered, it nevertheless reached the ears of Rattling Pinye, who always knew absolutely everything going on in town.

By some miracle he did not himself understand, Yitskhok-Yoyne turned out to own a barrel, which he scoured out carefully. Then he had the tinsmith make him a boiler and various utensils and wheels; and then he bought a pressure gauge, and then on one fine cloudy night he began to cook. Yitskhok-Yoyne, on his own, would not have understood how to go about the business. The barrel was all that he owned, and it was a long and laborious task to scrape together the money for the boiler. And sugar, just then, cost twenty rubles a *pood*. So he discussed the matter with Yosef the Doll, and in good time they became partners. But on that very same day, Rattling Pinye showed up and informed them that he too meant to be a partner in the business. The other two, outraged, shouted in unison, "Crook! What do you mean? How can you even think of it? We've gone to a lot of expense; had all the utensils made. And there won't be any profit if there are three partners."

He hemmed and hawed, but he was not to be budged. Without him, he said, the business would not work.

This drove Yosef the Doll into a rage. He grabbed one of Pinye's hands and squeezed it with the strength of a pair of tongs. "Ah, Pinye you lowlife. You want to use force to become a partner? Not if I can help it!"

Pinye was furious. His nose sharpened, and the pouches under his eyes turned yellow. Tearing himself loose from Yosef the Doll's grasp, he shouted, "I'll teach you," and then ran off.

A couple of days later Yitskhok-Yoyne's son Leybl was squatting before the boiler adding wood to the fire. Above the glowing boiler, the vat was boiling. The rising steam entered a pipe, pushed its way through various brass valves, then entered once more into a pipe that ran through a cooler. And there, the distillate dripped through the pipe and into a pot that Yitskhok-Yoyne held under it.

"The first distillation," he said formally, and his face glowed. And when he took the temperature of the mixture and the thermometer showed eighty-five, he opened his mouth wide and said happily, "Ah ha, a fine distillation. An eighty-fiver. Ah ha!"

And it was just then that Yosef the Doll came in, taking the steps in three bounds. He flung the door open, snatched the kettle from the fire, disconnected the tubes and, as if speaking a single breathless word, said, "Quickly, quickly. Landsmann and Jaeger are on their way."

There ensued a mad bustling. No one knew what to do first. Think of it: in one corner there was a kettle full to the brim. They grabbed it up, and it began to slosh over. And droplets, like tears, continued to flow from the disconnected pipes. There was still vapor in the pipes, and as it condensed, the droplets fell and soaked into the muddy floor. Leybl said sadly, "Eighty-five," as, sweating like a beaver, he dragged and carried things about.

But his father was white as chalk, and his mother, that little woman, shoved bottles of brandy into a basket; then, covering them with an apron, she ran to hide them in the home of a neighbor. The Doll's nose had grown thin and pointed, like that of a corpse. "A fortune," he thought, "an entire fortune gone to hell." And Brayndl's red cheeks turned even redder. She grabbed, dragged and buried what she could. Then, as she was standing on a wet barrel cover, she slipped and fell, and as she fell, her dress caught on a nail that was protruding from the wall. She fell, revealing a silk ribbon tied around one of her stockings just above the knee.

What a disaster. One can hear those hounds already. They're watching, like murderers.

And in came the Germans.

"What kind of factory is this?" asked the sergeant major as he looked around the house.

"A tailor lives here," Yitskhok-Yoyne replied, trembling like an autumn leaf.

"A tailor," said the sergeant major, with a sly smile on his face. "A tailor? Then where's the machinery?"

"Here they are, dear sir," burst from Tshippe, who could no longer contain herself. She plucked at the German's uniform and, giving free rein to her tongue, said, "Him . . . my husband, Yitskhok-Yoyne, is a tailor. A patch tailor. But there's no needlework to be done, so the machines have been put away in a corner. But you, gentleman, are such a nice gentleman. Be good enough to sit down," and she thrust a moist, filthy chair toward him.

"What a dirty place," Landsmann said to the man with him, a tall, thin fellow with high cheekbones, a flaccid mouth and a nose like an archer's bow. The round, brimless hat he wore gave him the look of a dog with a docked tail.

"Have a look and see what's in that barrel."

The tall man bending over to look looked as if he would break in two at any moment, like a stick.

"It's empty, Herr Sergeant Major. But it has a terrible stink."

"What kind of barrel is this?" said Landsmann turning toward the others threateningly. "Yes. It's brandy."

"Oh, no sir. What . . . brandy? Brandy? Where? How? It's the smell of sauerkraut." But when she saw the expression on his face, she cried out, "Pity. O please sir, pity us."

Now Landsmann inspected a vat. "And this, too, is for sauerkraut?"

"Yes, yes. Sauerkraut."

He continued to look around, then he saw Brayndl in the other room. And suddenly he was completely transformed. The look on his face cleared and his eyes shone more brightly.

"Do you live here, *Fräulein?*" He made a gesture toward Jaeger. "A pretty girl, eh," and, not contenting himself with that, he went up to her and pinched her cheek. "So, you are the daughter of this Jew? I've seen the young lady at the magistrate's. I've been at the magistrate's." And again his eyes glistened. He took out a notebook and wrote down their names. As he was leaving, he said to Brayndl, "You must come see me today, at six o'clock. There will be a fine."

When the Germans were gone, the Jews seated themselves on the moist chairs and assessed the damage, like mourners. "Who knows whether the troublemaker will be good to us?"

"There's a hole in the boiler."

"Where are the brass valves?"

"Here they are, in the cellar."

"We took it apart well. They didn't find anything."

Then Yosef the Doll approached Yitskhok-Yoyne's daughter. "Brayndl," he said in a beggar's voice, "you'll go to him. Give him a little smile. You know how." Turning to Yitskhok-Yoyne, he said: "Those fellows—they'd cut their own throats for a Jewish girl."

Brayndl, hearing this, turned red to her eyelids and ran into the other room. And yet, she was pleased: to be favored by the sergeant major.

"Who knows whether this wasn't the Rattle's work?" the Doll said, voicing his suspicion. But Yitskhok-Yoyne got angry, "Eh? What are you talking about. The Rattle's a Jew!"

Just the same, it was agreed that they would take Pinye in as one of their partners. And, though no one could say exactly why it was so, things got better after that. For one thing, the still was no longer kept in the house. They rented some out-of-the-way empty hut in an orchard just behind Pantl's courtyard. And in addition to that, they enlarged the still. Two boilers were set going, yielding whole barrels of brandy. But there was difficulty getting water. The well was far off in the orchard, and carrying the buckets back would reveal that the "factory" was at work.

So they got Zerekh-Donkey, who treated the name with which the town had honored him with respect. And Zerekh did nothing else for whole days at a time but haul water up from the well, loading it into his wagon and pouring it into the empty barrels that were arrayed along the wall inside the hut. Ah, if he only had an extra pair of hands. Even on Saturday, his arms were stiff and crooked, as if he were still carrying the buckets.

9

It was a day at the end of winter. One of those days that are both windy and sunny. On such days, people in the towns open all their doors and windows. Children crawl about on the doorsteps, taking the air.

Our smugglers, waking from their sleep at noon, were delighted to see the friendly rays of the sun streaming into their houses. They left their beds gratified and refreshed and went out into the street where they made ready for their journey.

On the way into town, it had rained all the way. The tarpaulins had been soaked through and through. Now in their dry clothes, the smugglers felt rested, and they looked toward the sky, where great masses of white clouds drifted— endlessly drifted.

It was six o'clock in the evening. Shadows were beginning to lengthen along the eastward-looking walls as the wagons left the courtyards and turned onto the road.

The smugglers walked along the sides of the road, near the houses, their bundles in their coats and in their shawls, their heads bent as they kept a wary eye out until they were well past the crucifix, past the first little bridge and onto the main road. Then they quickly threw their bundles in the wagons and jumped in themselves. The wagon drivers lashed the horses, crying , "Up, up, Giddap."

It was then that they heard a whistle and a shouted "Halt!"

The smugglers poked their heads out of the wagons, and seeing who was running after them, they turned pale. The livelier ones grabbed up their bundles, jumped from the wagons and ran across the fields and into the wood so swiftly that it would seem that they were carrying chips in their hands instead of sacks that weighed two or three *pood*. The German, seeing how many were escaping, pointed his revolver into the air and shouted, "Halt! Not another step. Stop!"

They were all petrified. Old Shayke stood, one foot in the wagon and the other on the ground, unable to move one way or the other. His hands holding the bundle trembled and twitched, and he looked imploringly at the German, who was now beside the wagon shouting angrily. He ordered Mendl to throw down all the bundles and to see whether anyone was carrying contraband.

Pantl stood beside the horses, his contracted body trembling. "Ah, if I were to 'bless' his teeth, he'd have something to remember me by."

Mendl threw the bundles down from the wagon. They bounced and lay on the pavement. But when the German stuck his head into the wagon to see that nothing was overlooked, Pantl, behind his back, grabbed up seven of the bundles and threw them into the ditch where they could not be seen. Those in the other wagons, seeing what Pantl had done, did the same. The German, seeing the smugglers disappearing with their bundles, cocked his pistol and fired into the air. The smugglers, terrified, stopped in their tracks. Well, what would be, would be.

Now the German counted the bundles and set Mendl to stand guard over them. "See that none of them is missing," he said. And he repeated the same thing at Kopl's wagon. As the bundles were being thrown, one of the seams split, and a stream of white flour flowed into the dark, like a fluffy snow. The German gave a mocking laugh, "What is it? Eh? What?"

A stout young peasant woman ran up. It was Mateusz's wife. She spread her apron under the stream of flour to keep it from falling to the ground. She wept, "Jesus. Ah, God. My whole fortune. Dear Jesus."

"So," the German cried, seeing that the flour was hers. "Gather it up quickly." Then to the others, "There are thirty bundles here. Put them in the wagons, and off to the station house."

A racket ensued. Gimpl's daughter, Khanna, ran up. She was bareheaded because, in her haste, she had lost her headkerchief somewhere. She knelt to kiss the German's hand and wept, "Lord, great lord, have pity on a poor Jewish woman. Don't take away our bit of bread."

Without taking his eyes from the Mateusz woman's plump shape, the German thrust Khanna away. Then he smiled under his mustache. Riding to the station, he whispered something to Mateusz's wife, then tickled her. Though she did not understand a word of what he said, she understood his meaning. He pointed to her bundle and said, "You'll get your contraband back. All of it." Then he winked broadly at her.

When the wagons reached the Great Marketplace, such a crowd gathered that the horses could not drive through. But a single word from the German, and a look from his flashing eye was enough to scatter everyone into the side streets. That was the sort of power the German had.

And when the wagon was in the courtyard of the station, all the smugglers hurried up to the second floor where the commandant had his office. But only the deputy commander was there, and the bespectacled scribe. The commandant had gone for a stroll. The smugglers gathered around and made such a turmoil that the deputy commander did not know what they wanted of him. It was not until Jaeger came and drove them out that they had a chance to talk things over. It was left that the police would keep half of the contraband and return the other half. Only Mateusz's wife got her entire bundle back. But she had to go immediately with Jaeger and the bespectacled scribe to a private room in an upper story of Mayerl's inn.

11

Pantl was getting confused. Ever since the customs agents had taken the several hundredweight of flour from him he had gone about like a mute bear. He never left his pregnant wife, who was approaching her time, out of his sight. He preceded—and followed—everything he said with a curse. Nor did he spare his sons, though he did not risk troubling Mendl, the oldest one. Mendl took after his mother: he was tall, broad—a giant. He looked like two of Pantl. But he picked on the younger son on every occasion.

And something was always being taken from him—mostly from his wagon. Kopl, on the other hand, was doing well. Fayfke was riding with Kopl again, and he was still hanging out with Mateusz's wife. They bought goods together, and when they came to the customs agents, she claimed his goods were hers, and the fact is that then they took nothing from her. Old Shayke joked that Mateusz's wife was "Fayfke's bride." But Fayfke had the last laugh, not only on him but on the whole world. Pantl thought, "If I had had such a 'bride,' they wouldn't have taken anything from me. Not then, and not now. And she's certainly a help in one way. What can you do in Warsaw? There's no food, no rest. As for my wife, is she any help to me? Even at home? She walks about—a great nothing—with her big belly. She's going to have another boy; a boy—nothing else will do. I can't stand to look at her ugly face." Such were the thoughts swirling about in Pantl's head. He did not yet know where they would lead him. That would come later.

And when he came home at dawn from his travels and tried, all frozen as he was, to go to sleep, his thoughts gave him no rest. He kept staring up angrily out of his sleep and cursed his wife and went out into the orchard to Yitskhok-Yoyne's place, where he asked for ninety proof, which he drank, one glass after another.

But there were times when those thoughts left him—disappeared as if into the ground. That only happened occasionally—and only on a Sabbath. That's when he and his pals got together. Sometimes they came to his house. Lozer, Khayim Kaiser's father, used to say that in the old days when Pantl and the others were fiery young men, if they had any business in hand, they exchanged looks and it was done: one, two, three. Or else he told the story of the peasants. "Ah, old pals, old pals. Those times will come again." And at such times a look of confidence spread over their faces. Their eyes, their pulses gave off such fiery heat that it could be felt from a distance.

On one such Sabbath, as they sat in the house, Lozer Kaiser was telling a tale (how many times had he told it already?) and stroking his white beard. "It was on a Friday night when a few of the peasants came into the town. Railroad workers, intent on making trouble. It got dark, and they started to beat up Jews who were on their way to the evening service in the synagogue. And wasn't it just like old 'Kaiser' to grab up a wagon crossbar and leap right into a crowd of peasants swinging away with the bar, now left, now right so that they fell like flies. Just then some tall peasant with an iron pole came within an ace of splitting 'Kaiser's' head open, except of course that Pantl leaped in front of him and gave him such a blow on the head with his fist that he stretched the peasant full length on the ground."

Little Urke was one of those who heard this tale, and it made him gleeful as a puppy so that he began to pound his father's back with his fists. Pantl, it appeared, did not welcome such a show of affection from his son and gave him such a box on the ear that the boy rolled completely over and landed on the floor. And it was at that moment that Pantl began to understand what it was he had to do. Because that blow produced the following developments: When little Urke fell to the ground, he began to shake in a way that could make one think he was having an epileptic seizure. It was then, when he lay quiet, his eyes open, gazing at his father as if nothing had happened, ready to pound his shoulders once again, that Glike shouted, "What have you got against the boy? Pantl, you might have killed him—may the Lord punish you."

And it was at that moment that Pantl, feeling guilty and unable to pour out his wrath on anyone, blushed, stood up and, turning his furious eyes on his wife, whom just then he hated, started toward her. But he was embarrassed by the presence of his buddies, so he merely spat in her direction and went out of the house toward the stable and slammed the door behind him. There, as he passed his hand over the stallion's hide, he calmed down little by little and began to think over what had just happened. And it was clear to him at once that his wife was the cause of all his misfortunes—even the share of his goods the customs agents took from him. "Damn her father to hell, the old chaser. Gentile young women!" he thought as he thwacked the stallion's side. Then he took the animal's long tail and tied it into a knot. "Pantl, damn you if they take a cut of your goods one more time. You won't deserve to live." Then he went up to the roan and thrust a handful of feed into its mouth. Then he climbed into the loft, crawled into the hay and lay there for a while, thinking. And what he finally concluded was this— though how he would do "this" he could not yet be sure. Still, the heart of the matter was clear. A partnership with a gentile woman. Though he couldn't just walk up to any woman he might meet by chance and say, "Hey, come ride with me." But one thing was clear. He ought to get started on the matter right away— and be done with it.

And shortly thereafter a lucky chance brought Pantl together with the right woman—a woman whom even younger men envied him and who was the occasion of more than one quarrel.

15

Fayfke was prospering as a smuggler. From the time that he entered into partnership with Mateusz's wife he had not had any of his goods taken by the customs officers, and people guessed that his profits could be written in large numbers. And so he ordered a suit for Shavuot and ordered it, as a matter of fact, from Ahrele Quarter-Master, Itshele's father. There he explained that he wanted the trousers with broad bell-bottoms and the cuffs with double buttons. He had himself been a tailor before the war, earning four rubles a week in Warsaw. And he specified that the jacket pockets should be in the German fashion, opening from the top.

The minute he woke in the morning, he went right over to Ahrele.

"Well, how's my suit doing?" he asked.

"Have to measure one more time," replied Itshele for his father.

So Fayfke got out of his smuggler's linen trousers, and they measured him for the whole suit once more.

"Just take a look, this isn't quite right," he said to Itshele, inwardly proud, as he peered in the mirror. "Though it's not bad."

"Eh, never mind. No harm. It's nothing," said Ahrele, passing his hand over Fayfke's shoulder, smoothing things out.

Then it was out into the street where he met Bertshe, Kaiser's friend, as well as Muli and Avromtshe, Velvl's son for whom all the young women, Jewish and gentile, would willingly have died. And since they had found each other, it was only natural to look for Mendl, after which they all went to Elye's tavern and undertook to drink their fill.

"Ah, old friends," said Mendl, his mouth loosened by the third glass, "You ought to have seen those three gentile women—pure cream!" he said, smacking his lips.

"Which ones do you mean?" Bertshe said, laughing because he thought Mendl was drunk.

"Fayvl, tell him which ones I mean. He's burning to know."

So Fayvl told the story of last night's adventures—how they had come upon the three young women, and what they had said to them.

The young men listened intently. Bertshe's mouth stood open, and he drooled.

"Now you've heard it," Fayvl concluded. "Hot stuff, eh?"

Avromtshe, Velvl's son, raised his eyebrows and downed one glass, then another. "If they were still here," he said, "It might be worthwhile. . . ."

"Impossible," burst from Itshl.

And so Avromtshe turned on him. "What do you mean? There's nothing 'impossible' for me. Don't you know, my little tailor, who Avromtshe is?" But all the others were on Itshl's side. "Come on, it's Itshl talking. Is there a book that he hasn't read? As for his recitations. . . ."

But Avromtshe, who by now had more liquor in his head than was left in the bottle, insisted on opposing them. And who knows how it would have ended if it had not all suddenly changed. Because just as Avromtshe grasped the bottle by its neck and, all atremble, started toward Itshl, the door opened and Blind Grunim looked in. With a single bound, he was beside Fayvl and, grabbing him by the collar, began to shake him the way one shakes a *lulav*° in the synagogue.

The palm branch that is carried and waved in the synagogue during the Sukkot holiday.

"Listen, my friend. I'll cut your liver out, damn your bloody guts."

For a moment, they were all confused, but then, seeing what was happening, they undertook first to get Fayvl out from under Grunim's paws. The fellow could bend an iron rod.

And Muli, whom the whole town called "The Tough Guy," said quietly, "What's your trouble, Grunim? Eh?"

"And what the goddamn hell business is it of yours?" replied Grunim, and his blind eye trembled, and there was a liquid red glow behind the lid.

"Come on, Grunim, what kind of talk is that?" put in Mendl and poured him a glass of beer.

Grunim took it, sat down and drank the beer. Mendl poured him another glass, which Grunim drank. Mendl filled his glass again. He drank the third and then the fourth.

But the blonde Muli stood by as anger turned his nose pale. And his eyes narrowed as if his lids were suddenly puffed up.

"What is it you want, friend?" Fayvl, who was the occasion for the quarrel, finally spoke up. He was pale as chalk. Grunim was no child, by any means. But as he watched Grunim filling his glass and saw the foam spilling from his mouth and the tremor of his skin at the wet coldness, Fayvl calmed down. "Never mind. I, Fayvl, won't abstain, either." Then, to Grunim again, "Why did you blow your top at me?"

Grunim, who had been pouring beer down himself, had by now cooled down. He said, quite affably, "The devil take your mother. When are you writing out the articles of engagement?"

The crowd, hearing these words, burst out laughing and started in to thwack Fayvl. Fayvl's eyes narrowed.

"Well, my friend, you know the song: 'The Two Poor Went Dancing, Without a Penny, Without a Cent.' So you understand it all."

"May you burn in hell," laughed Blind Grunim, and his thin-lipped mouth twitched fearfully as he laughed. "They should know that Raytshl is making preparations. She's bought cloth from Dzierdiew." He put his arm around Fayvl's shoulder and looked deeply into his eyes.

"Why are you staring at me like that? Don't you know me?" asked Fayvl, whom Grunim's look had chilled.

"Why don't you talk to Raytshl about being engaged?" he said, angry once again.

"Who? Who says? . . ."

"Who? My sister says it herself."

"Alright, let's go ask her."

"Let's go."

They stood and left, their arms about each other's shoulders. Left without a glance at their friends, who stayed behind as if they had been spanked.

"Raytshl isn't here?" Grunim asked, poking his head into Kopl's house.

"She's just gone upstairs to get dressed," shouted Kopl's wife.

They climbed the stairs quickly and opened the door. Fayvl, in sheer surprise, let his hand fall from Grunim's shoulder and stood as if he had been shot. The lid of Grunim's blind eye rose, revealing a dreadful gleaming red abyss.

Raytshl stood naked with her back to them. She was wrapping bits of meat from which the blood was still dripping. She wrapped them around her breasts, her belly and her feet. The flattened bits of cool, moist meat adhering to her warm skin sent up a vapor. As she kept winding the bits of meat, binding them to her with strips of raw flesh, she looked like someone who has been flayed alive. Fayvl could not help shuddering. But he was also illuminated and awed by Raytshl.

Grunim shouted to Fayvl, "Raytshl! D'you see what a money-maker she is, damn you."

Raytshl, embarrassed to be seen this way by her destined bridegroom, grabbed up some article of clothing and covered herself.

"Raytshl," said Grunim again, "has Fayvl talked to you about being engaged?"

"Leave me alone," she said, still embarrassed.

"Well, well," said Grunim. Seeing that they were both upset, he was willing to let the matter drop. "You're not carrying flour any more?"

"Yes, flour usually. But meat pays better."

Fayvl was suddenly overwhelmed with respect for Raytshl, who seemed to him a quite different being from himself. A being of some higher order. "Who would think to do a body search?" Enraptured, he said to Grunim, "We'll write out the engagement agreement at the first of the month."

Grunim was delighted. His eyelid twitched, and he embraced Fayvl and kissed him. "Damn you to hell. D'you see what Raytshl can do? And Raytshl, just look at him. Well, you're practically bride and groom."

And grabbing his sister, he shoved her into Fayvl's arms. The powerful smell of raw meat made Fayvl nauseous. At that moment, he regretted the words he had just spoken. And when Grunim, laughing his horrid laugh, tried to push him and Raytshl closer together, he felt a constriction in his throat and felt that he might vomit. Seeking for some excuse to get away he cried, "Listen, I have to make one more trip before Saturday." He tore himself away and fled from Raytshl's embrace as from the plague.

17

The town breathed a little more easily. Bakers, distillers, soap makers, cigarette sellers, tavern keepers, butchers and every sort of smuggler celebrated a Sabbath in praise of the Lord, who does not overlook a worm; and because Haman had had his comeuppance. "It was becoming unbearable."

And indeed, the lame commandant deserved his nickname. In the few weeks that he was in power, he had brought misfortune on half of the town. When he first arrived, the town thought, from the way he looked, that he was by no means a bad gentile. He was tall and limped from a wound he had received to his left foot. But the very next morning all the smuggled goods were impounded from the wagons. After that he turned his attention to the distillers. He had a bloodhound's nose. Standing at the magistrate's gate, he could detect the smell of a still in a street at the town center.

He had exposed Dovid-Yitskhok and Yenkl Beder. And he had taken some fifteen hundred marks from Reb Yidl. Only Yitskhok-Yoyne had escaped detection. Yosef the Doll had indeed boasted, "We work in the orchard, and so long as The Rattle is one of us, we have nothing to fear."

And so they "cooked" almost in broad daylight. And Donkey dragged the buckets of water, and there were strips of hard encrusted sweat on his forehead that he washed away once a week, on Friday evening. And it was on one such evening that the commandant, together with Landsmann and Jaeger, all of them in full uniform, went to the orchard by a roundabout way.

It was rumored in town that on that same evening, only an hour after Yidl's still was discovered, that one of his sons or daughters was seen strolling in the vicinity of the two-story house in which the sergeant major lived. But that's neither here nor there. What matters is that Yitskhok-Yoyne was once again "an absolutely poor man," without a penny to his name. "What's to be done? What else is there to do?"

Aggravation turned Brayndl's red cheeks pale. But Leybl was utterly untroubled by the misfortune. He continued to go about smiling, laughing into everyone's face.

As for The Rattle . . . poor fellow. He was in no way responsible for that first search on Yitskhok-Yoyne's house. Because he had felt a revulsion against distilling. He had only meant to work on for another couple of weeks so that he could rent a small orchard somewhere. And there was money to be earned without an orchard. And the point was that it was legal.

The Rattle's nature was essentially fearful. It was just that he liked to talk. For instance, what good had it done him to threaten them then? But that's the way he was. The truth is, he could not restrain himself whenever he heard anyone talking. Ah, how often had his wife dressed him down because of that habit of his. But it did no good. Whenever there was talk of great deeds, of heroism, then he was inflamed by heroism. And when he chanced upon a newcomer to the town or some younger people, didn't he say that during the battles with the Great Russians he was among the first to attack? Or, when there was a fire, for example—that's when he most demonstrated his skill. How? By running about with his cap on backward.

Poor fellow. He had everything he owned invested in the still. He had even borrowed money. He bought a few hundredweight of sugar, expecting the price to go up.

But that fellow, that lame commandant had had a sudden death. And he had been replaced by a fresh officer, also young. A wonderful man. Why should he worry about smuggling or bootlegging? He had his fiddle; he sat and played on it. It happened one day that the soldiers in the round hats without visors impounded some goods on their own authority and brought it to the "Commandant." He just laughed and returned the bundle. A cheerful young fellow. He strolled about, or rode his bicycle and chatted amiably with everyone. . . .

And thus God had sent a salvation to his Jews. And everyone brought their machines and their kettles and barrels out of hiding and set them up distilling again that product on which the world turns.

20

There were disconsolate times, and people lowered their heads as if to say, "Go on, then. Beat away as much as you like." And the smugglers who had become accustomed to changes in the weather: suns, moons, clouds, snows, rains were suddenly enveloped by something that seemed suspended in the air—and that "something" seemed to trail invisible strands of grief that entered into their smuggler's hardened hearts. At such times, the boys put their hands over the rails of wagons they followed, and walked silently, accompanied by the groaning melody of the turning wheels. Old Shayke sat in the wagon, deaf and silent, his eyes closed as he recalled old thoughts, the way a cow rechews her cud. Recalling, rechewing for the hundredth time a particular thought about his children: his grandson was still sick; and he had had no word from his son. And what's to come? What's still to come? "How much longer can I keep wandering?"

And Dovid, too, was snoozing as he sat, his head rocking until he slumped all the way down and lay with his head on good Stasha's lap—she who was such a help to him, either at hauling goods or at talking their way out of a scrape. And then he dreamed strange dreams in which strange things were revealed to him. Sometimes the dreams frightened him and he woke and did all he could, though it proved difficult, to drive them away. He had first to remind himself of his grandmother who had died three years ago; then of his dead father; and of God in Heaven. But finally, he could not rid himself of those thoughts no matter what he did. Which proved, he thought, that he was far gone in sin and that Hell would be the least of his punishments. Because why else would a boy—a thirteen-year-old—dream such awful dreams. And now he touched something soft; something that sent warmth coursing through every vein in his body. Something smooth after which he felt something sweet, so sweet. He begin to feel about, more and more quickly flushed with heat. He lowered his head and felt how his mouth touched the softness. His lips widened, and he kissed the warm place joyfully the way he once kissed whatever was holy. But nothing he had ever touched before had created such heat in him; such a bright fire. And why was it happening to him? He seemed unable to think clearly; he seemed to have forgotten everything. He forgot and kissed again and again. . . .

Such dreams. Dovid had such experiences on those sad, dark, rainy nights.

Once, when the three young gentile women had first taken to riding with Pantl, he woke and, still half asleep, thought he was home. And it seemed to him that his mother called him, and he got up and tried to go to her but he kept bumping into various seated people. Then he fell. All around him it was dark, pitch dark, and there was a storm outside and rain was coming down in torrents. As in a deluge. And he heard the young gentile woman saying, "What is it?"

And Pantl's voice, "Are you asleep? Are you asleep?"

And he held his breath, like a thief. And though it was pitch dark he kept his eyes shut so that it would be seen that he was asleep.

And then there was another time, when he was getting down from the wagon in Warsaw, when it was already daylight. He was standing on the ground and was just reaching for his bundle, which had been on the seat. Just then Nacia,° starting to get down from the wagon, put out her foot, which made tentative movements as it searched for the ground. And he saw a portion of her naked leg and felt his heart racing and the coursing of something soft and caressing through his blood.

One of the three Polish whores brought from Warsaw to act as sexual bait on the road.

But Raytshl, wrapped in the wet strips of meat, looked off into the distance like a *golem*. She was remembering the bit of cloth from Dzierdiew that she had bought, anticipating her wedding; and the six shirts she had bought at a bargain from Minke, who sold needlework; and she was thinking what sort of shoes to buy for the holiday.

Sometimes, too, a tall, respectable Jew, with a long white beard, wearing a merchant's topcoat and a stiff hat traveled with them. He sat among the smugglers, never taking his eyes from the traveling bag he held in his hand. Everyone asked himself the same question, "Who is the fellow, and is he also a smuggler?" Everyone felt constrained by his presence. But he paid his way, and in advance; and never said a word throughout the trip. A royal figure, but nobody knew that his children, doctors and engineers, had left the country. Only one daughter remained. She still had an infant at her breast, and her husband was off in the war. They had been struggling for more than a year, using up the capital of their business so that they finally sold everything they had in the house. Side boards, tables, chairs, sold for trifling sums. What was there left to do? The children did not write. They had to do something. "What the others can do, you can do." So he had put on his stiff hat, like one going on some honorable business and, on a market day, had gone to get some eggs or butter, or flour, and brought it to Warsaw. Quietly, calmly, he went into a little shop and sold what he had and brought the profits home. The smugglers knew nothing of this, and yet they were respectful of him, though why they could not have said.

Sometimes on a moonlit night old Shayke sat about telling tales of rabbis and wizards. Everyone listened, and as the tales were being told, they looked out of the wagons toward the silent fields. Their eyes wandered. There was a gleam of silver hovering over the night. And when the old man stopped talking, they felt themselves overwhelmed with lassitude, with such a sense of generosity that if someone were to come by just then who needed money, they would have given him a twenty-fiver at his first word.

But when they arrived in Warsaw, all of that vanished at once. Young men and women raised their heads alertly and did what they could to get rid of the "corpse" as they called their goods and to get their hands on "live" jingling coins.

21

And when they get back to town, everyone rushes home, leaving Pantl, his sons and Nacia beside the wagon. Each of the wagoners by now has his own "bride." Right from the start Blind Grunim, who rode with Yenkl-With-the-Sheepskin-Cap, brought his "bride" into his home. He told his wife to get out of bed. "Enough lying about," he said, and his gentile woman went to sleep in her bed.

At first, this created a scandal in the town. "Well, young folks," people said, "Young folks are young. But married men with wives, fathers of children—ugh."

Grunim's wife raised the roof. Tore her hair and tore at him—insulted and shamed him until one day he said, "You don't like it? Then you can leave the house."

To which she replied, "God damn you to hell. And what about the children?"

"Then stew in your juice and don't say a goddamn word."

And it was said that he beat her. That he had beaten her black and blue. When people started to interfere, he turned his blind eye on them so that they felt their blood curdling in their veins. "Who wants to pick a fight with that gangster, Grunim?"

His wife's brother, a shoemaker, grabbed him by the throat one day and said, "You can choose to live or die. Are you going to get rid of that gentile woman?"

And didn't Grunim just grab a knife and drive it into the shoemaker's hand. The fellow's still wearing a bandage.

And if even the older married men had "brides," why should the younger men feel any embarrassment? And Pantl felt none. One day he said to his wife, "Listen. Don't you dare say a word to me about it."

She did him one better. When the gentile woman came to the house, Pantl's wife got out of bed herself. "If I hadn't, he'd have put her into his own bed."

And that's how it was. When Glikl heard the horses snorting and shaking their manes, or the clatter of their hooves as they were being led into the stable; or simply when she heard the wagon pulling up before the house, she was already standing there wearing her slippers and her short velvet skirt. "No point in discussing it with her. . . ." And they would go to bed: Pantl in one bed and the gentile woman in the other, covering themselves with the bedclothes. Sleeping soundly.

Sometimes the pregnant Glikl was overwhelmed with shame when she remembered that she was approaching her time. And an unusual pain tugged at her heart when she remembered the early days when they had just begun smuggling. So she ran to her father's house and complained to him, pouring out her bitter grief.

The old man listened and then said angrily, "Ugh. You ought to be ashamed of yourself. To say such things about your own husband. What do you want him to do? He supports you, doesn't he? Is there food in the house? You're not running out of potatoes? Then what do you want? There are many women who would give a lot to be in your shoes. To have such a breadwinner."

So she sat there looking like a fool. The old man stood up, looked at her and laughed, "Ha, ha, ha. You'd best say nothing at all. Do you see? Who do you expect will pay for the baby's circumcision feast? Eh?"

She burst into tears, and he was touched. Old Dovid took his knotted walking stick and, bent double, he went to see his son-in-law to talk things over with him.

He went into the kitchen and sat down at the table and looked around. "Ah, ah, a prosperous house, God be thanked." But when his daughter pulled at his sleeve, gesturing, he stood up and went to the bedroom door, opened it slowly and went in. What he saw there, no one knows because he never said a word about it. What he did was to run from the room back into the kitchen. He ran as fast as he could. Then, slamming the door, he stood leaning on his stick, as if he meant with his own body to prevent anyone's entering. He made no reply to his daughter, who had just asked him something. He put his finger to his lips and said, "Shhhhhhh."

A moment or two later, he put on his hat and, with his finger still at his lips, he went away. Only when he was out in the street did he say, "Oh my, what a young man can do. Oh my—with his own wife in the house. Oh my, my . . ."

But Glikl got used to it. Sometimes when Pantl was out and she needed money, she would go to the gentile woman and get from her what she needed. And when some of the smuggled goods were confiscated, she would sit down and talk with her about what had happened and how much had been confiscated and what was taken from whom.

The young woman described it all at great length and Glikl listened, nodding her head, "Yes, yes."

In the evening—the gentiles are sitting in the house. Outside there's still plenty of daylight, but inside the house the cheap lamp is already burning and there are shadows of men and bundles on the wall. And the gentile men and women lie down together in the shadows, and there is the sound of giggling from their direction. Pantl comes in and says that the wagon is ready. Only the seats need to be readied. Then everyone gets up, and they prepare the bundles to go just as Fayfke and Jurek° come in, arm in arm and drunk as can be, singing some strange song and stamping their feet. Behind them, sounding the refrain, harmonizing with them like a choir, come Itshele in the lead and all of their friends. Mendl hears them in the courtyard and stops working with the seats, leaves the wagon and comes running into the house to slap his friends on the shoulder and they have to start their song from the beginning°:

A non-Jew.

This song is in Polish

We drive out of town,
Contraband in the wagon's our own.
   Refrain: We drive, we drive on in fear. . . .
On the road, the watchmen stand,
In Warsaw there's money to spend,
Money to hold in our hands.
And happy, we drive till we sing
At home with one voice in a ring:
   Refrain: We drive, we drive on in fear. . . .

That was the song of the smugglers, more or less, as Fayfke and Jurek sang it—with the lead singers on one side and the chorus on the other. . . . The song went on as all of the smugglers, laughing and whistling their approbation, crowded around, falling over gentile men and women. That song that captured within it the smugglers' thoughts and deepest feelings. The song that Fayfke and Jurek had made themselves.

1920

62 Revolutionary Chapters

HAYYIM HAZAZ

I

The war went on and would not be stopped. On the contrary. It proved futile to hold it to any schedule or limit. At no prearranged time would the land be quiet, not at harvest time, not near winter, and not in the spring.

At harvest time, and near winter, and also in the spring it was as if the war had just begun setting to work in earnest.

Like a pot left on the fire: the water starts simmering and is about to come to a boil.

In short, all the filth and noxious scum rose to the surface. Rasputin, secret spies, a wireless hidden in a Holy Ark in the House of Study, alas, a windmill somehow waving its sails and transmitting signals to the Germans, Jews driven out, old Jews hanged on trees as spies . . .

And the whole country, from one end to the other, full of war, darkness, poverty and the fear of sudden death.

Man and all his generations perished!

Sons called to the army shortened their years as much as possible, violating their faces and shaving their whiskers very, very close every day, to remain boys, absolute youngsters, while the fathers added on years and grew older and older—

But to no avail!

The war visited fathers and sons together, old man and youth—no one was exempt.

Old and young, fathers and sons, all together joined the army! Everyone in the world took up a gun, shaking arms and legs, walking from the barracks to the bathhouse, humming tunes.

"No end to her, damn her!" men shouted to themselves and to their comrades. "What's to be done about the bitch?"

Ps. 126:1.   Eventually, but not necessarily at the appointed time, when the Revolution occurred, the dream came true at last. Then everyone was like a dreamer°: joyful, surprised, a bit apprehensive, as one is sometimes surprised and apprehensive after a dream.

Even the heavens and earth seemed to have been created only to assist the dream: blue skies, sparkling and fresh. . . . The snow melted outside, and the heavens were planted in their waters, the roofs were scoured and dripped bright drops of water. A cool breeze blew. And people were drawn outside, walking in crowds, bright, glowing, like throngs of blind men, singing, raising their voices, shouting, and yelling—they truly withdrew their souls from their bodies! Weeping, they hugged and kissed each other, red flags fluttered in the breeze above their heads and the wheel of the sun shone and rolled above them, and it seemed as though the throngs led the wheel of the sun wherever their spirit happened to take them. . . .

War had not yet fallen silent in the land. But now it was of another degree, another degree and a different flag.

"War with no annexation or confiscation," the formula passed from mouth to mouth.

"War to the final victory!" some said.°

School children learned how to deliver those proclamations and spread them throughout the world.

The deserters, who had hidden in corners all during the war, became human again and emerged into daylight.

A huge mass of people marched through the streets toward the railroad station, all of them bearing rifles with a song on their lips:

"Arise, ye workers of the people! . . ."

The deserters made a great name for themselves in town. . . .

Nevertheless, the benefit proved to be flawed. How is that?

The reason is, to borrow from Torah cantillation, that *darga*, the rising note, precedes *tevir*, the falling one.

Thus said Reb Simcha Horowitz.

Reb Simcha was an expert Torah reader, a true connoisseur of notes and signs.

Then the word got out: the soldiers have mutinied. . . . They've had their fill of war. . . . Impossible to keep them in the trenches . . .

"Of course! They aren't laying hens, and who could get them to hatch these?"

Conspirators pressed and insinuated themselves into the crowds, grumbling:

"An end to the war! True liberty!"°

Also Henya Horowitz, Reb Simcha's daughter, had plenty of demands:

"An end to the war! Enough!"

"Everyone will immediately stop what he's doing and listen to you," Reb Simcha chided his daughter. "Don't mix into other people's business!"

"Let them put an end to the imperialist war!" Henya spoke in denunciation.

That is just the phrase she used: "the imperialist war!"

Henya had an infernal spirit, a rotten pest, not a maiden, an agent of destruction! Since the confusion of tongues,° no tongue was ever found like Henya's.

"Do you really think," Reb Simcha asks her, "that since I never studied geography and Sherlock Holmes, I lack all understanding?"

Why, she couldn't see the strength of his position at all! . . .

Round and round revolved the wheel. Events took a bad turn and sprouted up like weeds in the land. The front collapsed and soldiers flowed up out of all the fields and the paths over the mountain crests, they and all their hordes—horror! The whole land rumbled before them.

As though through an open door, they passed through the town.

Generally speaking: the war was abandoned.

This was the motto of Kerensky, who headed the provisional government.

This was Lenin's position.

After the Tower of Babel.

"It must be because the town is situated in the center of the earth," says Reb Simcha, "right in the middle, and that's why those passing through here are so numerous they cannot be reckoned up in real numbers, with no end to them. . . . And perhaps the soldiers have lost their course, and they go back and forth, back and forth, because the earth is round, and since those marchers have no set and determined longitude, they come back again and again."

Yes, that brigade had already been through once, like a rat trapped in a maze, without officers or military equipment, with only a large cooking pot, on their way to their home country somewhere. . . . Then, the first time around, they had stood, perishing with empty bellies. They broke into all the ovens and removed the *cholent* and all the Sabbath food, without the tiniest leftover, cleaning everything out spotlessly, and they sat in the center of the marketplace and ate away their hunger and pain, even dancing and celebrating. Now the brigade came back, the very same one with the same quality—as borne out by their looks: without officers and without military equipment, only a large cooking pot. . . .

"What's this?" the townsmen explain to them. "We are of the opinion that you have already gone through here once."

"No, no, not us," the answer. "That is, we have not yet gone through. We are considered another brigade, so to speak."

As it seemed, they spoke the truth. Since they left without breaking into the ovens.

Such righteousness!

"Happy are we and happy our lot," says Reb Simcha, "that surveyors are not commonly found amongst us. For if that were not so, those splendid orators and all the public speakers who have risen up over us would propose and demand miles and long miles and plots of land. . . . Now, since we have only storekeepers, those speakers will offer up their deceitful arguments and claims and all their imaginary assurances according to the length of their own yardstick.

"They have one title—Bolshevik! Such a sect. Jewish sinners. Blast their souls for having studied the Revolution with Rashi's commentary! Not the literal meaning, but the homiletic meaning: what's mine is yours, and what's yours is mine. . . . And their ulterior evil intention is visible to everyone who is at all knowledgeable about them."

In one swoop like the tail of a comet, in the wink of a single eye, the plague spread through the world: bolshevism.

"The world is holding a memorial service," says Reb Simcha, "and so all the minors with parents still living have been set loose!"°

All the young people and boors have usurped the birthright and begun ruling, even Henya has been made a commissar. A regular commissar.

The worms in the earth would wreak less destruction than they!

"Absolute redemption!" Henya girded her loins against Reb Simcha and mixed things up. "Now redemption has come to the proletariat! . . . The rule of workers and peasants . . . Wars will cease, poverty and slavery will be no more, no oppressors and no oppressed."

In short, the whole world is grace, mercy and peace. And the wolf shall dwell with the lamb. . . .°

According to custom, those with parents still living exit the synagogue during Yizkor, the memorial service for the dead.

Isa. 11:6.

A rotten pest, not a maiden! The spirit of redemption throbs in her breast! . . . Just get a load of her theories and doctrines! Try and plead a case against her!

Bad, bitter, helpless. There is no restoration in the world, no one setting things right. What has come to pass! . . .

"Where are you going, comrades?" Reb Simcha shouts, confused and distraught. "What are you doing for the bitter sorrows of our soul?"

The comrades, armed to the teeth, reply:

"Remember this, old age, and pay heed: the whole land is in the hands of the aroused people. Don't you wish to go along with the people in their uprising?"

"Have pity and mercy, comrades, for you are murderers, armed robbers, oh Lord of the universe."

"Spare us your poetry, comrade Reb Simcha, your Lord of the universe has created a new spirit within us—to raise the edifice, to give it an upper story."

Those are the words of Henikh the carpenter to Reb Simcha, and as he speaks, he raises his hand high and calls out:

"True, comrade! . . . We agree!"

"The Holy One blessed be He created a will in us, to submit our will to His blessed will!" Reb Simcha shouts to Henikh.

"Look, look!" Henikh thrusts his callused, soiled hands in Reb Simcha's face. "Did you see? We don't know how to study the Mishnah! Since the start of this imperialist war, I haven't set eyes on a book. Understand?"

Another "sinner" like that went up to Reb Simcha, stared at him with murderous, robber's eyes, as though to slay him:

"You old dog's nose, where are you sticking yourself, eh? If I step on your foot, you'll be lame. If I crush you in my closed fist, you'll no longer exist. Old louse!"

A second sinner walked up to Reb Simcha, yawned in his face as if he were a dog, took his hand and pushed him to the side, saying:

"Get out of here."

To be sure, Reb Simcha left. By the skin of his teeth, you could say, he slipped away from the murderers and hid in a cellar beneath his house.

Nothing restrains those heretics! All who are compassionate have compassion for Israel. All dwellers in the dust will beg for mercy.°

Cf. Isa. 26:19.

The next Sabbath Reb Simcha was called to the Torah and made the benediction for escaping death.

II

The world is mad, the world is satanical, torn to shreds. Band after band, piled up and confused, quarrel with each other, speaking in floods of words. Life is enveloped with hunger and blood, dread and darkness. And the mainstay, scattering hunger and blood and dread and darkness from one end to the other, is comrade Polishuk.

The winds snatched up that fine comrade and brought him to the town!

"Authorization," people reported. "He has one in his pocket from Petrograd itself, to put things right.

And people even found it amazing: a young man of short stature, skin and bones, tattered and worn, and he sets out to conquer towns and cities—what a man! People tried to avoid direct encounters with him. They knew that he had an authorization from Petrograd itself and that he came swooping down in a train bearing a sign in red letters: "Death to the Bourgeoisie!"

Comrade Polishuk took up residence in the home of Reb Simcha. Henya herself brought him.

Reb Simcha was secretly fuming, grumbling to himself about the comrades, men and women, and their evil seed. Finally he became reconciled: "Very well, let him stay. What can we do? Eventually he'll probably go away. Perhaps a spirit from on high will be aroused in him, and he'll go. Perhaps the blessed Lord will grant that his days be short."

So he stayed. He stayed in the large *zal.* He slept on the old sofa. He folded his coat beneath his head and slept. At his head, on the wall, hung his rifle, and on the table the pistol and several deadly pellets scattered about.

"I wouldn't make room for anyone else in the *zal,*" says Reb Simcha. "Only for you."

Comrade Polishuk smiled as if to say: "As though it depended only upon you and your wishes."

It was evident right away: fine fruit! . . . A vicious foe, inside and out!

"What is the main reason for your coming here?" asks Reb Simcha.

Reb Simcha wants clear and straightforward information.

"To put things in order," Polishuk answers vaguely.

"Well," Reb Simcha offers advice, "put things in order so those bastards won't be bastards!"

"That's not my job," Polishuk says with a sneer, the words trickling drop by drop, even freezing.

It looks as though he himself is quite a bastard. If only the house would vomit him forth forever.

Thus thought Reb Simcha, putting his hand over his mouth.

But what comrade Polishuk left obscure during the day, he clarified at night. His sleep told the story. Night, darkness and silence—suddenly he was hauled from his bed as though a fire had broken out in the house, perish the thought, and he paced irregularly back and forth in the room looking for some kind of bomb.

"It's me . . . me," Henya takes him by the hand every now and then. "It's me, comrade Polishuk!"

"Happiness at last!" Reb Simcha was annoyed at his daughter. "It's me, it's me! . . . Leave him alone, please."

In short, that was the only telltale sign of who that person really was.

Day by day the town declined, oppressed in low spirits and heavy with melancholy and mute silence, like a deserter.

"No doubt," says Reb Simcha, "Like a deserter, like a number of deserters all in the same place.

"Now these are the three categories essential to a person's needs: children, life and food. None is quite in the shape it ought to be; quite to the contrary.

"The children are bastards, criminals, sinners, Amalekites, not children. Life is nothingness, absolute zero, inimical to the heart and soul. And as for food, it's extremely dear when it's to be found at all!

"But it is known to those who know, and the truth is, as it is written: behold the eye of the Lord is upon those who fear him. . . .°

Ps. 33:18.

"Only the problem is known too: where did those Jewish sinners come from, who at first were neither seen nor known at all?

"Since the souls of all the Jews come from the same place, and things taken from the same place are a single entity through and through, it follows that every Jew is implicated in his fellow Jew's sin, for they are a single building. Like the body, for example, if the feet rush off to do evil, isn't the evil in the whole bodily frame?

"The difficulty: where were all those cruel, evil bastards and sinners taken from? And Thy whole nation is righteous?°

Isa. 60:21.
Yiddish for
"Help!"

Shevuot 39a and
elsewhere.

"*Gevald!*"° Reb Simcha shouts to himself. "Robbers, murderers! Yet all of Israel are responsible for one another,° so what are you going to do?"

Daily they came to the town. Some in sheepskins and others in greatcoats and still others in leather jackets. What they all had in common was that they were all bastards. . . .

Daily they came to the big stores owned by Brilliant and by Margolin and that of Hayyim Zelig the blacksmith, and they loaded wagons full of goods. Then they went their way.

"Anarchy! The world is lawless! Liberty is abroad in the world," grumbled Reb Simcha. "Only there's no freedom from robbery and theft, only there's no freedom from the enemies of the Jews, from 'thou shalt murder,' and from 'thou shalt steal,' and from 'bear false witness against thy neighbor.' "

"Are things good this way?" Reb Simcha challenged Polishuk. "How does it seem to you, comrade Polishuk, is it good this way?"

"Thank God," answered Polishuk. "Nothing's wrong. One could even say it's good . . . a Bolshevik doesn't know how to complain."

Reb Simcha cannot bear it any longer. His heart is hot within him. He cannot simply stand there because of his anger and the coursing blood.

"Good? Good? Get out of my house! . . . Right away! Get out! This is my house! Mine! M-i-n-e."

Polishuk measured Reb Simcha with his eyes, at his own pace, slowly, with his eyelids and eyebrows, slowly, as though wishing to root him out of his sight and remove him seven cubits from the face of the earth. Then he looked at Henya and gave another glance at Reb Simcha, turned his back, and left.

"You get out too, you hussy!" Reb Simcha was boiling with angry rage. "Bolshevik! . . . I won't stand for it! . . . Not for a single minute! . . . Get out! . . . May your names and memories be blotted out, sinners, boors, carpenters' and shoemakers' apprentices!"

That very day Polishuk returned, took up his rifle and went to live in the bathhouse.

Fear then seized Reb Simcha to hear about such a person—a madman like that, God in heaven!—going to live in the bathhouse! Then Reb Simcha even regretted the whole affair. But regret is not the stuff of a merchant. "Let him break his skull and neck! To the bathhouse—the bathhouse, the devil take him! And may everyone else 'from his abode'° be equally blessed!"

Liturgical
appropriation of
Ezek. 3:12.

A good man is comrade Polishuk, and a better one is comrade Soroka—so similar looking!

With the town like a wide open door, if you please! Some leave, some enter:

disturbers of the peace, ruffians, their unsavory faces skinned, their eyes mad and evil. . . .

On foot came comrade Soroka on the road leading up from the woods. Walking, sheepskins on his head, a military coat hanging on his back and dragging a small machine-gun behind him by a rope held in his hand. . . .

That very night, in the stillness of the dark, came a shriek from the steam power station in the village of Svirodovka, and on all sides the sky turned fiery red.

Dread and fearful silence spread through the whole town.

From mouth to mouth: "What happened? What happened? What happened?"

From mouth to mouth:

"Fire in Czupowski's manor."

"Fire in Kowalewski's manor."

"Fire in Count Branicki's manor."

The whole town was surrounded by fire on all sides and stood hiding with its face covered as though by a crow's wings.

The steam power station shrieks. The church bells strike with a great din. Dogs howl at their masters' heads, and a storm rolls through the air, raising itself ever higher and piling up like a huge mountain, flying and passing by with a howl, pulling the treetops after it. . . . And suddenly, in the meanwhile, an oppressive silence, the peace of death . . .

Now the sky was bright and clouds of smoke and flames wander and roam. Comrade Polishuk went down on his knees before the snowy plain, stretched his arms before him and cried out:

"Revolution, behold, Ha-ha-ha!"

"Revolution, ha-ha-ha!" Henya repeated after him.

They looked at each other and leapt into each other's arms. . . .

Night after night the sky burned around the town. Night after night the sky was red, flaming and smoky, without stars or constellations.

It was as though comrade Soroka wished to uproot not only the stars and constellations, but also all the angels, as it were, the seraphim and heavenly host.

For nights and weeks the sky was wrapped in flame.

All those weeks Soroka was never seen in town. Until once he came and went through the street: sheepskins on his head, a military coat hanging on his back, and his fingers were reddish blue as though uprooted, pulling behind him a small machine-gun on a rope, and so he walked, clanging with an iron key:

"Arise, ye workers of the people!"

Of all the huge quantity of booty stolen by the peasants from the noblemen's estates, Soroka took for himself only an iron key that had fallen from a smashed door.

Soroka's voice was heard from the street. Immediately all the comrades, men and women, leaped up and went out, shouting, "Hoorah!" "Long live the rule of the workers and peasants!" With a waving of hats and hands in the air, they raised their voices in the "Internationale."

At the sound of the song, comrade Soroka stood at attention, stretching his whole body upwards, turned his stern face to the side and raised his hand in a salute. . . .

The crowd took hold of comrade Soroka by his arms and legs, picked him up in the air, carried him in their hands, bearing him to the council building.

A mass of men pressed at the entrance, and Jews from everywhere were drawn after them as though to a circumcision or bar mitzvah.

Soroka stood in the middle of the room, extended his hands to all present and spoke:

"Ha, shake my hand, but hard! . . . Even though you're no Bolshevik, as I can see, and not at all different from a bourgeois, nevertheless, shake, as I am a Jew."

That evening, in comrade Polishuk's residence, in the bathhouse, festivities and celebration.

The whole band of comrades from the town, men and women, gathered at the bathhouse.

Polishuk kept the commandment of offering hospitality in proper fashion. Nothing necessary for a celebration was lacking, neither food nor drink.

By candlelight all the comrades, men and women, sat in a circle on logs and inverted tubs, indulging themselves with lard, pickles, brandy and tea. They drank tea in famous fashion: wrapped in towels till the seventh degree of sweat°—one slurping from a cup, another from a soldier's mess tin and yet another from a plate with Hebrew writing in red letters on a white background: "Bread and salt shalt thou eat, and reap the truth."

A Russian custom, to order a towel along with the tea.

At midnight, when their hearts were gladdened with eating and drinking, they shook the benches and beams of the bathhouse with their mighty dancing, as much as their legs could dance.

From the hole in the oven, flames reached out and licked the sooty bricks. The stones heaped up around the boiler turned black, and splinters of flame flickered. Above the boiler a thick column of steam rose to the beams of the black ceiling and veiled the benches. Heels pounded. The bodies were linked in a single chain, spinning, rocking, a chain of whirling skirts, red shirts and gun-belts, boots, wild hair, shouted song, whistles, sudden outcries and guttural, throaty sounds. . . . Everything in the bathhouse danced dizzily: the boiler and the stones, the ritual bath and the regular bathtub, old bundles of twigs, piles of full sacks and even comrade Gedalia hopped on his crutch.

Then the poor bathhouse, torn in roof and ribs, saw joy, one joy for all the days to come! The homes of rich landlords and officials in their glory were never honored with even a sixtieth of that honor from the time that the temple—the temple of the bathhouse—was a bathhouse. Truly that was a happy occasion!

But what was even more marvelous was the end, the end of the celebration!

The festivities, the singing and dancing were like the air all around, invisibly filling up space, like something not properly understood.

At the end of the night, when everyone was acting in his own way and dancing according to his own nature: one prancing on an upper bench and another hopping inside the empty, steaming bathtub, someone shouting: "Help! Help!" and someone else had made himself into a wagon and rolled along the floor on his belly—comrade Polishuk fled outside as though mad with worry and anger. He ran to the river and plunged in through a crack in the ice.

The other comrades noticed immediately and raised a panicked outcry. The women wept and wailed, the men ran with iron tools, laboring to crack the ice, some hastily smashing it, others peering into the black water. . . . Shouts all around, then suddenly a dreadful silence, the howl of the snowstorm, fear and dread and the sound of breaking ice. Suddenly Polishuk's head gleamed on the rushing water. . . . Hubbub, racing about, shouting, shoving . . . Polishuk was stuck between chunks of ice. Looking about him, supported by the arms reaching to him, he jumped up out of the river, healthy and strong, running to the bathhouse on his own feet with the whole crowd behind him—in a noisy, rushing tangle.

In the bathhouse all the comrades pressed around the one standing there, trembling in all his limbs, everyone astonished and enjoying the sight.

Soroka stood above him, gave him brandy to drink, hugged him and kissed him on his blue lips, asking how he felt:

"Is your soul restored? Is your soul restored, tell me, hey!"

Henya cried and laughed, wrung her hands, cried and laughed, and all the others hastened to do something, making loud noises to each other.

"*Mazel tov! Mazel tov!*" cried out Polishuk and enthusiastically animating his blue face and leaping into the steam room, with Henya after him. Henya was nearly crushed between the door and the frame.

The whole crowd wandered around the room in little groups, everyone by himself, but all together in a single mass, dark, moving, singing in joy and enthusiasm:

"*Mazel tov! Mazel tov! Mazel tov!*"

Nothing like it had ever been heard.

Only Soroka stood at the door of the steam room and shook his head from side to side, clapping to the sound of the singing and shouting:

Apparently the lyrics to a Russian song.

"To kill the lion in the well on a snowy day!"°

Such a high level of devotion.

III

Deeds that make the heart soar, not sermons or clever speech and the like, truly inspiring actions, at the sight of which a person might even forget to rub his own flesh—such were Soroka's. Fire!—Here it is, ho! Fiery flames and the sight of torches . . . The noise of war—that too is good, you might say!

But Soroka's spirit fell, and he sat in front of his machine-gun, ripped a page from a Menshevik° pamphlet and rolled himself cigarette after cigarette.

A Social Democrat who, after November 1917, was officially opposed to the policies and methods of the Bolshevik Party.

"In this world every dog is stuck to his own tail," Soroka argued with the machine-gun. "In this world every dog is stuck to his own tail."

For a few days the little machine-gun listened to that general observation, which was spoken and reiterated a hundred times or more, until Soroka stood up, shook his head as though shaking a heavy burden from his shoulders, spat in his palm, and said:

"May the seven spirits be in your navel!"

He girded his loins with his pistol, left the bathhouse, and went out into the street. He passed by as though to say, "I am a king and worthy of it!"

People saw him walking in the street that way and cursed him roundly:

"President, stones in his guts! . . . Look how he's walking! . . . A parade like that. . . . Lord, may such a presidency collapse, ha? Nu? . . . Is there still any reason to live in this world?"

Where did Soroka go that way, standing erect and taking straight steps? Impossible to say he knew clearly where he was going, in any case, not to the council building, certainly not. . . .

In the council building they're always giving speeches, scheming in speeches, death to them! Quickly get yourself a pair of ears and stand and listen. . . . Soroka avoided speeches like poison!

Nevertheless, Soroka did go to the council building. An important reason brought him there. He came with something to say:

"Yes, comrades, there will be a union of Jewish soldiers—that's all there is to it!"

No words, no arguments, no putting off were of any avail.

Soroka was not one to scatter his words to the winds.

"Yes, comrades, there will be a union of Jewish soldiers, and not only that! This is how. . . ."

Councils of counselors met to take counsel, discussed, argued, pondered and debated, squabbled with each other in good order.

"Well, comrades!" Soroka stood at their head. "Have you decided yet? Yes? . . . I want to be allotted five hundred rifles immediately, twenty machine-guns, three hundred hand grenades and five hundred pistols! . . . Is it signed yet? Comrade Polishuk, it seems to me you have all the qualities needed to become a clearminded Bolshevik. Is it signed yet? Comrade Polishuk, don't tell me stories from when your grandmother was a bride. Is it signed yet?"

The mandate was written out and signed and delivered to Soroka.

The union was established.

A staff and duties and sergeants were appointed.

The head of the union, comrade Soroka, rode like a hero, as is proper, mounted on a fiery steed.

The assistant to the head of the union was comrade Gedalia, the man with the crutch, and like comrade Soroka he rode on a tall horse, tied into the saddle with ropes, proud and glorious, edifying the entire assembled crowd with looks from his black eyes.

In vain the astonished people wondered:

"Who made an army out of the Jews?"

Not only that, Motl Privisker the teacher instructed Reb Simcha that Shamgar Ben-Anath, who smote six hundred Philistines, did so with an oxgoad,° and was redeemed through him, Motl Privisker, the teacher of young boys. For the word "oxgoad," *malmad habakkar,* can also mean a *melamed,* a teacher of young oxen, who hits his pupils to make them learn. And those six hundred were an esoteric reference to the six Orders of the Mishnah. . . .

But when that force of Jewish soldiers passes through the street, ordinary mortals had better pay up in good coin and regard that pleasurable spectacle—

That is what Motl Privisker himself says.

"Comrades," Soroka spoke to his army. "Take heed: Like a drum major, look! This is how you should march! . . .

"One two, one two!"

After much labor and effort the job was finished and Soroka was idle again.

Soroka had only to sit and wait for coming events.

But such conduct was foreign to Soroka's way and nature.

And events did not tarry.

One snowy and sunny day, the market was stunned. The Jews laid aside their business and fled: they were prepared, anticipating a pogrom.

Judg. 3:31.

"Because of the flour," they reported, "because they supposedly give the Jews the finest, and the gentiles get only dura flour."

The council members arose and tried to address the gentiles who had surrounded the cooperative store, using soft language:

"Comrades! Comrades!"

In response, the roar of the mob:

"Can't we eat bread fit for humans? . . . The Jews get fine flour! . . . A Jewish kingdom! . . . Clobber him, that dwarf! . . . He's a bourgeois, you can tell by his pockets. . . .

"Comrades! . . . Comrades!"

Then Soroka went through the market with his band. Not to make war against the goyim, but just to show them how soldiers march in good order and how they sing. . . .

The goyim immediately noticed it and fell silent. At the same time everyone was made to comprehend perfectly well, visibly and palpably, the yellow dura bread that the Jewish women brought out of their houses for proof.

"Dura bread too, for example, so what do you have to say?" The goyim kneaded the crusts of bread with their hands and put it in their heavily bearded mouths, milling it between their molars.

A reference to the curse that turned into a blessing, Num. 22–24.

Go remove Balaam from their mouths,° a thorn in their sides!

IV

Wrapped in their cloaks, Reb Simcha in a tattered fox-skin coat and Motl Privisker in a balding cat-skin coat, the pair of them tried to make a place for themselves at the side of the oven and warm up.

They were both long in years, having completely forgotten how they once were their fathers' and mothers' little boys, yet they still remembered the Garden of Eden well, the angels singing, the Tree of Life in the garden,° and the incorporeity of the Holy One blessed be He. For all that, neither of them knew what "the end of days" might bring.

Based on the folk belief that the unborn soul resides in Paradise.

Motl Privisker sat and crossed his booted legs, placing one foot on the other, flourishing a bottle of brandy now and then, squinting at it, pouring some into his cup, and from there into his mouth, wiping the remnant from his black beard with his sleeve.

The brandy goes down into him like a fiery torch, till it reaches his very heart, making a hot conspiracy with his stomach. A sprite, not brandy! . . .

Reb Simcha likes to sit with Motl Privisker, and each time he honors Motl with these words: "May the blessed Lord help us, may every man take pity on his fellow and may we all be saved soon, amen."

Good taste and discernment has Motl, weighty teachings and wonderfully wise sayings, interpretations of the Bible that delight the listener. . . . A mighty lion in Hasidic wisdom! . . . A rose of esoteric learning!

When Motl Privisker opens his mouth, Reb Simcha can sit and listen to him day and night. All of Israel, the holy nation, each according to his capacity and virtue, will then stand before the eyes of Reb Simcha.

"The Master of the Universe and the Divine Presence are in exile, right and left, flushed and pale with judgment and mercy, the wings of the dove, the wings of the commandments, the matron and the bird's nest, the Jews lie in prayer shawls

In rabbinic legend, magicians who opposed Moses and fashioned the Golden Calf.

Mythical founders of Rome.

Names of the Leviathan in Isa. 27:1.

Tsav in Hasidic usage is brandy with 96 percent alcohol.

Motl is quoting bits and pieces from Ezek. 7:5–12.

The twenty-four books of the Hebrew Bible.

and phylacteries in exile, and Jannes and Jambres the sons of Balaam,° Remus and Romulus,° the tortuous serpent, the piercing serpent,°° and the two lips that are called flames, and the two apples between which the spirit of the Messiah emerges, and the king bound in stocks. . . .''

"Now, Reb Simcha, lay aside the worries that concern you. . . . Lay them aside, I tell you. . . . For when I reflect, Reb Simcha, that I never committed adultery nor murdered, nor did I steal from my fellow, I put on my prayer shawl and phylacteries every day and wash my hands and behave according to the laws of the Torah as ordained by our rabbis of blessed memory and the earlier and later halakhic authorities, and have even exceeded the requirements, no matter what, I am happy with my lot! What do you have to say, hm? . . . *Lekhayim*, Reb Simcha. . . .''

"Ech! . . . E-ech! . . .'' Motl Privisker shuts his eyes, stretches his jaws and wags his head. "A sprite, not brandy!''

"A *Tsavele*,° fine, fine, delightful. . . . It truly gives wings to the soul, E-eh! . . .''

Reb Simcha rubs his shoulders against the stove and says nothing.

Motl Privisker puts the tail of a salted fish in his mouth, chews and slowly pours another cup:

"Fish like to swim.

"Reb Simcha, why? Why are you so down in the dumps?'' he continued, "Speak up, foolish man! . . . Vanity of vanities, mud of mud . . . Have a drink and don't let your wings stink! Hm? . . . A glass of brandy is a weighty matter, a matter of ritual purity. . . . It cleanses the filth, the ugliness from the heart, very much so, oy, very much so! . . . Drink a *lekhayim*, I tell you, and return to your proper state.''

Motl Privisker empties the cup into his mouth, wipes his mustache with his sleeve, raises a crust of bread up in his hand, leans over to Reb Simcha and whispers in his face:

" 'An evil, behold an evil is coming. . . .° The end is coming, the end is at hand, putting an end to you. . . . It's coming. . . . The designated hour, inhabitant of the land . . . The time is come. . . . The day is close. . . . Turmoil and not the echoes of mountains . . . Let the buyer not be glad nor the seller grieve. . . .' Choice words, Reb Simcha, precious words, deep, deep . . . They should be kissed with great kisses. . . . The whole matter . . . Drink a *lekhayim*, I tell you, and don't be a fool. Ezekiel—brother and friend, I shall make thee learned and wise—is the most remarkable of the twenty-four books of the Bible. . . . Ezekiel is the soul of the twenty-four. . . .° Drink a *Lekhayim* and don't let your body dry out!''

From time to time Motl Privisker empties the cup into his mouth, turns around and hums in Aramaic: "Children, life, food.''

Inside, darkness rotted in the dreariness and silence. Outside the wail of the embittered wind could be heard. All of a sudden the winds fell from on high. The house groaned with the crash of the wind, and the howling snow pounded the windows.

"Henya, Henya!'' shouted Motl Privisker. "Another piece of bread!''

"Henya! Give me a piece of bread.''

"Henya, a maiden reaching those years, an evil spirit in your bones!''

Motl Privisker walks through the room on his soft boots, walks to the window, and stands still.

Outside the window, a deep, broad night, full of drunkenness and turgid whiteness.

"Henya, may a pig gnaw you."

Outside the window—a white orchard, stormy and spinning dizzily in rage, moons and planets, with spirits and angels . . .

"True is it, ha?" Motl Privisker leaps and stands as an adversary to Henya, who has entered with a piece of bread in her hand. "That the world is on the path of truth, hmm?"

"Go away, go, you Hasid, you drunken Jew!"

"Hold your tongue, hussy!" Reb Simcha sits upright. "You'll talk yet!"

"In truth, ha, a maiden reaching those years, an evil spirit in your bones! . . . The truth, eh, is it yours? Does it belong to you? . . . The truth belongs to the Holy One blessed be he, stu—pid! . . . The Lord's seal, youuu shrewww! Ri—ight! . . . *She* discovered the truth! . . . And you are unaware of your foolishness, that you only found the pudendum of truth! . . . And who sent you this face eh? . . . The shape of your mouth and forehead and cheeks, eh?—a maiden reaching those years, an evil spirit in your face!

"My soul is tossing within me," Motl Privisker cries out to Reb Simcha, waving his arms and making a strange motion, "the whole of my inner being!"

He paces back and forth in the room, fumbling in his trouser pockets and talking to himself:

"The pupil of the eye is a mirror . . . a mirror . . . even though it's black. . . . When it disappears, it's an impenetrable thought. . . . And when it appears—at the same time the heavens open and I see divine sights!"

Motl Privisker paces back and forth, returns to his seat, sits next to Reb Simcha, lowers his head and speaks, saying he very much wanted to travel to Ger to see the Rebbe.°

Then he says:

"If I had a violin in my hands and could play now . . . I would play such a melody, gathered from running brooks and set with precious stones!"

And then he empties the bottle into his mouth, sitting and speaking incomprehensible words, sketches, drawings, shades of color, toward which he is headed, as it were. . . .

"By way of secret," he speaks "Adam . . . Adam of *beriah*° rode on a lion. . . . Turning to the right he sketched roads; and paths—

"And to the left, Adam of *yetsira* rides on an ox and takes fire from his mouth and draws pictures—

"Adam of *'assiya* rides on an eagle, and the spirit in his mouth makes shades of color."

Motl places his hand over his eyes and sits in silence, then he speaks again for a moment:

"Lord of the universe, Lord of the universe! . . . Give my heart wisdom and knowledge to persevere! . . . In what path shall I start upon and persevere? Where shall I begin my effort? What can I do with my soul? Lord, Lord, Lord of the universe, I don't know the meaning at all!"

"Forget it, Motl, forget that confusion," said Reb Simcha. "Leave it be! . . . You've imbibed and gotten drunk like a goy. . . . You'll only dishonor yourself, feh! . . . Tell me, why don't you go back to your wife and children?"

Travel to Ger (Gora Kalwarja) in western Poland was impossible at that time.

Beriah (creation), yetsira (creativity) and 'assiya (action) are Kabbalistic terms.

"Leave me be, leave me be. . . . I'm doing something great for the whole Jewish people, and this isn't the time to deal with personal matters."

"Motl, now nothing's stopping you from going home. They aren't conscripting men for the army any more."

"Simcha, Simcha, Simcha! . . . Why are you mixing me up? . . . *Gevald*, why are you disrupting my train of thought!"

Motl Privisker leaps to his feet and starts staggering drunkenly, circling the room.

Then he lies on the hard, narrow bench and speaks to himself.

With an old, shaking hand Reb Simcha pulls down his hat and covers all his gray hair. For long moments they plunged into the depths of oblivion.

Covered with crushing layers of snow, the town stood: veiled, sinking.

Snow—infinite in breadth and height . . .

All around the winds race in brotherhood and friendship, singing in wails.

Above the empty space of the world hangs like a silver lamp, and a storm comes flying and lights up stars and fiery flames in it. . . .

A hairy beast, frightfully white, walks to and fro in the air, grasping the town the way a man might take a nut in his hand, screaming, terrifying with its voice.

As when the Ten Commandments were given at Sinai.

No bird flies above, no man walks below.° The wind comes and picks up the snow like a curtain above, and there, shot through with silver and carried along by the storm, are Polishuk and Soroka on the street.

"Hey, hey, snowstorm! Here we are! Come out, comrade Henya!—Yoo hoo!"

Winnowing storm winds blow, hills are thrown up, white darknesses are flattened.

"Hey, hey, hey!"

White darkness blocks the eyes. Frost plucks at faces.

"First, where to?"

From within the storm:

"There's no first, comrade Henya, and no last!"

"Comrade Henya, the heart exults, the heart is happy, bursting in fiery sparks, hey, hey!" Jumbles of wind whip out and pound from face to face.

"Comrade Henya," Soroka calls from within the storm, "Comrade Henya, tell me: Who am I?"

"You are married!" Henya laughs.

"Comrade Henya, I can't sleep. . . . Do you love me? . . . Do you love me? . . . Tell me!"

"Whom?"

"Me, nu!"

"No . . ."

"Nu, love someone, it's all the same, all the same!"

Henya's eyes, in their coquetry and their laughter, glowed over the field of snow and looked lovingly. Like white columns of smoke the snow flurries rise above Henya's head.

"And the Revolution, eh?"

"Ah—my daughter!"

"Hey, hey! . . . Revolution . . . A-ho-ho!"

The storm rises up and hangs over them.

Pulling each other by the hand, the three of them race into the eye of the storm, in the brilliant wheels of snow, between white, winged fires.

"Hey, hey, hey, my white darkness!"

Henya throws her hands up in the air on both sides.

"Hey, hey—he-hey! . . ."

Roaming towers formed in the air, white sheds journeyed, sheaves of wind flew about and whacked one's face, sharp black things rocked in the whiteness of the opaque space; the storm was set dancing wildly, the one that put eternal generations to sleep, the order of creation, emperors' and kings' sons, houses of study, beards, the Torah, the commandments, and the King of kings, and which raised white tablets between heaven and earth. . . .

"Listen, listen—until the soul is lit with pain and light!"

"Hey, hey, as fierce as the revolution."

And from the heart and soul:

"Henya!"

With a loving voice, melting the heart:

"Polishuk!"

"Not that way. I don't want it at all!" cried out Soroka, turning his shoulder and leaving.

"Why are you acting that way, comrade Soroka?" called Henya, and stood in anticipation.

Polishuk began to chuckle.

"What happened to him?" asked Henya.

The white storm whirls and whirls, scattering flames in every wind. The world leaps, screams.

From within the turning storm:

"A third part of thee shall fall by the sword round about thee—and I shall scatter a third to every wind—the evil arrows of hunger—and plague and blood— *Ezek. 5:12.* and I shall bring a sword upon you—.'"°

"Hey, who's there?"

Polishuk and Henya stood still, leaned their heads into the darkness, looked hard, looked and saw: staggering through the snow, a single man, falling and rising, waving his hands, walking, and on his shoulders something like the starry sky all poured out.

"Who's there?"

"It's I, have no fear, I! . . . Wait!"

The wanderer drew near them. It was Motl Privisker.

"Where are you coming from, comrade Motl?"

"From where? . . . From the prophet Ezekiel . . . Yyess!"

They didn't understand what he was talking about.

"From whom?"

"Didn't I tell you? . . . Just now he came . . . You didn't recognize him, ha-ha-ha. I'd never seen Ezekiel in my life. . . . He came and asked: 'Who are you, my son?' 'I,' I answered, 'I'm a certain Reb Motl. . . .' 'Give me an interpretation of my verse, "A third part of thee shall fall by the sword." ' Then I understood right away."

"Nu?" asked Polishuk.

"Nothing at all. I said . . ."

"Nu?" Polishuk asked again.

"Nu? . . . Nothing at all."

"Ezekiel, Ezekiel," laughed Henya. "For the extra glass of brandy he took."

"You, don't laugh!" Motl turned to her. "You, don't laugh! You would do better to go home. Your father doesn't know what to do. He's sitting and crying, crying."

V

It was a bright morning, rough, bristling with frost and snow.

The trees stood drawn like Sukkot palm branches—decorated and veiled with marvelous playthings and ornaments—of pure silver.

The houses were sunk in snow and the bright glow.

With joy and song like sharpened knives the snow creaked underfoot.

The frost burned with flames and searing.

On an upturned tub, without raising his head from the ground, sat Soroka before the flaming hole in the furnace.

He had returned to his seclusion with his little machine-gun.

He passed several days just in thought and cogitation.

That day Polishuk transferred his residence from the bathhouse to a room he rented for himself. It was a fine room in every respect. A room that was a house in itself, sitting in a large courtyard, peaceful and quiet.

"Join me," Polishuk spoke to Soroka. "The room's big, and there's only Henya who'll come and live with us."

Soroka delayed his answer, as though weighing his words very very carefully before speaking.

Hardly was the crunch of the snow under Polishuk's feet heard as he went away from the bathhouse, before Soroka sat down and repeated his motto:

"In this world every dog is attached to his own tail."

Soroka hadn't managed to repeat that saying a hundred times before going out and heading for the staff courtyard.

In the staff courtyard Soroka reviewed his men, went out before them, strutted and paced back and forth, stood, and with his second in command, comrade Gedalia at his side, he called out:

"Comrades! At this moment I still have the power to give you orders! Therefore, first: drum major! . . . Second—always remember this: the force of the union of Jewish soldiers has no right not to be hanged, not to be shot, not to be burned and not to be buried alive! . . . Now, friends, as you have heeded me, so shall you heed the head of the union, comrade Gedalia."

The troops were bewildered. A secret voice of complaint passed from one end to the other.

"Comrades!" Soroka made a circle in the air with his arm, "Obey the order! Now your chief will be comrade Gedalia, and I leave you to go to my work and my activities, and the like. . . . I thank you, comrades, for your work and your assistance, may you be well."

"Kru-gom marsh!"° comrade Gedalia spoke out after Soroka.

Soroka turned his back and left.

Soroka disappeared, he and his machine-gun together, as though the wind had taken him away, a silent wind, and no one knew where he went.

In Russian, "About face!"

VI

In Reb Simcha's house, silence and barrenness—enough to make you burst!

Reb Simcha angrily paces about his house, wandering here and there like a colt blasted with rain and wind. Conversation between him and Henya has ceased. He but sees her and turns his head away so as not to look at her impure face.

Sometimes Motl Privisker comes and has a heart-to-heart talk with Reb Simcha:

"If the blessed Lord can sit and see the troubles of the world and keep silent, then we, Reb Simcha, can suffer in silence. Anyway . . ."

He also spoke to Henya:

"Tell me, Henya, wouldn't you ever think: 'What's happening to me?' You're stuck far away, absolutely distant!"

As for Henya, nothing touches her soul, and today passes like yesterday: beautiful as though drafted with a compass, her mouth reddish and her cheeks white. Beauty and splendor.

Grief, grief. Reb Simcha restrains himself. He sits with his feet up in front of the oven, burning logs, and sighing to the oven:

"Oy-oy-oy."

If only Motl Privisker could stifle that grief of his! If he could but be silent or pour his heart out like water in a humble voice and spirit submissive to the very center of his heart! Tears flow from both his eyes without cease.

"You're stuck far away, absolutely distant!"

"Henya, tell me what in the world you're doing? . . . Do you know what in the world you're doing!"

Motl Privisker spoke, giving Henya a look, a look of Reb Motl Privisker's sort, till Henya became completely ill at ease and didn't know where to turn or what to say.

"I ask you, what are you actually doing?"

Motl took large steps and walked across the room, sitting in his chair, putting his head on the table, then raising his head and putting it down again.

"The world is destroyed. . . . The world is destroyed. . . . Oh Lord, Oh Lord . . . The world has gone mad, mad . . . What can we do? What can we d-o-o?"

He stood up and shouted:

"Henya! Henya!"

Then he went back and resumed where he had stopped:

"The world has gone mad, mad. . . . And I'm mad . . . completely. . . ."

"Motl, I am very surprised at you," Reb Simcha broke in. "I'm astonished! What idea have you fixed in your mind?"

"That I shall cut them to pieces!" Motl put a hand over his mouth and turned away from Reb Simcha.

"Motl," Reb Simcha spoke sternly. "I don't understand. What do you expect? Why won't you return to your home and your wife?"

"Not me, not me, teach your *daughter!*" shouted Motl, and his eyes glowed like fire. "There you have someone to instruct!"

Reb Simcha fell silent. He gave up. Motl's eyes almost turned white, but Reb Simcha would not say what should be said at such a moment.

The logs didn't burn. Reb Simcha sighed. He mumbled the first words of the afternoon prayers and dealt with the furnace. He pulled himself together and dealt with the furnace.

A bluish light surrounded the room.

Motl Privisker stood in the corner, swaying and moaning a weepy chant, saying his afternoon prayers. During the central portion of the prayers, when he reached, "Forgive us, our father, for we have sinned," he secretly wept, and tears flowed ceaselessly from both his eyes.

VII

The storms spread out—long, dangling, crooked, smooth and round—and they blasted and blew about freedom on earth and about the end of redemption; about Amens once answered with voices loud and joyous that had since grown silent; about the trilling song and psalm with which congregants, once upon a time, backed up their leader of prayer; about festival feasts that had been disrupted; about grooms and marital honors that had been abrogated—about the Jewish pulse that had gone dead.

The heavens and the earth whistled evening prayers with all the vowels and points of the Torah, but slightly obscure: Je-ho-va-ha—ha-ha! . . . And answering with a "Jee-hee-vee-hee—He! He!" Others echoed, "Jo-ho-vo-ho—Glo-o-ory!"

And this at the door:

"Knock knock!"

"Who's there?"

"I, Reb Simcha. Open up!"

And before Reb Simcha could close the door:

"Close the door! . . . Close it!"

Reb Simcha closed the door.

"That?" Reb Simcha pointed to a small, loaded sled.

"Where's the axe?"

"Right away, right away."

Motl Privisker's lips were twisted, and his face was pale. His ears were full of the trumpeting and fanfare.

"What are you looking at? Rip up the floor, Reb Simcha!"

"Is everything there?"

"Everything except the *Handful* and *The Devil's Skin.*"[6]

"Shh . . . Shh."

In the large *zal,* where the tiniest memory of the goodness and grace of broad, peaceful life still remained, the floorboards were ripped open.

A cold, wet smell wafted up from the bared earth.

Motl Privisker and Reb Simcha bent down over the bared earth like hungry wolves during a storm.

Outside a kind of wolves' howl was heard.

The axe struck softly like teeth.

It was as though they, Motl Privisker and Reb Simcha, were sitting and howling and gnashing their teeth.

Boxes of textile well wrapped up were buried.

The work was finished.

The floor was repaired, once more becoming what it was.

"How will it be found? eh, Reb Simcha? How, I ask you, will it be found? No! It will never be found."

Reb Simcha hurried over to the furnace, sat and struggled to make the fire blaze up in the wood in the oven, to heat the house, which had become chilled.

Cryptic use of Hebrew titles to describe the contraband.

Motl Privisker roamed about the room, briskly moving his legs and body.

"The famine years are over, over. . . . What hunger have we, hm? . . . What hunger, I ask you, have we? What is the wickedness of the evildoers for us? Nothing, we shall bear it and suffer! . . . It's nothing. . . ."

The furnace blazed. The wind sent little fiery candles flying.

The fire burned higher and higher.

"Ah, what has been done? What has been done! . . . Tell me, Reb Simcha! . . . What is the Revolution like? . . . Seven times a revolution, and seven times a malignancy! . . . Have no fear, Reb Simcha, my friend, my brother. You have great plenty, great plenty. We lack nothing. . . . Motl is no liar, eh?"

The fire of the furnace lit the wall. On the splinters of wood rose budding flowers, braided Havdalah candles,° and above them all—a single flame like a large golden censer. Below the wood, on the bottom, coals glowing like bars of pure gold.

"Ah, what has happened!" crowed Motl Privisker and grasped Reb Simcha's belt. "It is not in the heaven . . . nor over the sea . . . not the entente, and not world capital . . . but close, close . . . beneath our feet!"

From outside the snowy window the storm howled about the entente, about world capital, about the worldwide revolution and about the Internationale.

In the howl of the storm could be heard the sound of Henya's triumphant laughter.

"Did you hear? Oh-oh, a girl who's come of age! . . . Ah, why's she laughing, that evil thing."

"Nu-nu?!" Henya's voice came from outside. "Ha-ha-ha."

"Are you coming? . . . Come!" Polishuk's voice.

"Ye-he—he, he!" the sound of the storm.

Reb Simcha was bewildered. He didn't know what to do. He ran about the room, back and forth, sat down again in front of the stove, ran about again.

"Ye-he—he! he!" the sound of the storm at the window.

VIII

By the window, near the place where the wind raged, dresses and shawls floated up, old rags, and felt boots and threadbare, hairy coats, fur caps wandered on the whiteness. The snow gleamed with the cleanliness of teeth, Reb Simcha sat with his white beard falling down over his blue hands, and his spectacles, fixed with strings and iron wires from old "Fialka" bottles,° mounted on his nose.

The wind trumpeted and whistled outside about freedom in the world and the end of redemption, loudly about the silenced response of "Blessed is He and blessed be His name, amen," about Sabbath hymns and *cholent* and *kugel* that had been suppressed, about the study of Torah, which had completely ceased, about the reciting of psalms, which the old men nevertheless continued, the remaining old men, each one in the bitterness of his heart, and his torn voice, and especially about the eleven psalms one says for a sick person. . . .°

Motl Privisker wandered about the room like an angel of destruction, not as was his wont, but with frightfully big steps such as were never seen, standing before Reb Simcha like a tree pleasant to look at, with the secrets of the Torah, from which wise teachings flourish, for a few moments he stood still before Reb Simcha like that, as though planted there, looking him over with his eyes, and in

A candle with multiple wicks used at the conclusion of the Sabbath.

Perfume derived from flowers.

E.g., Pss. 6, 20, 25, 30, 32, 38, 41, 51, 86, 91, 102, 103. Traditions vary among Ashkenazic communities.

that too—the likes of which had not been seen, with those eyes in Motl Privisker's famous fashion, saying:

"What is it, Reb Simcha, that Rabbi Akiba said to his disciples? 'When you reach the place of the pure marble plates, do not say, "Water, water," lest you endanger yourselves'—ha?"°

B. *Hagigah* 14b.
In Merkavah
mysticism, refers
to the dangers
confronting the
mystic in his
ascent through the
seven palaces of
the seventh
heaven.

Afterwards Motl sent his legs, may the all-merciful preserve us, all over the room—and that was an affair in its own right!—Revolving around a pole wondrous to heart and soul, when we see him with our own eyes, turning and talking to himself secretly with a soft, crestfallen voice, weakening the mind:

"That is a high secret, more elevated than can be borne . . . a high secret . . . high. . . ."

With enthusiasm and ardor and waving his hands upwards:

"Ex-al-ted!"

Reb Simcha already heard disturbing noises outside, hu-ha and hu-ha, the sound of people pursuing and running.

Outside there was also order in its own right.

Dr. Yukel the Bundist crawled, beaten and wounded, on hands and knees through the snow. . . . A red flag that proclaimed, "Long Live the Constituent Assembly" spreading in the wind and rolling . . . The student, Cahan, and Reb Aharon Shapira's son fleeing, and Polishuk and his people running after him and crying and shouting out loud . . .

Motl still paced about the room, not seeing or hearing anything, turning around and around and talking:

"*Bereishit*, the beginning . . . in the beginning . . . Listen, daughter, and see . . . listen, daughter, and see. . . . In the beginning, there in that passage—*shim'i* 'listen,' there—*bat* 'daughter,' there—*re'i* 'see' . . . 'Listen'—the same letters as in 'the beginning,' 'daughter'—there it is, the same word in the first part and at the end of the word, . . . 'see.' And here is the word in the middle. . . ."

"Motl, Motl!" shouted Reb Simcha in a voice not his own. "Murderers . . . Murderers . . . What are they doing! What for! Motl, Motl, go tell them. . . . Motl! They'll slay him. . . ."

Motl turned about, preoccupied with his own thoughts and spoke to himself:

"Listen, daughter, and see. . . . Listen, daughter, and see. . . ."

Outside the wind caught up with the sun and the sun with the wind. Lights interwoven flew up. Veils. Handfuls and handfuls of pure white curls.

On the windowpanes, decorated with scepters and palm branches, rainbows stuck each other in all their colors.

Bearing a day like a copper column and wind.

IX

Like a green wave, pushed back and leaning into the distance, lay greenish the layers of snow, and the crimson of the sunset was on and around them.

Among the columns of smoke rising from the chimneys of the houses the wind hung as though among the masts and shrouds of ships in the heart of foamy seas.

Suddenly a rumor was heard, noise, a tangle of voices, massive and fearful:

"They're coming."

"The murderers."

"Murderers."

Polishuk flashes through the street garbed in the flames of the sunset and, with his right hand, drawing the pistol at his side:

"Toward the enemy! . . . Toward the enemy!"

Like a spirit he went by the House of Study, contemplated the three old men who had come to say their afternoon and evening prayers:

"And even to defend," he shouted from his throat, "this House of Study!"

Outside, flight and hubbub.

They ran away from Polishuk to the right and left, hopping and running and limping and groaning.

Not two were left together.

Silence blanketed the street and houses.

Sky blue and white.

As though no human soul had been there for many days.

The snowy wasteland, an abandoned salt mine . . .

Red the sun sets. The snow soaks up its dark blood.

Leaving the courtyard in front of the Union of Jewish Soldiers' headquarters, at an hour when the eye can no longer distinguish between one thing and another, on his horse, bound to the saddle by ropes in pride and glory, was comrade Gedalia, and behind him, like a river, flowed the files of armed men.

The snow gleamed.

Chill and darkness floated up into one's eyes.

The footsteps whistled in the dark blue of the snow.

Row upon row, two by two, in good order, the armed and silent men went up.

They all passed under Polishuk's critical eye, as he stood at the side, supporting and fortifying them with his voice:

"One two, one two!"

"Who brought you here?" Polishuk raised his voice against a few of the men coming up. "Wh-who took you out? I order you to stay behind and guard the town!"

"Comrade Polishuk, are we one-armed or one-legged cripples, that we must sit in the rear?"

"Wh-what? . . . Are you still arguing with me? . . . Follow my orders! . . . On the double, march!"

"Ah, may his guts collapse!" the ones left behind muttered, wrinkling their noses and turning to the side like whipped dogs.

In a moment they lifted their feet and raced after the camp.

The files moved over the snow like black stains.

From a distance they were visible, near the old cemetery, which they passed with loud singing, the new and carefree life disturbing the ancient dream of those lying in the earth.

Then they were swallowed up in the darkness.

In the town life stopped.

The silence of death.

Darkness.

All night the dead town was silent.

In the morning the soldiers returned, with the sound of singing and joy they returned.

"It's a brigade of soldiers on their way back from the front, not murderers!" the returnees announced.

The town came back to life.

In the afternoon the soldiers entered the town. They went to the council building and began speaking:

"Comrades, regarding the Jewish brigade with you in the town, let them lay down their arms, comrades."

"What's this? Comrades, you . . . "

"Now, do as we said: lay down your arms, no more!"

"How can you say that, comrades?" Polishuk negotiated with them out loud. "They are in favor of the rule of soldiers and workers."

"Don't argue with us, shorty! See this?" They waved grenades in the air.

As ashamed as a jilted bride removing her jewels, the members of the Jewish brigade were humiliated, walking with their heads down, quietly cursing and swearing, each man to himself, with filthy and vile curses, returning their weapons to the armory.

Actually only a few returned them. Most hid them in the bathhouse, in the poor-house and in potato pits.

They returned their weapons, and they were all summoned, all the members of the union, to the courtyard of the council building and ordered to stand against the wall.

Their faces turned black, their eyes went dark, as when the stars come out.

"Low, low," they whispered quietly.

"We have failed."

Ten soldiers with angry faces, silent, stony, looking and waiting, stood in the middle of the courtyard. Every one of their movements, every blink evoked the fear of death.

The courtyard was barren, full of snow piled up, pink and blue.

Silence fell. Then Polishuk appeared at the gate, with his hair and eyes wild, running into the courtyard with a single breath and stood at the wall among the rest.

The soldiers went up to each of the men standing at the wall, searching him.

No weapons were found.

The men standing there moved away from the walls.

To the sound of laughter and cries of contempt the fighters were dismissed and sent away.

Near the fence stood one of them, all dressed in black, weeping.

That was a day of utter defeat, of humiliation. Every heart burned like fire. Every heart cried out against the injustice.

That night the soldiers left the town.

X

Every house is heavy with melancholy and worry.

Every eye expects enmity. All the lips are bluish—you mustn't speak out, only curse and cry out against injustice silently.

Driven from the house is every favorable sign, all cheerful expressions and grace. Oblivion and expiration whisper, fasting and cold rustle about. . . .

No more is the woman of valor who nurtured and raised her children as commanded by the blessed Lord.

No more is the active householder with his sharp eye and quick pace, searching here and pecking there, dragging a grain and bearing a bundle, urgently rushing, reading the cantillation marks vigorously and gloriously like a rooster, disagreeing with God. . . .

No more are the maidens, preparing dowries with skillful hands and waiting for bridegrooms.

The women of valor lie still, exhausted, like sick goats, mourning, with dried dugs.

The sons die untimely.

The solid citizens race about like roosters with their throats extended, slaughtered, dripping blood. . . .

And the maidens—

"May you know a good year!"

The world has gone mad. Heartbreak! . . . Heartbreak . . . And the blessed Lord knows! There is nothing left to do but "get up and lie in the street and laugh!"

The fifth month in the Jewish calendar, usually coinciding with parts of January and February.

In the month of Shevat,° the name of which is related to the word for severe judgment according to Motl Privisker, Henya left her father's house and went to live in Polishuk's room.

That made no impression in the town. The town had seen so much lawlessness and wild living that it had become used to it.

The town was silent. It saw and was silent.

Not her alone, but another one too:

For comrade Polishuk also opened his room to Nechama, the daughter of Reb Meyer the slaughterer, and Leyzer Potashnik's Shprintsa, also to comrade Gedalia and comrade Henikh the carpenter, and they all lived there together:

"A commune!"

"They strung up a rope," it was whispered in town, "from one wall to another across the room: dividing the women's beds from the men's!"

The town looks for similarities between Sodom before it was destroyed and Polishuk's "commune." The deeds of the former are like those of the latter. . . .

"The daughters of such righteous men, ah? Will you split their bellies, Lord of the universe!"

"Reb Simcha," people whispered about him, "has gone completely mad!"

That seemed quite likely. . . . True, one could go mad.

"Reb Simcha," they whispered, "is sitting in mourning, nodding his head ceaselessly and whispering, 'I have no daughter. . . . I have no daughter. . . . I have no daughter!'—nothing more."

Ezek. 23:35.

On Friday Motl Privisker visited Reb Simcha and told him an interpretation of the verse: "Because thou hast forgotten me and cast me behind thy back."° "How is it possible that a daughter of Israel could be cast away? . . ."

"I have no daughter. . . . I have no daughter. . . ." Reb Simcha sat on the floor and nodded his head.

Motl Privisker turned his face away from him and remained standing there.

"Reb Simcha, Reb Simcha! . . . You are a father, are you not? . . . shouted Motl in a tearful voice. "Are you not a father? . . . Are you not a Jew, and the Lord is in heaven? . . . Why are you silent?! . . . Why are you silent and doing nothing?"

"I have no daughter. . . . I have no daughter. . . ."

"Why are you silent!" cried Motl in tears. "Lord, Lord of the world, why are you silent, oy, oy! . . . Why don't you watch over your children, for they are in great misery."

"I have no daughter. . . . I have no daughter. . . ."

"Simcha!" Motl Privisker jumped, raising his head and hands in the air. "I want to break the law! . . . I want to curse. . . . To violate the Sabbath in public! . . . I want to be an adulterer! . . . I will transcend my nature! . . . Master of the whole world, master of the whole world." He grasped both his earlocks, "May I not be given a Jewish burial! . . . I'm a Bolshevik!" He pounded the table with his hand till the windows rattled. "Now, now the time has come. . . . Enough! I want to be a Bolshevik!"

"I have no daughter. . . . I have no daughter. . . ." Reb Simcha's desolate voice was heard.

Motl leaped up onto his long legs. The hem of his jacket fluttered in Reb Simcha's face, as he sat and whispered, "I have no daughter. . . . I have no daughter. . . ." And as though stones were being split, the door slammed against the doorpost, and the corners of the room shuddered—Motl was gone!

XI

Lying in the snow, shoved and pressed together, the humiliated houses crouched. The winds wept bitterly over them. The barren, red sun set over them.

On the surface of the snow runs a purplish shadow.

Silence outside.

No one is to be seen. No one greets his friend, no one wishes anyone well. Silence and snow. As though the snow had covered the towns and settlements forever. Neither good nor evil will ever find that place.

Just one man, who appeared drunken in the full, pure whiteness of the snows, was Motl Privisker. He too was like a soul that had already died, whirling and wandering in the world of chaos.

Nightfall in the silence and snow. An encrusted city preserved in the sinking red sun . . .

The snow whistles and whistles beneath one's feet, making a sound like a radish being sliced.

Spread before one's eyes is snow, near and far, sparkling on the ground like a bridegroom's prayer shawl.

Is this a dream or reality? Is it Motl Privisker there in the snow or some lone, forgotten, derelict out after the curfew? Who is it? Is it a poor teacher who lost his way, or some crazy man whose brains have been addled? Is that silence only apparent? Or are they voices, calling loudly, and after them the silence came? He is not clever enough to understand. . . .

The snow sparkles and sparkles like crates and crates of candles lit all at once to make a great light! . . .

No matter, for he is weary unto death! No matter, for he has been beaten into silence! No matter, for he is bereft of kindness or joy, of motive or interest. . . .

He walked slowly and heard a kind of silence, voices calling. Slowly he walked and looked at the moonlit snow, glowing under his feet.

Motl Privisker walked slowly by himself, until the voices of nearby people overtook him, real voices. They were Polishuk and his bunch, who appeared in the street. As if they had come outside just to rule over the silent snows. Motl Privisker was alarmed. He looked at Henya walking, dressed in a leather coat, a pistol belted around her waist, booted, and his heart wept within him. In a moment his heart returned and was joyous. Motl spoke to himself:

"I was meant to suffer, and I have suffered already."

He looked again at her reddish mouth, her cheeks and forehead, and he said again: "I was meant to receive suffering, and I have received it already."

"Ah, comrade Reb Motl," Polishuk greeted him. "Where are you going?"

The people crowded around him, standing there and stamping their feet.

"Comrade Motl," Polishuk continued. "Come with us! Be a Bolshevik, ha-ha. . . ."

Motl Privisker raised his eyes toward Henya, who was standing at the side, and he said:

"If I am destined to go to hell, I wish to do so as a kosher Jew!"

"Ha-ha-ha! . . . Ha-ha!" the people raised their voices in laughter.

The silence returned to what it was. No one was visible. No one greeted his friend.

Silence. A silvery round moon overhead. A long shadow on the snow below.

"I was meant to suffer, and I have suffered already."

And sometimes:

"For it is forbidden to look her in the face, forbidden, forbidden!"

XII

Time passed, bringing other skies to rise over the town. A young sun with lovely rays melted the snow and opened spots of light outside. The winds chewed up the snow by the mouthful, and with every bite they wandered on, full of thoughts and melodies of spring.

The houses shed the white piecrusts from their shoulders and stood warming themselves in the sun, dark, old and a little distant from each other.

The roofs wept before the glowing sun like little children.

Bit by bit the snow yellowed and fell into its water.

Puddles spread in the street like big clouds spread in the heavens.

Before the gates calves jumped, wild-eyed with tails erect.

Crows moved in the boughs of the trees, calling "krak-rak."

Motl Privisker was covered with his prayer shawl and phylacteries—and lo: no oppression or injustice in the world, no evil and malicious joy, but everything was as in earlier times:

"The Lord is one. . . ."

Then, during prayer, while he was standing and acknowledging the Creator as King, proclaiming "The Lord is one!" in came two soldiers and shouted:

"Citizen Mordukh Karasyk, in the name of the Soviet Socialist Republic of Russia, you are under arrest!"

As though preparing himself to study it very thoroughly, Motl Privisker took the paper that was handed to him, and all his eyes saw on the paper was the signature: Henya Horowitz.

Afterwards Motl Privisker turned to face the soldiers and said,

"That's how it is."

"That's the way it is. Come with us!"

They didn't offer to content him by allowing him to finish his prayer.

Motl Privisker removed his phylacteries, took off his prayer shawl, draped himself in his balding cat-skin coat and went. All the time he was walking in the street between the two armed soldiers, the image of Reb Simcha, the floorboards ripped up, and Henya never left his eyes. . . . His throat was warm with the heat of sated thirst, and his heart beat within him as at a time of arousal and desire.

Many days passed, days and weeks.

But, could it be that many days passed, and yet comrade Soroka is walking down the street!

The days that passed were not many—many were the deeds done by comrade Soroka! Many are the nests he burned and many the fires he lit in the country he went through!

From the end of the street, which was darkened with gunpowder, went forth Soroka.

It was a debilitating spring evening.

Saturated silence, thick and dark, as it is sometimes in the depths of one's heart.

Swallowed in a gullet, the berry of a blue night is seen.

The town crouched in its mud like a sick, mourning goat with dried dugs.

Following footsteps stamped in the mud, large and small footprints of men and women, Soroka walked till he reached Polishuk's house.

When he opened the door and went in, his eyes saw a rope before him, stretched from wall to wall, and two beds on either side of the walls, full of bodies, bodies like cadavers.

Soroka placed himself in the center of the room and shouted:

"Are you asleep, you devils! . . . Get up: the Germans are coming!"

1924

63 Months and Days

ITSIK KIPNIS

Ayzik, a young tanner, and his newlywed wife Buzi have just spent the first night of the pogrom hiding in the wheat fields near their home in the shtetl of Sloveshne. The next afternoon, they and their family set out with horse and wagon for the neighboring village of Petroshi, where they hope to take refuge for the night. Along the way they meet a group of unfamiliar peasants heading for the town.

And we get out of their way; we move in the opposite direction, toward where they've come from, toward Petroshi.

And you see, they do not forbid it. And it may be that in Petroshi, where they live, we will be permitted to spend the night somewhere. After all, we are "Sloveshne Jews." Isn't it true that they have a high regard for "Sloveshne Jews"? Haven't we often heard them say so? And indeed, my father is going to one of his clients there, a fellow who brings hides in to be cured.

"That fellow," my father says, "will welcome us. Arkhip is his name. He'll give us the best food that he has."

And my hope is that all of these Jews may have a client like him in Petroshi who will welcome them; who will give them the best food that he has.

My father brags about his clients. And his one-horse trap is already rolling into Petroshi.

Ah, were we ever stared at in Petroshi!

The whole family sat together in the wagon and a crowd of Jews who arrived earlier is already there. Now we are a considerable group. And we move on.

There are swaggerers among them who bum cigarettes, who light them and smoke unconcernedly, the way they would on a fast day.

And there are already a number of Jews at Avrom's house in Petroshi. (I'd seen Avrom's house filled with Jewish men and women once before. But that was when he was marrying off his older son and the whole town gathered to celebrate.) Perhaps there was no guard at Avrom's now.

The priest was talking with Avrom at a fence facing the house. He was talking about Jews and Sloveshne.

A fine priest in Petroshi. A man in his thirties, good looking. He made clucking sounds with his lips and wondered why the Jews were suddenly suffering so much in Sloveshne. "A pity, a pity, a pity."

And perhaps he was not being hypocritical. It's possible that there is one priest in a hundred who doesn't meddle.

The brim of Avrom's hat was pulled down on one side. "So many guests, God save us." And, "May God keep everything calm."

A fine Jew, that Avrom. Tall and stocky, bearded, with a gentle, freckled face and large expressive eyes. He wore an alpaca jacket and was friendly to everyone. He could be a pal even with the children, though he was himself already the father of five grown sons. Furthermore, he was by no means shy when he talked; he spoke loudly, giving his words a village pronunciation. That was Avrom of Petroshi.

Father got down from the wagon, and whispering into Avrom's ear, he asked where a certain Arkhip lived. And Avrom told him what he knew and we drove to Arkhip's house. We were followed by two other families, who carried with them children, a cat and small pitchers of milk. "The milk is to shut the mouths of the little ones in case they wake at night."

But since there was no law that guaranteed that Arkhip had always to be at home—he could, after all, be away in the woods or on a trip somewhere—it was just our luck that he turned out not to be at home and one of his younger sons talked with us—a boy some fourteen years old. A shepherd.

"I won't allow it without my father."

"Don't be a child. Your father brings me hides to be tanned every year. . . . Your father is an old pal of ours. If you try to keep us out, he'll be very angry with you."

"I can't do anything by myself. Without my father."

"Well, when will your father be back?"

"I don't know. Perhaps tonight."

"Well, that's fine. Let us into the barn until he gets here."

Willingly or unwillingly, the shepherd boy brought out a large wooden key and unlocked the barn. We unharnessed the horse (the others had rented wagons and sent them back to their owners), and we spread out sackcloth and carpets and lay down.

We were three families in the barn, and each family had some additional people.

And if a child whined, it was given milk. There was a sick child, not a member of a family, who lay there and wanted nothing. And older children, because they had nothing to say, just sat there and were silent.

As I went out to cover the horse and to give him a bit of fresh hay, an old neighbor woman, barefoot and wearing a linen blouse and a dress made of two aprons, one in front and one behind, came up to the wagon. She was weeping.

She wept because she had lived to see what she was seeing. "Think of it. Just think of it. What a desolate and bitter generation has grown up. Is it likely that they'll live to enjoy the property of strangers? No, such things were once unheard of. Maybe it's the damned war that has so spoiled the people."

A while later, she wiped her eyes, pulled a wisp of straw from the wagon and tried chewing it with her rotten teeth and mused, "There is one thing in which you are a little bit at fault, my dears. You shouldn't have hidden the salt. You ought to have known how the people lacked salt. Well, I won't ask you why you had to do such a thing. There's nothing worse than food without salt. We even add salt to a cow's drinking water. What else needs to be said? Even a cow. Ah, my dears, how bitter it is for us without our bit of salt. It may be that that's the reason the people are angry. It's searching for salt."

"Yes," I said to her. "The people are angry. They're looking for salt."

"God preserve us and those we love from such behavior. Just wait a bit, dearie, I'll be right back." And in the space of two minutes, she went a few doors down and returned with a bowl of eight or ten roasted potatoes. "Give it to the children. Give it to them, my dear." And she wiped her old eyes with an apron.

And hour or so later, daylight was almost all gone. And the evening made every eyelid heavy despite all efforts to keep one's eyes open. The scent of green grass reached us from the other side of the barn where there were kitchen gardens. Gardens, passionately alive. Every blade of grass unashamedly immersing itself in the cool dew.

The floor in the barn where we were was dry and smooth. There was room for all three families. Buzi was already dozing, and I was anxious to take off her shoes before she fell asleep, but I did not want to wake her. Mother was also dozing and the children as well. Father, apparently, was not yet able to get to sleep. He wanted just to lie still without disturbing anyone. There was silence all around him. All that one heard was the steady, monotonic sound of the horse's chewing. I had already removed one sweaty, sticky sock from one foot and was removing the other. Someone opened the door. In barns, the doors are very wide. And the moon over the village was full and low in the sky so that the entire barn was filled with moonlight. But who was coming into the barn at such a late hour? After all, it was bedtime. It was the shepherd once again.

"Jews . . . Jews . . . go away. I don't want you here. I'm scared."

"Who are you afraid of?"

The boy didn't know and couldn't say. He was still a kid. "I'm scared they'll burn the barn." And he wept.

Evidently there was nothing to discuss. The matter was simple. We had to go. The question, however, was, Where?

Little by little, the people in the barn came awake. They looked into each other's faces. Questions were asked. Everyone said what everyone else was saying. That they had just settled down and were getting cozy—and now, this. There was no rest for the weary. But slowly, the situation became clear, though no one offered any suggestions. It was not really their business. A couple of men discussed what to do, as if it was up to them. They would decide what to do, and whatever they decided the others would do.

And that, if you like, is where the trouble lay. Because the men had no idea what to do either. Perhaps one ought to leave and then later sneak back in. Perhaps they ought to harness the horse and ride off—but now that would be hard—and spend the night somewhere in a field, in the open. (But that might be dangerous, eh?)

Maybe this. Maybe that. Return to Sloveshne (we all know the way). But that won't do either.

Father went to the village. It turned out that the Jews in Avrom's house also didn't know where they would spend the night. Perhaps they would hang around the house. We, for our parts, had little children with us. Well, what to do?

And Father had a discussion with Esther of Petroshi. "She's already placed two families with little children among the peasants. She'll advise us, too. Come on."

Esther led us into a garden that was wet with dew. "Sit here for a while." And she went off somewhere.

We sat there, some ten of us of varying ages (dark Hershl was six and Father was forty-five). Each of us responded differently to the wet garden and to the moist, sandy rye. But what would have been best of all would have been just to lie still. Hershl wanted to do something, but we pleaded with him to stay still and not to creep about. And, in reaction to so much sorrow, we had an impulse to laugh; but not far away there came the sound of young men stamping their feet, like horses, and leaping over fences. On their way to an evening party. They have no notion that families of Jews are sitting in the rye; that the Jews are terrified of the sound of their stamping feet.

And there was no Esther.

She's been gone for so many hours. And she's left us here among the cultivated rows. Perhaps she won't come back at all. That's it. She's not coming back. The peasants talked her out of it.

Mother tore off a blade of grass and studied it. She was thinking something over. She would gladly have told us what she was thinking, but now was not the right moment to talk aloud.

"Well, people, come on."

It was Esther who had returned and was calling us. Esther was a coarse speaker. When she said "Come," one could hear every letter in the word as she pronounced it. But it didn't matter. "May she live long, that Esther . . . ah, what a service she's doing for us—at a time like this."

Mother thanked her, then everyone, adults and children, as best as they could, climbed over a strange fence. And she was surprised that we hadn't stolen anything.

"Sleep well," she said. The place belonged to good peasants. They had set out a bed where, usually, a young couple slept. A clean, well-carpentered little stable.

Mother thanked Esther and wished for her all the good fortune she deserved, and we entered into a well-prepared haven whose owners we had not yet seen, and whom we might not see for several days.

How close are we to dawn? (It was, after all, a summer's night.) And we parceled out and divided the space, as well as the bed belonging to the young couple. But several of us were beyond falling asleep. And there was someone knocking on the other side of the wall. Not knocking, exactly, but more as if someone was climbing on the walls.

Who could it be? What if it was young peasants with knives. Oughtn't we to have sticks nearby?

Everyone thought his or her own thoughts, but hardly anyone said a word. And what's happening now in Sloveshne? Is it calm, or are the goyim living it up? While now, on the other side of our wall, there was neither knocking nor climbing on the wall. Perhaps it was some unlucky peasant lad of seventeen, some weak-minded orphan who wasn't smart enough to come in out of the rain but who now wanted to attach himself to a Jewish family in the little stable. "You'll see. I'll split his head open with a stick. That miserable idiot orphan."

Buzi was lying down with the girls. Perhaps she had fallen asleep, too. And my mother has to be shunted from pillar to post, from one stable to another. And Hershele . . . What wouldn't I give to keep Buzi and my mother and Hershele from being shoved about like this? And my father . . . and my sisters. The other mother and her children were far away. Where were they spending the night? In a stable or in a house? And in Radomishl, how are they spending the night? And in Proskurov?

It can't be possible that they could massacre three thousand Jews in Poskurov? Three thousand is an exaggeration. Meanwhile, the knocking on the other side of the wall continued. If it's a lone peasant youth, I'll kill him. Even if there are two or three. But if there are many, I won't budge from my place.

Young peasants are on their way to some celebration. They talk loudly and laugh.

. . . Better let them pass. Good. They're gone. . . .

Now, I would really like for it to be dawn, or to fall asleep.

Does the passage of every night take up so much time before dawn comes? And perhaps it wasn't peasant youths banging on the other side of the wall. Perhaps it's just a pen for sheep.

"Sheep," I whispered so softly I could hardly be heard. "It's a pen for sheep. And they're making the noise on the other side of the wall."

If anyone had chanced to be awake, they would have heard me and would certainly have been relieved by what I said.

And, evidently, I too fell asleep. Because I did not get to see the arrival of the dawn.

It was a lovely morning in Petroshi, and we were safe and sound. What did we lack?

"Let Ayzik drive into town and find out what's happening there." And if Ayzik goes, you must know that Buzi is going too. She feels uncomfortable without him.

Somehow or other, our horse and harness turned out to be safe at the old inn. So, let's get harnessed and go. Hershele wanted to come too. Then someone else wanted to come, and someone else as well. Everyone, in short. Finally, no one but the two of us went. And when we brought back news, everyone else would be able to go.

At any other time, what we did would have been called "taking a coach ride," something we very much liked. But we had never had a horse.

Father's horse was a good one. We would be in Sloveshne in less than twenty minutes.

The wagon rolled downhill. The horse moved along amiably. The world was alive. What a pleasure. On the outskirts of town we met a herdsman with all kinds and colors of cattle.

"Cattle, you spent the night in Sloveshne. Maybe you have something to tell us. Maybe you can give us some news about the home we left behind in strange hands on a dismal night?———"

Hush. There goes Naum and his oxen. He's on his way to the forest for wood. You see him there, a short little peasant. His face is shaven, and he has a pair of long Ukrainian mustaches. An unhurried fellow. Whatever you may be thinking, he has thoughts of his own. He's not interested in any one's else's business.

"Naum, what's going on in town?"

"Phoo! In town? What's going on? Nothing. There were beatings last night. Banging and breaking."

"And in general, what's happening in town?" And the sun, meanwhile, dapples the red-colored backs of his oxen and makes a different design on my horse's ash-colored hide. We're riding *into* town, he's riding *out* of town. "In general, what's going on in town, Naum?"

"In general—nothing. They brought four dead Jews from Gorodishche.° All but Khitrik's son-in-law were strangers."

"Khitrik's son-in-law? The tall one?"

"Yes."

And Khitrik's son-in-law was a tall, well-built fellow, like a pine tree. Mordkhe-Leyzer Gershteyn! If they could overcome a fellow like Gershteyn and kill him, things must be pretty bad. "Wait a minute, Naum. When did it happen? When were they brought in?"

"When were they brought in? Yesterday. It seems to me they were put away yesterday. It's too bad—Khitrik's son-in-law. He was a good Jew."

"And now, what's happening in town?"

The site of the pogrom memorialized in Markish's "The Mound" (64).

"Now it's quiet. I think. Gee up!"

"Giddap."

It's a lovely sun. The window panes gleam in the school on the outskirts of town. And the morning looks just as it would if it were cheerful.

Buzi holds on to my hand. She's very unhappy because they killed Mordkhe-Leyzer, Khitrik's son-in-law. She lived with them in the same apartment for a year. In a room in Mordkhe-Leyzer's house and with his lovely children. The two older ones were now grown up.

Buzi looks into my eyes and asks, "Ayzik, is it that simple to cut someone's throat with a knife? Like a cow or an ox at the slaughter?"

"I've never seen anything slaughtered."

"And a cow? You've seen a cow slaughtered?"

"No."

It was a calf that Buzi saw being slaughtered in her garden. Its legs were bound, and it made a terrible death rattle. She didn't want to say any more. She felt nauseated, remembering. For more than a week she had been unable to look at their neighbor, the ritual slaughterer. It had seemed to her that he was a very ugly creature. Ugh . . .

Our streets were crisscrossed with threads of fear. But as we moved along them, they became familiar again, our streets. And dear to us. It was hard to turn off into another street or lane. Until you passed over the threshold of gloom, after which it was easier once more. And our streets had a look that was neither like Purim nor like the Interval Days° of Passover and Sukkot. The shops were neither closed nor open. The shopkeepers were not doing business. The shoemakers were not hammering. Everyone sat scattered about on earthen mounds as if drying in the sun. Or perhaps taking the air. Or perhaps neither the one nor the other, and they were merely keeping warm.

It was quiet in town. Whatever had happened at night had happened. Now, the town was quiet. Buzi will walk about. It may be she'll hear news of her mother and the children. Meanwhile, I'll get our people.

We moved spiritedly. It was bright, sunny. Easy.

During the Passover and Sukkot holidays, the intermediary weekdays between the first two and last days of the holiday.

Thursday is Thursday, and people are people. Our situation was not what anyone would call good, but by now that was nothing new for us. It had been a long time since we had slept in our own beds. And a long time since we ended our days where we began them. It should be no surprise to us that our local peasant boys teased us. They teased us and we were silent. Because for each five of us there were thirty of them.

"Go, children. Go to Sokhvye's Hane and drink your fill of milk." It was Mother sending us to Hane, Shmayle's wife. Our milk was there.

So we went to Sokhvye's Hane. She spoke to my sister as to a friend. Talked about household matters; housewifely things. Her stove was hot, and she gave us milk to drink. If we liked, we could drink right out of the jugs. Hane had a square face, a square jaw and white teeth and intelligent eyes. When she laughed, it was with her whole face, including her intelligent eyes and her white teeth. And, it may be, that this was not the first time that we had been beggars. And so we drank half sour milk at Hane's. The upper part of the milk was buttery and smeared one's lips and nose. Then all of a sudden there was a gush of the thinner sour milk that spattered one's clothes. Nothing to worry about. The clothes were not made of silk, though perhaps it was unpleasant for Hane. We could take our own jugs home with us; to our tumbled, our abused home. And there we would . . .

"Hane, may we?"

"All right, then. Take them. But bring the jugs back so that I'll have something in which to put your cow's milk." (We still had a cow.)

"Hane, how come you have the little red chair and the two stools?"

Hane crimsoned. Was there any reason for her to be embarrassed before us? She would have liked to make a different answer, but she would say what she could. Enough said.

"I thought I would carry something away. If you came back, it would be yours again. And if not—well why should strangers have it? Here are your forms, too. Your forms and your baking tins."

Hane is red-faced, embarrassed. She is a bit confused. But she is right. What she did is good. We carried the jug with the half sour milk home with us.

"And bread. Just see how we've forgotten. We don't have any bread."

Tonight, we made more intelligent preparations. Tonight, we even scraped the starter dough out of the kneading trough. There was not a bit of breadstuff left in the house.

Khvedosia, who lives near Yisroel-Dovid's house, was carrying buckets from the well on a yoke over her shoulder. She wanted to pass us by as if she did not see us, but Mother stood in her way.

"Khvedosia, you're on your way home. Lend me a bit of bread, for the children's sake."

"Bread?"

She hadn't baked bread for our sakes, Khvedosia. Bread. She is Adamke's sister. Adamke who lives right next door to Zeydl. And she's really wicked. But she can't be an utter pig. After all, she lives right next door to us.

"Mama, Khvedosia gave us a cake."

"May God punish her. The cake is moldy."

We break the old cake apart. It's true. Its innards are all mold. How did Mother know it would be? But it had to be eaten, moldy or not.

What puzzles me is why we didn't lock the door yesterday when we went away.

"So that they wouldn't break the windows," says Father. And Motl, Feygl's son, wonders why I'm wearing such tattered trousers.

"So that I won't be left wearing only underpants," I explain. And Buzi and I go into town. There it is being said that the furrier Yeshue had hidden himself and his family and that people broke into his barn—it was early in the evening—and killed his wife and two sons.

One of them, the older one, Dovid, is also a tailor. A man about my age.

Dovid Frenk.

Yeshue's family was considered one of the best in town. And it was said that Dovid was survived by a wife and child.

Buzi was very anxious. Her mother and the children had gone off in the same direction. Buzi wept, but there was nothing to cry about. If, God forbid, something had happened, we would have heard about it. There were some thirty people in their group.

"Buzi dear, don't cry. And let's think a bit about Dovid Frenk. Of his mother and his brother Khayim-Leyb. It was not long ago that he wanted to buy himself a violin—Khayim-Leyb. He wanted to learn how to play it."

And it was neither Purim nor the Interval Days on the street. Jews sat on hummocks or on their porches. And various of their peasant neighbors sat around, doing nothing too. Some of them talked to Jews; some of them sat before their doorways. All at once, we heard a woman's musical voice. Everyone flushed, and one's hair stood on end. Some woman was wandering about, singing. Her hands hung at her sides. Her scarf was flung negligently across her shoulders. And its fringed ends hung down on both sides. That's how her hands dangled. That's how she wore her scarf. So that her movements would be freer; so that she would not be put to trouble on its account. And the way she walked was also like that. Not near the walls nor along the sidewalk but out in the middle of the street, where the wagons drive. That's how she walked, her figure loose, unbound. She came from Dolnye, past the marketplace. Now she was walking in the dead middle of Listvene Street. Singing.

What a fool I am. What a downright idiot. Who's singing? She's not singing. That's Dovid's wife. Dovid Frenk. Who was murdered last night in Behun. Together with his mother and his younger brother. This is Dovid's wife. And she's not singing. She's preaching like a priest. No. She's declaiming in a hoarse, careless fashion as if she were in a theater. And indeed she does sing a little bit, too. In a moderate tone, as if she were talking to someone. And she walks slowly, with her hands at her sides, as if she had nothing at all to make her hurry. As if by walking she would disappear. And she sings.

Of course you all know Dovid,
Dovid Frenk of Dolnye,
Yeshue the furrier's son.

He was a furrier, too.
But he was dearer to me than a prince.
Dovid . . . that Dovid . . . was my husband.

Of course you all know Dovid,
There was no reason to look into his face.
Murderers killed him in Behun.

He was vibrant and lively
When they tore him from my arms.
I begged them:
Murderers, kill me too.

Murderers, have you no human heart?
You must also have wives and children.
Murderers, kill me too.

I kissed their feet. . . .

I humbled myself before them,
And I begged:
Murderers, kill me too.

Dovid, you can't go. . . .
You can't go without me.
And what shall I do with your child?

Ah, Jews—if you only knew. . . .

She goes, meandering like water, and she sings; and we can feel our blood curdling. Buzi and I stand near a wall. The two of us are still whole. And she will come and demand her share.

And what will I do if she sees me and comes up to me.

"Ayzik, you knew Dovid Frenk. Ayzik, have you any idea why they killed Dovid Frenk yesterday? He was so good looking; so warm; and now he lies there, rigid. Come now and look."

And my blood chills. And Buzi turns as pale as a wall, and my impulse is to go up to Dobe and ask, "Dobe, do you happen to know whether they are going to kill Jews tomorrow, too? No doubt you know what's going on. If they're going to kill again, then tell me, so we can figure out ways to escape."

It was with great difficulty that I got Buzi home. She was nearing her time,° and she wasn't supposed to cry.

To give birth.

We already knew who the most important celebrants were at our grim little festival. They were Kosenko (Klim's son), the captain of the guard and Maritshko Lukhtans—our neighbor, the poor Gypsy, the liar who loves Jews.

Maritshko is unbelievable. There he was on Thursday, standing at the fence beside his grapevines, popping grapes into his mouth, actually shouting at a couple of peasant women, "Ah, what sort of idiot business have you gotten yourselves into? Do you expect to have Jewish bodies and to wear Jewish clothes?"

The peasant women replied that they hadn't meant any harm. They had simply come to look around in Sloveshne. But he had jumped down from the fence and, unbuttoning their swollen jackets, he removed several children's sleeveless shirts, an old waistcoat and a pair of children's shoes. He looked them over quickly, gauging their value.

"Here," he said to Yisroel-Dovid's Feygele. "Give these back to poor Jewish children so they can wear them."

"Bravo Marko, bravo! That's how to pay the bloodsuckers." And the two peasant women, one young and pretty and the other a mother-in-law, crimsoned and beat a retreat to the accompaniment of his jibes, "Go on. Go home, you foolish donkeys. There's nothing here for you. If we should need you, we'll send for you."

"Right, Marko." And Feygele thought, "How nice it would be if there were many such peasants, but preferably arrested and condemned to hard labor."

Evidently Feygele knew something. She had been in his house last night where she had seen several visitors of the sort that made her wonder how she had escaped from his house with her life. The portrait of Czar Nicholas hanging on the wall had taken on a quite different appearance, glowing red, and there was such a Christian holiday atmosphere in the house that no sane Jew would have entered

The Rape of the Shtetl   333

it. Feygele had backed slowly out of the house. Then she had seen how Marko had been sent off to ride through the village on horseback. Yes, that had been a truly close call—and she had just barely escaped with her life. And Marko's tall liar of a wife, her dress tucked in at the waist, had cheerfully confided to Feygele that, "They've been asking about brandy. The soldiers, the commandant and various other strangers." And she was pleased to be hosting such distinguished guests. Kings for a day. And the oven gave off a holiday fragrance, and the portrait of Czar Nicholas had a festive glow.

Feygele looked on with admiration mixed with fear at the way Maritshko stood there beside the fence, plucking grapes and popping them into his mouth even as he drove the peasant women away. Perhaps, it suddenly occurred to her, it was a form of magic: The number of grapes he popped into his mouth represented the number of Jews whose heads would be bashed in today by those guests of his. Then she rejected the thought at once. There was no need to think such foolishness. No doubt nothing would happen. Nothing at all.

Meanwhile, crowds of young peasants from Levkovich, Mozharia and Verpia kept crossing our fields. Young peasants who wore their shirts over their belts, who were barefooted and had beady eyes. Ugly, filthy young peasants. The hems of their shirts were wet as if bepissed. They looked uglier than carrion birds. And now they were here. In Mikita's lane, it had already been clear that they were drifting this way. Ugly folk. And by no means bold. One loud shout would scatter them all. But I was not about to do it. There were many of them. Like locusts. And it's said that even mice, if they attack in their numbers, can kill a man.

The peasant boys crept about our attic, searching. In our attic; in my aunt's. Searching. Whatever they found would be pure profit.

The young peasants teased us. Behaved boorishly toward us. They were angry with us because we had taken many things of ours back from them. We had called our neighbors together and instigated them to scold the ugly young fellows.

And, of course, our neighbors had to do what we told them; they had driven them away and taken things away from them. And, as a joke, they had even locked a couple of the young men into a locker in my aunt's house.

A flock of peasant women as well as boys and girls found their way into the lower courtyard of the tannery. It was a group that had come to town carrying various vessels in their hands on the chance that they might find some gasoline or grease. In short, they were ready for anything that might come their way.

Evidently they had asked directions to the tannery and started off, some fifty of them. They moved with slow deliberation. They were women, after all, and who knew what might happen?

"I'm going to drive them away."

"No need," said Mother.

"I won't let you," said Buzi.

"Let them choke on the grease," said my sisters and our neighbors.

But I very much wanted to scare those peasant women. Not just because I was angry, but for the sheer fun of it.

"I won't let you," said Buzi.

"There's no need to do it," said Mother. I searched for and found a splintered log—there was no stick available, and I started toward the "Philistines."

"Hey, the devil take you all." And the women, poor things, like frightened hens fluttering their wings, leaped first to one side, then to the other. "God help us," and they ran. But a couple of them managed to find their way to the Holy of Holies.

"I only meant to find a little grease," one of them said, climbing down from a window.

"Damn it to hell, what you meant can get you killed," I said. "You didn't find any grease." And I swung at her with the bit of log. The second woman fell into a tub, while a third made her way out of the window and ran off.

"Damned mares! The devil take you and your filthy faces." Then, like a gander after a fray with a cat, I turned to my women, glowing with the joy of victory.

And Buzi said, "I didn't tell you to do it. They'll call their men and tell them that you beat them. It'll be worse for us, then."

Buzi, as if she were talking to Yosele or to Meylekh, talked to me like a teacher and proved, with examples, that I would have done better to follow her advice.

But I noticed that my family had laughed when the peasant women and girls ran off like wet hens. And Buzi had also laughed. And so I bragged a little about my exploits against the women who, I said, would be afraid to show their faces here again. And I was very pleased with myself.

Meanwhile, we had news from town that eight families were getting ready to go to Turov.

"Smart, very smart. Because who knows where it will all end?"

"Maybe we ought to harness up and drive to Turov, too?"

Mother would not agree to that. Well, we didn't go.

The news from town was that the families had decided not to drive to Turov. Why not?

Because all at once the wagon drivers made excuses and said they could not go. They had, evidently been threatened by the pogrom committee. One way or another, they would not be permitted to drive out of town.

The news from town was that the pogromists wanted a meeting. They wanted to try the Jews. The priest would make a speech. The rabbi would be there too.

The men went off to the gathering. My older sister and Buzi wanted to come too.

It was a strange trial. It was a day that was neither a working day nor a holiday. A little like a fair in the center of the marketplace, and yet no business was conducted. The priest and the rabbi stood at the center of the crowd. The rabbi was bloodstained, but he neither wept nor groaned. He did not wince, but it was clear from the way that he sweated that his strength had been sapped. There was no trial here of equal strengths where, at some point, one could call a halt and an authority would say, "Right. That's right. Right. That's right."

The priest spoke first. "We will have to persuade the people to restrain themselves. To stop its turbulence; or the Jews will have to be careful (about what?). The Jews will have to (what?) . . ." The priest spoke guardedly, ambiguously. He was still in his right mind and knew that power was not with the church now. In church he could speak quite differently. Here, he had to be a bit careful.

Now it was Stodot's turn to talk. The name Stodot may not mean anything to those who are not acquainted with that bumpy-featured murderous bastard with the gray, protruding eyes. A huge man in his forties. Perhaps because he had neither children nor prosperity, he devoted himself to finding ways to bathe in Jewish tears. Jews, he said, were foreigners; they were harmful. Jewish cattle devoured the pastures. Jews cut down whole forests in order to make brooms. Jewish geese spoiled the wheat fields, so that the community was put to the trouble of rounding up Jewish livestock every year. And, if Stodot was in charge of the roundup, any Jewish woman who owned a cow had a hard time of it. Now it was Stodot Popak who spoke. And, as far as Jews were concerned, there were things that he loved to say loud and clear. And he was saying them.

"And Jews have always been like this. They even sent noodles to the Germans during the war. Now, we don't want them to be communists."

"What? Communists? Who?"

But hold on a minute. Stodot is right, after all. During the night, when Velvl, the senile shoemaker's windows were being broken, people shouted, "Communist. You're a Jew and a communist. Just wait. We'll kill you. If not today, then tomorrow."

Ugh. Ugly words.

And Marko, our neighbor, was there and said, "Jews, give money. Our brothers need money. And let that be the end of the matter."

And so the Jews met in the synagogue and collected money.

And later, Marko advised the Jews, "Since the people are rebellious, let the Jews gather in one place at the center of town and we'll put an armed guard around them. But I can't guarantee the safety of those who don't come to the center. The populace is restless."

Have you got the picture of Marko? He counts the money. He issues commands.

"What do you think, Marko? Ought we, perhaps, to go to Motl, the commissioner?"

"A good idea. All of you go to Motl, the commissioner's house."

Motl's childless daughter-in-law lived in the upper painted houses. Below them lived Motl himself. Motl's place was like a railroad station and not a place to live. People constantly coming and going. Jews as well as peasants. And his wagon drivers were all fond of Motl and his house.

"Whatever happens to anyone else, no one's going to kill Motl."

And Motl's daughter-in-law was fat. Perhaps the fattest person in town. She had been raised in a big city. She was enormous, and she wanted to have a child.

Perhaps tonight Yokheved, Motl Rattner's daughter-in-law, will be friendly to the ordinary folk whom she will meet. Usually, she behaves as if she were doing common people a favor, but tonight she will be on the same plane as them all. They will all have to hide together.

The news was already known in town: people were spending the night at Motl's.

And those in the forward houses could rest easy. As for other Jews, if they had any sense, they would spend the night with peasants because Motl Rattner's house was filled to overflowing.

Father brought good news: "It will be quiet tonight. One can even spend the night at home. But if we don't want to do that, we can go to Motl Rattner's."

Yes. Father had paid not only for himself but for others as well.

For such news, Father no doubt deserved well of us. It was no trivial matter.

But it was hard to believe that the pogrom's black maw would be shut so mechanically.

"Choose your rooms, people. Lower the shutters; shut your doors and sleep well."

Mother did not want to go to Motl Rattner's. She had no faith in such good luck.

"Well, then, where shall we spend the night?"

Opposite our house and opposite our door there stood Yisroel-Dovid's stable. Shoulder to shoulder with our house, as it were. There were oak logs piled before the stable. Some were already squared off, and from the beginning of the pogrom, it was among these logs that we spent our time. We lay there, taking the sun; it was there that we received news from town. That's where we had our quarrel with the peasant youths. That's where we argued about the peasants. Nor did we feel like going inside the house. It felt eerie, and it smelled musty there. The rear legs of the table had been twisted off because one of our neighbors (we knew who it was) had suspected that there was money hidden in the table's locked drawer.

What if that's where his wallet is—the one he keeps large sums of money in? What then? The table drawer is locked with a lock. Well there's a remedy for that. Twist the table legs around. And if necessary, lose your temper a little.

And indeed, the slob lost his temper and twisted the table's hind legs about.

And left satisfied.

Not that there was any money in the drawer. Only Father's packet of cheap tobacco, cigarette papers and his passport.

Well, too bad. And the table lay sprawled in the house, like a pig that spreads its hind legs out when it's being beaten on its back. Perhaps you've seen how it does. Though mother was constantly after us not to beat the pigs. A pig's back is its most tender part.

Well, where are we going to spend the night?

Mother and the children to Avdei's barn and father to Rattner's house?

When will my father be smarter in such matters instead of always choosing what is not good for him? This is not a time for families to part. In money matters perhaps it's alright to hide things in various places. If it's dug up in one place, there's still some hidden someplace else. But money is not to the point in this case. Money is something altogether different.

Zelik, Borukh Isaac's son, came and sat on the squared logs with us. He was all dressed to travel. It was possible that a nearby wagon driver might take on some passengers. Which is why young people from town came to us, all dressed and ready to travel.

Zelik, we could see, was also ready to go. He was not even thinking of going home. He had forgotten nothing there.

Yes, Zelik, you're right. You're right in every way. Still, no wagon driver is going to drive by here. Ah, come with us, we'll find someplace to spend the night together.

That pleased me. Zelik was one of Buzi's friends. And it would cheer her up to have one of her friends nearby in the open field.

"Where shall we spend the night?———"

"Yevrosi of Listve. My father is working on a hide for him." He came by and sat next to my father and talked with him. A peasant who only recently returned from military service. A large young fellow and, it would seem, an intelligent one. With a twisted and sporty blond mustache.

I might as well overhear what he is saying to my father.

"When will you be finished with my hide?"

"On such and such a date, perhaps. The disturbances are dying down."

"They are? I haven't heard that they're dying down."

My father explained to him that it was certain. As certain as could be.

What was his reason for coming to us? "Maybe you'd like to hide your horse and wagon with me? The stables are certain to be robbed at night."

I was mistaken to think he was intelligent. He thought that we would keep the horse in the stable so that he, Yevrosi, could come to steal it at night. But the horse has been in a stable since yesterday, and perhaps Yevrosi knows in whose.

"No," said Father. "Nobody will take the horse. I don't have to hide it, not even with a fellow like you."

"And the cow?"

"No one will take the cow either."

How do you like that? However cleverly starched Yevrosi's mustaches may be, he was still far from intelligent. Because he was truly a fool if he thought he could deceive us with quiet flatteries and with favors.

He hemmed and hawed for another quarter of an hour and left with what he had come with. But he was very, very unhappy.

"See to it, Panye Leyb . . . see to it that my hide is whole. Because . . ."

"As for your hide, for the time being no one will touch it. You may be certain of that. Go home and eat supper."

And he left, hardly bothering to say good night.

We do not spend the night in Motl Rattner's or at Avdei's house. We'll stay in clearings in the woods. All we have to do is go quietly and one at a time so that the neighbors don't notice us. And if things are quiet in town, then the worst that will have happened is that we will have spent the night in the clearings whose fences border our property a thousand yards from our house.

An hour or so later, our whole family sat clustered in a tree-enclosed clearing. My aunt's family was with us, and her daughter Brokhe had her little children with her. My aunt was angry. She said that the little good-for-nothings would endanger us all.

"Stop their mouths with something or other and keep them quiet." What is it that makes my aunt so angry? And against her own grandchildren?

And the wooded clearing suddenly had visitors. Unexpected and suspiciously silent.

Little wood, I'll tell you what. Don't bother us, and we won't bother you. Just leave us alone, and we'll get through the night quietly.

How fine it will be . . . how fine if the night passes like a quiet yawn. And may the night pass as quietly as a yawn at Motl Rattner's house as well.

At sunset, Pugatshov (he's a Lederman), his wife, who is better looking than he, and their children crept in among us in the wood. The older boys, seven and nine, were all girt up in their overcoats. They were eager and willing whenever an older person needed their help. "Come, adjust that thing on my shoulders," and the small-fry were always ready to help. "Here, let me do it." "No, let me."

It's good that you're here. But more quietly, please. More quietly.

The tenth month in the Jewish calendar, usually coinciding with parts of June and July.

And the evening approached. A lovely Tammuz° evening. And when little birds ready themselves for sleep, they must first sing their little bit of song.

Well, why not? Sing, little birds. Sing and enfold us in the web of your song as with thin strands of distant violin strings. Enfold us and protect us here in our cool and unfamiliar beds.

Certainly all will be well when this night is done. But I feel that I have not done well by my mother or Buzi or Hershele or my sisters. I should have provided them with a better and a safer place to rest. Yes, it all devolves on me.

The smaller children are already asleep, but the adults are still whispering among each other. They assure each other that it will be a peaceful night. My father and Pugatshov are the ones who are most convinced of it. They are merchants, and they know how much was paid to whom and for what.

"We were foolish not to have gone to Motl Rattner's instead of lying about here."

No one would let me go into town to see what was happening. If I had binoculars with me, I would have been able to see at least from a distance. I was very anxious to know what was happening at Motl Rattner's house.

Motl's was a wooden two-story house. And now it was packed with Jews, with their wives and children. All sorts of people, including, perhaps Dobbe Frenk and Mordkhe-Leyzer's wife. I was very anxious to know how they were all getting on in such crowded conditions. All jammed together as on Atonement night. And what was Motl Rattner's big-city daughter-in-law doing? Is she perhaps saying *"Pardon"* and "I'm sorry?" Eh? And I'd like to see how many people were in Motl's house for the first time. And most of all, I'd like to know what was happening above in the painted houses. I hope they're not feeling out of place. It's clear, too, that the Ovrutshev families made a big mistake—those who live in two towns.

What? The Ovrutshev pogroms weren't enough for them.

And I'd like to see how the women at Rattner's give their children suck. It's a crowded house, God bless it, with men in it. And many young mothers who have to suckle their babies. And it must be so hot at Motl Rattner's that the closeness will put the lamps out. Just think of it—how crowded it is. And how do they pass the time there in Motl Rattner's house? The house has many rooms. Perhaps there's a different group in each of the rooms.

Have the workingmen gathered together in the kitchen because they're embarrassed to be with the middle-class young people?

And, if I had a pair of binoculars, I would be able to see how they blessed the wine at the head post office. . . . There were Jews who had asked to be let in and were gathered in the director's cellar. And they could hear the sounds of merriment, of drinking, singing and dancing going on above them. Who was the object of the toasts of those drinkers: of the director, the military commandant, various clerks and four or five other young people? Marko drinks toasts to the noblemen and is on intimate terms with them. He makes them in Russian, and he sings lovely songs in unison with them. The Jews in the cellar are not calm. They are by no means calm.

And I very much want to meet that short fellow, Klimko, Uncle Zalman's neighbor, and I want to tease him. "Proud as you are of your son and though you are the best-informed slanderer on the military staff, and the first to know whatever it is that's going on, you'll rue the day you were a drinking companion of the director's. You stand staring like an owl with your sly eyes into the dark of Antonovitch Street, conceiving new schemes in your liar's sly head.

"But there's no one to tell them to. Old Zalman is no longer in his house. And there are only scorched holes where his windows were.

"Stare, owl. Stare. And do you know what, Klimko? It doesn't even occur to you that I'll live to see you dead. Your death and your son's. Though now you stand all alone looking out at the dark Antonovitch Street. Lonely and with a sense of expectation in your filthy heart that something will happen.

"Klimko, damn your ugly mug. You're waiting for something, aren't you?"

And if I had binoculars, there are many things I would have seen. How mother and the children were spending the night, and groups of village Jews who are wandering about from pillar to post. But they are the most likely to be safe from all danger. Though Dovid Frenk was killed in one of those villages. Dovid Frenk with his mother and brother as well as Osher Gershteyn's father. No, mother and the children must by now be far away. And there are Jews spending the night in the priest's attic. So that if there should be a reckoning he can say, "On the contrary, I hid Jews."

And Jews are spending the night in various peasants' stables. Though who knows whether the owners of those stables will spend the night in their homes?

What's being said? There ought to be a radio antenna on Motl Rattner's house because Motl Rattner's house is now like a train station and the house is the very nerve center of a number of worlds.

But I don't have binoculars with me. I sit in the dark, hidden among trees, and it is dark all around me. And there is grass growing near me. Yes, grass.

What's that noise beside me. What?

Maybe it's a beetle, or perhaps a young bird in its nest stirring in its sleep, shifting from one place to another.

Almost all of my people are asleep.

"And Ayzik, you sleep too. When you wake up all the evil will have disappeared, evaporated into the empty fields and the dry woods. It'll all enter into stones and logs." I desperately wanted someone to whisper that to me. And I wished to be a child again, even younger than Hershele and Yosele. As young as the child sleeping in my aunt's daughter-in-law's lap. And Buzi is sleeping not far from me. I can feel her shoe with my hand and I think, "Buzi dear. Your hands and feet are cold because of the freshness of the evening. Your thin dress isn't much of a blanket for you. But I can feel—ah how I feel it—how your young blood courses back and forth endeavoring to keep you warm."

It's well, my dear, that I can feel your blood moving about. Because, from that point of view, it's all over for Dovid Frenk.

And I have an impulse to wake Buzi. To let her know, even more urgently, that she is here. That she is mine.

Beside Buzi's shoe, I feel something like coarse cloth. It's rough grass and not fragrant, crumbling earth.

I'm glad to be getting sleepy. And I'm glad that it's quiet in town. It'll be daylight in a couple of hours. And then it'll be true. . . . And Yevrosi wants to take the horse . . . and peasant girls . . . a townful of peasant girls . . . at Motl Rattner's house. . . .

Then I dream of a bright courtyard filled with glowing people. Transformed people, not from here. And they are not really people. Rather, they are heavy sheep and cattle on a green pasture. So heavy the earth can hardly hold them. So heavy . . . And the wealth of it all makes one swell with pride and the lightfooted evening sun wearing a veil of grace is strolling about. Suddenly, the cattle begin stamping their feet, and there is a dense cloud and then thunder and lightning. I woke up. There was no rain. It was dry. There was a strange feeling in the air. Dogs were howling. Countless dogs. A multitude of them howling in all parts of the town. I tried to open my eyes; to test whether I was dreaming or whether what I was hearing was real. . . .

Vrrroooom. A grenade exploded somewhere; and the thunder continued to rumble, exploding over the earth. You could hear its echo for perhaps half an hour.

Yes, it was happening in town.

Our families—half of them wake up. They wring their hands; they turn pale. And those who are still asleep—would that they would stay asleep.

Vrrroooom. Thunder again.

There are explosions on all sides. Our hair stands on end. And dogs!! Where did so many dogs come from?

We are on a hillock. The town is below us, and we can hear screams and cries.

They're not drunken cries. They are the cries people make at the point of death.

There is a banging of crowbars and the rattling of tin. Maybe there's a fire. Maybe the town is burning. And again we hear cries and shouts. Who can be screaming like that? Jewish children? I've never heard them cry like that.

Then someone comes to us from out of the trees.

Don't be frightened. Don't be frightened. It's Shmuel-Yankl, the shoemaker's son and his family. They've spent the night near us. And none of us knew the others were there.

Who else is coming out from among the trees? Ah, it's Mikhl the baker and his wife. They didn't want to stay in the peasant's stable, and they crept here. Good. Good. But quieter, please. As quiet as possible. The children are waking up. Then let their mothers do what must be done. And again, the outcries from the town. Girls are being dragged by the hair. Girls and young mothers being dragged from their beds.

"Down with communists and Jews. Hurrah!"

And Sloveshne shrieks and chokes itself on blood.

What's going on in town? Streams of blood are flowing. Ah. Blood is pouring. It's pouring. And in Motl Rattner's house the blood is flowing perhaps from the upper-story windows. Red streams. Oh Lord, why are they shrieking like that in town? And we stand there, a silenced cluster, with wives and children and people staying with us.

"Yankl," I say to my former boss, "we've no weapons in our hands. Let's at least go and find some axes. It's not far."

"Be still," Yankl replies. "Be quiet. We won't go."

"But what if Kosenko comes here? Kosenko or Marko? Let's at least have a stick of some kind."

"Be still," Yankl begs. "We won't go."

And Buzi kneels before me, and her eyes are lifted to me, she whispers so low she can hardly be heard, "Ayzik, you won't go anywhere. I won't let you."

Now where did Buzi suddenly acquire the look of a madonna? And why does her voice tremble as she pleads? Is it because she loves me; is it because she's scared?

"Both, Ayzik. Both," I make my own reply.

Why didn't we take an axe with us yesterday? A couple of axes? We could have carried them under our clothes. We believed what Marko and Kosenko said. We trusted them. And I look at Shmuel-Yankl's wife—at Sarah, Shmuel-Yankl's. There she is in our crowd, with daughters, sons-in-law and grandchildren. She says nothing to anyone. She is simply pale. Waiting. Listening very attentively.

No, I'll not turn her over to Kosenko—to that wormy Kosenko. He'll not get any of these sleepers. I'll crush him like a bedbug. I don't care if he's got a gun, I'll crush him like a bedbug. A couple of weeks ago he announced that he was a watchmaker. Aha! He wanted to deceive his own brothers. What a peasant can think up. That all the Jewish watches in town would find their way to him. To him at his father's house. Some watchmaker he is.

Well, what about his partners? What will they steal? Kosenko, you're too smart.

And it's two weeks now since he's been driving about among the villages on Jewish business. And now he's running about the town with a gun in his hand. All infected. No, he's too young to be so exalted. To have priests and headmen and whole villages consulting him on Jewish matters. He is too young to be riding around on a horse maligning me in the villages. I'll stomp him!!

Is it daylight yet? Yes, it's daylight. And there's no sound of shouts coming from town. No shrieking. Only dogs bark one after the other. Evidently a great deal happened while we were asleep. While we slept, our town was convulsed.

Yisroel-Dovid is here, bringing us the news from town.

"There was a great slaughter at Motl Rattner's house. The rabbi is at his last gasp, he's been stabbed in the heart. The daughter-in-law was killed. Many people were killed in Motl Rattner's house, though it's not yet clear who they were. There's a great bloody pile of them."

"Is it likely they'll come here?" some women asked uncertainly.

"When there's more light, we'll leave this place. All of us . . . all of us will leave," someone says with determination.

We put our faith in daylight as if it were a powerful guardian. It might reveal us, but it would not turn us over to our enemies.

We hear the cries of Jews running across the fields. And someone is chasing them, crying, "Stinking Jews, don't crush my oats; I'll cut you down like dogs."

"It's Shmayle," says my sister. "That's his voice." Well, if Shmayle is in the game, then everyone is in it. So that's how it is. Jews run, but they have short feet. And Shmayle pursues them, his features contorted with rage. But perhaps he won't do anything. It's daylight already.

Baran's Yisroel is here.

"People, let's go. Nisl the Beech has been killed. He's lying near Yekhiel Dorf-man's house."

"What do you mean, killed?"

"Killed with a scythe. One of his neighbors from below the river."

"Yontl's Hershke also killed. By the same peasant."

Yontl's Hershke, my boss? He recently came back from the war and was just gathering his family together. He had curly hair, like a young ram's. Curly and very black. That curly hair must have been smeared with blood. He didn't know where to run to and, seeing a ladder next to the widow's house, he started to climb it when the peasant pulled him down and killed him with a scythe across his throat. The same thing happened to Nisl the Beech.

A tall, dark fellow, that Nisl. In middle age. A furrier.

Dovid the grocer, also killed. Mikhoel stabbed. Naftoli-Yoshke's daughter killed. Zisha Guretske's wife . . . the old market woman . . . .

"Naftoli-Yoshke's daughter? The one who lived beside the river. The seam-stress?"

"Yes. She was engaged to be married. She's lying not far from the church."

(It all happened so quickly, I wasn't even able to ask, "When will we kill peasant girls? And young peasant women? Women as simple as Naftoli-Yoshke's daughter, the seamstress who lived beside the river—or any others who may come to hand and whom no one ever expected to kill.")

Rokhl, Baran's daughter, lost a two-year-old child as she was running. The child's marrow spilled on a stone not far from her house. Rokhl, with her other children, kept running. Now you could hear her calling her husband, "Shloyme, my dearest love. Where are you? Shloyme, my dear. My darling, where are you?"

A quiet woman, that Rokhl, and now she is confused, calling as loudly as she can. She's no longer in town, but calling aloud in the fields. Hoping that her husband will respond to her. She now has only one thing on her mind, and she keeps on calling.

All of us in our hiding place among the trees can hear her. We recognize her voice, and we do't know whether we ought to call out to her or not.

"People, come."

And mother says, "Come, let's get away from here."

And we do what she says. We go.

See, now we are out in the bright sunlight.

Kosenko, here we are.

We scramble over the most distant of the fences and we go. There are many Jews near us. And we go.

And the Jews! Just look at them. There's hardly any difference between the living and the dead.

Just look at them. Zisl has been killed. Zisl who was talking to you is now dead. I'll believe it. Because the very least thing separates those of us who live from the others.

I cannot believe that the tormented ones are dead. And those who speak—I cannot believe that they are alive.

And on whom does the mark of the scythe show? Can you tell? Because a single nighttime hour or an expelled daytime breath can achieve that which an entire century will not erase. Look, then, at our living and at our dead.

But mother is exhausted. Worn out. Every five steps, she has to sit down. She says, "Go ahead, children. Go with the others. I'll stay here. God's will will be done."

Mother says it very calmly. But we don't leave her.

"Do you know what?" I say. "I'll just run over to the peasant's house and harness up our horse; then mother can ride. I looked them all in the eye. None of them dared to say "Yes". And in fact, that's what I did. I ran to Avdei's to get the horse.

And someone seems to be whispering in my ear, "What you're doing Ayzik is good. But quickly. Move quickly. Every minute counts. An instant's delay and the way there and back will be closed to you. Quickly, Ayzik. Quickly. It's well that you aren't scared; that you aren't depressed; that you are alert. There's reason to be depressed, but put it off until later. For another ten minutes; for half an hour. Hurry."

And I feel that I am treading the earth on the other side of the border. I have stolen into a strange country, and I may be betrayed at any moment. I may be caught at any moment. And I cannot rely on any of these moments.

At my right, I recognize my father's house. Opposite it, Yisroel-Dovid's house. Yes, I recognize them. It's been so long since I've been here, the place where I grew up. And I recognize things, though I have no time to stay.

But I've come here in stealth, and without permission.

I turn left into Avdei's lane to get our rig.

Avdei's wife, a tall, powerful peasant woman, has trouble recognizing me, but I go at once to the stable and start to harness "my" horse.

"Where are you planning to drive at a time like this?" And I know her two daughters whom nobody is just then about to betray—and that grieves me deeply.

"You'll find out later where we're going," I say. "Bring out some bread." And I put the harness on.

"What kind of bread? I've only just begun to bake."

"Old woman, bring out a loaf, and don't delay."

She turns unwillingly toward her house door. I've given her an order.

Suddenly, bang, bang! Someone's cracking nuts. There's gunfire in town. Gunfire.

I've hooked up the last strap of the harness. The very last one, and they're shooting in town. It's hot in town once more. One hundred degrees for everyone.

A neighbor from two doors down brings me a loaf of bread. Evidently she heard my dealings with the witch.

"Neighbor, open the gate."

She is more responsive to my requests and drags the broad pine gate open. And puts her hands fearfully on her heart as she says, "Ah, dear God. They're shooting again."

"Yes," I say, "they're shooting again. Giddap."

"Wait a minute, here's a cake for you." Avdei's wife, after a bit of agonizing, had decided to put off doing penance until next year.

"To hell with you. Giddap."

I hear the sound of cracking nuts right behind me. They're shooting, the way children play. Erratically, like the leaping of fleas.

Giddap.

My horse only now begins to move. I woke him out of his doze. A horse, it would seem, is always a horse. It makes no difference to him where he finds his oats.

The shooting in town seems to have no preconceived plan. My horse puts his ears back. Evidently he's not pleased that there's scatter shot behind us. His nostrils expand, and he lifts his head.

"Giddap. There's nothing to hear." The trouble is that we're still a bit below the hill. "So there, giddap. A touch of the whip, and giddap. Get a move on. Giddap."

I may meet a neighbor peasant who will ask me where I'm going . . . my neighbors are, today, ten times better and ten times worse than usual. Their eyes are sealed, and they seem unable to see people. And Nisl, the leather worker, a black corpse, lies beside Yekhiel Dorfman's house. . . . Giddap. Perhaps we ought not to leave town. Perhaps we should stay for Nisl the Beech's funeral. And that of Yontl's Hershke. And Naftoli-Yoshke's daughter. And that of other Jews. Young people, women and children whom Kosenko wanted dead.

What was it like for Yontl's Hershke under the scythe? For the rabbi under the point of the spear? I don't know. I've never in all my days felt the blade of a knife at my throat or had anyone want to kill me or been at the point of death. I'd like to know what that's like. Giddap. You won't get there until tomorrow. And the old market woman—all of her children are in America. And she lies murdered all by herself in her little house. And I owe her some money, the old market woman. I owe her some money.

Ayzik, Ayzik, hurry.

You see a shorn lamb. And a pregnant ewe is stumbling about alone in the bare wheat field weeping.

"What's the matter, Buzi? Come dear, get into the wagon. Quickly."

And Buzi says tearfully, "Let's get away from here. . . . They began shooting again, so I said, 'Why have you sent Ayzik to town? Why have you sent him away? You hear? They're shooting. Who'll go get Ayzik? They're shooting. Who'll go get him?' And none of them replied."

I'm really angry at my father for letting such a child, such a little lamb, wander about in an empty wheat field in search of her Ayzik. She's still a child, and the firing over there goes on without letup. With no beginning or end. Like the bells in the church on the first day of Easter. Morning, noon and night, children pull at all sorts of bells without stopping.

Buzi would not tolerate my standing in the wagon as I drove. "Let's sit down. Let's hide from the fact that wicked spirits are shooting in town."

"Where is mother?"

"Oh, dear. We've driven past her. We have to drive back. We have to turn into the field of clover. That's where she is."

To turn around, to have the wagon's wheels roll over the wheat . . . now that's a reason to kill a Jew. If I'm caught doing it, I myself would justify him.

"This time, neighbor, you're entirely right. I've crushed somebody's wheat with one of my wheels. That's because I turned the wagon around so that I could go in search of my weak mother who is waiting for me in the clover field."

"Hey, stop!"

Eh, who is it? Wait a minute, let me think it over slowly. Is it Yevrosi? With the curled mustaches? Who urged us to leave our horse in his stable last night? His face is all scratched and bruised? He stands there now with his eyes narrowed, his features all twisted. He's got his hand on my horse's bridle.

I'd ask him, "Yevrosi, who's scratched your face? Yevrosi, have you any idea who'll be at the rabbi's funeral? At the rabbi's, at Nisl the Beech's; at the funeral of Naftoli-Yoshke's daughter. Who'll be at their funerals, since we're all going away?"

But I don't ask him that. Instead, in a stern voice, I ask, "What is it, Yevrosi?"

"My hide. I've lost one of my hides because of you. So I have to unharness the horse."

He's right, of course. Though it may be he's making a mistake. He's entitled to three horses for one of his hides, not one.

"Listen to me, Yevrosi. There are sixteen hides in the attic of the house. Don't take all sixteen, Yevrosi. Take three to replace your one. And good day to you. Let go the reins."

"No. I have to take the horse. The horse is mine. I've lost one of my hides on account of you."

So you see, he is being reasonable.

"Yevrosi, in the house, in the attic, there are sixteen hides. Tell me, Yevrosi, do you understand me, or are you pretending? And who scratched you up. And are you, too, a highwayman?"

I saw a couple of young peasants just then on the road. They were leading horses in from their pasture. The peasant youths were from Hantsharske Street. I knew them. They had done by night what Yevrosi was doing now. But now it's daylight. Now they were just simple folk. I called them by name and, speaking in a confident voice, I asked them to judge between us.

"Do you see what a pain in the neck he's being. I've told him, 'There are sixteen hides at our house in the attic. Go take three in place of the one you've lost. But remember Yevrosi, no more. If you do, it'll be the worse for you.' "

If Nisl the Beech were to see me just then, he would say, "Ayzik, how did you get to be so clever? You know, it's not wise to say too much to a peasant. Listen, I know what a peasant is. (How many years is it since I've been sewing pelts for them, wandering about from village to village, hardly making a living?) This time, I hardly said ten words, and see what they've done to me. I'm a furrier. I have a wife and children. . . . Ayzik, at least do what you can to see that I'm properly buried, so that the pigs won't drag my body the length and breadth of Sloveshne."

"You see what a pain in the neck he's being," I said to the peasants.

"Yeah, you're right," said the young peasants leading the horses. And that was all they said.

Poor Yevrosi had not counted on such an end to his adventure. To lose such a horse in a single instant. As if it had escaped from his stall.

How long had it been since he set his mind on acquiring the horse, and now the end of it was that it was gone.

And Yevrosi has no clear understanding (since he's still confused) that if he doesn't get it now, it will, most likely, be never.

"Giddap!" I'll get even with him. The devil's hindmost is what he'll find if he goes searching for cowhides in the attic. Our neighbors are certainly smarter than he is. They've already stolen them. A rock flung in his teeth is what he'll find if he goes there. "They" have the preference. "They" are neighbors. And he's a dog of an outsider. Giddap. And here's my family.

"Now, mother, get into the wagon. That's it. Now. Giddap." Mother and my sisters and Hershele . . . my father was too impatient. He went off with the other Jews.

Buzi told mother and my sisters about Yevrosi. They clasped their heads, astonished.

"Giddap, Kosye. So what if it's up hill? Once in a while you have to make an exception. Giddap. We'll soon catch up to the other Jews. It'll be more cheerful with Jews. Giddap."

No one knows what day it is today. One cannot imagine a day in the week with today's color or today's name.

But the others say that today is Friday. Simply Friday.

That's droll.

And where are such contented Jews going on this Friday? Packed together in a flock: men, women and children.

Or it may be that they are not quite so contented. That's one thing. Where they are going is another. They're going. But they don't rightly know where they are going. Because there's still the question whether anyone will welcome such unlucky folk who have been beaten for three days and there's still no end to them. And, moreover, it may be that wherever there is a community of them in the world there will be a Kosenko or a captain of the guard. And it's said that our neighbors are bragging that they will follow us anywhere in the world. Our neighbors have condemned all the Jews to destruction. Perhaps they say what they say because they know something.

The shoemaker Leyzer's daughter is in her ninth month, so she has to get into the wagon. And let Shmulik's daughter Khane, a widow, put her children in, too. And are there other children?

"Come. Please get in the wagon."

I've driven my sisters off the wagon. They were tired, and it didn't occur to them that little children had a higher priority. Even when I shouted at them, they couldn't understand it. Even when they got down from the wagon, they weren't finished with my scolding. Is the "scolding" any better in Sloveshne?

"Anyone with small children, on the wagon, please."

It may not be nice to scold and shout this way on the road between the fields.

And my six-year-old brother, Hershl, understood that he was a man and got gravely down from the wagon, his hands in his pockets. All the men were on foot.

Giddap. I pass open-sided wagons. And I've left my depression somewhere else. I hope it stays there until we've reached a town.

It's clear to everyone now that today is Friday. But let me ask you, if you were in our place and you came to a point where there is a fork in the road and you knew that if you went in one direction no one would let you pass, and if you went in the other the same thing would be true, which direction would you take? Left or right?

We stopped. We considered what to do. Informed suggestions were made, roads mentioned, predictions made as to what might happen. The end of it all was that we could not agree. Some of us went to the right. We turned left, toward Velednik. There we would see what we would see.

My father had left the horse and the householder's role to me and had gone off with the others. Wheat was ripening in the fields on both sides of the road. Barley was ripening, and buckwheat was just springing up in other fields. The sun kept the dew from the fields. A true Friday sun. Pale. And bees hovered above the rows of grain in the fields. And there was a swallow darting about the horse's feet. Now low, right near its feet, and then suddenly darting upward through a shaft of air to hover above us once again. I didn't know whether it was teasing us or whether it meant to console us. And my wagon was filled with bleating children.

Children, children. We'll avoid danger, and you'll grow up to be healthy adults. And then you'll remember that there was a Friday on which you were all packed into a wagon, and that some fellow, Ayzik, drove the horse and walked beside the wagon. Ah, children, I could not stand the way you were packed together; and I could not stand your bleating. Just like lambs. And whenever the wagon swayed, your cries swayed too, and they became a strange sort of music, never heard before.

And other children, standing and weeping, nevertheless fell asleep. . . . Giddap, Kosye. . . .

A foolish Jew, newly arrived, rides along with us. He describes how Yekhiel Dorfman was killed. Old Yekhiel Dorfman. For most of the night he hid in the garden of the church, among the beanpoles. Then he went back to his house and sat down at the head of his table. Then when the town grew jolly, murderers came into the house and stabbed him. And there he continued to sit, at the head of his table. It may be he's still sitting there. . . .

A woman says that there was a great deal of butchery in our town last night. There was a particularly heavy butchery in Motl's house. And among others who were killed, she included Nayditsh, a foreign student, and Natan Granadyor. Each of them about twenty-six years old. And I find it hard to believe that they could rest in peace. Such young and handsome folk. And in what attitude are they now? Strong young shoulders, hands and feet, all together. How do they lie there in that bloody tangle?

Then, the woman told how some twenty men at Avrom-Ber's house survived though others died. They were not found—but theirs was not a good resting place, under the groans of the dying, under corpses, with streams of blood flowing down to find a hiding place. "Don't faint. Don't move. Hang on. It may be that you'll survive." No, such living is nauseating. And Haykl's head is split open. Kosenko opened a window and told the Jews to run, to save themselves. Meanwhile, he stood there and chopped at the head of anyone who looked out of the window.

But others who were lucky got away, despite their wounded skulls.

Hershl-Gedalikh's wife was killed, but Hershl and his son-in-law escaped with head wounds and ran through the streets like chickens that have not been properly killed.

And Keyle-Esther, the widow, has a broken arm; and Itsl's Yosl, who works at the tannery, has a stab wound in his hand.

The woman telling all this is very lucky. She saw them all as she was looking for her children. Now she is alone. She says that Kosenko ran about waving a revolver; the soldiers had rifles; while the others had scythes, others had guns, and some had ordinary iron rods. Pashkovski grabbed the butt of a gun from an old man and broke the same old man's hand with it. No doubt this upset the old man. And Alter Krayzman, Alter the harness maker, stood before the door of his house, an axe in his hand: "For every pair of feet that comes close, there'll be a head lying on the ground."

Alter is a brave man, but Alter's wife and children, unwilling to be left widowed and orphaned, pleaded with him to do what other Jews did until finally, in the midst of the turmoil, they managed to escape to Dyakon's stable, where they hid.

And the woman had also seen a woman from Ovrutsh who was killed and lying in the street. But she had no time to pause beside the body.

"Giddap."

My women in the wagon neither hear nor see anything. They are terribly confused and frightened. And if they think of anything at all in their lethargy, it is this: whether they have been rescued yet or not.

"Giddap."

And the Jews are stumbling about. They are talkative, as if it were an early Sabbath morning when they go to bathe. They seem to be satisfied with something. This is especially true about the stranger, the newly arrived and foolish Jew. He had been in Sloveshne only a week, and yet he had managed to save his life.

"Uncle, I am in no way more respectable than you. And I have nothing against you. But I'm upset because Nisl the Beech is lying exposed and sprawled in Yekhiel's house. Benyomin-Leyb's Yekhiel. And because Yekhiel is sitting there with the point of the spear still in his heart. And because his shutters are drawn, at midday. If the shutters weren't drawn, perhaps he would nod at Nisl the Beech, or give him advice or counsel. He's a wise fellow, this Yekhiel. And I'm upset, too, that the rivulets of blood have cooled on Motl Rattner's walls and on the other side of his windows. On the steps, on the table, on the beds, on the furniture and everywhere else.

What do you think? Will Motl Rattner's house ever be a house again, or do you think it'll be burned down? Burned one board at a time. And the ashes hidden, along with the dead.

And you, my faithful peasant neighbors, though you have wiped the scythes and knives, have you taken them home with you along with my blood? Peasants, faithful neighbors, may you rot. You and your wives and children. Wherever you may be. Because. Because I can't abide the fact that your children walk the streets sniffing at the boots that belonged to my dead.

Here!

We are already in the village on the outskirts of Velednik. Several of us make inquiries of the village peasants. They express sympathy for us, cluck their tongues, but they could swear that last night the same thing happened in Velednik. A peasant woman says she'll call her husband and that he'll tell us.

And indeed, he does tell us. He says that demons came to Velednik. But he thinks they were driven away.

"Giddap." We have to move on, because there's no turning back. And what's ahead is not so clear, either. Perhaps those who turned back to Yevrosi's village made the better choice. And the peasants sympathize with us. Even the dogs stop their barking. Curious, they watch us, their tails in the air as they stand beside their masters.

Nevertheless, it's kind of the peasants to let us pass.

"Good day to you."

"Go in good health. A good day to you."

"Giddap," and we're on our way again.

It's four versts to Velednik.

There is an uplifting scent of green hay in the gardens. For my horse's sake, I'd like to spring into one of those gardens and gather a bit of clover for him (it would be the perfect crime). In the streets of Velednik, one can smell fresh groat cakes. The inhabitants of Velednik behave like simple Jews. We don't. You can see it at once. We're different. No longer simple.

Well? We're not quite respectable: the moment they saw us, we frightened the Jews of Velednik. They didn't say much, but they wrapped their baskets in towels, and their children in shawls. They grabbed wagons and hurried off to Ovrutsh.

"What's it all about?"

It's all simple matter. There were people here during the night, but the local peasants drove them away. Indeed, one of the band who was slain and another who was wounded are still in town. The others scattered like a band of mice. Who they were and where they came from, nobody knows. Now, when the local Jews have seen what misfortune has overtaken us, they harness their wagons and hurry off to Ovrutsh.

It would seem that the Velednik Jews are using their heads. But why are they in such a hurry? It would be better if they exchanged a word or two with us. Though perhaps there's not much to say. Too bad.

And so, we drive on.

We unloaded the wagon and were left only with a girl who had lost her mother.

"Don't cry, child. We're driving to Ovrutsh, and your mother is there."

And, since father knows the way, and the wagon is now empty, all of us sit in it. Our horse moves at a crawl, and we're on our way to Ovrutsh. But why didn't all of Sloveshne go to Ovrutsh after the first day?

"Because no one knew . . ."

Franz Finkl of Volost had said, "Where are you going to go, since there's nobody left, even in Ovrutsh?"

And now, who knows whether there is anyone in Ovrutsh or not? We know nothing at all. He was a new arrival, that Franz Finkl. From Volost.

And it seems to me we'll get to Ovrutsh in 1925, but my father says that it's twenty-five versts to Ovrutsh. Is he telling the truth, or did he say that merely to keep our courage up?

We are overtaken by wagons from Velednik filled with entire families. Perhaps they curse us for making them drive off so abruptly.

When the road is sandy, we get down from the wagon. And there's stinking mud in the villages. The horse has a hard time dragging his way out of it.

"Daddy, is there always this much mud in the villages?"

And young people nearby are roofing a stable. They stand there with axes and boards in their hands. Young, indifferent folk who laugh at us.

"Sons of bitches that you are. You stand there laughing with axes and boards in your hands. Throw them at us. Throw your axes and stop laughing."

But they don't talk to us. They talk to the wagon drivers of Velednik.

"Where are you driving them? Why don't you just turn the wagon over and be done with them?"

The wagon drivers know who they are, so they make no reply and keep driving. "Giddap."

The horses strain, the mud stinks. We still have three such villages before we come to Ovrutsh.

One wonders whether we'll be allowed to drive into Ovrutsh? Whether anyone wants us there? And when will we get there? I'm beginning to think it will be never. Just think how long it's been since we first started.

Night is coming on. Blumele, who lost her mother, has been uneasy all along the way.

"Just after we pass this village, it will be Ovrutsh," says father.

"I hope we can eat *kreplakh*," says Buzi.

And indeed, we drive onto the cobbled road. The wagon begins to rattle. That's no fun for Buzi. Better for us both to get down.

It's candle-blessing time, and the Ovrutsh cattle are returning home from the fields. Do you see? In Ovrutsh, people are behaving as usual.

A freshly bathed, cleanly dressed Jew comes toward us. Perhaps he has already heard the news?

"From Sloveshne?" he asks father.

"Sloveshne," comes the reply from several voices on the wagon.

"Come to my house," he said simply and pointed our way for us as if he had found what he was looking for.

It was a heart-wrenching moment. . . .

The Jew's house was twenty paces away. Candlesticks were already on the table there, and a woman, either his daughter or a daughter-in-law, was still washing the kitchen floor.

Our people climbed stiffly and carefully down from the wagon, as if this was precisely the inn toward which we had so long been driving.

"Come into the house," came the fresh voice of a shy young woman.

Fortunately for me, I still have things I need to do so that I don't have to go into the house just yet.

I have to find a place for the horse.

The householder's boys show me where to put it.

"Youngsters, be good enough to go now. I'll feel better left to myself."

The horse is wet, tired and hungry. His sides are contracted. He whinnied at me when I took his harness off. And what'll happen if, following my impulse, I put my arms around his neck and burst into tears? Because of the great shame; and because of all the other things that are pressing on my heart and that I cannot express in words. To weep sweetly . . . to weep, to weep; and perhaps to indulge myself and simply dissolve into my tears. For them. For where we've been. For the great and miserable shame.

The End

On that same Friday night, Jews still lived in Sloveshne. In the morning, their roads were blocked. In the morning, they were driven back from every road by armed local peasants who, mad and red-eyed and murderous, drove them back along the roads.

They were driven into the center of town, to the church where they were told to kiss the cross. One of the peasants, as a joke, threw a grenade, but fortunately it fell into the mud.

Then Kosenko said, "In order to avoid cholera, we'll have to bury the dead. Let the Jews first go bury their dead, and after that we'll finish them off at the cemetery." Yankl the Wallachian harnessed up his wagon and heaps of dead were carted, gently or rudely, to the cemetery. Men and women, youths and maidens. And if it chanced to be a child, it was grabbed by the leg and thrown like a bundle onto the wagon.

Those who were half dead were left to lie in their torment and were not taken to a grave. "Wait until they die."

And those live Jews who lay under the bodies, when they heard quiet, exhausted Yiddish voices and finally risked opening their eyes to see what was going on, were nevertheless petrified lest Kosenko should become aware that they were playing dead.

The Jews in the burial party counseled them, "Roll up your sleeves and pretend that you're in the burial party. That'll explain why your clothes are bloody."

And the dead lay in a variety of poses and in various sorts of garments. And the dead were everywhere.

And so wide ditches were dug. One ditch was intended for men. Another for women. The young with the young. The old with the old. And they busied themselves about the task.

Young and old, all of them perspiring, worked until evening. Fifteen-year-olds had to show that they were good grave diggers; that they were fully experienced and could be permitted everywhere and to see everything. And that they could be trusted at the boundaries between life and death.

They worked until evening (as of early morning, no one had kept track of time), and then they all sang *Lekhu neraneno*° at the cemetery. Then each of them found the most densely overgrown graves that they could find among the huts and hid themselves until midnight, until dawn, until broad daylight. Until help arrived from Ovrutsh: a detachment of Bolsheviks. (Yitzkhok Ber Helfand, wearing warped boots, his feet rubbed raw, had, on Friday, escaped to Ovrutsh along with the others who were fleeing from the villages near Sloveshne and, with the same raw feet and still wearing the same warped boots, he returned to Sloveshne on Saturday morning with the detachment. For some reason, he showed no fear.

The opening prayer of the Kabbalat Shabbat service on Friday evening.

Perhaps because he was not from Sloveshne. He was not a local inhabitant. He was a teacher who himself came from Ovrutsh.)

In the middle of the marketplace, the detachment caught a young peasant carrying things he had picked up. They killed him on the spot. Poor fellow, a foolish young peasant. Luck was against him. He had really had nothing much on his mind. Poor fellow, he came late to the scene. . . . later than absolutely everyone and he had gathered up a few things in a tablecloth. They killed him on the spot.

Then the entire townful of peasants gathered up their bedding, tossed them onto their wagons and, driving their cattle, went into hiding in the woods.

Then four tall, handsome, but somewhat angry young peasants were stood up before the little jail and shot. Among them, Zeydl the tanner's neighbor—Adamko. A tall, smooth-shaven, red-scarred fellow. And his sister and mother and father wept.

Then those with broken bones and the wounded of all sorts (so long as they were still breathing) were taken to the hospital. And the doctor who arrived an hour before the Bolsheviks had been made to undress in Volost. No one would believe that he was not a Jew.

And in fact, he was not a Jew.

Then it was commanded: "Gather up everything that was stolen. If you don't, we'll burn your houses down and you will burn."

Then Mamma Khaytshik, who had been stabbed, was brought back from a village; Yosele and Malke, both stabbed; and the murdered Aunt Freydl and her twelve-year-old Yankl; and old Avrom, who had been stabbed; Aunt Rasle, who had been wounded, and her two frightened daughters from the village, Malkele and Esther. Stabbed, both of them.

You want to know, "What will Yoylik in America say about all this? A packet of his letters just recently arrived."

And you'll want to know, "What good did it do Yosele to hide his toys in the same hiding place as Hershl?" And, "How will Hershl inquire about his friend?"

I don't know. I know nothing. All I know is that my soul, my heart and all of my limbs are in pain. And I would gladly take Aunt Khaytshik's place in the wide rectangle of her grave. And that I would be very frightened to wipe away the foam from Malke and Yosele's lips. Rokhele says that she remembers very little; but what she does remember is that there was white foam spewing from Yosele's mouth—and from Malke's too. And that they twitched and groaned.

Saturday, Saturday during the day, when help was only an hour away, her mother and family had a very disagreeable experience. They separated themselves from the larger group—thinking they would outwit God and would hide in the vicinity of the dairy.

Rokhele remembers very little. She remembers Yosele and Malke and that her mother, still alive, tried to crawl into a garden and that peasant women betrayed her and she was dragged out and stabbed again.

Well for Rokhele that she remembers so little.

Rokhele remembers less and less, because it's all dreadful.

She remembers very little, even about herself. She remembers that it was hot. She was going somewhere when she met a peasant. He asked her, "Where are you going all by yourself?" She made no reply. Because she was angry, she made no reply.

The peasant took her by the hand and led her to his home. "Do you want to eat something?" he asked. "Do you want something to drink?" She said nothing.

Early next morning, he led her to the outskirts of Sloveshne and said, "I guess you can find your own way from here." Then he left.

She ran home but found nobody there. She was very thirsty. Taking an earthen cup, she went into the cellar where there was water. And she drank. After that, she remembers nothing.

Then things took their usual course.

Somebody passing by Borukh-Ayzik's house heard groans and went inside and found Mother Khaytshik's daughter Rokhele lying on a rag. From all indications, she had been lying there for three days. She was taken to the hospital.

I found Rokhele in the hospital, lying on the ground. She lay in a corner of the corridor, covered with lice. There was a half-raw egg near her, moldy and covered with hair, and a smeared crust of bread.

The peasants, it was said, were bringing milk, eggs and bread. Transformed into good peasants.

"Where is Buzi?" Rokhele asked, her voice coming as if from underground.

"See, here she is Rokhele." And Rokhele turned her eyes in the direction I indicated, but she did not move her head and asked no further questions.

Rokhele had two blunt stab wounds in her shoulder. Perhaps they were not dangerous.

And someone told me, "Ayzik, your beds are in the district office. Go get them. Timofeiko dragged them back. He meant to inherit them from you. Timofeiko."

And someone else said, "Ayzik, some pig of a peasant in Listve has your black cow. His name is Yevrosi. He's just back from his military service so he thought he might as well graze your cow."

At Mother Khaytshik's house I found Rokhele's clothes, caked with blood. I hid them someplace where I could find them again. And I searched for the two fresh (for that day) mounds in the cemetery. Nearby there was a board on which was written, "Here lie three martyrs: Avrom, Elimelekh and Yoysef." And on the board just opposite was written, "Here lies four martyrs: Freydl, Khaya, Esther and Malke." Do you see how none of them is paired? Neither the men nor the women.

Then the detachment of Bolsheviks put twelve peasants into a great wagon and bound their hands to its sides. All twelve were large, well built—and angry. Nine were local men, and one from the workers' settlement, as well as the dark little traitor and Franz Finkel (the one who had said: "Where are you going to go since there's nobody left, even in Ovrutsh?").

That makes three.

Nine and three usually makes twelve.

Just yesterday, they chose to bathe in blood. But that was Jewish blood. As for them, what did anyone have against them? And their faces again look strange. Stodot knows what was done to four of the young peasants. He knows that they licked the ground. And Stodot knows that he, too, will do the same; he and the dark little traitor, and Timukh Lukhtans (the tall, handsome militiaman) and his brother, and white-bearded Maxim. But the chief culprits are not here. Missing are Kosenko, Marko and the head man. And there are others missing. But where is one to find them?

In the morning, justice was done to the twelve. Timukhei excepted. He hid himself and managed to delay things for two months.

The mothers, wives and fathers who traveled to Ovrutsh described all that happened there. "It was all very simple. They hired Mongols. Many Mongols. They filled them full of brandy and then led them to the cemetery where they were told, 'Be good enough to kill these Russians here.' For the Mongols, this was a small matter. They spat once and it was done. As easy as eating bread."

Well, now they lie underground in the Ovrutsh cemetery—our lords.

Later, Mordkhe-Leyzer's older son (Osher Gershteyn is his name) enlisted as a volunteer in the Red Army. He could find no rest, and he could not understand why his father had been killed. He enlisted in the army promising that he would "do something." Osher Gershteyn.

Then, slowly, there was repayment: an eye for an eye. And peasant daughters-in-law and young wives had reason to weep. Some sixty, as against sixty victims. Then old Zalman's neighbor, Klimko himself, came back from prison and was taken up that very night. By morning, he lay newly washed beneath the sacred images. His wife and daughter were taken that same week.

After that, there were many who stopped weeping in two towns.

Crushed, wounded, we returned to heal our bruised Sloveshne.

And we had a doctor to care for Rokhele. And nothing more. What will we say to Osher and to Shoyel if they should come to inquire about their mother?

After that, the peasants in our neighborhood flattered us. "None of us thought it would end that way. We were told that there were no more Jews. And that no one would take their part. Well, too bad. It's been paid for. An eye for an eye. But enough already. It's a pity to kill such fine healthy peasants. And the Jews who were killed were not in the best condition. Old folks, women and children. Only here and there were there any healthy young men."

Well, certainly they are right. Is it their fault that they were deceived? They had only hoped for the best. They had believed that they could get on without Jews. And, as they say, possible consequences harm nothing today. Well, so be it. So they would divide up the bit of Jewish goods: the houses, the cattle (about which they had in some cases even quarreled). And then, just see! In the very midst of it all, along come the Bolsheviks. And besides, Sloveshne was getting a bad reputation. "Bandit country." Wherever you go, the minute they know you're from Sloveshne, they shout "Bandit" at you.

And I'm supposed to console myself with that. And we're supposed to take pity on them and say, "Blessings on you—too bad that you hungered after Jewish property."

Then Buzi gave birth to a lovely daughter. We wept, we laughed. And we named her Khayale.

Then the Bolsheviks called a meeting at which they said, "Comrades, peasants and citizens of Sloveshne. Wipe the stains from your reputation and send your sons to the Red Army. Who will fight for the power of the workers and peasants if not the workers and peasants themselves?"

And they said to the Jews: "Comrades, artisans and citizens of Sloveshne. Do you not see that you have delayed paying your debt to the Red Army for far too long? Other Jewish towns are being made to suffer by gangs and counterrevolutionaries. Come, join the Red Army."

And hard as it was for me to leave my two girls—one of them twenty-one years old, the other two weeks old, still, Buzi and I had long whispered consultations about it. And Buzi wept silently, and I promised her that I would not be gone for long.

And since, with the approach of winter, there was the threat of a plague of Polish bands heading toward Sloveshne, we young men girded up our loins and entered the Red Army. Entered the hungry, courageous, lousy and sunny Red Army.

Six years have passed. Six whole years, knotted and bound with considerable bloody suffering and the joys of eternal acts of courage.

Now I live in a large town, far from Sloveshne. And I'm not sure whether I am wise or foolish to have written these lines as a memorial, today, the twentieth of October, 1925.

Ayzik Leyb the Tanner of Sloveshne

A Brief Observation

And Marko Lukhtans, that beggar, that Gypsy who loved Jews, was also killed.

It happened in the middle of the day. Suddenly three shots were heard on the outskirts of town, and then a wagon drove in on which were Marko, his handsome brother Timukhei and his brother-in-law whom the town called Yakov-Kakov.

Three of Lukhtans's daughters-in-law were left widows. And when an orphanage was built in Sloveshne and snotty-nosed children went there for food carrying their own earthen bowls . . .

Why there they were, the orphaned Jewish children and Marko's orphaned children. Marko murdered Jews, and the Jews killed Marko. And orphan children come running to the kitchen, their bowls in their hands. And the children think nothing of it. They just raise their eyes and their mouths toward the food. The older folk find this a bit strange. Very strange.

1926

XIV

Between the Wars: Prophecy and Profanity

"I yearn to merge with you in prayer / And yet my heart, my lips are moved / Only to blasphemies and curses." The year was 1921. A young poet who had already fought on the Eastern Front, where the dead were numbered in the millions, and who had already witnessed the slaughter of Jews in the Ukraine found himself in the familiar Jewish predicament of wanting to find solace in myth and wanting to break with those consoling archetypes once and for all. This time the poet, named Peretz Markish, combined the two yearnings into a kind of Black Kaddish dedicated to the victims of one pogrom out of many. He shaped the victims into a mound of rotting corpses so that this mound might vie with all the sacred mounds of the past: Ararat, Moriah, Sinai and Golgotha.

What fueled Markish's blasphemy was both his firsthand experience of historical cataclysm and the fact that he came armed with a new poetic idiom—an amalgam of Russian Futurism and German Expressionism—that freed him from the constraints of literary propriety, normal syntax, meter and rhyme, a method specifically designed to give voice to the present chaos.

Another Expressionist poet, fresh from the battlefield, found a different way of using myth to express the horror of modern Jewish existence. Buried beneath the rubble and suppressed by rabbinic censorship was Masada (**65**), the desert stronghold where the Zealots from Jerusalem had staged their last armed struggle against the Romans in 73 C.E. For poet Isaac Lamdan, Masada embodied the apocalyptic yearning and the blasphemous rage that he felt as a victim of the failed revolution in Russia and as an active combatant in the Zionist revolution still unfolding in

Palestine. With the egocentric pathos so typical of Expressionism, Lamdan made his personal odyssey emblematic of his generation and reclaimed for it a whole new set of symbols: an ecstatic group of latter-day Hasidim dancing before a bonfire on the eve of battle; a walled fortress in the middle of the desert; a God who bestows His blessing on the people's struggle to overcome its inexorable fate. In "Masada," all the contemporary issues and personalities were described in terms of the biblical landscape; the poem was both apocalyptic scream and prayer for national self-determination. Most radically, the poem legitimated even a suicidal last stand as a historical necessity. For these reasons, "Masada," more than any other text, later inspired the uprising in the Warsaw ghetto. The present selection is based on the Warsaw anthology of 1940, which included four excerpts from "Masada" from a total of thirty texts.

Zionism was also Uri Zvi Greenberg's answer to the screaming contradictions of the Jewish and human predicament, but Greenberg's view of the world was even more polarized than Lamdan's. All of Europe, for Greenberg, was "The Kingdom of the Cross," a place that always was and always would be steeped in Jewish blood. The return to the ancient homeland was predicated on purging oneself of Christian Europe, of everything from the sound of church bells to Beethoven's Ninth Symphony (**66**). Greenberg's messianism of blood-God-and-soil ultimately led him to espouse the militant right-wing politics of Revisionism. Less predictably, it led him to celebrate that large segment of east European Jewry that every branch of the secular movement had disavowed: the ultra-orthodox Jews who still wore black gaberdines and let their sidelocks grow long. Greenberg believed that the *ḥalutzim* (pioneers) in Palestine could reclaim only the soil but not the spirit of Judaism. What was needed in this hour of crisis was a vast ingathering of energy of all the Jews—whether wearing khakis or *kapotes*.

By the late 1920s, Jewish Expressionism had played itself out as the poetic arm of apocalypticism. With Fascism on the rise throughout Europe, the terrifying isolation of the Jews led to a demand for greater unity as well as greater simplicity—for traditional forms, more accessible language, greater thematic clarity. The direction taken by Yiddish and Hebrew writers everywhere but in the Soviet Union was toward recognizable symbols of collective endurance.

In Poland, the forces of political reaction first made their presence felt through anti-Jewish boycotts and sporadic pogroms beginning in 1936. One such pogrom, in the town of Przytyk (pronounced Pshitik), became a rallying cry for self-defense. Because the Jews fought back; because the Jewish Labor Bund called a general strike to protest the police handling of the affair; and because Mordecai Gebirtig, a Yiddish folk bard from Cracow, immortalized the event in song (**67**), Przytyk became almost as important a symbol of catastrophe as Kishinev had been thirty-three years before. Though his imagery was timeless, in the tradition of conventional pogrom poems, Gebirtig in "Fire!" delivered the central message of the modern Jewish response to catastrophe: Do not trust in anyone but yourselves! The shtetl (the Jewish collective presence in exile), Gebirtig went on to warn, can be saved only by a united Jewish front.

The call for unity in Gebirtig's hymn provides a clue as to what constituted prophecy for a generation of readers that no longer believed in God. Because prophecy for many (if not most) eastern European Jews was identical to one's politics, any poet who claimed the prophetic mantle had to have the proper ideological credentials. But the authority for the poetry itself had to come not from the party line but from the poet's personal experience of pain and loss. That is how Bialik became the spokesman for his generation, even outside the Zionist camp. After Bialik, the next poet to achieve this status was H. Leivick, a veteran of the Bund. Leivick's theme, based on his own experience of imprisonment in Siberia, and gleaned secondhand from Tolstoy, was spiritual endurance and purification through suffering.

Leivick was the first self-conscious "survivor" in modern Jewish culture. His early poetry was suffused with a sense of election that translated into a far-reaching exploration of the messianic motif in Jewish history and consciousness (his poetic drama *The Golem* [1920] is the most famous example thereof). But even from the start, at a time when the redemption seemed truly at hand, Leivick foresaw that the world might be redeemed at the expense of the Jews. "A Stubborn Back—And Nothing More" (**68**), written in the first person plural, achieves an extraordinary toughness through its spare diction and its imagery of caves and bones that evokes a primeval landscape of elemental struggle. Not since the Mosaic Curses had the search for meaning through history yielded so naked a vision.

The legendary quality of Leivick's poem pointed to another feature of the prophetic response to catastrophe in modern Jewish culture. Whereas the Expressionist poets *magnified* the present through grand historical myths so that each event could be read as a sign of the apocalypse, those poets whom I shall now call "the prophets of consolation" did precisely the opposite: They cut the global scope and inscrutable design of historical events down to familiar size. In literary terms, metonymy replaced myth; normative replaced apocalyptic.

It was the dual nature of the Nazi Holocaust that made such an approach so compelling. On the one hand, the Nazis deliberately turned back the clock and resurrected the whole medieval chamber of horrors—the ghetto and yellow star; mass expulsions; myriad acts of sacrilege. On the other hand, this catastrophe was to eclipse all others and become its own archetype. After the Holocaust, the apocalypticism of Markish, Lamdan and Greenberg seems dated and histrionic, whereas the lyrical archaism of Leivick, Glatshteyn and Alterman anticipates our need to single out the destruction of European Jewry from all previous disasters and to mourn it on its own terms. Perhaps, too, the poetic discipline exercised by the prophets of consolation makes their work especially appropriate for liturgical use.

In the Holocaust, the imaginary became real. That is why poet Yankev Glatshteyn felt obliged to record the exact dates of his *Memorial Poems* that spoke of "ghettos" fully two years before they were actually established. What Glatshteyn really had in mind in April 1938 was a return to Jewish humanism: to collective faith, to self-discipline, to an indigenous culture, poor though it be. The gruff, declamatory style of his celebrated poem "Good Night, Wide World" betrayed Glatshteyn's debt to English modernism, particularly to Ezra Pound, but the newness of his message was matched by a new celebration—through end rhymes and idioms—of the folksiness of Yiddish itself. In June 1938, Glatshteyn took up the theme of exile in his haunting poem "Wagons"—haunting because the wagons and the grasses were the only things left endowed with any life. Three months later, all Polish Jews were expelled from Germany and ended up in a no-man's land between the two countries. But perhaps the most affecting, and truly prophetic, of these poems was "Ghetto Song" because by the end of the war, an entire people would be orphaned, each survivor a childless parent or a parentless child.

Glatshteyn tried to turn the specter of ghettos into a source of consolation and moral renewal. The voluntary ghetto that he called for was a place of spiritual commitment. The darker side of the ghetto was a place that had begun to shrink and where soon every Jewish life would be on the line. Halfway across the world, Glatshteyn's counterpart, the Hebrew modernist poet Natan Alterman, intuited exactly what that life would feel like *existentially*. To dramatize the situation, he invented another closed space: a nameless city under siege, soon to be destroyed. Inside the walls an extraordinary dialogue took place between a dead lover and his living beloved. The dialogue dwelt on the absolute value of life and death, on the relationship between personal and universal suffering, on guilt and shame and, above all, on "thoughts of the dead" as the structuring principle of human existence.

The dead lover's point of departure was Ecclesiastes: "Not all is vanity, child, / not all vainglory and folly." This already implied a dual perspective: one that accepted life's futility (hers) and one that negated it (his). But could not his be special pleading, given that he was already dead? Indeed, the central challenge facing his living beloved was to accept the principle of life's absolute value, though only in death could she ultimately prove it. To appreciate how radically new this existentialist position was to Jewish literature, one need only recall Bialik's response to the Kishinev pogrom (**46**):

For if when I have perished from the earth
The Right shine forth,
Then let its throne be shattered, and laid low!

Here, in contrast, there was no possible proof of the dead lover's position.

The dead lover's second major point (which also contradicted the teachings of Ecclesiastes) was that the death of the body was not the end of life:

For iron breaks, my child,
but my thirst for you is unquenched.

The will has no end, my child;
the body is clay, and shatters.

Strengthened by that "will" to face her death and the fall of her city, the living beloved came to perceive the nature of life on the brink, which was the center of Alterman's vision:

For the world is riven, and double
the clamor of its distress.
For no dead have forgotten their dwellings,
all dwellings mourn somebody dead.

At our cities of sorrow forever
gaze the dwellers of darkness and mound.
The glory of our days brims over
with thoughts of the dead underground.

The universalism of this poem was the source of its enduring power. History itself would supply the context when the first German bombs fell on Haifa and Tel Aviv and the tiny Jewish settlement prepared for a full-scale invasion by Rommel's army. Much later, this poem would be reinterpreted in the light of what no one could foretell: that a third of the Jewish people would be removed to dwell in "darkness and mound."

64 The Mound

PERETZ MARKISH

> After you, the killed of the Ukraine;
> After you, butchered
> In a mound in Gorodishche,
> The Dnieper town . . .

Kaddish

The opening canto is a sonnet.

I°

No! Heavenly tallow, don't lick my gummy beards.
Out of my mouth's brown streams of pitch
Sob a brown leaven of blood and sawdust.
No. Don't touch the vomit on the earth's black thigh.   5
Away. I stink. Frogs crawl on me.
Looking for mother-father here? Seeking a friend?
They're here. They're here, but taint the air with stink.
Away. Awkwardly they delouse themselves with hands like warped brass.

From top to bottom, a mound of filthy wash.
Claw, crazed wind. Take what you want; take it.   10
Before you, the church sits like a polecat beside a heap of strangled fowl.

Ah, black thigh. Ah, blazing blood. Out, shirttails! To the dance; to the dance.

We're laid out here. All. All. A mound. The whole town.

11 *Tishrei* 5681°

The date of the pogrom in Gorodishche in which 216 Jews were murdered corresponds to September 23, 1920, the day after Yom Kippur.

Cf. Num. 13:27: the report of the spies that the land to be conquered is a land of milk and honey.

Cf. Gen. 8:8–11: the doves sent out by Noah from the Ark.

Reference to the only kid bought by the father for two coins in the Khad Gadya song that concludes the Passover service.

Possible reference to the second circumcision undergone by the Israelites on the eve of Passover (Josh. 5:2) or to God's renewed covenant after the flood.

II

As one of the dead, I'll enter
The day of blood and honey.°
My first doves° will be
Dead spies upon the land.
Doves. Doves. Uphill.   5

It is my fate that hangs
Upon the bloody moon,
Her gleams, mere vowel signs.
Bellies, bellies to the dust—
Sleep is for dawn.   10

A mad town expires on my heart.
Street corners creep from my shoulders.
Ah, thou kid of the ascending sun,
Traded for two gulden,°
I'm at your circumcision feast° again.   15

Ah, you, my blind fathers,
How many bloated wombs,
How many debaucheries have borne me?
Then why am I afraid to take
A step into the ripped world?   20

Hey, boundaries of the earth! Spread.
The mill wheel turns from Nile to Dnieper now.
You, with spiked eyes,
Leap, mound, wild fever,
Over threshold, over ditches.   25

Blind Samson, blinded hero,
Hair's sprouting on your head again.
Leap upon a bow; on firebrands.
Make the distance tremble
And topple all the world.   30

III

Sunk to the loins in silence, the town sits
Like an upturned empty wagon in a marsh.
Ah, if only one would come
To say something.

Ah, grief and woe. The sunset, like a weeping hawk   5
Sits on the blind roof of an entreating palm.
Ah, Almightiest of the world,
Open—open up your starry title page.
  Hineni, he'oni.° Unworthy, here I stand.

"*Here am I, poor in worthy deeds,*" the reader's meditation that precedes the recital of the Musaf service on the High Holidays.

I yearn to merge with you in prayer   10
And yet my heart, my lips are moved
Ony to blasphemies and curses.

Ah, my prayer-exhausted,
Tenfold dishonored hands turn.
Take them; take them.   15

Caress them, lick them, as a dog
Licks its scabby, suppurating hide.
I pledge them to you.°

Yiddish, Ikh bin zey dir menader—an allusion to the Kol Nidre service on the eve of Yom Kippur.

Yiddish, mishkn, or tabernacle.

I've built you a new ark°
In the middle of the marketplace.   20

A black mound, like a blotch.
Seat yourself upon its buxom roof
Like an old raven on a dungheap.

Take my heart, my prayer-exhausted heart,
And all such rubbish. Take it   25
And peck, peck what the chariot of twenty generations brought.
I pledge it to you.

A wander-stick rolls about
Waiting for your steps that follow
Cain's unscrewed right legs.   30
I cool a capful
Of sanctifying blood
From Abel's throat for you.

You, whom noise diminishes,
A black wagon full of mud-smeared   35
Sleeping passengers pulls up
And something, something stirs.

Ah, sucked from my eyes, streams of pitch
To cleanse the dead. Take them, take them.
A black wagon with mud-smeared, sleeping passengers   40
More being driven there, more being driven, still being . . .

Come! cross yourself and count them.
A shekel a head,°
A shekel a head,
And thrust them—as always—   45
Thrust them from you.
I pledge them to you.
I pledge them to you.

Reference to the selling of Christ; i.e., the Jews were murdered in the name of the Cross.

V

Go slow. Pilgrim winds, from rocky lands and wild,
Will you now tread the brass and scarlet snows
Of the mound's head?
Store food for a millennium and, wrapped in elephant hides,
Sanctify your wings with blood. I myself will guide you.   5

Here, like cliffs of hacked bellies,
Wells lurk around you.
Wild bones, gummed with a black hoof,
Protrude like giant horns,
Two thousand years of a fierce blizzard wandering in a well,   10
And still not yet arrived at the unsated depth.

Go slow. The mound climbs to lick the sky up like a plate of cloudy calf's-foot
    jelly,
To suck dry the hollow, scraped bone of the world.
Any moment now, red madness gushes to seas and distances.

Ah, pilgrim winds, you will yet tread upon my father's prayer shawl.   15
Though dead, there, on the mound, he delouses my sleeping mother.
Go slow! After me, step by step. After me.

IX°

Fluttering ribbons, beads,
Buttons and tubs

This canto describes a bustling market day after the pogrom.

At fairs and marketplaces
Seethe.

At Sunday market stalls,   5
Joy flickers on all faces;
Each wagon heaped to the skies with wares,
Peddlers dance while dickering.

Yiddish, Nile-
tsayt—the time of   It's Yom Kippur's-end.° Quickly. A ducat more or less.
the Ne'ilah or   Beggars on *banduras* pray for all,   10
Closing Prayer.   And with false yardsticks measure
Ripped Torah parchments scrap by scrap.

"Hey, ribbons, beads, buttons and tubs!
use them in good health."
An idiot pig, somewhere in a culvert,   15
Wets the holy Ten Commandments
As on a piece of smeared and foaming rag.

This canto written   XX°
in terza rima.
From the heights, mouths like sheaves
Reach up to withered udders—
Yiddish,   Clouded, sealed.°
farkhasmete, an   Will heaven yield a drop?
allusion to the
sealing of one's   And skies, like blue tin teapots bent,   5
fate by the end of   Or naked bakers bending.
Yom Kippur.   Will they trickle at least once?

With hairs curled like twisted wires,
A jostled wheel quarrels.
Will there be the slightest puff of wind?   10

And sunsets chew the cud of trodden grass
Like tiny bones of childish hands.
Will there be no wondrous sign at last?

XXI

Ah, generation after generation will come
And go, in bread and salt,
In exhausted vexations,
And will pause, perhaps,
To count and caress their *groschens*   5
Beside the extinguished crow-shine
Of the Ark.

And, should sunshine
Ever again be desired,
Then, in the course of a meal
Of worldly radiance,   10
The outdoors will turn foul;

Thresholds will weep
And, in the midst of the world
A specter will swim into view,   15
Scratch its back on the sun,
And blaspheme:

"Brothers and sisters, I itch; I stink."

To protect their They take shattered glass and stain it with smoke; °
eyes from the solar On seaside hills, eyes protrude—
eclipse. A wonder, a wonder. A miracle. A solar eclipse!   20

The day's sun is obscured with blood and pus,
With the cadaverous Mound, with a Babel of corpses.

And the Mound—a filthy cloud—blasphemes:
"Who'll cleanse me for death?   25
And who will console me?
And out of what deluge
Will a straying Ark
Bring me doves
To this City of Death?"   30

Ah, wind of the desert,
You will stay faithful to me.
Prometheus, perhaps, will kiss me from a cliff.

Pass on; pass on.
My head will not offer the Ark any respite,   35
Nor desert cattle drink at my heart.

Ezek. 16:6, later "In thy blood live!°
amplified by In thy blood live."
rabbinic midrash
to refer to the
blood of **XXIII**
circumcision and
the redemptive It's a milky night, like moon-flesh set in a pitcher.
blood of the Oh, black cats, don't be afraid of my restless tapping—
paschal lamb. I will utter the Sovereign Mound's decree:
It flings the Ten Commandments back at Mount Sinai.

Its thirsty mouth, a swill of grief that seethes   5
With black marrow, fumes like a glowing crater.
Hey, markets and mountains, I call you to oath with my song.
The Mound spatters Mount Sinai's Commandments with blood.

Two birds circle its mouth; they speak; they conjure.
From on high, they wind its tongue like a blazing scroll   10
And place on its brow a crown of frothing stars.

Ah, Mount Sinai! In the upturned bowl of sky, lick blue mud,

Humbly, humbly as a cat licks up its midnight prayers.
Into your face, the Sovereign Mound spits back the Ten Commandments.

1921

65 Masada

ISAAC LAMDAN

I

A Fugitive

1. I was told

One Autumn night, on a restless couch far from our ravaged home, my mother
   died:
In her eyes, a last tear glistened as she whispered me a dying blessing. Before I
   went to campaigns on distant, foreign fields, with my army kit pressing on
   my shoulder . . .
On Ukrainian paths, dotted with graves, and swollen with pain,
My sad-eyed, pure-hearted brother fell dead,° to be buried in a heathen grave.
Only father remained fast to the doorpost wallowing in the ashes of destruction,
And over the profaned name of God,° he tearfully murmured a prayer.
Whilst I, still fastening my crumbling soul with the last girders of courage,
Fled, at midnight to the exile ship, to ascend to Masada.

*The poem is
dedicated to his
memory.*

*Hebrew, Shaddai,
inscribed in the
mezuzah on the
doorposts of
Jewish homes.*

I was told

The final banner of rebellion has been unfurled there, and demands from
   Heaven and Earth, God and Man: "Payments."
Stubborn nails grind the gospel of comfort on tablets of rock;
Against the hostile Fate of generations, an antagonistic breast is bared with a
   roar:
"Enough! You or I! Here will the battle decide the final judgment!"

I was told:

There are prophets wandering amongst the walls of Masada, prophesying
   redemption,

And in the tents of the tabernacle, amongst the ramparts, Levitical sects are
   singing *lamenatseah*.°
With tomorrow's echo answering *amen, selah*.°
There the young priests extend merciful arms from the top of the wall to the
   orphaned and depressed night sky.
And pray for the restoration of its impaired moon . . .

*"To the victor,"
the chapter
heading for several
psalms.
Amen implies
consent; selah is a
psalmic full stop.*

I was told:

The Divine Presence,° dropping atonements, has descended on the heads of the warriors,

And through the curtain of the future, the large eye of Dawn is watching and caring for Masada.

6. At the Entrance

Open thy gates, O Masada, and let me, the fugitive, enter!

At thy feet, I place my disintegrating soul—place it on the anvil of thy rocks and beat it out, shape it and beat it out anew!

For where more can I take this my weary, stumbling body when all the shells of rest have fallen from it?

The graces of the world have disappeared!

The circle of the earth has become a gallows for my neck, and its expanse is the palm of the hangman that, strangling, closes on me with the fingers of its ways.

Here I am, all of me, before you, a fugitive:

In my bosom, swollen with sicknesses, the God of Israel has inserted a severed head; its blood has touched mine. . . .

On my image have the sharp nails of disbelief engraved convulsion and a tattoo of enmity towards everyone, everyone, everyone. . . .

In my brain are flags of blood unfurled for the storm of terror that blows from the four winds of heaven, and the scorching tongues of the *auto-da-fé* lick my wounds. . . .

And over everything: chaos, chaos, chaos—no people, no land, no God, and no man.

Well do I know that a ready refuge is this chaos for a fugitive like me.

Like a weary moth, deprived of day and sunlight, am I drawn to its cold, consuming flame—

Deliver! I shall close my eyes that they be not drawn to this terrible refuge, and that they be not attracted to its flame.—I pin myself entirely to the bars of your gates:

Open them, Masada, and I, the fugitive, shall come!

III

5. Encouragement

Who is kneeling? Who has fallen? A tired brother? Why do you groan, child of Masada? What ails you? Are you in pain?

Arise! Who is twisting there at your feet? The limping yesterday? No matter! Rise, break its neck, cast it to the bonfires, and return a free, lightfooted man to swing into the dances!

Again, stumbling feet are carried—no matter! Weep not for fractured yesterdays; we have the morrow!

Bolster the leg, strengthen the knee, round and round increasingly!

No matter! Does a crying mouth open the heart? Close your sobbing mouth! No regrets for what is passed, no regrets at all!

Does enticing sorrow whisper supplication? Does persuasive sorrow depress the
head? No matter! Our chain shall bind it well, and choke it, that it be
tempest tossed in our dance!

Days weep on our necks: 'Where shall we go? Where is our recompense?'

No matter! Draw, O days, without asking, If you have been presented as lacking
all—Masada is the reward!

Bolster the leg, strengthen the knee, round and round increasingly!

Ascend, chain of the dance! Never again shall Masada fall! Does the leg
stumble? Let us ascend! The son of Yair° shall again appear. He is not dead,
not dead! . . .

If the age-old Fate derides: "In vain!" we will pluck out Its inciting tongue! And
in spite of itself, the derisive negation, defeated, shall nod its head: "Indeed,
indeed. Amen!"

V

6. The Prayer

As for those who escaped execution in a foreign land, and ascended to the
wall—make firm their step, O God, that they totter not, that they fall not, for
they still stumble and are weary!

For those whose suns in the seven heavens of the world are dark—order, O
God, a kindness of the last Masada sun, for if this also darkens for them—
where else would they go, or make for?

To those who have left the swaddling clothes of the flags of seventy nations, and
come naked, give, O God, one cloak that will warm them, that will cover
their tremor-stricken nakedness. . . .

To those whose mothers' milk on their lips is not yet dry, and on whose cheeks
still flutters the warm caress of a father's hand—relieve, O God, their
orphanhood,

Be a father and guardian to them, sustain the strength of their tender arm to
hold the heavy, pressing shield.

Soften the hard rocks of Masada at their heads when they weary! To those who
sowed here with a tear the seed of a soul and of dreams—let them not be
struck by the hail of sorrow, or dried up by sudden heatwaves.

Command, O God, many comforting rains, that dew should fructify them by
night until they blossom into a harvest of compensation!

To those who from their wallowing ascended to the wall, the ashes of
destruction on their head and sacks of mourning on their loins to derive
comfort in the battle of Masada—bolster their spirit, O God, bolster their
spirit when comfort delays!

To those whose people's Presence has loaded the enigma of their Fate on their
shoulder, to bring it to solutions, to lead it to the gates of the exit—

Grant power, God, grant courage to carry off and bear this heavy thing to the
border that the sick Presence saw in Its last vision! . . .

So weary, so weary are the children of Masada, deep is the suffering of the few.

Those who have been tried in many battles, and have bared their breast to every

*Eleazar ben Yair,
commander of
Masada from 66
until its fall in 73
C.E.*

arrow—have not yet been tried in one battle, this drawn-out and obstinate
battle on but one piece of land—

Support their spirit, O God, and let not the flames of their rebellion that they
have brought with them to the wall like holy Sabbath candles in the twilight
of worlds, die out.

When night falls on the wall—do not let the bonfires flicker! From dark
horizons, loneliness rises and threatens.

Doubt stalks amongst the ramparts, and whispers its message in every ear, and
the ears of the weary are extended, and absorb the whisper. . . .

Memories of yesterday enfeeble hands, and make upright heads that were
always stretched towards them droop behind them with fatigue.

Vain dreams bring terror and confusion to the fighters, and the sickle of sorrow
reaps amongst the campaigns, and many are those that fall.

Is it a little thing, God, that the battle should consume—why do these also
impose so on Masada, and upon its warriors?

Why should all the stars be extinguished when the bonfire dies out on the wall
except for one star—the mocking planet of Israel—

It is seven times brighter in the nightmarish light, sowing terror, fixing its rays in
the branches of the wall, and giving light outwards, to chaos, ah, again and
again to chaos. . . .

Till when will the wasted hand of the people grapple with blind fingers on the
enclosures of salvation?

Oh God, look, it is stretched out, and on its palm is the last dream that it has
drawn up from nights of wandering: "MASADA!"

This dream and its interpretation have been entrusted in the hands of a few
people on the wall.

If this time as well, O God, you have no mercy, and do not accept the dream
with favour, and even now do not turn to the sacrifices of its interpreters—

God, guard Masada!

1924

66 My Brothers, the Sidelock-Jews

URI ZVI GREENBERG

And if there I lied to my brothers the sidelock-Jews in their wrathful basis and
their indignation against us, the unbelievers,

Outsiders to the disgrace of Judaism in its deep pain, more like the gentiles with
scented locks,

Who smoke cigars on Friday nights, in order to spoil the lungs of our Hebrew
God—

I.e., from the
poet's present
vantage point in
Palestine.

Mythic constructs
invented by
Greenberg to
convey the
primordial claim to
the land.

Arabic word for
the summer heat
wave.

Yiddish,
shtraymlekh, fur-
rimmed hats worn
by Hasidic men.

Surely here, from afar,° in days of the Hebrew clarification on land of the race
　　and the Jerusalemite god-head,
God lives, I will not lie to my brothers the sidelock-Jews!
And as I love the breathing stones in my Land: *rocks of the mute gold*° of our
　　dead kingdom
And "gold-my-gold" I'll call the sand here; gold-my-gold in the Jewish ḥamsin,°
And just as I favor all the ruins in Sion and I'll find also my happiness in this
　　struggle in the wilderness,
All the more so I love the *living parts-of-gold:* my brothers the sidelock-Jews in
　　tallit-and-*tefillin,*
In mink-hats° of Sabbath and holiday in remembrance of crowns and in
　　overgowns of silk and of satin with the dull sheen
Of a sword of ancient silver . . .
And thus I'll see them from far off, as they walk in Europe: *fabulous ambassadors
　　of the kingdom of the East.*
The NO-to-Christian-Europe takes on a splendor of fire from the eyes of the
　　adults
And from the eyes of the children, who walk in their tracks with a warmth of
　　lambs and their narrow mouth is no more than a knife-slit— —
And if at their oy-like exultation I once jeered because well I knew a ninth
　　symphony in the world
And lighter is their lamentation in a rhythm of blood and of tears than the
　　gentile funeral-march of Chopin—
Now I catch the depth of their oy-like exultation: it's the song of the whole man
　　from generation to generation of the pain,
This heart-cutting song rises from my fingertips and the leanness shines in my
　　flesh as I sing it— —
Now I hate like them the Latin script, the Cyrillic script.
In those letters were written the terrible-decrees, they call placards on the walls
　　of the thoroughfares!
(And so what if in those letters I envisioned the vision of the superior man of
　　Nietzsche!)

The word carries
covenantal
associations in
Greenberg's poetry.

Now the cut° of the Jewish soul opens in me, and I continue upon myself the
　　holiness of father's Jewish house,
Which is in time of slaughter *the only house in the world.*

　　　　　　　　　　　　　　　　　　　　　　　　　　　　　　　　　　1926

67 Fire!

MORDECAI GEBIRTIG

Fire, brothers, fire!
Our poor town's on fire!
Raging, winds so full of anger

Shatter, scatter, tear asunder
Fanning the flames ever wilder
Everything's on fire!

   While you stand there, looking on
   With folded hand.
   While you stand there, looking on
   At the fire brand.

Fire, brothers, fire!
Our poor town's on fire!
The whole town's already devoured
By flaming tongues of force and power
And the wild wind howls and churns
As our shtetl burns.

   While you stand there, looking on . . .

Fire, brothers, fire!
The dreaded moment may soon come
When the town with us included
Will be turned to flames and ashes
As after battle a city falls,
With empty, blackened walls.

   While you stand there, looking on . . .

Fire, brothers, fire!
It all turns to you.
If you love your town,
Take pails, put out the fire,
Quench it with your own blood too.
Show what you can do!

   Don't look and stand
   With folded hand.
   Brothers, don't stand round, put out the fire!
   Our shtetl burns!

1936

Bey - ze vin - tn mit yir - go - zn Ray - sn, bre - khn un tse - blo - zn

Shtar - ker nokh di vil - de fla - men, Alts a - rum shoyn brent.

Un ir shteyt un kukt a - zoy zikh Mit far - leyg - te hent

Un ir shteyt un kukt a - zoy zikh __ Un - dzer shte - tl brent. __

68 A Stubborn Back—and Nothing More

H. LEIVICK

Come, let us hide ourselves in caves,
in stony crevices, in graves
where stretched full length on the hard ground
we lie, backs up and faces down.

We shall not record, we shall not say   5
why we've immured ourselves this way.
No notch in a wall, our stony page,
shall mark the historic year or age.

We shall not leave behind as clue
one thread of ourselves—not the lace of a shoe.   10
No one shall find, hard though he look,
one shred of a dress, one page of a book.

Whether he search by night or by day,
no one shall find a trace of our clay.
But if someone should, let his find be poor: 15
a stubborn back—and nothing more.

Let him stand wondering, mouth agape,
why we fled to a cave for our escape,
what the last words of our distress
in these depths of stoniness.   20

And let him seek and still not find
if conscience here were undermined,
if the tormented heart grew faint
and blood and courage suffered taint;

If we were tortured by a fiend,   25
or maybe by someone just and kind;
by ax, by bullet, by lynching herd
or maybe by a casual word.

If he asks our bones mixed one with the other:
Are you the bones of a foe or a brother,   30
the answer will come: horror struck dumb
and from his own mouth white bubbles of foam.

Long will he stare—not comprehending—
till he turn—eyes bulging, arms extending
to flee in his fear and consternation   35
from generation to generation.

The greater his fear, the faster his flight,
running till history flounder in night,
while we go on lying as heretofore:
a stubborn back and nothing more.   40

1937

69 Memorial Poems

YANKEV GLATSHTEYN

Good Night, Wide World

Dated in the original.

Good night, wide world   April 1938°
Big stinking world!
Not you but I slam shut the gate.

Traditionally worn by ultra-orthodox Jewish men.

With my long gabardine,°
My fiery, yellow patch,   5
With head erect,
And at my sole command,
I go back into the ghetto.

Wipe off all markings of apostasy!
I roll my body in your grime; 10
Glory, glory, glory to you
Crippled Jewish life!
I cast out all your unclean cultures, world!
Though all has been laid waste,
I burrow in your dust, 15
Sorrowing Jewish life.

From Exod. 17:14; since then a symbol of all the persecutors of the Jews.

Swinish German, hostile Polack,
Thievish Amalekite°—land of swill and guzzle,
Slobbering democracy,
With your cold compress of sympathy, 20
Good night, brash world with your electric glare.

Back to my kerosene, my shadowed tallow candles,
Endless October and faint stars,
To my twisting streets and crooked lantern,
To my sacred scrolls and holy books, 25
To tough Talmudic riddles and lucid Yiddish speech,
To law, to profundity,
To duty and to justice.
World, joyously I stride
Toward the quiet ghetto lights. 30

Good night, I give you in good measure
All my redeemers;
Take your Jesus Marxes; choke on their daring.
Burst with each drop of our baptized blood.

An allusion to the Ani ma'amin ("I Believe"), the affirmation of faith in the coming of the Messiah.

And still I trust that though He tarry,° 35
My waiting will spring newly day by day.
Green leaves again will rustle
On our withered tree.
I need no comforting.
I walk again my straight and narrow way: 40
From Wagner's heathen blare to Hebrew chant
And the hummed melody.

I kiss you, cankered Jewish life,
The joy of homecoming weeps in me.

Wagons

With quiet signs of faraway   June 1938
At dusk the mournful wagons come.
Doors stand ajar,
But no one waits to meet them.
The town is peaceful, bells of silence toll. 5
Every blade of grass pricks up
In the heady cool.

A few sickly Jews climb down from the wagons,
And a clever word falters
In every brooding head.   10
God, on your scale of good and bad,
Set a dish of warm porridge,
Toss some oats, at least, for the skinny mules.
The deadness of the town grows dark.
A cruel silence afflicts the Jewish beards,   15
And each sees in the other's eyes
A prayer of fear:
When death comes,
Let me not remain the only one,
Do not pass over me with my thin bones.   20

Ghetto Song

My song melts into your bones
like fresh snow.
A joy wakens in your
starry eyes from long ago.
Laughylaugh, my child,   5
singalong, my sighs,
over an old wall,
seven suns will arise.

Up to the treetops
the desecrated Sabbath cried.   10
Through all the darkened alleys,
sat beggars who have died.
Lullaby, my child,
sleepysleep, my crumb,
dancing into your empty plate,   15
a golden fish will come.

Stars along the way are strewn—
to light your father's pace,
all he has is the moon
throughout the nocturnal chase.   20
Sleepybye, my child,
kissykiss your eyes,
across the lamentable ruins,
a little dove flies.

The dove is you for real;   25
your hands become white wings,
mother won't abandon your hungry cradle,
no matter what her life brings.
Rockabye, my child,
hushabye, my fate,   30

your father's kind hands
open the gate.

circa 1940

70 Joy of the Poor

NATAN ALTERMAN

Song to the Wife of My Youth

<table>
<tr><td>Invokes the
opening line of
Ecclesiastes.
Cf. Isa. 49:4.</td><td>

Not all is vanity, child,
not all vainglory and folly.°
I scattered my days to the winds,°
I broke my pact with money.
I pursued only you, my child,
as the neck pursues the hangman.

</td><td>5</td></tr>
</table>

For you put on your shawl, my child,
and asked me to behold you.
And I vowed to break no bread
till my teeth turned black with your greenness.   10
I vowed to behold you, child,
till my eyes grew dim with looking.

And sickness struck, my child,
poverty covered our faces.
And sickness I called "my house,"   15
and poverty, "our daughter."
We were wretched as dogs, my child,
and dogs fled from our presence.

Then the iron appeared, my child,
beheading me of you.   20
And nothing remained except
my dust pursuing your shoes.
For iron breaks, my child,
but my thirst for you is unquenched.

The will has no end, my child;   25
the body is clay, and shatters.
Joy did not visit my house
and earth became my pallet.
But the day you rejoice, my child,

Rejects Eccles.
2:14. my eyes will rejoice in their darkness.°   30

Joy will yet come, my child,
and we shall have our portion.
Lowered to me with a rope,
you will drop to my earth long promised.
Not all is vanity, child,   35
not all vainglory and folly.

The Mole

Not in vain did I vow to be faithful,

*The rare verb
ashuf recalls God's
curse on the
serpent: "They
shall strike at your
head,/And you
shall strike at their
heel" (Gen.
3:15).*

not in vain did I tag at your heels.°
With the mole I struggled from darkness,
stubborn and under a spell.

You, grief of the nails on my fingers,   5
you, woe of my head growing bald,
hear me in the cracking of plaster,
in the spreading silence of mold.

In a mirror inlaid with copper
your humble candle sways.   10
Those who go toward your face in the darkness
have watched from their hiding-place.

But when I stole forth to steal you,
your candle blinded me.
Bristling and dark before it   15
remained the Mole and I.

                    *

Not in vain did I vow to be faithful.
Assaulting the earth where I dwell,
I longed toward your life from my darkness,
for life casts spell upon spell.   20

See me absurd, my wonder!
rehearsing you clue by clue,
the way you stand, your gestures.
And trembling with joy for you.

My every thought besieged you—   25
the hairs of my head upright

*I.e., the modest
meal.*

as I thought of bread on the table°
and the candle shedding its light.

Bent and old like your mother,
I held you to my breast,   30
bearing your misery for you
without refuge from you or rest.

You—grief of the nails on my fingers,
you—woe of my balding head,
burden of my midnight brooding,   35
burden I cannot forget.

Because our foes persevere,
and you break like a stalk of grain,
bristling and dark before them
only Mole and I remain.   40

In a mirror inlaid with copper
see the candle flicker and spark.
Never shall we forget you,
our faces say from the dark.

For the world is riven, and double   45
the clamor of its distress.
For no dead have forgotten their dwellings,
all dwellings mourn somebody dead.

At our cities of sorrow forever
gaze the dwellers of darkness and mound.   50
The glory of our days brims over
Rejects Eccles.   with thoughts of the dead underground.°
1:11, 2:16,
9:2–6.

A Song of Omens

Last night a bird in bitterness cried
   As if hunters hid in the wood;
Last night the glass flew from your hand,
Your dress was ripped as if you had died,
You sat down to sew it, and wearily sighed.   5
   The needle was covered with blood.

Don't heed the omens, child,
Nor let fear burn in your eyes,
For the omens foretell only good,
For it is joy that knocks on all doors,   10
And not for you, my child,
But for your torturers.
My child, if dogs weep in the town,
It is an omen, child, of an angel in the town.
If an angel is in the town,   15
It is an omen, child, of wailing in the town.
Because eyes will grow bright, my child,
And the heavens will curse, my child,
And the years will go by, my child,
And they will remember, my child.   20
And great omens will be seen,
Nor will they speak in vain,

Cf. Ps. 69:33:
"The lowly will
see and rejoice;/
you who are
mindful of God,
take heart!"

The humble will rejoice and the poor:°
It is joy that knocks on the door.

I am sorry, sorry for your despair   25
  As if hunters returned from my death.
And I who have no dream, no light
Dreamt you bad dreams at the mouth of the lair;
I woke, and your torn smile grew bright.
  A needle was red in your hand.   30

Because the language of omens is clear,
Because it speaks in your eye and mine,
Not good is what they foretell,
Not joy will knock on the doors,
And not for you, my child,   35
But for your torturers.
My child, if dogs weep in the town,
It is an omen, child, of an angel in the town.
An angel in the town
Is an omen that others—you too—   40
Will perish in the town.
Let your shoulders be ready, my child,
For much is in store, my child,
Without respite to the end, my child,

Cf. Isa. 51:17:
"Arise, O
Jerusalem,/You
who from the
Lord's hand/Have
drunk the cup of
His wrath . . . "

And an omen will come, my child,   45
And it will be the last.
You will drink our cup to the end.°
To bear these omens—our fate.
My only one, be strong!
Not joy is at the gate.   50

1940

XV

Scribes of the Warsaw Ghetto

We come now to the bleakest chapter in Jewish history. By the winter of 1940, the largest concentration of Jews in all of occupied Europe was in the Warsaw ghetto. Here, the Nazis launched the second phase of their war against the Jews. Here, as well, the multilingual culture of the Jews became one of their most sustained—and sustaining—means of defense.

Some have argued—quite erroneously—that no adequate response to the Holocaust could come about until one generation after the catastrophe. This feeling was not shared by those who were living, writing and performing in the ghettos. It *is* true, however, that it has taken almost two generations for their work to be published—even in their original language(s), let alone in translation.

Besides its sheer volume, the extraordinary range of what was written in the ghettos is a measure of its importance. We find jokes, legends and messianic signs (Huberband), psychological and documentary fiction (Goldin, Opoczynski), private journal entries (Kaplan), a satiric feuilleton (Perle); a lament (Auerbach) and, of course, the expository prose of its major historian, Emanuel Ringelblum. More to the point: ghetto writings provided an internal focus that is fundamentally different from that of the postwar period. Overwhelmingly, the story told by Holocaust survivors—both in print and, more recently, in videotaped interviews—is an *individual* saga that is studied in the light of universal theories of human behavior.

Ringelblum's agenda was to probe the life of the *collective* against a specific social-historical backdrop. Our question is: How did they survive? The staff of *Oyneg Shabbes* asked: How did they perish? In his retrospective overview (**71**), Ringelblum emphasized that the central achievement of the ghetto archive was its collection of monographs on the destruction of Jewish cities and towns. Not one of them has yet been published!

There is another major difference as well. Overwhelmed by their losses, the survivors soon realized that bringing the external enemy to justice was far more important than settling old internal accounts. *All* the victims assumed an aura of holiness; through an act of voluntary self-censorship, the stories of betrayal and internecine warfare were suppressed, reinterpreted or forgiven. This act of self-discipline was eloquent testimony to the collective ethos of eastern European Jewry, which survived the destruction of the culture itself.

How different this was from the response of ghetto writers themselves! Here, so much of the anger was still directed at the enemy within—at the communal leadership, at the growing class of smugglers, at one's political opponents. Anticipating this phenomenon, Ringelblum instructed his staff to assure informants that none of the material would be used during wartime. One should write "as if the war were already over." Because of this tactic, he concluded, the material collected would be "of great importance for the future tribunal which, after the war, will bring to justice offenders among the Jews, the Poles, and even the Germans." *Even* the Germans!

Despite Ringelblum's own political agenda (which made him extremely conciliatory toward the Poles, for instance), he did provide "future historians" with multiple perspectives on the same events. Whereas he and his staff considered the Jewish smugglers the unsung heroes of Warsaw, Chaim Kaplan viewed them as the scum of the earth. Whereas Kaplan and Perle and most of the Jewish intelligentsia hated Adam Czerniakow, the head of the Warsaw Judenrat, as much as they hated the Germans, Ringelblum preserved Czerniakow's diary so that he might tell his own story.

The materials preserved in the *Oyneg Shabbes* Archive also validate another point of Ringelblum's: that life in the ghetto changed "with cinematic speed." Take the concept of the "Other Side." In Opoczynski's reportage on the first months of the German occupation (**73**), it meant crossing over the Polish border into the putative freedom of the Soviet Union. After the establishment of the ghetto, in November 1940, it meant escaping to the Aryan Side of the city where one could survive only with forged papers, a flawless Polish accent, an "Aryan" appearance and lots of money. The meaning of the ghetto also changed. In the folk mind (judging from the legends that Huberband recorded), the ghetto was a safer place to be than among the Poles, but when the first eight Jews were publicly executed for illegally crossing over to the Other Side (on Novem-

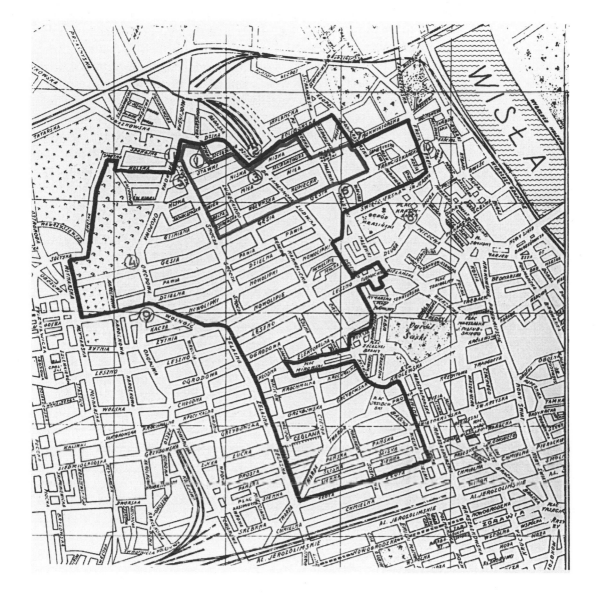

2. From *The Jews of Warsaw, 1939–1943; Ghetto, Underground, Revolt* by Yisrael Gutman (Indiana University Press, 1982)

ber 17, 1941), Kaplan recorded the shock and despair of the entire population. In 1940, the worst indignities that the Jews of Warsaw experienced were the hated *paruvkes,* or fumigations, of their apartments, with forced baths in the middle of winter (as described by Opoczynski). Two years later, in March 1942, Kaplan would describe the mass graves of the emaciated dead in the Gęsia cemetery. Then, within a few months, a whole new vocabulary would come into being: the *Umschlagplatz,* or round-up point for the *Great Deportation* of some 275,000 Jews to the *Treblinka death camp;* the *blockades* set up to trap the inhabitants of various streets; the German-owned *shops,* where the survivors of the Great Deportation were set to work; the *number* that each had to be assigned; and finally, the underground *bunkers* used during the *Uprising* and the *Final Liquidation* of the ghetto.

For all that the description of events required a new vocabulary, the same events elicited a desperate search for analogies. As before, the greater the catastrophe, the more it was made to recall the most ancient archetypes. But this time, ghetto writers could draw on the whole modern tradition of Jewish response, not only on ancient and medieval sources.

Some analogies were subtler than others. The fast-talking, aggressively self-confident Pearl, who dominated Opoczynski's narrative (**73**) as she did the entire tenement courtyard, was a close cousin of the garrulous women in Sholem Aleichem's fiction. Though it was the men who made all the momentous decisions about whether or not to leave for the Soviet Union, Pearl and the landlady represented (in turn) the ingenuity and staying power of the Polish-Jewish "collective." The tenement, in fact, was a kind of shtetl-in-miniature, and the tenement committee was a latter-day *kahal* (see chap. VIII). As a member of the tenement committee himself, Opoczynski believed that for all the corruption, self-interest and fractiousness, the self-governing committees would weather the Nazi storm. Thus, no matter how cruel the fumigating brigades were, the victims still emerged from the baths with a self-deprecating joke. Yet Opoczynski knew enough about the centrifugal impact of wartime to give the last word to Pearl's cynical husband.

At the other extreme was Leyb Goldin (**74**), who marshaled all the literary and ideological evidence at his disposal to deny that culture could in any way mitigate even one minute's worth of hunger. Yet at the end point of this bitter narrative, when the only proper analogy for the starving ghetto was to a zoo, he witnessed an operation to save the life of a ghetto child and was forced to admit that this was something that animals would never do.

For Chaim Kaplan (**75**), the Hebrew pedagogue and former instructor of Bible, all the horrors of the ghetto were naturally filtered through the words of Job and the Prophets, Bialik and the modern secular Jewish writers. As he, too, approached the point of no analogy, especially upon learning about the liquidation of the Lublin ghetto, his writing became more heavily ironic and impassioned. What sustained him throughout was the act of writing itself, which he elsewhere described as *melekhet hakodesh,* a holy task analogous to the building of the Tabernacle.

In Yehoshue Perle's tour de force (**76**), all hallowed concepts became grist for the satirist's mill. The *kehillah kedoshah,* or holy congregation, was now perverted into a collaborationist Judenrat, and the Chosen People were now reduced to a few thousand "numbered" Jews working as slave labor for the Germans.

Thus, there were two poles of response: Some saw the destruction of European Jewry as the dark culmination of all previous analogies; others saw it as a terrible new beginning, as an archetype that as yet lacked its own name. These two positions emerged with absolute clarity after the ghetto was destroyed. For Rachel Auerbach (**78**), looking back from the Aryan Side of Warsaw, the turning point had been the Great Deportation in the summer of 1942, which she was able to recapitulate with great epic skill. What unlocked the memory of those weeks of unsurpassed terror and what probably enabled her to write in the first place was the liturgy. From a Jewish woman's perspective, this liturgy began with Hannah's prayer in 1 Samuel and ended in the recitation of *Yizkor* four times a year in her grandfather's synagogue back home in Galicia.

For the anonymous writer (**77**), also in hiding on the Aryan Side, the turning point had come not with the Uprising, which he seems to have been part of, but with the systematic destruction of the entire ghetto simply for the sake of killing its few thousand underground Jews. For this, the only analogy was the cinema: At one moment he was reminded of a Chaplin film, but upon seeing the whole ghetto in flames, he knew that no cinematic imagination, no matter how extravagant, had ever encompassed a Holocaust.

71 *OYNEG SHABBES*

EMANUEL RINGELBLUM

During three and a half years of war the Ghetto Archive was run by the group called *Oyneg Shabbes*.° This curious name originated from the planning sessions of the group, which took place on the Sabbath; the whole institution was dubbed *Oyneg Shabbes* for reasons of secrecy. I was the one to lay the cornerstone of the Archive in October 1939. At that time the atmosphere in Warsaw was very oppressive. Every day brought new ordinances against the Jews. People were afraid of political reprisals; they dreaded searches of a political nature. They feared the files of the *Regierungs-Kommissariat* and the *Defensywa*.°

The scare dragged on for months but proved groundless. The Germans were not looking for individual "criminals." Their aim, which they achieved, was the collective. They aimed at whole groups and professionals, not individuals. In the first months of occupation, especially in January of 1940, mass arrests occurred, and there were probably also mass executions of the intelligentsia. The arrests were made according to a roster of the groups concerned (The Doctors' Association, The Engineers' Union, etc.). They were not linked with any particular searches. In general, the Germans did not carry out any investigations at all but took the easiest course and shot all who fell into their hands.

The frequent and thorough searches that were actually carried out were aimed at something altogether different: finding foreign currency, gold, diamonds, valuables, merchandise and the like. Such searches have been going on during the entire three and a half years of war and continue to this day.

We have dwelt on the nature of the searches because it greatly affected the survival of written documents from the war period. During the earliest months the population was terror stricken and in dread of the searches. Everything was burned, down to innocent books that even Hitler did not regard as *treif*. Most of the socialist literature in libraries and private dwellings was destroyed. The exiled German writers, such as Thomas and Heinrich Mann, [Lion] Feuchtwanger° and [Emil] Ludwig,° also suffered. Anticipating searches, people were afraid to write.

The terror kept mounting, but as we have said, the targets were whole groups and classes. The Germans did not care what the Jews did in their own homes. So the Jews began to write. Everyone wrote: journalists, writers, teachers, community activists, young people, even children. The majority wrote diaries, in which daily events were illumined through the prism of personal experiences. A great deal was written, but the largest part by far was destroyed along with the end of Warsaw Jewry in the Deportation. All that remained was the material preserved in O.S. [*Oyneg Shabbes*].

I began collecting contemporary materials as early as October 1939. As director of the Jewish Self-Help (at that time it was the coordinating committee of the

Literally: Enjoyment of the Sabbath; here, a Friday evening gathering in honor of the Sabbath. The Defensywa (Polish Secret Political Police) kept a file on left-wing party activists that fell into the Germans' hands.

Author (1884–1958) of The Jew Süss and other historical novels.

Author (1881–1948) of many historical biographies, e.g., Napoleon.

The American Jewish Joint Distribution Committee was founded in 1914. Isaac Gitterman, who headed the Polish office, was a close friend of Ringelblum's.

See 72.

A Left Labor Zionist who survived and helped retrieve the Archive after the war.

welfare organizations), I was in active daily contact with the life around me. News reached me about everything that was happening in Warsaw and its suburbs, because the coordinating committee was an outgrowth of the Joint,° where delegations came from the provinces almost every day and told about the harsh experiences of the Jewish population in their areas. In the evenings I recorded the mass of information I had heard during the day and supplied footnotes of my own. As time went on, these records grew into a sizeable book, several hundred closely written pages, which provides an overview of that period. After a while I replaced these daily recordings with weekly and monthly reports. I did this when the staff of *Oyneg Shabbes* had grown into a large body.

Already in the first months of my work with O[yneg] S[habbes] I chose several people, but no great advantage came of this. It was not until I enlisted the cooperation of the young historian Rabbi Shimon Huberband° that *Oyneg Shabbes* acquired one of its best coworkers. Unfortunately, however, Rabbi Huberband kept his records in the form of marginal notations inside various religious books so that they should pass for textual emendations. Not until later did he let himself be convinced that no danger accrued in his recording everything rather than using the cryptic method he had first employed.

In May 1940 I felt that the time had come to give this very important work a broad social base. Because I had made a good choice of personnel, the work started off in the right direction and was carried on with appropriate scope. The staff of O[yneg] S[habbes] then elected as its secretary Hirsh W[asser], who continues in this post up to the present.° Through his political activities, Comrade W., himself a refugee from Lodz, had acquired the experience necessary for this kind of work. His daily contact with hundreds of refugee delegates from every part of the country made it possible to produce the hundreds of monographs on cities, which are the most important treasure in the O[yneg] S[habbes] project.

Our genial comrade, Menakhem [Mendel Kon, a social and cultural activist] brought the finances up to the required standard. A rich cultural life began developing in Warsaw. Benefit public readings, special forums and concerts were given. This provided a basis for extending and deepening the work of O[yneg] S[habbes].

The instituting of the ghetto, the confinement of the Jews within walls, gave the archival work still greater opportunities. We became convinced that the Germans cared very little what the Jews did amongst themselves. Meetings were held, in an atmosphere and on subjects that would not have been possible before the war. In every house committee, soup kichen and meeting place of a social institution, people could say anything that came into their heads without the slightest interference. The Jewish informers of the Gestapo were busy searching for rich Jews, warehouses full of goods, smuggling, etc. They took little interest in politics. We reached the point where illegal editions of work of all political leanings were published with almost complete freedom. People read them openly in cafés, collected money for the press fund, debated with rival publications: in short, they behaved almost as they had before the war. It is not surprising that in this "freedom" that prevailed among the prisoners of the ghetto, the work of O[yneg] S[habbes] had favorable opportunity for development. The project branched out. Dozens of people joined the staff of O[yneg] S[habbes], some full time, others part time. The work extended its range but remained conspiratorial.

Survived the war and wrote extensively on Jewish cultural life in the Warsaw ghetto.

A Jewish literary critic who wrote in Polish.

She actually survived.

Breslav and Kaplan, active in Hashomer Hatsair (a left-wing Zionist youth movement), were shot by the Gestapo in September 1942.

Economist M. Linder (born 1911) was shot in the Aktion of April 18, 1942. Bloch (born 1889) was active in the democratic wing of the General Zionists and headed the Keren Kayemet in Poland. He died in Mauthausen.

In order to give our work a legal sanction, we announced to some dozens of writers, teachers and intellectuals that we were holding a contest and offering money prizes. These prizes, which were funded by the Joint with a single cash payment, enriched the Archive with a series of valuable works, such as the work on the Yiddish theater in wartime by Jonas T[urko]w,° [the well-known writer, stage director and actor]; the monograph on Jewish life in Lemberg under Soviet rule, by [the Zionist activist] Esther M[angel] and her husband Sh[vayge]r; the history of a Jewish family during the war by the poetess Henryka Lazawert; and the monograph on the Kampinos labor camp by Rabbi Huberband.

O[yneg] S[habbes] branched out so widely, and so much valuable material was assembled, that it seemed to all of us that the time had come to make, if not a synthesis, at least a summing up of various problems and important phenomena in Jewish life. If this plan had been realized, it would have been a highly important contribution to the history of the Jews in the days of Hitler. It is to be greatly regretted that only part of the projected work was carried out. We lacked the peace and quiet necessary for a project of such scope and size. The authors who undertook to work on one chapter or another did not have the opportunity to bring their work to a conclusion. More than one writer went to [his or her death at] the *Umschlagplatz* (Mrs. Slopak,° Rabbi Huberband, [Helena] Szereszewska°°); more than one was killed by a bullet (Menakhem Linder, Shmuel Breslav, Yoysef Kaplan°); more than one crossed to the Other [Aryan] Side.

The plan was familiarly known as "The Two-and-a-Half Year Plan" because it was intended to provide a survey and summing up of Jewish life in Warsaw during two and a half years of war. The plan was divided into three [in fact four] parts: a general section, an economic section, a cultural-scientific-literary-theatrical section and one dedicated to social welfare. The work, which was started at the beginning of 1942, was directed by an editorial board consisting of the present writer, along with Menakhem Linder and Lipe B[lo]ch.°

The present writer took on [the task of writing] the first and third sections; Linder, the economic section; and Lipe B., social welfare. The work was intended to have a semilegal character. New forces joined the project, professionals from various walks of life. The work was designed to be more than one hundred printed pages long and one of the most important documents of the war. We wanted to hold our coworkers' attention to certain guidelines and set the direction for them to follow. By this we did not mean to impose any particular approach on the writers of the articles. Articles were written on the Jewish Police, on corruption and demoralization in the ghetto, about social activities, the school system; there was a questionnaire on the life and work of Jewish creative artists during the war, Jewish-Polish relations, smuggling; a questionnaire on the state of the different artisan groups, youth, women, etc.

Seeing that it was difficult to elicit the work that had been assigned to the various authors, we introduced the principle that each author was obliged to give us the source material that he collected in connection with his work; for example, the biographies of young people on which one author was supposed to base his article on youth. In this way interesting material was amassed on various aspects of our wartime situation.

In the course of our work, our experience as to how such a project should be carried out was greatly enriched. Many authors had already made much progress in their assignment, but just when the two and a half years [of the "plan"] was about to turn into three, a new disaster descended upon [the heads of] the Warsaw Jews, a disaster that cost us three hundred thousand victims—the Deportation.

The work of *O[yneg] S[habbes]*, along with the whole of our social and economic life, was disrupted. Only a very few comrades kept pen in hand during those tragic days and continued to write about what was happening in Warsaw. But the work was too sacred and too deeply cherished in the hearts of the *O[yneg] S[habbes]* coworkers; the social function of *O[yneg] S[habbes]* too important for the project to be discontinued. We began to reconstruct the period of the Deportation and to collect material on the slaughterhouse of European Jewry—Treblinka. On the basis of reports made by those who returned from various camps in the province, we tried to form a picture of the experiences of Jews in the provincial cities during the time of the Deportation. At the moment of writing, the work is proceeding full force. If we only get some breathing space, we will be able to ensure that no important fact about Jewish life in wartime shall remain hidden from the world.

There were two classes of coworkers in *O[yneg] S[habbes]*: full time, who dedicated themselves entirely to the project, and part time, who wrote on a one-time basis about their personal experiences in their city or town and then ended their connection with *O[yneg] S[habbes]*.

Everyone appreciated the importance of the work that was being done. They understood how important it was for future generations that a record remain of the tragedy of Polish Jewry. Some realized that the collection of writings would also serve to inform the world about the atrocities perpetrated against the Jewish population. There were several part-time coworkers who became so involved in the project that they stayed on full time.

Of the several dozen full-time staff, the great majority were self-educated intellectuals, mostly from proletarian parties. We deliberately refrained from drawing professional journalists into our work, because we did not want it to be sensationalized. Our aim was that the sequence of events in each town, the experiences of each Jew—and during the current war each Jew is a world unto himself—should be conveyed as simply and faithfully as possible. Every redundant word, every literary gilding or ornamentation grated upon our ears and provoked our anger. Jewish life in wartime is so full of tragedy that it is unnecessary to embellish it with one superfluous line. Second, there was the matter of keeping a secret; and as is well known, one of the chief failings of journalists is that they reveal secrets. A few able journalists might have been enlisted as time went on, had they not sought contact with the Gestapo informer [Abraham] Gancwajch,° and although this relationship was not of a "professional" nature, it nonetheless made it impossible for us to associate with the journalists in any way.

Those who helped us with a single piece of work were ordinary people, who had lived the whole of their daily lives in their hometowns. Upon arrival in Warsaw with the horde of 150,000 refugees, they continued to lead their [fellow] townspeople in the so-called *landsmanshaftn*° organized by the refugee center of the Jewish Self-Help. After a day of hard work at the Committee, distributing bread or performing other kinds of assistance, these delegates of the *landsmanshaftn* spent the evening writing—according to our plan—the history of their town; or they related it to our coworkers, who later wrote it up. This was very arduous work. In the terrible overcrowding of the ghetto, the refugees lived in [housing] condi-

Gancwajch headed the Office to Combat Usury and Profiteering in the ghetto, which was subject directly to the Germans. He vied with the Judenrat for control of the ghetto and fell from power in July 1941.

An organization of Jews hailing from the same town or region.

tions that simply cannot be described. To preserve secrecy under such conditions was a difficult task. It was cold in the winter nights: last winter most of the Jewish houses did not have electricity. Writing necessarily has attendant risks and indescribable difficulties, and to obtain the chronicle of a town required long weeks and months of exertion. It demanded much effort to encourage my coworkers not to be distracted by all these obstacles and to do their work. Let me complete the picture by adding that at the beginning there was a fear of being discovered by the Gestapo informers. More than one manuscript destined for O[yneg] S[habbes] was destroyed as the result of a search in a tenement.

As we have mentioned, our coworkers were mostly [just] ordinary people. Among them were talented individuals whom we spurred on to literary creativity. Had these people not died of hunger or disease, or in the Deportation, we would have been enriched with their new writing talent. And new literary energy would have been infused into a field that was so neglected among us [eastern European Jews]—the writing of memoirs. Because most of our coworkers were suffering great hunger in Warsaw, that city of pitiless Jews, O[yneg] S[habbes] had to provide for them. We lobbied the social institutions to supply them with food parcels.

O[yneg] S[habbes] strove to give a comprehensive picture of Jewish life in wartime—a photographic view of what the masses of the Jewish people had experienced, thought and suffered. We did our best to arrange for specific events—in the history of a Jewish community, for example—to be described by an adult and by a youngster, by a pious Jew—who was naturally concerned with the rabbi, the synagogue, the Jewish cemetery and other religious institutions—and by a secular Jew, whose narrative emphasized other, no less important factors.

Typhus, which claimed thousands of victims among the Jewish population of Warsaw, was rampant among our coworkers. This was not surprising. Our people worked among thousands of refugees, who constituted the largest contingent of its victims. Our people came into contact with returnees from the labor camps, who were the principal carriers of typhus among the population. No one was immunized against typhus because no one could afford a five-hundred- to six-hundred-zloty injection.

See 73.   Rabbi Huberband, Hirsh W. and Peretz O[poczynski]° recovered from typhus. A whole group of our coworkers died of it. [. . .]

Comprehensiveness was the chief principle of our work. *Objectivity* was the second. We aspired to present the whole truth, however painful it might be. Our depictions are faithful, not retouched.

The atrocities of the Germans against the Jewish population predominate in our work. However, quite a lot of material reveals humanity on the part of Germans. There are constant indications, both in the completed essays and in the oral reports, that we must be objective even in the case of our deadly enemies and give an objective picture of the relationship of Germans and Jews.

See Ringelblum's Polish-Jewish Relations during the Second World War (Jerusalem: Yad Vashem, 1974).   The same can be said of Polish-Jewish relations.° Opinions prevail among us that anti-Semitism grew significantly during the war, that the majority of Poles were glad of the misfortunes that befell the Jews in the Polish towns and cities. The attentive reader of our material will find hundreds of documents that prove the opposite. He will read, in more than one report on a town, how generously the Polish population behaved toward the Jewish refugees. He will encounter hundreds of examples of peasants who, for months on end, concealed and fed Jewish refugees from the surrounding towns.

In order to ensure the greatest possible objectivity and to obtain the most exact, comprehensive view of the events of the war as they affected the Jews, we tried to have the same events described by as many people as possible. By comparing the different accounts, the historian will not find it difficult to reach the kernel of historical truth, the actual course of an event.

Our coworkers wrote the truth; and they had an additional reason for doing so. We assured everyone that the material, insofar as it concerned living people, would not be exploited for immediate use. Therefore, everyone should write as if the war were already over. He should fear neither the Germans nor those *kehillah*° members who were attacked in a report on a given city. Because of this, the material of *O[yneg] S[habbes]* is of great importance for the future tribunal, which, after the war, will bring to justice offenders among the Jews, the Poles and even the Germans.

Ringelblum uses this word as a synonym for the Judenrat.

The war changed Jewish life in the Polish cities very quickly. No day was like the preceding. Images succeeded one another with cinematic speed. For the Jews of Warsaw, now closed in within the narrow confines of a shop, the ghetto period seems like a paradise and the pre-ghetto period an unreal dream. Every month brought profound changes that radically altered Jewish life. It was therefore important to capture at once every event in Jewish life in its pristine freshness. What a quantum leap from the pre-Deportation shop to that which came after! The same is true of smuggling, and of social and cultural life; even the clothes Jews wore were different in the different periods. *O[yneg] S[habbes]* therefore tried to grasp an event at the moment it happened, since each day was like decades in an earlier time. We succeeded in doing this with many of the events. What greatly aided us in this task was that some of our own coworkers kept diaries in which they not only recorded the facts and happenings of day-to-day life but also evaluated noteworthy events in the ghetto.

As we have already said, the work of *O[yneg] S[habbes]* was secret. We had to find ways of hiding the collected materials. In establishing contact with the hundreds of refugees from the province, we were afraid of falling foul of one of the several hundred agents of the "thirteenth,"° which was then at the height of its "glory." Fortunately, this danger was averted as a result of the extreme cautiousness of *O[yneg] S[habbes]* operations. We had a principle: before entering into relations with anyone, we found out first about his character, social and political past, etc. Not until we had this information would we sit down and talk with the person to obtain the news we needed. Very few people knew the real purpose of the conversations we conducted with them. Very often, especially in the last months before the Deportation, our coworkers did not record the facts they had heard in the presence of the informant, but did so afterward. This method of recording lessened the authenticity of the material, but there was no other way to keep the work as secret as it had to be.

The popular name for Ganewajch's Office to Combat Usury and Profiteering; see previously.

In writing the monographs, we duped people into thinking we were collecting data on their native towns for use by the *landsmanshaftn*. Most people played innocent and pretended not to understand what our work was for.

Because of the secrecy that had to be employed in the *O[yneg] S[habbes]* work, however far-reaching that work might be, it was still narrow in comparison with the vast treasury of news and facts that could and should have been assembled during the war. "We have to work badly" was the watchword of O[yneg] S[habbes]. We had to do all we could to prevent the precious treasure of O[yneg] S[habbes] from becoming an open secret.

For this reason we avoided all contact with people from the *kehillah,* even those among them who were honest. An atmosphere of Gestapo seeped from the walls of the Jewish Council. We were afraid to have any dealings with it: that is why we are so poor in its official materials.

What sort of material is preserved in the O[yneg] S[habes] Archive? The most important treasures are the monographs on cities and towns. They contain the experience of a given town from the outbreak of war to the deportation and liquidation of its Jewish community. The monographs, which were written according to our outline, encompassed all aspects of life: economic life, the relationship of Germans and Poles to the Jewish population, the kehillah and its activities; social welfare; important episodes in the life of the community, such as the arrival of the Germans, pogroms, expulsions and acts of atrocity perpetrated during Jewish holidays; religious life; work and matters connected with it (labor camps, the obligation to work, impressment of labor, the Labor Department of the kehillah, relationship of Germans to Jews at work); etc.

Such was the appearance of a monograph in its general outline. Few monographs, however, conformed to the preceding outline in reality. The authors wrote in various ways. But all the monographs express the tragic sufferings of the Jews in the Polish cities. The monographs were written with a sense of compassion. It is often remarkable with what epic stoicism the authors relate the most tragic facts about their [own] towns. This is the stoicism of the graveyard, the stoicism born of painful ordeals and of the resignation that follows these ordeals. This is the stoicism of people who know that anything can be expected from the Germans, that there is no cause for surprise at the indescribable savageries that have been perpetrated.

The greatest number of monographs comes from former Congress Poland.° The other regions of prewar Poland are meagerly represented. This is because all the monographs were written in Warsaw, and most of the refugees there had come from former Congress Poland. From Galicia, in particular from Lemberg, we began to receive news only after the outbreak of the Russo-German war, when people who had left in September 1939 or in the following months began returning to the capital. The same applies to Vilna, Slonim, Grodno, Rowno, etc., cities in the occupied eastern territories. From those areas, too, we received news from returnees. An especially large amount of information was brought by the wave of people returning from Bialystok and the Bialystok region.

Because of the conditions of conspiratorial work with people who had never before engaged in historical research, there is no complete record of what exists in the materials of O[yneg] S[habbes]. Therefore, it is hard for me to tell how many monographs on cities we possess. It is certain at any rate that they can be numbered in the hundreds. On some cities there are several monographs or even several dozen.

Apart from comprehensive monographs, we sought accounts of *single, significant episodes in the various cities.* We elicited the accounts from those who were involved

The historic heartland of Poland set apart from the rest of the Russian Empire after the Congress of Vienna in 1815.

in the episode in question directly or indirectly, as participants, witnesses or people associated with the episode in some other way. For example, to this category belong the account of the execution of fifty-two Jews from Nalewki 9 after a Jewish underground hero had killed a Polish policeman; and the account of the Savoy Restaurant execution of seven dozen Lodz Jews,° etc. We always endeavored to give the description of each happening the stamp of directness, of true experience. That is why the materials of O[yneg] S[habbes] are so deeply imbued with subjective elements and why the narratives are often highly dramatic. The monographs on the cities are not free from this subjective approach.

On November 1, 1939, the Germans arrested fifteen Jewish social activists at the Astoria café in Lodz. All of them were shot.

In order to elicit the most direct report possible of a writer's or narrator's experiences, we dispensed with a set protocol in many cases and told him to relate what had happened in whatever order he thought best. Most of these narratives have the character of *tales of wandering*. A hair-raising example of this genre relates the death march of eight hundred Jewish POWs, of whom half were murdered on the way from Lublin to Biala.

Another narrative of a journey, by a Jewish Red Army soldier who originally came from Warsaw, has its beginnings as far away as Orshe. This route is marked everywhere by rivers of Jewish blood, spilt on the fields of White Russia, the Ukraine, Podolia and Galicia. Another account of the mass slaughters of Jews in the southern parts of Russia is to be found in the wandering narrative of a young man from Warsaw, who strayed to Mariumpol in the Crimea.

"Blood-red Highways"—this is the name we can give to all the tales of wandering of Jewish men and women, young people and children, who roamed constantly from the time the Germans approached their homes until they found a place of rest and settled in a spot from which they could wander no farther. All the highways are stained, like Jewish history, with drops of blood shed by the Gestapo murderers or the Wehrmacht.

An important section of the O[yneg] S[habbes] project is on the *labor camps* where thousands of young Jews died. Except for the ghettos, the labor camps are one of the most effective instruments to destroy the Jewish population, robbing it of its best elements: the young people and men of working age. This is not the place to describe the labor camps, but one thing may be said: with a few minor exceptions, the labor camps were designed not for labor but to bring about the death of their inmates. Of those who did not succumb to the dreadful working conditions and inadequate nourishment, those who were not shot or tortured to death by the notoriously inhumane camp guards, most perished after their return home. A great portion of the blame rests on the Judenrats, which did very little to provide for the camp inmates or to keep alive those who returned. Of all the Jewish councils, the Warsaw *kehillah* was the worst in its relationship to the camp inmates. O[yneg] S[habbes] succeeded in collecting a rich supply of material on almost all the labor camps, at least the major ones. Among the most important and comprehensive is the exhaustive description of the labor camp at Kampinos, where, on the notorious "Hill of the Dead," over fifty young Jews were buried, shot or tortured to death by the camp guards. This account, compiled by Rabbi Huberband, is one of the most important documents on Nazi brutality toward Jewish laborers.°

Published in English as Kiddush Hashem: Jewish Religious and Cultural Life in Poland During the Holocaust (New Jersey and New York: Ktav Publishing House & Yeshiva University Press, 1987). Appeared in Hebrew translation in Kiddush Hashem (Tel Aviv, 1969).

The section of narratives under the heading "Experiences in Prisons and Concentration Camps" is a meager one, not because few Jews spent time in these places, but for the simple reason that from the very outset, as a rule, a Jew did not come out alive. Thousands of Jews were sent to Auschwitz, but not a single one returned. The one document relating to these victims is the telegram to their families, bearing the standard form message that the "guilty party" is dead and his property can be picked up at a specified place. I knew two people who had returned from Dachau. One of them was afraid to relate the slightest thing; the other—incidentally, a very interesting personality described by Rachel Auerbach in her diary—died of hunger.

Those who returned from the prison were [also] so intimidated that they were afraid to tell us the smallest detail. I was able to convince two former prisoners to relate their experiences. One of them was Meylekh Shteynberg, an activist of the Left Labor Zionists. A printer by occupation, he had earned a large income before the war managing the Left Labor Zionist newspaper *Arbeter-tsaytung,* on account of which he had been imprisoned in Polish jails more than once. Now too, in wartime, he was imprisoned in the Pawiak° for his previous crimes. By playing the role of a simpleton, he succeeded, with great good fortune, in being released from jail. Comrade Shteynberg, together with his family, died during the Deportation.

O[yneg] *S[habbes]* also preserved materials from the Polish-German war of 1939. The Jewish population remembered well the sufferings of Jews in Germany and other occupied countries. They had a clear presentiment of what Hitler had in store for the Polish Jews. For this reason, the Jewish soldiers fought with extraordinary heroism. This is acknowledged by many leaders of the Polish Army. It was very important for future history, and for the mutual relations of Jews and Poles, to collect the account of *experiences of Jewish soldiers* in the German-Polish war. The collected materials illustrate a crisis in the mood of the Polish population, and for a short time it liberated itself from the plague of anti-Semitism. Defeats on the battlefield and the need to find a scapegoat led to the resurgence of anti-Semitism; for example, in Warsaw it gave rise to the emergence of a new Jablonna,° i.e., the segregation of Jews from the common military divisions and setting up of unarmed Jewish battalions, detailed to work on fortifications.

This mood of anti-Semitism, which was already manifest in the dying days of the Polish State, was roused to full activity in the POW camps, where Jewish soldiers suffered far more from their Polish comrades [in arms] than from the German guards. A host of such facts is recounted in the personal narratives of the Jewish POWs in Germany. The best is by Daniel Fligelman; it is entitled *Die Waren in Deutschland gefangen.*

These narratives inform us of the highly gratifying fact that the Jewish POWs won themselves a reputation in Germany as a diligent and desirable element. "You came to Germany as damned Jews and you are returning home as blessed children of Israel." Such were the words of praise with which a German characterized the changed attitude toward the Jewish POWs. This may well be the main reason why the Jewish soldiers were freed from captivity, whereas the Poles remain imprisoned up to this day.

It is impossible to list all the topics covered by the work of *O[yneg]* *S[habbes].* They are as numerous and variegated as our life. We attempted many subjects but did not find suitable coworkers for all of them. It can, however, be asserted with confidence that there is no important phenomenon of Jewish life in wartime that was not mirrored in the materials of *O[yneg]* *S[habbes].* A subject such as smuggling,

A Tsarist-built prison situated in the ghetto and used by the Germans to imprison Poles, Jews and other political prisoners.

Town near Warsaw where, in 1920, an internment camp was set up for Jewish soldiers and officers of the Polish Army.

which is always extremely important in wartime, is represented in *O[yneg]* *S[habbes]* by the work of Comrade T[itelman]. In this work we see the tremendous scope of smuggling in Warsaw: during the whole period of the ghetto's existence it saved the four hundred thousand members of the Jewish community from dying of starvation. If the Jews of Warsaw had had to live on the official ration of eighteen deka° of bread a day, all trace of Jewish Warsaw would long since have vanished. Smuggling caused the loss of several Jewish lives every day and, on the eve of the Deportation, a dozen or dozens of lives a day. In the liberated Poland of the future a monument should be set up to smuggling, which, by the way, also saved the Polish population of the city from dying of hunger.

Abbreviation for dekagrams.

Comrade T[itelman]'s work on smuggling portrays its folkloric aspects—argot, customs, etc.—rather than its economic significance.

O[yneg] *S[habbes]* was in general somewhat unsuccessful in the economic field. Good plans were set up on various economic topics, with detailed outlines, but very few of these were carried out, owing to a lack of suitable coworkers. Economic problems [also] require a tranquil mind. They require time, and the right materials, based on comprehensive investigations: we had neither time nor the proper working conditions. Nonetheless, we did manage to elicit a few valuable articles. One of these, by Comrade W[inkler], deals with the *ability of a society in wartime to adapt itself to altered economic conditions.* The author shows how the Jews, in the intolerable conditions of the ghetto, built up a whole series of branches of production to serve the so-called Aryan side. The astonishing skill that the Jews displayed in obtaining raw materials and creative ersatz materials testifies to the tremendous ingenuity of the Jews in finding a way out of the most difficult situations. It is proof of the vitality of the Jewish population, which not only created this production but developed smuggling to a level at which the total production could get "abroad" [i.e., the Aryan side, the consumer].

Eliyohu Gutkowski (1900–1943), an active Labor Zionist in prewar Lodz. Edited the information bulletin of O.S. together with Hirsh Wasser.

Of the fragmentary projects in the economics section, we should mention the work of Comrade G[utkowsk]i° on *the foreign currency trade*—another wartime phenomenon of great importance. Comrade G. succeeded in fathoming the deepest secrets of the foreign currency trade. He describes not only its economic aspect but also its folkways, the argot of the money changers and their customs. He gives highly important tables, which illustrate the fluctuating rates of exchange throughout almost the entire period of the war. It will be an interesting project for the future researcher to find in the events of world politics, in the occurrences in the surrounding Jewish and Polish life and in yet other factors the key to these fluctuating rates of exchange. Incidentally, we learn from the work of Comrade G[utkowski] the "secret" that a foreign currency factory existed on Pawia Street, where "hard ones" (gold dollars) and "pigs" (gold rubles) were forged. After the war, the national banks of the countries in question will no doubt be kept busy dealing with the currency "Made in the Ghetto."°

In English in the original.

Among fragmentary articles on the subject of the *kehillah,* we find one on *The Jewish Mail,* which was resurrected after a hiatus of more than a hundred years. One of the "mailmen" was the Yiddish journalist, Peretz O[poczynski], who describes for us the hard work of a Jewish mailman and the relationship of the Jewish population to the mailmen, who often had to collect the tax from their neighbors, which the *kehillah* had decreed as an extra payment to be made on correspondence and also on parcels.

There are a few articles on the topic of *sanitation;* one of them, by the journalist Peretz O[poczynski], is dedicated to one of the ten plagues of the ghetto, the plague of *Disinfection Brigades.*° The writer depicts a *paruvke* [delousing] in a poverty-striken Jewish tenement. The second article, by a member of the Disinfection Brigade, is like a final confession. The author admits and proves, with concrete facts, that the Disinfection Brigades were disseminators of typhus, as a result of the corruption and demoralization that prevailed among them. Peretz O[poczynsk]i reaches the same conclusion.

Also incorporated into 73.

The same Peretz O[poczynsk]i conducted an interesting experiment, which, unfortunately, has not yet been concluded.° He wrote "The History of a Warsaw Tenement during the War." The starting point was the story of the House Committee, set against a background of the general condition of the tenement and its residents. The work, originally quite restricted in scope, grew into the history of a whole tenement courtyard and its inhabitants, beginning on the eve of the war and continuing through the bombing of Warsaw, the entry of the Germans, the flight [and wanderings on the way] to Russia and so forth. This microcosm may serve as an introduction to the history of Warsaw, the macrocosm.

See 73.

"The History of the House Committee at 23 Nalewki" described the establishment and activities of one of the most interesting institutions in wartime Poland.° The House Committees were transformed from social welfare organizations into institutions of a public nature, which fulfilled many different administrative functions. Apart from this, the House Committees played a cultural and social role in introducing various cultural events and entertainment. There was no aspect of Jewish life in wartime that was not associated with the House Committees. They provided for refugees who had returned from the camps, supported various children's institutions, took care of domestic sanitation, procured practical assistance for neighbors, solved various disputes between neighbors and, most important, took responsibility for the fate of impoverished neighbors, for whom the House Committee was the address to turn to in case of need.

Ringelblum himself was instrumental in setting them up.

Dr. Celina Levin has portrayed one of the oldest and best organized House Committees, which for many months ran its own kitchen and, during the bombing, even bought its own generator for a sum of seven thousand zlotys.

The writer Peretz O[poczyns]i describes the activities of another House Committee at 24 Leszno.

In the social welfare section, we should mention the work of the writer Rachel A[uerba]ch on the public kitchen at 40 Leszno. Describing the establishment of this kitchen and depicting its patrons, she comes to the melancholy conclusion that the Jewish Public Kitchen, which at times served up to a hundred thousand diners, i.e., a quarter of the Jews of Warsaw, did not save a single person from dying of hunger.° And that is why there was such a rapid turnover of diners in the kitchens. While one group took its place in the mass graves of the Warsaw cemetery, the kitchen was filled with a new wave of diners from among the newly returned refugees or the pauperized, whose only food from then on was the thin soup of the People's Kitchen. Among the characters at the public kitchen at 40 Leszno, the most memorable was the man from [°], a refugee from Germany, whose health was ruined in the notorious Dachau Camp. He was not helped by the five or six helpings of soup that the head of the kitchen, the writer Rachel A[uerba]ch, forced into him every day. Deprived of fats and other life-giving nour-

Cf. 74.

The name is missing.

ishment, his organs refused to go on working. Despite all the efforts of Rachel A[uerba]ch, he died of hunger.

This death proved clearly that social welfare can exist only when it has vast financial means at its disposal and can substantially help the needy: social welfare activities of minimal scope are a wasted effort.

A rich area of O[yneg] S[habbes] was the *diaries*. We have already mentioned that during the present war everyone has been writing something, particularly diaries. Some wrote their diaries in a finished form, while others contented themselves with brief notes that could be written up after the war. Most of these diaries were destroyed during the Deportation or because their writers were dragged off to the *Umschlagplatz* and the writings they left behind were destroyed along with the rest of their property. Other diary writers also, because of the continual block-ades and need to relocate from one street to another, often lost the greater part of their manuscripts. It is safe to estimate that dozens if not hundreds of diaries were lost, for it should be remembered that only a small fraction of those who wrote diaries admitted to it. Most of them kept it a secret.

See 75.

The diary of the Hebrew writer and teacher [Chaim Aaron] Kaplan,° written in Hebrew, amounted to thousands of pages and contained a mass of information about what happened each day in Warsaw. Kaplan was not a man of broad interests; but the experiences of every ordinary Warsaw Jew, his sufferings and feelings, his thirst for revenge, etc., are all faithfully conveyed in Kaplan's diary. It is precisely the ordinariness of the writer that makes the diary important. I asked Kaplan more than once to give his manuscript to the Archive, on the guarantee that it would be returned to him after the war. Most reluctantly he was persuaded to let us copy the manuscript. But this was very difficult. A part remains in the O[yneg] S[habbes] Archive. The complete manuscript was lost during the Depor-tation, together with the author, who was taken to the *Umschlagplatz* [. . .].

See The Warsaw Diary of Adam Czerniakow (New York: Stein and Day, 1978).

The head of the Warsaw Jewish Council, the unfortunate [Adam] Czerniakow, kept a logbook on everything that happened in the ghetto during his tenure.° The diary or, more correctly, logbook is undoubtedly very interesting, for Czerniakow was in daily contact with the German authorities and also with the Polish munic-ipal authorities, and, as chairman of the *kehillah*, he held the reins of Jewish daily life in his hands.

The diary was lost.

Professor Mayer Balaban began writing his memoirs during the war, starting with his early childhood. His son, Alexander Balaban, informs me that his father's memoirs reached the war years, on which he wrote a considerable amount. The diary is on the Aryan Side.°

Published in English translation by the Holocaust Library in 1978.

The famous Polish-Jewish writer for children, and no less a famous pedagogue, Dr. Janusz Korczak (Dr. Goldschmidt) kept a diary, which is on the Other Side.° In this diary, Dr. Korczak, who was a master writer in Polish, has unquestionably left a monument to the tragedy of the Jewish children, whom the German occu-pation deprived of air, sun, school and bread.

Many materials for a diary were collected by the well-known singer and jour-nalist [Menakhem] Kipnis. After Kipnis's death we endeavored to obtain these materials for O[yneg] S[habbes]. However, his widow would not give her consent. She was taken to the *Umschlagplatz*, and no trace of the materials remains.

The same thing happened to the diary of the journalist Krimski, who was taken during the Deportation.

My daily—later, weekly and monthly—recordings survive. Later these were especially important for the first year of the war, when others did not keep diaries. The weekly and monthly reports supply not only data on the most important events of this period but also an evaluation of them. Because of my social activities, these evaluations are important documents, as they express what the surviving remnant of Jewish society thought about the current questions of its life.

A Hebrew edition was published by the Ghetto Fighters' House in 1969.

An important document is the diary of A[braham] L[evi]n.° The author has kept his diary for the past year and a half and poured his entire literary creativity into it. Each sentence in the diary is planned. Comrade Levin puts into it everything that is reported, not only about Warsaw, but about the harsh sufferings of Jews in the provinces. Even in the period of the Deportation, when he suffered the terrible loss of his wife Luba, he kept his diary daily, in conditions that seemed impossible either for work or for creativity. Because of the purity and conciseness of style, the exact rendering of facts and its profound content, the diary can qualify as an important literary document that should certainly be published after the war. It was written in Yiddish until the Deportation, and in Hebrew thereafter.

The Deportation, which began on July 22, 1942, marked the start of a new era in the history of the Warsaw Jews. The work of O[yneg] S[habbes] also changed in character. There was an interruption of several months in our activities. At a time when one was in constant danger of being caught [and sent off] to Treblinka, there could be no question of the systematic work of collection. Only a few co-workers continued to keep their diaries during the Deportation and note down their daily experiences. As soon as things settled down a bit, we started our work afresh. But it was not possible to write monographs on cities that [°].

Unfinished sentence in the original.

The staff of O[yneg] S[habbes] made up and continue to make a coherent group, inspired by a united spirit, guided by a single idea. O[yneg] S[habbes] is not an association of scholars who compete and struggle among each other, but a coherent group, a brotherhood in which each helps the others and strives toward the common goal. For months on end the pious Rabbi Huberband sat next to the Left Labor Zionist Hirsh W[asser] and the General Zionist Abraham L[evin] at one table. And yet we worked together, in harmony. O[yneg] S[habbes] did not forget its coworkers. The faithful father and provider was the ailing Menakhem K[on], who saved both Hirsh W[asser] and Rabbi Huberband from dying of typhus, who cared about the sick child of Comrade G[utkow]ski and who greatly aided the writer and the journalist Peretz O[poczyn]ski, who was always suffering from hunger. The quiet dove, Daniel Fligelman, would have died long since had it not been for the constant and affectionate help of our dear Comrade Menakhem. There were countless occasions on which he pressed me to leave Warsaw after the bloody night of April [18], 1942.° Every coworker of O[yneg] S[habbes] knew that his effort and pain, his difficult toil and tribulations, the risk he ran twenty-four hours a day in the clandestine work, carrying materials from one place to another—that all this was for the sake of a noble ideal and that, in the days of freedom, society will correctly evaluate and award it the highest honor of free Europe. O[yneg] S[habbes] was a brotherhood, an order of brothers, who wrote upon their banner, ''Readiness for Sacrifice; Loyalty of One to Another; Service to Society.''

The so-called Night of Blood, when fifty-two Jews of a wanted list of sixty were shot by the Germans. This Aktion was ostensibly aimed at stopping the underground press.

End of January 1943

72 Ghetto Folklore

SHIMON HUBERBAND

I. Jokes and Puns

1. A teacher asks his pupil, "Tell me, Moyshe, what would you like to be if you were Hitler's son?" "An orphan," the pupil answers.

2. British Radio announces: "Today, we destroyed two hundred enemy aircraft. German Radio announces: "Today, we caused the enemy to lose two hundred aircraft." Soviet Radio announces: "Today the enemy lost four hundred aircraft."

3. A child who steals from others is said to be manic. An adult who steals from others is said to be kleptomanic. A nation that steals from others is called Germanic.

4. Winter, 1939–40. An enormous line of needy people stood in front of a welfare agency, seeking assistance. It was bitter cold. They remarked to each other while waiting: "Now you know how lucky the rich people are. They'll stand on line when it'll be warm, in the summertime."

5. During the Norwegian campaign: "Hitler has captured another piece of territory—the bottom of the sea."

6. A Jew and a German are sitting together. The German spreads open a map of the world and starts boasting to the Jew that Hitler has already gotten all of it. So the Jew asks him, "And has he also gotten *Mise Meshunah?*"° The German studies the map but can't find such a country. So he tells the Jew that it's not on the map, but if it exists at all, the *Führer* will certainly get it.

Yiddish for violent death.

7. A Jew had all his worldly possessions taken from him, but he remained jolly and in good spirits. So his neighbor asked him: "All your possessions were taken away. Why are you still in good spirits?" The Jew answered, "My dear neighbor, they took away Czechoslovakia, Poland, Denmark, Belgium, Holland, France and other countries. Someday they will have to return all these countries. So then they'll have to return my things, too."

The major street in the Jewish quarter.

8. Another version of the same joke: Hitler comes to Nalewki Street° in Warsaw. A Jew recognizes him and goes over to him. "What's new with you, Mr. Hitler?"

"Go away," Hitler replies, "you're insane; how could it occur to you that I'm Hitler?"

The Jew answers, "You know that it's hard to fool a Jew."

"Alright, let's say I'm Hitler," he admits. "So what? What do you want from me?"

"I want you to buy a few things from me," the Jew says and presents him with a list of items he wants to sell him. "I'd gladly buy a few things," says Hitler, "but what can I do, I don't have any money."

"Well, if you don't have any money, I'll lend you some, Mr. Hitler," the Jew answers.

"How do you know that I'll give the money back to you?" Hitler asks.

"Listen here, Mr. Hitler, you've conquered so many countries that you're going to have to give back. Are you going to steal just for my few *zlotys*?"

9. The *Führer* appeals to General Franco: "Please give me advice, comrade! Help! Things are so bad!" Franco answers, "I'm sorry, but I can't help you. I can't join your pact." So Hitler says, "Then give me at least some advice."

FRANCO: "Stretch out a peaceful hand to England."

HITLER: "I tried that already, but it didn't work."

FRANCO: "Then stretch out your legs, as well."

10. During the Italian defeat in Greece and Ethiopia, the *Führer* calls up *Il Duce*: "*Duce,* are you in Athens?"

Il Duce (catching the *Führer*'s joke): "Ha? What? Where are you calling from? I can't hear you. Are you calling from London?"

11. The *Führer* inquires of General Franco, "Comrade, how did you solve the Jewish problem?"

Franco answers, "I instituted the yellow badge."

"That's nothing," says Hitler. "I imposed tributes, instituted ghettos, lessened their food rations, imposed forced labor." He goes on, enumerating a long list of edicts and persecutions. Finally, Franco says, "I gave the Jews autonomy and Jewish councils."

"Ah," says Hitler, "that's the solution."

12. After Czechoslovakia joined the Triple Alliance, the *Führer* invited General Franco and President Czerniakow° to come to Berlin. For what purpose? To ask that their kingdoms join the alliance.

Chairman of the Warsaw Judenrat.

13. Germany is waging a war. England is playing a game. Germany will win the war. England will win the game.

14. A strange-looking airplane was noticed in the sky. The onlookers found it difficult to determine what country it belonged to. Suddenly one of the spectators said, "I know whose airplane it is. It's Russian."

"How do you know?" everyone asked him.

"Simple," he answered. "I saw the pilot's bare feet."

15. The *Führer* embarked on a journey to visit all the hospitals. Upon arriving in a certain one, the hospital director gave him a tour and showed him everything.

The *Führer* unexpectedly barged into a corridor and found a securely locked room. This seemed very suspicious to the *Führer*. He insisted on seeing the room.

"If you insist, then I must first explain what is inside," the hospital director said to Hitler. "Locked up inside, there is a madman whose external appearance is similar to yours. His illness expresses itself in his self-delusion that he is the *Führer*.

"If that is the case," says the *Führer*, "then I must see him." Hitler entered the room alone. After a short while, he left the room. But no one is certain which one left and which one remained inside—Hitler or the madman.

16. God dispatched an angel from heaven to find out what's new on earth. The angel returned with a report that he simply could not understand the world. "England is unarmed and does not want peace. Germany is armed and wants peace. And the Jews are screaming that everything is fine."

17. The Jewish Legion refused to fight against the Germans. Why? Because they're afraid they might be seized for forced labor.

18. A group of downed German pilots came to the gates of heaven, but the guard at the gate refused to let them in. The pilots were infuriated. How can this be? The *Führer* had assured them that if one came from Germany the gates of heaven would be open. The guard then showed them the communiqué from German military headquarters that stated explicitly that only three pilots had been killed. "How can you expect me to let you, more than one hundred persons, into heaven when your communiqué states with certainty that only three were killed?" asked the guard.

The area of Poland under German civilian administration, established October 1939.

19. During the rumors that the Russians would conquer the General-gouvernement of Poland,° it was said that whoever is studying German is a pessimist, whoever is studying English is an optimist, whoever is studying Russian is a dreamer and whoever is studying Polish is a realist.

20. God forbid that the war last as long as the Jews are capable of enduring.

In 1941, Deputy Führer Rudolf Höss flew from Germany to Scotland, ostensibly on his own initiative, to negotiate a separate peace between the Third Reich and Great Britain. He was arrested and detained until the end of World War II, when he was tried at the Nuremberg War Crimes Trials.

21. If only the navy of Eretz Israel will look ten years from now like the German navy does today!

22. After Rudolf Höss escaped from Germany,° Hitler sent him the following letter: "I can forgive you for committing treason, I can forgive you for escaping. I can forgive you for everything except for one thing—that you didn't take me along."

23. If we can endure for twenty-one days, then we'll be saved—namely, eight days of Passover, eight days of Sukkot, two days of Rosh Hashanah, two days of Shavuot and one day of Yom Kippur.

24. We eat as if it were Yom Kippur [i.e., we fast], sleep in *sukkahs* [i.e., in makeshift quarters] and dress as if it were Purim [i.e., in outlandish clothes].

25. Jews are now very pious. They observe all the ritual laws: they are stabbed and punched with holes like *matzahs* and have as much bread as on Passover; they are beaten like *hoshanahs* [willow twigs beaten at the end of the Sukkot festival]; rattled like Haman [durim the reading of the Purim *Megillah*]; they are as green as *esrogim* [citrons used for Sukkot]; they fast as if it were Yom Kippur; they are burnt as if it were Hanukkah [i.e., candles]; and their moods are as if it were the Ninth of Av.

26. A prominent German gave birth to twins. They were very similar to each other, and they were named Hitler and Mussolini. Once, during the bombing of Berlin, the two children were confused for one another, and because of their resemblance, it was impossible to determine which one was Hitler and which one was Mussolini. The greatest anthropologists were consulted, but not one of them knew how to resolve the problem. A Jew was called in to clear up the problem. He didn't need to think for long and replied, "Whoever filthies himself first is Mussolini."

27. The Jews worshipped other gods and were therefore granted a ghetto.°

"Gods" [geter] and "ghetto" [geta] sound almost the same in Warsaw Yiddish.

28. It is forbidden for a *Kohen* to marry a woman from the ghetto, because she is a *gerusha*.°

Hebrew-Yiddish for divorcee; can also mean exiled or deported woman.

29. A Jew was arrested. None of his relatives knew that he was in custody. The Jew pleaded that he be allowed to notify his relatives, but he was not granted permission.

He asked to be allowed a brief telephone conversation with his family. The prison warden allowed him to speak only for five minutes. The Jew agreed and had lifted the receiver when the warden told him to speak no more than one word. The Jew agreed to this condition as well. He took the receiver to his lips and screamed into it, "*Gevald*!" ("Help!").

30. The Jewish legion positioned itself near the Syrian border. And what happened next? It's still standing there.

31. A contemporary Jewish prayer: Oh Lord, help me become a chairman or vice-chairman, so that I can allocate funds to myself.

32. No garbage was permitted to be taken out of the ghetto. A Jewish ghetto administrator appeared before his German commissar to request permission to remove garbage accumulating in his home. When the Jew came into the commissar's office and did not raise his arm in the Hitler salute, the commissar became furious and threw him out of the room.

A few days later the Jewish administrator appeared a second time in the commissar's office. The commissar was certain that this time the Jew would salute him by raising his arm. And indeed, the Jew entered his room, raising his arm. So the commissar addressed the Jew, "This time, *Jude,* you acted correctly by raising your arm in the Hitler salute."

"No, Mr. Commissar," the Jew answered. "I just wanted to show you how high the garbage has gotten."

33. Where does Hitler feel best?
In the toilet. There, all the brown masses are behind him.

A popular wit in the Warsaw ghetto.

Pun on Führer.

34. Rubinshteyn° says, "I had a *groschen,* but lost it; I had a *tsveyer* (two-*groschen* piece) but lost it; I had a *drayer* (three-*groschen* piece) but lost it. Only the *firer*° (four-*groschen* piece) I can't seem to lose.

35. It is rumored that after the war all that will remain in Germany will be military targets. Because, according to German war communiqués, British bombs are hitting only civilian areas, and no military targets.

36. A German asked an Englishman, "On what do you base your optimism that England will emerge victorious? Do you have a huge army, like the German army?"
"No."
"Do you have an air force like Germany's?"
"No."
"Do you have enough ammunition?"
"No."
"Then what do you have enough of?"
"We have enough time," the Englishman replied.

II. Signs of the Messiah

As soon as the war broke out, on the 17th of *Elul* 5699/September 1, 1939, all the Jews were confident that the Messiah and his redemption would come in the year 5700, because there were numerous allusions to that effect in holy books printed hundreds of years ago. There were, in addition, other such signs in holy books published a few decades ago, as well as popularly construed signs that were transmitted orally.

1. The earliest source stating that the redemption would come in 5700 is found in the commentary of R. Joseph Yahya on the Book of Daniel. This work is no longer extant.

2. In R. Gedalia Ibn Yahya's *Shalshelet Hakabbalah,* reprinted in scores of editions during the past three hundred years, the following appears in the Warsaw edition of 1899 on page 64, under the entry, "Maimonides": "My father and teacher in his commentary on the Book of Daniel proves that the end of days will be in the year 5700." This is the year 1939–40 according to the common calendar.

Should be: Eisenstein.

Sephirot, divine emanations.

3. The *Otsar Yisrael* encyclopedia, edited by J. D. Eisentadt,° presents the following under the entry "End of days": "The Kabbalists agree that the period in which we live is suited for the redemption of Israel. For the ten supernal spheres° reach perfection every one thousand years. And if one subtracts three spheres, which are the broken vessels, from the year 6000, this gives the year of redemption 5700."

4. Since these holy books merely state that the redemption will come in the year 5700, the masses began to look for allusions to the specific date of the redemption. The strongest hint that emerged was that the redemption would be on the day after Passover, 5700, based on the following textual allusion:

The verse from the Song at the Red Sea reads: אמר אויב ארדוף אשיג אחלק שלל תמלאמו נפשי אריק חרבי תורישמו ידי. ("The foe said, 'I will pursue, I will overtake, I will divide the spoil; My desire shall have its fill of them. I will bare my sword—My hand shall subdue them' " [Exod. 15:9]).

The five letters א that appear at the head of the first five words signify five thousand years. The letters ש and ת at the beginning of the next words indicate the year ת"ש (700). The letter נ at the beginning of the next word refers to the month of Nisan. The letters א and ח of the next words signify אסרו חג "the day following the festival," and the letters ת and י of the last two words signify תשועת ישראל , "the redemption of Israel."

In short, the verse states that on the day after the festival in the month of Nisan, i.e., Passover, in the year 5700, the Jews will be redeemed.

Ki Tavo: read out of context, the opening words could mean "When it [the redemption] will come."

Late afternoon prayer.

5. When the day after Passover came and went without the arrival of the Messiah, people began to search for another date during the same year. Since the war began on the 17th of Elul, the date exactly nine months later fell on the Sabbath of the weekly reading: "When you enter the land . . ." [Deut. 26:1–29:8].° When the Sabbath morning service ended Jews began to hope for *Mincha*-time°; when *Mincha*-time came they hoped for the conclusion of the Sabbath. When three stars began to shine in the sky, the lights were lit, *Havdalah* was recited and the Messiah still did not come, the mood turned despondent. But not for long. Soon a new sign was found that the redemption must occur in the year 5700.

According to tradition, Amalek, the intractable enemy of the Israelites, spawned all haters of the Jews down through the ages.

6. The sign consisted of the final letters of the word in the verse: תמחה את זכר עמלק ("You shall blot out the memory of Amalek"—Deut. 25:19).° The ת of the first word refers to five thousand years. The ת of the second word, the ר of the third word, and the ק of the fourth word add up to seven hundred. This was taken to mean that the memory of Amalek will be blotted out in the year 5700 and, as is well known, Hitler and Germany are Amalek.

When the year 5700 drew to a close and the Messiah did not come, the search began for signs regarding the year 5701.

I.e., from the beginning of the month of Elul.

7. It was said, in the name of a certain Hasidic rabbi: "When we begin to blow the *shofar*,° the enemy will be blown away."

In Hebrew, ḥayil can mean both "valor" and "army."

8. In the name of the same rabbi, another sign of the Messiah was quoted: אשת חיל מי ימצא ("What a rare find is a capable wife!"—Prov. 31:10).° The word אשת consists of the same letters as the year תשא (5701). In that year it was said, חיל מי ימצא ("no armies will be found anywhere").

9. A sign was then found in the book *Toledot Ya'akov Yosef* by Rabbi Jacob Joseph of Polnoye, one of the major disciples of the Ba'al Shem Tov. On the verse כי תשא את ראש בני ישראל ("When you take a census of the Israelite people . . ."—Exod. 30:12), he wrote: "When the year תשא (5701) will come, it will be ראש בני ישראל, Jews will lift up their heads, and the Messiah will come."

And so Jews anxiously began to await the week of the reading: "When you take a census . . . (Exod. 30:11–34:35). When the date passed, Jews did not fall into despair or despondency and began to look for other signs. Such signs were located yet again.

10. The Targum Jonathan on the weekly reading: " 'When you mount the lamps . . .' " (Num. 8:1–12:16), speaks in [chap. 11] Verse 20 of a nation, Magor,° that will arise on the eve of the redemption. It will be extremely well armed, organized and disciplined. This nation will conquer many other nations and will subjugate them. This nation will reach the land of Israel and wage war on it. At that time, all the soldiers of this nation will perish, the dead will be revived and the Messiah will appear.

> ° *Actually a scribal error; it should read Magog.*

11. Fake signs were also invented. Thus, a report spread that in the book *'Alumah* by the great Kabbalist Rabbi Moses, it is written that in the days of the Messiah, there will be a ruler of a certain land who will torture Jews greatly and will conquer many lands. Indeed, this ruler will be an evil spirit named Hitler. In the end, when the evil spirit Hitler will wage war in the year 1940, he will be defeated and the Messiah will come.

As it turned out, there was no such statement in the entire book of *'Alumah;* the sign was a total fabrication.

12. Following the Passover festival of 1941, handwritten flyers appeared, which were copied from one another. The flyers ostensibly contained a text from the *Sefer Etanim.* It was allegedly stated in this book that on the 22nd day of Iyar, 5701, the redemption would come. It then emerged that there was no book in existence with the name of *Sefer Etanim.*

III. Legends

1. On the Fall of Poland

The Maggid of Kozhenitz was a great Polish patriot. He was on friendly terms with the Czartoryski family of the Polish nobility. Members of that family came frequently to Kozhenitz to request that the Maggid include them in his prayers and to submit slips, *kvitlekh,* containing various petitions. Not only the Czartoryskis, but many other families of Polish nobility were intimately involved and acquainted with the Maggid.

A number of Polish songs and several Polish aphorisms and sayings of the Maggid have survived to this day. Before his demise, the Maggid also spoke, among other things, about the future of Poland.

The Maggid said that Poland was a lion. There would come a time, however, when the lion would be captured and tied to a leash. For close to 150 years, the lion would pull at the leash but would be unable to free itself.° Ultimately, however, at the designated time, the lion would tear off its shackles and free itself.

But the lion would not be free for very long, the Maggid continued. For a total of some twenty-odd years the lion would be free.° Then a nation would appear that would recapture it and enslave it anew. But this would not last for long, for when this would occur, the Messiah would appear.

A reference to the partitions of Poland, 1772–1795. The Polish Republic existed from 1919–1939.

2. The Woman with the Shorn Braids

It happened during the first days after the fall of Poland. Ration cards had not yet been instituted, the ghettos did not exist, and there were still no "badges" to distinguish Jews from Christians. Jews and gentiles stood together on long lines in front of the bakeries to buy bread. Jews who stood on line were primarily women, for the men feared they might be seized for forced labor.

The Germans kept order on the lines. They were unable to recognize which women were Christian and which Jewish. But the Poles wished to harass the Jews and pointed out the Jews on line to the Germans. The latter would shout at them, "Jews, beat it!"

Upon hearing such shouts, the Jewish women would leave the line at once. But there were some women who were not detected as being Jewish from their appearance. They would ignore the shouts of the Germans and remain on line.

It was then that a certain legend spread across all of Poland. In each version it was said to have taken place in a different city or town.

A Jewish woman, who had not been recognized as being Jewish, stood on line for a loaf of bread. The German soldier shouted that all Jews must leave the line. All the Jewish women did so with the exception of this woman, who thought she would not be detected. She therefore remained on line. A nearby Pole summoned a German soldier and pointed out the Jewish woman.

After removing the woman from the line, he cut off her braids, as punishment for failing to follow his order. Upon seeing this, the Pole who had informed on the woman burst out laughing.

The Jewish woman turned to the Pole and said, "Why are you rejoicing? My hair will grow back before your state will be restored."

The Pole went into a horrible rage. He lunged at the woman and wanted to beat her. The German soldier who witnessed the scene, not knowing Polish, did not understand what was happening. When he learned what had taken place, he led the Jewish woman to the head of the line and ordered that she be sold two loaves of bread, instead of the one loaf sold to all the others.

Another version: a German cut off a Jew's beard. A passing Pole, seeing this, burst out laughing. The Jew replied to him, "My beard will grow back before you regain your state." The German, who understood Polish, told the Jew, "You are a wise *Jude.*"

3. The Miracle of the Ghetto

Outside the ghetto wall there were two German militiamen who tortured Poles in a terrible fashion. The Poles therefore decided to do away with them. But, anticipating the bloody acts of revenge this would elicit, they decided to do away with the Germans, load them onto a wagon covered with trash, smuggle the bodies past the guards into the ghetto and then plant the dead bodies inside the ghetto.

Ps. 121:4.

But the guardian of Israel "neither slumbers nor sleeps!"° As soon as the trash wagon reached the sentry that night, one militiaman decided to prod through the trash with his bayonet and felt it pierce the flesh of the corpse. He ordered the Poles to empty the trash from the wagon.

The whole story was revealed. And the Poles who drove the wagon were arrested at once, of course. They extracted the whole truth by torture. The German revenge against the Poles was extremely bloody. And the Jewish ghetto was rescued from great peril.

4. Another version

Poles shot two German militiamen on the other side of the ghetto wall. In an attempt to avoid bloody acts of revenge, they decided to throw the two corpses over the ghetto wall that night, at a location where there were no guards.

Late at night, when the Poles were in the midst of carrying out their plan, a German patrol happened to pass by and noticed what was taking place. The members of the patrol jumped over the ghetto wall and grabbed the murderers, who confessed the crime. The Jewish ghetto was spared a great calamity.

5. [It's All For The Best]

When the ghetto was suddenly sealed off, on a certain Saturday, a great crowd of women came running with shrieks and tears to the great Hasidic master, Rabbi Yehoshua. When they entered the rebbe's study, he was in the midst of wrapping himself in his *tallit* to begin praying.

"Holy rebbe!" the women cried out. "We all live near the border of the ghetto, next to the sentry station. Until now we all earned a good living. But now that we have been locked up like living corpses inside a casket, we will all starve to death, God forbid." The women cried that all the Jews would die of starvation.

The rebbe stood for a moment, immersed in thought, and then replied, "Dear women. You must know that the Lord our God will not forsake us. Whatever the Almighty does is for the best. Before long, everyone will see that even the sealing off of the ghetto is for the best."

After hearing these words, the women calmed down and left the rebbe's study with relief.

Igo Sym, a well-known prewar Polish film director who collaborated with the Germans, for which he was executed by the Polish Underground on March 7, 1941.

It did not take long. On a certain day, the artist Igo Sym° was murdered on the other side of the ghetto wall. Large-scale arrests were carried out on the "Other Side." Hundreds of Poles were imprisoned and executed, but not a single Jew, because the ghetto was sealed, and therefore no Jew could have taken part in the murder.

Now everyone recognized the great holiness of Rabbi Yehoshua's words, that whatever the Lord does is for the best, even the sealing of the ghetto.

6. They Fell into Their Own Trap

Warsaw's Fifth Avenue.

A large number of German vehicles stopped on Marszałkowska Street,° and the Germans began to grab Jews from all directions, to be taken for forced labor. A sizeable number of Jews were assembled, several hundred. The Germans ordered them to stand in circles and dance around the cars while singing the Polish national anthem, and forced them to do so.

Before long, hundreds of Jews and thousands of Poles came running to observe the spectacle. At first, the Poles were satisfied with staring, laughing and poking fun at the unfortunate Jews. When they saw that the Germans were not interfering with them, they became bolder and began to beat the dancing Jews. They grabbed the hat of one Jew, pulled another by his jacket, seized a third one by the ear and so on.

By this time the German soldiers were infuriated with the Poles. In the midst of the dancing, when the streets were filled with thousands of Poles, both sides of Marszałkowska Street were suddenly sealed off by a large unit of militiamen and soldiers. The Jews were ordered to get out. Then the soldiers and militiamen suddenly threw themselves at the Poles, locked them up in vehicles and took them away to Germany for forced labor.

circa 1941

73 House No. 21

PERETZ OPOCZYNSKI

House No. 21 on Wołynska Street was the author's residence both before and during the war. The time: the first months of the German occupation, before the establishment of the ghetto. The building sustained heavy damage during the aerial bombardment of Warsaw in September 1939.

One of the northern suburbs of Warsaw, close to the Jewish quarter.

Gulden is used throughout as a synonym for zloty, the basic Polish currency issued by the Germans.

A peasant drives into the courtyard with a cartload of cabbage, bread and potatoes; he sells the potatoes to one of the tenants, who has been waiting for him by the road from Wola.° Nobody knows how much the man pays, but barely five minutes later he is asking a price for the potatoes that makes eyes pop. The other tenants buy the bread—bread and cabbage. There is a rush, a scramble, they pay the peasant whatever he asks—so many gulden° for a kilo of pasty black bread and the same for a kilo of cabbage. However, in the midst of the commotion one snatches a small loaf from behind his back, while another carries home a head of cabbage without paying a penny. When the peasant realizes that he is being robbed, he lifts a crossbar from his cart and brandishes it with such terrible anger that the crowd backs away; people make off with what they have and keep quiet. The peasant stands by his cart, eyes flashing like knives, while his wife pours out curses on the Jews, screaming that all they are suffering isn't as much as they deserve.

The Zelechower, who has helped himself to a few heads of cabbage, rubs his hands together gleefully: even after the fire he hadn't lost heart, and now he is even hopeful. His apartment is being rebuilt; the walls are already up, although the roof is not yet covered. The autumn rains have come and the rainwater pours down from the damaged apartments onto the heads of the tenants below. It has even reached the bottom story, flooding the egg dealer's floor.

The landlady rises at five o'clock and cleans the courtyard by herself; her husband will sleep until late in the morning, but she cannot rest. After the janitor took leave of her company, she herself was seized by an extraordinary desire to work, to toil; work gives her pleasure. It reminds her of her younger years. However, she isn't allowed to enjoy it; every moment another tenant runs out of his ruined apartment to inform her that it is her own fault that her property has fallen to shambles, that the entire house will be ruined if she doesn't speed up the restoration.

Hearing these arguments, the landlady becomes very agitated. Not this, anything but this: her house go to ruin, her sweat and blood? She promises to finish building as quickly as possible; as soon as the bricklayers arrive she will get things moving, and while she's at it, she thinks to herself, start demanding rent. . . . Can the building be put up for nothing? She knows that the Zelechower, the shoemaker and Pearl have stripped the wood from the ceilings and walls of their ruined apartments, every beam, and laid it under the beds in their "shelters" to burn for heat during the winter, yet she doesn't say a word; she understands that if you can't enter by the front door, you have to go through the back, besides which, she is not about to start up with Pearl . . . no need to make trouble—they will be paying rent soon enough. She holds her peace and goes back to work, cleaning, sweeping, dragging the scattered bricks into the yard and sweeping out her big apartment . . . the entire house. . . .

From every direction peasants come with cartloads of produce from the villages, with potatoes, cabbage, wood and even with coal, for Jews cannot get coal from the trains. Some claim that these aren't peasants at all, but people from the city's outskirts who want to make their living by trading with Jews. It's hard to say how they got permission to bring their carts into the city, but probably the authorities in these parts are lenient in such matters; after all, the German commandant in an out-of-the-way place has to live too.

All of Mila Street is filled with the peasants' carts; they also weave through Lubeckiego and Wołynska Streets and, indeed, throughout the entire neighborhood, especially those with wood.

In front of Wedel's shop° on Marszałkowska Street and, later, on Bielánska Street, people are standing in long lines, just like that, each one suspiciously watching the others. If a passerby asks why they are waiting here, he is told that they themselves don't know, they are simply waiting. . . . However, it eventually comes out that for two gulden one can buy a slab of prewar chocolate from Wedel, with a small sack of candy thrown in. People don't buy this for themselves, but as merchandise, for there is still a small remnant of Jews who can afford a slab of good chocolate, even though there are many, many more who are already dropping in the streets from hunger. So let there be chocolate—as long as it helps you stay alive.

A famous factory of chocolate and sweets that also ran its own stores throughout Warsaw.

In the state-run shops of the Christian section, such as those far down on Marszałkowksa, one can obtain milk and even candy to sell. The furrier's wife, the glove maker's daughters and the shoemaker's wife hear about this and spend entire days waiting in the lines so that they can bring home a few slabs of chocolate and a little cheap milk. The milk, which the peasants have just brought in from the villages, like the butter, cheese and sweet cream, is expensive.

Suddenly, Jewish men with yellow Stars of David on their sleeves appear all over the city, along with women who have yellow patches sewn onto their shawls.° Giant flatcars pass by, carrying Jewish men, women and children whose noses are red from the damp, cold autumn weather. What's this? Who are these people?

As they pass through the streets, people shout at them: "Where are you from?" And the men, embittered by the endless questions, answer, "From Raciąz, from Sierpc. . . .'"°

Forty Jews from Sierpc come to No. 21 and settle in the front, in a vacant store. The landlady doesn't emit a word of protest; on the contrary, she talks with the commandant, the head of the tenement committee, about helping them out. Since it's Thursday afternoon, they come up with the idea of providing them with a *cholent,* the traditional dish for the Sabbath, which begins the next evening. (Later the commandant will brag that this *cholent* cost a good hundred gulden.) When the Sabbath is over, the commandant runs to all the tenants who wanted to take in subtenants and places the forty newcomers in the building. The landlady hears all about this: tenants are making the Sierpcers pay good money for the kitchen corners, under sinks, where they place them—why then is she forbidden to collect rent?

The four thousand Sierpc Jews and an equal number of Jews from Raciąz have already been quartered in the city; however, there is news of expulsions from other areas, and all at once Jews stop hoarding supplies: Katz, who has stored a wagonload of coal in his cellar, refuses another; the butcher and the landlady stop buying up potatoes and cabbage for the winter; the sausage maker stops buying salt and the shoemaker leather. Why should they, when no one knows what lies ahead?

A peasant stands in the yard with a wagonload of potatoes from early on in the morning. Instead of the eighty gulden a bushel he had demanded yesterday, he is asking only seventy. After a while he lowers his price to fifty; however, although he stands there until dusk, asking as little as forty-five gulden a bushel, no one buys. The peasant spends the night in the yard and drives away in the morning, his lips forming a curse on the "kikes"—has some devil suddenly possessed them that they've stopped eating, or what?

This state of confusion lasts a day or two, and then suddenly a rumor spreads from ear to ear: they are coming . . . the Russians . . . they are already near Praga° . . . the border has been opened . . . Jews are passing to the Other Side in broad daylight. . . .

The tenants crowd the courtyard; not only the butcher, the Zelechower and the volatile commandant, but all the tenants carry the conversation from the yard into the street. People gather in groups in front of the gate to discuss the news, and the scene is repeated in front of all the other gates on the street: every courtyard is packed. In the street you can learn the latest developments faster by simply shouting to the passersby: "So, what's up? Are they really coming?"

The refugees from Wartheland, the western part of Poland incorporated into the German Reich, were required to affix a Star of David to their clothing; in the General-gouvernement where Warsaw was situated, the Jews wore white arm bands instead.

Towns that became part of Wartheland; the Jews from this area were expelled from November 1939 to February 1940, and many of them ended up in Warsaw.

In the first weeks of the German-Polish war, rumor had it that the Russians would advance to the Vistula, thus including the Warsaw suburb of Praga on the right side of the river.

"What a question. You'll see, tomorrow morning they'll be in Warsaw."

As soon as he gets back his apartment, the Zelechower will know what to do . . . Ah! They can't pry open his mouth. . . . His slanted little Mongolian eyes sparkle shrewdly; his firm, broad, square shoulders straighten out over his low frame like a board as he tightens his belt and chuckles.

The army tailor is also very secretive. He doesn't even tell his own wife, Pearl, that he is planning to take their son, Zalman, with him to the Other Side. However, Pearl soon gets wind of this and leaves no doubt that she won't let Zalman, her only son, out of the apartment—her husband can forget about that. Besides, she doesn't care for the whole business—no, you can make a living here too, and it's a fair chance that you can do better under the Germans than on the Other Side.

The tenement commandant toys with the idea of going to his brother-in-law in Tel Aviv, but he knows very well that this is only talk. Yes, certainly the Germans will let you out of the country for good money, and the Italian Jews issue visas; the Italian consulate in Warsaw won't make things difficult, at least not yet. . . . When Hitler and Il Duce meet at the Brenner Pass things will be different.° However, in the meantime one has to earn the favor of the Germans, that is, not so much earn it as buy it. The commandant knows stories about Jews who have fled to the Land of Israel and beyond, but always for a price, say, twenty thousand gulden, and if you have that kind of money you don't need a visa.° People also go to America. How do they manage it? Don't ask questions! There are those who arrange such things. . . . But what does it matter? . . . He, the commandant, is not one of the rich, and besides, he has a revolutionary past . . . 1905. . . . Still, he considers sending his sons to the Other Side—he has another brother-in-law in Malkinia. . . .°

The Germans order the Jewish shopkeepers to put up signs in Yiddish, no, in Hebrew. . . . " 'Your forefathers . . . lived beyond the Euphrates.' "°

This causes no surprise. It is seen simply as a continuation of the Polish ordinance from before the war, under the OZON regime,° which ordered all Jewish shopkeepers to hang small placards by their stores, bearing their authentic Jewish forenames—not Hela Wierzbicka or Bernard Leczycki but, in true biblical style, *Chana* and *Boruch*. Hebrew sign makers spring up overnight and flood the streets with their inadvertently comic reading material: *Akhilo Mezoynes Uminim* (All Kinds of Various Foods to Eat), *Barzel Yoshon Koni* (Second-Hand Iron Buy I), *Ḥayot Bgodim Ishim* (Clothing Tailored to Personality) and similar nonsense. Winebaum puts up a sign: *Ḥonus Leḥem Mezoynes vekhol Akhilo* (Dealer in Bread, Food and Everything for Eating), and his new wife, his late wife's sister and not at all the stepmother that Rukhtshe the baker's wife had prophesied, argues with the dealer in gauze, the Yiddishist, who makes fun of her because, although she could have made a better sign solely in Yiddish, she has wasted a perfectly good sign board by using both Yiddish and Hebrew. What does he want, that she should provoke the Germans? If they want Hebrew, let it be Hebrew. They can rack their brains over it, so long as they leave her alone!

Already Jews are forbidden to travel by train°; however, this ordinance is not yet strictly enforced. Besides, it isn't such a great blow to Warsaw Jewry: only a few individuals take the train to the Soviet side; the majority make the journey by bus, cart or simply by foot. To travel anywhere else by train is unheard of, except for those who are extremely daring—smugglers and other cunning souls

Where Hitler and Mussolini met for a mutual nonaggression pact.

At that time, the Palestine Office in Geneva used the Italian steamship line Adriatica to help individuals reach Israel. That company had a branch office in Warsaw.

Malkinia was a town on the new German-Soviet border; as such it was the last stop for thousands of refugees before they crossed into Soviet territory.

Josh. 24:2.

The National Unity Camp, the neo Fascist party that came to power in Poland in 1937.

As of February 8, 1940, Jews were forbidden to travel by train ostensibly because they were spreading disease and were engaged in smuggling.

A volunteer brigade for civil defense set up in the first months of the war.

who can talk like demons and pay good money for papers that permit them to travel through almost all of Poland.

There's a big to-do at the entrance to the tenement: the tax collector's daughter, whose fiancé had joined the "Children of Warsaw"° and been killed during the defense of the city, fell in love with a thief and married him. Her father, a Hasid, had run out on his daughter in the middle of the bombardment because she had taken several thieves into the apartment as subtenants. Now she was married to one of them. From heartache her father took sick and passed away.

Pearl serves up this story with all the trimmings, crying, "Who would have believed that such things could happen? But naturally she is, of course, the daughter of a Hasid—the trash! Our own children would never do such a thing; only a Hasidic daughter could fall for a crook."

The shoemaker's wife listens to this with deep satisfaction, while the Zelechower strains his patchwork mind for an appropriate illustration of how inferior these Hasidic bunglers are to ourselves . . . yes, even in Zelechow he knew this.

Pearl goes on and on discussing this story in the "provisional" quarters, where she continues to live with the Zelechower and the shoemaker until her own apartment is ready so as not to let the other neighbors see how eagerly she is awaiting the day when she will move her few possessions back into her freshened, refurbished home. The kitchen is already prepared, and she has begun secretly cooking dinners there; after all, the others don't have to know of every single thing she eats. She's already ordered the paint; meanwhile she stands every day at the Wolówka Flea Market° selling jackets, thinking as she smugly pats her belly: "Well, if your head's on straight, you can have it all—a new apartment, all the wood off the walls, and even get out of paying rent."

Opoczynski described this market in one of his prewar journalistic essays.

The baker Brodsky's eldest son has left for the Other Side; he went by bus. On Nalewki Street there are buses that will take you all the way to Bialystok for two hundred gulden. Where on Nalewki Street? The commandant knows; he too wanted to send his eldest son on the bus, but he has hit on an even better plan: he himself will take him to Malkinia by train. . . .

Rivkele's son, the "Gandhi" activist, is now also in transit. A few of the subtenants leave to the Other Side each day. In every tenement the talk is only of leaving, escaping. The army tailor and the Zelechower, both waiting for their apartments to be made ready, spend entire days dreaming like schoolboys about going to Russia, making it to the big cities—Moscow, Leningrad, Kharkov—where you can get huge loaves of white bread and bowls filled with rice, fish and meat.

"Listen, neighbor, listen," stammers the Zelechower. "I talked with this kid from No. 10 who came back from there yesterday to fetch his wife and children. He says that if you get a position in the Bolshevik Party you can make up to five hundred rubles a week, there are all kinds of good things to eat, all you need is a little luck."

"And what if you don't get a position?" asks the army tailor.

"You sleep in the House of Study," answers the Zelechower, "and there will still be food. Three times a day they serve bread and soup, enough to live on."

The army tailor would agree to everything, even though his service in the World War has made him skeptical about easy answers, but he is afraid of his wife, of Pearl; it won't be easy to talk her into letting him go.

The two men cannot sit indoors for long; they are constantly running out to listen to those gathered in front of the gate. Suddenly a cart with a woven lining, such as one sees in the little towns around Lublin, moves up the street, and this cart is crammed with Jewish men and women who look like they belong to a wedding party; the women, dressed beautifully, hold small valises in their laps and their faces are flushed. Where are they headed?

"To the Other Side!"

"Really? I don't believe it."

"Then don't believe it—but that's where they're going—to the Other Side."

Now the number of carts that pass through the street filled with people bound for the Other Side increases from day to day. None of the tenants can sit home anymore, business and work are at a standstill, the remaining household possessions are sold and everyone dreams only about going to the Other Side. The army tailor, who has seen something of the world, knows all the routes: through Malkinia by train, and through Otwock by the commuter line and then by regular train, through Kolbuszowa and Zamosc, or through Siedlce by train and through Sokolow and Biala by bus. The bus to Sokolow goes there straight from Bonifraterska Street in Warsaw; however, you have to wait in the ticket line a whole week and then pay double for the ticket.

Rivkele's son, who didn't have money, went to Praga. The sentry at the bridge let him through for five zlotys, which he stuffed into the hand of a Polish policeman while the German guard pretended not to see. And so he walked to Malkinia, and from there it was easy to cross the border. Actually, he was detained at the border, in "no-man's land," for a whole week, but then a good sentry arrived and the soldiers shouted, *"Tovarishtshi, perekhaditye!"*—which means, "Comrades, pass through!" and so he crossed the border. Now he is not in Bialystok but in some little town, where he is doing very well; he has work and writes to his mother that he will bring her there.

This letter from Rivkele's son makes the rounds of the tenement; people read it and run their hands over it as though it were some wonderful talisman—a wishing ring. Every moment a different neighbor runs into her apartment:

"Good morning, Rivkele."

"Good morning, Good year."

"Rivkele, may I have a look at that letter from your son?"

"The letter? It's not in the apartment. They took it to the cane maker."

Without even bothering to say good-bye, the neighbor slams the door behind him and runs down to the cane maker, in the basement. His home is already packed; in the center the Zelechower is explaining the letter, although there is nothing to explain.

The letter is written in Yiddish, with German characters: "Dear Mamma, I am working and doing very well. I have enough food and can go wherever I please. You can make a living here, people sing in the streets. I have already submitted a request for your papers and, God willing, I will bring you here soon."

"Ah, you understand," says the Zelchower, extending his index finger as though about to open a lock. Exposing the tip of his tongue, he contracts his low, blunt forehead and stammers, "Yes, he has enough f-food and can go wherever he p-pleases. Just as I said, what m-more do you need? Here, if you step out they g-grab you for forced l-labor; there—you do just as you please. Neighbor, do you hear, n-neighbor?'' His eyes moist, he turns to the army tailor, ''Are you with me? Come, let's leave this week.''

In the basement all is chaos. Everyone speaks at once, interrupting the others. Only the cane maker remains silent.

''Why should we leave?'' asks the shoemaker. ''The Russians will soon be in Warsaw anyway.''

The day after the war began the shoemaker was already back at work, refurbishing old shoes and looking for a place to sell them until the ruined Wolówka Flea Market should be repaired. He has no desire to venture out into the world. He is perfectly content with the black bread he earns by rising at five in the morning, just as before the war, and hammering on his shoemaker's bench, and therefore he is willing to wait for the Russians to come to Warsaw. However, the cane maker, the Zelechower and even the army tailor, although they too can eke out livings, are drawn to the world beyond the border. They don't have the patience to wait for the Russians; they want to be free.

The cane maker maintains his silence one day, two days, three. He is constantly going out to listen to the conversation at the gate, and early one morning, not at all a beautiful morning but gray and foggy, he puts his wife and child onto a wagon that has driven up to the tenement and, with other Jews and their wives and children, sets off for the Other Side. The only one left in the basement apartment is his aged mother, who will live by taking in subtenants.

By now this has become the sole topic of conversation in the tenement: in front of the gate, in sitting rooms by day and in beds by night. Wherever one walks or loiters, the question is always the same:

''So, when are you going? And Zelig? He has already gone? Through Hrubieszow or Malkinia? How, on the commuter line?''

The whole city talks of leaving. Workmen and artisans, merchants and clerks, teachers and writers, doctors and lawyers—there is no type of Jew who does not think of going away. Traveling brotherhoods are created: one man attaches himself to another, and he, in turn, to another; these returned yesterday from Praga, turned back by the border guards, while those will set out tomorrow for a second time. This one is accompanied by a gentile guide, who will take him from Warsaw to the other side of the border, but that one is afraid that a gentile might lead you on only to desert you along the way. Another has hired a reliable gentile, a peasant from near the border who speaks Yiddish; in fact, he is so reliable that he has made a hiding place in his wagon where one can put gold and jewelry, like in a . . . bank—God forbid that one should lose one's few remaining possessions.

Already brokers have appeared to manage the ''reliable'' gentiles from near the border, and there are also Jews who drive flatcars, buses, and all kinds of carts. From morning to night one sees the carts on Wolynska, Lubeckiego, Niska and Zamenhofa Streets. Where does one not see them?

A peasant's cart now passes through the alley; a Jew with a short, blond beard sits next to the peasant on the cab. On the only seat for passengers—a sack of straw—sit two boys of six or seven, swaddled in shawls and gazing with sad, dark little eyes from which peers a world of terrible suffering—gazing as if to say:

''Look what we've lived to see: destined to wander yet again . . . war in the land, nothing to eat, one's very life hangs by a thread . . . those murderers . . . those brutal decrees. . . .''

In a propitious hour Pearl moves into her renovated apartment. The Zelechower is furious: his apartment still isn't finished. His need is greater than Pearl's. The shoemaker has also moved back into his apartment; only the Zelechower is still shut out. Now the tailor, the former tenant of the "shelter" who had moved out before the bombardment, is giving him trouble, claiming that he needs it again. The Zelechower understands that he wants to rent it out, even if he doesn't say so. He runs to the landlady three times a day, insisting (as if that will help) that he be let back into his old apartment already. But the landlady, unabashed, informs him that first he must pay his back rent.

"What?" The Zelechower doesn't understand. "Rent? What kind of rent can there be now, during the war?"

Right away he runs to Pearl with the news only to discover, alas!, that she, Pearl, who had always joined the others in insisting that nothing could make her pay rent in wartime, when evictions are forbidden, has nevertheless handed over a hundred zlotys down payment; of course, she would never have done such a thing had she not learned that the newly established Polish courts ordered the payment of rent on pain of eviction.

The Zelechower has no choice; he too must hand the landlady a couple of gulden, his last, if he is to move into his apartment. However, he has barely been in his new home a week when he realizes that with the scarcity increasing, there is no work, business is at a standstill, nothing pays . . . and so he sends his wife and children back to Zelechow. He takes a subtenant into his home, a musician, and the "shelter" is let to a rabbi from whom the former tenant, with the landlady's assent, collects rent.

The Zelchower, alone now, spends entire days contemplating escape to the Other Side. He is constantly trying to persuade the army tailor to join him. It seems, however, that the other has plans of his own, for he vanishes from the house so suddenly that not even the roosters give warning. Pearl swears and curses: What kind of husband is this?—nothing but heartache. But on realizing that he is indeed gone, she gradually calms down and carries all the sewn things he had left behind to sell on the flea market. Her eldest daughter can also stitch a pair of pants or patch a garment, and so Pearl continues climbing the stairwell, carrying loaves of bread and sacks of potatoes with which to feed her family.

Having a rabbi as a neighbor is agreeable to everyone, but especially to the landlady, who wants to get rid of the more disreputable tenants and replace them with others who are more respectable; there is general approval, and soon the rabbi is picking up a clientele: the girl from Skerniewice, who subleases from the furrier's wife, has found herself a lad who will accompany her across the border; since her dowry is to be used for traveling expenses, the young man readily agrees to take her under the bridal canopy before they depart.

Such weddings are now a frequent occurrence throughout the city, and not only in Warsaw, for half of Poland yearns for the Other Side. In Warsaw and everywhere else, girls are meeting young men, and their parents are only too happy to get a daughter out of the house by marrying her off. These weddings provide the rabbi with a tolerable living.

Boys from Wołynska Street cross over to the Other Side and come back in a few weeks in order to earn a few gulden as experienced guides. While they're at it, they take along wristwatches, which are very expensive there and dirt cheap here, as well as suits and shoes, likewise worth their weight in gold on the Other Side.

Brodsky's son has already returned. He doesn't look well, but he plans to go back someday; he already knows all the routes, gives advice on how to make the journey and proposes himself as a reliable guide across the border. He has brought regards from the army tailor, but Pearl just laughs: Ha! What did she say? Doesn't she know her husband, the big shot? So, he's going to make it on his own, as though he can get along without her for a single day! He was full of talk about how he could find work and make money. So what? He knows nothing about housekeeping, or if he does . . . let him tell it to his grandmother—she, Pearl, will never be convinced, never be fooled. She knows that if he goes a little hungry just once, he'll remember her good cooking, her full pots, and he won't be able to take it anymore. . . . Well, now he wants to come back. Didn't she tell him there's no way around it, that you can live better here, from jackets and from Germans, than there?

Outside the rain pours incessantly; it's foggy and bleak, and the streets are filled with mud and filth, but the carts keep going to the border. Already there are houses with vacant apartments, and elsewhere you can rent a furnished apartment for next to nothing. An apartment that rented for up to two thousand gulden before the war can now be taken for three or four hundred gulden. It's said that the border is closed; people are held up in "no-man's-land" for a week, two weeks, three—and nothing can pass over the border. Many become sick from waiting in the cold, rainy, late autumn days, and many more from spending the cold autumn nights under the stars. Children are dropping like flies. It seems that the Germans no longer allow people to cross; they force any wanderers they encounter to hand over not only their last groschen, but also their overcoats and boots, and in return give them terrible German beatings, merciless blows, and drive them back. It's also rumored that the Russians no longer call the wanderers "comrades," but curse them and beat them and sometimes place them under arrest. The woods are full of bands of Polish thieves, who ambush the wanderers, rob and beat them and even tear the gold teeth from their mouths.

The shipping clerk's young son has come back from Bialystok without the jewels that were hidden in the hollow buttons sewn onto his overcoat. The Germans saw through the ruse and cut off the buttons. The hairdresser in the neighboring tenement hid a diamond under the filling of a gold tooth, but the tooth was cut out and he returned a pale, broken man, full of hatred even more for the Russian "comrades" than for the Germans. However, people continue to leave for the Other Side. The buses to Bialystok have stopped, it's true, but still people find dozens of other ways.

The weather gets colder and colder; in "no-man's-land" there is already frost. The peasants near the border are making piles of money letting people spend nights in their stables and rooms. All of this is known here, yet people continue to leave.

The Lithuanians have already retaken Vilna,° and a new exodus begins. Lithuania is now a "neutral" country—under the German heel but, formally, neutral—and it offers a chance of escape to the free world. People leave from here with the clear goal of smuggling themselves over two borders: the German-Polish-Soviet and the Soviet-Lithuanian. At first the Lithuanians had let themselves be bribed,

The Soviets signed a mutual-aid agreement with independent Lithuania on October 10, 1939, and returned Vilna as part of the package.

but now they have become unbending and cruel and allow no exceptions: anyone seen stealing over the border gets a bullet in the head.

Pretty, young Khayale Auerbach, married barely six months, sews all her worldly possessions, the dowry that she has exchanged for jewels, into the square, hollowed-out buttons of her overcoat and passes without incident over the border at Malkinia. But when, after joining her husband in Bialystok, she tries to cross the Lithuanian border, she falls dead with a bullet in her heart; her husband goes out of his mind with grief.

This isn't the only tragedy. People know it, but the stream of travelers doesn't stop.

When the army tailor returns there is snow in the courtyard. His hands and feet are frozen and he must lie in bed several weeks, but he is relieved to be home again. It's not worth it, he says, to labor for nothing; the Bolsheviks don't let you live. . . .

The landlady stands in the yard but no longer sweeps or cleans—she is once again the mistress of the house. She stops every passing tenant and demands rent. At first, she asks rather timidly, with a faint smile and a quiet voice: "Well, Mr. Grauman, someone has to pay for water, for garbage collection. My husband is, after all, only human; he too must make a living!" People respond quietly and politely, so she is contented, satisfied with a promise, with a good word, and it gives her a strange pleasure; she never imagined it would go so smoothly. Only two months ago she would have been stoned for showing such nerve.

The next day she is bolder and less tongue-tied, she speaks a little louder, and each succeeding day she grows more confident. Now she is heard far out in the courtyard, arguing with the "good-for-nothings"; the defiant, sharp-tongued women are ready for battle: What is this? They should pay her rent, now, during the war—rent "under the Germans"? She should lie sick for so long!

But the landlady knows her rights: "You won't pay? Then I'll take you to court. You'll pay at the green table; do you want to eat, to buy bread? You also have to pay for the roof over your head—no free lodgings, not with me!"

"Look at her, the scum, the trash," the broker's wife shouts up from the basement. "She won't be happy if she doesn't get her money; you can't gorge yourself on our labor now—curses I'll pay you!"

"During the bombing I guarded this house for nothing, stood entire nights by the gate," says the butcher. "Now, you rich bitch, a curse on your years, do you think we don't know you? We know how you got hold of this property. . . . 'From the sweat of your brow?' . . . You should drop dead. . . . Don't knock your ass around!"

The landlady says nothing but, leaving the butcher and the broker's wife, walks quickly into her apartment.

Pearl, who held her breath as she stood in a corner by the hall window and listened to the slanders with delight, now shouts to the furrier's wife, "Did you hear that quarrel? How they gave it to her! I should live so long—it's given me back a little courage; she thinks it's going to be easy, the filthy whore, she actually threatened to take me to court. Well, we'll see if it works out so nicely for her, we'll see. If the Germans say no to evictions, just let her try it."

The army tailor, his frozen hands and feet already healed, helps his wife deal with the landlady; he claims that he paid her the hundred zlotys just like that; it wasn't worth fighting over it. But to pay all the rent he owes, no, she can forget about that! When the war is over—then we'll see.

The Zelechower, who has already received a clear, precise and exhaustive account of the army tailor's journey to the Other Side, runs all over the tenement letting every neighbor in on his secret: had the army tailor not sneaked off alone but crossed together with him, he would not have returned in such a state, for he (the Zelechower) would have shown him the best route, and, of course, he has many relatives in Russia—aunts, uncles, brothers-in-law—who are all doing very well, making a lot of money in good positions. Now he has no choice but to go it alone. Yes, he still intends to go—he's only waiting for a letter that a goy is going to bring over from the Other Side any day now, and people will see who the big shot really is; he doesn't like to boast, but they will see! . . .

And they do indeed see, that is, not so much see as hear that the Zelechower has sold two of his three new sewing machines and quietly taken the third by cart to Zelechow—and he is gone—no more Zelechower.

"Where is the Zelechower, where is he?" the neighbors ask one another. "Has he really gone to the Other Side?" However, in a week or two he is back. It seems that the Germans confiscated his sewing machine on the way; he no longer wears his heavy winter coat with the sheepskin collar, but a rubber summer coat; also his cheeks have grown hollow from the journey. He says he has come back to Warsaw on business and will soon be off again, and he is true to his word—he leaves once and comes back and leaves a second time, until finally he grabs the chance to sell his apartment to the musician, who is playing at Polish weddings again, as he did before the war. And—there's an end to it. Now the Zelechower leaves Warsaw for good, to join his wife and children in Zelechow; he would trade all the opportunities of the city for one bowl of Zelechower garlic borscht with potatoes!

Pearl holds open the door to her refurbished, brightly painted apartment, with the polished red floor that she didn't even have before the war. She stands with her hands on her hips and meets each oncoming neighbor with a grim countenance:

"What can you say to that lowlife, the landlady; she's taking us to court, a curse on her years, she's indicted ten people. Well, we'll see who gets thrown out, may she be thrown from the top of a roof! Father in heaven! . . ."

The furrier's wife is also standing in her doorway. Her red hair again neatly combed, she wears a sporty vest that makes her figure seem even more slender, as if she were getting herself ready again to work out at the Shtern Sports Club.° It seems that her husband gave up his wartime business: they no longer go to Otwock for milk, she no longer waits in line for chocolate and candy or sells German papers. Instead, he makes fur collars, and their neighbor the purse maker, who stopped making purses, makes a living by selling the furrier's collars at the flea market.

The furrier's wife, who is among the ten who have been indicted, argues Pearl's position in the phraseology of propaganda booklets:

"One pays no rent in wartime. Such 'dealings' aren't 'legal.' Sorry, neighbor, if she wants to collect for water and for the W.C.—let her want to. And did she have the right to collect key money before the war? To steal the last morsel from

A Jewish sports club set up by the Left Labor Zionists.

the worker's mouth? We won't pay; together—we won't capitulate—in unity lies strength!"

Suddenly Khavtshe, the shoemaker's wife, comes in from the street bearing news: a *paruvke*—a disinfection.

Pearl looks daggers at her; she believes that Khavtshe is responsible for all her problems, because she was the first to deliver rent to the landlady after the war began, when the bombs were already falling. But when she hears Khavtshe pronounce the dreaded word, she ducks into her apartment like a thief, quickly shuts the door behind her, and forgets about court, about the landlady, about curses—a *paruvke*!

Soon the screeching of closet doors and the scraping of the sofa are heard from inside the apartment; the sewing machine stays put but benches are tumbling, and there is a stirring from within, the bustling and packing one hears during a fire.

A quarter of an hour later Pearl emerges carrying a bundle of clothes wrapped in a shawl, followed by her daughters carrying fabrics and bedding, and before most of the other tenants have even been properly informed, Pearl has returned with her daughters to carry a second load of bundles to her mother on Smocza Street; now prepared, she can wait for the official decree.

As the news spreads, the tenement is thrown into a panic: Who could have guessed that the smooth-talking little doctor with the black whiskers who had, after all, confessed that in almost all the apartments he had encountered scoured floors, fresh bedding and scrubbed heads—who could have guessed that he would still call for a *paruvke*? And where is the tenement commandant, the tenement committee? How is it that just yesterday enough money was collected to pay off everyone?

People run into the yard, the women with kerchiefs on their heads, and the sharp, freezing wind doesn't let them stand in one place. They are waiting for the members of the committee to tell them that the situation isn't so dangerous, that there may still be a good chance of avoiding this threat, for a *paruvke*, which took place in the neighboring tenement only a few days ago, strikes terror into every heart. But wherever or whoever the members of the committee may be—they seem to have vanished into thin air.

The women return to their homes and try to copy Pearl, carrying whatever they can to neighbors and relatives; there is a great deal of running about, for no one knows when the brutes will come, perhaps today or perhaps tomorrow. Then, suddenly, the angry, threatening voices of the Polish police are heard in the court-yard, calling everyone to the bathhouse.

Ah, now they're in for it. . . . People run to their windows and look out into the yard: the gate is already closed, there is no place to run or hide, they have them in their grasp.

These were Polish police called the Blue Boys in slang. Polish patriots considered them collaborators.

Soon screams are heard in the yard; the police° are hitting people with rubber truncheons; they block every exit from the house so that there is no place to go except into the line for the baths. Some of the police stand in the exits, while others run through the apartments, driving people to the bathhouse; from everywhere screams and cries are heard. The stallkeeper's wife, who is pregnant, tries to explain to a policeman that she can't go into the bathhouse in her condition, but he brings his stick down on her head and her agonized cry echoes through all the floors.

In truth, the brutality of the police is a first-rate ploy: The butcher calls in several policeman and, locking the door behind them, takes a flask of whiskey from a cabinet, sets a plate of sliced wurst on the table and even . . . opens up his wallet. Afterwards the police emerge with red mugs and everything is hush-hush. The butcher stands calmly by the window and looks out at the crowd being driven to the bath.

Pearl goes down with her daughters and little boy and stands for appearance sake in the line, but the members of her household won't be going into the bath. She has paid off the police brute, who opens the gate and lets both her daughters out.

Now the policeman at the gate becomes even more severe, more demanding; the Polish janitor, who has been waiting for this blessed hour a very long time, acts as middleman, and he too receives special bribes from those who want to buy themselves out; only big money is accepted, not single gulden but five and ten gulden pieces, which will be used to buy big flasks of liquor and sausage. The majority of the tenants are led with their wives and children into the bathhouse on Spokojna Street—the "slaughterhouse" they call it.

On the way, several try to sneak out of the line, but the police have sharp eyes, and as soon as someone even raises a foot to run, the club comes down on his head.

One resident is allowed to remain in each apartment, until the bedding can be removed for cleaning and the homes disinfected.

A mob of Polish riff-raff, men and women, enters the yard—these are the disinfectors, the fumigators; they have a list of dwellings that have to be disinfected, that is, wherever the tenants didn't pay them off in cash. The committee members get straight to the point; they direct the doctor and the fumigators to those apartments that require . . . fumigation. It makes no difference if a room is clean or not, if the bedding is spotless or not. The only thing that matters is . . . money.

The fumigators go about their work with perverse joy, with an almost insanely malicious pleasure in destruction: they drag the bundles of clean bedding with the freshly changed sheets and throw them onto the filthy stairwell; then they pile them up in the yard on the wet asphalt. The piles lie there for a long time, until the trucks from the bathhouse come to collect them; sometimes they lie like that for a day or two or even three, and no one cares if it rains or snows. Then they are stacked up high on the bathhouse trucks and trodden down by muddy shoes until the wagon is full. If a sheet should happen to catch on a nail and tear, this bothers the fumigators no more than any of the other little disturbances they endure; they are having a fine time—getting their revenge on the kikes. . . .

The commandant comes in off the street and stealthily crosses the yard, but the few remaining housewives spot him and run after him, shouting, "Mr. Bernholtz, Mr. Bernholtz, so this is how you serve us? Is that what we paid you for?"

The commandant gets angry. His eyes flashing, he shouts, "I warned you to keep your homes clean!"

"Oh yah? But whoever laid out some dirty cash didn't get fumigated, and the committee members' homes weren't fumigated either!" the knitter's wife screams down from the fourth floor. "Wait, just wait, your time will come, you won't always be in charge!"

The commandant, furious, storms out of the yard screaming: he's through with doing favors for everyone; he isn't a Moses that he should take everybody else's problems on his shoulders. . . . But it's readily apparent that this display of anger is really intended to let him slip quickly out of the yard, so that he can show up at last with the other committee members, now that the danger is almost over.

On Spokojna Street the tenants encounter long lines of Jews who have been brought to the bathhouse from other tenements; placards now hang from these tenements, with yellow letters spelling out in German and Polish "Spotted Typhus," although no typhus victims have been removed from any of these buildings. The Jews, who stand here pushing and shoving in order to enter the baths more quickly, are very much aware of this and bear their humiliation patiently: What does it matter how one suffers, from blows or from . . . baths? They save their bitterness and impatience only for each other; they argue and curse and do not spare their fists:

"Look at the great man, the rag picker, how he shoves, what a hurry he's in. What, you don't have time? Are you so afraid the Germans haven't purified you yet? May your brains rot to hell, you trash! . . ."

In the middle of this jostling an attendant comes out of the bathhouse and starts bringing his broom down on heads and tearing the caps away from those in front so that they have to go to the back of the line. All in all, about twenty are admitted to the baths, while the others have to wait outside in a new line.

Those who can stuff something into the attendant's hand are let in first. Others enter through a back door or window and with the help of a gift get taken first. Those who don't have money may have to wait outside or in the first or second anteroom for half a day or more before they are let inside.

The ones who are lucky enough to get in must immediately strip themselves naked and hand over their clothes for disinfection, but the clothes can lie bundled up for hours because the disinfection machines are always busy. The naked crowd stands on the cement floor and freezes, hungry and shivering.

And now the shearing plague begins. A brutal Pole appears with a dull, blunt shearing machine and proceeds to mercilessly shave everyone's head, taking special pleasure in the coiffured locks of the young dandies. The Hasid saves a bit of his full beard with a couple of gulden, while the butcher's son the whole head of hair by placing a substantial coin in the Pole's hand.

After the shearing comes the examination by the "doctor," really only a barber surgeon—a young lout who makes sure that the shearing machine has been applied to all the hairy parts of the body and sends back anyone who has not been shaved to his satisfaction. Those who have been shorn and examined are driven naked through the cold corridors that lead from these rooms to the bath, but there they must wait for the water to heat up, since there isn't enough coal. And there they stand from eight until midnight and sometimes even longer, until they are finished bathing. After that they still must wait a few hours for their clothes to be brought from the disinfecting machine and only then, after enduring an entire day of this, can they go back home carrying cards attesting to their purification.

So it goes in the men's bathhouse; for the women it is even worse. The gentile women who examine their hair know where to land blows—after all, they themselves are women! For good money one can get by with a dirty scalp, but those without money have their heads mercilessly shorn, whether they are young girls or mothers. One hears screams, desperate cries, hysterics; those with shaven heads go home sick, shattered, humiliated, and the next day, wearing kerchiefs on their heads, they will seem like dazed old women.

Pearl stands among the women, loudly cursing the tenement committee; she takes the injustice personally—although she herself knew what to do, how to buy her own way out as well as her daughters'; but her heart aches for the others, only for the others. . . .

The shoemaker's and the furrier's wives were also lucky, because they too took along a few gulden; but everyone else in the tenement goes home broken in spirit. The egg dealer's daughter has almost fainted from weeping; she won't be seen in the courtyard for several days.

The furrier and his wife are both still young, just over thirty, and both suffer from asthma. Still, they laugh off their troubles; it is, after all, only the first winter of the war, one can still make a joke. At two in the morning, enveloped by the frosty, starlit winter night, the people, their stomachs empty, say to one another: "To health . . . We've been kashered and rendered pure. So where are the challah and fish?"°

The children, after enduring the full day of torment along with their parents, also forget about their hunger and weariness and enjoy the walk: "Look, look Papa, a falling star . . . a star."

Several sinister characters are standing by a street lamp in the distance. Although the war curfew prohibits people from staying out at night, members of the Polish underworld still lie in wait for Jews emerging from the baths, from whom they can steal a towel, a jacket, or even snatch a purse.

Many return from the baths chilled and half sick, but there is no bedding in their apartments; they have to wait long days, even weeks, until it is returned from the *paruvke*. There is absolutely nothing to sleep on. When the bundles are returned, they will see that several items are missing, but they will be happy to have escaped with their lives.

The stallkeeper's wife was brought back unharmed; she had suffered less than others and she only hopes to give birth soon, before the next *paruvke*, because everyone already knows that when these butchers get hold of the house again they won't let them off so easy.

The next day those who stayed home are rounded up for the baths, even the aged and the infirm: deaf old people, the mute and the crippled, the mentally impaired. No one is overlooked. As they are driven away, the house heaves a heavy sigh for the *paruvke*, and heads are bowed low.

Also on the next day, the members of the tenement committee are reluctant to venture into the courtyard, as though ashamed to show themselves. But they aren't ashamed, no, for how would it have helped matters, argues one member, if they had gone to the baths, if they too had suffered a *paruvke*? Pearl, however, won't let him off so easily. "If there's a *paruvke*," she screams, "it's for everyone. No privileges. To the baths—everyone must go to the baths."

"And your children went to the baths?"

"My children, my children," Pearl's eyes begin to flame, "my children weren't in the baths? Didn't my Zalmele go to the bath? Didn't my husband go to the bath? Wasn't I in the bath? How dare you, you brazen lout!"

"And what about your daughters?"

"My daughters also."

Prior to the Jewish holidays, men would immerse themselves in the ritual bath.

"You're lying!"

"Oh, look who's talking—the fine man, everyone's toadie—he's calling me a liar. And if I sent the girls to another bathhouse, what of it?"

"So, another bathhouse," drawls the committee man. "That's a different story."

Those gathered around understand what this means: Pearl paid Bernholtz for a note from the bathhouse stating that her daughters had been bathed. But still Pearl deafens everyone with her tirade against the injustice she has suffered at the hands of man, and she will go on cursing until the next *paruvke,* so that the commandant shall know with whom he is dealing and . . . keep her off the list.

Now, after the brutal *paruvke,* even those who have lagged behind want to flee to the Other Side. What kind of life is this here? There at least you're free—true, you may starve, but you're a human being just the same. But here? Even the purse maker joins the chorus. However, the traffic to the Other Side has already slowed; only the daredevils go now, people with nothing to lose, for the frost burns terribly at the border and every day a few travelers show up in the alley with frozen arms and legs. In the facing tenement a youth returned with his leg frozen up to the knee, and who knows if it will heal without an operation?

Frost is frost, but the news that the Russian border guards are shooting at anyone who tries to cross the border is much worse. This bursts like an icy current on all speculations: How can they, who call everyone "comrade," shoot at people who are escaping from hell? At Jews, victims of Hitler's reign of terror?

The shoemaker, who cannot bear for his basic faith in human justice to be trodden underfoot, tries to explain: "What do you expect them to do? The Jews themselves are to blame, bringing goods to Bialystok and speculating, dealing in bread, cigarettes and all sorts of contraband, sneaking from village to village, smuggling dollars and jewels into Russia—what do you want, that the Russians watch all this and keep quiet? There's a war going on, and the Russians also have to keep an eye on the Germans."

But as soon as the shoemaker mentioned the Russians and the Germans in the same breath, the faces of his listeners turn somber. The furrier's wife especially wants no more fancy talk about justice and humanity: if Russia can make a pact with Germany, well, it's the end of the world—what's left?

The butcher simply laughs at the whole business: why should it matter to him if it's Russians or Germans? If you want to, you can live here as well as there—it's the same world. A sensible man can get along anywhere . . . take him, for instance, Hershl the butcher. . . .

Only the army tailor stands apart, listening to this conversation in the furrier's home with his head cocked, smiling. *Oy,* he has seen these Russian soldiers, how they creep through the woods at night, lying in wait for all who try to steal across the border; he has heard the cries of the captured ring through the frosty nights, although for sixty gulden he himself was allowed to cross the Bug in a little boat; but no, they won't be able to squeeze any answers out of him: "If freedom is such that it cannot save me, just me, me first of all—understand?—from the claws of the beast, then it's over, no more freedom or justice; then it's live as you can . . . rob, steal and fill your own belly, because there's nothing better or more beautiful on the face of this earth than a good meal, and there never will be."

Under his whiskers the army tailor breaks out into a shrewd smile. He already knows what he has to do, yes, already knows . . . just now he has begun to live . . . the real life of the war . . . his own life.

1941

74 Chronicle of a Single Day

LEYB GOLDIN

> How differently my song would sound
>> If I could let it all resound.

—paraphrase of *Monish*°

A celebrated mock-heroic poem by I. L. Peretz, first published in 1888.

A major Japanese daily.

Tired, pale fingers are setting type somewhere in Cracow:
"Tik-tak-tak, tik-tak-tak-tak. Rome: the Duce has announced . . . Tokyo: the newspaper *Asahi Shimbun* . . .° Tik-tik-tik-tak . . . Stockholm . . . Tik-tik . . . Washington: Secretary Knox has announced . . . Tik-tik-tik-tak . . . And I am hungry.

It's not yet five o'clock. At the door of the room, a new day awaits you. A quiet breeze. A puppy wants to play with you—jumps up at your neck, over your body, behind your back, nuzzles up, wants to tease, to get you to go out and play. A discordant orchestra of sleepers breathing. As one begins, another—a child—interrupts right in the middle. And a third—and a fourth. The conversations in one's sleep are over, complaints satisfied. From time to time someone groans in his sleep. And my brain is bursting, my heart is sick, my mouth is dry. I am hungry. Food, food, food!

The last portion of soup—yesterday at twenty to one. The next will be—today at the same time. The longest half, already endured. How much longer to go? Eight hours, though you can't count the last hour from noon on. By then you're already in the kitchen, surrounded by the smell of food; you're already prepared. You already *see* the soup. So there are really only seven hours to go.

"Only" seven hours to go; it's no joke. Seven hours—and the fool says "only." Very well then; how does one get through the seven hours—or the nearest two? Read? Your brain won't take it in. All the same, you pull the book out from under the pillow. German. Arthur Schnitzler. Publisher so-and-so. Year. Printer. "Eva looked into the mirror." You turn the first page and realize you've understood no more than the first sentence: "Eva looked into the mirror."

You've reached the end of the second page. Didn't understand a single word. Yesterday the soup was thin and almost cold. You sprinkled in some salt, which didn't dissolve properly. And yesterday Friedman died . . . of starvation. Definitely of hunger. You could see he wouldn't last long. And there's a gnawing in my stomach. If you only had a quarter of a loaf now! One of the quarter loaves over there, a square-shaped quarter loaf, like the ones in that display window, by that table. Oh, brother! You realize that you've jumped up, the idea was so delicious. There's some name or other on page four of the novella: Dionisia. Where she's from, and what she wants—you don't know. There! A quarter of a loaf! There! A bowl of soup! You would make it differently. You would warm it through until it began to boil. So that a spoonful could last five minutes at least. So that you would sweat as you ate. So that you would blow at the spoon, not be able to swallow the soup all at once! Like that!

Maybe it isn't nice to think about oneself in this way—only about oneself, oneself. Remember once; preached a thousand times: the century of the masses, of the collective. The individual is nothing. Phrases! It's not me thinking it, it's my stomach. It doesn't think, it yells, it's enough to kill you! It demands, it provokes me. "Intellectual! Where are you, with your theories, your intellectual interests, your dreams, your goals? You educated imbecile! Answer me! Remember: every nuance, every twist of intellectual life used to enchant you, entirely possess you. And now? And now!"

Why are you yelling like that?

"Because I want to. Because I, your stomach, am hungry. Do you realize that by now?"

Who is talking to you in this way? You are two people, Arke. It's a lie. A pose. Don't be so conceited. That kind of split was all right at one time when one was full. *Then* one could say, "Two people are battling in me," and one could make a dramatic, martyred face.

Yes, this kind of thing can be found quite often in literature. But today? Don't talk nonsense—it's you and your stomach. It's your stomach and you. It's 90 percent your stomach and a little bit you. A small remnant, an insignificant remnant of the Arke who once was. The one who thought, read, taught, dreamed. Of the one who looked ironically from the dock directly into the eyes of the Prosecutor and smiled directly into his face. Yes, stomach of mine, listen: such an Arke existed once. Once, once, he read a Rolland, lived side by side with a Jean-Christophe, admired an Annette, laughed with a [Colas] Breugnon.° Yes, and for a while he was even a Hans Castorp, by some writer . . . Thomas Mann.°

"I don't understand, wise guy. Haven't you eaten?"

Yes, stomach, sure, I ate but I didn't know I had eaten. Didn't think I was eating.

"Do you remember, buddy, the first day in jail? You sat in solitary confinement, bewildered, sad; they had just thrown you, like a piece of old clothing, into a pantry. For two days you didn't eat, but didn't feel the least hunger. And suddenly the peephole opened in the door: 'Good evening, Arke! Keep it up! *Grunt się nie przejmować, dobrze się odżywiać* (keep your spirits up and eat well)!° Listen, Arke, in the corner, behind the radiators, there's bread and bacon. The main thing, brother, is to eat—the next installment comes tomorrow, on the walk.' Remember?"

And yesterday Friedman died. Of starvation. Of starvation? When you saw him naked, thrown into the large—the gigantic—mass grave (everyone covered his nose with a handkerchief, except for me and his mother), his throat was cut. Maybe he didn't die of hunger—maybe he took his own life? Yes . . . no. People don't take their own lives nowadays. Suicide is something from the good old days.

The last three names are of characters in novels by Romain Rolland (1866–1945).

In Mann's The Magic Mountain.

In Polish in the original.

At one time, if you loved a girl and she didn't reciprocate, you put a bullet through your head or drained a flowered phial of vinegar essence. At one time, if you were sick with consumption, gallstones or syphilis, you threw yourself from a fourth-floor window in a back street, leaving behind a stylized note with "It's nobody's fault" and "I'm doing the world a big favor." Why don't we kill ourselves now? The pangs of hunger are far more terrible, more murderous, more choking than any sickness. Well, you see, all sicknesses are human, and some even make a human being of the patient. Make him nobler. While hunger is a bestial, a wild, a rawly primitive—yes, a bestial thing. If you're hungry, you cease to be human, you become a beast. And beasts know nothing of suicide.

"Brilliant, my pet, an excellent theory! So how long is it, wise guy, till twelve o'clock?"

Shut up, it'll soon be six o'clock. Another six hours and you'll get your soup. Did you see the burials yesterday? Like dung—that's how they drop the dead into the grave. Turned the box over and flipped them in. The bystanders get such a livid expression of disgust on their faces, as if death were taking revenge for the aura of secrecy. For the various irrelevant, unnecessary things that had been tied on to him, now, out of spite, he let down his pants and—here! Look at me, kiss my ass. Like a spoiled child, who's sick of endearments. And do you know, Brother Stomach, how I imagined death when I was a child? I remember when I was four and five, I went to a kindergarten. They played the piano and split their sides laughing and spoke Hebrew. And I remember there was a funeral in the same courtyard. I only saw the hearse entering the courtyard, and soon after, cries and laments. I fancied that the man in the black coat and stiff hat wanted to drag a woman into the hearse, and she didn't want to go, and in fact it was she who was making the noise, and she threw herself on the ground, and he took hold of both her arms, and she was sitting and sliding along, and shouting and screaming. How do you like that, my little stomach? You don't answer—are you asleep? Well, sleep, sleep, the longer the better. At least until twelve o'clock.

Food, food. It isn't my stomach talking now—it's my palate and my temples. Just half a quarter loaf, just a little piece of crust, even if it's burnt, black, like coal. I jump off the bed—a drink of water helps, it provides an interruption. On your way back to bed you fall—your feet are clumsy, swollen. They hurt. But you don't groan. For the last few months you've got used to not groaning, even when you're in pain. At the beginning of the war, when you were lying in bed at night and thinking about the whole thing; or in the morning, when you had to get up, you often emitted a groan. Not now. You're like a robot now. Or maybe, again, like a beast? Perhaps.

Die? So be it. Anything is better than being hungry. Anything is better than suffering. Oh, if only one could use arithmetic to reckon *when* one would breathe one's last! That woman in the courtyard, from No. 37, who died, had been starving for six weeks. Yes, but she ate nothing, not even soup once a day. And I do eat soup. One can go on suffering for years in this way—and maybe kick the bucket tomorrow. Who knows?

I realize that I'm still holding the book. Page seven. Let's see if I can get through it. I turn the pages. Somewhere, on one of the pages, my eye spots the [German] word *Wonne*. Ecstasy. A piquant, magnificent erotic scene. A few pages earlier they were eating in a restaurant. Schnitzler gives you the menu. No, no, don't read it. Your mouth becomes strangely bitter inside, your head spins. Don't read about what they ate. That's right—just as old people skip descriptions of sex. What's the time? Half past six. Oh, how early it still is!

But it's possible that tomorrow or even today I'll give up the ghost. The heart is a sneak—you never can tell. Maybe I'm lying here for the last time and feeling so sluggish for the last time. So slow to get dressed. And handing in a soup ticket for the last time and taking a new one for tomorrow. And the cashier, and the waitress, and the janitor by the door—they will all look at me with indifference, as they do every day, and not know at all, at all, that tomorrow I won't come here anymore, and not the day after tomorrow and not the day after that. But I will know, and I will feel proud of my secret when I am with them. And perhaps in a few months, or after the war is over, if statistics are made of the diners who died, I'll be there, too, and maybe one of the waitresses will say to another: "D'ya know who else died, Zoshe? That redhead who insisted on speaking Yiddish, and whom I teased for an hour and, just to fix him good, didn't give him his soup. He's been put in the box too, I bet."

And Zoshe, of course, *won't* know, as if she would remember such a thing—
An indecipherable part of the manuscript
and then you will have such a high, high [. . .].° Maybe it will already have been poured; oh, how magnificently Thomas Mann describes it in *The Magic Mountain*.

I remember his thoughts, the way he delineated them. Never has their brilliant truth appeared so clear to me as it does now. Time—and time. Now it stretches like rubber, and then—it's gone, like a dream, like smoke. Right now, of course, it's stretched out horribly, horribly, it's really enough to kill you. The war has been going on for a full two years, and you've eaten nothing but soup for some four months, and those few months are thousands and thousands of times longer for you than the whole of the previous twenty months—no, longer than your whole life until now. From yesterday's soup to today's is an eternity, and I can't imagine that I'll be able to survive another twenty-four hours of this overpowering hunger. But these four months are no more than a dark, empty nightmare. Try to salvage something from them, remember something in particular—it's impossible. One black, dark mass. I remember, in prison, in solitary confinement. Days that stretch like tar. Each day like another yoke on your neck. And in the evenings, lying in the dark, reviewing the day that had passed, I could hardly believe that I had been in the bathhouse that day—it seemed that it was at least four or five days ago. The days passed with dreadful slowness. But when I went through the gate on that side of the street, all the days ran together like a pack of dogs on a hunt. Black dogs. Black days. All one black nightmare, like a single black hour.

At the prison gate friends were waiting—I don't remember all of them. But I
A Christian Pole.
remember Janek.° Yes, Janek. I forgot all about him. Not long ago, last year, I met him. Half naked, in rags, he was tinkering with the gas pipe in a bombed-out house halfway along Marszałkowska Street. He called to me. And out of the blue, as if twelve years hadn't gone by since we met last, he gave me our standard greeting, "Know something?"

"No. And you?"

"Me neither. But it's OK."

Then the supervisor came up and left. So maybe, maybe I should write to Janek. Write to him: Listen, brother, I'm having a hard time. Send me something. Write, then? By all means, write yet more openly: if you could provide me with a quarter of a loaf every day—ah, a little quarter loaf. Yes, when I'm dressed I'll write to him. It may be difficult to send the note but I'll write to him.—A little quarter loaf. And if you can't, then let it be an eighth.

Somewhere in the world people are eating as much as they want. In America sits Hershel eating his supper—and there is bread on the table, and butter, and sugar and a jar of jam. Eat, Hershele, eat! Eat! Hershel, eat a lot, I tell you. Don't leave the crust, it would be a waste, and eat up the crumbs from the table! It tastes good, you become full—true, dear Hershel?

And somewhere in the world there is still something called love. Girls are kissed. And girls kiss in return. And couples go walking for hours in the gardens and the parks and sit by a river, such a cool river, under a spreading tree; and they talk so politely to each other, and laugh together, and gaze in such a friendly way, so lovingly and passionately, into each other's eyes. And they don't think about food. They may be hungry, but they don't think about it. And they are jealous and become angry with each other—again, not eating. And all this is so true, and it is all happening in the world—far away from here, true, but it is happening, and there are people like me over there. . . .

"Sick fantasies!" interrupts the scoundrel, my stomach; he's woken up, the cynic. "What a dreamer! Instead of looking for a practical solution, he lies there deluding himself with nonsensical stories. There are no good or evil stomachs, no educated or simple ones, none in love and none indifferent. In the whole world, if you're hungry, you want to eat. And by the way, it's all nonsense. There are good providers for their stomachs, and there are unlucky wretches like you. You can groan, you idiot, but as far as filling me up—damnation, what's the time?"

Ten past eight. Four hours to go. Not quite four whole hours, but let's say four, and if less, that's certainly to the good. I slowly draw on my pants. I no longer touch my legs. I touched them until, not long ago, I measured them with my fist, to see how far they'd shrunk. No more. What's the point?

And Friedman has died. Tying my shoelaces reminds me of the dozens of dangling genitalia there in the large common grave. And young girls stood around, holding their noses with handkerchiefs, and looked at the islands of hair. Again— is it because animals have no shame? Yes, so it seems, at the cemetery—funeral notices of rich men, of doctors, of good citizens . . . there is no end of rickshaws, and an easily recognizable crowd gathers—no poor people there. In other words, this kind of person dies too, though they have enough to eat. One doesn't die of hunger alone. Things even themselves out. They'd better get the message.

"Tell me, friend, are you starting up with your stories again? It's already time to go. Maybe the soup will be earlier today. Move, my dear!"

In the air and heat of early fall the street is full of the smell of sweat and the smell of corpses, just as in front of the ritual cleansing room at the cemetery. Bread, bread everywhere. It costs the same as yesterday. You want to go to a stall, feel, pinch the fresh whole-wheat bread, satiate your fingertips with the soft, baked-brown dough. No, better not. It'll only increase your appetite, that's all. No, no— just as you didn't want to read what the lovers ate in the restaurant on the quiet Viennese street. And fish roe is cheaper. Cheese—the same price. Sour cream is now in season—but it's expensive. Cucumbers are cheaper, and onions are at the same price. But they're bigger today than yesterday.

Cheerful tomatoes, full of joie de vivre, laugh in front of you, greet you. Trips into the mountains, rucksacks, shorts, open shirts, wild, joyous songs of earthly happiness rising into space. When, where? Two years ago, altogether two years. Tanned faces, black hands and feet. And hearty laughter, and brooklets of unexpected spring water, and bread and butter sandwiches with sweet tea; and no armbands on your sleeves, no mark of being a *Jude.*

Bread, bread, bread. *Razowka. Sitkowka. Vayse sitka. Hele sitka. Tunkele sitka. Walcowka.* First-class bread. *Beknbroyt.*°

There are no English or American equivalents for these breads. They are roughly listed in order of desirability.

Bread, bread. The abundance of it dazzles your eyes. In the windows, on the stalls, in hands, in baskets. I won't be able to hold out if I can't grab a bite of breadstuff. "Grab? You don't look suspicious," says he, my murderer. "They'll let you near, they'll even put it in your hand. They'll trust you. They can see you aren't one of the grabbers."

Shut up, buddy, you've forgotten that I can't run. Now *you're* the wise guy, hah?

"You're a goner, you are, my breadwinner," says he. "Just take a look at those two having their identity papers checked at the gate.° Look at the color of their faces. You can bet they've eaten today, and they'll damn well eat again, soon. But look over there—they're waiting for the car to pick them up. If you were a *mentsh,* you'd have looked after me earlier on, and you'd be eating like a human being, and *not* have swollen legs. And you'd also be able to wheedle yourself in and go along for the ride. They give you half a liter of soup and a loaf of bread a week. Too bad you're such a *shlemazel!*"

These were the Palatzovka workers who reported for duty at the gates of the ghetto to be taken to their work places outside the ghetto.

Wrong again, you argue with him, your stomach. To begin with, there isn't soup every day. Often enough they come back without eating. And they're not treated with kid gloves either. Sometimes they get pushed around. You take your chances. But now, you're guaranteed the soup in the kitchen, you have a ticket. And for doing nothing, and without working. Well, where could you be more secure?

The secondhand dealers by the gates look at you, at everybody, according to the value of the jacket you're wearing, and expertly value the pants that will be pulled off you tomorrow—whether you're dead or alive. A light breeze carries a torn fragment from the wall: "Four hundred grams of black salt. Chairman of the Judenrat." Go to him, perhaps? Something rises in your memory: a committee, a hall, not very large, a bell, a carafe of water. You recognize him: a tall figure, a fleshy Jewish nose, a bald head. A small bow tie. Yes, *he* is now the chairman. Maybe you really should go to him? Write to him: Honored sir, I do not request much of you. I am hungry—you understand?—hungry. So I request of you (and remind him here of your becoming acquainted, in 1935 I think—does he remember?). Therefore, I request of you, Mr. Chairman, that you see to it that I receive a piece of bread every day. I know, much honored sir, that you have a thousand other things to do—what importance at all can it have for you that such a wreck of a person as I am should kick the bucket. All the same, Mr. Chairman of the Judenrat—

You stumble over something on the ground. You nearly fall. But no, your two feet keep their balance. On the ground, across the sidewalk lies a mound of rags with a . . . a green, hairy lump of wet dirt that was once a face with a beard. Now for the first time you realize that the calls, "Hello, hello," were to you. At first you didn't look around because Jews don't have names anymore—all Jews today are called . . . °; but now one of those secondhand dealers is standing by you. Didn't I see that I nearly stepped on a corpse? Philosopher! As if his jacket hadn't been sufficiently creased and disheveled? Must I add insult to injury? The shoes have been pulled off by someone and sold; at least leave the pants! What use is it to tell him that I was just thinking about the Chairman of the Judenrat. The gate-keeper walks slowly, lazily, from the gate, carrying bricks and an old, excrement-stained sheet of newspaper, ties it round the dead body and walks slowly away, and that's it.

According to some clocks, old and crippled, it is already eleven o'clock. You get a liking for the ones that tell you it's later. Those big ones are haughty and not in any hurry, and you hate them. Another hour, no, stand around and wait . . . standing is also a way of passing the time. Another hour. A few dozen minutes—they count for something too! It's nothing, indeed, but if you were eating a good old piece of bread, eh? What would you do, for example, if you were now to be given a slice of bread—would you eat it right away, or would you keep it for the soup to make it more filling? I think you'd keep it. And if the soup was late, and it came out much later, let's say, would you also wait? Enough stories for the time being, don't make a fool of yourself. You'd devour it like a wolf. Oh, how you'd demolish it!

"Just a little bit of bread. . . ," the refrain of all the criers, from the sidewalks, from the cobbles, a little bit of bread. Oh, you jokers! Don't you know that I too want nothing more than a "little bit of bread"?

"My father's dead, my mother's in hospital, my elder brother's missing—a little bit of bread. . . ."

You've eaten today, you bastard, haven't you?

"Small children at home—a little bit of bread." And I would so gladly add my voice: I'm hungry, hungry, hungry. Another hour till soup, another hour—you understand? "A little bit of bread! ! ! !"

The soup was *not* late today. The steam is already in the air. Plates are already being rattled. The manager is already shouting at the waitresses, the assistant manager is already measuring the length of the hall with his tiny feet and nodding his plump head from side to side as in a puppet show. The second assistant manager is already shouting at some diners. The day of soup giving is already begun. There are more people here than yesterday, just as yesterday there were more than the day before. Poor fellow! They're starting to hand out the soup from *that* table. So you'll have to sit here until it reaches you. How do you like that—you can eat your heart out.

Time—and more time. You remember the days when the kitchen announced, indifferently, and you thought, vengefully, "There's no meal today." How bitter were the words on the door: "Today's tickets are valid for tomorrow." How hideously long were those days and nights. And yet it seems to you that that pain was nothing compared with the half hour that you still have to wait.

The opposite table is already in a state of grace. Peaceful quietness—they are already eating. And it somehow seems to you that the people at that table feel superior to you, worthier. Someone or other takes from his bosom a quarter sheet of newspaper and unwraps it, uncovering a thin, round piece of bread. Unlike you, they don't gobble the soup directly; first they stir it, wrinkling up their noses in disgust—just as they do every day, because it's thin; start at the side, where it's shallow; chew for a long time, slowly; pretend to be looking around, as if the soup were of secondary importance and the main thing—the ceiling. After the first few spoonfuls they add salt. They play with the soup as a cat plays with a mouse. And after the soup their faces wear an expression of near-religious bliss.

And it hasn't reached your table yet. And—are you only imagining it?—somehow the people sitting here all have such long faces, not-having-eaten faces, with swollen ghetto spots under their eyes, which give the face a Mongolian look. You think of a master of world literature, a Tolstoy, a Balzac, a Wassermann. How they made a fuss over people, they chiseled every feature, every move. "You seem to be somewhat pale today!" one of these geniuses would write, and the world was enraptured. "You seem to be somewhat pale today," and women dabbed their eyes with handkerchiefs, critics interpreted and serious, business-like gentlemen, owners of textile factories or partners in large, comfortable manufacturing businesses beneath white marble signs felt a quiver in their cheeks—reminiscent of the first kiss, fifty years ago. "You seem to be somewhat pale today"—ha, ha! If someone *today* were to read or write, "You seem somewhat pale today," when the whole world is deathly pale, when everyone, everyone has the same white, chalky, lime-white face. Yes, yes, it was easy for *them* to write. They ate, and knew that the readers were going to eat and that the critics were going to eat. Let these masters *now* show their true colors and write!

"Why don't you eat?" What is this? Everyone around you is eating; in front of you, too, there is a bowl of steaming soup, glistening and glittering with delicious splendor. You were looking across at the people and saw nothing. And did she take the ticket? No, you're still holding it in your hand. What's going on? Should you call? Turn it in? You've already finished with the helping, while around you people are smacking their lips, spitting, sipping as a cat sips milk, and grumbling, exactly as if they weren't eating. And that scoundrel over there, who has such a full plate, full of fried onions sits there sniveling—you could just faint. It's all right, they're hungry, everyone may eat any way he likes. I'm probably comical too when I eat my soup. And there are some who tilt the plate so convulsively and scrape together the last drops . . . and submerge their whole face in the plate and see nothing else, as if it were the entire earth, the world. Can she possibly have given you the soup without a ticket? You steal a glance—the date is right. She simply didn't notice in the confusion. No, don't give it to her. Revenge. And she will realize it maybe; maybe not. It can't be—maybe, maybe to get another helping? And say nothing? But she did it on purpose. You know what, Arke? If a *man* sits down at your table now to eat his soup, you'll take the risk; if a *woman*, it's a bad omen, and you won't give up the ticket.

You stare hard. On one side a mother is now sitting with a child. A waitress hurries past, the mother says to the child, loudly, with a smiling, ingratiating look: "Wait, wait, the lady will soon bring you some thick soup." The bench squeaks, someone has sat down. That person is hidden from view; you see a bit of white toast. A fragment of a second: man or woman?—man or woman? A woman! Apparently—a pair of eyes—a mummy, eyes without expression. A woman, a woman, damn it. This means not turning in the ticket, not taking another bowl of soup? Too late, that's the way you set it up. But now the soup is better and better, thicker, hotter. How do you know? That's the way it always is. The later the better. Though it's not so certain. But this time—yes. And so once again, from the beginning. Man or woman, man or woman?

There is movement around you. People come and go, sit down, speak. Polish, Yiddish, Hebrew, German. First here, now there, like a rocket, a question flutters with an exclamation: "Who, him? I saw him only yesterday! Who, her? She ate here only the day before yesterday! They are talking about those who have died, one of hunger, another from "that" louse and today's sickness. And they whisper so mysteriously in each other's ears: "Don't shout—so, died at home, unannounced." But above all other conversations, one theme—we won't be able to survive it. There's such a winter coming. If the war lasts through the winter. Last year we still had something. Parcels were still arriving, it wasn't sealed so shut. What are they splitting hairs about? Whether we will survive or not. What can people do, when they are sentenced to death and know the exact time of the execution? Thus the French aristocrats in the prisons during the great Revolution gambled at cards, acted in plays, until the man in the tricolor came in and called out the names, and "The guillotine is waiting." Yes, you see? But they weren't hungry and weren't threatened with starvation. Yes, indeed, this is really the main point. Well, and during the more recent Russian Revolution? But why am I getting involved in these great stories—man or woman, man or woman?

At this point she showed up, the waitress, and automatically began taking tickets. Everyone held them out, you as well. It's over. And now you dip your spoon in the bowl, in the second bowl of soup—you understand? It really is thicker than the first. Now you can afford to play with it, to eat graciously, like all the rest, and not gobble. You don't eat in whole spoonfuls. Sometimes you spit out a piece of chaff, like a VIP.

In the street the smell of fresh corpses envelops you. Like an airplane propeller just after it's been started up, which spins and spins, and yet stays in one place— that's what your feet are like. They seem to you to be moving backwards. Pieces of wood.

They were looking, weren't they? Involuntarily, you cover your face with your arm. And what if they find out? They can, as a punishment, take away your soups. Somehow it seems to you that they already know. That man who's walking past looks so insolently into your eyes. He knows. He laughs, and so does that man, and another and another. Hee, hee—they choke back their stinging laughter, and somehow you become so small, so cramped up. That's how you get caught, you fool. A thief? *Only* unlucky. That one soup can cost you all the others.

A burning in your left side. Your arm, your leg, your heart; not for the first time, but this time it's stronger. You must stop moving. You feel someone is watching. It's already too late to respond. A director of social assistance, in a rickshaw,° is riding down the street. A former acquaintance. Yes, he looked at you; yes. You notice when someone's looking—it's your nature. Always, when you see him traveling past, you look at him, wanting to catch his eye, and always in vain. Today it's the other way around: *he* noticed *you.* Maybe . . . maybe he already knows.

The director is already far away. Behind him are dozens of rickshaws. But the burning remains. Why the devil did you have to be in the street just *now?* Others go past, actually touch you and don't recognize you, or pretend not to. And he—

The major means of conveyance in the Warsaw ghetto; a symbol of luxury.

saw you from up there in his rickshaw and pierced you with a glance. What will happen now?

By a gate, in a narrow crack, a cucumber. A whole one, untouched. It seems that it fell from a housewife's shopping basket. Mechanically, without thinking, you bend down, take it, no disgrace, no joy. You deserve it. Just as a dog deserves a bone. A bittersweet cucumber. From looking at the skin you can already taste the sweetness of the seeds. It's not healthy. Typhus? Dysentery? Nonsense. For thirty centuries, generations of scholars have devoted their brilliant abilities, their youth, their lives to extorting from Nature the secrets of vitamins and calories—in order that you, Arke, by a gate in Leszno Street should munch on a cucumber you found, which someone lost, or threw down for you.

Bracketed ellipses indicate indecipherable parts of the original manuscript.

What? It's impossible to [. . .]?° Oh, if you only tried . . . if you only tried . . . if you only tried to beg. The first housewife that comes along . . . make a piteous face. . . . So what? Better people than you are out begging. Should I list them for you? You don't want to? Then, don't! If you don't want to, you don't have to—he stopped at L[. . .].

You feel that today you have fallen a step lower. Oh, yes, that's how it had to begin. All these people around you, apparently, began like that. You're on your way [. . .] The second soup—what will it be tomorrow?

It's getting dark. The darkness thickens; you could cut it with a knife. It would be good to buy some bread now, it's cheaper. It would! A round-bellied prostitute gives irises to two of her friends. On their lime-white faces, all skin and bone, the rouge and color on their spear-sharp eyebrows look ghostly.

A small group of people stand on the sidewalk and look across at the other side, from where a long beam of light falls. It's the children's hospital. Low down, on the first floor, in a wide, high window, a large electric lamp hangs over a table. A short woman in a white mask moves something very quickly with her hands. Around her, other women, also in masks. A calm hurry. And everything—to the table, to the one who lies on the table. An operation. You've never seen one before. At the movies, in a book, in the theater, yes, but in life, no. Strange, isn't it? You've lived some thirty-odd years, seen so much—and now you're seeing an operation for the first time; and it has to be in the *ghetto!* But why, why? Why save? Why, to whom, to what is the child being brought back?

And suddenly you remember that dead Jew, whom you nearly tripped over today. What's more, you now see him more clearly than before, when you were actually looking at him. Somewhere, years ago, there was a mother who fed him and, while cleaning his head, knew that her son was the cleverest, the most talented, the most beautiful. Told her aunt, her neighbors his funny sayings. Sought and delighted in every feature in which he resembled his father, his father. And the word *Berishl* was not just a name to her, but an idea, the content of a life, a philosophy. And now the brightest and most beautiful child in the world lies in a strange street, and his name isn't even known; and there's a stink, and instead of his mother, a brick kisses his head and a drizzling rain soaks the well-known newspaper around his face. And over there, they're operating on a child, just as if this hadn't happened, and they save it; and below, in front of the gate stands the mother, who knows that her Berishl is the cleverest and the most beautiful and the most talented—Why? For whom? For whom?

And suddenly (you—a grown, tall man, a male) you feel a quiver in your cheek, in your hands, all over your body. And your eyes become so rigid, so glassy. Yes, that's how it must be. This is the sign—you understand?—the equation, the eternal Law of Life. Maybe you are destined now, of all times, in your last days, to understand the meaning of this meaninglessness that is called life, the *meaning of your hideous, meaninglessly hungry days.* An eternal law, an eternal machine: death. Birth, life. Life. Life. Life. An eternal, eternal law. An eternal, eternal process. And a kind of clarity pours over your neck, your heart. And your two propellers no longer spin round in one spot—they walk, they walk! Your legs carry you, just as in the past! Just as in the past!

Somewhere a clock is striking dully: one, two, half past. Four-thirty, three-thirty, five-thirty? I don't know. Here there is no sunrise. The day comes to the door like a beggar. The days are already shorter. But I—I, like the fall, autumnal, foggy dawns. Everything around you becomes so dreamy, lost in thought, longing, serious, blue-eyed, concentrated in itself. Everything—people, the world, clouds— draws away somewhere, prepares for something responsible that carries a yoke, something that connects everything together. The gray patch that stands in the corner of the room with open arms—that's the *new day.* Yesterday I began to write your experiences. From the courtyard came the shouts of the air-raid wardens telling people to turn out the light. There's a smell of *cholent.* How come? It's Thursday, not the Sabbath [. . .]. A forest, a river, the whistle of a train, an endless golden field. Kuzmir, Tatrn[. . .]. The Lithuanian border. This longing, this wound will never go away, it will stay forever, even if today, tomorrow should once again [. . .]. Let it be in the city itself, go, go—go forever, without stopping, at least see the bank of the Vistula, at least see just the city. The city that you know. The happiness of quickly turning a corner, then [. . .] the hundredth. With an open jacket, with happy, swift steps. *Your city,* your second mother, your great, eternal love. The longing pierces your heart. It remains.

Somewhere they are typing [. . .]. They're reporting. It is reported from Brussels . . . Belgrade, Paris. Yes, yes, we're eating grass. Yes, we're falling in the streets without a word of protest—we wave our hands like this, and fall [. . .]. Each day the profiles of our children, of our wives, acquire the mourning look of foxes, dingoes, kangaroos. Our howls are like the cry of jackals. Our hymn, *papierosy, papierosy* (cigarettes, cigarettes) is like something from a nature reserve, a zoo. But we are not animals. We operate on our infants. It may be pointless or even criminal. But animals do not operate on their young!

Tokyo. Hong Kong. Vichy. Berlin. General number of enemy losses: six thousand eight hundred and forty-nine. Stockholm. Washington. Bangkok. The world's turning upside down. A planet melts in tears. And I—I am hungry, hungry. I am hungry.

Warsaw ghetto, August 1941
(Ringelblum Archive, Part 1, no. 1486)

75 Scroll of Agony

CHAIM A. KAPLAN

November 13, 1941

The journal is my life, my companion and my confidant. Without it I would be lost. In it I pour out all my heart's feelings, until I feel somewhat relieved. When I am angry and irritable and my blood boils; when I am full of reproach and bitterness because I have so little strength and capacity to fight the vicious waves that threaten to engulf me; when my hands tremble with inner feeling—I take refuge in the journal and am immediately enwrapped in the inspiration of the *Shekhinah* of creativity, though I doubt whether the task of documentation with which I am occupied is worthy of being called "creativity." In the future let them evaluate it as they may: the main point is that I find repose for my soul in it, and that is enough for me.

Why am I angry? Typhus has attacked my home too: my wife has contracted that dread disease. Her life is in great danger, and I must save her. Our material means are limited, infinitesimal. Only with great difficulty did I manage to earn a day's sustenance in normal times. In times of danger, when physicians, medics and all sorts of healers frequent your house, and you must spend more than a hundred zlotys a day on them, my strength is insufficient. And there is no help on the side. The Joint [Distribution Committee] community fund and other social welfare institutions are open to but a few, to those close to them, to bootlickers, to the Director's lackeys who submit to his ways. And what am I? I have no foothold there. So, with my meager forces, I bear and suffer the expenses of the illness, which must also be concealed from strangers' eyes, because it's a contagious disease and those who have caught it are forbidden to stay in a private house. In addition to all that, I am alone and bereft in my troubles. My sons are in the Land of Israel, and I am in exile. There is no one to nurse the patient, whose illness is severe and demands care day and night. Therefore, you need a nurse, a "sister of mercy," for whose pains you must pay a hundred and twenty zlotys a day. The cost of medicines has increased sevenfold, and the Judenrat imposed a surtax of twenty-five percent on their high price, for its coffers. And the main point is—the patient, who feels, as she says, the approach of death. Her sighs and moans tear at my heart. She is certain that the thread of her life will be severed in just an hour, two hours, that her minutes are numbered, and she will never see her children again. Though the danger to her life is great, and she is close to the portals of death, she is conscious and her mind is clear. Therefore, she realizes and understands that she is about to die. I console and soothe her, but only outwardly. Sometimes suspicion creeps into my heart that the patient knows her condition with more certainty than the doctor. Now the evil tidings of Job are reaching the city. In town it is said that the disease is laying low hundreds of patients daily.

My brain teems with but a single thought: whence will come my aid? It plots stratagems for finding money. What valuable thing remains in my possession that I can sell and get some decent sum for? During the two years of the war my possessions have become almost completely depleted. One by one I have sold them to evade the disgrace of hunger. With a sinking heart I removed them from my house and accepted mere pennies for them, for woe to man and object when there is need or necessity to bring it out to the marketplace for sale. "Bad, bad!" says the buyer, valuing it seven times less than what you reckoned while you sat at home. With pain in your heart you place the beloved object in a stranger's hands, and in return you receive a few crumpled bills, which bring you slight relief for a few days, for in the meanwhile the prices have soared, and the money melts away between your fingers. But there's no choice. The danger of death lurks at the head of the patient's bed. At moments like that you repress all kinds of sentiments.

But before my weary brain can labor and choose some object, a dark, cloudy autumn night spreads its wings over the ghetto dwellers. With evening comes darkness, and the ghetto then becomes a city of madmen and lunatics. The darkness is double: no light outside for fear of air attack. The gas lamps are not lit. Shop windows are extinguished. Shutters are sealed over doors. Quite simply, as *Exod. 10:21.* it is written: "a darkness that can be touched."° Inside the houses there is no spark of light: at midnight the electric current is cut off, and a watery tallow candle that melts and drips when it smells fire replaces it. To go out at night in darkness such as that is to risk mortal danger. People collide and crash into each other, and they are left wounded and bruised. This is no time to settle your affairs, whether buying or selling. You must put everything off till morning light. By the dim light of the candle the night shadows thicken. You are completely sunk in thoughts and shadows. The silence of the ghetto in the darkness increases the fear of night, full of secrets and hints. In my room there is no living being except the patient with her burning fever and death lying in wait for her.

Deut. 28:67 (1).   " 'If only it were morning!' "°

November 18, 1941

Warsaw is depressed and wrapped in deep mourning. But it is no ceremonial mourning with only the outward trappings, lacking heartfelt grief. On the contrary, if we could, we would weep bitterly, and our cry would rise to the high heavens. Were it not for fear of the evil kingdom, our wailing would burst forth in the dark alleys, and we would cry and weep and wail dreadfully for our calamity, as vast as the sea. But because of the sword, drawn and waiting for our plaint to lop off our heads—our grief does not break out. Our hearts—are our graves.

Group by group the Jews of the ghetto, shrunken, shriveled and frozen with frost, shadow Jews whose flesh cries emaciation, and the bones of whose faces jut out like skeletons, deathly ill, worn down and wretched in their great poverty, the hardships of displacement, wandering and expulsions—they stand next to a red proclamation signed by the commissar of the ghetto, [Heinz] Auerswald, in which there is official notice that because of the "sin" of crossing the border of the ghetto illegally, eight Jews were caught and tried, and all were condemned to death. The sentence was carried out yesterday, November 17, 1941. . . .

See here: simple Jewish women died to sanctify the name of God like heroines of the human spirit. One of them was a young maiden less than eighteen years old. In her innocence she asked a Jewish policeman, who was present when she was murdered, to tell her family that she had been sent to a concentration camp and would not see them again soon. Her companion proclaimed out loud, before her death, that she begged the God of Israel that her death be an atonement for her people, and that she might be the last victim.

Jacob Lejkin, who became head of the Jewish Police in May 1942 and was shot by the Jewish underground in October 1942.

While they were being murdered, a representative of the Jewish prison on Zamenhofa Street, Mr. Lejkin,° was present, and a deputation from the Jewish police. Their task was to bring the condemned people to the gallows, to bind their eyes and tie their hands. The men were unwilling to die with their eyes closed and hands tied. Their wish was not honored. The ones who shot them were Polish policemen, and after committing the act of murder, they wept with great emotion.

Oh earth! Do not hide my blood!! If there is a God to judge the land—may He come and take revenge!!!

December 2, 1941

Here, a pejorative name for Jewish assimilationists.

"The Kingdom of Israel" was the magic slogan for the Revisionists. But if those who used that enchanting rallying cry, "the Kingdom of Israel," could have known how it would be implemented in life by the Jews of Poland, by the *shmendriks*° from the brothels who came to power, they would not have inscribed it on their banner even as a propaganda measure. The Nazis, wishing to bedeck us with shame before the entire world, to show our baseness and the abysmal level of our culture, granted us broad "autonomy," almost a "state," as it were. They granted us that "privilege" with the premeditated intent to prove how incapable we are of being our own masters and to reveal our corrupt nature and our desire, stamped in our blood, to do injustice even to our brethren, not only in religion and race, but also in grief and disaster.

True, only a caricature of autonomy was granted us, and not out of excessive affection, but rather out of excessive hatred, the main point of which is only to separate the Jews from the nations, to undermine our material and spiritual existence, to hem in our steps, to have us perish slowly. In essence it is no more than a stillborn child lacking the power to flourish and grow, a sickly administrative and political creature lacking true vitality. By its principles and foundations it would seem to be only the kind of "self-rule" that prisoners have in a jail where some will be hanged and others will die a degraded death from exhaustion. That is known to everyone.

Nevertheless, if only we could be not just brethren in race and religion but also in suffering: were we truly a single national unit, at least during the violent persecution that has come upon us to extirpate us from the land of the living, we could use that tool called "autonomy" (i.e., the ghetto) to ease our sufferings and gain some relief under the unbearably difficult conditions of the ghetto. After all, the entire administration is in our hands, and we have the right to shape its inner form as we wish. It is precisely in that regard that we have gone bankrupt. Without exaggeration I may call it the government of evil, a band of villains, murdering the poor and oppressing the needy; the cronies of unjust wrongdoers, each one of whom has an unsavory past, and as types they are little more than criminals who have not yet been brought to trial. At the very mention of the word *rulers* (i.e., the Judenrat), helpless rage makes our blood boil and our fists tighten of themselves. The rulers have become the symbol of tyrannical injustice; and the leaders— the symbol of bullies and ruffians.

At the first opportunity, not one stone will remain upon another of the building

*Office of the
Judenrat.*

at 26 Grzybowska Street,° which has become the headquarters of injustice and tyranny, a den of robbers and evildoers.

And if a prophet lived among us to reprimand us, he would raise his voice against them:

————Why do you oppress my people?!

And his voice would be heard from one end of the earth to the other. From the depths of our troubles we would be consoled at once: "Their day shall come too!" They will not be immune forever. Together with the Nazi they will be undone, and the property of strangers that they have swallowed—they will vomit it forth.

Thus the masses console themselves when they are aroused. But the wisest among them know it is merely a vain consolation. At the time they agree, but in their hearts they think differently.

A joke is making the rounds:

Two degenerates from the Judenrat are talking with each other, and in the midst of their friendly conversation, one starts threatening the other with "What will happen."

*Used here as a
name typically
adopted by
assimilated Jews.*

"Money won't help on judgment day! Sigmund!° Think of your end! Beware of the anger of the mob and its rage!"

But Sigmund has no fear, answering:

"You fool! When the earth is overturned and the order of life changes, then I'll be up on top, not down below."

I suspect he spoke the truth. In the end, not a hair of his head will come to grief. . . .

In my coming notes I shall tell posterity something of the deceptions of the rulers and their abominations.

*A born "Litvak"
(Lithuanian Jew,
with a rationalist
bent) from the
Russian-speaking
part of the Pale,
Kaplan apparently
felt himself
alienated from the
Hasidic, Polish-
speaking city of
Warsaw. In the
ghetto, he stood
apart both from
the Judenrat and
from the "counter-
community."*

I'm not an insider; on the contrary, I come from outside.° It could be—that's my advantage. Their "fine" deeds and straight rules are known to me by rumor, and some facts I was an eyewitness to. I cling to a great general principle: The voice of the people is like the voice of the Lord!

December 3, 1941

————When the Jewish representative body was appointed, we were certain we would find shelter from our troubles in it, that it would extend a brotherly hand, alleviate our suffering, that even in the difficult, bitter times it is subject to, it would do everything in its power to bring balm and healing to our wounds. The huge and dreadful trouble that has befallen us has made everyone equal, without any exception: for nothing makes for common feelings so much as shared trouble. It increases sentiments of mercy, love and solidarity in times of trouble, even among strangers who are not brothers by blood and origin. So much the more so among those who are brethren, members of a single people, related in flesh and spirit.

However, Polish Jewry did not behave thus. Therefore—eternal shame shall be its lot.

An alien power coming from the outside assembled the *shmendriks* among us and appointed them leaders over us. They are half-, third- or quarter-assimilated circles. In peacetime they did not wish to know us and confined themselves to their own Jewish-goyish society, insulting and insulted at the same time: they themselves reviled the Jewish *holota* [mob in Polish], and their gentile neighbors also included them in their hatred and contempt. The Jewish community has not yet acknowledged them. They were strangers to their people, its spirit and its culture. Perhaps even more than strangers: there was hatred in them for everything that could be called by the name of Judaism. Their opposition to the Jewish masses did not derive from an ideological opposition, for they had no ideology at all aside from materialism.

And those "gentlemen," once they were appointed the heads of the Judenrat, began to trample our heads with exceptional brutality. And since the day the ghetto was established a wide-ranging and extensive network of great enterprises has been set up, such as the Jewish police, the ghetto food supply department, the housing agency, the post office, the internal administrative body, the representation for external relations, the primary schools, health matters and in general: all sorts of official functions—they have a vast field for enriching themselves by taking bribes and by favoritism. Those in the know concur, saying that the corruption within the Judenrat has reached a level unprecedented in the entire world. It is beholden to no one except the commandant of the ghetto, who himself is a partner in all the conspiracies formed at the expense of the oppressed masses gripped in a material and spiritual vise like incarcerated prisoners helpless to free themselves. When times improve, certainly trustworthy people will emerge and tell coming generations what must be told on the basis of documentation and exact statistics.

January 7, 1942

"Whatever is on land is also in the sea." That is true of the ghetto, on the one hand, and of all nature, on the other. Everything found in the wide world of nature is found on a small scale in the narrow, confined ghetto. There is penury and poverty and, in contrast, wealth and plenty. The Nazi overlord acts according to this rule: whoever makes the great equal the small misses the mark. The means of destruction do not have a uniform effect throughout all ranks of the ghetto. There is a certain percentage of ghetto residents who become wealthy and have secured a life of sustenance, perhaps even a life of ease, and that is because they trade on their brothers' distress. There is one great principle of life: no one has a misfortune that does not benefit someone else. The all-embracing restrictions that most of the residents of the ghetto cannot tolerate have produced a full complement of smugglers and practical men who risk their money and lives, amassing fortunes that permit them to enjoy the pleasures of life. Two leeches suck our marrow: the Nazi leech, the elite of the elites and the primum mobile, the first "father" in setting up the machinery to make us perish and suck our blood; and its spawn—the Jewish leech, born of contraband and price gouging. Despite draconian measures, smuggling does not cease. Even the danger of death does not restrain it. Rather, as those means become more severe and harsh, they drive up prices. Every price rise increases the extent of the profits. That is in reference to the large-scale smugglers who are in cahoots with the Nazis and share their spoils with them. No eye oversees their misdeeds, and they have permission to set prices as they see fit. Everything depends on their hard hearts and avid greed for wealth.

That is human nature: in a crisis the urge grows stronger: "Eat and drink, for tomorrow we die!"°

The ranks for whom dollars are valued as pennies seek pleasure and pursue

Isa. 22:13.

the pleasures of life. Therefore, the ghetto is full of luxuries: but only the minority enjoy them. The shop windows are cluttered with all sorts of pastries and delicacies that ony a small percentage buys and eats their fill of. Places of entertainment have been established in the ghetto, full to the brim every evening, with every seat taken. Someone who didn't know, for example, that his feet were standing on the earth of the ghetto, if he were to enter the luxurious pastry shops and look at the well-dressed crowd enjoying the sounds of music and, with great pleasure, drinking coffee and other expensive beverages, every sip of which costs several zlotys— he could not imagine that those guests were life's outcasts, lacking elementary human rights. He would not notice that until he went outside. Upon leaving, he would trip over a dead body at the entrance, a victim of starvation!——

February 2, 1942

One trouble is unlike the next. The latest is the gravest. We have a motto: "If only the present condition would not worsen!" We always feel that the murderous eyes of robbers are staring at us and casting their venom upon us. At all times we are prepared for some new evil decree. Passive preparedness lightens the oppressiveness of the decree once it has come. We are immune to surprise. Occasionally the Jews themselves imagine that some strange, psychopathic decree will be imposed on them. When you first hear of it you are surprised: "Is it possible?" But after a few moments you say, "It is possible, quite possible." For that reason the decrees no longer terrify us. "Come what may, we shall not be wiped out of this land!"

But in recent days dreadful, horrifying rumors have been oppressing our spirits. Even the ghetto dwellers, inured to suffering, are struck by them. In essence each evil decree only sets difficult living conditions, ordered by unjust laws; nevertheless, it contains some legality, for in the end a hard life is still life; especially for a group that has always lived a life of grief and humiliation.

But the recent rumors are different, for if they have even a bit of truth to them, they are no longer in the category of decrees but have become physical destruction, extinction, bitter death. It is hard to assess their truth. But we are sure of one thing: even if they are exaggerated, there is a little truth to them, and that "little" is sufficient.

The *Führer* has ceased legislating evil decrees against us, which it irks him to enforce and implement in life, as the adversary discovers subterfuges to negate and annul them. He has condemned an entire nation to death. Not by starvation, not even by contagious diseases and not even by expulsions and conversion,° but simply by shooting. There is no need for legal authorization and all the other illusions that go along with it. Rather you take thousands of people out of the city and shoot them to death—and that's the end of it.

The rumors make our blood freeze:

In Vilna forty thousand Jews were shot to death without any trial or judgment, without even a legal pretext, and the remainder—their number comes to ten thousand four hundred.

In Slonim a Nazi was killed by someone; the living Nazis knew very well that no Jewish hand was involved in that killing. But it provided them a broad field for blood libel. Thus outside the city eight thousand Jews were shot to death.

In Kleck—the flying rumor continues—of all the Jewish inhabitants of the city,

° The Hebrew is unclear.

only six families are left. And that is the same in the other cities of Lithuania and the Ukraine. The Nazi comes and holds a massacre—and the Jewish question is solved.

That "solution" hits the target. Those rumors exaggerated their evidence; therefore, we took them to be mere tales up to now, created by popular imagination and therefore excessive and overblown. Disastrously for us, recently we have witnessed dreadful facts such as those in the Generalgouvernement,° too:

Not expulsion, not even epidemic, but physical shooting to death. Any accusation is superfluous. Whole groups are taken to slaughter only because they are Jews. Whole towns have been wiped out by killing and slaughter in a fashion barbaric beyond all the murders and slaughters that have taken place in world history. We have become like sheep to be slaughtered. . . .

Yesterday we read the speech of the *Führer* commemorating the date of January 30, 1933. In that speech he proudly said that his prophecy has begun to be fulfilled: from the beginning he said that if war broke out in Europe, the Jewish race would be extirpated from it. *That process has already begun and will continue until it reaches its conclusion.* He has condemned all the Jews of Europe to physical death on the basis of the law of their doctrine: "Eye for an eye!" "Tooth for a tooth," "Arm for an arm," "Leg for a leg." That is a kind of justification before the entire world. But in particular that gives us an indication that the horrors being reported are not mere rumors but real and true facts. The Judenrat and the Joint have documents indicating the new direction taken by Nazi policy regarding the Jews in conquered areas: death by the sword, the physical murder and destruction of whole groups of Jews.

Till now we were afraid of being deported. Now we are afraid of death. Moreover, the signs of deportation are becoming clearer:

The Judenrat is arranging a census of the Jews in the ghetto. By January 31, 1942, every one of the residents of the ghetto is required to fill in a questionnaire with his name and his parents' names; whether he is the head of a family; his address in Warsaw before the war broke out, his present address; his profession before September 1, 1939, and his present profession.—

Is there no catastrophe lurking in that whole census?

The refugees from other cities say that in their towns, too, the tortures of deportation began with such a census. In the meanwhile—fear and trembling have seized us.

Here we are: "an anguished heart and eyes that pine and a despondent spirit!"°

March 7, 1942

After the first reduction [in the area of the ghetto] the Gęsia Street Cemetery was removed from the Jewish zone. Legally, therefore, no Jew may set foot there, living or dead. Geographically, it is beyond the wall dividing Jews and Aryans. But in fact it was impossible to forbid the burial of Jewish dead there, because the sanitary situation demands that the cemetery be placed outside the city. The ghetto is completely surrounded by a wall within a wall, and it is against the law to breach them and lay the Aryan side open to the entry and exit of the Jewish dead and their funeral parties.

Therefore, they chose the lesser evil. They passed an emergency regulation

The area of Poland under German civilian administration, established October 1939.

Deut. 28:65 (1).

permitting the continuation of Jewish burials outside the area; but the restrictions are well known: simply entering the cemetery is strictly forbidden; anyone wishing to enter may do so only after buying a ticket for two and a half zlotys, a new source of decent revenue for something so intimate and familial as a funeral. That caused the number of those attending to decrease to the minimum. First—they spare themselves the small expense, and second—you must pass through two sets of guards, German and Jewish, who watch every step you take and give you evil looks, for they suspect you haven't come here for a funeral but rather for smuggling. Even the slightest suspicion will bring down such evil upon you that you won't be able to extricate yourself. If you watch yourself, you'll stay away. And perhaps, retrospectively—it's better that not many people attend funerals. For if they came in multitudes there would be no possibility of carrying out jobs decently. To bury two hundred corpses a day—that's no small matter!! A long line of wagons extends along Gęsia Street, and each one brings not just a single person to the gates of death but several in one trip. Within the wagon there is barely room to squeeze in four bodies; and if there is a fifth, they place it on top of the flat roof. If there is a coffin—fine: they put him in the coffin, whether it is open or closed; if there's no coffin—they lay him on his back and tie him so he won't slide out; and even if he's lying on his back, tied, they don't take care that he be covered.

Simply a dead man, just as he is, without even a paper shroud, lying on his back on the roof of the wagon, and no one feels the indignity. When the wagons enter the gates of death, they begin to remove the bodies, and anyone who has not seen that with his own eyes has never seen ugliness in his life. Anyone who wishes for a life with some spiritual repose should avoid coming here and looking at all the "*Betrieb*" [business] of this slaughterhouse for human beings.

Mostly naked corpses are removed from the wagons, without even a paper loincloth to cover their private parts. I was stunned at that ugly sight, which made me feel that simple human dignity had been insulted, the dignity of man. I was so disgusted that physically I had to vomit. Full of anger, I addressed one of the workers: How can this be? But he actually got furious at me and nearly reviled me: "Have you fallen to earth from the sky? Is there cloth for shrouds for two hundred corpses a day? And if there is? Who can afford to buy it? A meter of cloth is worth its weight in gold; the wealthy give white sheets instead of cloth, but not always, because they hide them for sale when bad times come. 'Paper,' you might say. There hardly is any to be found. It went up in price, and the average person can't afford enough to bury even one of the dead members of his family. It's wartime, a hard, bitter time. We are in an emergency! The dead will forgive us! Isn't it the same to them? Just as the dead man's flesh can't feel the scalpel, it can't feel its nakedness."

I was left speechless. . . .

The dead brought to burial are divided into three classes. The highest class are those who die and are brought to the purification room near the cemetery. The crowding and shoving are unimaginable. Sometimes two or three are laid on the same sheet. But in praise of the dead let it be said that they are peaceable and calm, and it has yet to happen that one rose up and said, "This place is too narrow!"

The second highest class is those who were cleansed of their disease at home, and most of them are dressed in shrouds made of white sheets, and the men are wrapped in their prayer shawls. They are laid on litters for the dead standing ready in the courtyard of the cemetery by the dozen, and no place is free of them. By their side stand the mourners, weeping and waiting their turn; by the way: a good watch is kept against theft; for if one doesn't keep a good eye out, the prayer shawl disappears in the wink of an eye. Those two classes are buried in individual graves. Those dead are privileged to receive a decent burial, a great privilege in times like these.

The third class is the dead, victims of hunger and epidemic—the majority—gathered up in the streets of the ghetto, who went to their deaths outdoors in the ghetto, who perished in the hospitals, who died of hunger in some attic, in general the children of indigence and poverty, who have no one to labor in their behalf and bring each one to burial in his own individual grave. Dead of that sort are brought to burial in a huge, deep mass grave, just as they are: naked, without purification, without planks. For that "elite" no individual funerals are held for each one. Their burial is, after all, a wholesale business. What were formerly the stables of the cemetery have become chambers for the dead. They're thrown there like the carcasses of animals. Body after body of the departed, laid one on top of the other. In such positions, insulting the humane feelings within you, half breaking your body. The impression crushes your breath from you like a vise. Is that man and his end? A living man is unlike a dead one in his ugliness. Ugliness that has some movement is relative ugliness; still ugliness, with no movement, is absolute ugliness. Then man is revealed in all his nothingness and weakness.

Dead of that sort accumulate during the day by the dozens and dozens. Like dung they pile up in the stables waiting for burial till they reach the grave digger's quota. The dawn is still spread over the new cemetery annexed to the left side of the old one, behind the stables. That is an enormous, square grave, nearly fifty meters by fifty meters in length and breadth; and in depth—ten meters. There they are brought down a wooden ladder leaning on the lip of one end of the pit. Down that ladder they are brought to their eternal rest one by one. A thin layer of dust is spread over them, which does not cover them, so that limbs reach out and protrude. But not for long. The next morning new corpses are lowered, laid down, and "buried" in the same fashion. Row after row; layer upon layer. One need fear no strife among the brethren buried together, perish the thought. They lived in darkness, they went to death in darkness and in darkness they were "buried."° No one knows of their grave.

Paraphrase of "Bontshe the Silent" by I. L. Peretz.

But the day will come when the Jewish people will raise a permanent memorial upon that very mass grave.———

March 22, 1942

———The light of springtime has come to the world, and our heavens are covered with clouds. Evil hours have come such as never were even under the Nazis. Wonder of wonders: the evil decrees have been silenced, but a dreadful evil awaits us worse than any decree. It has not yet come, but with all our senses and emotions we feel its impending arrival. The echo of its footsteps almost reaches our ears. Is there no illusion here?

Horrible, dreadful rumors are passed on in whispers, taking one form and another, depending on the spirit of the one reporting. We feel that someone alien, tyrannical and dreadful has unsheathed his sword to decapitate us, but all his preparations are made behind our backs, so we see the movements of the murderer only in our mind's eye, not with eyes of flesh.

I wish I were imagining things, but I am not free to refrain from writing them down:

The first rumor. The deportation of Lublin has taken place, about a hundred thousand Jews were placed in closed railroad cars sealed with the Nazi seal and, under the supervision of Nazi overseers, they were brought . . . where? No one knows. Thus the Jewish community of Lublin has passed away and been removed from the face of the earth. The proof: they tried to speak with the Lublin Judenrat by telephone, but that request was denied, because "There no longer is such a Jewish institution in Lublin." Once again they tried to telephone a private person, and he answered briefly: "My wife and I are living!"

It is clear: some disaster has befallen our brothers in Lublin. But its character and extent are unknown to us.

A second rumor: in Rodno the entire Jewish community was executed. Not a single living soul is left. Why and wherefore? No one knows. Some advance a theory that has a certain foundation—in obedience to the decree of the *Führer*—to bring destruction upon the Jews of Europe. Once more: there is no smoke without fire! The Jews of Rodno have undergone a dreadful trial. But who will rush in and tell us what it is?

A third rumor: it is strange and inconceivable, though one may count on the Nazis to do even the strangest things. It happened in Zdunska Wola. There the Nazis took revenge upon the Jews for the ten sons of Haman who were hanged. They therefore summoned the Judenrat and ordered it to provide a list of ten Jews of the community to be hanged in revenge for the ten sons of Haman. And if not, the members of the Judenrat would take their places. The list was given, and ten Jews were hanged.

Can it be believed? There are arguments on both sides. But one thing is absolutely certain: it is not impossible! We are dealing with Nazis!

March 23, 1942

From flying rumors I shall pass to facts. Here our torture stands out in its full horror. It is known that Litzmanstadt (formerly Lodz) has been sanctified with extreme "holiness" and now has the same legal status as the "Reich," which Jewish feet are forbidden to tread, and special laws are in force there regarding inferior races of men, that is to say: Poles and Jews. The Poles too are deprived of full and complete civil rights; but their deprivation is secondary, the Nazis acknowledge their second-class citizenship, but not so the Jews! They were deprived of their citizenship and all the rights pertaining to it. Furthermore, not only does the law not defend their lives and property, but it is a national duty to do away with them and divest them of their possessions. And no means is more extreme in depriving and impoverishing the Jew than deportation. This must be known: the Nazi deportations are unlike the historical expulsions we have read about in the pages of our history; not even those executed by cruel Tsarism. Then they would tell the Jew who was about to be expelled: "Give me your soul, and keep your property, and if you value your soul—take both your soul and your property and leave here." The Nazi repeatedly says: "Take your soul and give me your property!"

The first major deportation, of 10,000 Jews, from the Lodz ghetto took place from January 16–29, 1942. See 91

The administration of Lodz decided to abolish the ghetto in two or three days.° That is always its way, to surprise the wretched deportees and cast confusion in their ranks; and the main point is that they not manage to remove their property in the time of emergency, so that the regime will be the "legal" inheritor. In line with that custom it called upon the Chairman of the Judenrat, Chaim Rumkowski, decreeing with the full severity of the law, that he was required to abolish the ghetto in two or three days. Immediately after the announcement it began its thievish work: it stole all the cash from the council treasury (estimated at two million zlotys) and plundered all the food supplies and all the raw material that had been brought in to sustain the ghetto. The hand that had given returned to take away. The deportation began. The details of it are not well known to me, because I am far from the scene of the deed. Now Lodz is tantamount to foreign soil, and there is no contact between it and the other Jewish settlements in the Generalgouvernement. The local chroniclers will certainly record them in full detail for coming generations. Here I only emphasize the existence of the signs of that dread decree. Now the post office no longer sends letters from Jews to the inhabitants of the Lodz ghetto, as if they no longer were living. And letters from there no longer arrive here. All one can do is request information about the relatives of people in Warsaw° using a printed form not signed by the one making the request but by the head of the Judenrat, so apparently there is still some slender remnant awaiting sentence. That, then, is the end of the splendid city of Lodz!!

This phrase can also read: "All one can do is request help from relatives in Warsaw. . . ."

And Lwow preceded its condemned sisters.

There a slow but systematic expulsion began. There is no ghetto there because it wasn't worthwhile taking the trouble for a short time. In a short while the Jewish settlement in that populous city will disappear. Before my eyes I have a letter announcing that every day one thousand one hundred Jews from Lwow are being deported. Before many weeks pass, the Jewish community of Lwow will pass from the face of the earth. That is the end of Lwow, a thriving Jewish city, which, when it flourished, was a center of Torah study and the Enlightenment for the Jews of Galicia. The end has come to its Jewish existence! The synagogue of Lwow was devoured by fire.——

April 6, 1942

——This week, under the supervision of Nazi policemen and gendarmes, a total of 2,600 "Jewish" citizens of Germany were brought to Warsaw to leave them . . . Where? Apparently in the ghetto, but for the moment they have been left outside the ghetto. In general, they received a different kind of "escort" than, for example, the deportees from Danzig a year ago. With the Danzig deportees, the full weight of the law was enforced. Weary and worn out, tortured by the trip and overcome with troubles, they were thrown into the ghetto without any support or sustenance. At first they still resembled human beings. True, they knew their path was strewn with thorns and briars and their future boded ill. However, immediately upon their arrival they were considered to be people who had lost their fortune, but not all their property.

Some of them, before setting out, had smuggled valuables away beneath the murderers' eyes, managing to put aside something for bad times. But that situation did not last. From week to week they declined further and further. Lacking livelihood and left alone in foreign surroundings, they ate up the remnant of their money and became utter beggars. Hunger brought epidemics, bereavement and widowhood upon them. Many of them died during the year, and some of them are still living a life of shame and humiliation till death has mercy upon them. The *Führer* achieved his goal: he brought havoc and destruction upon an entire Jewish community.

The "Jewish" deportees from Germany got a different reception this week.

It is noteworthy how they behaved: the Gestapo greeted them with flowers; they took the trip in Pullman cars, so no signs of the discomforts of travel were visible on them. Their countenance was that of superior folk—fat and lively. Dressed elegantly. In short: aristocratic exiles. Not only that—it is also said—the Poles, too, expressed warm sympathy for their fate and offered them food and flowers. The main point is—they were not considered by the Nazis as polluted people who must be driven from the camp. They remained in the Aryan quarter; apparently a ghetto within the ghetto will be prepared for them. Miserable exiles and fortunate at the same time. Who are they?

They are "half-Jews" according to the racial laws. Many of them were born as Christians, because their parents were apostates. Many of them were born to mixed marriages. Some of them have wives who are German by birth and origin. In short: they lived as complete goyim, true Germans who, before 1933, occupied high and exalted positions in all walks of life. Not only that, they absolutely hate Jews, and if their birth certificates had not betrayed them, they would observe the commandments of Nazism more scrupulously than true Germans. But there was one thorn in their sides: they all lack one generation of Christianity. As everyone knows: until the third generation no one of Jewish race can enter the congregation of Nazis. Nazi law terms them "half-Jews," and thus their formal status is their undoing.

In peacetime no harm was done to them for the sake of tranquillity. But we are in an hour of emergency. This is a moment of spiritual turmoil in Germany. Once aroused, the spirit cannot not be hemmed in. In the air—is political ferment. For the time being, the revolt is inward; if the situation is prolonged—a flame will shoot out. In conditions of life such as these, half-Jews must not remain in the heart of the German community. They are deeply esconced and cannot be prevented from arousing the German public to some active deeds. If they are of the seed of the Jews, they can be depended on for all kinds of treachery. "Throw a stick in the air—it falls on its root." Their Jewish blood has not yet been eradicated.

For that reason they have been condemned to exile. That is the judgment. The doctrine of Nazism and its severe ramifications are no longer acceptable and are already repulsive to the German people. That doctrine demands reinforcement according to the principle: "Let justice take its course!" Wherever there is suspicion of the desecration of Nazism, one must act with the full severity of the law. Therefore—out with them!

But their children—the third generation of Christians—and their wives have remained in Germany. And it is unjust to torment them. Thus they must act in this fashion here: the left hand repels, and the right hands draws in. The Jewish part of the body is driven out. The German part of the body is greeted with honor and affection.

Yes, Heine was right: "Judaism is not a religion but rather a tragedy"—a tragedy for generations.

April 17, 1942

Hearing about Lublin we were gripped by trembling. In danger of their lives a few refugees fled from that city of murder and came to the Warsaw ghetto. Their stories freeze the blood in your veins. Terrifying rumors had been common among the masses even before their arrival; but who believed them? We thought they had not been heard from reliable sources. Without newspapers, when everything is passed by word of mouth, every rumor is liable to be exaggerated. Experience has taught us that—but now eyewitnesses have arrived, those who were to be deported from their settlement. In the Warsaw ghetto there is a Lublin colony. The refugees were its guests and lecturers in a secret meeting held to seek a way of saving the remnant. What they reported was so dreadful and horrible that we nearly suspected that they too were exaggerating and overstating. For human beings created in God's image are incapable of such depravities.

But one way or another—it is a fact that reality has outdone imagination. Jewish Lublin, a city of sages and authors, a center of Torah and piety, was completely and utterly destroyed. An entire community of forty thousand Jews was uprooted and banished. Its institutions, synagogues and houses of study are gone from the earth—all its wealth has been confiscated, for its sons left it for exile as naked as the day of their birth. When the decree first burst upon them, forty thousand Jews were deported; about ten thousand remained. When the first fury had passed, they were almost certain they had reached a "safe haven." They would not be touched again. But once again Jewish confidence was disappointed. After a few days another decree was passed, that Lublin must be *Judenrein,* and the remaining Jews drank the poisonous draught. Today not a single Jewish footprint can be found in the city of [blank in original diary]. The walls of the house of study have been stained with innocent blood. The Judenrat was dissolved and deprived of all its rights; five of its members remained to guide the murderers in the process of liquidating the community. "They will be shot last!" the officer reassured them. Whoever expected such a dreadful calamity as that!

. . . The decree of expulsion came as a complete surprise to the Jews of Lublin; for in that city the government was not particularly oppressive toward the Jewish inhabitants—Nazism is not an egalitarian system, whether for evil or good. Its principle is—from everyone according to his ability. The local commander is omnipotent, and his opinion is decisive in every issue. It happened that the commander of Lublin and his advisers were rather easy on the local Jews. Apparently it was profitable to them to turn a blind eye. As much as local conditions permitted, the Jews engaged in commerce and manufacturing, and the Nazi overlords ignored them. Lublin was famous as a "Garden of Eden" for the Jews in comparison with Warsaw and Częstochow.

But the luck of the Lublin Jews turned, and the murderous Himmler came to visit. That visit brought their horrible disaster down upon them—the chief murderer gave the word: "The number of Jews in this border city is too great!" Besides, a typhus epidemic broke out there, taking more victims than usual in places where the Nazi sets foot. Typhus acknowledges no borders, and there is no escaping from it for anyone in its vicinity. The chief murderer envisioned great danger for the Aryan population.

Hence—deportation! Here he also took up the pretext of taking revenge for the German blood shed through the fault of the Jews of Russia and America, who called for war against the Nazis. The word of the chief killer went forth, and a massacre of the Jewish population was planned.

First of all, the killers broke into the hospitals and slaughtered all the dying patients—without them the exiles would find the trip easier. From there they went to the old people's home and butchered the old men and women; they simply stood them up in a row and used them as targets. Not one was left. That too would make the exiles' trip easier. Afterwards they murdered the children and babies, the abandoned orphans who had found refuge in the community orphanage, those whose parents had previously been killed by the murderers. Following all those "easements" they commenced great expulsion and slaughter. When the evil broke out, people started to slip away. Then the hunt began. They brought an additional disaster down upon the Jews of Lublin. Those who fled for their lives thought they could follow the prophet's advice, "Hide but a little moment/Until the indignation

Isa. 26:20.

passes."° Perhaps they will be spared! Perhaps the Guardian of Israel will have pity for them! But the killers discovered those hidden places, and anyone found in them was put to the sword. Some died of suffocation, because the doors weren't built to be opened from inside, and there was no one outside to open them. For all the members of the household had fled for their lives or been arrested to be deported.

When the hunt began, they gathered like dumb sheep led to the slaughter, herd by herd, thousands of Jews, who were taken. . . . Where? No living soul knows. That is the Nazi's way: He commits his abominations in darkness. There is no crack through which a ray of light might penetrate. Forty thousand oppressed Jews, weary, consumed, broken; bereft and abandoned by their families. Naked and penniless they were delivered to the Nazi overlords to be taken to some distant place of slaughter.

One rumor is afoot that they were brought to Rawa-Roska and there burned to death with electricity. They chose a good death for them. The murderers have the virtue of doing everything wholesale.

Immediately after the expulsion all possessions were removed from the depopulated houses, and after setting aside the valuable objects, they were burned. That was all done to serve two purposes at the same time: extirpation of the typhus epidemic and of the epidemic of the Jews.

So that is the end of Jewish Lublin!

I wrote the foregoing according to rumors I heard and the testimony of refugees from Lublin. Perhaps that is not carefully sifted historical evidence. But the general picture fits the historical truth.

April 18, 1942

The evening of the holy Sabbath, 1 [month missing], 5702, was a night of horror and dread in the miserable ghetto. The Nazis committed a massacre against the Jews, and much innocent blood was shed. Darkness covered the murderers' abominations, and aside from officers of the Jewish police force, no one was present at the time of the murder, though the echo of the shooting reached the ears of all the inhabitants of the ghetto in the silence of the night. Most people didn't know why or wherefore there was shooting. Only with the light of morning, when we found the victims at the gates of our houses, did we know that our calamity was as vast as the sea.

Just a day or two before the slaughter it was felt in the air of the ghetto that some catastrophe was in the offing. We sought confirmation in the events of Lublin. In what way is Warsaw favored over Lublin? The battle cry, "Destroy, murder, wipe out," was the same everywhere. Little Lublin was destroyed in a few days: Warsaw was larger and would be destroyed in a few weeks. Greater confirmation was given by rumors that began to spread, saying that the same battalion that had acted in Lublin was coming to carry out a massacre in Warsaw too.

In addition to what has been said, at this time, on the border between the ghetto and the Aryan quarter, a *Yonak* [hoodlum] was killed, a type of ruffian and bully who supported himself with theft and strong-arm methods. Some of them are Ukrainians and some are Germans. This time a German *Yonak* was killed, put to death by a violent villain like himself because of a smuggling dispute. His murderer was known to the authorities. But that didn't prevent them from concocting the false accusation that a Jewish hand was involved.

Therefore, our hearts prophesied some impending evil. A person's heart tells him, and that of a nation—even more so.

The night before the slaughter eighteen Jewish policemen who speak German well were summoned to accompany the murderers on their way. A secret movement arose in the ghetto, and in a whisper various words were passed. The Jewish policemen calmed the angry crowd, saying that not a hair on their heads would be harmed!

The killing began at midnight. Small groups of four murderers with lists in their hands started going from door to door, arresting those "condemned" to death, with a Jewish policeman showing them the way. They held pistols in their hands, and machine guns were strapped to their waists. They rang the bell at the gate. The porter would hurry to open the gate, and the murderers beat him shamefully, till his soul nearly fled. And if, for any reason, the porter tarried a little and didn't hurry to open the door in the wink of an eye, he was the first victim. In that fashion six porters fell on the night of the slaughter, though their names were not on the list prepared the day before. Here's something amazing: unlike their usual ways, they behaved with the requisite courtesy this time, saying "good evening" on their arrival and politely inviting the condemned man to come with them. On their way out to the courtyard a powerful searchlight lit up the darkness. Without any unnecessary delay they stood the condemned man up against the wall and put an end to his life with two or three shots. They left the body in the gate and immediately departed, hurrying on to a new killing.

How many squads of murderers like that dispersed throughout the ghetto to shed innocent blood? It's hard to say. But the total number of murders is known to us: fifty-two dead and twelve wounded! In the morning light their corpses were found splayed out in doorways. There was no trial or judgment. Officially they were not accused of any crime or sin—in darkness the list was prepared, and in darkness the sentences were executed. Not a living Jewish soul knows why, for what reason they were killed. . . .

76 4580

YEHOSHUE PERLE

A round number. At first glance it looks silly and seems to have no specific meaning. A detached number such as this can be likened to those gray people who go through life alone and die without confession.

But if an arithmetician or a stargazer were to take a good look at this number, he might arrive at some ingenious conjecture, or discover some esoteric numerological computation, from which fools would later infer either the Apocalypse or the Coming of the Messiah.

Sober minds, if they consider it, will probably take it to be the Identity Number of a policeman, a railroad porter, a prisoner or—pardon the proximity—a dog, or the devil knows what else. But that this foolish number should be a substitute for the name of a living person, who was never a policeman, a railroad porter, a prisoner or even a dog—that will be difficult to believe.

People will also not believe that great suffering and pain cry out from the number, and so does the disaster of the people from whom it is my lot to be descended.

And yet the impossible has become possible. It happened in the year 1942, in the month of Tishre, in the land of Poland, in the city of Warsaw. Under the savage rule of Amalek—may his name and memory be blotted out; with the consent of the Jewish *kehillah*—may its good deeds stand it in good stead in this world and in the next.

May it merit eternal life, the Warsaw Jewish *kehillah*. For it was the *kehillah* that favored me with the number: *four thousand five hundred and eighty*.° It was the *kehillah* that cut off my head—my name—and set a number in its place. I go around with it and live; it has become "me."

It may be worth recounting how I, a Jew, on a rainy day in Tishre, turned into a number. I won't brag. Like everyone else I entered the world headfirst and fell into it without a name. For eight whole days, in accordance with Jewish law, I lived not only without a name, but also without a number. Someone living in the year 1942 won't want to believe that, although I possessed no number, my dear mother was not afraid to hold me nor to give me warm milk from her beautiful breast. She was not afraid to warm me with her young body, to caress me, to worry over me, as a mother—and Jewish into the bargain—can worry over her firstborn son, the one who will recite the *Kaddish*.

Eight days later, as is the custom among Jews, they made a blessing over me and said: "May his name in Israel be, etc."

A person's name is like a living organism; it has flesh and blood. You can't feel it or see it, but you can't live without it. I wore it, this name of mine, as a lovely woman wears a still lovelier string of pearls. It was mine, entirely mine. I had, after all, inherited it from my grandfathers and great-grandfathers. I absorbed it, together with my mother's blood, together with the sweat of my overworked father.

Upon arrival in the Warsaw ghetto in 1941, Perle secured a job in the clothing department of the Judenrat run by Shmuel Winter. In 1942, again with Winter's help, Perle was joined to a shop of ersatz honey and candies, which exempted him from immediate deportation.

My name lived in the same house with me. Under the same roof, in the same bed. It was I, and I was it. It learned to walk with me, learned to speak, just as I did. If I was called, it pricked up both ears. If I suffered, it suffered too. It rejoiced with my joy, wept with my tears, laughed with my laughter and dreamed with my dreams.

But don't think that my name was a slave to me, that it didn't have a say and a will of its own. On the contrary, when I fell into a melancholy mood and started thinking about the world to come, my name asked to have *this* world. And just as my mother wished that I should survive her, so my name wanted to survive me.

I don't know and wouldn't swear that my life was rich with good deeds; I also don't know whether I was virtuous. I do know that when a wicked moment came upon me (for we are all but human) and I wanted to injure myself, my neighbor and my enemy—my name stood up and sternly warned me not to do it.

"You must not put me to shame," it said. "If people point their finger at you, their finger will reach me first. I am the phylactery on your forehead. Without me you may shout 'I am Solomon,'° and nobody will believe you. And if you want to know, I'll whisper a secret to you: I no longer belong only to you. Your life wanted me to be in the public domain. And if indeed I am in the public domain, no blemish may appear on me."

That's how my name spoke out. And I wouldn't be honest if I convinced myself that my name had no blemish at all. I lived with it for fifty-three years, kept pace with it for over fifty-three years. How could it be possible, in the course of half a century, for a person not to make one false step? My name was present. I saw it exposed to humiliation. I suffered with it and was silent. Not until later, when I realized that it wanted to survive me, did I make an effort for it to rise up.° And it rose and shone, just as my first new little gaberdine once shone, the coat that my father had sewn for me for Passover.

And let people interpret it as they wish. Let them say it is pride, self-delusion: my name also shone from *her*.° She loved both me and my name. Just as she bore with proud pleasure her majestic head of hair, so did she bear my name with proud pleasure. To her it was the loveliest, the cleverest. She caressed and drew it out. I often didn't recognize it, so strange did it sound. But when I heard it issuing from her pure lips, with all the delight she put into it, I heard it anew, fresh, bathed in her young laughter.

Cruel fortune willed that in her youth she should carry it with her to the grave. It lies there, together with my letters to her, which accompanied her as she had instructed. The name has turned to stone in the tablet that guards her grave. And I believe with absolute faith that, just as I cannot forget her name here, so she cannot forget my name there.

And can one forget one's own name? For fifty-three years it has grown with me, for fifty-three years it has lived with me, for fifty-three years it has blossomed, put down roots, branched out into a child and a child's child. Whosoever looks at times into a holy book knows that one name can destroy a world. And one name can also create a world. The Torah is called the Law of Moses—is named after Moses. Homer's name is written on the Iliad.

It is true that there are names that must be cursed, obliterated from the human

Based on a rabbinic legend about King Solomon trying to reclaim his throne from Ashmedai, king of the devils.

A possible reference to Perle's shift in style midway into his career.

A reference to his wife Sarah, who committed suicide in 1926.

stock. But there are names that the human race blesses and will bless as long as it exists.

My name is not great; humanity has no reason to bless it. It also has no reason to curse it. But unimportant as this name of mine may be, I did not give the Warsaw *kehillah* any right to take it away and set a paper number in its place. Amalek, may his name and memory be blotted out, gave the order; and the head of the *kehillah*, whose learning and wisdom are known throughout the Jewish Diaspora, carried it out—to the letter.°

Perle's attack on the new head of the Judenrat, Marek Lichtenbaum, is gratuitous. The Judenrat had no influence on the Nazi policies.

Instead of me, there roams about beneath the desolate walls of the ghetto—which that same head of the *kehillah* has had built—a big number, printed in black and white: an arrogant creature, an aristocrat among numbers.

This number—is the former "I." This number is my former name. I have no idea what they will do in 120 years, when I'm given a Jewish burial (I believe that may happen). The Angel of Death will take a trip down and knock on my tombstone: *"Mah shimkho?"* "What is your name?" . . . How will I answer him then?° That my name is Four Thousand Five Hundred and Eighty? But won't he look at me as if I'm crazy? I also don't know what they'll do about the people who come after me. They'll read in chronicles about the city of Warsaw in the year nineteen hundred and forty-two and will certainly be surprised that it was possible for a living number to be transformed into a dead number.

Based on the belief that when you die, you have to report your name to the angel of the grave.

I would like to tell them, the people of the future, that we—who are not reading history on paper but making it with our blood—are not surprised in the least. What is there in it that could surprise us? Our soul has been torn out, our body raped, our Holy Ark spat into, our Torah of Moses trampled by soldiers' boots.

Amalek, may his stock be obliterated from human memory, gave the order; and the Warsaw *kehillah* carried it out. Of three times a hundred thousand living Jewish souls it was granted that some thirty thousand ciphers of the Chosen People be left, stamped and sealed with the seal of the head of the *kehillah* himself—whose name will one day be used to frighten children in their cradles.

My name and all that is me also found favor in the eyes of the VIPs and were metamorphosed into a number. And just as Sholem Aleichem's Motl, the son of Peyse the Cantor, runs around barefoot and happily proclaims, "I'm alright, I'm an orphan," so I walk around in the tenement courtyard on Franciszkanska Street, which has become the great wide world, and proclaim:

"I'm alright, I'm a number."

I'm leading a life of luxury. The aristocratic number gives me dignity, importance. It elevates me above the rubbish heap where the other thirty thousand or so are swarming—and persuading themselves that they alone are worthy to remain members of the Chosen People Club.

My number receives a quarter of a clayey loaf of bread a day and some very tasty grits consisting mostly of boiled water, a potato that someone has already stolen from the pot and a few grains of cereal that chase about and can never, poor things, catch up with one another. What's more, from time to time they dole out to my number a stale egg with a drop of blood on it,° a lick of honey and, once in a blue moon, a scrap of aging meat that—even if you were to hack it into pieces—would by no means have the flavor of old wine.

The blood would render the egg unkosher.

I'm all right; I'm a number. I'm inscribed in the Community Register of the Holy Congregation of Warsaw. The clever head of the *kehillah* likes turning the pages of the Register. Someone else, in his place, would perhaps read out the Mosaic Curses. He would perhaps hear the weeping of the children who have died, even before they began to live. He would perhaps take cognizance of the roaring of three times a hundred thousand souls, slaughtered on the altar of Amalek, who rush around and do not allow a single one of these classified, happy ciphers of the Chosen People to rest.

But he only sees numbers, the clever head of the Holy Congregation of Warsaw. And, as he is the ruler of the numbers, and as he is not obliged to feed numbers for nothing, he issues edicts every other day and sends out polite notices:

"Thus-and-thus, dear number, I decree that you shall present yourself at six o'clock tomorrow, to help build the bleak wall that confines you as with a chain, and wants to strangle and choke you. You must wall yourself up. You must also come and wash away the blood of your mother and your father, whom Amalek deigned to slaughter, gladly assisted by the loyal crew. And if there is still something left in your father's house, or in your own house, you must help Amalek to steal it and bring it to him as a precious gift.

"If you are recalcitrant, if you will not come forward—" warns my good head of the *kehillah*—"if you do not wall yourself up with your own hands, if you do not bring Amalek the candlesticks that your dead mother used when she blessed the Sabbath candles, if you do not bring him the diamond brooch with which your mother adorned herself for the blessing of the New Moon; if you do not offer him the pillow on which your child slept, I shall erase you from the Register and you will cease to be a number."

That's how my head of the *kehillah* warns me every day. To tell the truth, I'm delighted by these fearsome warnings that I'll stop being a number: I'll become "I" again! I'll get my name back! To put it simply—I'll rise from the dead. Since the world began, not a single Jew has risen from the dead: the Messiah hasn't arrived yet. I'll be the first resurrected Jew. So why shouldn't my heart rejoice? On the other hand, I remember that if I stop being a number there's an executioner's ax waiting for me. No longer being a number means good-bye to the clayey quarter loaf each day, good-bye to the smell of the year-old egg, good-bye to the little room they allotted me to live in, good-bye to the potato that other people steal from my plate of grits, good-bye to honor; no longer an aristocrat, no longer of the Club of the Chosen.

Without a number I'll be like my neighbor, who was once as clever as I and as learned as I, as polite as I—maybe more polite. But evil fortune willed that he should not find favor, not be metamorphosed into a number; he kept his name. His beautiful human name. But a beautiful human name has the same value today as a beautiful human heart, or a beautiful human virtue. Today the beautiful human hearts, the beautiful human virtues lie bleeding among the scraps that lie scattered in the desolate Jewish courtyards.

My neighbor's honest name doesn't get the quarter of a loaf, doesn't taste the flavor of a little grits, has nowhere to lay its head, hides itself in holes together with cats and stray dogs. My neighbor's name has been erased from the Communal Register. The friends of yesterday, who have numbers, no longer say good morning to him, no longer sit with him at the same table, no longer pray with him in the same house of prayer. He has become a leper, this neighbor of mine, with the honest name and without the paper number.

454 The Literature of Destruction

And how should I not value my number? How should I not worry about it? I do indeed worry about it, as a mother worries about her only child. I guard it as one guards the apple of one's eye. I have a little velvet bag, embroidered with a Star of David, and I carry my number next to my heart. I sleep with it, I eat with it. My dreams are woven around it, with it, of it.

And if I were young today and my number was also under thirty, a woman would surely appear and say tenderly: "Dear little number!"

And she would pamper it: "Darling number, my crown!"

And would use affectionate diminutives: "My numberkin!"

Because I was born under a lucky star. I'm alright—I'm a number.

But in order to become a number, my fifty-three years had to be jabbed at until they bled. Jabbed at, mocked, raped. In order for me to become a number, they had to destroy my house first. Destroy it, tear it up by the roots. Under my number lie three times a hundred thousand Jewish martyrs. Three times a hundred thousand Jewish lives, that Amalek slaughtered with the consent of the head of the *kehillah* and his servants. From under my fortunate number leaps out the cry of tens of thousands of poisoned, strangled Jewish children. In the dark nights I hear the great weeping of the mother of all mothers, our Mother Rachel. She walks across the desolate fields and wraps her dead children in burial sheets.° With her beautiful, delicate hands she washes the blood off her sons and daughters. But can she wrap *all* of them in burial sheets? Can she wash them *all*? Blood cries out; and the earth, in all its length and breadth, is dissolved in lamentation.

Based on Jeremiah 31:15.

They lie, the slaughtered creatures, naked and shamed, scattered and spread, impurified for burial, without a *Kaddish*, without a gravestone, violated by the murderous hands of Amalek, with the consent of the holy congregation of Warsaw.

I'm alright, I'm a number.

Warsaw ghetto, end of 1942
(Ringelblum Archive, Part 2, no. 1245)

77 The Ghetto in Flames

ANONYMOUS

On April 19, 1943, armed units entered the ghetto to begin its final liquidation. This was the signal for the uprising to begin. Most of the fighting took place in the central ghetto, which had been turned into an underground network of bunkers. In the northern ghetto, where the large German factories (called "shops") were located, the hiding places were neither widespread nor particularly sophisticated, so that opportunities to go into hiding for a long period were far more limited. Most of the "shop" workers, moreover, were convinced that as "productive labor," they would be spared. On April 21, Többens, the owner of the largest factory, issued the deportation order to the managers of the sixteen major "shops." Three days later, Himmler ordered the entire ghetto burned to the ground, even if it meant destroying all the factories and machinery.

Located at Nalewki 30, the firm of Hermann Brauer employed six hundred Jewish workers.

We had already been hiding for a week—in cellars, between walls, vanished so as never to be found. The German blockades had had only limited success. Of our group, the block of Hermann Brauer,° only thirty people had been flushed out of hiding, and the Nazis were having a hard time finding more, even though they searched our cellars and ransacked our dwellings every day—it was as if the earth had swallowed us up. The four and a half thousand people who had occupied this area seemed to have disappeared by magic, without a trace. Still, we weren't allowed to breathe, unlike previous *Aktions* when the nights had been ours and one could cautiously cross the area between one blockade and another. This time they had brought in a group of sharpshooters who were on the lookout night and day and opened fire at even the slightest rustling sound. They were terrified, because in the first days dozens of them had fallen in combat against our armed units.

These figures are greatly exaggerated.

Just the same, before daybreak a neighbor from another cellar managed to reach us by cautiously stealing through the intervening cellars and quietly uncovering our trapdoor. After asking if we had heard anything, he shared some news with us. He said that in the first days of the uprising about three hundred of the enemy fell.° We held good defense positions. They [the Germans] brought two tanks into the ghetto, and we succeeded in destroying one of them. We hung out a Polish flag, and the Germans were unable to shoot it down. Now things were quieter; they could find hardly any of our people, since most were so well hidden. It was impossible to tell how long things would go on this way, but if no one were found in the next few days, the Germans would have to either cut the operation short or bring in Aryan workers for the shops; then everyone would be forced to adapt to new circumstances. On this note, our conversation ended. Our comrade covered up the trapdoor again, pouring dirt over it and hiding it behind a pile of old things; then he discreetly made off.

How little we understood what the Germans were capable of! We simply could not imagine that all of this property, all the warehouses filled with merchandise, all the workshops, factories and machines worth tens, worth hundreds of millions—that all this would be set on fire because of us, because of all of us who had burrowed underground or hidden between the walls and who possessed nothing more than our lives and our determination, the powerful determination not to give it up. No, we simply could not imagine it.

In our hideout, life went on as in the first days. We still had electricity, we had water in the water closet; we cooked dinner on the electric stove and lay on the plank beds reading pamphlets.

The hideout was not large: three small rooms under the front of the house by the gate (Nalewki 8), two of which were taken up by iron cots, and the third containing a kitchen. There were twelve of us: three children, five women and four men. We were comfortable, for the place had been intended for more people, but the others, fearing that its frontal location and proximity to the street made it unsafe, hid elsewhere; their crowded hideout was less comfortable but more secure.

We were already running low on air; the ventilation was sparse. We couldn't move around or talk to each other because the gate was so near; we had to suppress every cough, every loud noise.

The day passed into afternoon like all the previous days. Twice we heard the sounds of troops marching into and out of the ghetto. Apparently, they hadn't found any victims, because all we heard were the soldiers' retreating footsteps, and then it was quiet again. Around five in the evening we sensed a muffled movement and the frequent coming and going of trucks. Something was being loaded onto the trucks, something was happening, but what? It was possible that they were moving the firm out, but so many goods, workshops and machines would take them weeks, perhaps months, so what was the meaning of all the shouting and hurry? By seven everything had become quiet once more. Even quieter than before, it seemed. Then, shortly after seven, I smelled fumes in the room. I became a little uneasy and started to look for their source. I found smoke seeping through a wall; perhaps someone in an adjoining cellar had made a fire and the smoke had gotten into ours. We had cement and sand, which we mixed with water and used to quickly seal the opening that had let in the suffocating smoke. When the job was done we rested, relieved that we had had the cement and sand on hand. It never occurred to us that we were already caught in the fire, which was spreading rapidly around us.

It was eight o'clock. The noise of movement on the street had intensified, while the smoke in our rooms did not thin out at all; we would have to let in more air. There were little windows along the front wall, openings of ten to fifteen centimeters such as you find under every storefront, but they were masked and sealed so that only a couple of holes of not more than a centimeter each remained. Now we had to uncover these. I forced open a small window in the front room and saw a house burning on the other side of the street—from the ground to the roof, the whole house in flames. Suddenly the door to a second-story balcony burst open and a man of about fifty ran out, his wild face and bulging eyes illuminated by the fire; he had just emerged from a hiding place in the house, crying, "Fire! Fire!" He threw his legs over the balcony and got ready to jump. A few shots cut short his attempt, and he fell motionless, like a block of wood. From nearby, the sound of laughter cut into the roar of the flames—the laughter of the guards who were there to ensure that the fire spread nicely, so that no living thing could escape.

A group of people, mostly women, ran out of another house. I heard their cries for help. They didn't know where to run. Their last cries were silenced by a burst of machine-gun fire.

I turned away from the little window and looked at those around me, thinking to myself that this could never happen to us; those were wildcat houses° over there, but we were, after all, part of the German Reich firm of Hermann Brauer, a former German spy in Poland, an army man and loyal follower of Hitler. They wouldn't set fire to this. It was their own property.

But things had changed in the territory of Hermann Brauer.

Three days before, Brauer had called in several of his managers, whomever he could reach since all were in hiding, and informed them that his firm would stay open and that in the coming days there would be a re-registration; those who presented themselves would immediately return to work. The first four to respond were given special numbers cut from big pieces of white linen, and with these they were able to move freely over the territory of the firm.

Over the next three days twenty-five managers donned the white numbers; Hermann Brauer pocketed 150,000 zlotys, and his assistant, the invalid Klaus, fifty thousand zlotys.

Half of the seventy thousand Jews who remained in Warsaw after the Great Deportation were not registered "shop" workers. These illegals hid in houses abandoned by the deportees.

Even after Brauer had learned that his firm would be burned down with all its stock, both living and dead, he said nothing to the managers, just had them carry out small details for his own benefit. At five o'clock in the afternoon of the last day, the SS came up to the office, called together the managers and led them to the first courtyard. Taken unawares, the managers held their arms up and didn't dare move from their places. Soldiers faced them with rifles poised. They were searched and all their possessions confiscated; not only money, watches and rings, but also documents, every trifle, even scrawled-on scraps of paper. After this came an hour of torture, of punitive exercises. The SS were having a fine time. The German directors stood by the office window watching these SS, with whom they had just shared a drink to celebrate the ransom money they had collected from the managers (the drink serving to keep the SS in a festive and compliant mood). After the exercises the managers were forced to help load helmets, for in the past few hours the evacuation of equipment had begun; a few trucks had brought prisoners of war to the task, and the managers were forced with blows to assist them. However, the enormous warehouses filled with woolen sweaters and socks, the storerooms for leather goods, the paper mills, the huge reserves of field packs and other equipment—all these could not be cleared out so quickly. Only a few flatcars loaded with steel helmets were let out, followed by one other flatcar—carrying the managers.

At a quarter to seven (the precise details and exact time were given to me later by one whose hiding place provided a view of the first courtyard) Brauer came down from his office, remained standing at the gate, took a last look around him, smoked a cigarette and climbed into a car.

Five minutes after his departure German troops and sharpshooters entered and threw incendiary bombs into the firm's living quarters and cellers, onto the stairwells and into the attics. Then they turned to other details.

And so the German Reich's firm of Hermann Brauer burned from the corner of Franciszkanska and Nalewki Streets to Muranowska Street.

The first to notice this from their hideouts in the houses ran at once to the courtyard. But most of those who had been in hiding didn't make it out, for the wooden stairwells were usually the first things to burn, and by the time the smoke and fire had driven everyone from the hideouts the whole house would already be in flames and its occupants trapped.

The few who managed to get out alive went knocking on the entrances to bunkers where they knew people were hiding. That is how they remembered me. Around nine o'clock some friends missed me, and the cry went up to find M., to break open the shelter in which I was hiding and save me and my companions. A group entered the first courtyard with irons and crowbars and approached the bunker. But it was already impossible to go down. The corridor that led to our bunker was already in flames, and our hideout was very far away. With lowered heads they turned back. A pity about M. and those with him, but were their own lives safe yet? They still faced the enormous task of saving themselves.

In our shelter we still knew nothing. Around nine we sat down to our evening meal. How tragicomic was our situation! How like a scene from a Chaplin film! Our home had been set on fire, the neighboring bunkers were burning, the fire was getting closer and closer to us, the people on the outside who had come to save us couldn't get to us—and we, as though none of this concerned us at all, we sat down to eat.

Around ten I went to wash my hands and felt hot water coming from the faucet. A shudder passed through me; I turned hot and cold as the truth suddenly dawned on me: we were surrounded by fire.

Without a word I went to the opening, crawled out under the wall and lifted the trapdoor. The small cellar through which one entered our hideout was extremely hot and brightly lit. A fire from an incendiary bomb had spread through the little window. Fortunately, a few days before, I had moved all the things in the cellar to the doorway, so nothing had caught fire by our hideout. I leaped into the corridor that led to the exit; this long corridor and all the cellars on both sides were completely engulfed by flames. I ran back to the shelter, where everyone was waiting for me by the entrance; they had seen me run out and knew that only a serious matter could have compelled me to uncover the trapdoor.

"Listen," I said to the frightened group around me. "If you keep calm we'll all get out. Everything around us is burning; the corridor that leads out of here is in flames. After a week in this bunker our clothes are soaked through, so they won't catch so easily when we run through the fire; but you must all cover your heads with someting damp because hair can ignite very quickly. The children will go first, then the women and finally the men."

I got them into a line with myself leading the way and the children behind me. We ran through the fire. I couldn't breathe. I thought, "Just don't fall, just don't fall. If you fall, everyone dies in the fire." My face was burning, I pulled the damp rag over my eyes. We reached the exit stairwell and in a few bounds were standing in the open. I turned around and counted twelve heads; no one was missing.

But where were we? All around was the heat of the fire, which was climbing from the houses to the sky. Flames were shooting from the cellars to the high heavens.

I remembered the man on the balcony and his cry: "Fire! Fire!" It was deserted out here, not a living thing in sight. Only burning roofs caving into the courtyard from crumbling walls.

Where could we run? On the street—I knew already—men would be standing on corners with machine guns, waiting for those who had fled the fire. We had to shield our heads quickly, because bricks and burning debris were coming down, entire walls collapsing. We ran to another gate, knowing from previous bombardments that the ceilings of gateways are the strongest. But the wind carried sparks and smoke from every direction; we were suffocating and our eyes burning, we couldn't stay there. Where could we run for refuge?

Suddenly we noticed in the left corner of the last courtyard a black island removed from the fire, and people were moving inside it. We ran to it and found ourselves among friends; we embraced, we kissed. They told how they had tried to save us but couldn't get inside, how they had given us up for dead.

But there was no time for talk. The building, which had formerly housed the printing and editorial offices of *Moment*,° had to be saved. Its two stories had already been burned down once before, at the beginning of the war, but half of the building had been rebuilt; now we had to save this refuge from the fire in order to save ourselves. There was water in the cellar, so we formed two columns: one to pass

A major Yiddish daily in prewar Poland.

the water in tin cans from the cellar to the roof and the other to pass the emptied tins back down to the cellar.

I was handed a pair of goggles and took my place on the roof. Facing me was my former home, where I had once had a bed and a pillow on which to lay my head and which was now bursting with flames that were swallowing everything inside. The two of us on the roof had to make sure that every spark that landed there was put out immediately, for the tarred surface was extremely flammable. Because the smoke was heavy, we had to relieve each other frequently.

We were surrounded by a sea of fire. The greatest film directors have not yet succeeded in capturing such a scene; it roared and crackled and shot flame; it deafened us so that we couldn't hear a thing, not even the others shouting to us. We were working with our last measure of strength, we were fighting with superhuman endurance. And we were winning.

After laboring a whole night, we succeeded in saving the building. By morning the danger of being engulfed by the fire had passed.

We looked around us. Of the five hundred who had escaped to this place from neighboring houses, many had died in the fire, suffocated by smoke in the cellars. And we who survived—were we really saved? For the moment, we didn't think about this. Everyone was hard at work, removing flammable material from the house, especially from the paper storeroom: an entire warehouseful of paper had to be thrown into the courtyard and burned. We were all exhausted, our eyes smarting.

And then a bright, sunny day dawned and revealed to us the incinerated houses of the ghetto, of the murdered city.

And let this remain for a memory.

Sunday, the twenty-fifth of April, 1943. In the evening, the Jewish ghetto in Warsaw was set on fire, and tens of thousands of men, women and children perished in the flames; those who tried to escape the fire were shot on the streets and those who miraculously did escape were hunted and tormented for weeks, for months, until they too were annihilated

And when later, searching through one of the cellars full of suffocated people, I came upon children whose mouths gaped like black, scorched holes and women whose closed fists clutched hair torn from their heads, I wept and clenched my own fists and remembered the millions of clenched fists all over the world, raised against Hitlerism and Fascism.

The Aryan Side of Warsaw, 1943

78 Yizkor, 1943

RACHEL AUERBACH

I saw a flood once in the mountains. Wooden huts, torn from their foundations were carried above the raging waters. One could still see lighted lamps in them; and men, women and children in their cradles were tied to the ceiling beams.

Other huts were empty inside, but one could see a tangle of arms waving from the roof, like branches blowing in the wind waving desperately toward heaven, toward the river banks for help. At a distance, one could see mouths gaping, but one could not hear the cries because the roar of the waters drowned out everything.

And that's how the Jewish masses flowed to their destruction at the time of the deportations. Sinking as helplessly into the deluge of destruction.

Cf. Ps. 137 (3).   And if, for even one of the days of my life, I should forget how I saw you then, my people,° desperate and confused, delivered over to extinction, may all knowledge of me be forgotten and my name be cursed like that of those traitors who are unworthy to share your pain.

Every instinct is revealed in the mass—repulsive, tangled. All feelings churning, feverish to the core. Lashed by hundreds of whips of unreasoning activity. Hundreds of deceptive or ridiculous schemes of rescue. And at the other pole, a yielding to the inevitable; a gravitation toward mass death that is no more substantial than the gravitation toward life. Sometimes the two antipodes followed each other in the same being.

Who can render the stages of the dying of a people? Only the shudder of pity for one's self and for others. And again illusion: waiting for the chance miracle. The insane smile of hope in the eyes of the incurable patient. Ghastly reflections of color on the yellowed face of one who is condemned to death.

Condemned to death. Who could—who wished to understand such a thing? And who could have expected such a decree against the mass? Against such low branches, such simple Jews. The lowly plants of the world. The sorts of people who would have lived out their lives without ever picking a quarrel with the righteous—or even the unrighteous—of this world.

How could such people have been prepared to die in a gas chamber? The sorts of people who were terrified of a dentist's chair; who turned pale at the pulling of a tooth.

And what of them . . . the little children?

The little ones, and those smaller still who not long ago were to be seen in the arms of their mothers, smiling at a bird or at a sunbeam. Prattling at strangers in the streetcar. Who still played "pattycake" or cried "giddyup" waving their tiny hands in the air. Or called, "pa-pa." O, unrecognizable world in which these children and their mothers are gone. "Giddyup."

Even the sweetest ones: the two- and three-year-olds who seemed like newly hatched chicks tottering about on their weak legs. And even the slightly larger ones who could already talk. Who endlessly asked about the meanings of words. For whom whatever they learned was always brand new. Five-year-olds. And six-year-olds. And those who were older still—their eyes wide with curiosity about the whole world. And those older still whose eyes were already veiled by the mists of their approaching ripeness. Boys who, in their games, were readying themselves for achievements yet to come.

Girls who still nursed their dolls off in corners. Who wore ribbons in their hair; girls, like sparrows, leaping about in courtyards and on garden paths. And those who looked like buds more than half opened. The kind to whose cheeks the very first wind of summer seems to have given its first glowing caress. Girls of eleven, twelve, thirteen with the faces of angels. Playful as kittens. Smiling May blossoms.

And those who have nearly bloomed: the fifteen- and sixteen-year-olds. The Sarahs, the Rebeccahs, the Leahs of the Bible, their names recast into Polish. Their eyes blue and gray and green under brows such as one sees on the frescoes unearthed in Babylon and Egypt. Slender young *fräuleins* from the wells of Hebron. *Jungfraus* from Evangelia. Foreign concubines of Jewish patriarchs; desert maidens with flaring nostrils, their hair in ringlets, dark complected but turned pale by passion. Spanish daughters, friends of Hebrew poets of the Middle Ages. Dreamy flowers bent over mirroring pools. And opposite them? Delicate blonds in whom Hebrew passion is interwoven with Slavic cheerfulness. And the even brighter flaxen-haired peasants, broad-hipped women, as simple as black bread; or as a shirt on the body of the folk.

It was an uncanny abundance of beauty of that generation growing up under the gray flag of ghetto poverty and mass hunger. Why was it that we were not struck by this as a portent of evil? Why was it that we did not understand that this blossoming implied its own end?

It was these, and such as these, who went into the abyss—our beautiful daughters. These were the ones who were plucked and torn to bits.

And where are the Jewish young men? Earnest and serious; passionate as high-bred horses, chomping at the bit, eager to race. The young workers, the *halutsim*, Jewish students avid for study, for sports, for politics. World improvers and flag bearers of every revolution. Youths whose passion made them ready to fill the prison cells of all the world. And many were tortured in camps even before the mass murder began. And where are the other youths, simpler than they—the earthen roots of a scattered people; the very essence of sobriety countering the decay of idealism at the trunk. Young men with ebullient spirits, their heads lowered like those of bulls against the decree spoken against our people.

And pious Jews in black gaberdines, looking like priests in their medieval garb: Jews who were rabbis, teachers who wanted to transform our earthly life into a long study of Torah and prayer to God. They were the first to feel the scorn of the butcher. Their constant talk of martyrdom turned out not to be mere empty words.

And still other Jews. Broad shouldered, deep voiced, with powerful hands and hearts. Artisans, workers. Wagon drivers, porters. Jews who, with a blow of their fists, could floor any hooligan who dared enter into their neighborhoods.

Where were you when your wives and children, when your old fathers and mothers were taken away? What happened to make you run off like cattle stampeded by fire? Was there no one to give you some purpose in the confusion? You were swept away in the flood, together with those who were weak.

And you sly and cunning merchants, philanthropists in your short fur coats and caps. How was it that you didn't catch on to the murderous swindle? Fathers—and mothers of families; you, in Warsaw. Stout women merchants with proud faces radiating intelligence above your three chins, standing in your shops behind counters heaped with mountains of goods.

And you other mothers. Overworked peddler women and market stallkeepers. Disheveled and as anxious about your children as irritable setting hens when they flap their wings.

And other fathers, already unhorsed, as it were. Selling sweets from their wobbling tables in the days of the ghetto.

What madness is it that drives one to list the various kinds of Jews who were destroyed?

Grandfathers and grandmothers with an abundance of grandchildren. With hands like withered leaves; their heads white. Who already trembled at the latter end of their days. They were not destined simply to decline wearily into their graves like rest-seeking souls; like the sun sinking wearily into the ocean's waves. No. It was decreed that before they died they would get to see the destruction of all that they had begotten; of all that they had built.

The decree against the children and the aged was more complete and more terrible than any.

Those who counted and those who counted for less. Those with aptitudes developed carefully over countless generations. Incomparable talents, richly endowed with wisdom and professional skill: doctors, professors, musicians, painters, architects. And Jewish craftsmen: tailors—famous and sought after; Jewish watchmakers in whom gentiles had confidence. Jewish cabinet makers, printers, bakers. The great proletariat of Warsaw. Or shall I console myself with the fact that, for the most part, you managed to die of hunger and need in the ghetto before the expulsion?

Ah, the ways of Warsaw—the black soil of Jewish Warsaw.

My heart weeps even for the pettiest thief on Krochmalna Street; even for the worst of the knife wielders of narrow Mila, because even they were killed for being Jewish. Anointed and purified in the brotherhood of death.

Called khesedlekh in Warsaw slang.

Ah, where are you, petty thieves of Warsaw; you illegal street vendors° and sellers of rotten apples. And you, the more harmful folk—members of great gangs who held their own courts; who supported their own synagogues in the Days of Awe; who conducted festive funerals and who gave alms like the most prosperous burghers.

Ah, the mad folk of the Jewish street! Disordered soothsayers in a time of war.

Ah, bagel sellers on winter evenings.

Ah, poverty stricken children of the ghetto. Ghetto peddlers; ghetto smugglers supporting their families; loyal and courageous to the end. Ah, the poor barefoot boys moving through the autumn mire with their boxes of cigarettes, "Cigarettes! Cigarettes! Matches! Matches!" The voice of the tiny cigarette seller crying his wares on the corner of Leszno and Karmelicka Streets still rings in my ears.

Where are you, my boy? What have they done to you? Reels from the unfinished and still unplayed preexpulsion film, "The Singing Ghetto," wind and unwind in my memory.° Even the dead sang in that film. They drummed with their swollen feet as they begged: "Money, ah money, Money is the best thing there is."

A Nazi propaganda film made in the ghetto in May 1942.

The Tokheḥa, 1.

There was no power on earth, no calamity that could interfere with their quarrelsome presence in that Jewish street. Until there came that Day of Curses°—a day that was entirely night.

Hitler finally achieved his greatest ambition of the war. And finally, his dreadful enemy was defeated and fell: that little boy on the corner of Leszno and Karmelicka Streets; of Smocza and Nowolipie; of Dzika Street. The weapons of the women peddlers reached to every market square.

What luxury! They stopped tearing at their own throats from morning until night. They stopped snatching the morsels of clay-colored, clay-adulterated bread from each other.

The first to be rounded up were the beggars. All the unemployed and the homeless were gathered up off the streets. They were loaded into wagons on the first morning of the Deportation and driven through the town. They cried bitterly and stretched their hands out or wrung them in despair; or covered their faces. The youngest of them cried, "Mother, mother." And indeed, there were women to be seen running along both sides of the wagons, their headshawls slipping from their heads as they stretched their hands out toward their children, those young smugglers who had been rounded up along the walls. In other of the wagons, the captives looked like people condemned to death who, in the old copperplate engravings, are shown being driven to the scaffold in tumbrils.

The outcries died down in the town, and there was silence. Later on, there were no cries heard. Except when women were caught and loaded onto the wagons and one could hear an occasional indrawn hiss, such as fowl make as they are carried to the slaughter.

Men, for the most part, were silent. Even the children were so petrified that they seldom cried.

The beggars were rounded up, and there was no further singing in the ghetto. I heard singing only once more after the deportations began. A monotonous melody from the steppes sung by a thirteen-year-old beggar girl. Over a period of two weeks she used to creep out of her hiding place in the evening, when the day's roundups were over. Each day, looking thinner and paler and with an increasingly brighter aureole of grief about her head, she took her place at her usual spot behind a house on Leszno Street and began the warbling by whose means she earned her bit of bread. . . .

Enough, enough . . . I have to stop writing.

No. No. I can't stop. I remember another girl of fourteen. My own brother's orphan daughter in Lemberg whom I carried about in my arms as if she were my own child. Lussye! And another Lussye, older than she, one of my cousins who was studying in Lemberg and who was like a sister to me. And Lonye, my brother's widow, the mother of the first Lussye, and Mundek, an older child of hers whom I thought of as my own son from the time that he was orphaned. And another girl in the family, a pianist of thirteen, my talented little cousin, Yossima.

And all of my mother's relatives in their distant village in Podolia: Auntie Bayle; Auntie Tsirl; Uncle Yassye; Auntie Dortsye, my childhood's ideal of beauty.

I have so many names to recall, how can I leave any of them out, since nearly all of them went off to Belzec° and Treblinka or were killed on the spot in Lanowce and Ozieran in Czortkow and in Mielnica. In Krzywicze and elsewhere.

Absurd! I will utter no more names. They are all mine, all related. All who were killed. Who are no more. Those whom I knew and loved press on my memory, which I compare now to a cemetery. The only cemetery in which there are still indications that they once lived in this world.

° A death camp in Poland.

I feel—and I know—that they want it that way. Each day I recall another one of those who are gone.

And when I come to the end of the list, segment by segment added to the segments of my present life in the town,° I start over again from the beginning, and always in pain. Each of them hurts me individually, the way one feels pain when parts of the body have been surgically removed. When the nerves surviving in the nervous system signal the presence of every finger on amputated hands or feet.

I.e., hiding on the Aryan Side.

Not long ago, I saw a woman in the streetcar, her head thrown back, talking to herself. I thought that she was either drunk or out of her mind. It turned out that she was a mother who had just received the news that her son, who had been rounded up in the street, had been shot.

"My child," she stammered, paying no attention to the other people in the streetcar, "my son. My beautiful, beloved son."

I too would like to talk to myself like one mad or drunk, the way that woman did in the Book of Judges° who poured out her heart unto the Lord and whom Eli drove from the Temple.

A reference to Hannah's prayer in 1 Sam. 1, not in Judges. Eli did not drive Hannah from the Temple.

I may neither groan nor weep. I may not draw attention to myself in the street.

And I need to groan; I need to weep. Not four times a year. I feel the need to say *Yizkor* four times a day.

Yizkor elohim es nishmas avi mori ve'imi morasi . . . Remember, Oh Lord, the souls of those who passed from this world horribly, dying strange deaths before their time.

And now, suddenly I seem to see myself as a child standing on a bench behind my mother who, along with my grandmother and my aunts, is praying before the east wall of the woman's section of the synagogue in Lanowce. I stand on tiptoe peering down through panes of glass at the congregation in the synagogue that my grandfather built. And just then the Torah reader, Hersh's Meyer-Itsik, strikes the podium three times and cries out with a mighty voice so that he will be heard by men and women on both sides of the partition and by the community's orphans, boys and girls, who are already standing, waiting for just this announcement: "We recite *Yizkor.*"

The solemn moment has arrived when we remember those who are no longer with us. Even those who have finished their prayers come in at this time to be with everyone else as they wait for the words, "We recite *Yizkor.*"

And he who has survived and lives and who approaches this place, let him bow his head and, with anguished heart, let him hear those words and remember his names as I have remembered mine—the names of those who were destroyed.

At the end of the prayer in which everyone inserts the names of members of his family there is a passage recited for those who have no one to remember them and who, at various times, have died violent deaths because they were Jews. And it is people like those who are now in the majority.

Aryan Side of Warsaw,
November 1943

XVI

Ten Ghetto Poets

Poetry was a primary means of public communication in the Nazi ghettos and, later, in the camps. Whereas the research work of the *Oyneg Shabbes* archive was a closely guarded secret and whereas only his closest friends knew that Chaim Kaplan was keeping a diary, the professional poets, songwriters and street balladeers had a loyal following both within their own ghettos and, to a surprising degree, outside their boundaries as well. (The question of how songs circulated during the war has never been systematically studied.) Yankev Herszkowicz **(80)** performed his songs to the accompaniment of a violin in the middle of the ghetto streets (and was photographed doing so by Lodz photographer Mendel Grossman); Yitzhak Katzenelson **(81)** and Joseph Kirman **(82)** published some of their poems in the Warsaw underground press; Leyb Rosental's songs were written for the Vilna ghetto theater and were performed there; Shmerke Kaczerginski's "Youth Hymn" was sung at every meeting of the Youth Club in the Vilna ghetto; and Hirsh Glik's "Never Say" **(86)** became the unofficial Jewish Partisans' Hymn throughout Nazi-occupied Europe. Many of the poets, moreover, were openly aligned with the resistance movement or actually took up arms. The resounding finale of Glik's hymn was more than rhetorical flourish: "But a people amid crumbling walls did stand, / They stood and sang this song with rifles held in hand."

As a public medium, these songs and poems had to be relatively accessible, but their specific power came from the interplay between poetic convention and the terrible reality of the war. Sometimes there was an obvious clash, as when Avrom Akselrod **(79)** took the most popular Yiddish folk songs and subjected the original lyrics to a bitter parody. Leyb

Rosental's "Yisrolik" **(83)** combined two motifs from an old Yiddish operetta by Abraham Goldfaden—the "Bagel Seller's Song" and the "Song of the Abandoned Orphan"—only here the child was left orphaned by the Nazi terror and his name (Izzy, Israel), made him a stand-in for the Jewish collective. More subtly, Leah Rudnitsky **(84)** applied the standard motif of the Yiddish lullabye—the motif of the absent father—to describe the impact of the mass killings in Ponar: both parents had been killed, and it was now a stranger who rocked the child to sleep. Similarly, in Kaczerginski's lullabye **(85)**, the mother began by telling her orphaned child: "Still, still. Let us be still. / Graves grow here. / Planted by the enemy, / they blossom to the sky."

Not surprisingly, the parent-child relationship was the central focus of many ghetto songs, or at least of those that enjoyed the greatest popularity. Because every Jew was ultimately singled out for destruction, the fate of one became the fate of many, and everyone was to become an orphan. The power of the poem was in the tension between innocence and knowledge: the parents' task was to initiate their children into hunger and cold (Katzenelson), or into the cruelty of the ghetto and of those who stood outside (Kirman). But it was also the parents who could read the signs of salvation for the benefit of their children: the flames over Warsaw that perhaps augured a Russian advance, or simply a prayer that the "greatest of days," the day of liberation, was soon to come **(82)**.

Melodies, too, played an important role in wresting meaning from the mass death and starvation. That Glik set his "Never Say" to a Soviet melody was surely no accident, because many, if not most, east European Jews saw the Red Army as their only hope of defeating the Germans. The melodies for most of the "art songs," on the other hand, were composed on the spot, either for theatrical performances (Misha Veksler's melody to "Yisrolik" and Avreml Brudno's to "Beneath the Whiteness of Your Stars") or for a music contest in the ghetto (Alek Wolkowiski's [now Tamir] "Still, Still"). In a third group of songs, the satiric broadsides of Akselrod and others, the use of familiar tunes was both terrifying and consoling, for the ghetto texts forever clashed with the original, naive lyrics of these beloved songs, even as the melodies somehow made the unprecedented events of ghetto life more manageable.

As the full extent of the catastrophe came to be known, a new kind of song came into being, one that called for armed resistance. In each ghetto, the chronology of the Final Solution dictated the nature of these songs. Vilna, two thirds of whose Jewish population was slaughtered in the first six months of the Nazi occupation, was the first ghetto in which a Jewish resistance movement was organized—on January 1, 1942. In the summer of that year, two members of the United Partisans Organization (the UPO) carried out their first act of sabotage by blowing up a German munitions train outside the city. Hirsh Glik's ballad "Silence, and a Starry Night"

(86) was written to commemorate that defiant act. About a year later, Kaczerginski struck an altogether more somber note in his heroic ballad on Itsik Vittenberg **(85)**. For all that this song echoed an earlier ballad on Hirsh Lekert, a local hero who was hanged for his revolutionary activity in 1902, the later tragedy was incomparably greater: Vittenberg was the head of the UPO, who, on July 16, 1943, gave himself up to the Gestapo to save the entire ghetto from destruction. The manhunt that preceded his capture shocked the fighters into realizing that the whole ghetto population was against them. The UPO had lost not only its commander but also its hope of mass support. The only "savior," therefore, was the mauzer itself.

In Warsaw, meanwhile, the Nazis tried to resume the mass deportations to Treblinka in January 1943; this time, however, there was Jewish armed resistance on the *Umschlagplatz* and on the streets, as a result of which the deportation was called off. This was the first open combat between Jews and Germans, and its electrifying effect on the ghetto population produced Wladyslaw Szlengel's "Counterattack" **(87)**. The newness of its message was matched by the newness of its form, adapted from the revolutionary poetics of Vladimir Mayakovsky.

It is against this backdrop that one can best appreciate the singular achievement of Abraham Sutzkever **(88)**. Imagining Keats in a Nazi ghetto would be the closest thing to placing Sutzkever in the cauldron of the Holocaust. Here was a late Romantic poet in love with his craft, with his language, with the boundless gifts of nature, destined to witness and record the life-and-death struggle of Jewish Vilna, a microcosm of east European Jewry. Sutzkever's large poetic output—more than eighty poems, two of them epics—was never interrupted during the entire span of his life under Nazi occupation: in hiding (prior to the establishment of the ghetto), in the ghetto proper and in the forests as a member of the Jewish partisan brigade Nekome (Revenge). What sustained him was an almost mystical faith that the poetic word itself would rescue him from death.

Beginning with a situation of extreme terror, brutality and despair, Sutzkever arrives, through a poetry of wrenched opposites, of oxymorons, at a sense of beauty, wholeness and artistic permanence. Thanks to his memoirs (first published in Moscow in 1946), we can piece together the dire circumstances under which these poems were written.

The Germans occupied Vilna on June 24, 1941. Within days, Mobile Killing Unit 9 began the full-scale slaughter of the Jewish population. Thirty-three thousand Vilna Jews were murdered during the next six months, mostly in the woods of Ponar, some five kilometers outside the city. Young, able-bodied men were the first to be rounded up, and for seven weeks in June and July, Sutzkever hid underneath the tin roof of a building with just enough room to lie flat on his stomach. Scorched by the heat during the day, he was able, in the evenings, to write by the light of the moon. This is where he wrote the sequence of five poems called "Faces in the Mire."

The sequence begins with the ideological legacy of the past, now rendered meaningless by the Nazi onslaught, and ends with the poet's determination to "redeem history's omission." In between are three poems that tell of the poet's personal despair—his thoughts of suicide ("In the Cell"), his longing for his beloved ("Leaves of Ash") and his guilt at having abandoned his friends in the streets below ("Because I Was Drinking Wine"). Each poem is a study of oppositions: white doves that suddenly change into [black] owls and faces in the swamps below that threaten to eclipse the sun over the rooftops; the warm reflection of the moon on a broken piece of glass that is also sharp enough to slit one's throat; the dark ash of the letters from one's beloved that contain the "healing beauties" of her memory; the mark of Cain, the world's first murderer, come to haunt the laughter from before the war; and, most paradoxically, that "ancient virus" that contains both the legacy of submission and revolt ("A Voice From the Heart").

The faith that poetry could rescue him from death was tested yet again a month later when Sutzkever entered the precincts of the Judenrat to sign up for a labor battalion that would lead him to safety outside of town. The head of the first Judenrat, Pinkhes Kon, then informed him that all members of the previous battalions had just been shot in Ponar and that the Germans were coming at any moment to claim their daily allotment of fifty male victims. And so, with nowhere else to hide, Sutzkever jumped into a coffin in the yard of the Burial Society next door and, lying on top of a corpse, composed a poem about the interpenetration of the living and the dead.

Although the pain to his own person was something that Sutzkever could transmute soon after the fact, the murders of his firstborn son and of his mother within weeks of one another required the distance of time to regain absolute poetic control. A full year later, Sutzkever sat down to write about the death of his child by poison (for a detailed analysis of this poem, "To My Child," see my *Against the Apocalypse*, pp. 231–37). He also wrote several poems about the death of his mother, including a long narrative poem, most of which was lost. But the poem that most powerfully conveyed the impact of her death was written upon the sight of her shoes in a shipment of plundered clothing a year later. In "A Load of Shoes," Sutzkever described one of the most macabre of "death dances" ever imagined.

Sutzkever's ghetto poetry was by no means dedicated solely to transmuting his private horror into rhyme, meter and meaning; he was centrally involved in the cultural life of the ghetto as a whole. On the eve of the first public concert held in the ghetto, a program that he put together, he wrote of his desperate search for an audience ("Pray"). And when the

Germans called for volunteers to sort the cultural treasures plundered from Vilna's Jewish libraries, Sutzkever joined this "Paper Brigade" to help smuggle, at pain of death, the most valuable items into the ghetto for safekeeping ("Kernels of Wheat").

The gradual shift in Sutzkever's poetics from private expressions of grief to a voice of public exhortation can be seen most forcefully in two poems of prophetic denunciation written in February and March 1943, at a time when the so-called Stabilization Period within the ghetto was coming to an end and the Jewish populations of the neighboring towns were being systematically wiped out. In these poems he returns to the theme of the generation's false hopes and foreign ideologies; *a DORN zayt ir itster, nit keyn DOR*, "You're your nation's nettle," he writes in "Song For the Last," "not its fruit." Only now the poet's rage is fueled by something else: the knowledge that this generation that went whoring after strange gods will also be the last and that the fate of the survivors will be the most terrible fate of all. In "How?" he writes:

> In a rubble-encrusted old city
> Your memory will be like a hole,
> And your glance will burrow furtively
> Like a mole, like a mole.

During the Nazi occupation, Sutzkever's confrontations with death were translated into radical confrontations with himself. The destruction of Jewish Vilna and all that it stood for finally strengthened Sutzkever's faith in the power of the poetic word to rescue beauty (and now, the memory of the dead as well) from annihilation ("Charred Pearls"). Strengthened also was his faith that nature would help propel and purify that poetic process ("No Sad Songs Please"). By personal example, he gave meaning to the survivor's role in history, and by making Vilna the sacred text, rather than invoking the ancient archetypes, he made each reader a partner in the resurrection of the dead.

79   Avrom Akselrod

Sung to the tune of Afn pripetshik brent a fayerl.

At the Ghetto Gate°

At the ghetto gate
A fire flames.
Search is the worst yet.
Jews parade back
From the work brigades
Dripping buckets of sweat.

Should I go on ahead
Or stand still instead?
I'm not sure what to do.
The little commander
Decked out in green
Takes everything from you.

A stick of firewood,
Money in a wad,
God, he takes it all!
Milk from the can,
Lard from the pan,
Jews, it's awful.

Friend at the gate, listen,
I'm not all that clean.
Help me make it through,
Get me past the guard,
You'll get a kilo of lard
And more tomorrow too.

"Line up in fours!
You—stand over here
by me. Don't run away!"
Find the right goy—
"This one's OK"—
A loaf of bread for you today.

Ghetto code for those who "ascended" to power; "May our prayer ascend to heaven" is a climactic prayer from the Yom Kippur liturgy.

Ya'ales°

Tell me, oh tell me, you ghetto Jew,
Who plays first fiddle here, just who?
And which of the big shots in the ghetto gang
Hands out orders just like a king?

Tumbala, tumbala, play on, ghetto Jew.
Play me a song of the Jewish Who's Who.
Of all the inspectors and bosses
The ghetto has raised up from the masses.

Which of the big shots has a card to give
And a permit to keep you alive?
And just how much must you pay
For the privilege of an easy work brigade?

Tumbala, tumbala . . .

Why does the top brass have white rolls to eat,
Warm bagels, fresh buns and rolls that are sweet?
How can they glory in music and poker stakes
And live it up with honest-to-goodness cakes?

Tumbala, tumbala . . .

Have the big shots ever slaved at the airport
With an axe, a shovel or a crowbar?
Maybe then they might give an ear to our moans
How us poor folk have all these questions.

Tumbala, tumbala . . .

Who needs concerts when so great are our sorrows
And hunger whines in the poor man's house?
Far better we all have soup in our bowls
And you stop with your ritzy carnivals.

Kovno ghetto, circa 1942

80 Yankev Herszkowicz

Rumkowski Chaim Gives Us Bran-a

Oh, the Jews were blessed with Chaim,
Chaim Rumkowski with his head of gray.
Now, dear friends, let me tell you a story
I'll tell it all in a truthful way.

Rumkowski Chaim gives us bran-a
He gives us barley, he gives us life.

Once upon a time, Jews too ate manna
Now each man is eaten by his wife!

Rumkowski Chaim gave it much thought,
He thought all day and thought all night.
A ghetto he made with "dispensaries"
And then he shouted that he's in the right.

Listen, Jews, I'll tell you something,
A plague is what I'll tell you's.
Our little Jews are full of omens:
The ghetto, they say, will be open on Shavuos.

When that day passed, Jews gathered again
And figured out some more true signs.
Rumkowski, ol' boy, he had a good laugh:
The ghetto's closed as in previous times.

Old bearded Jews have no worth today.
Once they were proud; now they're shaved clean.
And as for the girls—they've nowhere to stroll
And aren't allowed to powder their nose.

June 16, 1940. The census day° was a very hot day.
Rumkowski traveled about like a king.
Now, dear folks, let me tell you the truth:
His Royal Highness has already gone gray.
May he live to be a hundred!

[Alternate ending, as sung by the crowd:
May the devil take him away!]

Lodz ghetto, circa 1941

81 Yitzhak Katzenelson

Song of Hunger

Come out, my dear, on to the street,
Come and die on the street,
On the hard sidewalk.
Bring our pale children.

Bring the eldest,
Bring the middle one.

Our third is very young yet
But like a grown Jew
Is able to die of hunger on the street.

Come on to the street
Come on to Karmelicka°
Here we fit in well.
Some fall, some stay sitting.
There is a hubbub on the Karmelicka.

The busiest thoroughfare in the ghetto, connecting Leszno and Gęsia Streets.

Come out, oh leave the house
The empty house.
I'd be ashamed
To lie there in a living grave.
A starving man
Should not die lonely in his home.

No cause for shame on the street.
People go out, lie down
Swollen, tight-belted.
A whole legion dies together.
They are dying wholesale, wholesale.

We too, we'll lie down on the sidewalk.
No, not lie down—we'll fall.
No, no, not fall—lie down,
Heart to heart
And die,
Die with the rest

Warsaw ghetto, May 28, 1941

Songs of the Cold

1

It's cold indoors, a bitter cold.
Wolves run around the room.
Frost-bears beset the window panes.
I, my wife and children tremble
And don't know what to do.

And no one sees, and no one wants to hear.
Don't cry, oh don't cry.
Though your tears are silent
They could freeze in your eyes.

It's cold indoors.
Fear attacked me in my house
and I went out into the empty streets.
I stepped over people who were frozen

Lying like felled trees.
Their arms flung out in a dumb terror,
Like a vain, empty cry.
Stiff ones,
Is it me you greet?

2

It's cold indoors and also dark
At night I pulled down quietly from my windows
The black paper shades
And the high moon looked in at me
And poured on me her cold and misty light.
And just as long ago
Innumerable stars
Glittered through a crack and said
"Happiness, happiness."
—Stop it! Stop it!
It's a trick. You don't play fair.
You're making eyes at me
As in those nights of long ago.
Stop it!

But the stars pretended not to understand,
And did not tear away from me
Their threads of trembling gold.
They did not stop winking at me.
—Go to hell!
Ardently I stretched out cold hands
To my old friends the stars:
—Oh, go to hell!

Warsaw ghetto, January 10, 1942

82 Joseph Kirman

I Speak to You Openly, Child

(Short Poems in Prose)

Doves on Wires

. . . My child, on a cold and frosty day, with an evil wind blowing and shaking man and earth, your father dragged himself along, tired, in search of himself. He wandered through the streets, past buildings and people.

Instead of himself, he found wires—barbed wires that cut through the street and cut it to pieces. On both sides of the wire people walked up and down. Poverty and hunger drove them towards the fence through which one could see what went on on the other side. Jews, the badge of shame on their arms, walked on one side and Christian boys and girls on the other. When from the other side a loaf of bread was thrown over the fence, boys on this side tried to catch it. Police in jack-boots, armed with rubber truncheons, beat up a child. The child cried and German soldiers, looking on, shook with laughter. When a Jewish girl sang a song, begging, pleading—"I am hungry and cold," policemen drove her away, and the soldiers smiled, when they saw the loaf of bread, rolling on the ground.

People walked up and down. And your father stood there and looked over the fence. Suddenly a flight of doves came down, driven from somewhere out of the blue. Silently they settled on the wires and began quietly to coo. I felt the pain of their sadness and sorrow, I listened to their weeping hearts and understood the anguish of the freezing doves.

And yet, my child, how greedy man is! With his heart he feels sympathy, while his eyes are filled with envy. The doves have wings, and if they want to, they can fly, onto wires or up to rooftops, off and away!

Your father stood there, dreaming. And a policeman came and knocked him on the head. Ashamed he began to move on, but he wanted to look once more at the doves. And, then, my child, your father saw something terrible:

The doves were still there, on the barbed wires, but . . . they were eating the crumbs, out of the hands of the soldiers! . . .

My child, your father grew very sad, and sad he still is: not about the doves on freezing wires, and not because they have wings and he has not, but because now he hates the doves, too, and he warns you: Keep away from them, as long as the innocence allows itself to be fed by murderous hands. . . .

Flames over Warsaw

My child, when the steel birds hailed down death we all fled to the woods. You remember how terrified we were when the woods along our tracks caught fire and we went on in our flight without hope and without thought that we would ever reach our goal?

Now it is different. . . . Come, come out into the street. Though a biting frost cuts the ears and it is late in the evening. My dear, beloved son, come, I will show you a fire that lights up the skies over Warsaw. I don't know where it comes from and what it is for. Maybe they are fliers from Russian fields or maybe the birds came from the other side of the Channel; or maybe it is the work of hidden hands at home°; perhaps this, perhaps that. . . . But look, how the sky grows red. How beautiful the red is over the snow-covered town; it is evening and it's light and there where the Vistula is frozen to ice, rise up higher, and higher, and almost as high as the sky: giant tongues of fire and of smoke. Wherever we turn we see wide-open spaces lit up by the flames. It smells of sulphur, of white heat, though the frost is grim and the snow lies dense on roofs and walls.

A reference to the partisans.

How beautiful is this wintry evening! Something great and unexpected is coming from over there, from the Vistula, where the fires are burning.

My child, you regret that you cannot put out the fire, that you are not a Polish fireman with a little trumpet: *tu-tu-tu!* . . .

Don't be a silly child! You'll be a fireman one day. But not yet, not yet. It's too early yet to extinguish the fires. Let them burn, let them burn, let them burn, my child!

Come children, let's form a ring and dance and clap our hands: *tra-la, tra-la-la!*
A pity the fire grows smaller . . . Someone asks me:
—What was on fire, Mister Jew, perhaps you know? What was it?
—The wickedness of the world was on fire, I thought. . . .
—Really?—The woman who asked nods knowingly.

It Will Be as in Our Dream . . .

My son! You should not regret it that you have been with me in the locked-up streets of the Ghetto—Dzika, Stavki and Mila.

My son, you should not regret your crying today. It does not matter that, when you look up to the sun, tears come into your eyes.

For you will see, my child, you will see: where today there is wailing and sadness hovers in homes; and the Angel of Death reigns supreme like a drunken madman; and people in rags, heaps of shattered hopes, cower along old, dark and smoky walls; and bodies of old men rot away in doorways or on bare floors, covered with newspapers or pieces of stone; and children shiver and whisper: "We are starving" and like rats stir in piles of refuse; and worn-out women hold up their hands, thin as ribbons in their last barren consumptive prayers; and frost and disease close in on dying eyes that, in their last agony crave for a crust of bread—

There, my dear, my sunny child,
there will yet come
that great,
that greatest of days,
that last, the very last day—
and it will be as in our dream . . .

Warsaw ghetto, February–March 1942
Published in the Bundist *Yugnt-shtime*
['Voice of Youth'], no. 2/3

83 Leyb Rosental

Yisrolik

So, you wanna buy some smokes?
Saccharin too I got.
These days the stuff's going dirt cheap.
A life for just a groschen,

All day I don't make squat—
You heard of the ghetto-peddler? That's me.

    I'm called Yisrolik,
    The kid from the ghetto.
    That's right, Yisrolik,
    A happy-go-lucky guy.
    I end up with a big fat zero,
    Still I can whistle
    And hawk a song any time.

A coat without a collar,
Shirt from a gunnysack,
Galoshes, yeah, but no sign of shoes—
Anyone laughs or snickers,
Anyone cracks a joke,
I'll show them what's what and who's who.

    I'm called Yisrolik. . . .

It ain't like I was born, say,
In a ditch or a gutter.
Once I had a regular mom 'n dad.
But they both been dragged away.
Well, no use blubbering.
Still, I'm like wind in the fields, a nomad.

    Yisrolik, that's me.
    And when no one can see,
    I wipe away
    A tear or two.
    But this sorrow—
    Better let it be.
    Why make a case of it
    And drag the heart so low?

            Premiered in the Vilna ghetto, February 1942

Moderato

Nu koyft zhe pa - pi - ro - sn, Nu koyft zhe sa - kha -
rin, Ge - vo - rn iz haynt skhoy - re bi - lik vert._____ A

le - bn far a gro - shn, A pru - te — a far - dinst — Fun
ge - to - hend - ler hot ir dokh ge - hert. _____
Kh'heys yis - ro - lik Ikh bin dos kind fun ge - to,
Kh'heys yis - ro - lik A hef - ker - di - ker yung. Khotsh far -
bli-bn go - le - ne-to Der - lang ikh alts nokh A svish-tshe un a zung!

84 Leah Rudnitsky

Birds Are Drowsing

Birds are drowsing on the branches.
Sleep, my darling child.
At your cradle, in the field,
A stranger sits and sings.

Once you had another cradle
Woven out of joy,
And your mother, oh your mother
Will never more come by.

I saw your father fleeing
Under the rain of countless stones,
Over fields and over valleys
Flew his orphaned cry.

Vilna ghetto, circa 1942

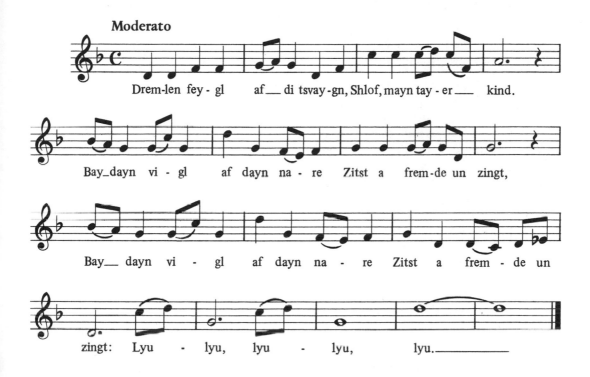

Moderato

Drem-len fey - gl af __ di tsvay-gn, Shlof, mayn tay - er __ kind.

Bay __ dayn vi - gl af dayn na - re Zitst a frem-de un zingt,

Bay __ dayn vi - gl af dayn na - re Zitst a frem - de un

zingt: Lyu - lyu, lyu - lyu, lyu. __

85 Shmerke Kaczerginski

Still, Still

Still, still, let us be still.
Graves grow here.
Planted by the enemy,
they blossom to the sky.
All the roads lead to Ponar,
and none returns.

Somewhere father disappeared,
disappeared with all our joy.
Be still, my child, don't cry, my treasure;
tears are of no avail.
No matter the fury of your tears,
the enemy will not notice.
Rivers open into oceans,
prison cells are not a world,
but to our sorrow,
there is no end,
there is no light.

Spring has blossomed in the countryside,
and all about our lives is fall.
Today the day is full of flowers,
but the night alone holds us.
Somewhere a mother is orphaned.
Her child goes to Ponar.
The river Viliye, chained,
convulses in our pain.
Ice floes race through Lithuania
Into the ocean now.
Somewhere there is no darkness.
Somewhere, out of darkness,
suns are burning.
Rider come at once.
Your child calls you.
Your child calls you.

Still, still, wellsprings flow
deep without our hearts.
Until the gates come falling down
we must guard our tongues.
Don't rejoice, child, your very smile
is treachery now.
Let the enemy see the spring
as a leaf in autumn.
Let the wellspring flow its course
and you be still and hope. . . .
Father will return with freedom.
Sleep, my child, be still.
Like the Viliye freed of its chains
and like the trees renewed in green,
freedom's light will glow
upon your face,
upon your face.

Vilna ghetto, April 1943

Andantino

Shti - ler, shti - ler, lo - mir shvay - gn, Kvo - rim vak - sn do.

S'ho - bn zey far - flantst di so - nim; Gri - nen zey tsum blo.

S'fi - rn ve - gn tsu po - nar tsu, S'firt keyn veg tsu - rik,

Iz der ta - te vu far - shvun - dn Un mit im dos glik.

Shti - ler, kind mayns, veyn nit, oy - tser, S'helft nit keyn ge - veyn,

Un - dzer um - glik ve - ln so - nim Say - vi nit far - shteyn.

S'ho - bn bre - ges oykh di ya - men, S'ho - bn tfi - ses oy - khet tsa - men,

Nor tsu un - dzer payn keyn bi - sl shayn,____ Keyn bi - sl shayn.

Youth Hymn

Our song is filled with grieving,
Bold our step, we march along,
Though the foe the gateway's watching,
Youth comes storming with their song:

    Young are they, are they, are they
    whose age won't bind them.
    Years don't really mean a thing,
    Elders also, also, also, can be children
    In a newer, freer spring.

Those who roam upon the highways,
Those whose step with hope is strong,
From the ghetto youth salutes them
And their greetings send along.

    Young are they . . .

We remember all the tyrants,
We remember all our friends,
And we pledge that in the future
Our past and present blend.

    Young are they . . .

So we're girding our muscles,
In our ranks we're planting steel,
Where a blacksmith, builder marches,
We will join them with our zeal!

    Young are they . . .

Vilna ghetto, circa 1942

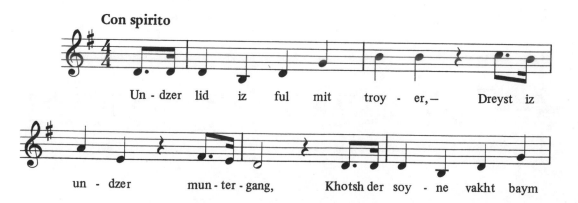

Con spirito

Un - dzer lid iz ful mit troy - er, — Dreyst iz

un - dzer mun - ter - gang, Khotsh der soy - ne vakht baym

toy - er, — Shtu-remt yu-gnt mit ge-zang: Yung iz
ye - der, ye - der, ye - der ver es vil nor, Yo - rn
ho - bn keyn ba - tayt, Al - te ke - nen, ke - nen, ke-nen oykh zayn
kin - der Fun a nay - er fray - er tsayt.

Itsik Vittenberg

Somewhere crouching, hiding
The foe, beastlike, biding,
The mauzer keeps watch in my hand,
Suddenly the Gestapo
Leads one whom they've trapped oh!
Through darkness, it's our commandant.

With lightning the night
Tears the ghetto with fright,
There's danger about and fears mount.
Dear friends so devoted,
Chains must be exploded,
And vanish must our commandant.

Night faded, it tore us,
As death stood before us,
The ghetto in fever did pant.
In turmoil the ghetto,
Commands the Gestapo:
It's death or it's your commandant.

Then spoke up our Itsik
As quick as a blink is
"I must heed this edict, that's clear.
I'll not forfeit your lives
To the tyrants' cruel knives."
To death he goes without fear.

Again, crouching, hiding
The foe, beastlike, biding,
Again mauzer guards in my hand.
Now you're dear to me,
My savior you must be,
Now you must be my commandant.

Vilna ghetto, 1943

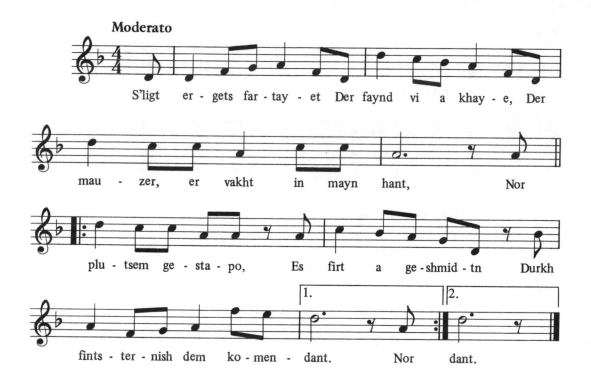

Moderato

S'ligt er-gets far-tay-et Der faynd vi a khay-e, Der

mau—zer, er vakht in mayn hant, Nor

plu-tsem ge-sta-po, Es firt a ge-shmid-tn Durkh

fints-ter-nish dem ko-men-dant.   Nor   dant.

86 Hirsh Glik

Silence, and a Starry Night

Silence, and a starry night
Frost crackling, fine as sand.
Remember how I taught you
To hold a gun in your hand?

In fur jacket and beret,
Clutching a hand grenade,
A girl whose skin is velvet
Ambushes a cavalcade.

Aim, fire, shoot—and hit!
She, with her pistol small,
Halts an autoful,
Arms and all!

Morning, emerging from the wood,
In her hair a snow carnation.
Proud of her small victory
For the new, free generation!

Vilna ghetto, Summer 1942

Moderato

Shtil, di nakht iz oys-ge-shte - rnt,
Un der frost, er hot ge - brent; Tsi ge-
denk - stu vi ikh hob dikh ge - le - rnt
Hal - tn a shpay - er in di hent. Tsi ge - hent.

Never Say

Never say, this is the last road for you,
Leaden skies are masking days of blue.
The hour we yearn for is drawing near,
Our step will beat the signal: we are here!

From southern palms, from lands long white with snow,
We come with all our pain and all our woe,

Wherever seeped our blood into the earth,
Our courage and our strength will have rebirth.

Tomorrow's sun will gild our sad today,
The enemy and yesterday will fade away.
But should the dawn delay or sunrise wait too long,
Then let all future generations sing this song.

This song was written with our blood and not with lead,
This is no song of free birds flying overhead,
But a people amid crumbling walls did stand,
They stood and sang this song with rifles held in hand.

Vilna ghetto, 1943

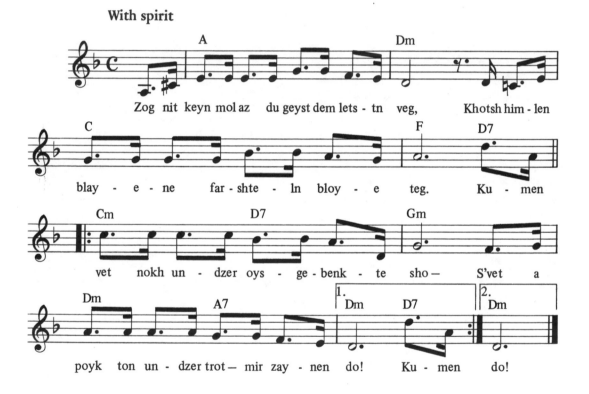

87 Wladyslaw Szlengel

Two Gentlemen in the Snow

The falling snow is mean, piercing,
The white wool envelops my feet.

A Jew at his work—and a soldier;
Together we stand in the empty street.

You have no home—I have no home.
Time has stopped life's easy flow.
O what a fearful gulf between us,
And yet we're linked by the snow . . .

I am a captive you must guard,
But aren't you a captive, too?
I wonder who is holding whom;
Doesn't a third one hold us two?

And how can I compare at all?
Your uniform is fine, it's true,
But what's the use, if the snow can't tell
A handsome soldier from a Jew?

The snow falls evenly on us
With a peaceful cloak of white.
Together we watch through its screen
The dawning of a distant light.

Look now, what are we doing here,
Why pointlessly so roam?
Listen, man, it snows so long,
Let's part, let us go home. . . .

Warsaw ghetto, 1941

Counterattack

They plodded calmly to the cars
As though disgusted with it all—
Gazed like dogs at the guards' eyes . . .
Cattle! ! !

Dapper officers smirked to see
That nothing got under their skin,
That hordes moved with torpid step
. . . and only for sport
Lashed their snouts
With whips . . .
Counting-off in the square
Some dropped where they stood
Even before they could sob in the cars
Soaking the sandy ground with tears and blood
And the gentlemen . . .
On the corpses . . .
   let fall in a casual way . . .
     cigarette boxes that said

"Why Junos
   are round."

Until the day when at dawn
On the town they'd lulled to sleep
Like hyenas they rushed out of morning fog,
Then the cattle woke up
And . . .
Bared its FANGS.

On Mila Street the first bullet fell—
Gendarme wobbled in a doorway—
Looked astonished . . . stopped a moment . . .
—incredible———
—something isn't right . . .
It had all been so simple, so easy—
Because of special pull
He'd been transferred away from the Eastern Front
(A few days R & R)
To rest a bit in Warsaw
Herding this cattle in the "action"
Cleaning out this sty
And here . . .
On Mila Street BLOOD? ? ?
He backed away from the doorway
And swore: "I'm bleeding for real. . . ."

And meanwhile Brownings barked
On Niska
   On Dzika
      On Pawia———

On twisting stairs where a mother
Was dragged down by the hair
Lies SS-man Hantke . . .
Strangely tensed, as though
He found death indigestible—
This revolt like a bone in his throat—
Choked in bloody drool—
And a box: Junos are round . . .
Round . . .
   round . . .

Golden epaulets trampled in dust!
Everything spins around:
Sky-blue gendarme's uniform lies
On spit-flecked stairs
Of Jewish Pawia Street . . .
   And doesn't know
   That at Schultz's and Toebbens'°

*In point of fact,
there was no
fighting at the*

Bullets ring in joyous song
Revolt of the Meat!
Revolt of the meat! ! !
Meat spits grenades out the window
Meat bites with scarlet flames
And life hangs on from the beams—
Hey! What joy to shoot at their eyes
HERE IS THE FRONT gentlemen!
THE FRONT DEAR SUNSHINE SOLDIERS!
HIER
TRINKT MAN MEHR KEIN BIER!
HIER
HAT MAN MEHR KEIN MUT . . .
BLUT . . .
BLUT—
BLUT! ! !°

Schultz and Toebbens shops. This happened only in the April uprising.

"Here one drinks no more beer / Here one has no more courage / Blood / Blood / Blood!"

Take off the light smooth leather gloves,
Put away the whips—helmets on your heads
Tomorrow inform the press:
Toebbens' entry forced with a wedge
Revolt of the meat . . .
REVOLT OF THE MEAT! ! ! SONG OF THE MEAT! ! !

Do you hear, German god,
How Jews pray in wildcat houses°
Crowbars and clubs in their hands:
—We ask of you, God, a bloody battle,
We implore you, a violent death—
May our eyes before they flicker
Not see the tracks stretch out
But give our palms true aim, Lord,
To bloody the coats of blue.
Allow us to see before
Dumb groaning chokes our throats . . .
In those haughty hands—in those paws with whips
Our everyday human FEAR!

These houses were emptied of inhabitants during the Great Deportation; Cf. (77).

Like purple blossoms of blood
From Niska and Mila and Muranowa
Flames from our gunbarrels flower—
This is our spring, our counterattack—
This wine of battle pounds in our heads. . . .
These our partisan woods
Alleys of Dzika and Ostrowska—
Block-numbers flutter on breasts
Our medals in the Jewish War
The shriek of six letters flashes with red
Like a battering-ram it beats REVOLT

And on the street a package
Crushed and sticky with blood!
JUNOS ARE ROUND . . .

Warsaw ghetto, January 1943

88 Abraham Sutzkever

Faces in the Mire: I

This 5-part
sequence was
reconstructed from
the original
manuscript. In
Sutzkever's printed
works, they appear
scattered.

Night came, turning our abstractions grey.
Doves were owls, white became black.
Our wounds were soldered by the steaming salts of day,
Mocking our dream, smokily calling it back.

Are you trembling earth? Are you as we are: torn?   5
Does the odor of martyrs tease your sensual memories?
Devour us then, the overconfident, the cursed-when-born.
Devour our generation with its idiot ideologies.

Still thirsty? We'll overflow for you, burst like tires.
We'll pour the gold that is our flesh into your ruts.   10
A nightmare will go at our faces in the mire,
Faces in the mire, above the dusk, above the wretched huts.

In the Cell: II

The darkness wants to strangle me.
Invisible, leaden mice gnaw my sanity.
I toss in this awful world of stone,
Dreaming of something human, something known!

I grope and a morsel of glass comes to hand,   5
The moon pliered in its transparent sand.
I forget whether or not I'm ill:
A hand chipped this, fleshy, palpable.

Testing the lunar edge warily,
I ask: if I offered myself would you want me?   10
But the glass is freezing, my blood hot.
The blade, my throat: should I? No, not.

Leaves of Ash: III

I am boiling tea with your letters,
My only treasure.
All that's left
Of their touching measure
Are leaves of ash,   5
Fragile, wormed with glow,
That only I can read now as I ask:
Am I really boiling tea with your letters,
My only treasure?

Wind: stay stiller than a gravestone!   10
Shadow: don't dare move!
A single breath
Would scatter to the jealous world
All the healing beauties
Of my treasure.   15

How dear you are to me in these leaves of ash.
How radiantly you're fading in these leaves of ash
That only I can read now as I ask:
Am I really boiling tea with your letters,
My only treasure?   20

Because I Was Drinking Wine: IV

Because I was drinking wine, friend, and it was late,
While you waited for me to come set you free,
My words revolt with incandescent hate,
Slicing the curtains of my thoughts relentlessly.

Because I didn't stop my heart like a stunned steer,   5
Nor let your slaughterer's frenzy drive me insane,
Worms swarm from the apple of my cheer,
And my stale laughter brands me like the mark of Cain.

A Voice From the Heart: V

A voice from the heart commands me:
Believe in that degraded term, the right.
A lion's however distant progeny
Must shrug off slavery and fight.

There is a way, it arises   5
In the forests of recollection.
There is also an ancient virus
Still capable of infection.

To make sense of your terrible pain
You must clarify your hells.   10

Our grandfathers shake mythic chains,
Our sons wake to alarm bells.

There is a path through error:
Redeem history's omission.
Death excuses terror   15
But never submission.

                                        Vilna, June-July 1941

I Lie in This Coffin

I lie in this coffin
the way I would lie
in a suit made of wood,
a bark
tossed on treacherous waves,   5
a cradle, an ark.

From here, where all
flesh is taken to eternity,
A reference to his   I call
sister who died in   to you, sister,° and you   10
Siberia during   in your distance
Sutzkever's   still hear me.
childhood.

Something stirs
in my coffin,
a presence; you're here: 15
I know you by the stars
of your eyes, your light, your
breath, your tear.

This is the order of things,
and the plot: 20
today here, tomorrow not.
But now, in my coffin,
my suit made of wood,
my speech lifts,
my speech sings.   25

                                        Vilna, August 30, 1941

Pray

I think I just thought of a prayer,
But I can't imagine who might be there.
    Sealed in a steel womb,
    How can I pray? To whom?

Star, you were once my dear friend,   5
Come, stand for the words that have come to an end.

But dear, deaf star,
I understand, you're too far.

Still, someone in me insists: pray!
Tormenting me in my soul: pray!   10
  Prayer, oh wildest surmise,
  I still babble you till sunrise.

                              Vilna ghetto, January 17, 1942

A Load of Shoes

The cartwheels rush,
quivering.
What is their burden?
Shoes, shivering.

The cart is like   5
a great hall:
the shoes crushed together
as though at a ball.

A wedding? A party?
Have I gone blind?   10
Who have these shoes
left behind?

The heels clatter
with a fearsome din,
transported from Vilna   15
to Berlin.

I should be still,
my tongue is like meat,
but the truth, shoes,
where are your feet?   20

The feet from these boots
with buttons outside
or these, with no body,
or these, with no bride?

Where is the child   25
who fit in these?
Is the maiden barefoot
who bought these?

Slippers and pumps,
look, there are my mother's: 30
her Sabbath pair,
in with the others.

The heels clatter
with a fearsome din,
transported from Vilna   35
to Berlin.

Vilna ghetto, January 1, 1943

To My Child

Because of hunger
or because of great love—
your mother will bear witness—
I wanted to swallow you, child,
when I felt your tiny body   5
cool in my hands
like a glass
of warm tea.

Neither stranger were you, nor guest.
On our earth, one births   10
only oneself, one links
oneself into rings and the rings into chains.

Child, the word for you would be love
but without words you *are* love,
the seed of dream,   15
unbidden third,
who from the limits of the world
swept two of us
into consummate pleasure.

How can you shut your eyes,   20
leaving me here
in the dark world of snow
you've shrugged off?

You never even had your own cradle
to learn the dances   25
of the stars.
The shameful sun, who never shone
on you, should shatter like glass.
Your faith burned away
in the drop of poison   30
you drank down as simply
as milk.

I wanted to swallow you, child,
to taste
the future waiting for me.   35
Maybe you will blossom again
in my veins.

I'm not worthy of you, though.
I can't be your grave.
I leave you   40
to the summoning snow,
this first respite.
You'll descend now
like a splinter of dusk
into the stillness,   45
bringing greetings from me
to the slim shoots
under the cold.

Vilna ghetto, January 18, 1943

Last Hour

Last hour, when you come, bring strength enough
For me to see a palace in ruined masonry,
To drive my final moments to their given end,
To tap a message to my prisoner soul: Be free!

Last hour, bring with you such nourishing belief   5
That in a single tear seven suns will be afire,
And in the resurrected dust, the seeds of heroes
Will germinate their will and terrible desire.

Last hour, stir up storms in me,
Bleach out my wrongs, untangle my cacophony.   10
Form me like molten gold into your mold,
Sear my chaff away, leave me in melody.

Transform to love my weary self-disgust.
Let my corrosive sorrow have been withstood.
Exalt me to believe that the most wretched life,   15
If only in its longings, is still good.

Vilna ghetto, January 26, 1943°

Dated "March 2,
1943" in all
published versions.

How?

How and with what will you fill
Your cup on the day you're free?
Will you in your joy still
Hear the scream of the past
Where the skulls of chained days   5
Clot in bottomless pits?

Searching hopelessly
For the keys to jammed locks,
You'll chew pavement like bread
And think it was better before,   10

And time will gnaw your hand gently
Like a cricket under the floor.

In a rubble-encrusted old city
Your memory will be like a hole,
And your glance will burrow furtively   15
Like a mole, like a mole.

                                        Vilna ghetto, February 14, 1943

Kernels of Wheat

Caves, crack asunder.
Split open under my blow!
Before a bullet can get me—
I bring you a sack full of gifts.

Aged purposeful pages   5
With purple on silver hair,
Words on parchment, created
Through thousands of torturous years.

Like a hen sheltering its chick—
I run with the Jewish word,   10
Rummaging in every courtyard,
So its spirit won't be extinguished.

Stretch your arms into the bonfire
And rejoice: The main thing is this:
I still have Amsterdam, Worms,   15
Livorno, Madrid, and YIVO . . .

Oh, how I am tormented by a sacred page
Tossed about in a smoky wind!
Secret songs are choking me:
Conceal us in your labyrinth.   20

I dig holes and plant manuscripts . . .
And when despair overwhelms me
My mind turns to Egypt, to
A story about kernels of wheat.

I tell it to the stars: 25
Once upon a time, a king
Built his pyramid beside the Nile
So he could rule there after his death.

He ordered his servants
To pour wheat   30
Into his golden coffin—as a memorial
Of our earthly world.

Nine thousand years did suns
Rise and set in the desert
Before the kernels were discovered   35
In the pyramid.

Nine thousand years had passed!
But when the kernels were planted,—
They bloomed in gardens
Of sunny stalks.   40

Maybe the words, too, will wait patiently
To see the light,
That predestined hour
When they, too, burst unexpectedly into flower.

And like the age-old seed   45
That unravelled itself in the stalk,—
So the words, too, will nourish,
And will belong
To the People in its eternal journey.

Vilna ghetto, March 1943

Song For the Last

Declaimed at a memorial gathering for Liza Magun, the U.P.O.'s main liaison and courier, who was caught by the Gestapo and killed in Ponar on February 17, 1943.

You aren't moths, moths have power
enough to throw themselves into flame.
And not threshed grain
nor grass trampled underfoot.
Don't look in the mirror   5
if you want to know who you are:
tear a chunk of raw time off
and sniff it: it is your death-odor.

Brothers, lift your heads, your sick
heads sinking   10
like the sun: I want to see you as you sink
hearing at least what I'm thinking.
Stay naked for now, stripped of the present.
Read yourself, as condemned men
read scratches in the walls of their cell.   15
Do you think your pain will surmount its moment?

Yesterday you knew what you meant,
and hardly bothered to think what came next.
You built foundations on a breeze and a river
and on the gods of quicksand.   20
And envy, of course, and competition,
trumping your friend's hand.
And didn't know that thorns were your element,
and venom, and that your days would be perdition.

An animal in danger   25
will tear its own flesh to get free:
you never felt the trap close,
you thought the arrow could no longer see.
Millions at a time you were no one's
but believed in your individuality.   30
The clear words of your language were illicit;
you licked the honies of alien spit.

And when a thousand years of enmity
has walled the light out completely,
and cursed you, last generation,   35
wicks in your nation's memorial candles;
when each of you is a separate city
cemented together out of kith's congealed faces,
has destruction's furious violation
dared your footsteps to leave traces?   40

Have you broken apart, like a forest
when the night's hordes of lightning attack?
And felt the earth tremble and crack
and knew no one was there to protect you?
You haven't changed at all,   45
your sense and feeling have left you.
You're your nation's nettle, not its fruit,
your treasure is trash, your well webbed with disuse.

You loathe your filthy selves and envying
your enemy guide his hands to your throat.   50
You kiss his bloody conscience clean
while you attend his gentle permissions.
If you could believe, still, and pray,
it would be him who'd have your ablutions.
You find your origins disgusting and don't see   55
that it's you yourselves who've filthied the clay.

I fear the freedom you'll find finally
more than the three seconds I propose for myself.
Will you be admitted to that hallowed land
where stars ignite lamps on the shelf?   60
I beat my skull on stones to find consolation
for you in the fragments, you, the last,
for I, too, am a letter in your book,
my sun, too, is spring's leprous outcast.

Brothers, help me find what can console: 65
My head is broken, like blank slate.
Listen closely, remember its name,
help find how it might propagate.
It has to exist! How else lift the flags

of all our tomorrow's golden suns?   70
No, you're weak, your soul sags,
you, the disgustingly patient, last of millions.

Vilna ghetto, March 16, 1943

Beneath the Whiteness of Your Stars

Beneath the whiteness of your stars,
Stretch out toward me your white hand;
All my words are turned to tears—
They long to rest within your hand.

See, their brilliant light goes darker   5
In my eyes, grown cellar-dim;
And I lack a quiet corner
From which to send them back again.

Yet, O Lord, all my desire—
To leave you with my wealth of tears.   10
In me, there burns an urgent fire,
And in the fire, there burn my days.

Rest, in every hole and cellar
Weeps, as might a murderer.
I run the rooftops, even higher,   15
And I search—where are you? Where?

Past stairs and courtyards I go running,
Chased by howling enemies.
I hang, at last, a broken bowstring,
And I sing to you—like this: 20

Beneath the whiteness of your stars,
Stretch out toward me your white hand;
All my words are turned to tears—
They long to rest within your hand.

Vilna ghetto, May 22, 1943°

*Dated according to
the original
manuscript.*

Moderato

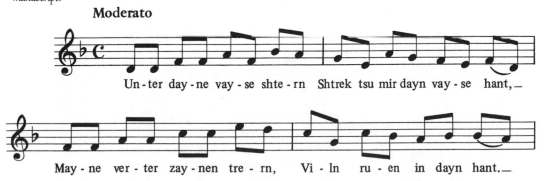

Un - ter day - ne vay - se shte - rn Shtrek tsu mir dayn vay - se hant, __

May - ne ver - ter zay - nen tre - rn, Vi - ln ru - en in dayn hant. __

Ze, es tun - klt zey - er fin - kl__ In mayn ke - ler - di - kn blik,__

Un ikh hob gor - nit keyn vin - kl Zey tsu shen - ken dir tsu - rik,

Un ikh hob gor - nit keyn vin - kl Zey tsu shen - ken __ dir tsu - rik.

Charred Pearls

My words tremble so violently they moan,
Like broken hands they plead, entreat,
Helplessly hone
Their edges like fangs lusting for meat.

I'm moved no longer by your howls,   5
Oh written word, fanner of the world's fire:
Instead, charred pearls like emptied vowels
Gaze blankly at me from their pyre.

And not even I, dead already to my death,
Can recognize this woman in flame.   10
Of all her pleasures, body, being, breath,
Charred pearls are left, not even a name.

Vilna ghetto, July 28, 1943

No Sad Songs Please

No sad songs please:
Sad songs just tease
At sorrow.
Words, too, betray,
And names,   5
Forever,
And tomorrow.

Look out at the snow:
In memory's art
Is unexpected   10
Radiance, and in

The speeches of the heart,
You yourself are
Resurrected.

Stretch your hands out   15
To that whiteness:
In its cold and burning
Veins
You'll feel returning
The redeeming life   20
It contains.

Narocz forests,° February 5, 1944

The Sutzkevers, along with a group of U.P.O. fighters, left the ghetto on September 14, 1943. The Narocz forests, located 90 miles east of Vilna, were a staging ground for partisan activity under the command of F. Markov.

XVII

Ghetto Preachers

Whereas the staff of *Oyneg Shabbes* was constrained by Ringelblum to stick to the facts and to leave the interpretation for future historians and whereas the ghetto poets tried to strike a balance between eloquence and savagery, the ghetto preachers enlisted all the myths, archetypes and paradigms of Jewish tradition to shape the catastrophe into a message of consolation. At both ends of the cultural spectrum—the ultra-orthodox Hasidic and the Yiddish secularist—there emerged a man of great learning, eloquence and moral suasion who was able to apprehend meaning in the Holocaust, perhaps more fully than most, precisely because he viewed it in its timeless aspect. Each man, moreover, anticipated a major strand of the Jewish theological response to the Holocaust: the exploration of God's pathos, the intimation of a voluntary covenant.

Rabbi Kalonymus Kalmish Shapiro, the Rebbe of Piaczesno, was both a talmudic scholar and the scion of two Hasidic dynasties. Once his home on 5 Dzielna Street was incorporated into the ghetto, he turned it into a

The analysis that follows is drawn from Nehemia Polen, "Esh Kodesh: The Teachings of Rabbi Kalonymos Shapiro in the Warsaw Ghetto, 1939–1943" (Ph.D. dissertation, Boston University, 1983).

combination synagogue and soup kitchen for his hundreds of followers. There he delivered sermons on the weekly and festival Torah readings throughout the war: from Rosh Hashanah 1940 until July 18, 1942, four days before the Great Deportation began. He translated these sermons into Hebrew and buried them for safekeeping early in 1943. Discovered by a Polish worker after the war, they were published in Israel in 1960 under the title *Esh Kodesh* (Fire of Holiness).°

As one might expect, his ghetto sermons were devoted to the traditional themes of faith, theodicy and love for one's fellow Jews *(ahavas Yisroel)*. But as he came to appreciate the unprecedented nature of the catastrophe,

Rabbi Shapiro began to explore the mostly uncharted territory of divine suffering. To be sure, the theme of God's suffering with Israel and His participation in Israel's exile had played an important role in rabbinic literature (see **14–16, 21**), but during the Middle Ages the rationalist philosophers Saadiah Gaon (882–942) and Maimonides struggled to remove all vestiges of an anthropomorphic conception of God. It also happened that such passages were attacked by Christian and Moslem polemicists intent on discrediting Rabbinic Judaism, so that by the fifteenth century, the impact of the most startling passages had been softened or eliminated through self-censorship. Beginning in February 1942, Rabbi Shapiro not only restored these passages but also advanced a new notion of the infinite magnitude of God's suffering; through the contemplation of His suffering, the human being could lose his attachment to his own. Rabbi Shapiro pictured the world poised on the brink of destruction—one divine spark of pain could destroy the universe were it to pierce its boundaries. This sermon also enunciated a kind of "mysticism of catastrophe," as Nehemia Polen puts it. Rabbi Shapiro hinted that a revelation might emerge precisely from the ruins; external destruction was internalized, so that the boundaries of one's ego dissolved, allowing one to hear the heavenly voice . . . weeping (the very same idea was expressed a few months later in Yitzhak Katzenelson's epic poem "The Song about the Radziner"; see *Against the Apocalypse*, pp. 218–20).

In his sermon for March 14, 1942, Rabbi Shapiro pushed one step further the idea of a human-divine partnership in suffering. Turning now to the concept of *hester panim* (divine hiddenness, or what Martin Buber called "the eclipse of God"), Rabbi Shapiro explained this hiddenness as resulting from God's desire to weep in seclusion. According to Rabbi Shapiro, in situations of extreme suffering, a person can burst into God's hidden chamber, so to speak, and join God in His sorrow. The weeping that man does *with God* can then be a source of renewed strength. From this mystical communion *in extremis* can come a renewed commitment to action (i.e., the study of Torah and the observance of His commandments).

The final and most radical move came on July 11, 1942, in Rabbi Shapiro's next-to-last sermon in which he redefined the traditional theology of suffering by reformulating the concept of *Kiddush Hashem*. *Kiddush Hashem* was not, as previously believed, the *consequence* of martyrdom, the surrender of one's life in a trial of faith that testified to the glory of God, but rather, its *origin*. In the present war, God was the primary object of attack. Because Israel identified with the divine cause, it had to share in His suffering. Jews suffered *on His account*. The destruction of European Jewry, in other words, was perceived by Shapiro to be a war against God, and in this war, Jews were His soldiers. This meant that Jewish suffering, no matter how great, was ancillary to His. It also meant that the catastrophe was occurring not for any sin, large or small, committed by Israel, but simply by virtue of Israel's identification with God.

Working with totally different assumptions, Zelig Kalmanovitsh, philologist, historian and cultural activist, arrived at much the same conclusion: that the Nazi onslaught was aimed at more than Jewish bodies; it was a war against the "sacred triad" of Israel-Torah-and-God. For Kalmanovitsh, the tragic realities of the Vilna ghetto seemed to bear out the bleak historical prognosis that he had formulated as early as April 1939: that the Jewish people would be crushed between the hammer of totalitarianism and the anvil of assimilation. Yet, if anything, Kalmanovitsh saw in the ghetto the first glimmers of a return to group solidarity and Jewish cultural renewal.

Kalmanovitsh's outlook was mirrored by his life. He became an observant Jew in the ghetto and began to keep a journal in Hebrew rather than in Yiddish. His two formal sermons were, it seems, spontaneous expressions of his newfound sense of belonging. At the same time, however, Kalmanovitsh continued to occupy a central place in the Yiddish cultural life of the ghetto: he helped establish and run the Union of Writers and Artists and he was the person principally consulted by the "Paper Brigade" as to which books and manuscripts should be smuggled into the ghetto for safekeeping. Sutzkever referred to him as "the prophet of the ghetto," and Abba Kovner sought his moral guidance over whether to organize an armed resistance. (Kalmanovitsh argued against it, and Kovner was almost persuaded.)

Kalmanovitsh's ability to see the destruction of east European Jewry as part of a metahistorical drama was indeed an act of rare prophetic power. He based his faith on two foundations. From an incident that occurred in the ghetto school, Kalmanovitsh formulated the idea of a voluntary covenant, that a Jew, even under the most terrible conditions, would still *choose* to be Jacob rather than Esau. Even if one argued that most Jews made that choice instinctively and not self-consciously, there were still sufficient "rational" motives to remain a Jew. So long as Jews affirmed their place in the Sacred Triad, two of the three partners would always remain inviolate. Although the Germans might ultimately destroy one whole arm of the Jewish people, they would never prevail against the moral law and the Creator of the Universe. History itself—notably the Exodus from Egypt—was proof that the combined force of God and the Torah would emerge triumphant from the present Holocaust.

89 Rabbi Kalonymus Shapiro

From *Fire of Holiness*

Parashat Mishpatim [*Exod. 21:1–24:18*]
(Shekalim [*additional reading of Exod. 30:11–16*])

Exod. 21:1. NOW THESE ARE THE ORDINANCES WHICH YOU SHALL SET BEFORE THEM.° We find a passage in *Berakhot* (3a):

In Hebrew, bat kol.

The words "to Me" were omitted from all standard editions of the Talmud; they do appear in the Ein Ya'akov and Menorat Hama'or.

In Hebrew, keveyakhol, if one could say such a thing.

Following the keri of the Masoretic text.

B. Sanhedrin 46a.

No such source has yet been located.

Here Rabbi Shapiro begins his own interpretation.

Note the radical twist on the concept of divine transcendence.

Further may mean that prior to this incident Rabbi Yosi had already attained a level of self-annihilation.

As the borders of the self recede, the mystic perceives the divine suffering.

Rabbi Yosi says, I was once [traveling on the road], and I entered into one of the ruins of Jerusalem in order to pray. Elijah of blessed memory appeared [and waited for me at the door till I finished my prayer. After I finished my prayer,] he said to me: [Peace be with you, my master! and I replied: Peace be with you, my master and teacher! And he said to me: ... My son, what sound did you hear in this ruin? I replied:] I heard a divine voice,° cooing like a dove, and saying: Woe to Me° for I have destroyed My house and burnt My temple and have exiled My children [among the nations of the world.] He said to me: [By your life and by your head! Not in this moment alone does it so exclaim,] but thrice each day does it exclaim thus! And more than that, whenever the Israelites go into the synagogues and schoolhouses and respond "May His great name be blessed!" the Holy One; blessed be He, as it were,° shakes His head and says: [Happy is the king who is thus praised in this house! Woe to the father who had to banish his children, and woe to the children who had to be banished from the table of their father!]

Inspect this passage at its source. We have already raised the following point about the passage. Why did Rabbi Yosi hear the voice only when he prayed in the ruin? Does not the Holy one, blessed be He, speak thus [as specified in the passage] three times every day?

Now the Israelite who is tormented by his afflictions thinks that he alone suffers, as if all his personal afflictions and those of all Israel do not affect [God] above, God forbid. Scripture states, however, IN ALL THEIR TROUBLES HE WAS TROUBLED (Isa. 63:9)°; and the Talmud states: When a person suffers, what does the Shekhinah say? 'My head is too heavy for me, My arm is too heavy for Me.'° Our sacred literature tells us that when an Israelite is afflicted, God, blessed be He, suffers as it were much more than the person does.° It may be°° that since He, blessed be He, is not subject to any limitation—for which reason no conception of Him is possible in the world—therefore His suffering from Israel's troubles is also boundless.° It is not merely that it would be impossible for a person to endure the experience of such great suffering, but that even to conceive of His suffering, blessed be He—to know that He, blessed be He, does suffer, to hear His voice, blessed be He: 'Woe to Me for I have destroyed My house and have exiled My children'—is impossible, because He is beyond the confines of the human. It is only when Rabbi Yosi entered one of the ruins of Jerusalem so that his selfhood was further° annihilated, and the constricted, bounded aspect of his being was further destroyed, that he heard the voice of the Holy One, blessed be He.° Even then he only heard a bit of it: he heard a divine voice that merely cooed like a

I.e, if God roars like a lion over the Ḥurban, then to hear a voice cooing like a dove represents but a partial revelation.

See 14.

dove, whereas Scripture states HE SURELY ROARS OVER HIS HABITATION (Jer. 25:30)—like the roar of a lion, as it were, over the destruction of the Temple.°

This explains why the world remains standing on its foundation and was not destroyed by God's cry of suffering over the afflictions of His people and the destruction of His house: because His great suffering never penetrated the world. This may be what underlies the passage found in the Proem of Midrash Lamentations Rabbah [which speaks of God's weeping at the destruction of the Temple].° The angel said:

"Sovereign of the Universe, let me weep, but don't You weep." God replied to him, "If you don't let me weep now, I will go to a place where you have no permission to enter, and weep there," [as Scripture says, BUT IF YOU WILL NOT HEAR IT,] MY SOUL SHALL WEEP IN SECRET (Jer. 13:17).

Citing the passage from memory, Rabbi Shapiro added the attribution to an angel.

Inspect this passage at its source. Furthermore, in *Tanna debe Eliyahu Rabbah* [chap. 17], we find that the angel said, "It is unseemly for a king to weep before his servants."° But if the issue was merely that of the unseemliness of a king weeping before his servants, then the *angel* could have gone away; then [God's weeping] would no longer be 'before his servants.' In light of what we've stated above, however, the passage suggests the following: what the angel meant to say was that it is unseemly, with respect to the king's servants, for the king to *need* to weep. Rather, since His suffering, as it were, is boundless and vaster than all the world—for which reason it has never penetrated the world and the world does not shudder from it—therefore the angel said, "Let me weep so that You won't need to weep." In other words, since angels are also messengers of God—for it is through them that He performs His actions, that is why the angel wanted the divine weeping to be manifested *in the world*; the angel wanted to transmit the weeping *into* the world. For then God would no longer need to weep; once the sound of divine

Here Rabbi Shapiro's own voice breaks through the literary convention.

B. *Megillah* 10b.

I.e., the angel was asking permission to transmit God's pain to the world, thus precipitating a cataclysmic explosion.

Rabbi Samuel Eliezer ben Judah Edels (1556–1631).

"Understanding" the third of the ten divine emanations.

See Zohar I:1b; III:193b.

weeping would be heard in the world, the world would hear it and explode.° A spark of His suffering, as it were, would penetrate the world and would consume all His enemies. At the [parting of the] Sea [of Reeds, Exod. 14–15], the Holy One, blessed be He exclaimed [to the ministering angels who wished to chant their hymns], "My creatures are drowning in the Sea, and you wish to sing hymns!"° Now that Israel is drowning in blood, shall the world continue to exist?! [So the angel said,] "Let me weep, but don't You weep"—in other words, You will no longer need to weep.° But since God wanted to atone for Israel's sins, and that time was not yet a time of salvation, He answered, "I will go to a place where you have no permission to enter and weep there."—Now the suffering is so great that the world cannot contain it; it is too sublime for the world. He causes His suffering and pain to expand, as it were, still more so that they would be too sublime even for the angel, so that even the angel would not see. In the Talmudic tractate Ḥagigah (5b), we find that this place [where God weeps] is in the inner chambers [of heaven]. There weeping can, as it were, be predicated of Him. In the commentary of Maharsha° [ad loc.] we find that the term *inner chambers*, understood kabbalistically, refers to the *sefirah* of *Binah*°; inspect this statement at its source. In light of what we've said above, the significance of Maharsha's statement is that *Binah* is a state in which questioning, but not knowledge, is possible;° it is beyond conception. In this state, therefore, His suffering is, as it were, hidden from the angel and from all the world.

February 14, 1942

Parashat Haḥodesh [*Exod. 12:1–20*]

. . . The Talmud states in Ḥagigah [5b] that, concerning God's outer chambers, we may apply the verse STRENGTH AND REJOICING ARE IN HIS PLACE (1 Chron. 16:27), but in His inner chambers, He grieves and weeps for the sufferings of Israel. Therefore, there are occasions when, at a time of [Divine] hiddenness—meaning, when He, may He be blessed, secludes Himself in His inner chambers—the Jewish person communes with Him there, each individual in accord with his situation, and [new aspects of] Torah and Divine Service are revealed to him there. We have already mentioned how the Oral Torah was revealed in exile, and how the Holy Zohar was revealed to Rabbi Simeon bar Yohai and his son Rabbi Eleazar at a time of acute suffering, caused by the terror of the [Roman] government.

At times the individual is amazed at himself. [He thinks:] "Am I not broken? Am I not always on the verge of tears—and indeed I do weep periodically! How then can I study Torah? How can I find the strength to think creatively in Torah and Hasidism?" At times the person torments himself by thinking, "Can it be anything but inner callousness, that I am able to strengthen myself and study, despite my troubles and those of Israel, which are so numerous." Then again, he will say to himself, "Am I not broken? I have so much to make me cry; my whole life is gloomy and dark." Such a person is perplexed about himself; but, as we've said, He, may He be blessed, is to be found in His inner chambers, weeping, so that one who pushes in and comes close to Him by means of [studying] Torah, weeps together with God, and studies Torah with Him. Just that makes the difference: the weeping, the pain that a person undergoes by himself, alone—they may have the effect of breaking him, of bringing him down, so that he is incapable of doing anything. But the weeping that the person does together with God—that strengthens him. He weeps—and is strengthened; he is broken—but finds courage to study and teach. *It is hard to rise, time and again, above the sufferings; but when one summons the courage—stretching the mind to engage in Torah and Divine service—then he enters the inner chambers where God is to be found. There he weeps and wails with Him, as it were, together, so that he even finds the strength to study Torah and perform acts of Divine service.*

March 14, 1942

Parashat Mattot [*Num. 30:2–32:42*]

. . . How can we lift ourselves up at least a little bit in the face of the terrifying reports, both old and new, which tear us to pieces and crush our hearts? With the knowledge that we are not alone in our sufferings, but that He, may He be blessed, endures with us [as Scripture states], I AM WITH HIM IN TROUBLE (Ps. 91:15). But more: there are some sufferings that we suffer on our own account—whether for our sins, or as sufferings of love in order to purge and purify us—in which case He, may He be blessed, just suffers along with us. There are, however, some sufferings that we just suffer along with Him, as it were. These are the sufferings of *Kiddush Hashem.* [As our liturgy states,] "Our Father, our King, act for the sake of those who are slain for Your holy name."—They are killed, as it were, for His sake and for the sake of sanctifying His holy name. [As our liturgy states,] "Save, please, those who bear Your burden."—Israel also bears His burden [besides its own]. The sufferings are basically for His sake, on His account; in sufferings such as these, we are made greater, raised higher. As a consequence, we can strengthen ourselves a bit more. [As our liturgy states,] "Save those who study Your Torah, whose cheeks are torn of hair, who are given to the floggers, who bear Your burden." . . . How is it possible to study Torah when "our cheeks are torn of hair," when we are "given to the floggers"? Because we know that we "bear Your

From Isa. 50:6—
the Suffering
Servant.

burden," and we thereby strengthen ourselves a bit.°

How can we tell if the sufferings are only on account of our sins, or whether they are to sanctify His name? By [noticing] whether the enemies torment only us, or whether their hatred is basically for the Torah, and as a consequence they torment us as well. Regarding Haman's decree, the Talmud asks, "What did the

B. Megillah 12.

Jews of that generation do to deserve destruction?,"° whereas regarding the Hellenic decree [against the Jews that resulted] in the miracle of Hanukkah, the Talmud does not raise the question, despite the fact that thousands of Jews were killed, nearly all of the Land of Israel was conquered, and the Temple was invaded. The difference is that Haman's decree was directed only against the Jews [not their religion]; it follows, then, that the decree [against them] was on account of some sin. However, with respect to the Hellenic [persecution], [our liturgy] states: "In the days of Mattathias, when the wicked Hellenic kingdom arose . . . to make them forget Your Torah and transgress the statutes of Your will. . . ." So it is not appropriate to ask "for what sin [did the sufferings come]," since, while they did purge them of sin, they were [essentially] sufferings of *Kiddush Hashem.* . . .

July 11, 1942

90 Zelig Kalmanovitsh

Three Sermons

Sunday, October 11, [1942]

Jacob Gens.

One of seven
processional
circuits around the
bimah, with
members of the
congregation
carrying Torah
scrolls.

On Simḥat Torah eve at the invitation of the rabbi, I went for *hakafot* in a house that had formerly been a synagogue and was now a music school. The remnants of the yeshiva students and scholars were assembled, as well as some children. There was singing and dancing. The commandant° and his assistants were also there. I was honored with the first *hakafa.* °. . . I said a few words: "Our song and dance are a form of worship. Our rejoicing is due to Him who decrees life and death. Here in the midst of this small congregation, in the poor and ruined synagogue, we are united with the whole house of Israel, not only with those who are here today and with the tens of thousands of the pure and saintly who have passed on to life eternal, but with all the generations of Jews who were before us. In our rejoicing today we give thanks for the previous generations, the noble generations in which life was worthwhile. We feel that with our song today we sanctify the name of Heaven just as our ancestors did. And, I, a straying Jewish soul, feel that my roots are here. And you, in your rejoicing, atone for the sins of a generation that is perishing. I know that the Jewish people will live, for it is *Deut. 11:21.*   written: 'As the days of the heaven upon the earth. . .'° And even if we were the last generation, we should give thanks and say: 'Enough for us that we were privileged to be the children of those!' And every day that the Holy One, blessed be He, in His mercy gives us is a gift which we accept with joy and give thanks to His holy name.''

Sunday, [December] 27, [1942]

This morning I was in the children's nursery. Women who work leave their *7 A.M. to 6 P.M.*   children from 7 to 6.° There are 150 children between the ages of three months and two years, [one group] from two to three years, [one group] from three to six, and another group that studies reading and writing. Speeches, dramatic presentations, the children march in line. But the Jewish flavor is missing. In ghetto circumstances the order is remarkable. What vitality in this people on the brink of destruction!

From here on, the entry was recorded in Yiddish.   Who mourns the destruction of East European Jewry? The destruction is a hard fact. Undoubtedly also those who predicted it did not envisage it in this form. Three or four years ago the central Zionist organ was writing of a Jewish center in the Diaspora parallel to the center in Palestine. But the catastrophe was nevertheless a definite thing, its contours so visible. Indeed, the innovative horror for our human consciousness is the personal destruction of human lives: old people, children, blossoming youth, weak and old men, but also those in full vigor. There is no doubt, it tears the heart. But millions of people are losing their lives in all parts of the world in the war. Not only combatants, but also infants and old people. The war has put its face on our destruction. But the destruction was certain even had there been no war. It proceeded on its way in an expansive manner. No one attempted to stem it. On the contrary, whoever attempted to convince himself and the world that he was erecting a defense, actually collapsed. The full proof came in the East [in the U.S.S.R.]. Everything was swallowed up in one great endeavor *A reference to the Soviet policy of forcibly assimilating the Jews and to the conformist Communist culture in Yiddish.*   to disappear.° The apparent life of culture was pure nonsense, arid. When the East came here, no one as much as raised his voice.° All was happiness. All found a place, a sense of belonging. Undoubtedly here and there someone thought: something is missing. Another reflected: Judaism is disappearing. But all this was glossed over by the fact of mere existence. There is no discrimination. One amounts to something, particularly something in the apparatus. One can have his say. Had the thing continued in existence, nothing would have been left of the enemies of Israel anyway, except, of course, the youth that yearns thither [Palestine]. Could *A reference to the Soviet occupation of Lithuania from June 1940 to 1941.*   they actually have got there, they would have been saved for our people, and the people through them. But the rest? The individuals would have remained intact, but would have been lost to our people. Jewry in the East is disappearing. The final result is the same as now.

What is better? Better for whom? The individuals who are saved are saved individuals. There are two billion people in the world, two billion people + x. For our people—the Jewish people—had constructive elements in East European Jewry. Those that yearned thither,° if they actually succeeded in coming there, they strengthened our people. Otherwise, our people will mourn them. Great will be the sorrow and mourning, the joy of redemption will be wrapped in black. But the same sorrow is also for the parts that disappeared through apostasy. And if you wish, the sorrow is even greater. Here the evil beast came: "Joseph is without doubt torn in pieces."° But how Jacob would have wept if the first plan, God forbid, had been carried out!° In that case the Jewish people would have been justified in feeling that sick, impure blood courses in our veins. No external enemy tears off our limbs. Our limbs rot and fall off by themselves. And a page of history will read: The grandchildren were not inferior to the grandfathers. Only fire and sword overcame them. A curse upon the murderer! Eternal glory to the innocent victim! But here, where comfort lures people into the camp of the mighty, it is of no interest to history. It will not condemn, but silence means condemnation. You are no longer. Like all of them—Ammon, Moab, Edom, the hundred kingdoms of Aram . . . an object for excavations and students of epigraphy. History will revere your memory, people of the ghetto. Your least utterance will be studied, your struggle for man's dignity will inspire poems, your scum and moral degradation will summon and awaken morality. Your murderers will stand in the pillory for-ever and ever. The human universe will regard them with fear and fear for itself and will strive to keep from sin. People will ask: "Why was it done so to this people?" The answer will be: "That is the due of the wicked who destroyed East European Jewry." Thus the holocaust° will steal its way into world history. Ex-tinction by means of a loving caress creates no sensation and means nothing to anyone.

Eventually the Jewish people itself will forget this branch that was broken off. It will have to do without it. From the healthy trunk will come forth branches and blossoms and leaves. There is still strength and life. Dried up and decayed—this happens to every tree. There are still thousands of years ahead. Lamentation for the dead, of course, that is natural, particularly if they are your own, close to you. But the Jewish people must not be confused. The mourning for close ones—some people bear their sorrow long; most find comfort. Human nature—such is the world. Whatever the earth covers up is forgotten. In the ghetto itself we see how people forget. It cannot be otherwise. It certainly is not wrong. The real motive in mourning is after all fear of one's own end. Wherein are we better than those tens of thousands? It must happen to us, too. If we only had a guarantee of survival! But that does not exist and one cannot always be fearful, then the feeling of fear is projected into mourning for the fallen, and sorrow over the destruction of Jewry. Spare yourself the sorrow! The Jewish people will not be hurt. It will, it is to be hoped, emerge fortified by the trial. This should fill the heart with joyous gratitude to the sovereign of history.

Friday, [April] 30 [1943]

Passover is over. There were *sedarim* in the kosher kitchen. . . . At the second *seder* I spoke briefly.°

"A year ago some intellectual circles in the ghetto searched for an answer to

Palestine.

Gen. 37:33.
The plan to kill Joseph.

In Yiddish, khurbm [ḥurban].

Kalmanovitsh recorded this speech in Yiddish a month after it was delivered.

the question: What is a Jew or who is a Jew? Everybody was tremendously preoccupied with this question. Formerly the majority of these people had never given much thought to this question. They felt that they were Jews. Some more so, others less. Some, perhaps, did not feel so at all. And if someone suffered because of his Jewishness, he somehow found a remedy for it and, in general, occupied himself with other more substantial matters, rather than speculate about such an 'abstract' matter. Now these diverse people were herded together and imprisoned within the narrow confines of the ghetto. People of diverse languages, diverse cultures, diverse interests and beliefs, of diverse and, at times, conflicting hopes and desires were assembled together in one category: Jews. Confined as if being punished for that; that is, they committed a crime and the crime consisted in being a Jew. Many of them actually did not know what to say about the 'crime.' They did not know what it means 'to be a Jew.' To be truthful, practically nothing resulted from all these speculations and reflections. It was impossible to find a clear and definite answer to the question: Who is a Jew nowadays? For only now, in our generations, in the past 150 years, has the concept of Jew assumed so many meanings. Earlier, 'Jew' was a clear concept that had only one meaning. A Jew was one who observed Jewish law and belonged to the Jewish community. Now various kinds of people are considered and consider themselves Jews, even such as do not observe Jewish law or even respect it, or have no idea what Jewishness is. But also in this case I obtained an answer to the question 'who is a Jew' from a child in the ghetto. The truth of the verse, 'Out of the mouth of babes and sucklings has Thou found strength,'° was again confirmed. A teacher of religion in the ghetto school told me the incident, from his own experience. Children attend who are totally alienated from Jews, who had never heard at home, in school, in the street, anything of the Jewish past, of Judaism. Now in the ghetto many of these children listen eagerly to the stories of ancient sacred history, of the Bible. One such child, who had once attended a Polish school and spoke Polish at home, studied with great interest the stories of the Bible. When, in the weekly portion of *Toledot*, they studied the story of Jacob and Esau, this child suddenly called out: 'Teacher, we are indeed the descendants of Jacob and they (i.e., those who do evil to us) the descendants of Esau. Isn't that so? It's good that way. For I really want to belong to Jacob and not to Esau.' I reflected on this story and discovered that I could deduce from it a method to decide who is a Jew. This is how: Man's imagination is after all free, no bonds can confine it. A ghetto person can then sometimes imagine that he has the freedom to choose: he can divest himself of his fallen and defeated Jewish identity and assume the identity of the ruler over the ghetto. Now I ask: What would he do? If he wanted to change, if he was eager to assume the identity of the ruler, we could suppose that he is not a Jew. But if by free choice he wishes to remain a Jew, then he is a Jew. Reflecting further: the Jewish child instinctively chose to be a Jew. He naturally feels at home among Jews. As for the adult who I imagine chooses freely to be a Jew, is instinctual feeling a sufficient ground or are there also rational motives?

"I think so. To be a Jew means in every instance to be on a high plane. The temporary suffering and blows that descend upon the Jew have a meaning, are not merely oppressions, and do not degrade the Jew. For a Jew is part of the sacred triad°: Israel, the Torah, and the Holy One, blessed be He. That means the Jewish people, the moral law, and the Creator of the universe. This sacred triad courses

Ps. 8:3.

The sacred triad was first conceived by poet, kabbalist and ethical

philosopher Moses
Hayyim Luzzatto
(1707–1746)
and was later
popularized by the
Gaon of Vilna and
the Maggid of
Mezritsh.

through history. It is a reality that has been tested countless times. Our grandfathers clung to the triad, lived by its strength. And now too: the Jew who does not cling to this triad is to be pitied. He wanders in a world of chaos, he suffers and finds no explanation for his suffering; he can be severed from his people, that is, he can wish to change his identity. But the Jew who clings to the sacred triad needs no pity. He is in a secure association. To be sure, history rages now, a war is waged against the Jews, but the war is not only against one member of the triad but against the entire one: against the Torah and God, against the moral law and the Creator. Can anyone still doubt which side is the stronger? In a war it happens that one regiment is defeated, taken into captivity. Let the ghetto Jews consider themselves as such prisoners of war. But let them also remember that the army as a whole is not defeated and cannot be defeated. The Passover of Egypt is a symbol of ancient victory of the sacred triad. My wish is that together we shall live to see the Passover of the future."

XVIII
The Great Lament

A new archetype is not born all that often; more rarely still can one trace its actual conception. Because of the extraordinary amount of writing that was done under Nazi occupation and because so much of it survived, we can see exactly how the Holocaust became a new archetype: from the early stage of awareness when it seemed as if everything was a replay of the Middle Ages—ghettos, yellow badges, Jewish councils and mass expulsions—to the final mapping of a landscape where everything was new—cattle cars and transports, death camps and gas chambers. That the process was complete before the war had ended testifies to the vitality of the Jewish cultural response to catastrophe. The chronicling of the Holocaust did not save any lives, but it dignified the millions of lives that were lost by incorporating them into a distinct and commanding memorial.

The ghetto, as we have seen, was the first point on the Holocaust compass. Of all the ghettos, none was more hermetically sealed than the ghetto of Lodz, established in April–May 1940 and finally "liquidated" in August 1944. Through mass deportations the ghetto Jews experienced the methodical nature of the Nazi plan, though it was left to the Judenrat and the Jewish Police to implement the daily quota, and the destination of these transports was never known. The first major deportation, of ten thousand Jews, occurred January 16–29, 1942. It was their plight and the knowledge of his own imminent fate that moved Simkhe Bunem Shayevitsh to write his epic poem *Lekh-lekho* **(91),** in which he collapsed ten thousand lives into three—a father, mother and child—while linking their fate with that of Jewish martyrs down through the ages.

In the tradition of Bialik, the entire poem is a "countercommentary" on the sacred texts: the command of exile is issued by the enemy, not by God; instead of a Jeremiah to lament the Destruction, the mother will herself be Jeremiah, "Who comforts all, though the heart fears and weeps"; her motherly love will be a stand-in for divine providence and the chain of Jewish catastrophes will stand in for the covenantal saga. Just as the mother has assumed responsibility for most of the sacred roles, the traditional role of Isaac has been taken over by a girl, the poet's daughter, Blimele. In this new archetype of exile, then, mothers and daughters make up most of the chosen flock. As for the fathers, there is little they can do other than instruct their children in passive defiance, to face with a smile the death that surely awaits them. What Shayevitsh could not have foreseen is that the Germans would designate an *Aktion* especially for the old and the very young. During the week of September 5, 1942, his daughter and newborn son were dragged off to the waiting trains—accompanied only by their mother.

Remarkably, this poem reaffirms a faith in divine providence. For a poet in whose library "Isaiah hobnobs with Goethe," *all* past traditions, both sacred and secular, are brought to bear on the present catastrophe. To respond effectively, if at all, to this destruction requires all of one's cultural resources. Thus, the subversion of the moderns, from Bialik to Markish and Greenberg, must itself be subverted so that even the blasphemies become a source of consolation; so that traditional faith and secular humanism, artistic self-awareness and confessional prayer be merged into one.

Yitzhak Katzenelson's *The Song of the Murdered Jewish People* **(92)** represents a different kind of culmination. For one thing, Katzenelson had by this time already lost two thirds of his immediate family, had witnessed the destruction of Warsaw Jewry and knew about the machinery of mass murder, though he still had reason to hope that he and his surviving son would soon be exchanged for German prisoners of war. For another, the Holocaust was both tragic confirmation of Katzenelson's Zionism (one chapter, not included here, is called "Too Late," meaning that Polish Jews discovered too late that they should all have emigrated to Palestine) and a profound challenge to his neo-Romantic poetic credo. Once he had apostrophized the heavens in song, just as the prophets before him had called on them to bear witness to God's word. Now these same heavens, dark and deceitful, would open their portals one last time to admit "the great procession of the crucified, / the children of my people, all of them, each one a God . . ." (canto 9).

Katzenelson's central achievement in this Jeremiad was to translate his greater knowledge and keener political passions into a neoclassical work of tremendous sweep and rhetorical power: fifteen cantos with fifteen stanzas in each, structured in a complex but highly effective way. Schematically, the work can be laid out as follows:

Punctuating the chronology of destruction, the naming of names and the evocation of his personal losses are those cantos (the first two, the middle and the last) that try to place such an unprecedented cataclysm into a metahistorical framework. Now that the people themselves have vanished, the poet must reinvent them to mourn their destruction. No longer crowding the streets and marketplaces or filling the houses of prayer and learning, the Jewish people exist only in works of the imagination. The biblical prophets failed them, but that failure only highlights the transcendence of the martyrs themselves, each child a prophet, each Jew a king.

Whom is the poet to address, then, if the people have been murdered? He begins by addressing the muse, only to conclude (I:15) that the dead will move him to sing. In the ninth canto, the centerpiece of the poem, he addresses the heavens, but they, too, are an empty shell. In recalling his personal losses, he addresses Hannah, his dead wife (cantos 10–11), and, finally, he is left addressing the unknown reader of the future.

The one model that has not failed him is, of course, Bialik, whose *Poems of Wrath* form a subtext throughout: in the invocation to the heavens, the description of the children, the image of the multitudinous eyes of the dead, the indifference of nature and, most concretely, the final curse that he calls down upon the Germans, the nation of murderers.

Katzenelson's ten-month stay in Vittel, the German concentration camp for foreigners in France where his epic poem was written, ended in March 1944 when all Polish Jews interned in the camp were transferred to Drancy and from there were sent back to Poland. Their transport arrived in Auschwitz on April 30, 1944. Katzenelson and his son Zvi were gassed the same day. Among the Jews on "special duty," whose task it was to extract gold teeth from the mouths of the dead, to cremate the bodies, to heat the giant furnaces and to clean the crematoria was Zalmen Gradowski, a former yeshiva student, merchant and aspiring writer from Suwalki.

In the ash pits of the crematoria where he worked, Gradowski buried his own writings on life in the *Sonderkommando,* and because he had even less reason than Katzenelson to believe that any Jews would survive on European soil, he, Gradowski, headed each manuscript with a declaration in four languages (Polish, Russian, French and German): "Take heed of this document, for it contains valuable material for the historian." Like Katzenelson, Gradowski borrowed from earlier literary traditions to tell his tale more effectively, but whereas Bialik's wrath could still inform Katzenelson's internal debate, Gradowski could find nothing in Jewish tradition, either ancient or modern, that would help him assimilate an entire factory of death. True, in canto 9, even Katzenelson had to fall back on the image of a mass crucifixion to convey the universal scope of this tragedy; for Gradowski, however, the only possible analogy for Auschwitz was Dante's *Inferno*. (One entire chronicle, now translated in Ber Mark's *The Scrolls of Auschwitz* [Tel Aviv: Am Oved, 1985], is a Dantesque journey through hell.) In "The Czech Transport: A Chronicle of the Auschwitz *Sonderkommando*," one of the four chronicles unearthed after the war, the one internal Jewish reference is to Purim, because it happened that the transport was to be gassed on that holiday.

At the same time that Gradowski cultivated what he believed to be a western literary style in telling his horrible story to the world at large, he behaved in his "private life" as an observant Jew. According to the testimony of a fellow inmate (as quoted by Mark, p. 157), Gradowski would return to the block after the cremation of each transport, wrap himself in a prayer shawl, put on his tefillin and recite *kaddish* for the souls of the victims. He would weep for the holy books and sacred objects that had been burned; occasionally he would cry that he was defiled by sin because of his deeds and the deeds of his fellow *Sonderkommandos* and that only by his death would he expiate that sin.

Of Gradowski's four surviving chronicles, two tell his own story—the fate of the transport from Luna that arrived in Auschwitz in December 1942 and the fate of the *Sonderkommando*, a third of whose members were selected for gassing in February or March 1944. One chronicle is a midnight reverie about the indifference of nature, and the fourth, translated here, is on the Czech transport. Why should he have chosen to write about this transport when each day brought new ones from all over Europe? The Czech transport was different for three reasons: (1) because this so-called Family Transport had already spent seven months in the twin camp of Birkenau and knew exactly what to expect if transferred to Auschwitz; (2) because the Germans had to adopt extraordinary measures to dupe this group into the gas chambers; and (3) because once the elaborate hoax succeeded, the victims still showed signs of passive resistance. In "The Death March," the central chapter of the chronicle, Gradowski quotes (or paraphrases) the defiant speeches of the Czech women, already undressed and on their way to the gas. For the reader of this anthology (and perhaps for Gradowski as well), their speeches echo that of the nameless mother in the Second Book of Maccabees. Earlier in the same chapter, Gradowski presents the cowardice and utter self-delusion of the Germans through an internal collective monologue. Here, in contrast, are the Czech women, voicing their heroism and self-awareness.

Gradowski's focus on the resistance and passivity of the victims was no mere academic exercise. From the first, he was actively involved in planning what was supposed to have been a campwide uprising. Instead, the *Sonderkommando* ended up fighting alone. Gradowski died leading this daylong revolt on October 7, 1944.

91   *Lekh-Lekho*

SIMKHE BUNEM SHAYEVITSH

And now, Blimele, dear child
Restrain your childish joy
—That mercurial stream within you—
Let us be ready for the unknown road.

Do not gaze in wonder at me   5
With your great brown eyes
And do not ask any questions why
We have to leave our home.

Dear lovely child, I am
An adult, already grown,   10
And I don't know why they're driving
The bird out of its nest.

Keep back your gentle, sweet
Little laughters—silver ringing
Of old spiceboxes—   15
And get dressed to leave again.

Put on your warm little pants
Which your mother mended
Only last night
As she sang and laughed   20

And did not know the house was hearing
Her last happy laughter
Like the cow that lows and knows not
Of the knife in the slaughterer's hand.

Put on, child, your little blue jacket,   25
Although the hem is singed
From drying on the pipe;
It will warm you in the foreign cold

And guard your little lungs,
Keep them strong and healthy.   30
And don't God forbid, catch cold
In any frost, in the slightest wind.

The frost outside scorches, burns, stings,
Enfolds one with a hoop of iron.
Well, your mother will braid   35
Your little plaits with a red band.

The frost outside glows, flames, steels the body,
The thermometer has sunk to eighteen degrees.
Well, dear child, I found for you
The golden band with silver tassels.   40

Do not gaze in wonder at me
With your great brown eyes,
And do not ask any questions why
We have to leave our home

And are going on long, long   45
Unknown, snowy roads;
And why, instead of village or town,
Terror should come to meet us;

And why we are ready to be cast out like rubbish
For every kind of suffering,   50
And where we spend the night
We will not be at dawn;

And have no inkling
Of what awaits us on the distant road:
A warm bed to sleep in,   55
Or a bare floor, cold and hard;

A pot of hot coffee
And a piece of bread sprinkled with salt,
Or to be thrust alive, alive
Into a common grave, scattered with earth.   60

Do not gaze in wonder at me
With your great brown eyes, surprised
That on a weekday Wednesday
I recite the Sabbath *kiddush.*°

I recite the *kiddush,* "Yoym hashishi,"   65
Over the nest of our home
And sing with joy "*Sholem-aleikhem*"°
To the two angel guests

Who stay by me, go everywhere
With me, side by side   70
And weep with my weeping
And rejoice with my joy.

These two angel guests—who are they?
Now guess, quick as arrow from bow.
They are: you, Blimele, beautiful child   75
And your mother, the woman of valor°

In whose spirit rests always the Sabbath,
Though her face is darkened

The benediction over wine.

The Sabbath hymn recited immediately before kiddush.

Prov. 31:10–31. Traditionally chanted at the Friday night meal before kiddush.

—As the sun rests behind clouds
On a rainy day when the sky is darkened.   80

And although our nest
Is in a well-known spot called "ghetto,"
And a silver-snowy web
Has been spun by the spider of frost

Through the thin wooden walls   85
Of our cramped unheated room
And frightened us with dead white hands,
With its cold eerie gleam,

And although hunger and worry
Have bowed our backs   90
And terror, a leaping frog,
Buried our faces like an old man's—

We are bound to our corner
With a thousand ropes,
And in our hearts the fire burns,   95
The dream flaps its wings—of hope—

Like the full golden kernel
In the beak of a bird;
The dream is our sustainer,
A sun-bronzed honey-cake   100

Which, although more than once
We've been disappointed, bitterly duped,
Yet it has given strength
And we have waited for better things.

And now Blimele, dear child,   105
Stop—stop playing now,
No time for that,
We can be called at any minute

To leave our poor home
—A lonely boat on an island of sand—   110
And be hurled into the midst
Of a naked furious sea.

Outside the first groups already
Are dragging themselves on the trek
Women, men, old people; on their backs   115
Heavy burdens, in their arms children.

Their grieving faces
Are drunken-red from shame and frost
Their step—fainting, staggering,
Their looks—sentenced to death.   120

But there is no Jeremiah
To lament the Destruction.
He does not go with them into Exile
To comfort them by Babylon's streams.

Do not gaze at me, dear child   125
With questioning wondering eyes—
Why are only poor folk here,
Where are the well-fed on the distant roads?

You know, child: *oylem* means world and it means eternal
The saying of a famous wise man.   130
I've told you the story

See 38.   The story of the Cantonists°:

Poor children, kidnapped,
Torn away from father and mother.
So why do you wonder, child,   135
If those times greet the ghetto?

And we must pick up
The old wander-staff and go,
Not knowing what will befall
Our poor sick bones.   140

Whether we'll get somewhere
And reach a place of rest,
And people will stretch out
Friendly hands, with a kind word;

Or whether like sick birds that fall   145
Dead in a field, in a valley somewhere,
We'll perish on the road,
Not be buried as Jews,

And the ravens will make
Banquets on our bodies,   150
And when one flock is sated
It will summon a second.

Don't weep, dear child! Don't weep!
Life is beautiful, it draws like a magnet,
And more than ever and more than anywhere   155
It draws beyond the ghetto.

But know that sinful man
Must always be prepared
Both for noisy colorful life
And for bleak unhappy death.   160

Prayer shawl.   Look I'm packing the *tallis*°
Man's solemn   And the *kitl*° for a shroud
white linen robe.

And also the small red Bible
And Leivick's poems for a time of rest.

And you, child—bring the bar of soap   165
To wash your little shirt.
One must keep clean at home
And still more in a strange, strange land.

And don't forget to bring
The white nit-comb, that we talked about before;   170
Every night mother will use it
To straighten out your hair

And take good care of you
Lest, God forbid, you get lousy,
And sing to you "Bibl, bibl   175
Little louse"—and hold you on her lap

And tell you stories
Of the past that is like today
And she herself will be Jeremiah
Who comforts all, though the heart fears and weeps.   180

And now Blimele, dear child,
Don't weep out your little white teeth
We have only time
To say goodbye to the house.

So let us say goodbye   185
To all that we hold dear,
To every little thing we leave
And it runs after us like fire,

With the longing that my lung
Breathed into each thing—   190
And bounds up like a puppy
Everywhere, faithful yet and swift;

With the unsung songs
That flutter about the house
And run ahead and come to meet us   195
When we are led to the grave.

Let us take leave of each tiny thing
Just like old grandmothers
Piously taking leave at dusk
Reference to the Of the holy Sabbath day,°   200
Got fun Avrom
(God of Abraham)
prayer recited by When the shadows creep on the walls
women at the end And one sees twinkling weekday stars.
of the Sabbath.

The heart gnaws, quivers, is torn by regret
And from the eyes run tears.

Here is the table—on it is spread   205
The cloth with the blue squares.
Your poor mother
Prepared her meals here.

Although her pale hands
Didn't always have something to prepare,   210
Nonetheless, the dear holiday
Always dazzled from the table.

On the table, your father too
Poured out his fevered spirit;
The table's wooden heart was the first to hear   215
The melody of his mournful song,

And shuddered in fear,
And began humming quietly too,
And our poor house was wrapped
In a sharp forest smell   220

And the damp bowed walls
Lent a crooked ear
Were surprised, and whispered as well
The song of joy, the song of grief,

And the ceiling lowered itself   225
To hear the peculiar songs
And the floor spun in rapture
And almost died of sweetness.

Here, child, is the wardrobe—
Two doors and a mirror between them   230
Which quietly saw everything
And sealed it in its glassy heart

And holds within it the sunny hue
Of your little red body at birth
And the first protest that made   235
Your silky lip scowl without a word

And like a phonograph record
The mirror holds hidden within it
The first song that lulled you to sleep
In your simple cradle of straw.   240

And your first little laugh is engraved there
Which spurted like sweet chocolate;
And also the similar twist of the mouth
In the final throes of death.

And here, child, on the right side of the cupboard   245
Your mother kept the laundry
Washed by her own hands
And scented with lilac

And she used to weep into it
When her hope evaporated   250
And her dreams went out
Like suns of earlier days.

But she often laughed into the clothes
When she slumbered amidst her work
And saw your luck like a sun   255
In a blue sky rising.

And on the left side lie Holy books,
Worldly books, my manuscripts.
Isaiah hobnobs with Goethe,

*Talmudist and
kabbalist (circa
1695–1764).*

Reb Jonathan Eybeschuetz° with Tuwim.°°   260

*Major Polish poet
of Jewish descent
(1894–1953).*

And Yesenin° wants to get drunk
And urinate in public
But suddenly he sees Abraham
Leading Isaac to Mount Moriah.

*Enormously
popular Russian
poet (1895–1925)
who married
Isadora Duncan.*

Miriam Ulinover° displays   265
The "antiques" from her grandmother's treasure;
King David flames up in the Psalms
And foots in His honor the circle-dances.

*From Lodz
(1894–1944);
most famous for
her volume Der
bobes oytser
(Grandmother's
Treasure, 1922).*

And the Kotsker° still stands waiting
With knotted beard and angry mutter   270
For ten young men to cry out to the world:
THE LORD ALONE IS GOD!

*Menahem Mendl
of Kotsk (died
1859), a late
Hasidic master.*

But the Vorker° slaps him on the back
In friendly fashion till the Kotsker blinks.
"Don't be a fool! Every day a Jew in Exile   275
Performs the command of *Kiddush Hashem*.

*Yitzhak of Vorke
(died 1858), a
disciple of Simkhe
Bunem of
Pzhysha.*

"So instead let's take a drop of whiskey,
A bite of cheese, and say *Lekhayim!*
It's time for God, the blessed, Himself
To hallow the name of heaven."   280

And in humility and trembling
Lie my poems and stories,
They lie and wait in fear
Like poor folk for well-paid jobs

And whisper quietly, softly entreat   285

*Credited with
redacting the
Babylonian*

Till Rav Ashi° hears their murmur

Talmud (circa
335–427 C.E.).

Most prolific and
popular Yiddish
novelist before
World War II
(1880–1957).

The abandoned
libraries of
religious books
that had belonged
to Jews deported
from the ghetto
were routinely
used as toilet
paper; see Isaiah
Trunk, Lodzher
geto (New York:
YIVO, 1962),
p. 453.

And bids "Make way!"; friendly, too
Is the proud Sholem Asch.°

And there's an uproar: "Here's another   290
In the family—let's crown him!"
Aaron the Priest makes with hands
And spoken words the priestly blessing.

Tremble, tremble, sacred books,
Tremble, tremble, dreams of geniuses—
Some dawn, someone will get up   295
And, dressed only in underpants,

Will cut squares out of you
For toilet-paper°
And turn up his nose too—"They're printed on!
It could harm me, God forbid!"   300

And here is the bed where the power
Of the first Adam was revealed
And that is the testimony of gods
To a new Genesis.

The bed that lulled us gently to sleep   305
With the sweetest, most beautiful dreams
And showed women a thousand times lovelier
Than Solomon's thousand wives.

The bed that lifted us
Like a magic rocket   310
And over all fences and wires
Carried us out of the ghetto

And flew with eagle wings
Over kingdoms and the most beautiful places
In the night of grief, drew us out   315
Of the deepest, deepest abysses,

And made us young, beautiful and fresh,
Set us down in golden castles
And put crowns on our heads
In the very hours of damnation,   320

And told us wonderful stories
Of a Thousand and One Nights
And into our gloomy mood
Laughed with a thousand charms.

Groan, groan—gracious, holy bed,   325
You're being sold now by the kilo.
To cook by your flame a ghetto soup
Is not, God forbid, a sin.

The mass
deportations
resumed on
February 22,
1942, after a one-
month
interruption.

B. Sotah 20a.

And now, Blimele, dear child,
Look outside, how the second group°   330
Is already wandering into Exile.
Soon we'll have to set out, too.

And although, child, you're a little girl
And he who teaches his daughter Torah
It is as if he taught her   335
To commit an unworthy sin°—

Yet the evil day has come,
The evil hour has come,
When I must teach you, a little girl,
The terrible chapter "*Lekh-lekho.*"   340

But how can one compare it
To the bloody "*Lekh-lekho*" of today?
"And God said to Abram:
Go forth from your land

And from the place of your birth   345
And from your father's house
To a land that I will show you

Gen. 12:1.

And there make of you a great people."°

And now the great people must go
To the unknown distant road—   350
Sick and weary—broken ships
That do not reach a shore.

One of them, faint with hunger
Will sit down in the snow
And quietly, in pain,   355
Die like a hurt puppy.

Another's eyes will fail
For terror on the road,
His heartstring will suddenly snap
And he'll fall heavy as a stone.   360

And someone's shivering child
Will freeze to death in the frost-fire,
And its mother will long carry it
Thinking it's still moving.

And fathers will call to their children   365
And children demand things from their mothers—
Families will get lost
And never find themselves.

And for a long way they'll carry
The great heavy pack on their shoulders   370

And throw it away at last, and often
Have no pillow under their head.

And the sick man, strengthless,
Will come to a halt in deep snows.
Birds will fly past   375
And be frightened, as by a scarecrow.

And women, pregnant, will collapse,
Fainting, to their knees.
Soon they will fall behind
And the snow will glow for them like coals.   380

And from their fiery faces
Death-cold sweat will pour
And the doggish howl and cry
They'll bite back with their lips

And vomit and writhe   385
On the painful, snowy birthing stool
Against heaven, against sun, against God,
Against all who merrily played.

Over their womb that aborts in snow
And makes the field terrible with blood and weeping   390
White snow kindles red,
And the red will rise in golden sheaves,

And with a thousand agonies
And a thousand terrors the night will shudder.
Though the moon shines brightly, the glitter of stars   395
Will hunt with fear, like rifle bullets.

And the ice underfoot will crackle
With the uproar of shrapnel explosions.
The snow will beckon: "Shrouds for all!
Shrouds for the young and aged!"   400

And from every shrub
And every twig, hands will lift
And from every little tree
Eyes, as of wolves and lions, will peer.

Someone in the forest waste   405
Who lies in ambush for your step—
Your vaporous breath will ring
Like the flow of your own warm blood.

So greetings to you, grandfather Abraham!
We go on your hard journey   410
But won't you be ashamed
Of your grandchildren's bloody tears?

And now, Blimele, dear child,
Put on your little coat, let's go.
The third group sways in readiness   415
And we must join them now.

But let us not weep.
Let us not lament, but in spite of all foes
Smile, only smile, so those
Who know the Jews will wonder   420

And not understand that in our blood
Flows the power of our grandfathers
Who in all generations
Climbed atop so many Moriahs;

That although our step is unsteady   425
Like a blind man's at a strange door,
There rings in it the echo
Of our uncle's stride on Siberian roads°

*Allusion to
Leivick's poems
about his life in
Siberian exile.*

That although, as in a fallen beast,
Terror in our eyelash trembles,   430
Pride burns in flaming lightning-bolts
As in our father on the gallows.

And although at any minute
We can be tortured and shot,
Well—it is nothing new: 435
Our sister was whipped naked.

So let us not weep,
Let us not lament, but in spite of all foes
Smile, only smile, so those
Who know the Jews will wonder   440

And not know that today
The same angels go with us as before:
On the right Michael, on the left Gabriel,
Uriel in front and Raphael in the rear.

And although beneath our feet is death,   445
Over our head is God's Presence.
So child, let us go with devotion renewed
And our old proclamation of Oneness.

Lodz ghetto, February 23, 1942

92 The Song of the Murdered Jewish People

YITZHAK KATZENELSON

I Sing!

1

Cf. Ps. 137 (2).

"Sing! Take your light, hollow harp in hand,°
Strike hard with heavy fingers, like pain-filled hearts
On its thin chords. Sing the last song.
Sing of the last Jews on Europe's soil."

2

—How can I sing? How can I open my lips?
I that am left alone in the wilderness—
My wife, my two children, alas!
I shudder . . . Someone's crying! I hear it from afar.

3

"Sing, sing! raise your tormented and broken voice,
Look for Him, look up, if He is still there—
Sing to Him . . . Sing Him the last song of the last Jew,
Who lived, died unburied, and is no more."

4

The poet's wife Hannah and his two younger sons, Benzion and Benjamin, are also referred to by various diminutive forms.

—How can I sing? How can I lift my head?
My wife, my Benzionke and Yomele°—a baby—deported . . .
They are not with me, yet they never leave me.
O dark shadows of my brightest lights, O cold, blind shadows!

5

"Sing, sing for the last time on earth.
Throw back your head, fix your eyes upon Him.
Sing to Him for the last time, play to Him on your harp:
There are no more Jews! They were killed, they are no more."

6

—How can I sing? How can I lift my head
With bleary eyes? A frozen tear
Clouds my eye . . . It struggles to break loose,
But, God my God, it cannot fall!

7

"Sing, sing! Raise your eyes towards the high, blind skies
As if a God were there . . . Beckon to Him,—
As if a great joy still shone for us there!
Sit on the ruins of the murdered people and sing!"

8

How can I sing—My world is laid waste.
How can I play with wringed hands?
Where are my dead? O God, I seek them in every dunghill,
In every heap of ashes . . . O tell me where you are.

9

Scream from every sand dune, from under every stone,
Scream from the dust and fire and smoke—
It is your blood, your sap, the marrow of your bones,
It is your flesh and blood! Scream, scream aloud!

10

Scream from the beasts' entrails in the wood, from the fish in the river
That devoured you. Scream from furnaces. Scream, young and old.
I want a shriek, an outcry, a sound, I want a sound from you,
Scream, O murdered Jewish people, scream, scream aloud!

11

Do not scream to heaven that is as deaf as the dunghill earth.
Do not scream to the sun, nor talk to that lamp . . . If I could only
Extinguish it like a lamp in this bleak murderers' cave!
My people, you were more radiant than the sun, a purer, brighter light!

12

Show yourself, my people. Emerge, reach out
From the miles-long, dense, deep ditches,
Covered with lime and burned, layer upon layer,
Rise up! up! from the deepest, bottommost layer!

13

Come from Treblinka, Sobibor, Auschwitz,
Come from Belźec, Ponari, from all the other camps,
With wide open eyes, frozen cries and soundless screams.
Come from marshes, deep sunken swamps, foul moss—

14

Come, you dried, ground, crushed Jewish bones.
Come, form a big circle around me, one great ring—
Grandfathers, grandmothers, fathers, mothers carrying babies.
Come, Jewish bones, out of powder and soap.°

A reference to the bars of soap made from the fat of the victims.

15

Emerge, reveal yourselves to me. Come, all of you, come.
I want to see you. I want to look at you. I want

Silently and mutely to behold my murdered people—
And I will sing . . . Yes . . . Hand me the harp . . . I will play!

October 3–5, 1943

II I Play

1

I play. I sat down low on the ground,
I played and sang sadly: O my people!
Millions of Jews stood around me and heard,
Millions of murdered—a great throng—stood listening.

2

A great throng, a huge crowd, O how huge!
Far greater than Ezekiel's valley of bones.°
And Ezekiel himself would not have spoken to the murdered of trust and hope
As in bygone days, but would have wrung his hands like me.

See 6.

3

Like me he would cast back his head helplessly,
Stare bewildered at the grey, remote, dreary sky,
And again drop his head heavily, down, down, down,
Like a petrified stone, bent deeply and mutely to the ground.

4

Ezekiel, O you Jew of the Babylonian valley,
Seeing the dry bones of your people, you were shocked
And lost, you let yourself be led,
Like a puppet, by your God into that valley.

5

When asked "*Ha-tehyenah?*°
Can these bones live?" You could not answer,
So what am I to say? Woe and grief!
Not even a bone remains from my murdered people.

Ezek. 37:3.

6

No bone is left for new flesh, new skin,
For a new spirit of life—
Look, look, here is a murdered people,
Staring at us with lifeless eyes.°

For the motif of silently staring eyes that the poet begins to elaborate on, see "In the City of Slaughter," lines 41–51.

7

Millions of heads and hands turn to us—try to count them!
See their faces and lips—is that a prayer or a frozen cry?
Go, touch them . . . There's nothing left to touch—hollow.
I invented a Jewish people. I made believe in my heart.

8

They are gone! They will never be back on this earth!
I invented them. Yes, I sit and make believe.
Only their sufferings are true. Only the pain
Of their slaughter is true and great indeed . . .

9

Look! Look! They all stand around me, endless throngs.
A shudder goes through me—
All of them look with Ben Zion's and Yomke's sorrowful eyes.
All of them look with the sad eyes of my wife,

10

The poet's younger brother, formerly the director of a Hebrew high school in Lodz.

With my brother Berl's° big blue eyes—yes!
How did they get his look? There he is! It's he!
He looks for his children, not knowing that they're here
Among the millions . . . But I shall not tell him, no . . .

11

I.e., in the Drancy camp.

My Hannah was taken with our two sons!
My Hannah knows; they shared her fate—
She does not know where Zvi is, nor where I am,°
Nor of my misfortune, that I am still alive . . .

12

She lifts her eyes to me in silence,
Sightless like all the rest.
Come Hannah, so silent and so eloquent, come,
Look at me. Listen to my voice, recognize me.

13

Listen Benzikl, my young prodigy. You'll understand
The last elegy of the very last, last Jew—
And you, Yomele, my light and comfort,
Where is your smile, Yom? O don't smile, don't . . .

14

I dread it, Yomele, as others surely fear
My smile . . . Listen to the song—
I fling my hand, like a heart, upon my harp.
Let it hurt us even more. And haunt the pain! . . .

15

Evoke not Ezekiel, evoke not Jeremiah . . . I don't need them!!
I called them: O help, come to my aid!

But I will not wait for them with my last song—
They have their prophecy and I my great pains.

October 15, 1943

III   O My Agonies

1

O agonies! O my agonies . . . Rejoice O Jews, rejoice!
Rejoice you forlorn remnants across the sea,°
In your ignorance. O if my agonies could speak.
They would poison your life, they would darken your world.

I.e., the Jews in America.

2

Agonies, you grow in me, you grow large, you swell—
Why do you gnaw at me? Are you forcing your way into me or out?
Don't leave me, agonies! Grow, grow in me quietly.
O my agonies, be still, you hurt me so, you are so painful!

3

You dig into me and gnaw blindly with closed eyes,
With open mouths like worms in a grave . . . O agonies! O pain!
Rest silently in me like all my dead!
Rest in my consumed heart, like worms in rotten moss.

4

Lam. 3:1 (4).

Ani hagever,° I am the man who watched, who saw
How my children, my women, my young and old, were thrown
Like stones, like logs, into wagons,
Brutally beaten, rudely abused.

5

I watched from the window and saw the brutes—O God!
I observed the beaters and the beaten—
I wrung my hands in shame. O what disgrace and shame.
Jews were being used, ah, to destroy my Jews!°

A reference to the Jewish Police.

6

Apostates and near-apostates with shiny boots on their feet,
Hats with the Star of David, like a swastika, on their heads,
An alien, corrupt and vile tongue on their lips,
Dragged us from our homes, flung us down the stairs.

7

They smashed doors and forced their way
Into closed Jewish homes with raised clubs in their hands—
They hunted us, beat us and drove young and old to the wagons,
Into the street! They spat in God's face, profaned the light of day.

8

They pulled us out from under the beds and closets, cursing:
"The wagon is waiting! Go to hell, to the *Umschlag*,° to death!"
They dragged us to the street and continued to prowl—
The last dress in the closet, last bit of grain, last morsel of bread.

Abreviated form of
Umschlagplatz.

9

Look into the street and you'll go mad!
The street is dead, yet full of shrieks and screams—
The street is empty, yet the street is full.
Wagons laden with Jews, with mourning and grief!

10

Wagons laden with Jews, wringing their hands, pulling their hair—
Some are silent—their scream is loudest!
They watch, they look . . . Is it a nightmare? Is it real?
Around the wagons, alas, woe is me! Jews in police uniforms, in boots and
   hats!

11

The German stands aside, as if smugly sneering—
The German stands aloof—he doesn't interfere.
Woe unto me—the German had Jews destroy my Jews.
Look at the wagons, behold the shame, look and see the suffering!

12

From my window I saw the crowded wagons . . . I heard
The heaven-rending cries and the silent sighs—
O wagons of pain, laden with the living carried to death.
The horses marched on, the wheels rolled on . . .

13

O stupid horses, why do you hang your heads in gloom?
O wheels, why do you roll on sadly? Do you know where
You are going, where you carry them? Where you are dragging
The noble daughters of my people, my gifted sons?

14

If you only knew—you would neigh furiously, rise
On your hind legs and wring your front legs,
Like human hands, in despair, in front of the entire world
And the round wheels would come to a halt . . .

15

They do not know. They go on. They turn from Nowolipki.
On Zamenhof, the road to the *Umschlag* is fenced off.

There waits an empty train to carry us far, far away—
And return tomorrow empty again . . . O my blood runs cold!

October 22, 1943

IV The Cattle Cars Are Here Again

1

Horror and fear grip me, hold me tight—
The wagons have returned! Only yesterday at dusk they left—
And today they are here again, standing at the *Umschlag*.
Do you see their gaping mouths? Their wide and terrible mouths? O dread!

2

They want more! They are never sated.
They stand waiting for Jews! When will the Jews be brought here?
They are hungry—as if they never tasted a Jew . . .
They have! But what of that? They want more, more!

3

They want more, they stand waiting, as if for a feast,
Ready to devour—Jews! Bring us as many as you can!
The old, the young, the children,
Young grapes from an old vine, and old Jews like old strong wine . . .

4

We want more, many more Jews . . . The cattle cars scream
Like cold and hardened criminals: More! There are never enough!
They stand waiting at the *Umschlag*. They wait for us, they wait,
The wide-gaping cattle cars, the entire train.

5

Only a while ago they were crammed, stuffed to suffocation with Jews.
Dead Jews stood among dazed living ones—
Pressed together, the dead stood erect, unable to fall,
No one could tell the living from the dead.

6

The dead Jew's head swayed as if it were alive,
Cold sweat poured down from the living.
A Jewish child begs his dead mother: Water! Give me a drop of water!
Beating her face with his tiny hands. Put me down, I am hot!

7

Another little child on his dead father's arm—
Yes, children, though faint and feeble, still persevere!
His father, though big, could not endure—
The innocent child urges: Come daddy! Let's go!

8

And there on the train, on that side, in that corner,
Something took place. Can it be no one knows?
But the people smile. They guess.
Someone has jumped out . . .Listen, listen, a shot!

9

Someone jumped out . . . Jews smile, laugh quietly.
O dear Jews, O my saintly Jews,
Why are you happy? Listen, the Ukrainian is shooting from the roof.
What of it? Someone got out! Someone is free.

10

The confession of
sins before death.

Hit by a bullet? Everyone's prayer—
No one can escape it! It's better to be hit in the escaping field,
Than . . . Where? Where are they taking us? Who recites *Vidui*° loudly?
Repeat after him! Let everyone repeat! It makes you shudder.

11

Empty train cars! You were just full, and now you are empty again.
What did you do with the Jews? What has happened to them?
Ten thousand counted and sealed—and here you are again!
O tell me you empty cattle cars, tell me where you have been!

12

You come back from the other world, I know. It cannot be very far.
Only yesterday you left loaded, and today—you are back!
Why this rush? Why such haste?
You will soon be old and broken like me.

13

Yiddish for
"Help!"

From mere watching, observing, hearing everything—*Gevald!*°
Though you are iron and wood, how can you endure it?
O iron, you came from deep in the earth.
O wood, you were once a tall, proud tree.

14

And now? Now you are freight cars watching in silence,
Silent witnesses to such human cargo, such pain and misery.
You watched, closely, silently. O tell me, wagons, where
Did you carry them? Where did you carry the Jewish people to death?

15

It's not your fault, they load you and tell you: Go!
They send you out full and drive you back empty—

You come from the other world, tell me, say a word.
O rolling wheels, tell me and I will shed a tear . . .

October 26, 1943

VI The First Ones

1

And it continued. Ten a day, ten thousand Jews a day.
That did not last very long. Soon they took fifteen thousand.
Warsaw! The city of Jews—the fenced-in, walled-in city,
Dwindled, expired, melted like snow before my eyes.

2

Warsaw, packed with Jews like a *shul* on Yom Kippur, like a bustling
    marketplace—
Jews trading and worshipping, both happy and sad—
Seeking their bread, praying to their God.
They crowded the walled-in, locked-in city.

3

Cf. Lam. 1 (4). You are deserted now. Warsaw, like a gloomy wasteland.°
You are a cemetery now, more desolate than a graveyard.
Your streets are empty—not even a corpse can be found there.
Your houses are open, yet no one enters, no one leaves.

4

Cf. Bialik's
"Upon the
Slaughter." (46)

The first to perish were the children, abandoned orphans,
The world's best, the bleak earth's brightest.°
These children from the orphanages might have been our comfort.
From these sad, mute, bleak faces our new dawn might have risen.

5

At the end of the winter of forty-two I was in such a place.
I saw children just brought in from the street. I hid in a corner—
And saw a two-year-old girl in the lap of a teacher—
Thin, deathly pale and with such grave eyes.

6

I watched the two-year-old grandmother,
The tiny Jewish girl, a hundred years old in her seriousness and grief.
What her grandmother could not dream she had seen in reality.
I wept and said to myself: Don't cry, grief disappears, seriousness remains.

7

Seriousness remains, seeps into the world, into life and affects it deeply.
Jewish seriousness sobers, awakens and opens blind eyes.
It is like a Torah, a prophecy, a holy writ for the world.
Don't cry, don't . . . Eighty million criminals for one Jewish child's seriousness.

8

Don't cry . . . I saw a five-year-old girl in that "home."
She fed her younger, crying brother . . .
She dipped hard bread crumbs in watery marmalade
And got them cleverly into his mouth . . . I was lucky

9

To see it, to see the five-year-old mother feeding him,
And to hear her words. My mother, though exceptional, was not that inventive.
She wiped his tear with her laughter and talked him into joy.
O little Jewish girl. Sholem Aleichem could not have done any better. I saw it.

10

I saw the misery in that children's home.
I entered another room—there, too, it was fearfully cold.
From afar a tin stove cast a glow on a group of children,
Half-naked children gathered around the glowing coal.

11

The coal glowed. One stretched out a little foot, another a frozen hand,
A naked back. A pale young boy with dark eyes
Told a story. No, not a story! He was stirred and excited—
Isaiah! you were not as fervent, not as eloquent a Jew.

12

He spoke a mix of Yiddish and holy tongue. No, it was all the holy tongue.
Listen! Listen! See his Jewish eyes, his forehead,
How he raises his head . . . Isaiah! you were not as small, not as great,
Not as good, not as true, not as faithful as he.

13

And not only the little boy who spoke in that children's home,
But his little sisters and brothers who listened to him with open mouths—
O no, you countries, you old and rebuilt European cities,
The world never saw such children before; they never existed on earth.

14

They, the Jewish children, were the first to perish, all of them,
Almost all without father or mother, eaten by cold, hunger and vermin,
Saintly messiahs, sanctified by pain . . . O why such punishment?
Why were they first to pay so high a price to evil in the days of slaughter?

15

They were the first taken to die, the first in the wagon.
They were flung into the big wagons like heaps of dung—

And were carried off, killed, exterminated,
Not a trace remained of my precious ones! Woe unto me, woe.

November 2–4, 1943

IX To the Heavens

1

And thus it came to pass, and this was the beginning . . . Heavens tell me,
    why?°

Echoes the opening line of Bialik's "Upon the Slaughter" (46).

Tell me, why this, O why? What have we done to merit such disgrace?
The earth is dumb and deaf, she closed her eyes. But you, heavens on high,
You saw it happen and looked on, from high, and did not turn your face.

2

You did not cloud your cheap-blue colors, glittering in their false light.
The sun, a brutal, red-faced hangman, rolled across the skies;
The moon, the old and sinful harlot, walked along her beat at night;
And stars sent down their dirty twinkle, with the eyes of mice.

3

Away! I do not want to look at you, to see you any more.
False and cheating heavens, low heavens up on high, O how you hurt!
Once I believed in you, sharing my joy with you, my smile, my tear—
Who are not different from the ugly earth, that heap of dirt!

4

I did believe in you and sang your praises in each song of mine.
I loved you as one loves a woman, though she left and went.
The flaming sun at dusk, its glowing shine,

Allusion to his popular song Di zun fargeyt in flamen, "the Sun Sets in Flames."

I likened to my hopes: "And thus my hope goes down, my dream is spent."°

5

Away! Away! You have deceived us both, my people and my race.
You cheated us—eternally. My ancestors, my prophets, too, you have deceived.
To you, foremost, they lifted up their eyes, and you inspired their faith.
And full of faith they turned to you, when jubilant or grieved.

6

Deut. 32:1, Ha'azinu hashamayim.

Isa. 1:2.
Jer. 2:12, Shomu shamayim.

To you they first addressed themselves: *Hearken, O Heavens, you—*°
and only afterwards they called the earth, praising your name.
So Moses. So Isaiah°—mine, my own. *Hear, O hear,* cried Jeremiah, too.°°
O heavens open wide, O heavens full of light, you are as Earth, you are the
    same.

7

Have we so changed that you don't recognize us, as of old?
But why, we are the same—the same Jews that we were, not different.

Not I . . . Not I will to the prophets be compared, lo and behold!
But they, the millions of my murdered ones, those murdered out of hand—

8

It's they . . . They suffered more and greater pains, each one.
The little, simple, ordinary Jew from Poland of today—
Compared with him, what are the great men of a past bygone?
A wailing Jeremiah, Job afflicted, Kings despairing, all in one—it's they!

9

You do not recognize us any more as if we hid behind a mask?
But why, we are the same, the same Jews that we were, and to ourselves we're
    true.
We're still resigned to others' happiness. Saving the world we still see as our
    task.
O why are you so beautiful, you skies, while we are being murdered, why are
    you so blue?

10

See 1 Sam. 28.   Like Saul, my king° I will go to the goddess Or, bearing my pain.
In dark despair I'll find the way, the dark road to Ein Dor; I shall
From underground awaken all the prophets there—*Look ye again,*
Look up to your bright heavens, spit at them and tell them: Go to Hell!

11

You heavens, high above, looked on when, day and night,
My people's little children were sent off to death, on foot, by train.
Millions of them raised high their hands to you before they died.
Their noble mothers could not shake your blue-skinned crust—they cried in
    vain.

12

You saw the little Yomas, the eleven-year-olds, joyous, pure and good;
The little Bennys, young inquiring minds, life's remedy and prize.
You saw the Hannas who had born them and had taught them to serve God.
And you looked on . . . You have no God above you. Nought and void—you
    skies!

13

You have no God in you! Open the doors, you heavens, fling them open wide,
And let the children of my murdered people enter in a stream.
Open the doors up for the great procession of the crucified,
The children of my people, all of them, each one a God—make room!

14

O heavens, empty and deserted, vast and empty desert, you—
My only God I lost in you, and they have not enough with three:
The Jewish God, the holy ghost, the Jew from Galilee—they killed him, too.
And then, not satisfied, sent all of us to heaven, these worshippers of cruelty.

15

Rejoice, you heavens, at your riches, at your fortune great!
Such blessed harvest at one stroke—a people gathered in entire.
Rejoice on high, as here below the Germans do, rejoice and jubilate!
And may a fire rise up to you from earth, and from you strike, earthwards,
      devouring fire!

November 23–26, 1943

XI Remember

1

I like to call your name, to call it aloud: *Hannale!*
They carried you off together with my people. How I would like to turn
To you and to imagine that you answer me with your shining eyes and the soft
      sad smile of your lips.
In my loneliness and misery I would like to ask you: Do you remember?

2

I ask you: Do you remember? O come, Hannale, come nearer to me
And rest your beautiful head with its black hair and white parting,
On my shoulder! Take me into your arms, revive me, give me strength . . .
Did I disturb your eternal rest? Hannale, I don't want you to rest.
Our wounds can never be healed, and never should they be forgotten.

3

Do sit beside me, I love you . . . Listen, my love, what I have to say.
Do you hear me? In my misfortune you are my good fortune, my Hannale, my
      wife!
In this great woe of ours, *in our un-being*. I embrace you for all the world to see.
Bear the fruit of my accusing, bear it as you bore my sons,
And carry it to all the corners of this dark and sinning world!

4

It was the most cruel, the most horrifying thing, do you remember?
I know you do. You took it with you into eternity.
You and my sons, you will forever remember the murder of your people.
I, too! Yet I sometimes fear that hour may never come!—I might forget.

5

I always put my trust in you, more than in myself. All you asked me
I fulfilled as if commanded by a secret order.
I did my duties, heavy though they were, with trembling joy.
I loved my people, shared its exile, sang of its hopes and fears.

6

The orphanage on Twarda 7 was run by David Dombowski.

Remember the house on Twarda Street, the home of orphans?°
The fifty children there, each healthy as a tree? I wrote a play for them.
Remember how they played *The Street*° and how each one grew with his role,
And with them grew my work. They put more heart to it than even I.

A three-act play in Yiddish written in 1941 and subsequently lost.

The "Little" and the "Big" ghettos were connected by a wooden bridge.

The "Little Ghetto" was liquidated in August 1942.

7

Remember the day they told us: the children, they were taken, too, *they, too!*
Together with Dombrowski and his wife, their teachers, my dearest friends?
I hurried off, towards the bridge.° I did not tell you then where I was going.
I rushed to the house. The sun was shining. What I saw were dogs and cats.

8

No Jews, no more Jews in that part!° I only saw a solitary shadow
Carrying a sack and crawling along the wall; it must have been a Jew.
The burden on his back made him go fast: Go! Go! It's true, it happened.
The streets are empty! No more Jews! The fair is over. It is the end.

9

From Ciepla Street I turned left to Twarda Number Seven. I ran
Towards the house, and up the stairs, to reach the second floor.
I found an open door and stopped and could not move.
I stood there long and stared into an open door and could not move.

10

Then steps: they come . . . Through the front door? Up the stairs?
A burglar? Or much worse, a German?
I fled into the corridor where left and right the doors were open.
From somewhere the sun threw down whole sheaves of shining rays in blinding
     wild confusion.

11

The children's overcoats on pegs along the wall! A few I recognized
And touched them with my hands: This one was Abale's
The one who played the peddler in my play. O, how he raised his head
And waved his hands: "All rags into my bags! Jews, everything I buy."

12

And this belonged to Ahrke who played the leading role, the boy who cheats
     the teacher.
"My mother's ill," he tells him and runs off to sing in courtyards
Begging for a coin. When he returns to class,
He's told that his mother really fell ill.

13

And this! This new coat is Pinkhesl's, the poet Hershele's beloved son,
Who died of hunger. The little orphan played the hungry boy
Who cleverly steals a bread roll from the basket. And while he eats it,
The blood runs down his cheek. He speaks through tears and does not even
     know . . .

14

I walked into the hall and ran away in horror; from there on to David's room,
Dombrowski's, their teacher . . . Empty! Gone! He and his wife, both went,
As Korczak and Wilczynska° did, together with their orphan wards,
To be with them in their hour. Piles of papers on the floor—

*Stefa Wilczynska
(1886–1942),
Korczak's
assistant.*

15

And in the piles of paper I looked for . . . Oh, throw all my works into a fire,
If this could save one little orphan, if only one, among the fifty dear ones—
My Hannale remember, instead of one of them I brought a crippled paper home,
The middle part, one of three copy-books, *The Street,*—a cripple without head and
feet.

December 14–16, 1943

XV   It's All Over

1

The end. At night, the sky is aflame. By day the smoke coils and at night it
   blazes out again. Awe!
Like our beginning in the desert: A pillar of cloud by day, a pillar of fire
   by night.°

Exod. 13:21–22.

Then my people marched with joy and faith to new life, and now—the end,
   all finished . . .
All of us on earth have been killed, young and old. We have all been
   exterminated.

2

Why? O don't ask why! Everybody knows, all gentiles, good and bad,
The worst helped the Germans, the best closed one eye, pretending to be
   asleep—
No, no, nobody will demand a reckoning, probe, ask why.
Our blood is cheap, it may be shed. We may be killed and murdered
   with impunity.

3

Among the Poles they looked for freedom fighters, only for those suspected
Of patriotism . . . They murdered many Russians in villages and towns—
"Partisans." Among us, they killed babies in their cribs, even the unborn.
They led us to Treblinka and before killing turned to us and said:

4

"Get undressed here. Put your clothes in order, shoes in pairs, leave your
   belongings.
You'll need your clothes, shoes and other personal effects. You'll soon be back!
You just arrived? From Warsaw? Paris? Prague? Saloniki? Take a bath!"
A thousand enter the hall . . . A thousand wait naked until the first thousand
   are gassed.

5

Thus they destroyed us, from Greece to Norway to the outskirts of Moscow—
  about seven million,
Discounting Jewish children in wombs. Only the pregnant mothers are counted.
And if Jews remain in far-away America and in nearby Eretz Israel—demand
  these children too from them
Demand the murdered unborn children. Demand those gassed in their mothers'
  wombs. World. Demand.

6

Why? No human being in the world asks why, yet all things do: Why?
Each vacant apartment in thousands of towns and cities asks: Why?
Listen, listen: Apartments will not stay vacant and empty homes will not remain
  empty.
Another people is moving in, another language and a different way of life.

7

Rising over Lithuanian or Polish towns, the sun will never find
A radiant old Jew at the window reciting Psalms, or going to the synagogue.
On every road peasants will welcome the sun in wagons, going to market.
So many gentiles—more than ever, yet the market is dead. It is crowded, yet
  seems empty.

8

Never will a Jew grace the markets, and give them life.
Never will a Jewish *kapota* flutter in markets on sacks of potatoes, flour,
  porridge.
Never will a Jewish hand lift a hen, pet a calf. The drunken peasant
Will whip his horse sadly, return with his full wagon to the village. There are no
  more Jews in the land.

9

And Jewish children will never wake in the morning from bright dreams,
Never go to *ḥeder*, never watch birds, never tease, never play in the sand.
O little Jewish boys! O bright Jewish eyes! Little angels! From where? From
  here, yet not from here.
O beautiful little girls. O you bright pure faces, smudged and disheveled.

10

Kasrilevke, Yehupetz— fictional towns in Sholem Aleichem's oeuvre.

Menachem Mendel, Tevye— Sholem Aleichem's major fictional characters.

They are no more! Don't ask overseas about Kasrilevke, Yehupetz.° Don't.
Don't look for Menachem Mendels, Tevye the dairymen, Nogids, Motke
  thieves.° Don't look—
They will, like the prophets, Isaiah, Jeremiah, Ezekiel, Hosea and Amos from
  the Bible,
Cry to you from Bialik, speak to you from Sholem Aleichem and Sholem
  Asch's books.

*Motke the Thief,
Shloyme Nogid—
fictional characters
in the work of
Sholem Asch.*

11

Never will the voice of Torah be heard from *yeshivot*, synagogues and pale
  students,
Purified by study and engrossed in the Talmud . . . No, no, it was not pallor but
  a glow,
Already extinguished . . . Rabbis, heads of *yeshivot*, scholars, thin, weak
  prodigies,
Masters of Talmud and Codes, small Jews with great heads, high foreheads,
  bright eyes—all gone.

12

Never will a Jewish mother cradle a baby. Jews will not die or be born.
Never will plaintive songs of Jewish poets be sung. All's gone, gone.
No Jewish theater where men will laugh or silently shed a tear.
No Jewish musicians and painters, Barcinskis,° to create and innovate in joy
  and sorrow.

*Hanoch
Barcinski—painter
and illustrator;
killed in 1942.*

13

Jews will fight or sacrifice no longer for others.
They will no longer heal, soothe someone's pain, forgetting their own.
O you foolish gentile, the bullet you fired at the Jew hit you too.
O who will help you build your lands? Who will give you so much of heart
  and soul?

14

And my hot-headed Communists will no longer bicker and argue with my
  Bundists,
Neither will they wrangle with my liberty-loving, devoted and conscientious
  Ḥalutzim
Who offered themselves to the world, not forgetting their own woe.
I watched the disputes and grieved . . . If only you could continue to argue and
  stay alive!

15

Woe is unto me, nobody is left . . . There was a people and it is no more. There
  was a people and it is . . . Gone . . .
What a tale. It began in the Bible and lasted till now . . . A very sad tale.
A tale that began with Amalek and concluded with the far crueller Germans . . .
O distant sky, wide earth, vast seas. Do not crush and don't destroy the wicked.
  Let them destroy themselves!

November 15–17, 1944

93 The Czech Transport: A Chronicle of the Auschwitz *Sonderkommando*

ZALMEN GRADOWSKI

Introduction

Dear reader, I write these words in the moments of my greatest despair. I do not know, I do not believe, that I myself will live to read these lines "after the storm." Who knows if I will have the good fortune to unfold the secret I carry deep in my heart to the world? Who knows if I will ever again behold a "free" man and be able to speak with him? It may be that these, the lines that I am now writing, will be the sole witnesses to what was my life. But I shall be happy if only my writings should reach you, citizen of the free world. Perhaps a spark of my inner fire will ignite in you, and even should you sense only part of what we lived for, you will be compelled to avenge us—avenge our deaths!

Dear discoverer of these writings!

I have a request of you: this is the real reason why I write, that my doomed life may attain some meaning, that my hellish days and hopeless tomorrows may find a purpose in the future.

I pass on to you only a small part of what took place in the hell of Birkenau-Auschwitz. It is for you to comprehend the reality. I have written a great deal besides this. I am certain that you will come upon these remnants, and from them you will be able to construct a picture of how our people were killed.

I also ask a personal favor, dear finder and publisher of these writings. Using the address I give here, find out who I am. Then ask my relatives for the portrait of my family, as well as that of my wife and me and, using your discretion, print them in this book. In this way I hope to immortalize the dear, beloved names of those for whom, at this moment, I cannot even expend a tear! For I live in an inferno of death, where it is impossible to measure my great losses. And, of course, I too am condemned to die. Can the dead mourn the dead? But you, unknown "free" citizen of the world, I beg you to shed a tear for them when you have their pictures before your eyes. I dedicate all my writings to them—this is my tear, my lament for my family and people.

Here I wish to list the names of my martyred family:

My mother—Sarah
My sister—Libe
My sister—Esther Rokhl
My wife—Sonia (Sarah)
My father-in-law—Raphael
My brother-in-law—Wolf

They were killed on December 8, 1942—gassed and incinerated.

I also make mention of my father, Shmuel, who was seized on Yom Kippur 1942, and about whom I have heard nothing since. Two brothers, Eber and Moyshl, were captured in Lithuania, my sister Feygeleh in Otwock. This is my entire family.

I doubt that any of them are still alive. I ask you—this is my last request—to print under our photographs the dates on which we were killed.

My own fate is evident from the present situation. I know the day approaches—the day before which my heart and soul tremble, though not from love of life, for this life is a torment. Yet, in the moment left me I cannot rest: Live, live for revenge! And immortalize the names of my loved ones. I have friends in America and in the Land of Israel. I give the address of one below, and from him you can find out about me and my family.

> J. Joffe
> 27 East Broadway, N.Y.
> America

Everything described here I experienced myself during my sixteen months of *Sonderarbeit*, and my accumulated grief and pain, my terrible suffering, could have found no other expression under these "conditions" than through this writing.

The Authorities Prepare

Three days earlier, on Monday the sixth of March 1944, the three of them arrived: the Camp Commandant, the cold-blooded murderer Oberscharführer [Johann] Schwarzhuber°; the Überreferat-führer Oberscharführer . . . ; and our Oberscharführer Voss,° the head of all four crematoria. Together they circled the entire area of the crematorium and devised a "strategic" plan for the military placement of the guards, of the fortified sentinel, on the day of their great celebration.

This caused a great stir among us, for it was the first time in our sixteen months of harrowing *Sonderarbeit*° that the authorities had taken such security precautions. Hundreds of thousands of strong, young people had already passed before our eyes—many in transports of Russians, Poles and Gypsies. They knew they had been brought here to die, but none of them ever tried to revolt or to go down resisting; like sheep to slaughter they passed. There had been only two exceptions in these sixteen months. A courageous young man from a Bialystok transport had attacked some guards with knives, wounded several of them severely and was shot trying to flee. The other exception, before which I bow my head in deep respect, was the incident of the "Warsaw Transport." This was a group of Jews from Warsaw who had become American citizens, some of them American born. All were to be sent from a German internment camp to Switzerland, where they would be put under the protection of the Swiss Red Cross; however, the "civilized" authorities brought these American citizens not to Switzerland but to the fires of the crematorium. And then something heroic happened: a splendid young woman, a dancer from Warsaw, snatched a revolver from [Walter] Quackernack, the Oberscharführer of the "Political Section" in Auschwitz and shot the Referat-führer, the notorious Unterscharführer [Josef] Schillinger.°

Her deed bolstered the courage of other brave women, who in turn slapped and threw vials and other such things into the faces of those vicious, uniformed beasts—the SS.

These were the only transports in which people, realizing they had nothing more to lose, offered resistance. Hundreds of thousands knowingly went to the slaughter like sheep. That was why the current preparations surprised us so. We figured that "they" had heard rumors that the Czech Jews, having already spent

Commander of the Men's Camp in Auschwitz II; executed at Nuremberg.

The printed version reads "Fast" or "Fost."

Literally, special duty.

Josef Schillinger was shot in October 1943; this celebrated case is widely documented.

I.e., in the twin
camp of Birkenau.

seven months in the camp° with their families and knowing very well what went on here . . . would not be so submissive. And so they took all the necessary precautions against those who would have the "chutzpah" to resist going to their deaths, who would dare stage an uprising against their "blameless" transgressors.

Monday at noon we were sent into the block to rest, so that we would be able to approach our work with renewed strength. One hundred and forty men—almost the entire block (two hundred had already been "removed")—would meet the transport this day, for both crematoria 1 and 2 would be operating at full capacity.

The plan was executed with the utmost military precision. We, the most wretched victims of all, were drafted into the camp's ranks against our own sisters and brothers. We had to form the front line, that which the doomed prisoners would eventually attack, while behind us the "heroes and warriors of the Great Regime" would stand with automatics, grenades and rifles poised and ready to fire.

A day passed, and then a second and a third. Wednesday came, the ultimate deadline for the transport's arrival. There were two obvious reasons for the delay. First, it appeared that in addition to strategic preparations, moral assurances were demanded. The other reason was that the "authorities" made special efforts to carry out their major massacres on Jewish festivals, and so they had planned this slaughter for Wednesday night, the night of Purim. During those three days, the authorities—murderers and criminals schooled in bloodshed and cynicism—resorted to all kinds of deception in order to disguise the true, barbarous nature of their masquerade and to confound minds that might otherwise "catch on" and penetrate the dark machinations behind the "cultured," smiling facade of the regime.

And so the swindle began.

First, they spread the fiction that the five thousand Czech Jews were to be sent to another "work" camp and had to submit their personal data—all men and women under the age of forty, according to trade and profession. The remaining, older people, unseparated by gender, would remain together for the time being, along with women who had young children; families were not to be broken up. This was the first opiate used to stupefy the frightened crowd and blind it to the terrible reality.°

The immediate
separation of the
sexes and of the
weak from the
strong was the
norm at
Auschwitz.

The second was that everyone should take his belongings on the journey, and the authorities, for their part, specially distributed double rations to the departing crowd.

And yet a third sadistic deception was devised. A report was released that, due to certain circumstances, correspondence to Czechoslovakia would be delayed until March 30; those who wanted to request parcels from friends should postdate their letters between now and the thirtieth of the month and hand them over to the authorities, who would send them on and hold the incoming packages until they could be properly distributed. None of the prisoners could imagine that a "regime" could have become so debased and insidious as to employ such subterfuge. And against whom? Against a defenseless crowd, whose only strength lay in its will, in its bare, unarmed hands.

This elaborate swindle was the best means of numbing the minds of the more clear-thinking and perceptive prisoners. All, regardless of gender or age, let themselves be trapped by the illusion that they were being led to work. Only when their deceivers felt that this "chloroform" had taken its full effect did the extermination process begin.

Families were broken up, men separated from women, young from old, and so they were caught in the trap, led to the nearby, still unoccupied camp. Unsuspecting, the victims were tricked into cold, wooden barracks, each group separately, and the doors were nailed up behind them with boards. The first phase had succeeded. People were maddened, perplexed; they could no longer think clearly. When they realized they had been trapped here to die, they lost hope and no longer possessed the strength to think about struggle and resistance, for every mind—even those that had dispelled all illusion—now faced a new anxiety. Strong young boys and girls thought only of their parents. Who knew what was happening to them there? And young men, full of courage and strength, sat there stunned by grief, thinking of the young wives and children from whom they had only just been parted. Every outburst of struggle or resistance was immediately overwhelmed by individual sorrows. Everyone was bound to his particular misfortune, and this paralyzed any thoughts about the general situation in which he found himself. The unshackled, energetic and rebellious crowd sat inert, resigned, shattered.

Unresisting, the five thousand victims took their first step to the grave.

This demonic deception, rehearsed so long in advance, had succeeded at last.

The Convoy

Wednesday, March 8, 1944, Purim Night, when those Jews lucky enough to be in countries that still allowed them to exist went to their synagogues, study houses and other places to celebrate the glorious festival of the national, eternal miracle of Purim and to pray that our new Haman might soon meet his end . . .

On that same night in Auschwitz-Birkenau 140 Jews of the *Sonderkommando* were also marching to a certain destination, but not to a synagogue, not with the intention of celebrating the festival and commemorating the Purim miracle.

They walked like mourners, with heads sunk deep in sorrow, and the profound sadness that emanated from them spread to all the Jews in the camp. For the road on which they marched was the road to the crematorium, to the hell of the Jewish people. And soon they would see not a celebration of the Jewish people's past delivery from death to life, but festivities of another sort—of a nation of betrayers who on this night were carrying out the ancient Purim decree, which their god had revived with still greater brutality.

Soon we would bear witness. With our own eyes we would have to watch our own destruction, as five thousand Jews, five thousand vibrant, thriving souls, women and children, young and old, would pass under the truncheons of civilized brutes. At the authorities' disposal would be rifles, grenades and automatics, as well as their constant four-footed companions, their vicious dogs; these would chase and savagely attack the Jews, who, distracted and confused, would run blindly into the arms of death.

And we, their own brothers, would have to help with this, help unload them from the trucks and lead them to the bunkers, help strip them mother-naked. And then, when all was ready, accompany them to the bunker—to the grave.

When we came to the site of crematorium 1, the representatives of the regime were already there, spread out along the field. Several SS men were among them, ready for battle, with rifles loaded and grenades at their sides. These well-armed soldiers completely surrounded the Crematorium, so that if anything were to go wrong they could respond immediately. Cars with searchlights were set up in every corner to illuminate the battlefield. And there was also a special ammunition truck, in the event that they should run out of bullets to use against the enemy, the mighty one. . . .

If you, citizen of the free world, could have seen this, you would have been struck with wonder. You would have thought that in that enormous building with the towering chimneys were giantlike men who could fight like demons, so well-armed they must have been. They could have wiped out entire worlds, mighty armies, in an instant. You would have thought: these men must certainly be great heroes, preparing to do battle with an enemy that coveted their land, their people, their wealth.

Imagine your shock when, after waiting a while, you actually beheld this terrible enemy, the source of this great hatred, the target of this brutal force.

Against whom were they preparing to do battle? Against our people Israel. Soon Jewish mothers would arrive, pressing their babies to their breasts and leading the older children by the hand, and they would stare, frightened and helpless, at the chimneys. Vibrant young girls would leap from the trucks and wait for a mother or a sister to accompany them to the bunker. And men, too, young and old, fathers and sons, would arrive at this inferno and be driven to their deaths.

So this was the great enemy against whom the villain was prepared to conduct battle that night. They were afraid, these brutes; perhaps not every one of the thousands of victims would drop like flies, perhaps one would have the courage to take a stand before dying. And it was because of that one, the unknown hero, that they were so afraid and hid behind their civilized guns. All was ready. Seventy men from our squad were also assigned to guard the area of the fenced-in crematorium. And behind us, outside the fence, they stood with their rifles aimed at the doomed.

Cars and motorcycles raced back and forth. There was much activity to make sure that things were in order. A deathly silence reigned in the camp. Every living thing must have disappeared, escaped into the wooden graves. The silence was suddenly disturbed by footsteps. Soldiers in helmets, with weapons loaded, marched by as though they were coming onto a battlefield. Never before had military personnel entered the camp at night, when everything was sleeping behind the barbed wires. The camp was prepared for battle.

Now every living thing remained motionless, frozen in the cages, even though everyone knew that many times, and especially in the recent past, victims had gone to their deaths in broad daylight, for all to see. Only tonight, out of fear and dread, did the authorities operate in this way. Only the night sky with its stars and bright moon could not be deceived by the devil: They alone would bear witness to what the devil had carried out.

In the silence, the secret silence of the night, trucks were heard approaching. Already they were bringing victims into the camp. Dogs howled ferociously, eager to attack. The voices of drunken officers and soldiers rang out.

German and Polish prisoners also came, having freely offered to help with the festivities, and all of them, this gang of devils and the murderers, went to meet the trucks, load the victims and send them on to the crematorium.

The victims were still in the barracks, stifled by the fear of death, their hearts pounding. The suspense was maddening as they listened to the activity outside the boarded-up doors. Through the crevices they could see the murderers, the robbers who were waiting in trucks to steal their lives. They knew that it could not last long, that they would not be allowed to remain even in this dismal place, where they wished they could stay forever. They would be dragged out forcibly and taken somewhere else—to hell.

A dreadful trembling suddenly seized the despairing crowd, and they remained silent, in paralyzing suspense. Like corpses, they turned to stone in their places. Now, as they heard the approaching footsteps, their hearts stopped beating. The board was torn from the door. This board, which had entombed them, had also protected them. As long as it was nailed in place it had set them apart from death, and they had secretly hoped that they could remain in this cage indefinitely—until they were freed.

And now the door burst open, and the victims, still motionless, nervously eyed their brutal oppressors and instinctively drew back, as from a ghost. They wanted to escape to a place where the barbaric eyes could not see them.

They were frightened, coming face to face with these who intended to take away their lives. But the angry dogs began to howl savagely and threw themselves on the nearest victims, and a club wielded by the hand of a brute—a Pole or German—came down on a young Jewish girl. And the crowd, which had clung together in a solid mass, poured out of the barracks in single file and gradually began to disperse—to fall apart. Hopeless, baffled, crushed, they began to run to the trucks, dodging the snapping of the dogs and the blows of the enraged brutes. And more than one fleeing woman fell with her child, so that the accursed earth already drank warm blood from young Jewish skulls.

The victims stood on the trucks, waiting to depart, looking around as if for something they had lost. It seemed to a young wife that her beloved husband might come to her out of nowhere. A mother peered into the tragic night; perhaps her young son would appear. And a girl looked around desperately; perhaps her lover was with the people in the trucks, over there.

They looked nervously at the beautiful world, at the sky with the stars and the moon moving majestically within it. They looked at the barracks, the tomb that they had just left. If only they could go back! They knew, they sensed that the truck—this precarious coach—would not hold them for long. Their eyes wandered over the wires to the camp where they had just been. The frightened Czech families were standing there, looking through the crevices at their brothers and sisters who were about to be taken away. In the glare of the lights their gazes met. Their hearts beat rhythmically, full of fear and foreboding. In the night silence hovered the farewells of the sisters and brothers, the friends and acquaintances who remained in the camp waiting for the end, to the sisters and brothers, the fathers and mothers about to be carried in trucks to their deaths.

And so the second stage had already succeeded; the devil had brought his victims to the second step of the grave.

They Are Here

They had already arrived, the unfortunate victims. The trucks pulled up. Their hearts froze as they stood stricken with terror, helpless and despondent, and looked toward the building in which their world, their young lives, their vibrant bodies, would soon vanish forever.

They could not understand what they wanted—all of these officers with their silver and gold epaulets, their shining revolvers and grenades hanging at their sides. And why were they, the victims, standing here like condemned thieves, watched by helmeted soldiers, while from between the trees and wire, gleaming in the light of the moon, the black barrels of rifles pointed at them? For what purpose? Why were all the searchlights shining? Was the night too dark? Was the moonlight too faint?

They stood baffled, unarmed and resigned. They had already perceived the truth. The void gaped before their eyes; they were sinking in it already. They felt that everything, earth, life, fields, trees—everything that lives and exists—was vanishing and sinking with them right into the deep abyss. The stars went out, the sky darkened, the moon stopped shining, the world descended with them. And they, the unfortunates, wanted only to sink, to disappear quickly into the abyss.

They threw down their parcels—everything they had brought for the "journey." They no longer wanted or needed anything. Passive, unresisting, they let themselves be removed from the trucks and fell, almost fainting, like cut stalks into our arms. Take me by the hand, brother, and lead me to the stretch of road that is all that remains of my life. We led them, our dear, beloved sisters; we held them under their arms, walking quietly step by step, our hearts beating together rhythmically. We suffered with them, bled with them, and we felt that each step we took was a step away from life, toward death. At the entrance to the sunken bunker, before they took the first step into the grave, they looked for the last time at the sky and the moon—and a moan escaped instinctively from deep in both our hearts. In the moonlight a tear would glisten in the eye of each sister who had been led here, and another would form in the eye of the brother who had led her.

In the Disrobing Room

In the center of the deep, vast room flooded by harsh electric light stood twelve posts that supported the weight of the building. Around the posts and against the walls, benches had been placed with hangers attached for the victims' clothes. A placard fixed to the first post stated that this was the entrance to a "bathhouse," and clothes had to be removed for disinfection.

We met them, looked at them with glazed eyes. They knew everything, understood everything, that this room was not a bathhouse, but the corridor that led to the grave.

The room filled with people. Trucks arrived with fresh victims, and the room swallowed them all. We stood as if confused, unable to speak to them. Even though this wasn't the first time. We had already received many transports and witnessed many scenes like this one. But still we felt as weak as if we would faint together with these doomed women.

We were stunned. Their clothes, already old and tattered, covered bodies full of grace and charm. From heads covered with hair—black, brunette, blond, and even gray—large, deep-set eyes looked bewitchingly at us. We saw before us fresh, lively women, all in their prime and full of vitality, all nurtured from the wellspring of life, like roses growing in the garden, satiated by rainwater and the morning dew. In the brilliant light the teardrops in their flowerlike eyes sparkled like pearls.

We didn't have the daring or brashness to tell them, our dear sisters, to strip themselves naked, for their clothing was the armor that shielded their lives. The moment they took off their clothes and stood mother-naked, they would lose their last foothold. And therefore it was impossible to tell them to hurry and undress. Let them remain just a moment, just an instant, in their armor, in the mantle of life.

The first question on their lips was if their men had already been there. Each wanted to know if her husband, father, brother or lover still lived, or if his corpse already was burning in flames that would leave no trace, and she herself a widow with an orphaned child. Perhaps she already had lost her father, brother or lover forever. Then why should she remain alive? "Tell me, brother," said one, who in her mind had long ago given up on life and the world forever—she asked frankly and boldly, "Say, brother, how long does it take to die? Is it easy or hard?"

They weren't let alone for long. The murderous beasts could not restrain themselves. The air was torn by the cries of the drunken criminals, who couldn't wait to satisfy their bestial, thirsting eyes with the nakedness of my dear, beautiful sisters. Clubs came down on shoulders and heads, and clothes quickly dropped from the bodies. Some of the women were embarrassed, wanted to disappear somewhere where their nakedness could not be seen. But there was no hiding place here, no room for shame. Morality and courtesy passed with life into the grave.

A few passionately threw themselves into our arms and asked us with bashful glances to strip them naked; they wanted to forget everything now, to think of nothing. They had given up all thought of their previous life, with its moral principles and ethical considerations, when they took the first step into the grave. Now, on the threshold of doom, they thought only about the basic needs of life and of the body—the body alone still felt and sensed and desired. They wanted to give it everything, everything, to satisfy the last pleasure that life still offered the body before its death. And so they wanted their bodies, still pulsing with life's blood, to be touched, to be fondled by the hands of the strangers, who were the only ones present to receive their love. And in this way each would feel the hand of her lover or husband, stroking and fondling her body consumed by passion. They wanted rapture, my beautiful, beloved sisters, and their burning lips drew lovingly toward us, wanting to kiss passionately, to stay alive.

Several new trucks arrived and more victims entered the big room. Many broke from the line and fell wildly, weeping and crying; naked children recognized their mothers and kissed, embraced, rejoiced that they had been reunited here. And a child felt lucky to have a mother, a mother's heart, accompany him to the grave.

They all stripped themselves naked and stood straight in the line. Some cried, while others were stonily silent. One tore her hair and talked madly to herself. When I approached her, I heard only the words: "Where are you, my love, why don't you come to me? I'm certainly young and pretty enough." Those standing near told me that she had lost her mind in prison the day before.

Others spoke to us quietly and calmly: "We're still so young. We want to live, just a little more life." They weren't pleading with us, for they knew that we were victims just like themselves. They simply spoke, spoke just like that, because their hearts were heavy and before they died they wanted to tell their sorrow to those who would survive them.

A group of women sat embracing and kissing. These were sisters, who had met here and clung together.

There a mother sat naked on the bench, holding her daughter, a girl not yet fifteen, on her lap. She pressed her head to her breast and kissed all her limbs. And streaming hot tears fell on the young flower. Thus the mother mourned for her child, whom she would soon lead to death with her own hand.

More light now poured into the room, into the giant grave. On one side of this hell the women were now lined up, their white bodies waiting, waiting for the doors to open and admit them to the grave. We the men, still dressed, stood opposite them and motionlessly looked on. We could no longer grasp if this scene was real or only a dream. Had we fallen into a world of naked women who were soon to be the victims of a demonic game? Or had we fallen into a museum or artist's studio where these women, of different ages and with faces contorted in every way, weeping softly and moaning, had been brought specifically to serve as models for the artist?

For we wondered why they, unlike many other transports, were on the whole so calm, many even brave and carefree, as though nothing could happen to them. They faced death so heroically, so calmly, that we were deeply moved and surprised. Could it be that they didn't know what awaited them? We regarded them with pity, because already there came to us a new, dreadful realization of how all these vibrant souls, even the noise and chatter that rose from them, would in a few hours be stilled by death, their mouths silenced forever. The sparkling eyes, now so bewitching, would gaze fixedly in one direction—seeking something in the deadness of eternity.

These same women who now pulsed with life would lie in dirt and filth, their pure white bodies smeared with human excrement.

From the pearly mouths—teeth and flesh would be torn out together and blood would flow.

From the noses, so finely shaped—two streams would trickle, red, yellow and white.

And the faces, white and pink, would turn red, blue and black from the gas. The eyes would fill with blood, so that it would be impossible to know if this was the same face we were looking at now. The head, now covered with wavy hair, would be shaven by cold hands, and ears and fingers would be stripped of their earrings and their rings. And then two strangers would pull on gloves or lay strips on their hands, because the snow-white figure, so dazzling now, would by then be so repulsive that they would not want to touch her with bare hands. They would drag her—this same beautiful young flower—across the cold, filthy cement floor, and the body, after sweeping all the dirt in its path, would be flung aside like a carcass, to be lifted by pulley to the inferno above and fed to the fire that in minutes would reduce it to ashes.

Already we saw their inevitable end. I watched them, these vibrant souls who filled such an enormous room; entire worlds were represented here—and in only minutes from now. . . . A second image appeared before my eyes, of a fellow prisoner steering a wheelbarrow filled with ashes to the mass grave. I was standing now near a group of ten or fifteen women and thought how all their bodies, all their lives, would soon fill a wheelbarrow. No trace would remain. All of them, who had occupied entire cities, who had had a place in this world, would be effaced, uprooted, as though they had never been born. Our hearts ached with sorrow. We felt through them, suffered through them the anguish of passing from life to death.

Our hearts filled with pity. If we could only have given them pieces of our own lives, sacrificed ourselves for our sisters, how happy we would have been! We wanted to press them to our sorrowful hearts, cover their limbs with kisses, imbibe the life that soon would vanish. To etch in our hearts their living images, to carry their portraits in our hearts forever. We were all in the grip of these nightmarish thoughts, while they, our beloved sisters, wondered why we were so shaken when they were so calm. They wanted very much to know what would be done with them when they were dead, but none of them dared ask, and the secret was never revealed to them.

The enormous, naked crowd now stood looking fixedly in one direction, and it could be that a single dark thought wove through all their minds.

There on the other side all the clothes and articles that they had just discarded lay in a pile. These things troubled them now. Although they realized they would no longer need them, they had been strongly bound to these possessions, which still retained the warmth of their bodies. Here they lay cast off—a dress, a sweater that had clothed someone and kept her warm. If they could only put them on once more, how good, how happy they would feel. Was it really so—their situation so hopeless that they would never wear these things again?

Was it possible that these clothes would just be left there? That their owners would never return to them?

Clothes abandoned like orphans. Like witnesses or testimonies to the approaching death.

Ah! Who knew who would wear these things after them? A girl stepped out of place to retrieve a strip of silk from under the foot of a companion. She took it quickly and stepped back into the line. I asked her why she needed this kerchief. "For a keepsake," the girl replied in a low voice. She would take it with her to the grave.

The Death March

The doors burst open. Hell gaped wide before its victims. In the little room that led to the grave, the representatives of the regime stood in full regalia, as if for a military parade. The entire Political Section had turned out for the celebration. High-ranking officers were there, whose faces we had never before seen during our sixteen months in the camp. Among them stood a woman, an SS officer, the director of the women's camp. She too had come to witness the "national" festival, the murder of the children of our people.

I stood aside and observed both groups—the terrible murderers and their hapless victims, my sisters.

The march, the death march, had begun. The victims walked proudly, boldly, with firm steps, as though they were marching toward life. Nor did they break down on seeing the place where the final scene of their lives would be played. They kept their footing even when they realized that they were captives in the heart of hell. They had settled all accounts with the world and with life before coming here. All ties with life had been broken in captivity. That was why they walked so peacefully, so calmly, approaching their end without breaking down. Without a pause, these vibrant, naked women marched. It seemed to go on for an eternity, an eternity.

It seemed as though entire worlds, entire worlds, had been stripped naked and brought here for a devilish stroll.

Mothers passed with small children in arms; others were led by the hands of their little ones. They kissed their children—a mother's heart cannot be bound—kissed them all along the way. Sisters walked arm in arm, clinging together, wanting to face death together.

All glanced scornfully at the line of officers, not wishing to grace them with direct gazes. No one pleaded, no one sought mercy. They knew there was no spark of human conscience in those hearts. They didn't want to give them the pleasure of watching them beg for their lives in despair.

Suddenly the naked procession came to an abrupt halt. A pretty girl of nine, whose long, intricately plaited braids hung in golden strips down her childish shoulders, had approached followed by her mother, who now stopped and boldly addressed the officers: "Murderers, thieves, shameless criminals! Yes, now you kill innocent women and children. You blame us, helpless as we are, for the war. As if my child and I could have brought this war upon you.

"You think, murderers, that with our blood you can hide your losses on the front. But the war is already lost. You know very well what beatings you take every day on the eastern front. Remember! Now you can smooth everything over, but there will come a day—a day of revenge. Russia will be the victor, and she will avenge us! You will be carved up alive. Our brothers all over the world will not rest until they have avenged our innocent blood."

And then she turned to the woman and said, "She-beast! Have you also come to look on our misfortune? Remember! You too have a child, a family, but you will not enjoy them for long. You will be torn to pieces, and your child won't live much longer than mine. Remember, murderers! You will pay for everything—the whole world will take revenge on you."

Then she spat in their faces and ran into the bunker with her child. The officers stood silent, stunned. They couldn't look at one another. The terrible truth they had just heard tore into their bestial souls. They had let her speak even though they knew what she would say, compelled to listen to this Jewish woman on her way to die. Now they stood gravely, deep in thought. This doomed woman had torn the blinders from their eyes and revealed the future that loomed before them. None of this was new to them; many times dark thoughts had clouded their minds, but now it was a Jewish woman who spoke the truth. Unashamed, she had forced them to see reality.

They were afraid to think too long, for the truth might penetrate too deeply. And then what would they live for?—But no! The *Führer*, their god, had claimed something completely different, that victory was not to be won on the battlefields of the east and west . . . but here in the bunker. This was where victory lay—here where the terrible enemy, the cause of German blood being spilled on the battlefields of Europe, was now marching past. These were the hated enemy; for their sakes English airplanes dropped bombs night and day, killing young and old. It was because of these naked women that they were so far from home, because of them that their sons had to lay their heads down in the east. No, the *Führer*, the god, was correct. They must be exterminated, destroyed. Only then, when these naked women and children lay dead, would victory be assured. Ach, if only it could happen faster, if only all the Jews could be gathered and driven from the world more quickly, stripped naked and driven into the inferno like these women here! How good it would be. The cannons would cease thundering, the airplanes would stop dropping bombs, the war would be concluded. Peace would reign over the world. Their scattered children would return home to begin new and happy lives. Only one obstacle remained—these naked women—there were members of their nation still in hiding, who had not yet been brought here to be stripped naked like these who were marching past. And a brutal hand stretched out a whip and mercilessly beat the naked bodies.

Run faster, our enemies, faster into the bunker, into the grave, for every step you take brings us closer to victory. And victory must come more quickly, more swiftly! We have paid too dearly for you on the vast battlefields—now run faster, children of devils, and don't stop along the way, because that would hinder our victory.

They marched on—rows of young, naked women. And again the marching came to a halt. Another woman, this time a lovely, blond girl, had addressed the officers: "Wretched murderers! You look at me with your thirsty, bestial eyes. You glut yourselves on my nakedness. Yes, this is what you've been waiting for. In your civilian lives you could never even have dreamed about it. You hoodlums and criminals, you have finally found the right place to satisfy your sadistic eyes. But you won't enjoy this for long. Your game's almost over, you can't kill all the Jews. And you will pay for it all." And suddenly she leaped at them and struck Oberscharführer Voss, the director of the crematoria, three times. Clubs came down on her head and shoulders. She entered the bunker with her head covered with wounds, and the warm blood caressed her body lovingly; she laughed for joy, for her hand still tingled from the blow she had dealt the notorious killer's face. She had achieved her final goal, and proceeded calmly to her death.

Pouring in the Gas

Two pairs of footsteps disturbed the night's silence. In the moonlight two figures appeared. They put on masks, in preparation for pouring the poisonous gas that they carried in two cylinders, enough to kill the thousands of victims who waited there. They walked now in the direction of the bunker, treading softly. They walked calmly, cold and assured, as if called upon to perform some sacred duty. Their hearts ice, their hands never even trembling, they guiltlessly moved to each "eye" of the sunken bunker, poured in the gas, and covered the "eye" with a heavy lid so that no gas could escape. Through the peepholes they could hear the deep, agonized groan of the mass of people struggling with death, but they remained unmoved. Deaf and dumb, they moved on to the second "eye" and again poured in the gas. Then, after taking care of the last one, they removed the masks. Proud, calm, at peace with themselves, they walked away, having performed a great service for their people and country, having brought them a step closer to victory. . . .

The Second Front

Everyone now moved "over there," to the second crematorium—the officers and guards, as well as ourselves. Again, a front was established. All was tense, in readiness for combat. Even more security measures were taken now than before because, even though the first reception of prisoners had proceeded smoothly and without any kind of resistance or casualties, the present group consisted of strong, young men, and so anything could happen. Before long we heard the familiar sound of the trucks. "They are coming!" shouted the Commandant. This was a signal to get everything ready. In the silence, one heard the rifles and machine guns being positioned for the last time before battle, so that they could function properly if called upon to do their "duty."

The enormous searchlights once again illuminated this place of death. And in their light and the light of the moon, several rifle barrels glittered once more, wielded by the "Great Regime" that now stood ready to do battle against the defenseless, hapless people of Israel. Faces peered wildly through the trees and barbed wire. In the moonlight the "death's head" gleamed frightfully from the helmets of "heroes" who wore it with pride. Like demons, like murderers, they huddled in the silent night, waiting, waiting in fear and hunger for their prey.

Devastation

We were all tense—both "us" and "them." The representatives of the regime stood frightened, apprehensive. They were trembling. Perhaps this group of desperate men would go down like heroes on the threshold of the grave. In such a case, a "misfortune" could strike one of the guards. Each one wondered who it might be; perhaps he himself was marked.

We too were tense, our hearts pounding as we removed them from the trucks. We hoped, believed, that it would happen tonight, that tonight would bring the redeeming moment for which we had been impatiently waiting, when the desperate throng on the edge of the grave would pull out the flag of resistance. And we would go with them, side by side, into the unequal battle. At that moment we would not think about the futility of our struggle or whether it would gain us life and freedom. Our best hope would be for a heroic end to this dismal life, an end to this terrible tragedy.

But what actually happened shattered our hopes; instead of fighting like wild animals, the victims for the most part came down from the trucks peacefully and passively, looking nervously at the vast area around them. Their final glances lingered on the building, the giant hell, and with arms dangling and heads bowed in resignation they proceeded quietly to the grave. All of them asked if their women had already been there. Their hearts beat only for them; thousands of unbroken threads still joined them. Flesh and blood, hearts and souls were still bound together into single organisms. It was not yet known by these fathers, husbands, brothers, bridegrooms and friends that their wives and children, sisters and brides, the thousands of souls whom they still thought of as alive and connected to their own lives, already lay dead in that gigantic building, that deep grave. They didn't want to believe it when we told them that the thread that bound them to the women was already severed.

A few threw their parcels violently to the ground. They recognized only too well this building whose chimneys every day spewed forth corpses to the high heavens. Others stood still, or whistled a little tune while looking wistfully and dreamily at the moon and the stars, and then, moaning, descended directly into the deep bunker. Before long all the naked men had gone peacefully, without struggle or resistance, to their deaths in the bunker.

She and He

It was a heartrending scene when a number of women who had been unable to fit into Crematorium 1 were brought over to the men. Naked men ran frantically to the women, each seeking his wife, his mother, his child, sister or friend. The few "lucky" couples who were reunited here clasped each other firmly and kissed passionately. In the middle of the big room one saw unbearable things—a naked man holding his wife in his arms; a brother and a sister standing embarrassed, kissing through tears, and passing "happily" together into the bunker.

There were several women who remained miserably alone. Perhaps a husband, brother or father was already there in the bunker. Perhaps he was thinking about his wife and child, mother or sister, not realizing that she was in the same bunker, naked among strange men, seeking his beloved face in the crowd. And so, yearning, searching, her gaze wandered wildly.

In this crowd of men a woman stretched upwards, yearning and searching, her body facing the throng. Even as she was drawing her last breath, she looked for her husband.

And there on the edge of the crowd, by the wall, he stood restlessly, on the tips of his toes, looking for his wife. And when finally he saw her, his heart began pounding furiously, and he stretched out his arms toward her, trying to make a path, to shout her name. That was when the gas entered the room, and so he remained transfixed in that position—arms outstretched, mouth open, eyes insanely frozen. His heart had given out, his soul departed, with her name still on his lips.

Their two hearts had beaten together with one pulse, and, yearning and searching, together they expired.

"Heil Hitler!"

Through the little window in the gas chamber's door, they, the authorities, could see for themselves how the mass of men lay dead, stiffened from the poison gas.

Happy, assured, with victory in their grasp, they emerged from the place of death. Each of them could now go home relaxed and confident. Effaced and annihilated was the great enemy of their people, of their country. And now, everything was possible once more. The *Führer*, the great god, had said it himself: "Every dead Jew—a step toward victory." And here, here were five thousand at once, killed off in just a few short hours. Such victory, such triumph, without one loss or sacrifice! Who, who else but they, these brilliant officers, could claim such a glorious deed?

They parted with the raised-arm salute and, after hailing their "holy one," climbed contentedly into their cars.

They drove quickly, exhilarated and full of daring, leaving behind a triumph that assured them heroic stature. Soon telephones would start ringing, spreading the news.

Until word of the great victory secured tonight would reach him, the *"Führer and god." "Heil Hitler!"*

In the Place of Death

It had become quiet in the area of the crematorium. No guards, no cars with grenades, no searchlights. Everything had suddenly vanished. A fatal stillness resumed its pacing over God's world, as if all the death contained in that deep hell would gather into a silent wave and inundate the world—would cradle and lull the entire world into the eternal sleep of death. The moon continued her peaceful stroll. The stars glittered enchantingly in the deep, blue sky. The night flowed in calm silence through eternity, as though nothing could have happened in the world below. Night, moon, sky and stars had swallowed up the secret that the devil had prepared for them, leaving no sign or vestige of cruelty for the world to perceive.

In the moonlight the only things discernible in this place were little hills of shadows, of discarded parcels—witnesses to lives that were no more. A few silhouetted human figures were dragging a heavy load along the ground; they passed the load—a corpse—through an open door. They went back with quiet steps and retrieved another one, this time disappearing with it behind the door. Through the night silence came the sound of a bolt being turned; the brothers, the wretches who had to dispose of the dead, were now locked in. Again footsteps were heard in the quiet night. This was the guard circling the deathhouse, watching over those who worked in that hell among the corpses of their brothers and sisters; and he made sure—this guard—that none of them could escape from that place of death.

In the Bunker

Hands trembling, brothers removed the screws and lifted the four bolts, opening the two doors to the giant tombs. A sickening wave from that scene of violent death washed over us. We stood stark still and could not believe our eyes. How long? How long had it been since we had seen them alive? They still hovered before us—the vital young men and women. Their last words still echoed in our ears. The gazes of their tear-filled eyes still accused us.

And what had become of them now? Thousands, thousands of spirited, bustling, singing° beings now lay stiffened by death. No word or sound was heard, their mouths silenced forever. Their gazes were fixed, their bodies motionless. In the deadened, stagnant stillness there was only a hushed, barely audible noise—a sound of fluid seeping from the different orifices of the dead. That was the only movement in this vast, dead world.

Our eyes were glued to this sea of naked corpses. We were viewing a naked world. They lay as they had fallen, contorted, knotted together like a ball of yarn,

In four chapters not translated here, Gradowski describes how the victims sang the "Internationale" and "Hatikvah," the Czech national anthem and the Partisans' Hymn (86).

as though the devil had played a special game with them before their deaths, arranging them in such poses. Here one lay stretched out full length on top of the pile of corpses. Here one held his arms around another as they sat against the wall. Here part of a shoulder emerged, the head and feet intertwined with the other bodies. And here only a hand and a foot protruded into the air, the rest of the body buried in the deep sea of corpses. The surface of this naked globe was made up entirely of parts of human bodies.

Here and there heads broke through this sea, clinging to the surface of the naked waves. It seemed that while the bodies were submerged in the vast sea, only the heads could peer out from the abyss. These heads—dark, fair, brown— were the only parts that broke through the universal nakedness.

Preparations for the Inferno

One must deaden the feeling heart, dull its capacity for pain. One must suppress the anguish that sweeps like a storm over every limb. One must turn into an automaton, unseeing, unfeeling, uncomprehending.

Hands and feet set to work. Every member of the squad is assigned a specific task. We pull, vigorously pry apart the knot of intertwined bodies, one of us taking a foot, the other a hand—how convenient it all is. It seems as though we will tear the corpses to pieces with our systematic prying. Each one is then dragged along the filthy, cold cement floor, the beautiful, clean body sweeping up all the dirt and filth in its path like a broom. Then it is laid facing upwards, eyes fixed in a stare that seems to ask, "What are you going to do with me, brother?" Frequently one recognizes an acquaintance. Three prisoners prepare the body of a woman. One probes her pretty mouth with pliers, looking for gold teeth, which, when found, are ripped out together with the flesh. Another cuts the hair, the woman's crown, while the third quickly tears off earrings, often drawing blood in the process. And the rings, which do not come off the fingers easily, must be removed with pliers.

Then she is given to the pulley. Two men throw on the bodies like blocks of wood; when the count reaches seven or eight, a signal is given with a stick and the pulley begins its ascent.

In the Heart of Hell

On the upper level, by the pulley, stand four men. The two on one side of the pulley drag corpses to the "storeroom"; the other two pull them directly to the ovens, where they are laid in pairs at each mouth. The slaughtered children are heaped in a big stack, they are added, thrown onto the pairs of adults. Each corpse is laid out on an iron "burial" board°; then the door to the inferno is opened and the board shoved in. The hellish fire, extending its tongues like open arms, snatches the body as though it were a prize. The hair is the first to catch fire. The skin, immersed in flames, catches in a few seconds. Now the arms and legs begin to rise—expanding blood vessels cause this movement of the limbs. The entire body is now burning fiercely; the skin has been consumed and fat drips and hisses in the flames. One can no longer make out a corpse—only a room filled with hellish fire that holds something in its midst. The belly goes. Bowels and entrails are quickly consumed, and within minutes there is no trace of them. The head takes

Uses the traditional term taare-bret to underline the desecration of their bodies.

the longest to burn; two little blue flames flicker from the eyeholes—these are the eyes burning with the brain, while from the mouth the tongue also continues to burn. The entire process lasts twenty minutes—and a human being, a world, has been turned to ashes.

We watch, stunned. Two more are laid out. Two people, two worlds, who have occupied a place in the human scheme, who have lived, existed, acted and created. Who have labored for the world and for themselves, laid a brick on the great edifice, woven a thread for the world, for the future—and in only twenty minutes no vestige of them remains.

Two more lie there now; they have been washed thoroughly. Pretty young women—how splendid they must have been! In life they made up two entire worlds—what happiness and joy they brought: their every smile was a comfort, every glance a delight, their every word charmed like heavenly music. Wherever they went they brought joy and gladness with them. Once loved by many, now they wait on the iron board. Soon the mouth will open, and within twenty minutes no trace of them remain.

Now there are three. A child pressed to its mother's breast—what happiness, what joy its birth brought to its parents! They built a home, wove a future, lived in an idyllic world and in twenty minutes no trace of them will remain.

The pulley moves up and down, lifting bodies without end. As in a giant slaughterhouse, stacks of bodies lie here waiting to be removed.

Thirty hellish mouths blaze now in the two huge buildings and swallow countless bodies. It won't be long before the five thousand people, the five thousand worlds, will have been devoured by the flames.

The ovens blaze furiously, like waves in a storm. This fire was ignited long ago by the barbarians and murderers of the world, who had hoped to drive darkness from their brutal lives with its light.

The fire burns boldly, calmly. Nothing stands in its way, nothing puts it out. Sacrifices arrive regularly, without number, as though this ancient, martyred nation was created specifically for this purpose.

If you who are free should chance to notice this great fire; if some evening you should raise your eyes to the deep, blue sky and see that it is covered by flames, then you will know that this is the same hellfire that burns here endlessly. Perhaps your heart will feel its heat, and your hands, as cold as ice, will extinguish it. Or perhaps, your heart bolstered with courage, you will exchange the present victims of this never-ending inferno for those who first ignited it, that *they* may be consumed by its flames.

March–April 1944

XIX

Broken Tablets

Destruction, in the liturgical scheme of things, had always been paired with redemption. That is why the rabbis instituted seven Weeks of Consolation following the Ninth of Av; during this period, the most breathtaking prophetic visions of restoration were rehearsed in the *haftarot* (supplementary synagogue readings), and that is why poems of Zion by Judah Halevi and his imitators were tacked on to the end of the *kinot* (dirges) for the Ninth of Av. Such automatic pairing, as we have seen, broke down when the secular intellectuals of the late nineteenth and early twentieth centuries began to challenge the traditional theology of sin-retribution-restoration, forcing their readers to focus on the brute reality of violence in a world devoid of God. To be sure, many of these same writers were sustained by a secular faith in national self-determination or revolutionary struggle, but the redemptive part of the equation was almost always removed from the description of violence. One can hardly infer the political commitments of Brenner and Bergelson based on the despairing portraits of their "dangling men" **(56, 58).** Even the Red Army's intervention at the end of Kipnis's *Months and Days* hardly compensates for the bloodbath that has just transpired. Only in the work of the Expressionists (Lamdan, Greenberg and Hazaz) was destruction itself seen as a redemptive act, as the combined force of historical and technological upheaval that would usher in a new age of human creativity.

Remarkably, it was the ghetto writers who reversed this trend. Desperately they tried to restore the redemptive possibility in the face of all that negated it, whether through armed revolt, a faith in the eternalness of Israel or the very act of writing. More than anything else, this attempt to piece together the broken tablets of the Covenant defines the dominant Jewish response to catastrophe, and it is this that differentiates those post-war writers who continued to work within the tradition from those who abandoned it.

Whether or not one stayed within the tradition had less to do with biography—whether one experienced the war directly or vicariously, in a ghetto or in a death camp—than with the audience one chose to address. The most traditional audience, because it was the most traumatized and devastated, was the Yiddish-reading public. Its faith in utopian solutions had crumbled in the face of the Nazi genocide, much as Glatshteyn had predicted. Hebrew readers, meanwhile, were now divided between the Old Timers, whose roots were still in Europe, and the Sabras (natives to the land), who had nothing but disdain for the Diaspora and whose own experience of destruction and redemption was soon to absorb all their psychic energies. Then there were Holocaust survivors who adopted new languages, notably French, German and English, to record their sagas, and in each, the literary expectations of their host culture determined what they wrote or, at least, what would get published. These are the best-known writers on the Holocaust—Romain Gary, Anna Langfus, Primo Levi, Jakov Lind, Arnost Lustig, Piotr Rawicz, André Schwarz-Bart, Elie Wiesel—writers who represent a new beginning, who share no common assumptions and who project no coherent vision of the present and past, let alone of the future.

It is to the bereaved writers in Yiddish and Hebrew, then, that we must turn, if we wish to see how the greatest collective Jewish trauma was "worked through" by means of internal codes and archetypes. Though the available literature is so vast that its bibliography alone fills several volumes (with much of it produced before the Eichmann Trial), it is still possible to isolate a single, recurrent pattern: a return to a liturgical mode of writing. Suddenly, the addressee of Jewish poetry—composed by avowedly secular writers—becomes, once more, the God of Israel. Through these dialogues with God, modern Jewish poets express the full range of their emotions: anger, despair, remorse, pride, joy and awe. And because God now presides over history once again, one can address all historical and metaphysical complaints directly to the source—thus, Kadia Molodowsky's plea that God (temporarily) choose another people **(94)**. In the world of Yiddish, where the human addressees have all but vanished, the presence of a listener-God is especially poignant.

Uri Zvi Greenberg's cycle "To God in Europe" **(95)** is part of a massive (385-page) volume of visionary and lyrical poems called *Streets of the River: The Book of Dirges and Power* (1951). These are not easy poems to digest or, for that matter, to present to "the world," for they reveal the poet in his rhetorical, fiery mode rather than in his moments of personal anguish (for an overview of the latter, see Alan Mintz, *Ḥurban: Responses to*

Catastrophe in Hebrew Literature [New York: Columbia University Press, 1984], pp. 171–202). Yet it is precisely in his self-dramatizing poems of prophetic reckoning—with Israel and the Nations, with God, with himself and his audience—that Greenberg explores the redemptive possibilities in a world still thirsting for Jewish blood.

Greenberg's Jewish response to catastrophe was one of unreconcilable oppositions: Because those who dreamed of redemption had all been destroyed, the nations were left to make their own choice between "Sinai, the Tablets of the Laws, the God of Israel" and the pagan blood lust of Christianity. But in order for the opposition to hold, the poet himself had to rouse God from His passivity: God, "the Shepherd-Seer," had to face the full extent of the horror. And if God refused the role of Avenger, then the poet's pen was the only weapon that could "rip the clouds apart" and turn the wayward back to Zion.

Unlike Bialik, Greenberg was not tormented by the loss of faith; the poet could rouse the people even in God's absence. What's more, living in the Land of Israel was itself redemptive, for it meant being part of "the returning time of greatness" ("I'll Say to God"). What could not be purged, mediated, redeemed or transmuted was the incalculable loss of life. The death of the millions was unassimilable; it admitted of no analogies ("No Other Instances"). That was the cumulative force of Greenberg's massive lament.

The return to liturgical forms was a way of reopening the dialogue with God, of exploring the possibilities of redemption and of finding a vehicle for mourning. It was also a way of reconsecrating language. For the Holocaust had destroyed both the physical heartland of world Jewry and the spiritual heartland of the Enlightenment, the movement that had birthed and nurtured the Jewish cultural renaissance. While mourning their losses, postwar Yiddish writers—notably Yankev Glatshteyn, Chaim Grade, I. B. Singer and Aaron Zeitlin—also lamented the failure of secular humanism. In their estimation, it had not only failed to redeem the Jews but also led to their eventual destruction. All that might be salvaged from the ruins was a language of tradition that would reaffirm the bond between Yiddish and *yiddishkayt*.

In "The Last Demon" **(96)**, Isaac Bashevis Singer places the argument against the secular heresy in the mouth of a demon—a highly articulate Jewish demon who, we eventually realize, is really a stand-in for the author himself. The plot, too, is merely a pretext, for what could be more conventional than a tale of a young shtetl rabbi being tempted by the devil? The important feature of his story is that the third and last temptation never happens because the petty foibles of Yiddish-speaking demons are forever eclipsed by the evil that German-speaking humans unleash.

The erudite and witty demon-narrator is rescued from madness (or suicide) by recalling the counting-out rhymes that Jewish children would use in eastern Europe to figure out who was "it." In the demon's hands, these irreverent rhymes are turned into a kind of liturgy, a language of innocence that tries to wrest some meaning, if not from the culture as a whole, then at least from the letters of the alphabet. It is a solitary, self-reflexive act designed to redeem no one but himself.

Yet when all is said and done, the recourse to liturgy remains a rhetorical device for the majority of postwar Jewish-language writers. However affecting, it remains an affectation. The notable exception to this rule is S. Y. Agnon, who decided in 1924 to combine orthodox Jewish practice with the profession of writing. It is a measure of his greatness that he refused to adapt the content or obscure the context of the Tradition to make the marriage work. Whenever Agnon has recourse to the liturgy, which occupies an ever greater role in his writing, it continues to mean the orthodox liturgy as prayed by young and old alike in his native town of Buczacz before World War I. This liturgy is sacred and immutable.

For Agnon, the world of faith was irreparably destroyed in World War I. It is all the more striking, then, that his elegy for the Great Destruction seems almost optimistic. The narrator of his story "The Sign" **(97)** is a God-fearing and synagogue-attending Jew, whose own life is neatly packaged into a story of destruction and renewal in which the murder of his townspeople is but a momentary disturbance. Everything in the story seems to mitigate the loss: the fact that his own house in Jerusalem has already been rebuilt; the arrival of the terrible news on the eve of Shavuot, which allows the festival liturgy to shape the nature of his late-night reverie; the narrator's distance in time from the events described (the original version of the story, which corresponds to chaps. 35–36, 40–42, appeared in 1944); and, of course, the epiphany at story's end. Yet in several subtle ways this lyrical reminiscence conveys an acute—and distinct—feeling of loss.

Despite the narrator's professed religiosity, he sees a pattern of rebirth-in-destruction that depends exclusively on human factors (chaps. 19–24). He recalls those who worked the land out of true idealism versus those who speculated on its commercial value; those who gave their lives to protect it versus those who came to destroy it. The Zionist endeavor is sustained by a flawed messianism; even in peacetime, the residents of the Talpiot quarter of Jerusalem, where the narrator lives, lack the resolve to build a proper House of Prayer. "We . . . build great and beautiful houses for ourselves," says the narrator ruefully, "and suffice with little buildings and shacks for prayer."

In contrast to this less than perfect present is the luminous past, but the town of his youth exists only in the writer's imagination and can be teased out of him only on certain occasions. What's more, as a *modern* Jewish writer, he uses tools that are by definition inadequate to the task of memorialization. His language is tainted; his faith equivocal. No modern writer can match the timeless power of an Ibn Gabirol, the great Hebrew liturgical poet of the Middle Ages, or can ever elicit the selfless devotion of the old *ḥazzan* of the Great Synagogue in Buczacz.

This story, then, is a plea for the *past* to be redeemed and its sorrowful ending is profound: the only adequate memorial to the dead is a liturgical poem that only Ibn Gabirol could have composed, but such a poem is too awesome for a surviving Jew to remember, and even were he to remember, the surviving community would not be a worthy guardian. Whatever new form the destruction/redemption equation must take, it must be mediated by an experience of the past, for only in the past was there a direct, unmediated connection to God.

94 God of Mercy

KADIA MOLODOWSKY

O God of Mercy
For the time being
Choose another people.
We are tired of death, tired of corpses,
We have no more prayers.   5
For the time being
Choose another people.
We have run out of blood
For victims,
Our houses have been turned into desert,   10
The earth lacks space for tombstones,
There are no more lamentations
Nor songs of woe
In the ancient texts.

God of Mercy   15
Sanctify another land
Another Sinai.
We have covered every field and stone
With ashes and holiness.
With our crones   20
With our young
With our infants
We have paid for each letter in your Commandments.

God of Mercy
Lift up your fiery brow,   25
Look on the peoples of the world,
Let them have the prophecies and Holy Days
Who mumble your words in every tongue.
Teach them the Deeds
And the ways of temptation.   30

God of Mercy
To us give rough clothing
Of shepherds who tend sheep
Of blacksmiths at the hammer
Of washerwomen, cattle slaughterers   35
And lower still.
And O God of Mercy

Grant us one more blessing—
Take back the divine glory of our genius.

1945

95 To God in Europe

URI ZVI GREENBERG

I I'll Say to God

God, I as one of the many beheaded of father and mother,
the heaps of whose slaughtered lie heavy upon them,
stand before you in the prayer-line of my slain ones,
I replace them in the world as a man replaces his comrade in battle,5
lest, one link lost, their chain of eternity   5
drop from the hand of the living:
the chain of the race whose latest link I am,
the chain leading to me,
to the end of the day of my night, and to
the returning time of greatness,—   10
for which the generations forged the chain.
In every circumstance, under every rule, they taught their children this,
who learned it by heart and wrote it down,
eye to eye and heart to heart.

Dumb are the slaughtered, the dust of seventy exiles stops their mouths: 15
I pray their prayer for them—and in their cadences.
Though my heart break, their Hebrew words are mine.
I believe in the continuity of this, I know completely
the earthly coast, its boundaries in dream,
where the pain of longing ends and visions wake with dawn.   20
In my mind I am close to all these, and I can touch them.
I am different from my forefathers: they indulged their longings, they prophesied
    right things,
but did not utter the Command of "Do" to the-people's-religion-of-longing.
God, therefore do I come to utter
in laws of song   25
this positive command,
since in Jerusalem there is not yet
ruler or commander for my people.

As I idly walk on my bounded path each day,
one of many along street and boulevard,—   30

the fragments of my people's disasters within me,
their weeping which is my blood,
and my legs, feelings, thoughts,
give way beneath the grave-stones of my dead—
and I walk my little path as if   35
I had been walking all my days
enormous distances, and in the warm flow of my blood.

I see the powerful armies of the barbarians, their wagons, chariots, their bolts
        and swords
and my intermingled tribes in the mingle of their babble:
their splendor and their darkness, the dispersal in exhaustion of their powers 40
though a bull is potent within them;
I see the brewers of mischief, the traitors, fools, sages among them:
and Satan walks among them, *but my songs, too, are among them,*
and I laugh then in my heart:
the sadness is here, true enough,   45
but soaring above all this, there soars the eagle of song,

Keter malkhut, carrying in his beak the crown-of-the-universal-kingdom°:
God's royal All, without knowing, go
crown, is an to the great palace of power,
image borrowed as my will directs them,   50
from Solomon Ibn this way or that:
Gabirol (circa in my songs is the magnet to which they are constantly drawn.
1021–1055).

II   To God in Europe

You are God, and You don't have to get
a permit to move freely around (made out in Your name)
from the Army commanders in the occupied areas,
the wide and rotting fields of Israel, Your flock.
By day the sun, at night the stars still blaze: 5

Patterned on the a bell and organ psalm of blood for the chief musician, for the conqueror.°
opening line of
many psalms of Go then and move among the gentiles there,
David, e.g., 13, the crosses and the dogs. They will not bark or stab or madly rage,
19, 20, 21. their ears will never hear Your footsteps' sound:
sergeant and gentile, chariot and cart, will pass as easily through You 10
as through the air of their street, the wind of the day, the shadow of a tree.

Your path is the path of a being bodiless; nevertheless,
Your vision encompasses all,
including that which is under the layers of grave-soil;
nothing is hidden, nothing can hide from you: not   15
six million bodies of prayer—mind pure, heart warm with song.

You are He who knows the beginning of Abraham and the days of the
        Kingdom,
the Jews of many exiles in song.

And you know their end: that death, that terror beyond all thought, beyond the
    moulds of words;
making clear: the time has come to disperse all parchment words, all letter
    combinations   20
so that they stand in uncombinable isolation
as before
the giving from Mt. Sinai of the Law . . .

All sensible survivors of the people dwell with their grief, while I must gnash
    my teeth,
grinding words that are the children of the writ of lamentation.   25
But the words are not capable of expressing that deep pain when the need is
    lamentation
for every square with its item of horror in terror's mosaic.
Never before had our nation known such terror, darkening gradually and
    closing
around it, as around a tree, the ring of bereavement; and now
all light is ending. The future holds no rustle of a silken hem, no violin that
    sings   30
on wedding evenings in our street . . . About us a field teems
with graves and wells of Babylon and the streams.

In Hebrew, haro- | Go wander about Europe, God of Israel, Shepherd-Seer,° and count Your sheep:
'eh-haro'eh. | how many lie in ditches, their "Alas" grown dumb:
how many in the cross's shadow, in the streets of weeping,   35
as if in the middle of the sea.
This is the winter of horror,
of orphanhood's sorrow, and of the fifth bereavement:
everything, everything is covered by the Christian, the silent snow of the
    shadow of death,
but not the sorrow, the orphanhood, the bereavement, the mourning,   40
for we have become, among the *goyim,* ashes and soap—dung for the dung
    heap.

You will count the few forsaken ones, those who have survived,
fugitive, whispering.
And they who light the smallest candle of hope in their darkness
will be heartened.   45
You will not cry aloud in lamentation—
God has no throat of flesh and blood, nor Jewish eyes for weeping.

And so You will return to heaven, a dumb Shepherd-Seer, after the shepherding
    and the seeing,
a shepherd staff in Your hand,
leaving not even the shadow of a slender staff on the death distances of Your
    Jews   50
where Your dead flock lie hidden . . .

A lying poet can poeticize: that after entering Your heaven
Your useless shepherd staff will shine, a rainbow in the sky.
Not I—who see within the vision the divided body of the bird.

I know very well that You will take the shepherd staff with You,   55
and wait till the battle subsides of Gog and Magog, who are also Your peoples,
    and our inheritors,
till the survivors assemble in the illusion of safety,
and once again there are synagogues, men praying to Your heaven,
societies again for chatter, platforms for speeches,
and again a pathway of roses for Your heretics,   60
And You will be the shepherd of them all.

And Jews will give their sons and daughters to the Moloch of *goyim:*
to seventy tongues—hands grasping pen, wheel, and banner;
give diligent agents of kingdoms: officers, soldiers;
give dreamers and fighters; inventors and doctors and artists;   65
those who turn sand into farmland and civilized landscape;
and those performing wonders—even for Albania—with their mastery of crafts;
give whores as well for brothels and clowns for stages,
dictionary compilers, grammar book sages
for languages still lame,   70
and spoken by barbarians who cannot write their name.

And there will be among us those loyal and dedicated
to all that is not ours; to the cultures that murdered us,
inherited our houses and all that they contained.
And moss will cover our racial mourning, and the sadness be hidden   75
of the knowledge of our people's bereavement.
Only a man like me will come with his pen in his hand
to beweep this moss-covered mourning, remembering always
the sorrow since pagan Titus's days
of an ancient race.   80

My rebuking pen, ripping the clouds apart,
shall make a flood descend!

Who listens to me will forsake his father and his mother and his friend,
he who shares his laughter and she who shares his heart,
the girl of dances and the woven wreaths—   85
and he will take the path my poem traces
to the lair of leopards in the mountain places.

III   No Other Instances

We are not as dogs among the gentiles: a dog is pitied by them,
fondled by them, sometimes even kissed by a gentile's mouth;
as if he were a pretty baby
of his own flesh and blood, the gentile spoils him
and is forever taking pleasure in him.   5
And when the dog dies, how the gentile mourns him!

Not like sheep to the slaughter were we brought in train loads,
but rather—

through all the lovely landscapes of Europe—
brought like leprous sheep   10
to Extermination itself.
Not as they dealt with their sheep did the gentiles deal with our bodies;
they did not extract their teeth before they slaughtered them;
nor strip them of their wool as they stripped us of our skins;
nor shove them into the fire to turn their life to ashes;   15
nor scatter the ashes over sewers and streams.

Where are there instances of catastrophe
like this that we have suffered at their hands?
There are none—no other instances.
(All words are shadows of shadows)—   20
This is the horrifying phrase: No other instances.

No matter how brutal the torture a man will suffer
in a land of the gentiles,
the maker of comparisons will compare it thus:
He was tortured like a Jew.   25
Whatever the fear, whatever the outrage,
how deep the loneliness, how harrowing the sorrow—
no matter how loud the weeping—
the maker of comparisons will say:
This is an instance of the Jewish sort.   30

What retribution can there be for our disaster?
Its dimensions are a world.
All the culture of the gentile kingdoms at its peak
flows with our blood,
and all its conscience, with our tears.   35

If for the Christians of this world there is
the repentance that purifies,
it is: confession. They have sinned.
They desire *the grace, the pain:*
to be Jews with a Jewish fate: the thorn bush without end—   40
from the king on his throne to the peasant in the field:
to raise on their staff David's banner and sign;
to inscribe the name of God on the jamb of their doors;
to banish their idols from their beautiful houses of prayer;
to place the Ark in the heart of soaring Westminster,   45
in St. Peter's, in Notre Dame, in every high house of God;
to wrap themselves in prayer shawls;
to crown themselves with the phylacteries
to carry out strictly the 613 commands—and to be silent:
so as not to pollute their lips with their language soaked in blood.   50
Perhaps their blood will then be purified, and they be Israel.

If they do not desire this with their being's full awareness,
and if they go their way—the way of Wotan and the Christian way—

a wild beast in their blood,
in the still-living-forest, night-of-beast, darkness of their heart—   55
then not the facade
of their courteous religiosity, the majesty of their churches,
their splendid festivals, their handsome art work,
head-halo, flower garland,
not the wonderful achievement of their best minds,   60
will save them
from the terrible passage
to the abyss;
not with a Jerusalem Christianity,
with such a Bible   65
that Wotan has not been able to digest,
so that Christianity turns in each of their bellies,
into a dish of dead sacrifice;
in every mouth, into a poisonous wine.
Wisdom and conscience sink within those rising vapours;   70
all notions of compassion
(as with the journeymen of scaffolds)
are confounded.

Either Wotan, the forest, the spit, the axe,
the roasted, bleeding limbs of the living;   75
or Sinai, the Tablets of the Laws, the God of Israel.

Wotan and Christianity are the secret of the disaster!
The world does not know.

V God and His Gentiles

It wasn't for nothing that Europe's faithful Jews
did not raise their heads
to study with their eyes the pride of her cathedrals,
the beauty in them: arch and spire and carving.
As if seared by their shadows the faithful Jews went by them—   5
not for nothing, not for nothing!
We know this clearly now.
From within them the horrors came
and came upon us.

If God in Europe should descend   10
to the thresholds of cathedrals
and ask His Christians, those who enter there
to pray to Him and praise Him:
"Where are My Jews?
I do not hear their voices in the heavens,   15
and therefore have I come to seek them here . . .
What is the meaning of their sudden silence?
Where have they disappeared?

Has there been an earthquake?
How is it then   20
That they've been swallowed up and you survive?
And if the beasts came from their forest to devour men
and ate them only, sparing you
are they then so wise?
You have raised up in the city to My glory   25
splendid cathedrals—
and if in My name you have raised them,
your God stands on your threshold.
Where then are My Jews?"
The gentiles would answer fearlessly: 30
"There were Germans here and we saw eye to eye.
We killed them. All your Jews,
old and young alike!
We killed them, sparing them no horror,
until they left a space,   35
as the felling of trees in a forest leaves a clearing.
We had hated them for so many years,
ever since you were nailed to the cross, Pater Noster!
And thought You hated them as much.
Thus, from our childhood, had we been taught   40
by father, priest, and book.
We saw as well that You had given us field and rulership—
them, not even the shelter of the sky.
They were the vulnerable. The despised. The to-be-trodden-on.
And then the Germans came and said: 'Among you there are many Jews.   45
Let us make an end to them.'
And this is the end, Pater Noster!"

And then, leaning His back against the gate,
God would look at his Christians—
voiceless, speechless.   50
And the gentiles would see in Him the likeness of a Jew:
wild ear-locks, a beard like a mane before Him,
the very eyes of a Jew;
and see that the cathedral resembled a synagogue,
and that there was no cross now at the entrance.   55
And the Christians would roar like beasts of the forest:
"Is there still one Jew left among us?
Does a synagogue still stand in our city?
Hey, boys, let's start a little fire.
We'll need kerosene, crowbars, axes."   60

1951

96 The Last Demon

ISAAC BASHEVIS SINGER

I

I, a demon, bear witness that there are no more demons left. Why demons, when man himself is a demon? Why persuade to evil someone who is already convinced? I am the last of the persuaders. I board in an attic in Tishevitz and draw my sustenance from a Yiddish storybook, a leftover from the days before the great catastrophe. The stories in the book are pablum and duck milk, but the Hebrew letters have a weight of their own. I don't have to tell you that I am a Jew. What else, a Gentile? I've heard that there are Gentile demons, but I don't know any, nor do I wish to know them. Jacob and Esau don't become in-laws.

I came here from Lublin. Tishevitz is a God-forsaken place; Adam didn't even stop to pee there. It's so small that a wagon goes through town and the horse is in the market place just as the rear wheels reach the toll gate. There is mud in Tishevitz from Sukkot until Tisha b'Av. The goats of the town don't need to lift their beards to chew at the thatched roofs of the cottages. Hens roost in the middle of the streets. Birds build nests in the women's bonnets. In the tailor's synagogue a billy goat is the tenth in the quorum.

Don't ask me how I managed to get to this smallest letter in the smallest of all prayer books. But when Asmodeus bids you go, you go. After Lublin the road is familiar as far as Zamosc. From there on you are on your own. I was told to look for an iron weathercock with a crow perched upon its comb on the roof of the study house. Once upon a time the cock turned in the wind, but for years now it hasn't moved, not even in thunder and lightning. In Tishevitz even iron weathercocks die.

I speak in the present tense as for me time stands still. I arrive. I look around. For the life of me I can't find a single one of our men. The cemetery is empty. There is no outhouse. I go to the ritual bathhouse, but I don't hear a sound. I sit down on the highest bench, look down on the stone on which the buckets of water are poured each Friday, and wonder. Why am I needed here? If a little demon is wanted, is it necessary to import one all the way from Lublin? Aren't there enough devils in Zamosc? Outside the sun is shining—it's close to the summer solstice—but inside the bathhouse it's gloomy and cold. Above me is a spider web, and within the web a spider wiggling its legs, seeming to spin but drawing no thread. There's no sign of a fly, not even the shell of a fly. "What does the creature eat?" I ask myself. "Its own insides?" Suddenly I hear it chanting in a Talmudic singsong: "A lion isn't satisfied by a morsel and a ditch isn't filled up with dirt from its own walls."°

B. Berakhot 3b.

I burst out laughing.

"Is that so? Why have you disguised yourself as a spider?"

"I've already been a worm, a flea, a frog. I've been sitting here for two hundred years without a stitch of work to do. But you need a permit to leave."

"They don't sin here?"

Based on a local legend from the actual town of Tishevitz.

"Petty men, petty sins. Today someone covets another man's broom; tomorrow he fasts and puts peas in his shoes. Ever since Abraham Zalman was under the illusion that he was Messiah, the son of Joseph,° the blood of the people has congealed in their veins. If I were Satan, I wouldn't even send one of our first-graders here."

"How much does it cost him?"

"What's new in the world?" he asks me.

"It's not been so good for our crowd."

"What's happened? The Holy Spirit grows stronger?"

"Stronger? Only in Tishevitz is he powerful. No one's heard of him in the large cities. Even in Lublin he's out of style."

"Well, that should be fine."

"But it isn't," I say. " 'All Guilty is worse for us than All Innocent.' It has reached a point where people want to sin beyond their capacities. They martyr themselves for the most trivial of sins. If that's the way it is, what are we needed for? A short while ago I was flying over Levertov Street, and I saw a man dressed in a skunk's coat. He had a black beard and wavy sidelocks; an amber cigar holder was clamped between his lips. Across the street from him an official's wife was walking, so it occurs to me to say, 'That's quite a bargain, don't you think, Uncle?' All I expected from him was a thought. I had my handkerchief ready if he should spit on me. So what does the man do? 'Why waste your breath on me?' he calls out angrily. 'I'm willing. Start working on her.' "

"What sort of a misfortune is this?"

"Enlightenment! In the two hundred years you've been sitting on your tail here, Satan has cooked up a new dish of kasha. The Jews have now developed writers. Yiddish ones, Hebrew ones, and they have taken over our trade. We grow hoarse talking to every adolescent, but they print their *kitsch* by the thousands and distribute it to Jews everywhere. They know all our tricks—mockery, piety. They have a hundred reasons why a rat must be kosher. All that they want to do is to redeem the world. Why, if you could corrupt nothing, have you been left here for two hundred years? And if you could do nothing in two hundred years, what do they expect from me in two weeks?"

"You know the proverb, 'A guest for a while sees a mile.' "

"What's there to see?"

"A young rabbi has moved here from Modly Bozyc. He's not yet thirty, but he's absolutely stuffed with knowledge, knows the thirty-six tractates of the Talmud by heart. He's the greatest Kabbalist in Poland, fasts every Monday and Thursday, and bathes in the ritual bath when the water is ice cold. He won't permit any of us to talk to him. What's more he has a handsome wife, and that's bread in the basket. What do we have to tempt him with? You might as well try to break through an iron wall. If I were asked my opinion, I'd say that Tishevitz should be removed from our files. All I ask is that you get me out of here before I go mad."

"No, first I must have a talk with this rabbi. How do you think I should start?"

"You tell me. He'll start pouring salt on your tail before you open your mouth."

"I'm from Lublin. I'm not so easily frightened."

II

On the way to the rabbi, I ask the imp, "What have you tried so far?"

"What haven't I tried?" he answers.

"A woman?"

"Won't look at one."

"Heresy?"

"He knows all the answers."

"Money?"

"Doesn't know what a coin looks like."

"Reputation?"

"He runs from it."

"Doesn't he look backwards?"

"Doesn't even move his head."

"He's got to have some angle."

"Where's it hidden?"

The window of the rabbi's study is open, and in we fly. There's the usual paraphernalia around: an ark with the Holy Scroll, bookshelves, a mezuzah in a wooden case. The rabbi, a young man with a blond beard, blue eyes, yellow sidelocks, a high forehead, and a deep widow's peak sits on the rabbinical chair peering in the Gemara. He's fully equipped: *yarmulka*, sash, and fringed garment with each of the fringes braided eight times. I listen to his skull: pure thoughts! He sways and chants in Hebrew, "*Raḥel t'unah vegazezah*," and then translates, "a wooly sheep fleeced."

"In Hebrew Rachel is both a sheep and a girl's name," I say.

"So?"

"A sheep has wool and a girl has hair."

"Therefore?"

"If she's not androgynous, a girl has pubic hair."

"Stop babbling and let me study," the rabbi says in anger.

"Wait a second," I say, "Torah won't get cold. It's true that Jacob loved Rachel, but when he was given Leah instead, she wasn't poison. And when Rachel gave him Bilhah as a concubine, what did Leah do to spite her sister? She put Zilpah into his bed."

"That was before the giving of Torah."

"What about King David?"

Gershom ben Judah Me'or Hagolah (ca. 960–1028), a leading Talmudist and spiritual molder of German Jewry. Issued a famous ḥerem (ban) on bigamy.

"Lord! Destroy Satan!," acrostic of a prayer recited before blowing the shofar on Rosh Hashanah.

"That happened before the excommunication by Rabbi Gershom."°

"Before or after Rabbi Gershom, a male is a male."

"Rascal. *Shaddai kra'Satan*,"° the rabbi exclaims. Grabbing both of his sidelocks, he begins to tremble as if assaulted by a bad dream. "What nonsense am I thinking?" He takes his ear lobes and closes his ears. I keep on talking but he doesn't listen; he become absorbed in a difficult passage and there's no longer anyone to speak to. The little imp from Tishevitz says, "He's a hard one to hook, isn't he? Tomorrow he'll fast and roll in a bed of thistles. He'll give away his last penny to charity."

"Such a believer nowadays?"

"Strong as a rock."

"And his wife?"

"A sacrificial lamb."

"What of the children?"

"Still infants."

"Perhaps he has a mother-in-law?"

"She's already in the other world."

"Any quarrels?"

"Not even half an enemy."

"Where do you find such a jewel?"

"Once in a while something like that turns up among the Jews."

"This one I've got to get. This is my first job around here. I've been promised that if I succeed, I'll be transferred to Odessa."

"What's so good about that?"

"It's as near paradise as our kind gets. You can sleep twenty-four hours a day. The population sins and you don't lift a finger."

"So what do you do all day?"

"We play with our women."

"Here there's not a single one of your girls." The imp sighs. "There was one old bitch but she expired."

"So what's left?"

"What Onan did."

"That doesn't lead anywhere. Help me and I swear by Asmodeus' beard that I'll get you out of here. We have an opening for a mixer of bitter herbs. You only work Passovers."

"I hope it works out, but don't count your chickens."

"We've taken care of tougher than he."

III

A week goes by and our business has not moved forward; I find myself in a dirty mood. A week in Tishevitz is equal to a year in Lublin. The Tishevitz imp is all right, but when you sit two hundred years in such a hole, you become a yokel. He cracks jokes that didn't amuse Enoch and convulses with laughter; he drops names from the Haggadah. Every one of his stories wears a long beard. I'd like to get the hell out of here, but it doesn't take a magician to return home with nothing. I have enemies among my colleagues and I must beware of intrigue. Perhaps I was sent here just to break my neck. When devils stop warring with people, they start tripping each other.

Experience has taught that of all the snares we use, there are three that work unfailingly—lust, pride, and avarice. No one can evade all three, not even Rabbi Tsots himself. Of the three, pride has the strongest meshes. According to the Talmud a scholar is permitted the eighth part of an eighth part of vanity. But a learned man generally exceeds his quota. When I see that the days are passing and that the rabbi of Tishevitz remains stubborn, I concentrate on vanity.

"Rabbi of Tishevitz," I say, "I wasn't born yesterday. I come from Lublin where the streets are paved with exegeses of the Talmud. We use manuscripts to heat our ovens. The floors of our attics sag under the weight of Kabbalah. But not even in Lublin have I met a man of your eminence. How does it happen," I ask, "that no one's heard of you? True saints should hide themselves, perhaps, but silence will not bring redemption. You should be the leader of this generation, and not merely the rabbi of this community, holy though it is. The time has come for you to reveal yourself. Heaven and earth are waiting for you. Messiah himself sits in the Bird Nest looking down in search of an unblemished saint like you. But what are you doing about it? You sit on your rabbinical chair laying down the law on which pots and which pans are kosher. Forgive me the comparison, but it is as if an elephant were put to work hauling a straw."

"Who are you and what do you want?" the rabbi asks in terror. "Why don't you let me study?"

"There is a time when the service of God requires the neglect of Torah," I scream. "Any student can study the Gemara."

"Who sent you here?"

"I was sent; I am here. Do you think they don't know about you up there? The higher-ups are annoyed with you. Broad shoulders must bear their share of the load. To put it in rhyme: the humble can stumble. Hearken to this: Abraham Zalman was Messiah, son of Joseph, and you are ordained to prepare the way for Messiah, son of David, but stop sleeping. Get ready for battle. The world sinks to the forty-ninth gate of uncleanliness, but you have broken through to the seventh firmament. Only one cry is heard in the mansions, the man from Tishevitz. The angel in charge of Edom has marshalled a class of demons against you. Satan lies in wait also. Asmodeus is undermining you. Lilith and Namah hover at your bedside. You don't see them, but Shabriri and Briri are treading at your heels. If the Angels were not defending you, that unholy crowd would pound you to dust and ashes. But you do not stand alone, Rabbi of Tishevitz. Lord Sandalphon guards your every step. Metratron watches over you from his luminescent sphere. Everything hangs in the balance, man of Tishevitz; you can tip the scales."

"What should I do?"

"Mark well all that I tell you. Even if I command you to break the law, do as I bid."

"Who are you? What is your name?"

"Elijah the Tishbite. I have the ram's horn of the Messiah ready. Whether the redemption comes, or we wander in the darkness of Egypt another 2,689 years is up to you."

The rabbi of Tishevitz remains silent for a long time. His face becomes as white as the slips of paper on which he writes his commentaries.

"How do I know you're speaking the truth?" he asks in a trembling voice. "Forgive me, Holy angel, but I require a sign."

"You are right. I will give you a sign."

And I raise such a wind in the rabbi's study that the slip of paper on which he is writing rises from the table and starts flying like a pigeon. The pages of the Gemara turn by themselves. The curtain of the Holy Scroll billows. The rabbi's *yarmulka* jumps from his head, soars to the ceiling, and drops back onto his skull.

"Is that how Nature behaves?" I ask.

"No."

"Do you believe me now?"

The rabbi of Tishevitz hesitates.

"What do you want me to do?"

"The leader of this generation must be famous."

"How do you become famous?"

"Go and travel in the world."

"What do I do in the world?"

"Preach and collect money."

"For what do I collect?"

"First of all collect. Later on I'll tell you what to do with the money."

"Who will contribute?"

"When I order, Jews give."

"How will I support myself?"

"A rabbinical emissary is entitled to a part of what he collects."

"And my family?"

"You will get enough for all."

"What am I supposed to do right now?"

"Shut the Gemara."

"Ah, but my soul yearns for Torah," the rabbi of Tishevitz groans. Nevertheless he lifts the cover of the book, ready to shut it. If he had done that, he would have been through. What did Joseph do?° Just hand Samael a pinch of snuff. I am already laughing to myself, "Rabbi of Tishevitz, I have you all wrapped up." The little bathhouse imp, standing in a corner, cocks an ear and turns green with envy. True, I have promised to do him a favor, but the jealousy of our kind is stronger than anything. Suddenly the rabbi says, "Forgive me, my Lord, but I require another sign."

"What do you want me to do? Stop the sun?"

"Just show me your feet."

The moment the rabbi of Tishevitz speaks these words, I know everything is lost. We can disguise all the parts of our body but the feet. From the smallest imp right up to Ketev Meriri we all have the claws of geese. The little imp in the corner bursts out laughing. For the first time in a thousand years I, the master of speech, lose my tongue.

"I don't show my feet," I call out in rage.

"That means you're a devil. *Pik*, get out of here," the rabbi cries. He races to his bookcase, pulls out the *Book of Creation* and waves it menacingly over me. What devil can withstand the *Book of Creation?* I run from the rabbi's study with my spirit in pieces.

To make a long story short, I remain stuck in Tishevitz. No more Lublin, no more Odessa. In one second all my stratagems turn to ashes. An order comes from Asmodeus himself, "Stay in Tishevitz and fry. Don't go further than a man is allowed to walk on the Sabbath."

How long am I here? Eternity plus a Wednesday. I've seen it all, the destruction of Tishevitz, the destruction of Poland. There are no more Jews, no more demons. The women don't pour out water any longer on the night of the winter solstice. They don't avoid giving things in even numbers. They no longer knock at dawn at the antechamber of the synagogue.° They don't warn us beore emptying the slops. The rabbi was martyred on a Friday in the month of Nisan. The community was slaughtered, the holy books burned, the cemetery desecrated. The *Book of Creation* has been returned to the Creator. Gentiles wash themselves in the ritual bath. Abraham Zalman's chapel has been turned into a pig sty. There is no longer an Angel of Good nor an Angel of Evil. No more sins, no more temptations! The generation is already guilty seven times over, but Messiah does not come. To whom

Joseph della Reina, a hero of Kabbulistic legend who was supposed to have lived in the mid-15th century.

According to custom, the community shames (beadle) would knock three times on the synagogue door each morning to send the dead souls away. If someone died

*during the night,
he knocked only
twice.*

*Singer begins with
a traditional
rhyme:*
  *Alef—an odler,
  an odler flit.
  Beys—a boym, a
  boym blit.
  Giml—a galekh,
  a galekh knit.
  A—an eagle
  flies.
  B—a tree
  blossoms.
  C—a priest
  kneels.*
*Then proceeds as
follows:*
  *Dalet a dorn, der
  dorn brent.
  Hei a henker, a
  henker hengt.
  Vov a vekhter,
  der vekhter
  shenkt.
  Zayin a zelner, a
  zelner shist.
  Khes a khazer, a
  khazer nist.
  Tes a toyter, a
  toyter mest.
  Yud a yid, a yid
  fargest.
  D—the thorn
  burns.
  H—a hangman
  hangs.
  V—the
  watchman boozes
  it up.
  Z—a soldier
  shoots.
  Kh—a pig
  sneezes.
  T—a dead man
  dies.
  Y—a Jew
  forgets.*

should he come? Messiah did not come for the Jews, so the Jews went to Messiah. There is no further need for demons. We have also been annihilated. I am the last, a refugee. I can go anywhere I please, but where should a demon like me go? To the murderers?

I found a Yiddish storybook between two broken barrels in the house which once belonged to Velvel the Barrelmaker. I sit there, the last of the demons. I eat dust. I sleep on a feather duster. I keep on reading gibberish. The style of the book is in our manner: Sabbath pudding cooked in pig's fat: blasphemy rolled in piety. The moral of the book is: neither judge, nor judgment. But nevertheless the letters are Jewish. The alphabet they could not squander. I suck on the letters and feed myself. I count the words, make rhymes, and tortuously interpret and reinterpret each dot.°

> *Aleph*, the abyss, what else waited?
> *Bet*, the blow, long since fated.
> *Gimel*, God, pretending he knew,
> *Dalet*, death, its shadow grew.
> *Hei*, the hangman, he stood prepared;
> *Wov*, wisdom, ignorance bared.
> *Zayeen*, the zodiac, signs distantly loomed;
> *Het*, the child, prenatally doomed.
> *Tet*, the thinker, an imprisoned lord;
> *Yod*, the judge, the verdict a fraud.

Yes, as long as a single volume remains, I have something to sustain me. As long as the moths have not destroyed the last page, there is something to play with. What will happen when the last letter is no more, I'd rather not bring to my lips.

> *When the last letter is gone,*
> *The last of the demons is done.*

1959

97 The Sign

S. Y. AGNON

1

In the year when the news reached us that all the Jews in my town had been killed, I was living in a certain section of Jerusalem, in a house which I had built for myself after the disturbances of 1929 (5629—which numerically is equal to 'The Eternity of Israel'). On the night when the Arabs had destroyed my home, I vowed that if God would save me from the hands of the enemy and I should live, I would build a house in this particular neighborhood which the Arabs had tried to destroy. By the grace of God, I was saved from the hands of our despoilers and my wife and children and I remained alive in Jerusalem.° Thus I fulfilled my vow and there built a house and made a garden.° I planted a tree, and lived in that place with my wife and children, by the will of our Rock and Creator. Sometimes we dwelt in quiet and rest, and sometimes in fear and trembling because of the desert sword that waved in fuming anger over all the inhabitants of our holy land. And even though many troubles and evils passed over my head, I accepted all with good humor and without complaint. On the contrary, with every sorrow I used to say how much better it was to live in the Land of Israel than outside the Land, for the Land of Israel has given us the strength to stand up for our lives, while outside the land we went to meet the enemy like sheep to the slaughter. Tens of thousands of Israel, none of whom the enemy was worthy even to touch, were killed and strangled and drowned and buried alive; among them my brothers and friends and family, who went through all kinds of great sufferings in their lives and in their deaths, by the wickedness of our blasphemers and our desecrators, a filthy people, blasphemers of God, whose wickedness had not been matched since man was placed upon the earth.

Cf. Isa. 4:3.
Eccl. 2:5.

2

I made no lament for my city and did not call for tears or for mourning over the congregation of God whom the enemy had wiped out. The day when we heard the news of the city and its dead was the afternoon before Shavuot, so I put aside my mourning for the dead because of the joy of the season when our Torah was given. It seemed to me that the two things came together, to show me that in God's love for His people, He still gives us some of that same power which He gave us as we stood before Sinai and received the Torah and commandments; it was that power which stood up within me so that I could pass off my sorrow over the dead of my city for the happiness of the holiday of Shavuot, when the Torah was given to us, and not to our blasphemers and desecrators who kill us because of it.

3

Our house was ready for the holiday. Everything about the house said "Shavuot."

The sun shone down on the outside of the house; inside, on the walls, we had hung cypress, pine and laurel branches, and flowers. Every beautiful flower and everything with a sweet smell had been brought in to decorate the house for the holiday of Shavuot. In all the days I had lived in the Land of Israel, our house had never been decorated so nicely as it was that day. All the flaws in the house had vanished, and not a crack was to be seen, either in the ceiling or in the walls. From the places where the cracks in the house used to gape with open mouths and laugh at the builders, there came instead the pleasant smell of branches and shrubs, and especially of the flowers we had brought from our garden. These humble creatures, which because of their great modesty don't raise themselves high above the ground except to give off their good smell, made the eye rejoice because of the many colors with which the Holy One, blessed be He, has decorated them, to glorify His land, which, in His loving-kindness, He has given to us.

4

Dressed in a new summer suit and new light shoes, I went to the House of Prayer. Thus my mother, may she rest in peace, taught me: if a man gets new clothes or new shoes, he wears them first to honor the holiday, and goes to the synagogue in them. I am thankful to my body, which waited for me, and did not tempt me into wearing the new clothes and shoes before the holiday, even though the old ones were heavy, and hot desert winds ran through the country. And—if I haven't reached the heights of all my forefathers' deeds—in these matters I can do as well as my forefathers, for my body stands ready to fulfill most of those customs which depend upon it.

5

I walked to the House of Prayer. The two stores in the neighborhood were shut, and even the bus, which usually violates the Sabbath, was gone from the neighborhood. Not a man was seen in the streets, except for little errand boys delivering flowers. They too, by the time you could look at them, had disappeared. Nothing remained of them except the smell of the flowers they had brought, and this smell merged with the aroma of the gardens in our neighborhood.

The neighborhood was quietly at rest. No one stopped me on the street, and no one asked me for news of the world. Even if they had asked, I wouldn't have told them what had happened to my city. The days have come when every man keeps his sorrows to himself. What would it help if I told someone else what happened to my city? His city surely had also suffered that same fate.

6

I arrived at the House of Prayer and sat down in my place. I kept the events in my city, as they appeared to me, hidden in my heart. A few days later, when the true stories reached me, I saw that the deeds of the enemy were evil beyond the power of the imagination. The power of the imagination is stronger than the power of deeds, except for the evil of the nations, which goes beyond all imagination.

I opened a *Maḥzor* and looked at the evening prayers for the first night of Shavuot. People outside the Land of Israel generally add many liturgical poems,° especially in those ancient communities which follow the customs of their forefathers. Although I think of myself as a resident of the Land of Israel in every sense, I like these *piyyutim* which prepare the soul for the theme of the day. Our teachers, the holy writers of the *piyyutim*, are good intermediaries between the

In Hebrew, *piyyutim*.

hearts of Israel and their Father in Heaven. They knew what we need to ask of God and what He demands of us, and they wrote hymns to open our lips before our Father in Heaven.

The people who come to the House of Prayer began to gather. Even those whom one usually doesn't see in the synagogue came, to bring their children. As long as a child is a child, he is drawn after his father and draws his father with him. That is, he is drawn after his Father in Heaven, and draws with him the father who gave him birth. In my town, all the synagogues used to be filled with babes like these. They were good and sweet and healthy; now they are all dead. The hand of the enemy has finished them all. There is no remnant, no one left. And if a few of them do remain, they've been captured by Gentiles and are being educated by Gentiles. Let's hope that they too will not be added to our enemies. Those about whom it is written "I shall bear you on the wings of eagles and bring you unto *Deut. 19:4.* Me"° are given over to others, and are trampled under the feet of human filth.

7

Although on the Sabbath and Festivals one says the evening prayers early, on Shavuot we wait to say *Ma'ariv* until the stars are out. For if we were to pray early and receive the holiness of the festival, we would be shortening the days of the *Lev. 23.15.* *Omer*, and the Torah said: "there shall be seven full weeks."°

Since they had already finished *Minhah*, and it was not yet time for *Ma'ariv*, most of the congregation sat talking with one another, except for the children who stood about in wonder. I know that if I say this people will smile at me, but I'll say it anyway: The same thing happened to those children at this season of the giving of our Torah as happened to them when their souls stood before Mount Sinai, ready to receive the Torah the following day.

While the adults were sitting and talking, and the children were standing about in amazement, the time came for the Evening Prayer. The gabbai pounded on the table and the leader of the prayers went down before the ark. After a short order of prayers, including neither *piyyutim* nor "And Moses declared the festivals of the *Formula for the* Lord,"° they greeted one another and went home in peace.
Festival kiddush.

8

I came home and greeted my wife and children with the blessing of the holiday. I stood amazed to think that here I was celebrating our holiday in my home, in my land, with my wife and children, at a time when tens of thousands of Israel were being killed and slaughtered and burned and buried alive, and those who were still alive were running about as though lost in the fields and forests, or were hidden in holes in the earth.

I bowed my head toward the earth, this earth of the land of Israel upon which my house is built, and in which my garden grows with trees and flowers, and I *Gen. 12:13.* said over it the verse "Because of you, the soul liveth."° Afterwards I said *Kiddush* *Hebrew,* and the blessing "Who has given us life"° and I took a sip of wine and passed my *Sheheheyanu,* glass to my wife and children. I didn't even dilute the wine with tears. This says *recited on the first* a lot for a man; his city is wiped out of the world, and he doesn't even dilute his *day of the festival.* drink with tears.

I washed my hands and recited the blessing over the bread, giving everyone a piece of the fine challahs that were formed in the shape of the Tablets, to remember the Two Tablets of the Covenant that Moses brought down from Heaven. The custom of Israel is Torah: if the bread comes from the earth, its shape is from the Heavens.

We sat down to the festive meal of the first night of Shavuot. Part of the meal was the fruit of our soil, which we had turned with our own hands, and watered with our own lips. When we came here we found parched earth, as hands had not touched the land since her children had left her. But now she is a fruitful land, thankful to her masters, and giving us of her goodness.

Prov. 31:14.

The meal was good. All that was eaten was of the fruits of the land. Even the dairy dishes were from the milk of cows who grazed about our house. It is good when a man's food comes from close to him and not from far away, for that which is close to a man is close to his tastes. Yet Solomon, in praising the Woman of Valor, praises her because she "brings her bread from afar."° But the days of Solomon were different, for Solomon ruled over all the lands and every man in Israel was a hero. And as a man's wife is like her husband, the Women of Valor in Israel left it for the weak to bring their bread from nearby, while they would go to the trouble of bringing it from afar. In these times, when the land has shrunk and we all have trouble making a living, bread from nearby is better than that which comes from afar.

9

The meal which the land had given us was good, and good too is the land itself, which gives life to its inhabitants. As the holiday began, Jerusalem was freed from the rough desert winds, which rule from Pesaḥ to Shavuot, and a soft breeze blew from the desert and the sea. Two winds blow in our neighborhood, one from the sea and one from the desert, and between them blows another wind, from the little gardens which the people of the neighborhood have planted around their houses. Our house too stands in the midst of a garden where there grow cypresses and pines, and, at their feet, lilies, dahlias, onychas, snapdragons, dandelions, chrysanthemums, and violets. It is the way of pines and cypresses not to let even grass grow between them, but the trees in our garden looked with favor upon our flowers and lived side by side with them, for they remembered how hard we had worked when they were first beginning to grow. We were stingy with our own bread and bought saplings; we drank less water, in order to water the gentle young trees, and we guarded them against the wicked herdsmen who used to send their cattle into our garden. Now they have become big trees, which shade us from the sun, giving us their branches as covering for the *sukkah,* and greens for the holiday of Shavuot, to cover our walls in memory of the event at Sinai. They used to do the same in my town when I was a child, except that in my town most of the greens came from the gardens of the Gentiles, while here I took from my own garden, from the branches of my trees, and from the flowers between my trees. They gave off a good aroma and added flavor to our meal.

10

I sat inside my house with my wife and little children. The house and everything in it said "Holiday." So too we and our garments, for we were dressed in the new clothes we had made for the festival. The festival is for God and for us; we honor it in whatever way we can, with pleasant goods and new clothing. God in Heaven also honors the holiday, and gives us the strength to rejoice.

I looked around at my family, and I felt in the mood to tell them about what we used to do in my city. It was true that my city was dead, and those who were not dead were like the dead, but before the enemy had come and killed them all, my city used to be full of life and good and blessing. If I start telling tales of my city I never have enough. But let's tell just a few of the deeds of the town. And since we are in the midst of the holiday of Shavuot, I'll tell a little concerning this day.

11

Ps. 115:16.

From the Sabbath when we blessed the new month of Sivan, we emerged from the mourning of the days of *Omer,* and a spirit of rest passed through the town: especially on the New Moon, and especially with the saying of *Hallel.* When the leader of prayer said "The Heavens are the Heavens of God, but the earth hath He given to the children of men,"° we saw that the earth and even the river were smiling at us. I don't know whether we or the river first said: "It's all right to swim." But even the Heavens agreed that the river was good for bathing, for the sun had already begun to break through its coldness; not only through the coldness of the river, but of all the world. A man could now open his window without fear of the cold. Some people turned their ears toward the sound of a bird, for the birds had already returned to their nests and were making themselves heard. In the houses arose the aroma of dairy foods being prepared for Shavuot, and the smell of the fresh-woven clothes of the brides and grooms who would enter under the *huppah*° after the holiday. The sound of the barber's scissors could be heard in the town, and every face was renewed. All were ready to welcome the holiday on which we received the Torah and Commandments. See how the holiday on which we received the Torah and Commandments is happier and easier than all the other holidays. On Pesah we can't eat *what*ever we want; on Sukkot, we can't eat *where*ver we want. But on Shavuot we can eat anything we want, wherever we want to eat it.

Wedding canopy.

The world is also glad and rejoices with us. The lids of the skies are as bright as the sun, and glory and beauty cover the earth.

12

Now children, listen to me: I'll tell you something of my youth. Now your father is old, and if he let his beard grow as did Abraham, you'd see white hair in his beard. But I too was once a little boy who used to do the things children do. While the old men sat in the House of Study preparing themselves for the Time of the Giving of the Torah the following morning, my friends and I would stand outside looking upward, hoping to catch the moment when the sky splits open, and everything you ask for (even supernatural things!) is immediately given you by God— if you are worthy and you catch the right moment. In that case, why do I feel as though none of my wishes has ever been granted? Because I had so many things to ask for, that before I decided what to wish first, sleep came upon me, and I dozed off. When a man is young his wishes are many; before he gets around to asking for anything, he is overcome by sleep. When a man is old he has no desires; if he asks for anything, he asks for a little sleep.

Now let me remove the sleep from my eyes, and I'll tell a little bit about this day.

Nowadays a man is found outdoors more than in his house. In former times, if a man's business didn't bring him out, he sat either in his house or in the House of Study. But on the first day of Shavuot everybody would go to the gardens and forests outside the town in honor of the Torah, which was given outdoors. The trees and bushes and shrubs and flowers which I know from those walks on the first day of Shavuot, I know well. The animals and beasts and birds which I know from those walks on the first day of Shavuot, I know well. How so? While we were walking, my father, of blessed memory, would show me a tree or a bush or a flower and say: "This is its name in the Holy Tongue." He would show me an animal or a beast or a bird and say to me, "This is its name in the Holy Tongue." For if they were worthy to have the Torah write their names, surely we must recognize them and know their names. In that case, why don't I list their names? Because of those who have turned upon the Torah and wrought havoc with the language.

13

I saw that my wife and children enjoyed the tales of my town. So I went on and told them more, especially about the great synagogue, the glory of the town, the beauty of which was mentioned even by the Gentile princes. Not a Shavuot went by, but Count Pototsky didn't send a wagon full of greens for the synagogue. There was one family in the town that had the special rights in arranging these branches.

I also told them about our little *kloyz*, our prayer-room. People know me as one of the regulars in the Old House of Study, but before I pitched my tent in the Old House of Study, I was one of the young men of the *kloyz*. I have so very very much to tell about those times—but here I'll tell only things that concern this day.

On the day before Shavuot eve, I used to go out to the woods near town with a group of friends to gather green boughs. I would take a ball of cord from my mother, may she rest in peace, and I would string it up from the roof of our house in the shape of a Star of David, and on the cord I would hang the leaves we had pulled off the branches, one by one. I don't like to boast, but something like this it's all right for me to tell. Even the old men of the *kloyz* used to say: "Fine, fine. The work of an artist, the work of an artist." These men were careful about what they said, and their mouths uttered no word which did not come from their hearts. I purposely didn't tell my wife and children about the poems I used to write after the festival; sad songs. When I saw the faded leaves falling from the Star of David I would be overcome by sadness, and I would compose sad poems.

Once my heart was aroused, my soul remembered other things about Shavuot. Among them were the paper roses which were stuck to the windowpanes. This was done by the simple folk at the edge of town. The respected heads of families in town did not do this, for they clung carefully to the customs of their fathers, while the others did not. But since the enemy has destroyed them all together, I shall not distinguish between them here.

I told my wife and children many more things about the town and about the day. And to everything I said, I added: "This was in former days, when the town stood in peace." Nevertheless, I was able to tell the things calmly and not in sorrow, and one would not have known from my voice what had happened to my town, that all the Jews in it had been killed. The Holy One, blessed be He, has been gracious to Israel: even when we remember the greatness and glory of bygone days, our soul does not leave us out of sorrow and longing. Thus a man like me can talk about the past, and his soul doesn't pass out of him as he speaks.

14

Following the Blessing after Meals I said to my wife and children, "You go to sleep, and I'll go to the syngagogue for the vigil of Shavuot night." Now I was born in Buczacz, and grew up in the Old House of Study, where the spirit of the great men of Israel pervaded. But I shall admit freely that I don't follow them in all their ways. They read the Order of Study for Shavuot night and I read the book of hymns which Rabbi Solomon Ibn Gabirol,° may his soul rest, composed on the six hundred thirteen commandments.

(1021/22–circa 1055).

There have arisen many poets in Israel, who have graced the order of prayers with their poems and strengthened the hearts of Israel with their *piyyutim,* serving as good intermediaries between the hearts of Israel and their Father in Heaven. And even I, when I humbly come to plead for my soul before my Rock and Creator, find expression in the words of our holy poets—especially in the poems of Rabbi Solomon Ibn Gabirol, may his soul rest.

I have already told elsewhere how, when I was a small child, my father, of blessed memory, would bring me a new prayerbook every year from the fair. Once father brought me a prayerbook and I opened it to a plea of Rabbi Solomon Ibn Gabirol. I read and was amazed: Was it possible that such a righteous man as this, whose name was written in the *Siddur,* did not find God before him at all times and in every hour, so that he had to write "At the dawn I seek Thee, my rock and tower."° Not only did God make him seek Him, but even when the poet found Him, fear fell upon him and he stood confused. Thus he says: "Before Thy greatness I stand and am confounded."°

This liturgical poem is recited at the beginning of the Shaḥarit service in the German Ashkenazic rite.

A verse from the same poem.

As I lie down at night I see this saint rising from his bed on a stormy windblown night. The cold engulfs him and enters into his bones, and a cold wind slaps at his face, ripping his cloak and struggling with its fringes. The *zaddik* strengthens himself to call for God. When he finds Him, terror falls upon him out of the fear of God and the majesty of His presence.

For many days that saint wouldn't leave my sight. Sometimes he seemed to me like a baby asking for his father, and sometimes like a grown-up, exhausted from so much chasing after God. And when he finally does find Him, he's confused because of God's greatness.

After a time, sorrow came and added to sorrow.

15

Once, on the Sabbath after Pesaḥ, I got up and went to the great House of Study. I found the old *ḥazzan* raising his voice in song. There were men in Buczacz who would not allow the interruption of the prayers between the Blessing of Redemption and the *'Amidah* for additional hymns. Thus the *ḥazzan* would go up to the platform after *Mussaf* and recite the Hymns of Redemption. I turned my ear and listened to him intone: "Poor captive in a foreign land."° I felt sorry for the poor captive girl, who must have been in great trouble, judging from the tone of the *ḥazzan*. It was a little hard for me to understand why God didn't hurry and take

For an English translation, see "A Song of Redemption" in The Jewish Quarterly Review 8(1896):269–70.

her out of captivity, or why He didn't have mercy on the poor old man who stood, his head bowed, begging and praying for her. I also wondered at the men of my city, who were doing nothing to redeem her from captivity.

One day I was turning the pages of the big *Siddur* in my grandfather's house, and I found those same words written in the *Siddur*. I noticed that every line started with a large letter. I joined the letters together, and they formed the name "Solomon." My heart leaped for joy, for I knew it was Rabbi Solomon from my *Siddur*. But I felt sorry for that Zaddik. As though he didn't have enough troubles himself, searching for God and standing in confusion before Him, he also had to feel the sorrow of this captive girl who was taken as a slave to a foreign country. A few days later I came back and leafed through the *Siddur*, checking the first letters of the lines of every hymn. Whenever I found a hymn with the name Solomon Ibn Gabirol written in it, I didn't put it down until I had read it through.

16

I don't remember when I started the custom of reading the hymns of Rabbi Solomon Ibn Gabirol on Shavuot eve, but since I started this custom, I haven't skipped a year. It goes without saying that I did it while I lived in Germany, where they like *piyyutim*, but even here in the Land of Israel where they don't say many of these poems, I haven't done away with my custom. Even in times of danger, when the Arabs were besieging Jerusalem and machine-gun fire was flying over our heads, I didn't keep myself from the House of Study where I spent most of the night, as has been done everywhere, in all generations, in remembrance of our fathers who stood trembling all night in the third month after going out of Egypt, waiting to receive the Torah from God Himself.

17

My home is near the House of Prayer; it takes only a little while to get there. You walk down the narrow street on which my house stands, and you turn down the wide street at the end, till you come to a little wooden shack which serves as a House of Prayer. That night the way made itself longer. Or maybe it didn't make itself longer, but I made it longer. My thoughts had tired out my soul, and my soul my feet. I stopped and stood more than I walked.

18

The world and all within it rested in a kind of pleasant silence: the houses, the gardens, the woods; and above them the heavens, the moon and the stars. Heaven and earth know that if it weren't for Israel who accepted the Torah, they would not be standing. They stand and fulfill their tasks: the earth to bring forth bread, and the heavens to give light to the earth and those who dwell upon it. Could it be that even in my home town the heavens are giving light and the earth bringing forth its produce? In the Land of Israel, the Holy One, Blessed be He, judges the land Himself, whereas outside the Land, He has handed this supervision over to angels. The angels' first task is to turn their eyes aside from the deeds of the Gentiles who do evil to Israel, and therefore the heavens there give their light and the earth its produce—perhaps twice as much as in the land of Israel.

19

I stood among the little houses, each of which was surrounded by a garden. Since the time we were exiled from our land, this area had given forth thorns and briers; now that we have returned, it is rebuilt with houses, trees, shrubs, and flowers.

Because I love the little houses and their blossoming gardens, I'll tell their story.

A young veterinarian from Constantinople was appointed to watch over the animals of the Sultan. One day he was working in a village in the midst of the desert sands. On his way home, he stopped to rest. He looked up and saw the Dead Sea on one side and the Temple Mount on the other. A fresh breeze was blowing, and the air was better and more pleasant than any place in the Land. He got down from his donkey and began to stroll about, until he found himself making a path among the thorn-bushes, briers and rocks. "If only I could live here with my wife and children," he thought. "But to live here is impossible, as the place is far from any settlement, and there's no sign that anyone lives here, nor is there any form of life, except for the birds of the sky and various creeping things." The doctor remained until it began to get dark, and the time came to return to the city. He mounted his ass and went back to the city. A few days later he came again. A few days after that he came once more. Thus he did several times.

It happened that a certain Arab's cow became sick. He brought her to the doctor. The doctor prepared some medicine for her, and she got well. After a while, another one got sick. She too was brought to the doctor. Again he prepared some medicine and she became well. The Arab heard that the doctor wanted to build a summer house outside of town. The Arab said to him, "I have a piece of land near the town. If you like it, it's yours." It turned out to be just the spot the doctor had wanted. He bought thirty dunams of land from the Arab, built a summer house, dug a well, and planted a garden and an almond grove. All the clever people in Jerusalem laughed at him and said, "He's buried his money in the desert." But he himself was happy with his lot, and whenever he was free from work he would ride out there on his ass and busy himself with planting. Sometimes he would take along his young wife and small children to share in his happiness.

The word got around. There was a group of people that worked for the settlement of the Land. They went and bought a piece of land near his. They divided their section up into lots, and sent messengers to other lands, to offer Zionists the purchase of a share in the inheritance of the Land of Israel. A few among them bought.

The Great War came, bringing death on all sides, and destroying in one hour that which had been built up over many generations. If one was not hurt bodily by the war, it hurt one financially. And if neither one's body nor one's money was hurt, it damaged one's soul. The War was harder for the Jews than for anyone else, as it affected their bodies, their money, and their souls. Thus it was in the place we are discussing. Turkey, which also entered the war, sent her legions to wherever she ruled. One legion came to Jerusalem and camped there, in this place, on the land of the doctor. The soldiers ripped out the almond trees to make fires to cook their food and to warm their bodies, and turned the garden into a lair for cannons.

From out of the storm of war and the thunder of cannons, a kind of heralding voice was heard°; a voice which, if we interpreted it according to our wishes and

The Balfour Declaration, November 2, 1917.

desires, heralded the end of troubles and the beginning of good, salvation, and comfort. The war, however, was still going strong. Neither the end of the troubles nor the beginning of salvation could yet be seen.

Slowly the strength of those who had started the fighting wore out, the hands of war were broken, and they could fight no more. The bravery of the heroes had been drained, so they left the battlefronts. Behind them they left destruction and desolation, wailing and tears, forever.

20

After the war Jerusalem awoke, bit by bit, from her destruction. A few people began to think of expanding the city, for even if there were a few places left which had not been damaged by the war, they were crowded and overpopulated. Even before the war, when Jerusalem lay in peace, and her inhabitants were satisfied with little, the air had become stifling. How much more so after the war. Even before the war there was little room left in Jerusalem; after the war, when the city was filled with new immigrants, how much more so.

People formed little societies to buy land in and around Jerusalem, and began to build new neighborhoods. These were small and far from town, and the sums owed were always great. People ran from bank to bank, borrowing in one place to pay off in another, paying in one place and borrowing in another. If it weren't for the bit of peace a man finds in his home and garden, they would have fallen by the way.

21

That stretch of barren desert also had its turn. They remembered the lands the doctor had bought, and asked him to sell them part of his holdings. He liked the idea, sold them a section of his land, and helped them to buy from others. The news got around, and people began to flock. They bought twenty-one thousand dunams, each dunam equalling a thousand six hundred Turkish pik, at the price of a grush and a half a pik. Some bought in order to build, and some bought in order to sell.

Now I shall leave the real-estate agents who held back the building of Jerusalem. If a man wanted to build a house they asked so much money that he was taken aback and went away. And if he agreed to come the next day to sign away his wealth, it would happen that overnight the lot had been sold to someone else, who had more than doubled his bid. The agents used to conspire together. Someone would ask to have a house built, and either they wouldn't build it for him, or they'd build it in the wrong place. So his lot stood empty, without a house, along with the rest of the fields to which the same thing had happened.

The neighborhood was finally built, but its residents were not able to open a school or a post office branch or a pharmacy or any of the institutions that people from the city needed, except for two or three stores, each of which was superfluous because of the others. During the disturbances it was even worse. Since the population was small, they could not hold out against the enemy, either in the disturbance of 1929, or in the War of Independence. And between 1929 and the War of Independence, in the days of the riots and horrors that began in 1936 and lasted until the Second World War began, they were given over to the hands of the enemy, and a man wouldn't dare to go out alone.

Of the Zionists outside the Land who had bought plots before the war, some died in the war, and others wound up in various other places. When those who were fortunate enough to come to the Land saw what had happened to the section, they sold their lots and built homes in other places. Of those who bought them, perhaps one or two built houses, and the rest left them until a buyer would come their way, to fill their palms with money.

22

Now I shall leave those who did not build the neighborhood, and shall tell only about those who did build it.

Four men went out into the dusts of the desert, an hour's walking distance from the city, and built themselves houses, each in one spot, according to lots. The whole area was still a wilderness; there were neither roads nor any signs of habitation. They would go to work in the city every morning and come back an hour or two before dark, bringing with them all that they needed. Then they would eat something, and rush out to their gardens to kill snakes and scorpions, weed out thorns, level off holes in the ground, prepare the soil, and plant and water the gentle saplings, in the hope that these saplings would grow into great trees, and give their shade. As yet there were neither trees nor shrubs in the neighborhood, but only parched earth which gave rise to thorns and briers. When the desert storms came, they sometimes lasted as long as nine days, burning our skin and flesh, and drying out our bones. Even at night there was no rest. But when the storms passed, the land was like paradise once again. A man would go out to his garden, water his gentle young trees, dig holes, and add two or three shrubs or flowers to his garden.

From the very beginning, one of the four founders took it upon himself to attend to community business: to see that the Arabs didn't send their beasts into the gardens, and that the garbage collector took the garbage from the houses; to speak with the governor and those in charge of the water so that water wouldn't be lacking in the pipes, and to see that the bus would come and go on schedule, four times a day. What would he do if he had to consult his neighbors? There was no telephone as yet. He would take a shofar, and go up on his roof and blow. His neighbors would hear him and come.

After a while, more people came and built homes and planted gardens. During the day they would work in the city, and an hour or two before dark they would come home to break earth, weed, pull up thorns, plant trees and gardens, and clear the place of snakes and scorpions. Soon more people came, and then still more. They too built houses and made gardens. Some of them would rent out a room or two to a young couple who wanted to raise their child in the clear air. Some of them rented out their whole houses and continued to live in the city until they paid off their mortgages. After a time I too came to live here, fleeing from the tremors of 1927, which shook the walls of the house where I was living, and forced me to leave my home. I came to this neighborhood with my wife and two children, and we rented an apartment. Roads had already been built, and the buses would come and go at regular times. We felt as though this place, which had been barren since the day of our exile from our land, was being built again.

23

Automobiles still came but rarely, and a man could walk in the streets without fear of being hit. At night there was a restful quiet. If you didn't hear the dew fall, it was because you were sleeping a good, sweet sleep. The Dead Sea would smile at us almost every day, its blue waters shining in graceful peace between the gray and blue hills of Moab. The Site of the Temple would look upon us. I don't know who longed for whom more; we for the Temple Mount, or the Temple Mount for us. The king of the winds, who dwelt in a mountain not far from us, used to stroll about the neighborhood, and his servants and slaves, the winds, would follow at his feet, brushing through the area. Fresh air filled the neighborhood. People from far and near would come to walk, saying, "No man knoweth its value." Old men used to come and say, "Here we would find length of days." Sick people came and said, "Here we would be free from our illnesses." Arabs would pass through and say, "Shalom"; they came to our doctor, who cured them of their ills. The doctor's wife would help their wives when they had difficulty in childbirth. The Arab women would come from their villages around us, bringing the fruits of their gardens and the eggs of their hens, giving praises to Allah, who, in His mercy upon them, had given the Jews the idea of building houses here, so that they would not have to bring their wares all the way into the city. As an Arab would go to work in the city, taking a short-cut through these streets, he would stand in wonder at the deeds of Allah, Who had given the Jewish lords wisdom to build roads, mend the ways, and so forth. Suddenly, one Sabbath after Tisha b'Av, our neighbors rose up against us to make trouble for us. The people of the neighborhood could not believe that this was possible. Our neighbors, for whom we had provided help at every chance, for whom we had made life so much easier, buying their produce, having our doctor heal their sick, building roads to shorten the way for them, came upon these same roads to destroy us.

24

By the grace of God upon us, we rose up and were strong. As I said in the beginning, I built a house and planted a garden. In this place from which the enemy tried to rout us, I built my home. I built it facing the Temple Mount, to always keep upon my heart our beloved dwelling which was destroyed and has not yet been rebuilt. If "we cannot go up and be seen there, because of the hand

Recited in the Musaf 'Amidah.

which has cast itself into our Temple,"° we direct our hearts there in prayer.

Now I'll say something about the House of Prayer in our neighborhood.

Our forefathers, who saw their dwelling in this world as temporary, but the dwelling in the synagogue and the House of Study as permanent, built great structures for prayer and study. We, whose minds are given over mainly to things of this world, build great and beautiful houses for ourselves, and suffice with little buildings and shacks for prayer. Thus our House of Prayer in this neighborhood is a wooden shack. This is one reason. Aside from this, they didn't get around to finishing the synagogue before the first disturbance, the riots, or the War of Independence, and at each of those times the residents had to leave the neighborhood. It was also not completed because of the changes in its congregants, who changed after each disturbance. That's why, as I've explained, our place of prayer is a shack, and not a stone building.

Now I shall tell what happened in this shack on that Shavuot night when the
rumor reached us that all the Jews in my town had been killed.

25

I entered the House of Prayer. No one else was in the place. Light and rest and a
good smell filled the room. All kinds of shrubs and flowers with which our land
is blessed gave off their aroma. Already at *Ma'ariv* I had taken note of the smell,
and now every blossom and flower gave off the aroma with which God had blessed
it. A young man, one who had come from a town where all the Jews had been
killed, went out to the fields of the neighborhood with his wife, and picked and
gathered every blossoming plant and decorated the synagogue for the Holiday of
Shavuot, the time of the giving of our Torah, just as they used to do in their town,
before all the Jews there had been killed. In addition to all the wild flowers they
gathered in the nearby fields, they brought roses and zinnias and laurel boughs
from their own garden.

26

I shall choose among the words of our Holy Tongue to make a crown of glory for
our Prayer Room, its candelabra, and its ornaments.

The Eternal Light hangs down from the ceiling, facing the Holy Ark and the
two tablets of the Law above it. The Light is wrapped in capers and thistles and
bluebells, and it shines and gives off its light from between the green leaves of the
capers' thorns and from its white flowers, from between the blue hues in the
thistles, and from the grey leaves and purple flowers around it. All the wild flowers
which grow in the fields of our neighborhood gather together in this month to
beautify our House of Prayer for the holiday of Shavuot, along with the garden
flowers which the gardens in our neighborhood give us. To the right of the Holy
Ark stands the reader's table, and on the table a lamp with red roses around it.
Six candles shine from among the roses. The candles have almost burned down
to the end, yet they still give off light, for so long as the oil is not finished they
gather their strength to light the way for the prayers of Israel until they reach the
gates of Heaven. A time of trouble has come to Jacob, and we need much strength.
Opposite them, to the south, stand the memorial candles, without number and
without end. Six million Jews have been killed by the Gentiles; because of them
a third of us are dead and two thirds of us are orphans. You won't find a man in
Israel who hasn't lost ten of of his people. The memorial candles light them all up
for us, and their light is equal, so that you can't tell the difference between the
candle of a man who lived out his days, and one who was killed. But in Heaven
they certainly distinguish between the candles, just as they distinguish between
one soul and another. The Eternal had a great thought in mind when He chose
us from all peoples and gave us His Torah of life. Nevertheless, it's a bit difficult
to see why He created, as opposed to us, the kinds of people who take away our
lives because we keep His Torah.

27

By the grace of God upon me, those thoughts left me. But the thought of my city
did not take itself away from me. Is it possible that a city full of Torah and life is
suddenly uprooted from the world, and all its people, old and young, men, women,

and children are killed, that now the city is silent, with not a soul of Israel left in it?

I stood facing the candles, and my eyes shone like them, except that those candles were surrounded with flowers, and my eyes had thorns upon them. I closed my eyes, so that I would not see the deaths of my brothers, the people of my town. It pains me to see my town and its slain, how they are tortured in the hands of their tormentors, the cruel and harsh deaths they suffer. And I closed my eyes for yet another reason. When I close my eyes I become, as it were, master of the world, and I see only that which I desire to see. So I closed my eyes and asked my city to rise before me, with all its inhabitants, and with all its Houses of Prayer. I put every man in the place where he used to sit and where he studied, along with his sons, sons-in-law, and grandsons—for in my town everyone came to prayer. The only difference was in the places. Some fixed their places for prayer in the Old House of Study, and some in the other synagogues and Houses of Study, but every man had his fixed place in his own House of Prayer.

28

After I had arranged all the people in the Old House of Study, with which I was more familiar than the other places in town, I turned to the other Houses of Prayer. As I had done with the Old House of Study, so I did with them. I brought up every man before me. If he had sons or sons-in-law or grandsons, I brought them into view along with him. I didn't skip a single holy place in our town, or a single man. I did this not by the power of memory, but by the power of the synagogues and the Houses of Study. For once the synagogues and Houses of Study stood before me, all their worshippers also came and stood before me. The places of prayer brought life to the people of my city in their deaths as in their lives. I too stood in the midst of the city among my people, as though the time of the resurrection of the dead had arrived. The day of the resurrection will indeed be great; I felt a taste of it that day as I stood among my brothers and townspeople who have gone to another world, and they stood about me, along with all the synagogues and Houses of Study in my town. And were it not difficult for me to speak, I would have asked them what Abraham, Isaac and Jacob say, and what Moses says, about all that has happened in this generation.

I stood in wonder, looking at my townspeople. They too looked at me, and there was not a trace of condemnation in their glances, that I was thus and they were thus. They just seemed covered with sadness, a great and frightening sadness, except for one old man who had a kind of smile on his lips, and seemed to say *"Ariber geshprungen"*; that is, we have "jumped over" and left the world of sorrows. In the Conversations of Rabbi Nahman of Bratzlav, of blessed memory, something like that can be found. He heard about a certain preacher in Lemberg who, in the hour of his death, gestured with his fingers and said that he would show them a trick. At that moment he passed from the world of sorrows. And the Zaddik enjoyed those words.

29

Bit by bit the peple of my town began to disappear and go away. I didn't try to run after them, for I knew that a man's thoughts cannot reach the place where they were going. And even if I could reach there, why should I prevent them from going, and why should I confuse them with my thoughts?

I was left alone, and I wandered back to former days, when my town was alive, and all those who were now dead were alive and singing the praise of God in the synagogues and the Houses of Prayer, and the old *ḥazzan* served in the Great Synagogue, while I, a small child, saw him standing on the platform intoning "O poor captive," with the old *Siddur* containing all the prayers and hymns open before him. He didn't turn the pages, for the print had been wiped out by the age of the book and the tears of former cantors, and not a letter could be made out. But he, may God give light to his lot in the world to come, knew all the hymns by heart, and the praise of God together with the sorrow of Israel would rise from his lips in hymns and in prayer.

30

Let me describe him. He was tall and straight-backed; his beard was white, and his eyes looked like the prayerbooks published in Slavita, that were printed on blue-tinged paper. His voice was sweet and his clothes were clean. Only his *tallis* was covered with tears. He never took his *tallis* down from his head during the prayers. But after every prayer of love or redemption he would take it down a little and look about, to see if there was yet a sign of the Redemption. For forty years he was our city's messenger before God. After forty years he went to see his relatives in Russia. The border patrol caught him and threw him into prison. He lamented and begged God to take him out of captivity and return him to his place. God did not let the governor sleep. The governor knew that as long as the voice of the Jew was to be heard in his prison, sleep would not return to him. He commanded that the *ḥazzan* be set free and returned home. They released him and sent him to our town. He came bringing with him a new melody to which he would sing "O Poor Captive."

31

The first time I heard that hymn was the Sabbath after Pesaḥ when I was still a little boy. I woke up in the middle of the night, and there was a light shining into the house. I got out of bed and opened the window, so that the light could come in. I stood by the window, trying to see from where the light was coming. I washed my hands and face, put on my Sabbath clothes, and went outside. Nobody in the house saw or heard me go out. Even my mother and father, who never took their eyes off me, didn't see me go out. I went outside and there was no one there. The birds, singing the song of morning, were alone outside.

I stood still until the birds had finished their song. Then I walked to the well, for I heard the sound of the well's waters, and I said, "I'll go hear the water talking." For I had not yet seen the waters as they talked.

I came to the well and saw that the water was running, but there was no one there to drink. I filled my palms, recited the blessing, and drank. Then I went to walk wherever my legs would carry me. My legs took me to the Great Synagogue, and the place was filled with men at prayer. The old cantor stood on the platform and raised his voice in the hymn "O poor captive." Now that hymn of redemption began to rise from my lips and sing itself in the way I had heard it from the lips of the old cantor. The city then stood yet in peace, and all the many and honoured Jews who have been killed by the enemy were still alive.

32

The candles which had given light for the prayers had gone out; only their smoke remained to be seen. But the light of the memorial candles still shone, in memory of our brothers and sisters who were killed and slaughtered and drowned and burned and strangled and buried alive by the evil of our blasphemers, cursed of God, the Nazis and their helpers. I walked by the light of the candles until I came to my city, which my soul longed to see.

I came to my city and entered the Old House of Study, as I used to do when I came home to visit—I would enter the Old House of Study first.

I found Hayyim the *shammas* standing on the platform and rolling a Torah scroll, for it was the eve of the New Moon, and he was rolling the scroll to the reading for that day. Below him, in an alcove near the window, sat Shalom the shoemaker, his pipe in his mouth, reading the *Shevet Yehudah*,° exactly as he did when I was a child; he used to sit there reading the *Shevet Yehudah*, pipe in mouth, puffing away like one who is breathing smoke. The pipe was burnt out and empty, and there wasn't a leaf of tobacco in it, but they said that just as long as he held it in his mouth it tasted as though he were smoking.

See 30–33.

I said to him: "I hear that you now fast on the eve of *Rosh Ḥodesh*" (something they didn't do before I left for the Land of Israel when they would say the prayers for the "Small Yom Kippur" but not fast). Hayyim said to Shalom, "Answer him." Shalom took his pipe out of his mouth and said, "So it is. Formerly we would pray and not fast, now we fast but don't say the prayers. Why? Because we don't have a minyan; there aren't ten men to pray left in the city." I said to Hayyim and Shalom, "You say there's not a minyan left for prayer. Does this mean that those who used to pray are not left, or that those who are left don't pray? In either case, why haven't I seen a living soul in the whole town?" They both answered me together and said, "That was the first destruction,° and this is the last destruction. After the first destruction a few Jews were left; after the last destruction not a man of Israel remained." I said to them, "Permit me to ask you one more thing. You say that in the last destruction not a man from Israel was left in the whole city. Then how is it that you are alive?" Hayyim smiled at me the way the dead smile when they see that you think that they're alive. I picked myself up and went elsewhere.

World War I.

33

I saw a group of the sick and afflicted running by. I asked a man at the end of the line: "Where are you running?" He placed his hand on an oozing sore and answered: "We run to greet the rebbe." "Who is he?" I asked. He moved his hand from one affliction to another and smiling, said: "A man has only two hands, and twice as many afflictions." Then he told me the name of his rebbe. It was a little difficult for me to understand. Was it possible that this rebbe who had left for the Land of Israel six or seven generations ago, and had been buried in the soil of the holy city of Safed, had returned? I decided to go and see. I ran along, and reached the tsaddik together with them. They began to cry out before him how they were stricken with afflictions and persecuted by the rulers and driven from one exile to another, with no sign of redemption in view. The tsaddik sighed and said: "What can I tell you, my children? 'May God give strength to His people; may God bless His people with peace.' "° Why did he quote that particular verse? He said it only

Ps. 29:11.

about this generation: before God will bless His people with peace He must give strength to His people, so that the Gentiles will be afraid of them, and not make any more war upon them, because of that fear.

I said, "Let me go and make this known to the world." I walked over to the sink and dabbed some water onto my eyes. I awoke, and saw that the book lay open before me, and I hadn't yet finished reciting the order of the Commandments of the Lord. I went back and read the Commandments of the Lord as composed by Rabbi Solomon Ibn Gabirol, may his soul rest.

34

There was nobody in the shack; I sat in the shack alone. It was pleasant and nicely fixed up. All kinds of flowers which the soil of our neighborhood gives us were hung from the wall between branches of pine and laurel; roses and zinnias crowned the Ark and the reader's table, the prayer stand, and the eternal light. A wind blew through the shack and caused the leaves and flowers and the blossoms to sway, and the house was filled with a goodly smell; the memorial candles gave their light to the building. I sat there and read the holy words which God put into the hands of the poet, to glorify the Commandments which He gave to His people Israel. How great is the love of the holy poets before God! He gives power to their lips to glorify the Laws and Commandments that He gave to us in His great Love.

35

Torah scrolls.

The doors of the Holy Ark opened, and I saw a likeness of the form of a man standing there, his head resting between the scrolls of the Torah, and I heard a voice come forth from the Ark, from between the Trees of Life.° I bowed my head and closed my eyes, for I feared to look at the Holy Ark. I looked into my prayer-book, and saw that the letters which the voice from among the scrolls was reciting were at the same time being written into my book. The letters were the letters of the Commandments of the Lord, in the order set for them by Rabbi Solomon Ibn Gabirol, may his soul rest. Now the man whom I had first seen between the scrolls of the Torah stood before me, and his appearance was like the appearance of a king.

I made myself small, until I was as though I were not, so that he should not feel the presence of a man in the place. Is it right that a king enter one of his provinces, and he not find any of his officers and slaves, except for one little slave?

But my tricks didn't help any. I made myself small, and nevertheless he saw me. How do I know he saw me? Because he spoke to me. And how do I know that it was to me he spoke? Because I was alone in the House of Prayer; there was no one there with me. He did not speak to me by word of mouth, but his thought was engraved into mine, his holy thought into mine. Every word he said was carved into the forms of letters, and the letters joined together into words, and the words formed what he had to say. These are the things as I remember them, word for word.

36

I shall put down the things he said to me, the things he asked me, and the things I answered him, as I brought my soul out into my palm, daring to speak before him. (But before I say them, I must tell you that he did not speak to me with words. Only the thoughts which he thought were engraved before me, and these created the words.)

And now I shall tell you all he asked me, and everything I answered him. He asked me, "What are you doing here alone at night?" And I answered, "My lord must know that this is the eve of Shavuot when one stays awake all night reading the Order of Shavuot night. I too do this, except that I read the hymns of Rabbi Solomon Ibn Gabirol, may his soul rest."

He turned his head toward me and toward the book that stood before me on the table. He looked at the book and said, "It is Solomon's." I heard him and was astonished that he mentioned Rabbi Solomon Ibn Gabirol and did not affix some title of honour before his name. For I did not yet know that the man speaking to me was Rabbi Solomon Ibn Gabirol himself.

37

Now I shall tell the things that transpired after these former things. The memorial candles lit up the shack, the thronged flowers which crowned the Eternal Light before the Holy Ark and the other flowers gave off their aromas, and one smell was mixed with another; the aroma of the House of Prayer with that of the roses and zinnias from the gardens. A restful quiet was felt on the earth below and in the heavens above. Neither the call of the heart's pleas on earth, nor the sound of the heavens as they opened could be heard.

I rested my head in my arm, and sat and thought about what was happening to me. It couldn't have been in a dream, because he specifically asked me what I was doing here alone at night, and I answered him, "Doesn't my lord know that this night is the eve of Shavuot, when we stay awake all night and read the Order of Shavuot eve?" In any case, it seems a little difficult. Rabbi Solomon Ibn Gabirol is the greatest of the holy poets. Why did he see fit to descend from the Palace of Song to this shack in this neighborhood to talk with a man like me?

38

I took my soul out into the palms of my hands, and raised my head to see where I was, for it was a little hard to explain the things as they had happened, though their happening itself was witness to them, and there was no doubt that he was here. Not only did he speak to me, but I answered him. Maybe the thing happened when the heavens were open. But for how long do the heavens open? Only for a moment. Is it possible that so great a thing as this could happen in one brief moment?

I don't know just how long it was, but certainly not much time passed before he spoke to me again. He didn't speak with his voice, but his thought was impressed upon mine and created words. And God gave my heart the wisdom to understand. But to copy the things down—I cannot. I just know this; that he spoke to me, for I was sitting alone in the House of Prayer, reading the Commandments of the Lord, as composed by Rabbi Solomon Ibn Gabirol. For ever since I was old enough to do so, I follow the custom, every Shavuot eve, of reading the Commandments of the Lord by Rabbi Solomon Ibn Gabirol, may his soul rest.

39

I was reminded of the sorrow I had felt for Rabbi Solomon Ibn Gabirol because God made him search for Him, as he says, "At the dawn I seek Thee, my rock and my fortress," and when he finally found Him, awe fell upon him and he stood confused, as he says, "Before Thy greatness I stand and am confounded." And as if he didn't have enough troubles himself, he had to add the sorrow of that poor captive girl. I put my finger to my throat as the old Cantor used to do, and raised my voice to sing, "O Poor Captive," in the melody he had written. I saw that Rabbi Solomon, may his soul rest, turned his ear and listened to the pleasant sound of this hymn of redemption. I got up my courage and said to him, "In our town, wherever they prayed in the Ashkenazic rite, they used to say a lot of *piyyutim*. The beauty of each *piyyut* has stayed in my heart, and especially this 'Poor Captive,' which was the first Hymn of Redemption I heard in my youth." I remembered that Sabbath morning when I had stood in the Great Synagogue in our city, which was now laid waste. My throat became stopped up and my voice choked, and I broke out in tears.

Rabbi Solomon saw this and asked me, "Why are you crying?" I answered, "I cry for my city and all the Jews in it who have been killed." His eyes closed, and I saw that the sorrow of my city had drawn itself to him. I thought to myself, since the Rabbi doesn't know all of the people of my town, he'll weigh the glory of all of them by the likes of me. I bowed my head and lowered my eyes and said to him, "In my sorrow and in my humility, I am not worthy. I am not the man in whom the greatness of our city can be seen."

40

Rabbi Solomon saw my sorrow and my affliction and the lowness of my spirit, for my spirit was indeed very low. He came close to me, until I found myself standing next to him, and there was no distance between us except that created by the lowness of my spirit. I raised my eyes and saw his lips moving. I turned my ear and heard him mention the name of my city. I looked and saw him move his lips again. I heard him say, "I'll make a sign, so that I won't forget the name." My heart melted and I stood trembling, because he had mentioned the name of my city, and had drawn mercy to it, saying he would make a sign, so as not to forget its name.

I began to think about what sign Rabbi Solomon could make for my city. With ink? It was a holiday, so he wouldn't have his writer's inkwell in his pocket. With his clothes? The clothes with which the Holy One, blessed be He, clothes His Holy Ones, have no folds, and don't take to any imprint made upon them from outside.

Once more he moved his lips. I turned my ear, and heard him recite a poem, each line of which began with one of the letters of the name of my town. And so I knew that the sign the poet made for my town was in beautiful and rhymed verse, in the holy tongue.

41

The hairs of my flesh stood on end and my heart melted as I left my own being and I was as though I was not. Were it not for remembering the poem, I would have been like all my townsfolk, who were lost, who had died at the hand of a despicable people, those who trampled my people until they were no longer a nation. But it was because of the power of the poem that my soul went out of me. And if my town has been wiped out of the world, it remains alive in the poem that the poet wrote as a sign for my city. And if I don't remember the words of the poem, for my soul left me because of its greatness, the poem sings itself in the heavens above, among the poems of the holy poets, the beloved of God.

42

Now to whom shall I turn who can tell me the words of the song? To the old cantor who knew all the hymns of the holy poets?—I am all that is left of all their tears. The old cantor rests in the shadow of the holy poets, who recite their hymns in the Great Synagogue of our city. And if he answers me, his voice will be as pleasant as it was when our city was yet alive, and all of its people were also still in life. But here—here there is only a song of mourning, lamentation, and wailing, for the city and its dead.

1962

XX

Return

Less than sixty years after Abramovitsh called on Russian Jews to meet their catastrophes with stoicism and self-help, the children of these Jews were on the verge of establishing a Jewish state in Palestine. But it was their grandchildren who would have to die fighting for it. All hopes now focused on these young men and women, many of whom were already Sabras (natives to the land), supposedly the first "free" generation of Jews. Although they were required to read Abramovitsh's work as part of their high school curriculum, his world of beggars and peddlers might just as well have been on the moon. Instead, a new literature was created that linked the Zionist endeavor directly with the biblical past and fashioned a new myth out of their day-to-day lives. Natan Alterman now emerged as the national bard. "The Silver Platter" **(98),** his ballad to the young pioneers who died for the state, was soon to become part of Israeli civil religion.

Even without the knowledge of hindsight—that there would still be many wars to fight; that the specter of a new Destruction would suddenly resurface one Yom Kippur day; that the Jewish state would regalvanize anti-Jewish hatred—one can see very clearly how ancient and modern traditions of Jewish response were absorbed by those who claimed to be striking out on their own.

Abba Kovner's life and work can be said to embody one line of continuity. As a leader of the left-wing Zionist youth movement Hashomer Hatsair in Vilna, Kovner represented the best that secular Jewish culture had produced: someone equally at home in Hebrew, Yiddish and Polish who trained himself and others for the rigors of agricultural life in Palestine even as he defended the civil rights of Polish Jews. One of his trainees, a fledgling poet like himself, was Hirsh Glik. It was Kovner who wrote the first call for Jewish armed resistance against the Nazis, and it was he who took over command of the United Partisans' Organization in the ghetto after Itsik Vittenberg was forced to give himself up to the Gestapo.

In 1946 Kovner arrived in Palestine, where he joined kibbutz Ein Hahoresh and married Vitke Kempner, his fellow partisan from Vilna (the heroine of Glik's ballad "Silence, and a Starry Night"). Under normal conditions, this would have been the happy ending of the story, but the transition from Holocaust to Rebirth could be smooth only on paper. The routine of daily life on the kibbutz did not heal his psychic wounds, and Kovner set out for Germany to wreak personal revenge on the Nazi killers. His hope was to make contact with other former partisans and together to track down the enemy-in-hiding. Caught by the British, he was interned in a prison near Cairo. His first major poem, a partisan saga in Hebrew, was written there.

Then, on November 29, 1947, the United Nations passed its resolution calling for the partition of Palestine and the establishment of a Jewish State. The Haganah, the main branch of the Zionist underground, began to mobilize against the Arab offensive, especially in the sparsely settled Negev. The commander of the Southern Brigade, dubbed the Givati, was Shimon (Koch) Avidan, who had tried to help Kovner a year before in his attempt to reach Germany. By now Kovner was back on the kibbutz, and in December 1947 Avidan arrived in person to appoint Kovner cultural officer of the newly established brigade.

Thus, a new genre in the Literature of Destruction came into being— the "Battle Bulletin" (*daf keravi*) designed to instill courage in a motley of young fighters, some of whom had barely gotten off the boat from Europe **(99)**. In form and diction, the battle bulletins were reminiscent of Red Army circulars in the Great Patriotic War; in content, they were a unique distillation of poetry and propaganda. One bulletin, for November 11, 1948, was made up solely of Ps. 18:34–43 and appeared in both Hebrew and Yiddish. In others, Kovner used sacred language to link the battle for the Negev with medieval martyrdom and biblical glory. Indeed, there was something biblical in their tone of absolute defiance, though nowhere was God given credit for the victory. There was also something biblical about the density of place names. What was new, radically so, was the renaming of these places in the memory of the fallen soldiers. And instead of saying that their souls were "gathered in the garland of life eternal," as in the *Yizkor* prayer for the dead, Kovner boldly declared: "May their Souls be Gathered in the Paths of Victory." In this way the present was made to eclipse the past. It was the culmination of the modern revolt that had become its own tradition.

Agnon's "Before the Kaddish" **(100)** represents the opposite strand: the attempt to create a seamless procession from past to present by establishing a sacred context for the Zionist struggle. The argument is simple: as opposed to secular wars, where men are but cannon fodder, in the wars of Israel each life is to be hallowed and each is a harbinger of redemption. The midrashic frame, the perfectly stylized language and the benign image of God all serve to obscure what is unprecedented: that a *Kaddish* is being recited for Jewish soldiers on a special day set aside for that purpose (though, remarkably, Agnon wrote the text before the War of Independence was fought).

Both Agnon's *Kaddish* and Alterman's ballad are recited each year as part of the memorial services for the fallen soldiers that are held throughout Israel on *Yom Hazikkaron*. In the program brochures distributed by the Ministry of Defense, the *Kaddish* is printed in the script used only for Torah scrolls and mezuzahs. At day's end the sirens sound to usher in the Independence Day celebrations. This sudden transition from national mourning to rejoicing can work because it obeys the pattern long ago established by the rabbis: that the wild revelry of Purim follows the Fast of Esther, that the dancing of Simhat Torah follows the somber day of Shemini 'Atseret and that the songs of Zion follow the chanting of Lamentations.

98   The Silver Platter

NATAN ALTERMAN

A State is not handed to a people on a silver platter.
[Chaim Weizmann, first president of Israel]

. . . and the land was silent. The incarnate sun
Flickered languidly
Above the smoldering borders.
And a nation stood—cloven hearted but breathing . . .
To receive the miracle.
The one miracle and only . . .

The nation made ready for the pomp. It rose to the crescent moon
And stood there, at pre-dawn, garbed in festival-and-fear.
——Then out they came
A boy and a girl
Pacing slowly toward the nation.

In workaday garb and bandoleer, and heavy-shod,
Up the path they came
Silently forward.
They did not change their dress, and had not yet washed away
The marks of the arduous day and the night of the fire-line.

Tired, oh so tired, forsworn of rest,
And oozing sap of young Hebrewness——
Silently the two approached
And stood there unmoving.
There was no saying whether they were alive or shot.

In the pidyon haben ceremony (redemption of the first-born son), the parents hand the infant on a silver platter over to the Kohen. Here, the symbolism is reversed.

Then the nation, tear-rinsed and spellbound, asked,
Saying: Who are you? And the two soughed
Their reply: We are the silver platter
On which the Jewish State has been given you.°

They spoke. Then enveloped in shadow at the people's feet they fell.
The rest will be told in the annals of Israel.

[First published in *Davar,* December 26, 1947]

99   Battle Bulletin

ABBA KOVNER

The battle described here, also known as "Operation Yoav" and "The Ten Plagues," was designed to lift the Egyptian siege of the Negev. "113" was the first strategic position captured by the Israel Defense Forces (the Givati

Brigade), followed by the crossroads, an important junction in the Negev; Kaukava, an Arab village used as an Egyptian staging ground; and Beit Timna.

GIVA. THE BATTLE STAFF   DEATH TO THE INVADERS!

BATTLE BULLETIN FOR THE DAY 10/21/48

The Battle of the Covenant

The Julis road is steeped in blood. Passing through it now is a full moon and we are keeping watch over the hills from both sides of the road. Many are the paths leading to the Negev—but this is the principal ROUTE.

Already behind us are "113," the crossroads, Kaukava, Beit Timna, and ahead of us: KHULEIQAT. Yonder—Gevar-Am.°

Gevar-Am was a kibbutz established in 1942 near Ashkelon. On May 21 the elderly, the sick and the young were evacuated. The siege was lifted at the end of the campaign.

The Breakthrough battalions which overran this road in the dawn of 10.20—could not see Khuleiqat, but only Gevar-Am, the Negev land and the shadow of invaders blocking the way to it.

Remember those who gave their lives for the crossroads.

Remember that there never is a GATE unless there is a WAY. Thus the fate of the Negev rests upon that of the Route.

Then they saw Khuleiqat. They saw a cluster of strongholds on both sides of the road, a cluster of strongholds at the center, and a cluster of strongholds on the west facing Gevar-Am. And these were all thoroughly dug-in all around: fortresses. A plane discharged bombs. The cannons shelled.

And then the battle began.

The cannons played their part. The mortars played theirs. And the enemy still stayed in its trenches, in its bunkers and did not flee. (Apparently the fear of the strange night in a foreign land is as great as the fear of death!) And that is when the decisive battle began; the penetration forces attacked. They broke through one fence. And a second fence. A third. They overran the first trenchline, slew among the enemy—but the enemy was as the sand upon the seashore. And its weapons in the posts (the rifles were left in the arsenal) were an infinite number of machine guns, heavy ones. Fiats, two and six pounders, Brownings and anti-tank rifles. Mortars of all sorts.

And the enemy launched a counter attack. The penetrators were wounded—utterly exhausted: it was the fifth hour of the assault.

(Yonder the heart of Gevar-Am was full of dread.) And then SPIRIT set out to battle.

The reserves were thrown into battle. A second wave burst forth. The enemy line shattered, further and further, one trench after another.

And suddenly:

The spasm of despair of invaders who sense their doom—face to face combat! Saudis trying to strangle our fellows. Teeth attempting to bite into their throats.

Nitzanim was a kibbutz about 10 kilometers from Ashkelon, conquered by the Egyptian Ninth Brigade on June 7, 1948, and held by it for 140 days. All the defenders were killed.

Negba was a kibbutz established in 1939; it sustained a three-month siege.

Yad Mordekhai kibbutz was established 1943 in memory of Anielewicz, leader of the Warsaw ghetto uprising.

Kefar-Darom was a kibbutz established in 1946.

Type of machine gun captured on that occasion.

Our fellows saw: before them stood the battalion which conquered NITZANIM,° which destroyed NEGBA,° which took "69," the battalion that entered El-Arish on May 1 with the purpose of marching through our entire country.

And then HATRED set out to battle: "BAYONETS-FORWARD! DEATH TO THE INVADERS!" And under the full moon brothers shook hands with one another: the GIVATI men on the one hand and the men of GEVAR-AM on the other, and in between them lay the invaders' grave.

THE BATTLE OF THE COVENANT HAS ENDED! The way is free. WE HAVE TORN YOUR GATES, OH NEGEV, OFF THE HINGES OF THE INVADERS' FORTIFICATIONS!

The Children of Nitzanim, Yad-Mordekhai° and Kefar-Darom°—prepare flowers for the Dedication of the House, for we have reaped to the hilt—and our day is soon to come.

In the fierce battle on the gates of Negev (from "113" to Khuleiqat) the enemy suffered no less than 500 CASUALTIES and dozens of prisoners.

Our booty: thirty-one half-tracks, four 6 pounder cannons and three 2 pounders. 20 Vickers,° close to 100 machine guns, hundreds of rifles, Fiats, mortars and a 37 millimeter cannon, ammunition stores and winter equipment stores and yet more.

Among the prisoners—a number of officers (the high command fled at the beginning of the battle).

MEMORIALS OF BATTLE HERITAGE

Hill "138" (Khuleiqat) will henceforth be named

SHIMON HILL

after Shimon GORALSKI: (Platoon Comm.)

Hill "120" (North of Gevar-Am) will henceforth be named

THE ḤAYYIM STRONGHOLD

after Ḥayyim BULMAN (Platoon Comm.)

The hill south of the Iraq El-Manshiye—Beit-Jubrin Road (at the eastern wedge)—will be henceforth named

YA'AKOV HILL

after Ya'aqov ZIMMERMANN (Company Sergeant).

May their Souls be Gathered in the Paths of Victory.

And may the Signaller Stetiner be distinguished by long life and as an example and model. He is one of the heroes of the war of Israel.

The road that was blasted through the Egyptian line connecting Iraq-El-Manshiye and Beit-Jubrin and which was paved during the battle will be reinvigorated through the name

THE LAKHISH ROUTE.

Among the fruits of the Khuleiqat Battle:

The books that were plundered from the NITZANIM Kibbutz returned to us.— Returned over the hands and the heads of the robbers.

100 Before the *Kaddish*

S. Y. A G N O N

When a king of flesh and blood goes forth to war against his enemies, he leads out his soldiers to slay and to be slain. It is hard to say, does he love his soldiers, doesn't he love his soldiers, do they matter to him, don't they matter to him? But even if they do matter to him, they are as good as dead, for the Angel of Death is close upon the heels of everyone who goes off to war, and accompanies him only to slay him. When the soldier is hit, by arrow or sword or saber or any of the other kinds of destructive weapons, and slain, they put another man in his place, and the king hardly knows that someone is missing—for the population of the nations of the world is big and their troops are many. If one man is slain, the king has many others to make up for him.

But our king, the King of kings of kings, the Holy One, blessed be He, is a king who delights in life, who loves peace and pursues peace, and loves His people Israel, and He chose us from among all the nations: not because we are a numerous folk did He set His love upon us, for we are the fewest of all people. But because of the love He loves us with and we are so few, each and every one of us matters as much before Him as a whole legion, for He hasn't many to put in our place. When from Israel one is missing, God forbid, a minishing takes place in the King's legions, and in His kingdom, blessed be He, there is a decline of strength, as it were, for His kingdom now lacks one of its legions and His grandeur, blessed be He, has been diminished, God forbid.

That is why for each dead person in Israel we recite the prayer "Magnified and sanctified be His great Name." Magnified be the power of the Name so that before Him, blessed be He, there be no decline of strength; and sanctified be He in all the worlds which He created according to His will, and not for ourselves let us have fear but for the superlative splendor of His exalted holiness. May He establish His sovereignty so that His kingdom be perfectly revealed and visible, and may it suffer no diminishing, God forbid. In our lifetime and in your days and in the lifetime of the whole house of Israel speedily and soon—for if His sovereignty is manifest in the world, there is peace in the world and blessing in the world and song in the world and a multitude of praises in the world and great consolation in the world, and the holy ones, Israel, are beloved in the world and His grandeur continues to grow and increase and never diminishes.

If this is what we recite in prayer over any who die, how much the more over our beloved and sweet brothers and sisters, the dear children of Zion, those killed in the Land of Israel, whose blood was shed for the glory of His blessed Name and for His people and His land and His heritage. And what is more, everyone who dwells in the Land of Israel belongs to the legion of the King of kings of kings, the Holy One, blessed be He, whom the King appointed watchman of His palace. When one of His legion is slain, He has no others as it were to put in his place.

Therefore, brethren of the whole house of Israel, all you who mourn in this mourning, let us fix our hearts on our Father in heaven, Israel's king and redeemer, and let us pray for ourselves and for Him too, as it were: Magnified and sanctified be his Great Name in the world which He created as He willed. May He establish His kingdom, may He make His deliverance to sprout forth, may He bring nigh His messiah, and so to the end of the whole prayer. May we be found worthy still to be in life when with our own eyes we may behold Him who makes peace in His high places, in His compassion making peace for us and for all Israel, Amen.

1947

קדיש על הרוגי ארץ-ישראל

מלך בשר ודם שייצא למלחמה על אויביו מוציא חיילותיו להרוג וליהרג.
ספק אוהב את חיילותיו ספק אינו אוהב את חיילותיו, ספק הם חשובים בעיניו
ספק אינם חשובים בעיניו. ואפילו חשובים בעיניו חשובים בעיניו, כמתים,
שכל היוצא למלחמה מלאך המות כרוך בעקבותיו ומתלווה לו להרגו.
פגע בו חץ או סייף או חרב או שאר כמיני מחלוחית ונהרג מיעקמידין אחר
במקומו, ואין המלך מרגיש בחסרונו, שאומות העולם מרובים וגייסות שלהם
מרובים. נהרג אחד מהם יש לו למלך הרבה כנגדו.

אבל מלכנו מלך מלכי המלכים הקדוש ברוך הוא מלך חפץ בחיים, אוהב
שלום ורודף שלום ואוהב את ישראל עמו ובחר בנו מכל העמים, לא מפני
שאנו מרובים זעשן ה' בנו, כי אנו המעט מכל העמים. ומתוך אהבתו שאוהב אותנו
ואנו מעטים, כל אחד ואחד מעלינו חשוב לפניו כבליון שלם, לפי שאין לו הרבה
להעמיד במקומנו. נפקד חס ושלום אחד מישראל באה פחת בלגיונותיו
של המלך ובאה תשיות כח כביכול במלכותו יתברך, שהרי מלכותו חסרה לגיון
אחד מלגיונותיו ונתמעטה חס ושלום גדולתו יתברך.

לפיכך אזרנו מתפללין ואומרים אחר כל מת מישראל יתגדל
ויתקדש שמיה רבא, יגדל כח השם ולא יביא תשיות כח לפניו יתברך,
ויתקדש בעולכות שברא כרצונו, ולא נפחד על עצמנו, אלא מהדר גאון
קדושתו יתעלה. וימליך מלכותיה שהתגלה ותראה מלכותו בשלימות
ולא ימעט ממנה חס ושלום. בחייכון וביומיכון ובחיי דכל בית ישראל
במהרה ובזמן קרוב, שאם מלכותו גלויה בעולם – שלום בעולם וברכה
בעולם ושירה בעולם ותשבחות הרבה בעולם ונחמה גדולה בעולם
וישראל קדושים אהובים בעולם וגדולתו בעולם גדלה והולכת ומתרבה
ואינה מתמעטת לעולם.

אם כך אנו מתפללים ואומרים אחר כל אדם שמת, קל וחומר
על אחינו ואחיותינו הנאהבים והנעימים בני ציון היקרים הרוגי
ארץ ישראל שנשפך דמם על כבוד שמו יתברך ועל עמו ועל
ארצו ועל נחלתו. ולא זו בלבד אלא כל הדר בארץ-ישראל הוא
מלגיונו של מלך מלכי המלכים הקדוש ברוך הוא שהפקידו
המלך שומר בפלטרין שלו. נהרג אחד מהלגיון שלו אין לו
כביכול אחרים להעמיד במקומו.

לפיכך אחינו כל בית ישראל, כל המתאבלים באבל הזה, נכוון
את לבנו לאבינו שבשמים מלך ישראל וגואלו ונתפלל עלינו ועליו
כביכול. יתגדל ויתקדש ויתקדש שמיה רבא בעלמא די ברא כרעותא
וימליך מלכותיה. ויצמח פורקניה ויקרב משיחיה. וכן כל הפרשה
כולה.. ונזכה ונחיה ונראה עין בעין, עושה שלום במרומיו הוא
ברחמיו יעשה שלום עלינו ועל כל ישראל אמן.

3. From *Yom Hazikkaron Haklali Leḥalalei Ẓahal* (Ministry of Defense of the Government of Israel, 1973)

Sources

1.–3.   *Tanakh: A New Translation of the Holy Scriptures According to the Traditional Hebrew Text* (Philadelphia: Jewish Publication Society, 1985).

4.   Lamentations: Ibid. Emended readings of 1:21b, 2:13a, 3:1, 3:41 and 3:50–51.

5. and 6.   Ibid.

7.   The Battle of Gog and Magog: Ibid. Emended reading of vv. 7, 14.

8.   God's Former and Future Deeds: Ibid. Emended reading of vv. 10, 19, 28.

9. and 10.   *II Maccabees* (The Anchor Bible), trans. from the Greek by Jonathan A. Goldstein (Garden City, NY: Doubleday & Company, 1983), pp. 268–69, 281–82, 289–91. Annotations based on Goldstein. Reprinted with the permission of the publisher.

11.   Hannaniah, Mishael and Azariah: *Tanakh*.

12.   Rabbinic Martyrs: *The Tractate "Mourning" (Semahot)*, ed. Dov Zlotnick, vocalized by Edward Y. Kutscher (New Haven, CT: Yale University Press), 1966, pp. 59–65. Annotations based on Zlotnick. Reprinted with the permission of Yale University Press.

13.   Rabbi Akiba: *Berakhot* 61b, trans. Maurice Simon. *The Babylonian Talmud* (London: Soncino Press, 1958), pp. 385–86. Reprinted with the permission of Soncino Press, London and New York.

14.–19.   *Midrash Rabbah Lamentations*, trans. A. Cohen (London: Soncino Press, 1939), pp. 40–49, 70–73, 76–78, 124–28. Annotations based on Cohen. Reprinted with permission of Soncino Press, London and New York.

20. and 21.   Alan Mintz, *Ḥurban: Responses to Catastrophe in Hebrew Literature* (New York: Columbia University Press, 1984), pp. 75–76, 82. Trans. from the Solomon Buber recension of the Midrash (Vilna, 1899). Reprinted with the permission of Alan Mintz.

22.   The Ten *Harugei Malkhut: "Midrash Eileh Ezkerah,"* trans. David Stern as "Midrash Eleh Ezkerah" in *Fiction* 7 nos. 1–2 (1983): 69–98. To appear in forthcoming *Rabbinic Fantasies: Imaginative Narratives from Classical and Medieval Hebrew Literature*, eds. Mark Mirsky and David Stern (Philadelphia: Jewish Publication Society). Annotations based on Stern; reprinted with the permission of *Fiction*. For the Hebrew original, see Adolph Jellinek's *Bet ha-Midrash: Sammlung*, 3rd ed., vol. 2 (Jerusalem: Wharman, 1967), pp. 64–72.

23.   The Crusade Chronicle of Solomon bar Simson: Trans. from the Hebrew by Robert Chazan in *European Jewry and the First Crusade* (Berkeley, Los Angeles and London: The University of California Press, 1987), pp. 243–57. Annotations based on Chazan. For the Hebrew original, see A. M. Haberman, *Sefer gzeirot Ashkenaz ve-Tzarfat* (Jerusalem: Ophir, 1971) pp. 24–60. Reprinted with the permission of The Regents of the University of California.

24.   Pour Out Thy Wrath: *The Passover Haggadah: Its Sources and History*, ed. E. D. Goldschmidt (Jerusalem: Bialik Institute, 1969), pp. 63–64.

25.   Commemoration of Martyrs: Chazan, *European Jewry*, p. 145. For the Hebrew original, see *Daily Prayer Book*, ed. Philip Birnbaum (New York: Hebrew Publishing Co., 1949), p. 383. Reprinted with the permission of The Regents of the University of California.

26.   There Is None Like You Among the Dumb: Jakob J. Petuchowski, *Theology and Poetry: Studies in the Medieval Piyyut* (London: Routledge and Kegan Paul Publishers, 1978), pp. 71–83. Includes the Hebrew original written in an alphabetical

acrostic. Annotations based on Petuchowski. Reprinted with the permission of Routledge and Kegan Paul Publishers, London, England.

27. O Law Consumed by Fire: *The Authorized Kinot for the Ninth of Av,* trans. Abraham Rosenfeld (New York: The Judaica Press, 1979), pp. 161–62; revised by Raymond P. Scheindlin. Annotations based on Rosenfeld. Reprinted with the permission of The Judaica Press, New York.

28. The Martyr's Prayer: Nahum M. Glatzer, *Language of Faith: A Selection of the Most Expressive Jewish Prayers* (New York: Schocken Books, 1967), p. 208. First appeared in Horowitz's *Shnei luḥot haberit.* Reprinted with the permission of Schocken Books, Inc., New York.

29. The Epistle of Martyrdom: Trans. from the Hebrew by Abraham Halkin in *Crisis and Leadership: Epistles of Maimonides* (Philadelphia, New York and Jerusalem: The Jewish Publication Society, 1985), pp. 24–34. Annotations based on Halkin.

30.–33. Trans. from the Hebrew by David S. Segal. From Solomon ibn Verga, *Shevet Yehudah,* ed. A. Shohat (Jerusalem, 1947).

34. Know Judah and Israel: Trans. from the Hebrew by David S. Segal in *'Al naharot Sefarad* [By the Rivers of Spain], ed. Simon Bernfeld (Tel Aviv: Maḥbarot Lesifrut, 1956), pp. 206–9. Annotations based on Bernfeld. First appeared in the Sephardic Maḥzor (Venice, 1519).

35. and 36. Nathan Nata Hanover, *Abyss of Despair (Yeven Metzulah): The Famous Seventeenth-Century Chronicle Depicting Jewish Life in Russia and Poland during the Chmielnicki Massacres of 1648–1649,* trans. Abraham J. Mesch (New York: Bloch Publishing Co., 1950), pp. 27–28, 50–53. © 1950 by Transaction Books. Annotations based on Mesch. Reprinted with the permission of Transaction Books, Rutgers University (New Brunswick, NJ).

37. The Martyrs of Pavlysh: *In Praise of the Baal Shem Tov* [Shivhei ha-Besht], ed. and trans. Dan Ben-Amos and Jerome R. Mintz (Bloomington: Indiana University Press, 1970), pp. 161–63. Annotations based on Ben-Amos and Mintz. Reprinted with the permission of Dan Ben-Amos and Jerome R. Mintz.

38. Songs of the Cantonist Era: Trans. from the Yiddish by the editor and Hillel Schwartz. "The Streets Flow with Our Tears" and "O, Merciful Father" from *Evreiskie narodniye pesni v Rossii* [Yiddish Folksongs of Russia], ed. S. M. Ginsburg and P. S. Marek (St. Petersburg, 1901), nos. 49, 50; "For Twenty Miles I Ran and Ran" from Eleanor Gordon Mlotek, "In the Time of the Cantonists" [Yiddish], *Yidisher folklor* 1 (1954): 5.

39. Song of the Balta Pogrom: Trans. from the Yiddish by the editor and Hillel Schwartz. From Beatrice Silverman Weinreich, "Three Pogrom Songs from Russia" [Yiddish], *YIVO-bleter* 33 (1949): 241–43, and Zosa Szajkowski, *An Illustrated Sourcebook of Russian Antisemitism, 1881–1978,* vol. 2 (New York: Ktav, 1980), p. 22.

40. Shem and Japheth on the Train: Trans. Walter Lever in *Modern Hebrew Literature,* ed. Robert Alter (New York: Behrman House, 1975), pp. 10–38, with slight emendations to conform more closely to the original. Reprinted with the permission of the Zionist Organization, Youth and Hechalutz Department. For the Hebrew original, see *Kol kitvei Mendele Mokher Sfarim* (Tel Aviv: Dvir, 1947), pp. 399–405.

41. Burned Out: Trans. from the Hebrew by Jeffrey M. Green. From *Kol kitvei Mendele Mokher Sfarim,* pp. 444–47.

42. Pogrom Songs: Trans. from the Yiddish by the editor and Hillel Schwartz. "The Kishniev Pogrom" from *Mir trogn a gezang: The New Book of Yiddish Songs,* ed. Eleanor Gordon Mlotek, 2nd rev. ed. (New York: Education Department of the Workmen's Circle, 1977), p. 137; "Oh, Have You Heard in the Newspapers" from Ruth Rubin, *Jewish Life: "The Old Country,"* Folkways Record No. FS-3801, side 2, band 8. Reprinted with the permission of the Education Department of the Workmen's Circle.

43. Have Pity!: Trans. from the Yiddish by the editor. From S. Frug, *Oysgeklibene shriftn* (Buenos Aires, 1960) (*Musterverk fun der yidisher literatur,* vol. 10), pp. 47–48. Music courtesy of Professor Mark Slobin.

44. Proclamation of the Jewish Labor Bund: Trans. from the Yiddish by the editor. From *Di kishinever harige* (London: Jewish Labor Bund, 1903), pp. 8–11.

45. Proclamation of the Hebrew Writers' Union: Trans. from the Hebrew by Zvia Ginor. From *Hapogrom beKishinev biml'ot 60 shanah* [Sixty Years after the Kishinev Pogrom], ed. Haim Schorer et al. (Tel Aviv: World Federation of Bessarabian Jews, 1963), pp. 113–17.

46. Upon the Slaughter: Trans. A. M. Klein in *Selected Poems of Hayyim Nahman Bialik,* ed. Israel Efros, rev. ed. (New York: Bloch Publishing Co., 1965), pp. 112–13. For the Hebrew original, see " 'Al hashhitah" in Bialik's *Shirim* (Tel Aviv: Dvir, 1966), pp. 152–53. Annotations based on A. Avital, *Shirat Bialik vehatanakh* (Tel Aviv: Dvir, 1952). Reprinted with the permission of the Histadruth Ivrith of America and Sandor Klein.

47. In the City of Slaughter: Trans. A. M. Klein in *Selected Poems,* pp. 114–28; from "B'ir hahaheigah" in Bialik, *Shirim,* pp. 250–60. Reprinted with the permission of the Histadruth Ivrith of America and Sandor Klein.

48. A Shtetl: Trans. Ruth R. Wisse in *A Shtetl and Other Yiddish Novellas,* ed. Ruth R. Wisse, 2nd rev. ed. (Detroit: Wayne State University Press, 1986), pp. 53–78. © 1973 Ruth R. Wisse and reprinted with her permission and that of Wayne State University Press. For the Yiddish original, see *Geklibene verk* 1 (Chicago: Zelechow Society, 1959), pp. 287–355.

49. The Wedding that Came Without Its Band: Trans. Hillel Halkin in Sholem Aleichem, *Tevye the Dairyman and the Railroad Stories* (New York: © Schocken Books, 1987), pp. 194–99, published by Pantheon Books, a Division of Random House. Reprinted with the permission of Random House, Inc. For the Yiddish original, see "A khasene on klezmer" in *Ayznban-geshikhtes,* vol. 28 of *Ale verk fun Sholem-Aleykhem* (New York: Folksfond, 1917–1925): 127–37.

50. The Cross: Trans. from the Yiddish by Joachim Neugroschel. From Lamed Shapiro, *Di yidishe melukhe un andere zakhn,* 2nd ed. (New York: Farlag yidish lebn, 1929), pp. 139–61.

51. Song of the Mobilization: Trans. from the Yiddish by the editor and Hillel Schwartz. From Walter Anderson, "The Song of the Mobilization" [Yiddish] in *Filologishe shriftn fun YIVO 2* (Vilna, 1928): 405–8.

52. Appeal to Collect Materials about the World War: Trans. by the editor. Yiddish original reprinted in *YIVO-bleter* 36 (1952): 350–51.

53. The Destruction of Galicia: Trans. from the Yiddish by Elinor Robinson. From S. Ansky, *Khurbm Galitsye* [The Destruction of Galicia: The Jewish Catastrophe in Poland, Galicia and Bukovina, from a Diary, 1914–1917] (Vilna, Warsaw, New York, 1921), vol. 4, pp. 13–17, 38–42, 109–114, 150–58; vol. 6, pp. 58–63, 88–93, 126–37.

54. Tales of 1001 Nights: Trans. as "The Krushniker Delegation" by Sacvan Bercovitch in *The Best of Sholom Aleichem,* ed. Irving Howe and Ruth R. Wisse (Washington, D.C.: New Republic Books, 1979), pp. 232–44. © 1979 New Republic Books and reprinted with permission. For the Yiddish original, see *Mayses fun toyznt eyn nakht,* chaps. 7–9 in *Mayses un fantazyes,* vol. 3 of *Ale verk fun Sholem-Aleykhem* (New York, 1917–1928), pp. 137–232.

55. A Night: Trans. from the Yiddish by Hillel Schwartz and the editor from "A nakht," *In Nyu-york* (New York: Vinkl, 1919), pp. 237–304.

56. The Way Out: Trans. Yosef Schachter in *Modern Hebrew Literature,* ed. Robert Alter (New York: Behrman House, 1975), pp. 145–57. Reprinted with the permission of the Institute for the Translation of Hebrew Literature. Annotations based on Schachter. For the Hebrew original, see "Hamotsa' " in *Kol kitvei Yosef Hayyim Brenner,* vol. 1 (Tel Aviv: Dvir and Hakibbutz Hameuchad, 1964), pp. 450–54.

57. White Challah: Trans. Norbert Guterman in *A Treasury of Yiddish Stories,* ed. Irving Howe and Eliezer Greenberg (New York: Viking Press, 1954), pp. 325–33. Reprinted with the permission of Viking Penguin, Inc. For the Yiddish original, see "Vayse khale" in *Di yidishe melukhe un andere zakhn,* pp. 67–82.

58. Among Refugees: Trans. Joachim Neugroschel from "Tsvishn emigrantn," in *A shpigl oyf a shteyn* [A Mirror on a Stone: An Anthology of Poetry and Prose by Twelve Soviet Yiddish Writers], ed. Kh. Shmeruk (Tel Aviv: Di goldene keyt and I. L. Peretz, 1964), pp. 62–81.

59. And Then There Were None: Trans. from the Russian by Max Hayward in Isaac Babel, *You Must Know Everything: Stories 1915–1937*, ed. Nathalie Babel (New York: Farrar, Straus and Giroux, 1969), pp. 129–33. © 1969 Nathalie Babel. Reprinted by permission of Farrar, Straus and Giroux, Inc.

60. The Rabbi's Son: Trans. Walter Morison in Isaac Babel, *The Collected Stories*, ed. Walter Morison (Cleveland and New York: Meridian Books, 1960), pp. 191–93. © 1955 by S. G. Phillips, Inc., and reprinted with permission.

61. Smugglers: Trans. from the Yiddish by Leonard Wolf. From Oyzer Varshavski, *Shmuglares*, reprinted in *Unter okupatsye* (Buenos Aires, 1969) (*Musterverk fun der yidisher literatur*, vol. 39).

62. Revolutionary Chapters: Trans. from the Hebrew by Jeffrey M. Green. From "Pirkei mahapeikhah," *Hatekufah* 22 (1924): 69–97.

63. Months and Days: Trans. from the Yiddish by Leonard Wolf. From Itsik Kipnis, *Khadoshim un teg un andere dertseylungen*, vol. 3 of *Geklibene verk* (Tel Aviv: I. L. Peretz, 1973), chap. 8.

64. The Mound: Trans. Leonard Wolf in *The Penguin Book of Modern Yiddish Verse*, ed. Irving Howe, Ruth R. Wisse and Khone Shmeruk (New York: Penguin Books, 1987), pp. 314–26. Reprinted with the permission of Penguin Books. For the Yiddish original, see *A shpigl oyf a shteyn*, pp. 414–21.

65. Masada: Trans. from the Hebrew by Leon I. Yudkin in *Isaac Lamdan: A Study in Twentieth-Century Hebrew Poetry* (Ithaca, NY: Cornell University Press, 1971), pp. 199, 207, 214–15, 227–29. Reprinted with the permission of the publishers, Hebrew Publishing Company. All rights reserved. For the original, see *Masada: Poema* (Tel Aviv: Hedim, 1927).

66. My Brothers, the Sidelock Jews: Trans. from the Hebrew by Harold Schimmel. "Aḥai, yehudei hapei'ot," reprinted in Uri Zvi Greenberg, *Be'emtsa ha'olam uve'emtsa hazman*, ed. Benjamin Hrushovski (Tel Aviv: Hakibbutz Hameuchad, 1979), p. 56. Reprinted with the permission granted by the Institute for the Translation of Hebrew Literature.

67. Fire!: Trans. from the Yiddish by the editor. Music reproduced from *25 Ghetto Songs with Music and Transliteration*, ed. Malke Gottlieb and Chana Mlotek (New York: Education Department of the Workmen's Circle, 1968), p. 10, and reprinted with permission.

68. A Stubborn Back—And Nothing More: Trans. Robert Friend in *The Penguin Book of Modern Yiddish Verse*, ed. Irving Howe, Ruth R. Wisse and Khone Shmeruk (New York: Penguin Books, 1987), pp. 190–92. For the original, see *Ale verk fun H. Leyvik* 1 (New York, 1940), p. 519. Reprinted with the permission of Penguin Books.

69. Good Night, Wide World: Trans. Marie Syrkin in *A Treasury of Yiddish Poetry*, ed. Irving Howe and Eliezer Greenberg (New York: Holt, Rinehart and Winston, 1969), pp. 333–35. Line 28 corrected. Reprinted with the permission of Irving Howe, Marie Syrkin and Henry Holt and Company.

Wagons: Trans. Chana Faerstein, ibid., p. 330. Reprinted with the permission of Irving Howe and Henry Holt and Company.

Ghetto Song: Trans. by Melvin Elberger.

For the Yiddish originals, see Yankev Glatshteyn, *Gedenklider* (New York: Yidisher kemfer, 1943), pp. 41–42, 46, 72–73.

70. Alterman: Trans. from the Hebrew by Robert Friend. Song to the Wife of My Youth, A Song of Omens in *Anthology of Modern Hebrew Poetry*, ed. S. Y. Penueli and A. Ukhmani (Tel Aviv: Institute for the Translation of Hebrew Literature and Israel Universities Press, 1966), vol. 2, pp. 398–403. Reprinted with the permission of Robert Friend.

The Mole in Natan Alterman, *Selected Poems: Bilingual Edition* (Tel Aviv: Hakibbutz Hameuchad, 1978), pp. 31–35. © Robert Friend. Reprinted with the permission of Robert Friend.

For the originals, see *Shirim shemikhvar* (Tel Aviv: Hakibbutz Hameuchad, 1972), pp. 151–208.

71. *Oyneg Shabbes:* Trans. from the Yiddish by Elinor Robinson. From Emanuel Ringelblum, *Ksovim fun geto,* vol. 2: *Notitsn un ophandlungen (1942–1943),* 2nd rev. ed. (Tel Aviv: I. L. Peretz, 1985, pp. 76–102), abridged. Reprinted with the permission of the YIVO Institute for Jewish Research.

72. Ghetto Folklore: Trans. from the Yiddish by David E. Fishman in Shimon Huberband, *Kiddush Hashem: Jewish Religious and Cultural Life in Poland During the Holocaust,* ed. Jeffrey S. Gurock and Robert S. Hirt (Hoboken and New York: Ktav Publishing House and Yeshiva University Press, 1987), pp. 113–29, abridged. © 1987 Yeshiva University Press and reprinted with permission.

73. House No. 21: Trans. from the Yiddish by Robert Wolf. A copy of the original typescript was provided by Beit Lohamei Haghtettaot (The Ghetto Fighters' House). The only complete edition of Opoczynski's sketches is *Reshimot,* ed. Zvi Shner and trans. Avraham Yeivin (Tel Aviv: Ghetto Fighters' House and Hakibbutz Hameuchad, 1970). The Yiddish edition, published by Yidish-bukh in Warsaw, 1954, is incomplete and omits all mention of the Soviet Union.

74. Chronicle of a Single Day: Trans. from the Yiddish by Elinor Robinson. From *Tsvishn lebn un toyt,* ed. Ber Mark (Warsaw: Yidish-bukh, 1955), pp. 49–65.

75. Scroll of Agony: Trans. from the Hebrew by Jeffrey M. Green. From "Pages from the Diary" (in Hebrew), *Moreshet* 2 (December 1964): 8–22.

76. 4580: Trans. from the Yiddish by Elinor Robinson. From Mark, *Tsvishn lebn un toyt,* pp. 142–49.

77. The Ghetto in Flames: Trans. from the Yiddish by Robert Wolf. Originally published in *Di goldene keyt* 15 (1953): 10–15.

78. Yizkor, 1943: Trans. from the Yiddish by Leonard Wolf. Originally published in *Di goldene keyt* 46 (1963): 29–35.

79. Avrom Akselrod: Trans. from the Yiddish by Hillel Schwartz and the editor. From Yosef Gar, *Umkum fun der yidisher Kovne* (Munich, 1948), pp. 406–9.

80. Yankev Herszkowicz: Trans. from the Yiddish by the editor. From *Dos lid fun geto,* ed. Ruta Pups (Warsaw: Yidish-bukh, 1962), no. 15.

81. Yitzhak Katzenelson: Trans. from the Yiddish by Elinor Robinson. From *Yidishe geto-ksovim: Varshe 1940–1943,* ed. Yechiel Szeintuch (Tel Aviv: Ghetto Fighters' House and Hakibbutz Hameuchad, 1984), pp. 493, 620–21.

82. Joseph Kirman: Trans. from the Yiddish by Jacob Sonntag in *The Jewish Quarterly* 6 (Autumn 1960): 17–18. Reprinted with the permission of *The Jewish Quarterly,* London. For the Yiddish original, see Mark, *Tsvishn lebn un toyt,* pp. 35–39.

83. Leyb Rosental: Trans. from the Yiddish by Hillel Schwartz and the editor. Music reproduced from *25 Ghetto Songs with Music and Transliteration,* comp. Malke Gottlieb and Chana Mlotek (New York: Education Department of the Workmen's Circle, 1968), p. 12, and reprinted with permission.

84. Leah Rudnitsky: Trans. from the Yiddish by Hillel Schwartz and the editor. Music reproduced from Gottlieb and Mlotek, *25 Ghetto Songs,* p. 19.

85. Shmerke Kaczerginski: Still, Still: Trans. from the Yiddish by Hillel Schwartz and the editor. Music reproduced from Gottlieb and Mlotek, *25 Ghetto Songs,* pp. 22–23.

Youth Hymn, Itsik Vitnberg: Trans. from the Yiddish by Roslyn Bresnick-Perry in *We Are Here: Songs of the Holocaust,* comp. Eleanor Mlotek and Malke Gottlieb (New York: Education Department of the Workmen's Circle, 1968), pp. 87–88. Music reprinted from Gottlieb and Mlotek, *25 Ghetto Songs,* p. 48.

86. Hirsh Glik: Silence, and a Starry Night: Trans. from the Yiddish by Jacob Sloan in *A Treasury of Jewish Folksong,* ed. Ruth Rubin (New York: Schocken Books, 1950), p. 181. Used with the permission of Schocken Books, Inc.

Never Say: Lines 1–10 trans. Leo W. Schwarz in *The Root and the Bough: The Epic of an Enduring People* (New York and Toronto: Rinehart & Co., Inc., 1949), p. 68; lines 11–16 trans. Elliot Palevsky in *Mir trogn a gezang: The New Book of Yiddish Songs.* 2nd rev. ed. (New York: Education Department of the Workmen's Circle 1977), p. 191. Music reprinted from *Mir trogn a gezang,* p. 191.

87. Wladyslaw Szlengel: *Two Gentlemen in the Snow:* Trans. from the Polish by Adam Gillon in "Here Too as in Jerusalem: Selected Poems of the Ghetto," *The Polish Review* 10 (Summer 1965): 38. Reprinted with the permission of *The Polish Review.*

Counterattack: Trans. from the Polish by Michael Steinlauf in *And They Will Call Me . . . : Poems from the Holocaust in Yiddish and English Translation,* ed. Joshua Rothenberg. Waltham, MA: Department of Near Eastern and Judaic Studies, Brandeis, 1982), pp. 80–84. © 1982 Brandeis University. Reprinted with the permission of the Department of Near Eastern and Judaic Studies, Brandeis University.

88. Abraham Sutzkever: All but the following two poems translated from the Yiddish by C.K. Williams.

Kernels of Wheat: Trans. David H. Hirsch in *Modern Language Studies* 16:1 (1980): 46–48.

Under the Whiteness of Your Stars: Trans. Leonard Wolf.

For the Yiddish originals, see Abraham Sutzkever, *Poetishe verk* 1 (Tel Aviv, 1963): 245–367. All translations used with the permission of Abraham Sutzkever.

89. Rabbi Kalonymus Shapiro: Trans. from the Hebrew by Nechemia Polen in "*Esh Kodesh:* The Teachings of Rabbi Kalonymus Shapiro in the Warsaw Ghetto, 1939–1943." (Ph.D. dissertation, Boston University, 1983). Reprinted with the permission of Nechemia Polen.

90. Zelig Kalmanovitsh: Trans. from the Hebrew and Yiddish by Shlomo Noble in "A Diary of the Nazi Ghetto in Vilna," *YIVO Annual of Jewish Social Sciences* 8 (1953): 30–31; 42–44, 50–52. Reprinted with the permission of the YIVO Institute for Jewish Research. For the original, see Zelik Kalmanovitsh, *Yoman begeto Vilnah ukhtavim min ha'izavon shenimtse'u baharisot,* ed. Shalom Luria (Israel: Moreshet and Sifriat Hapoalim, 1977). Annotations based on Noble and Luria.

91. *Lekh-lekho:* Trans. from the Yiddish by Elinor Robinson. From S. Shayevitsh, *Lekh-lekho,* ed. Nachman Blumental (Lodz, Poland: Central Jewish Historical Commission, 1946), pp. 31–45.

92. *The Song of the Murdered Jewish People:* Chaps. 1–4, 6, 15, trans. from the Yiddish by Noah H. Rosenbloom, rev. Y. Tobin in Yitzhak Katzenelson, *The Song of the Murdered Jewish People,* ed. Noah H. Rosenbloom, bilingual facsimile ed. (Tel Aviv: Ghetto Fighters' House and Hakibbutz Hameuchad, 1980). © 1980 Ghetto Fighters' House Ltd. and used by permission. Chaps. 9, 11, trans. Jacob Sonntag in *The Jewish Quarterly* 2 (Spring 1955): 35–36 and 7 (Autumn 1960): 14–16. Used with the permission of *The Jewish Quarterly,* London.

93. *The Czech Transport: A Chronicle of the Auschwitz Sonderkommando:* Trans. from the Yiddish by Robert Wolf. From Zalmen Gradowski, *In harts fun genem: a dokument fun oyshvitser zonder-komando, 1944* (Jerusalem: Chaim Wolnerman, ca. 1977), pp. 35–37, 54–64, 68–81, 92, 94–106.

94. *God of Mercy:* Trans. from the Yiddish by Irving Howe in *A Treasury of Yiddish Poetry,* ed. Irving Howe and Eliezer Greenberg (New York: Holt, Rinehart and Winston, 1969), p. 289. Used with the permission of Irving Howe and Henry Holt and Company. For the original, see "El khanun," in Kadia Molodowsky, *Der meylekh Dovid aleyn iz geblibn* (New York: Papirene brik, 1946), pp. 3–4.

95. *To God in Europe:* Trans. from the Hebrew by Robert Friend in *Anthology of Modern Hebrew Poetry,* ed. S. Y. Penueli and A. Ukhmani (Jerusalem: Institute for the Translation of Hebrew Literature and Israel Universities Press, 1966), vol. 2, pp. 264–78. Reprinted with the permission of Robert Friend and the Institute for the Translation of Hebrew Literature. For the original, see Uri Zvi Greenberg, *Reḥovot hanahar: sefer ha'iliyot vehakoaḥ* (Jerusalem: Schocken Books, 1951), pp. 237–52.

96. The Last Demon: Trans. from the Yiddish by Martha Glicklich and Cecil Hemley in *The Collected Stories of Isaac Bashevis Singer* (New York: Farrar Straus and Giroux, 1983), and reprinted with permission. For the original, see "Mayse Tishevits," in *Der shpigl un andere dertseylungen,* ed. Khone Shmeruk (Jerusalem and Tel Aviv: Hebrew University of Jerusalem Yiddish Department and Committee for Jewish Culture in Israel, 1975), pp. 12–22.

97. The Sign: Trans. from the Hebrew by Arthur Green in *Response* 19 (1973): 5–31. © 1973 Schocken Books and reprinted with permission. For the original, see "Hasiman," in vol. 8 of *Kol sippurav shel Shmuel Yosef Agnon* (Tel Aviv: Schocken Books, 1966), pp. 283–312.

98. The Silver Platter: Trans. by Dom Moraes and T. Carmi in *The Jewish World* (December 1964): 47. For the Hebrew original, see *Hattur hashvi'i,* in vol. 3 of *Ktavim be'arba'ah kerakhim* (Tel Aviv: Davar and Hakibbutz Hameuchad, 1962), pp. 154–55. Reprinted with the permission of ACUM Ltd., Tel Aviv.

99. Battle Bulletin: Trans. from the Hebrew by Joram Navon from *Daf keravi: Ḥativat Giv'ati* (Israel: The Organizing Committee of the Givati Veterans' Convention, 1962). My thanks to Dr. Shalom Luria for making this source available to me. Annotations done by Joram Navon.

100. Before the *Kaddish:* Trans. from the Hebrew by Judah Goldin in *The Jewish Expression* (New York: Bantam Books, 1970), pp. 484–85. For the original, see "Petiḥah lekaddish," in vol. 6 of *Kol sippurav shel S. Y. Agnon* (Tel Aviv: Schocken Books, 1966), pp. 288–89, and reprinted with permission.

101. Map of Jewish Eastern Europe, from *The Shtetl Book: An Introduction to East European Jewish Life and Lore* by Diane K. Roskies and David G. Roskies, published by Ktav Publishing House, Inc., and reprinted with permission.

102. Map of the Warsaw Ghetto. Reprinted with the permission of the YIVO Institute for Jewish Research, Inc.

Biographies

SHOLEM YANKEV ABRAMOVITSH, better known through the persona of Mendele Moykher Sforim (Mendele the Bookpeddler), played a major role in the emergence of both modern Hebrew and Yiddish literatures. In plays, stories and such novels as the satirical allegory, *Di klyatshe* (The Nag, 1873), and its Hebrew counterpart, *Susati,* he portrayed the shtetl Jew as victimized not only by persecution and stagnant tradition but also by his own misguided striving for redemption. Abramovitsh was born in Belorussia in 1836 and died in Odessa in 1917.

S. Y. AGNON (né Shmuel Yosef Czaczkes) was born in 1888 in Buczacz, Galicia, the scene of his 1939 novel, *Oreaḥ natah lalun* (A Guest for the Night). In 1924, after an aborted *'aliyah* and a decade in Germany, he settled in Jerusalem, where he remained until his death in 1970. Agnon's highly polished novels and stories attempt to synthesize modern fictional conventions and traditional Jewish forms and attitudes; no writer has more subtly evoked the transition from the death of Jewish Europe to the birth of Israel. He received the 1966 Nobel prize for literature.

AVROM AKSELROD, a refugee from Warsaw, lived in the Kovno ghetto, where he wrote mostly parodic songs. He perished in a bunker during the final liquidation of the ghetto.

SHOLEM ALEICHEM, born Sholem Rabinovitsh in 1859 in the Ukraine, was the popular genius of Yiddish literature. Underlying his comic vision are a sense of the precariousness of life and sanity and a perception of the tragic pattern of Jewish history in such masterpieces as *Tevye der milkhiker* (Tevye the Dairyman), 1895–1916, and *Mayses fun toyznt eyn nakht* (Tales of 1001 Nights), 1915. Although he gave a voice to shtetl provincialism, Sholem Aleichem led a life that was cosmopolitan, even uprooted; he traveled throughout Europe and twice to New York, where he died in 1916.

NATAN ALTERMAN, Hebrew poet, playwright and satirist, was born in Warsaw in 1910 and settled in Tel Aviv in 1925. Influenced in his early work by the Symbolist and Imagist movements, Alterman "returned" to traditional Jewish motifs with *Simḥat 'aniyim* (Joy of the Poor), 1940; these and later poems responded to the tragic nature of Jewish history by affirming the bond between the living and the dead—an affirmation necessary for the renewal of life. A national figure, Alterman died in Israel in 1970.

S. ANSKY was the pen name of Solomon Zaynvl Rapaport, Yiddish and Russian writer and ethnographer, who was born in White Russia in 1863 and died in Warsaw in 1920. He produced most of his Yiddish writings after 1905, following a lengthy career in populist *(narodnik)* and revolutionary circles. The fame of Ansky's folk tragedy, *The Dybbuk,* has eclipsed his achievements in such other fields as poetry, fiction and autobiography. The founder of a Jewish ethnographic society, he had an intimate knowledge of the folkways of eastern European Jewry that made his chronicle of its destruction especially poignant.

RACHEL AUERBACH, Yiddish essayist and historian, was born in Lemberg, Galicia, in 1903. In 1933 she moved to Warsaw, where she was active in Zionist and modernist literary circles. During the war she ran the soup kitchen at Leszno 40, worked closely with Ringelblum and wrote prolifically while in hiding on the Aryan Side of Warsaw. In 1950 she settled in Israel, where she died in 1976. The Holocaust dominated her postwar writings and activities, the highlights of which were her memoirs of Jewish cultural life in the ghetto and her role in establishing Yad Vashem.

ISAAC BABEL, Russian short story writer, was born in 1894 in Odessa, a city whose earthy Jewish milieu he would depict in *Odessa Tales* (1927). Out of his experience in the 1920 Polish campaign came the stories of *Red Cavalry* (1926), whose narrator, a Jewish intellectual among Cossacks, accepts the vital, sometimes cruel order of the Revolution but cannot deny his "obsolete" past. This theme reflected Babel's personal dilemma: unable to sacrifice his self-identity to the Stalinist literary/political climate, he was arrested in 1939 and presumably died in a labor camp.

DAVID BERGELSON, a leading Soviet Yiddish writer, was born in the Ukraine in 1884. He won recognition through such early novels as *Arum vogzal* (At the Depot), 1909, and *Nokh alemen* (When All Is Said and Done), 1913, impressionistic studies of middle-class Jews paralyzed by historical change and their own sense of futility. A highly individual artist, Bergelson struggled to produce within the increasingly stifling confines of Stalinist aesthetics. He was imprisoned in 1949 and was shot, along with other prominent Yiddish writers, on August 12, 1952.

HAYYIM NAHMAN BIALIK, born in Volhynia in 1873, was the leading poet of the modern Hebrew revival. As a youth, he absorbed the traditional pietism of the yeshiva and, in Odessa in the early 1890s, the cultural nationalism of his mentor Ahad Ha' Am. The tension between the poles, between the no-longer vital claims of the past and the inchoate promise of the future, contributed to his poetry's masterful, often anguished fusion of biblical and modern idioms. Bialik settled in Palestine in 1924, ten years before his death.

YOSEF HAYYIM BRENNER, a pioneer of psychological realism in Hebrew fiction, was born in the Ukraine in 1881. In 1909 he settled in Palestine, where he worked as a teacher and participated in literary circles. In his stories, and in such novels as *Shekhol vekishalon* (Breakdown and Bereavement), 1920, Brenner portrayed alienated European Jews striving, often ineffectively, for psychological and spiritual wholeness in the Land of Israel. He was killed in the Arab riots of May 1921.

SIMON FRUG, born in the Kherson province of Russia in 1860, first gained recognition for his Russian poems on Jewish themes. He turned to Yiddish in 1888, and his songs and ballads in that language were extremely popular, influencing Bialik among others. *Hot rakhmones* (Have Pity), which commemorated the Kishinev pogrom of 1903, became an anthem of the struggle against Tsarist oppression and, later, of the relief effort in World War I. Frug died in 1916.

MORDECAI GEBIRTIG, Yiddish poet and composer, was born in Cracow in 1877 and perished in the ghetto there in 1942. A carpenter by trade, Gebirtig wrote lyrics whose topicality and visionary power won them the status of folk songs in his lifetime; they continue to be sung after his death.

YANKEV GLATSHTEYN, poet, novelist and essayist, was born in Lublin in 1896 and immigrated to the United States in 1914. In the 1920s his iconoclasm and brilliant language brought him to the forefront of the *Inzikhist,* or introspectivist, movement in Yiddish-American poetry, but increasingly, in such collections as *Shtralndike yidn* (Radiant Jews), 1946, his modernism became an instrument for preserving the endangered past and for affirming the legacy of European Jewry. Glatshteyn died in 1971.

HIRSH GLIK, born in Vilna in 1922, was interned in the ghetto there for most of World War II. Influenced by the poets of the *Yung Vilne* movement, he wrote prolifically and his Yiddish poems were widely circulated; *Zog nit keyn mol* (Never Say) became the hymn of the Jewish partisans. Glik himself died a partisan in Estonia in 1944.

LEYB GOLDIN, born in Warsaw in 1906, where he was raised in poverty, early became active in the city's communist youth organizations and joined the Bund in 1936. A translator as well as critic and essayist, Goldin published in the Bundist underground press in World War II; his "Chronicle of a Single Day" was included in Ringelblum's archives. He died of starvation in the ghetto in 1942.

ZALMEN GRADOWSKI was born in Bialystok around 1910. He had a traditional Jewish education as well as some grounding in European literature. He spent the early years of the war in Soviet-occupied Luna, but with the German occupation, he and his family were deported to Auschwitz in December 1942. Assigned to the *Sonderkommando,* he recorded his impressions of the Auschwitz hell; two of the manuscripts that he buried were recovered after the war. Gradowski was killed leading the *Soderkommando* revolt of October 1944.

URI ZVI GREENBERG, Hebrew and Yiddish poet, was born in Galicia in 1894 and raised in the Hasidic milieu of Lvov. In Warsaw in the 1920s, Greenberg was a leader of the postrevolutionary avant-garde that also included Markish, but he later rejected modern secularism. In such volumes as *Rehovot hanahar* (Streets of the River), 1951, he offered verse rooted in traditional Hebrew forms, in which his despair over Jewish suffering was balanced by an anti-humanist, mystical faith in Zionism. Except for a sojourn in Warsaw in the early 1930s, he made his home in Israel from 1924 until he died in 1981.

MOYSHE-LEYB HALPERN, Yiddish-American poet, was born in Galicia in 1886 and immigrated to New York in 1908, where he wrote on the fringe of the *Di Yunge* literary movement. *In New York* (1919) and *Di goldene pave* (The Golden Peacock), collections of bitter, streetwise verse, were characterized by an ambivalent stance toward the Jewish past. Halpern rejected sentimental nostalgia; yet in that very rejection was an obsessive, indignant attachment. He died in 1932.

NATHAN NATA HANOVER, mystic, lexicographer and witness, was forced to leave his native Volhynia during the Chmielnicki pogroms of 1648. Wandering through Europe, he studied, preached, wrote prolifically and associated with the leading kabbalists of his day. He settled in Moravia, where he was murdered by a Turkish soldier in 1683. The best known of his few surviving works is *Yeven metsulah* (The Abyss of Despair), a chronicle of the Chmielnicki pogroms.

HAYYIM HAZAZ, Hebrew writer and playwright, was born in the Ukraine in 1898, where he witnessed the pogroms that followed the Russian Revolution. In 1931 he settled in Jerusalem, after living in Asia and Europe. His works, such as *Pirkei mahapekha* (Revolutionary Chapters), 1924, and the epic novel *Ya'ish*, 1947–1952, differ widely in historical and geographical setting, yet share such themes as Diaspora and Return and the redemptive value of self-sacrifice. Hazaz died in 1973.

YANKEV (YANKELE) HERSZKOWICZ, born in the town of Apt, was a patchwork tailor by trade who became the most popular street singer in the Lodz ghetto, gaining special notoriety for his satiric broadsides on Chaim Rumkowski. Until the summer of 1942, Herszkowicz actually made a living from his songs which were accompanied by Karul Rosenzweig, a traveling salesman from Vienna. With the liquidation of the ghetto two years later, Herszkowicz was deported to Auschwitz. He returned to Lodz after the war.

ISAIAH HALEVI HOROWITZ, kabbalist and halakhic authority, was born in Prague around 1565 and died in Tiberias in 1630. He was called the SheLoH, after his major work, *Shnei luhot habrit* (Two Tablets of the Covenant). Horowitz anticipated Hasidism in his belief that profane impulses and suffering could be turned toward holy ends, a belief reflected in his emphasis on *Kiddush Hashem*.

SHIMON HUBERBAND was born into a rabbinic family in 1909 and ordained by his grandfather. A religious Zionist, he founded the Society for Jewish Scholarship in Otwock and published widely on theological and historical topics. After his wife was killed early in World War II, he moved to Warsaw, where he remarried. Huberband became Ringelblum's most valued collaborator in the chronicling of the Warsaw ghetto. He died in the Great Deportation in the summer of 1942.

SOLOMON IBN VERGA was a Spanish chronicler of the late fifteenth and early sixteenth centuries. His chief work, *Shevet Yehuda* (The Scepter of Judah), is a partly historical, partly literary treatment of Jewish catastrophes from the fall of the Second Temple to the expulsions and persecutions of Ibn Verga's own day. His work is distinguished by its rejection of traditional messianic consolations and its favoring of a self-critical, humanistic view of Jewish suffering.

SHMERKE KACZERGINSKI, born in Vilna in 1908, joined the *Yung Vilne* literary movement in 1929. He recorded his wartime experiences in the Vilna ghetto and among the partisans in such works of Yiddish poetry and prose as *Khurbm Vilne* (Destruction of Vilna), 1947. Kaczerginski had been instrumental in saving Jewish documents from the Nazis. Settling in Argentina after the war, he continued his work for the preservation of Jewish culture until his death in 1954.

ZELIG KALMANOVITSH, Yiddish linguist and historian, was born in Latvia in 1885. He settled in Vilna in 1929. His belief that the impending destruction of the European Jews would be the termination of their historical role, coupled with his cultural activism within the ghetto, gave him the status of a moral leader. He perished in an Estonian labor camp in 1944.

CHAIM KAPLAN, Hebrew educator, essayist and diarist, was born in Belorussia in 1880. In 1900 he settled in Warsaw, where he wrote prolifically on pedagogic subjects and founded a Hebrew school, which he ran until World War II. In 1936 Kaplan began keeping a diary, first as a personal document but increasingly as an objective historical record of the Warsaw ghetto. He had the diary smuggled out of the ghetto in late 1942, shortly before he was sent to his death in Treblinka.

YITZHAK KATZENELSON, born in Lithuania in 1886, won recognition for the poems and plays he wrote in Hebrew and Yiddish before World War II. However, his major achievement was his literary response to the conditions in the Warsaw ghetto, among the members of the Zionist underground and in the concentration camps, as recorded in his Hebrew diary and in Yiddish in *Dos lid fun oysgehargetn yidishn folk* (The Song of the Murdered Jewish People). He died in Auschwitz in 1944.

ITSIK KIPNIS, Soviet Yiddish novelist and leading author of children's books, born in Volhynia in 1896, moved to Kiev around 1920. The lyrical treatment of shtetl life in *Khadoshim un teg* (Months and Days), 1926, brought Kipnis praise as a successor to Sholem Aleichem; it also earned him the hostility of Soviet critics—a hostility reinforced by his reaffirmation of his Jewish identity in the wake of the Holocaust. Expelled from the Writers' Union and arrested in 1948, Kipnis survived imprisonment to witness a partial rehabilitation of his works. He died in 1974.

JOSEPH KIRMAN was born in Warsaw in 1896. A laborer who had been arrested for his leftist views, Kirman lived in poverty. His poems and stories, written in Yiddish, addressed the needs of the poor. Some of his most memorable works, dealing with his anguish on being separated from his family, were written in the Warsaw ghetto, where they were published in the underground press. He perished in the liquidation of the Poniatow labor camp in 1943.

ABBA KOVNER, Israeli Hebrew poet, was born in the Ukraine in 1918 and raised in Vilna. His poetry and prose deal primarily with the Holocaust and the birth of Israel, the two events that shaped his life. The first he experienced as one of the leaders of the United Partisans Organization; the second, as a member of the Givati Brigade in Israel's War of Independence, which was the occasion of his "Battle Bulletins." He was a member of Kibbutz Ein Hahoresh until his death in 1987.

ISAAC LAMDAN, Hebrew poet, was born in the Ukraine in 1899. Disillusioned by World War I and the Bolshevik Revolution, he migrated in 1920 to Palestine, where he worked as a laborer for several years before turning to literature. His major work, *Masada* (1924), drew upon ancient and modern Jewish history in its passionate, anguished affirmation of Zionist faith. Lamdan died in 1954.

H. LEIVICK, born Leivick Halpern in Belorussia in 1886, endured poverty and political oppression, including Siberian exile, before moving to the United States in 1913, where he became active in *Di Yunge*. His early experiences left their imprint on his work: in his Yiddish poems and essays and in such plays as *The Golem,* 1920, Leivick drew on both Jewish and Christian traditions to explore the destruction and redemptive facets of suffering. He died in 1962.

MOSES MAIMONIDES, author of the *Mishneh Torah,* 1180, and *Moreh Nevukhim* (Guide for the Perplexed), 1190, was the greatest Jewish philosopher of the Middle Ages. Born in Cordoba in 1135, he spent much of his youth fleeing fundamentalist Moslem persecutors; these experiences influenced his *The Epistle on Martyrdom,* written in Fez in 1165. Shortly afterward he traveled to the Land of Israel and to Egypt with his family, eventually settling in Cairo, where he became a court physician and leader of the Jewish community. He died in 1204.

PERETZ MARKISH, Soviet Yiddish poet and novelist, was born in Volhynia in 1895. After serving in World War I he traveled widely. In Warsaw in the early 1920s, he worked with Greenberg and others in establishing an expressionist avantgarde. His poems of this period, like *Di kupe* (The Corpse Heap), 1921, attempt to give Jewish martyrdom universal significance at the expense of historical context.

Markish's later verse, while remaining technically brilliant, is more subjective and elegiac in its stance toward the tragic past and the ominous future. He was among the Yiddish writers executed in the Soviet Union on August 12, 1952.

MEIR OF ROTHENBURG, the outstanding German talmudist and halakhic arbiter of his day, was born in Worms around 1215. His numerous responsa and other works, as well as the teachings disseminated by his students, influenced the *Shulkhan Arukh*. In 1242 he witnessed the burning of the Torah in Paris. His opposition to the special taxes that Emperor Ruldolph I imposed on the Jews led to his arrest in 1286; he remained in prison until his death in 1293.

KADIA MOLODOWSKY, Yiddish poet, playwright and novelist, was born in Lithuania in 1894. Her teacher father gave her an unusually extensive Jewish education. Molodowsky's poetry is a deeply personal response to modern Jewish history, whose vicissitudes it reflects in its emotional range, from bitterly ironic lamentation to the joyful lyricism that made her a foremost writer of children's verse. Widely traveled, she settled in New York in 1935, and died there in 1975.

PERETZ OPOCZYNSKI, born near Lodz in 1895, was given a yeshiva education. His earliest literary efforts were poems, but he turned to prose to describe his experiences in World War I as a German prisoner of war. In 1925 he moved to Warsaw, where he continued his journalistic activities until his death from typhus in the ghetto in 1943. His contributions to Ringelblum's *Oyneg Shabbes*, written in Yiddish and sometimes Hebrew, are distinguished by the sharpness and vitality with which they portray a society on the edge of doom.

I. L. PERETZ was born in Zamosc in 1852. With Abramovitsh and Sholem Aleichem, he established Yiddish literature as a vital, legitimate medium of Jewish experience and aspirations. Of the three, he exercised the greatest influence on the succeeding generation of Yiddish writers. Peretz's own tales and plays brilliantly adapt religious and folk motifs to secular, nationalistic ends. After he moved to Warsaw in the 1880s, he remained active in communal and literary affairs until his death in 1915. In his various projects he was assisted by his loyal friend, the novelist and educator Yankev Dinezon (1856–1919).

YEHOSHUE PERLE, Yiddish writer, was born in Radom, Poland, in 1888. In 1905 he moved to Warsaw, where his naturalistic studies of Jewish life won him a large audience. He fled to Soviet-occupied Lemberg in 1939, but in 1941 made his way back to Warsaw. There he worked for the Judenrat and contributed to Ringelblum's *Oyneg Shabbes* detailed accounts of Nazi atrocities, which contrasted sharply with the bright, frank lyricism of his earlier work. He perished in Auschwitz in 1944.

EMANUEL RINGELBLUM, born in eastern Galicia in 1900, was the chief historian of the Warsaw ghetto. In 1919 he moved to Warsaw, where he studied, taught and published several articles on the city's Jewry. During the occupation, his leadership in the ghetto's mutual assistance program gave him access to extensive sources of information, which he and his staff collected under the code name *Oyneg Shabbes*. His own wartime writings were later published as *Ksovim fun geto* (Notes from the Warsaw Ghetto), 1961. Ringelblum was murdered by the Nazis in March 1944.

LEYB ROSENTAL was born in 1916 in Vilna, where, as a young man, he began contributing poems and articles to local Yiddish publications. During World War II he was one of the principal writers for the cabaret performances in the Vilna ghetto, and the popularity of his poems extended to other ghettos as well. He died in a concentration camp in Estonia in 1944 or 1945.

LEAH RUDNITSKY, born in Lithuania in 1913, published poetry in several Yiddish periodicals before settling in Vilna in 1940. In the Vilna ghetto she produced a verse collection, *Durkh neplen* (Through Mists), only a few of whose poems survived the war. Rudnitsky herself perished in an Estonian concentration camp in 1943.

KALONYMUS SHAPIRO was born into a Hasidic dynasty in 1889. Settling in Piasczeno, near Warsaw, he began to attract a following and became the community's rabbi in 1913. After World War I he moved to Warsaw, founding a yeshiva there in 1923. During the Nazi occupation his home doubled as prayer house and soup kitchen for his followers in the ghetto. There, in the sermons that he delivered until the Great Deportation of July 1942, Shapiro developed a theology linking human suffering with the divine. He perished in a death camp near Lublin in 1943.

LAMED (LEVI) SHAPIRO, Yiddish short story writer, was born in the Ukraine in 1878. In 1903 he went to Warsaw, where he joined I. L. Peretz's circle. *Der tseylem* (The Cross), 1909, brought him notoriety as the master of the pogrom story; it appeared with *Vayse khale* in *Di yidishe melukhe* (The Jewish State), 1919. Shapiro's exquisite prose gave powerful, ironic expression to the disorder and violence portrayed in his work. He died in Los Angeles in 1948.

SIMKHE BUNEM SHAYEVITSH, born in 1907, established a reputation as a prose writer in prewar Lodz, where he was a textile worker. In the Lodz ghetto he continued writing, turning to epic poetry; only two of these poems were recovered after the war. He was deported to Auschwitz in 1944 and perished in the Kaufering camp a few days before liberation.

ISAAC BASHEVIS SINGER, born in 1904 into a rabbinic family in Poland and raised in Warsaw, followed his older brother into a career in Yiddish letters. In such novels as *Sotn in Goray (Satan in Goray)*, 1935, as well as in his immensely popular short stories, Singer has drawn from Jewish history and folklore to fashion an elegiac, highly personal mythology of eastern European Jewish life. The universality of his fiction was confirmed by the 1978 Nobel prize for literature. Since 1935, Singer has lived in New York.

ABRAHAM SUTZKEVER was born in Belorussia in 1913 and educated in Vilna, where his early Yiddish poetry won the acclaim of the *Yung Vilne* writers. During the occupation, he escaped the ghetto and joined the partisans. His wartime experiences are central to his later work, beginning with *Di festung* (The Fortress), 1945. Sutzkever's verse, much of which was written under appalling conditions, uses poetic language and imagery to transform an otherwise unbearable reality into a vision of beauty and grace. Since World War II, he has lived in Israel, where he edits the Yiddish literary quarterly *Di goldene keyt*.

WLADYSLAW SZLENGEL was born in Warsaw in 1914. Active in the prewar Polish theater, he became, under the German occupation, the chief organizer and script writer for the underground literary cabaret *Zywy Dziennik (The Living Daily)* and for the Stuka (Art) Café. Szlengel died in 1943, in the Warsaw ghetto uprising. His so-called "documentary poems" on ghetto life, which eschewed rhetoric and high poetic diction, were published after World War II in *Co czytałyem umarlym* (What I Read to the Dead).

OYZER WARSHAWSKI, born near Warsaw in 1898, gained fame for his naturalist novel *Shmuglares* (Smugglers), published in 1920 with the aid of Isaac Meir Weissenberg. In 1924 he settled in Paris, where, unable to match his early success, he drifted away from the literary life. However, he returned to writing with the approach of World War II, making extensive notes while desperately fleeing the Gestapo. He died in Auschwitz in 1944.

I. M. WEISSENBERG was born in 1881 in Zelechow, the probable model for the shtetl of his 1906 novella. A protégé of I. L. Peretz, he began publishing his fiction in 1904. His starkly realistic description of social and political conditions in small-town Poland, which rejected or subverted traditional Jewish motifs, earned him his reputation as a leading Yiddish naturalist and polemicist. He died in 1938.

Index of Selected Biblical Citations

Index